Edward M. Hodges

Hodges American Bank Note Safe-Guard, 1865

Edward M. Hodges

Hodges American Bank Note Safe-Guard, 1865

ISBN/EAN: 9783742800374

Manufactured in Europe, USA, Canada, Australia, Japa

Cover: Foto ©knipser5 / pixelio.de

Manufactured and distributed by brebook publishing software
(www.brebook.com)

Edward M. Hodges

Hodges American Bank Note Safe-Guard, 1865

HODGES'

AMERICAN BANK NOTE

SAFE-GUARD;

GIVING FAC SIMILE DESCRIPTIONS OF UPWARDS OF

TEN THOUSAND BANK NOTES

EMBRACING EVERY GENUINE NOTE ISSUED IN THE

UNITED STATES AND CANADA.

REVISED AND CORRECTED,

And Arranged Geographically and Alphabetically.

THE MOST EFFECTUAL DETECTER OF

SPURIOUS, ALTERED AND COUNTERFEIT BILLS

EVER PUBLISHED.

THE ONLY WORK OF THE KIND EXTANT.

PUBLISHED BY

EDWARD M. HODGES.

NEW YORK:

1865.

NEW ENGLAND MUTUAL LIFE INS. CO.,

All over and above the actual liens and charges against the Company, returned in cash to all the insured, every five years, thus making it purely mutual. Last Cash Dividend, 30 ℔ cent.

COMPANY'S BUILDING.

This Company has never failed to make large dividends, and pay them in cash. An uniform prosperity and economy have marked its course since its organization—a period of twenty years.

BOSTON & NEW YORK. ORGANIZED, 1843.

BRANCH OFFICE, METROPOLITAN BANK BUILDING,

No. 110 BROADWAY, N. Y.

CAPITAL - - - TWO MILLIONS, ONE HUNDRED THOUSAND.
SURPLUS - - - - - - - - - - - ONE MILLION.

Last dividend paid *in cash to all* the policy holders, 30 ℔ cent., amounting to over $100,000, and making nearly $1,000,000 thus paid since the company began business. The past year, 1861, notwithstanding the adversities of the times, was one of marked prosperity.

WILLARD PHILLIPS, Pres. B. F. STEVENS, Sec.

Economy, care in its risks, and prudent investments characterize this Company. The last report of the Insurance Commissioners, comparing this company with all the principal companies, makes this the *leading company in the United States, in surplus and economy.*

This Company being purely mutual, insures at the lowest possible rates; and, if the premiums paid exceed the *actual* cost, the surplus is returned to the parties insuring.

Every five years, at the time of declaring the dividends, the business is, as it were, closed, so that its actual position and solvency are made manifest at that time; and the surplus funds are divided *pro rata*, among all the insured. This guards the assured against any possible loss from inefficiency on the part of the Company, and is a sure guaranty as regards the future.

The terms of payment are peculiarly advantageous to the insured. Premiums can be paid annually, semi-annually, quarterly, or one half of the first five annual premiums on life policies loaned to the insured, if desired.

Insurances may be effected for the benefit of married women, beyond the reach of their husband's creditors. Creditors may insure the lives of their debtors.

Documents of an interesting character, showing the benefits of the mutual plan, explaining the different forms of policies and the manner of making payments, furnished gratis, upon application, by mail or otherwise, to

JOHN HOPPER,
Agent and Attorney for the Co.,
(Metropolitan Bank Building) 110 Broadway, New York City.

ENDORSEMENTS

Of the Leading Bank Note Engravers of the Country, in Favor of this Work.

OFFICE OF THE NATIONAL BANK NOTE COMPANY,
New York, December 19, 1861.

E. M. Hodges, Esq.: Sir—We have examined the copy of your "Bank Note Safe-Guard" submitted to our inspection, and cheerfully recommend it as a work of unquestionable utility, well deserving the patronage of bankers, merchants, and tradesmen, throughout the country. As the merits of your work are very apparent, it will, doubtless, receive the liberal patronage of all who have occasion to handle paper money.

Yours, &c.,
J. MACDONOUGH, Secretary.

OFFICE OF DANFORTH, WRIGHT & CO.,
New York, March, 1859.

E. M. Hodges, Esq.:

Sir—Your "Bank Note Safe-Guard" seems to possess unequalled merit, in the detailed description it gives of all Genuine Bank Notes; and combined with the "Journal of Finance and Bank Reporter," you certainly offer a work of great utility, as a protection against frauds in paper currency.

Respectfully yours,
DANFORTH, WRIGHT & CO.

OFFICE OF RAWDON, WRIGHT, HATCH & EDSON,
New York, March, 1859.

E. M. Hodges, Esq.:

Sir—Having examined the plan proposed in your "Bank Note Safe-guard," for enabling the public to detect Spurious and Altered Bank Notes, by furnishing accurate descriptions of the Genuine Notes of all the Banks of the country, we take pleasure in expressing our approval of the same, as affording a simple and effectual protection against that species of fraudulent paper money.

Respectfully yours,
RAWDON, WRIGHT, HATCH & EDSON.

OFFICE OF WELLSTOOD, HAY & WHITING,
New York, March, 1859.

E. M. Hodges, Esq.:

Sir—We regard your "Bank Note Safe-Guard" as a work that should receive the most favorable attention from all who are accustomed to handle Bank Notes. The facility with which Altered, Spurious, or Counterfeit notes can be detected, is such that the most inexperienced can scarcely go astray. And we have no hesitation in commending the work to the public as one which is much required, and as fully accomplishing its object.

With best wishes for the success of your efforts to prevent imposition, through the medium of your publication,

We remain, truly yours,
WELLSTOOD, HAY & WHITING.

OFFICE OF THE NEW ENGLAND BANK NOTE CO.,
Boston, March, 1859.

E. M. Hodges, Esq.:

Sir—Allow me to express to you my unqualified opinion in favor of your "Bank Note Safe-Guard." The simplicity of it is what I most admire; the most inexperienced of the great mass, who are in the habit of taking Paper Currency can at once detect an altered or spurious note, which are much more dangerous than counterfeits, and more numerously in circulation.

You have my best wishes for its success, believing it to be the best work of its character ever published.

ISAAC CARY, Agent.

New York, March, 1859.

E. M. Hodges, Esq.:

Sir—We take great pleasure in endorsing Mr. Cary's opinion of your "Bank Note Safe-Guard," and in recommending it as a work of the greatest utility.

Respectfully yours,
TOPPAN, CARPENTER & CO.

OFFICE OF THE AMERICAN BANK NOTE CO.
New York, March, 1859.

E. M. Hodges, Esq.:

Sir—Attempts at literal imitation, or counterfeiting, in the present advanced state of Bank Note Engraving, are of unfrequent occurrence, most of the notes represented in Bank Note Detectors and Reporters being either Spurious or Altered Notes.

Spurious Bank Notes merely retain the name of the Bank and place of issue—not always using the true name of the President and Cashier, and are made up of devices unlike those of the genuine notes, a want of familiarity with which, on the part of the public, being counted on in perpetrating these frauds.

Your "Bank Note Safe-Guard," supplies a desideratum in a manner so simple and so easy of reference, that there can be no danger of suffering from Spurious or Altered Bank Notes, if brought to the test of comparison which it furnishes.

Respectfully yours,
JOCELYN, DRAPER, WELSH & CO.

TERMS.

The SAFE-GUARD sent by mail to all parts of the Country on receipt of $3 0
The Journal of Finance and Bank Reporter, including Hodges' Gold and Silver Coin Chart Manual,
and Safe-Guard, Weekly Issue ....
Semi-Monthly $6 00
Monthly $5 00
.... $4 00

INDEX

TO THE

BANK NOTE SAFEGUARD.

The Figures Enclosed in Brackets Denote the Denomination of Notes

IMITATED AND PHOTOGRAPHED!

SPECIAL NOTICE.—In consequence of the removal of certain Banks, particularly in the Western States, some will be found differing from the index bearing the *original* place of location; and a few banks, part of the plates of which have the *original location*, while the remainder of the plates of the *same Banks* have the place of *removal* on them. The *Index* contains their place of location at the time of the publication of this work. For a complete list of all Broken, Worthless and Retired Banks see JOURNAL OF FINANCE AND BANK REPORTER.

MAINE.

NEW HAMPSHIRE.

VERMONT.

MASSACHUSETTS.

RHODE ISLAND.

CONNECTICUT.

NEW YORK CITY.

NEW YORK STATE.

NEW JERSEY.

PENNSYLVANIA.

PHILADELPHIA CITY BANKS

PENNSYLVANIA COUNTRY BANKS.

DELAWARE.

MARYLAND.

DISTRICT OF COLUMBIA.

WEST VIRGINIA.

LOUISIANA.

OHIO.

INDIANA.

ILLINOIS.

KENTUCKY.

MISSOURI.

MICHIGAN.

IOWA.

WISCONSIN.

MINNESOTA.

CANADA.

NATIONAL CURRENCY.

U. S. TREASURY.

THE

SAFE-GUARD.

This work is at length thoroughly completed, being now arranged GEOGRAPHICALLY AND ALPHABETICALLY, thereby obviating the only objection there ever was to it. The notes of such Bank are all on one page, and it is but the matter of a moment to find any note required. This work has cost us many years of toil and expense, and we now present it to the public, with the assertion that no work was ever published that is of greater utility for commercial purposes. It is of interest and importance to every individual, of every age, condition, or sex, who handles a dollar of the miscellaneous and precarious paper currency of our country.

The paper money of the United States is of such infinite varieties of design and execution, that the artful and accomplished counterfeiter can sport upon and defy the perception of the great majority of our people. And the frequent and cruel impositions so repeatedly practiced upon the honest and credulous, have derived their impunity from the fact that other works and Detectors have only attempted to direct attention to the spurious and counterfeit, while, in our SAFE-GUARD ALONE, has the idea been developed of minutely describing the genuine Bank notes.

A new counterfeit, or spurious Bank note, is prepared by a rogue, who, with his numerous accomplices and confederates, distribute and circulate their issue simultaneously in different and distant localities. These notes (not being described in the Reporters and Detectors) being readily taken by the unsuspecting, and by the imperfect judges, in a short time obtain an extensive circulation: and days, weeks, and, in some instances, months have elapsed, before the VIGILANT Bank Note Reporters have informed the community that they have been fearfully victimized. This, being at last exposed, but not until he has reaped a rich harvest from his first issue, the counterfeiter again takes the plate to his haunt and alters it to some other bank or denomination, and may do the same thing again and again, and each time with impunity and profit, before the Detectors can act as an efficient check on his proceedings.

But the SAFE-GUARD always, and in every case, acts as a check and preventative against these impositions and frauds, by describing every GENUINE Bank note, and every part of every note, dissecting and analyzing all denominations of all notes, of every Bank, organized and doing business in the United States and British North America, showing each note, made up of different designs, vignettes, &c.; each denomination differing so materially, that no one of the notes could be altered to another and larger denomination, without the certainty of an immediate detection on reference to the *fac-simile* of the plates (in the SAFE-GUARD) of the particular bank on which such fraud has been perpetrated Herein is exemplified the great superiority of the SAFE-GUARD over all Reporters and other Bank Note Detectors.

Spurious, altered, or raised notes are by far the most numerous class of bad money, and bear no resemblance to the genuine. They are detected at a glance by reference to the SAFE-GUARD, there being therein portrayed a perfect Daguerreotype of the genuine notes; the dress and design of which are as unlike the spurious as is light to darkness.

Counterfeits, or *fac-simile* notes, are comparatively rare. They are intended to resemble and imitate the true, and calculated to circulate where the genuine are well-known, but can be more easily detected, by close inspection, than any other class of bad bills. Very few of this description are in circulation. Nine-tenths of the bad bills in circulation being altered, raised, or spurious. On reference to our Reporter this will be seen.

Within a few years, photograph imitations have made their appearance. They can be detected by applying cyanide of potassium, which turns the bills [illegible].

In a word, THE SAFE-GUARD detects all PAST, PRESENT, and FUTURE spurious, altered, and raised notes, and is of more value, protection and security to the commercial interests of the country, than all the Detectors, Bank Note Lists, and other works which, up to this [illegible] been published. In fact, THE SAFEGUARD is almost indispensable; FOR IT GOES AHEAD OF, AND ANTICIPATES THE COUNTERFEITER, cutting off his success, while the Reporters and Bank Note Lists but follow AFTER, and to use a homely but forcible expression, "can only lock the stable after the horse is stolen."

We have herein endeavored to show the utility and importance of this work, and with the promise *that it shall be always correct to the date of its issue*, we are satisfied to send it forth to the public on its own merits.

On another page will be found commendations from *all the first class* BANK NOTE ENGRAVING COMPANIES in the Union, endorsing HODGES' AMERICAN BANK NOTE SAFE-GUARD. This testimony, together with the approval and patronage of nearly every Banker and Broker in America, at once stamps it as the most valuable publication of the times—indispensable to every well-regulated counting room or business place.

No Person is authorized to act as Agent, unless having the Publisher's Printed Receipts and written authority.

E. M. HODGES.

HODGES'

AMERICAN BANK NOTE

SAFE GUARD

MAINE.

Left	Centre	Right
Spread eagle and shield. 1	Portrait of Washington, two females, sickle and sheaf of wheat at the left; milkmaid and cows at the right. ALFRED BANK, Alfred, Me.	1 Female, eagle and shield.
Female. 2	ALFRED BANK, Alfred, Me. Harvest scene.	2 Portrait of Franklin.
Portrait of Websier. Three and 3	Locomotive and train of cars. ALFRED BANK. Alfred, Me.	3 Female seated on a bale.
V and Five Farmer sitting under a tree.	ALFRED BANK. Alfred. Me. Signing of the "Declaration of Independence."	V Female with sickle, and an Indian woman.
State Arms. X, 10, Ten	ALFRED BANK, Alfred, Me. Indian, spread eagle, and two horses; factories and steamboat in background.	10 Female drawing water at a wall.
XX Milkmaid.	Man on **seback, farmhouse and drove of cattle. ALFRED BANK, Alfred. Me.	20 Female, eagle and shield.
50	Title of Bank. Three female figures. Female	50

MAINE.

Left	Centre	Right
100 Two females; shield between.	ALFRED BANK, Alfred, Me.	100 C 100
1	Vig. Female on either side of a shield; steamboat on left, train of cars on right. 1 AMERICAN BANK Hallowell, Me.	1 Female Portrait.
2 2	AMERICAN BANK Hallowell, Me. Ship building 2 Locomotive and car.	2 Cupid and a sea monster.
3 Female with balances in one hand, wreath in other, eagle by her side.	AMERICAN BANK, Hallowell, Me. Female and swan in water. 3	3 Two females.
Female reclining; eagle, globe, &c., steamer and ship on left. 5	5 AMERICAN BANK. Hallowell, Me.	5 Figure 5 and five females.
Female feeding an eagle from cup. X	Spread eagle, steamer on left; public building on right. AMERICAN BA**-d, Hallowell, Me.	10 Portrait of Washington.
Female. XX	Vig. Capitol at Washington. AMERICAN BANK. Hallowell, Me.	20 Man beside a capstan, and barrels behind.

MAINE.

Left	Centre	Right
50 Man; capstan behind.	Female. State Arms. Female. AMERICAN BANK, Hallowell, Me.	50 Female with pole, cap, shield, etc.
100 Man with grain cradle.	Vig. Ships, steamboats, vessels, &c., city in distance. AMERICAN BANK, Hallowell, Me.	100 Female with rake
1 Boy with rake, fork, and canteen; also dog.	AUBURN BANK, Auburn, Me. Train of cars, load of hay, men, cattle, &c.; in distance train of cars on bridge, city, &c.; in extreme distance city, bridge, water, &c.	1 Two females, one engaged at table, the other with horn in hand; chickens, &c.
Female reclining with scales. 2	Two men, horse, dog, cattle, and sheep. 2 AUBURN BANK, Auburn, Me. Loading hay.	Female erect with sword and scales.
Male portrait 3	Wharf scene—train of cars, depot, horses and carts, canal boats, vessels, men, buildings, steam boat, &c. AUBURN BANK. Auburn, Me. Cow and calf.	3 Male portrai:
V Female portrait.	Five gold dollars with three cupids above them; hunter seated on right; Indian female on left; cars in distance. AUBURN BANK, Auburn, Me.	5 Female portrait.
Female portrait. 10	Female seated; on her right is ten gold dollars; in front of her nine cupids making offering to her; steamboat and cars in distance. AUBURN BANK, Auburn, Me.	X Female seated with sheaf.

20	View of large public building; horses, carriages males, females, &c., in front.	20
	AUBURN BANK, Auburn, Me.	
XX	Female seated.	Female portrait,

Female erect leaning on anchor; ship in storm in distance.	Spread eagle; U. S Capitol on right, and steamship on left.	50
	AUBURN BANK, Auburn, Me.	Female reclining with balances, &c.
FIFTY		

C	Blacksmith shoeing a horse, forge, &c.; a jackass tied to anvil; locomotive on left.	100
Portrait of a boy.	AUBURN BANK, Auburn, Me.	
100	Two horses	Portrait of Webster.

	AUGUSTA BANK, Augusta. Me. This Bank uses the old Perkin's Stereotype plate, which has the denomination printed in fine letters all over the bill.	

ONE	1 Large ship	1
Mechanic and sailor with flag, quadrant and sledge, right.	B'K OF COMMERCE. Belfast. Me.	Man chopping a tree.
		ONE

TWO	Large steamer	2
Two females supporting sheaf of wheat.	B'K OF COMMERCE TWO DOLLARS Belfast. Me.	TWO
	Beehive	

3 Sailor seated on ground near barrel, bales, etc., ship on right in distance. State Arms.		3
	B'K OF COMMERCE THREE DOLLARS	
3	Belfast, Me.	Female seated
	Ducks	

V	Vig. Spread eagle, on either side flags with the names of the different States.	5
	B'K OF COMMERCE. Belfast, Me.	
FIVE	Genus.	Female.

X	Ship building.	10
	BANK of COMMERCE Belfast. Me	
Dog's head.	Female head.	TEN

TWENTY	XX Two females with scroll, liberty pole and grain, cornucopia at their feet; care crossing bridge on right; vessels on left.	20
Indian with bow and arrow, sail boat near him; vessel in distance.	BANK of COMMERCE Belfast, Me.	Bridge.
	Female head.	

1	1 Female seated with right hand on eagle and left on shield safe by her side.	Large figure 1 and full length female.
Med. Head.	BANK OF CUMBERLAND Portland, Me.	
1		

1	BANK OF CUMBERLAND, Portland, Me.	1
Propeller.	Sailor and farmer on either side of shield on which is deer and tree.	
ONE		

2	Title of Bank.	2
	Female erect, apparently reading to three others seated.	

2	2 Female seated on safe with cornucopia &c., farmer plowing on right; building &c., on left.	Large figure 2 and full length female.
Med. Head.	BANK OF CUMBERLAND, Portland, Me.	
2		

	Steamboat and other vessels.	3
	Title of Bank.	
3		Liberty.

3	Figure 3 and three cupids therein. Sportsman, female and child seated, train of cars on right; log house on left.	Large figure 3 and full length female.
Med. Head.	BANK OF CUMBERLAND, Portland Me.	
3		

5	Female seated with sprig in left hand; eagle, shield, sheaf, train of cars, &c., on right, town ocean and vessels on left.	5
Female seated with sledge; cog wheels &c., buildings in distance.	BANK OF CUMBERLAND, Portland, Me.	Portrait of Washington.

Sailor with flag; bale, hhd., anchor and quadrant	Shield on which is figures 10; on right farmers seated with sickle, and man on horseback, and negro driving drove of pigs; on left female, rudder, safe and steamboat.	10
TEN	BANK OF CUMBERLAND. Portland, Me.	Female Portrait.

XX	20 Vessels sailing, &c. XX	20
Male portrait	BANK OF CUMBERLAND, Portland. Me.	Male portrait
20		XX

50	Steamboat, schooners, sloops, &c; Female seated with spear and shield.	50
Male portrait	BANK OF CUMBERLAND, Portland, Me.	Male portrait
FIFTY		FIFTY

100	C Ship under full sail on ocean, two vessels in back. ground. C	100
Portrait of Van Buren.	BANK OF CUMBERLAND. Portland. Me	Male portrait
100		100

500	Vig. Same as hundreds. 500	500
Portrait of Van Buren.	BANK OF CUMBERLAND, Portland. Me	Portrait of Jackson.
500		500

1000	Vig. Same as 50's. Female seated with spear and shield.	1000
Portrait of Jackson.	BANK OF CUMBERLAND. Portland. Me.	Portrait of Van Buren.
1000		1000

Washington.	Farm yard scene, farmer and drover.	1
	BK. OF SOMERSET, Skowhegan, Me.	Goddess of Liberty, globe and Declaration of Independence.
1	Man plowing.	

Cattle, sheep, etc.	Maine logging scene in winter.	2
	Title of Bank.	
2	Female with scales, etc.; ship	Jefferson.

Clay.	Boot and Shoe manufacturing scene.	3
	Title of Bank.	
3		State Arms.

Train of cars; city in distance.	Head of Webster.	5 and FIVE
	Title of Bank.	Large 5, eagle and Goddess of Liberty; head of Washington and "FIVE."
5	FIVE	

Franklin.	Blacksmith shoeing a horse; train of cars in distance.	10
	Title of Bank.	
10	Blacksmith & locomotive.	Vulcan.

TWENTY	Vig. Landscape; locomotive in background; city, train of cars, etc., in distance; farmer plowing, cattle, etc.	20
Jackson.	Title of Bank.	
20	Load of hay.	Female churning

Goddess of Liberty, crown and wreath.	Indians and whites trading.	50
	Title of Bank.	Male portrait
50	Man cradling grain.	FIFTY

Left	Centre	Right
Goddess of Liberty. 100	Spread eagle; U. S. capitol; steamship in distance. Title of Bank. Agricultural Implements.	100 Male portrait
1 Female with tablet.	Female portrait BANK of THE STATE of MAINE, Bangor, Maine. State Arms.	ONE Female in a nearly nude state.
2 Portrait of female.	Title of Bank. State Arms; with agricultural implements and products.	2 Portrait of female.
3 Female gathering flowers	A man watering horses at a trough, and woman feeding swine; farmhouse and buildings. Title of Bank. State Arms.	3 Boy gathering corn.
Female seated with sickle and figure 5. FIVE	Title of Bank. State Arms.	Female seated and holding out figure 5. FIVE
Ship, brig, and schooner. X	Portrait of Gen. Taylor. Title of Bank.	10 State Arms 10
20 20	Title of Bank. Female seated, eagle and globe and word "America" thereon. State Arms.	20 Washington.
50 Med. head. 50	Title of Bank. State arms, female on either side; in distance steamboat and train of cars.	50
C	Shipping; city in the distance. Title of Bank. State Arms.	100 Spread eagle.
	B'K of WINTHROP, Winthrop, Me. This Bank uses the old Perkin's Stereotype plate, which has the denomination printed in fine letters all over the bill.	

Left	Centre	Right
Indian standing erect with bow and arrow.	ONE Vig. Sail vessels; light house in background. BATH BANK, Bath, Me. Dog.	1 Portrait of little girl.
TWO Dog's head.	Vig. Indian paddling canoe accompanied by two squaws, shrubbery and mountains in background. BATH BANK, Bath, Me. Ducks.	2 Female reclining on bale of mdse.
3 Sailor and blacksmith.	3 Vig. Eagle, and female partly disrobed. 3 BATH BANK, Bath, Me. Dog.	3 Large sail vessel, other smaller ones, &c.
FIVE State arms. V	Vig. Large sail vessel; smaller ones on either side. BATH BANK, Bath, Me. Female head.	5 Portrait of Webster.
TEN Portrait of boy.	Vig. Log rolling; three persons, another felling a tree; cattle in background, &c. 10 BATH BANK, Bath, Me Beehive.	TEN Group of three females representing Agriculture, Commerce, &c
XX Sailor seated	Vig. Ship building; ships on stocks, &c. factory on left. BATH BANK, Bath, Me. Beehive.	20 Miniature view of little girl.
50 Female gazing on ocean; vessel, etc.	BATH BANK, Bath, Me State arms; sailor and farmer either side.	50 Female with flower.
100	One Hundred Dollars Sailor with trumpet on vessel. 100 BATH BANK, Bath, Me.	100 Hunter drinking from brook.
ONE	Vessels. 1 BELFAST BANK, Belfast, Me.	ONE Female. ONE
2 TWO 2	Ship and other vessels. 2 BELFAST BANK, Belfast, Me.	TWO Female. TWO

Left	Centre	Right
THREE	Reaping scene. 3 BELFAST BANK, Belfast, Me.	THREE Steamer. Figure 3, and word "Three."
FIVE	Female holding drapery over a figure 5. V BELFAST BANK, Belfast, Me.	5 Ship under sail.
The word "Five" and letter "V."	Female holding rake and sickle; sheaf of grain, machinery, &c. Large V with female. BELFAST BANK, Belfast, Me.	5 Washington
X	Signing the Declaration of Independence. X BELFAST BANK, Belfast, Me.	X Locomotive and car.
1	Factory and train of cars. 1 BIDDEFORD BANK, Biddeford, Me.	1 Female.
2	Aurora and the hours. 2 BIDDEFORD BANK, Biddeford, Me.	2 Steamship.
3	Female seated. 3 BIDDEFORD BANK, Biddeford, Me.	3 Head. THREE
5	Man ploughing with horses. Female, cupid, V. BIDDEFORD BANK, Biddeford, Me.	5 Female.
10	Two ships under sail. Ship and X BIDDEFORD BANK, Biddeford, Me.	TEN Head of Washington. TEN
20 Female.	XX Eagle. XX BIDDEFORD BANK, Biddeford, Me.	20 Ship.

FIFTY
Female
FIFTY
50 Man and horse. 50
BIDDEFORD BANK, Biddeford, Me.
FIFTY
Female.
FIFTY

The figures 100 with the words "one hundred" running across.
Portrait.
Horses, wagon, wharf and shipping.
BIDDEFORD BANK, Biddeford, Me.
The figures 100 with the words "one hundred" running across.
Portrait.

ONE
Indian crouching with gun.
Moonlight scene; fishing schooners, etc.
BUCKSPORT BANK, Bucksport, Me.
1
Boy's portrait.

ONE
Indian kneeling on the bank of river with gun in his hand.
ONE
Drove of wild horses, two more prominent than others.
BUCKSPORT BANK Bucksport, Me.
1
Portrait of a boy.

TWO
Two females holding a bundle of grain over their heads, a sickle in the left hand.
BUCKSPORT BANK, Bucksport, Me.
2 TWO 2
2
Ship; light house and vessels seen in the distance.

THREE
Spread eagle over the banners of the different States.
Head of a dog.
BUCKSPORT BANK, Bucksport, Me.
3
Portrait of girl resting on right arm, left hand over her eyes to shield from light.

FIVE
Sailor erect and blacksmith seated
Fleet of Vessels; light-house in the distance.
BUCKSPORT BANK, Bucksport, Me.
5
V

TEN
Female with sheaf.
Marine view; ship, schooner and other vessels under sail,
Title of Bank.
X
State Arms.

TEN
Female with a sickle in right hand, left hand holding a bundle of grain on her shoulder.
Three ships on the stocks, steam mill, &c.
BUCKSPORT BANK, Bucksport, Me.
X
State Arms.

20
Light-house, small vessels, steam boat, and train of cars.
BUCKSPORT BANK, Bucksport, Me.
Bee hive
20
Sailor with quadrant in right hand.

L
Three dogs.
BUCKSPORT BANK, Bucksport, Me.
Santa Claus riding over the top of houses by moon light.
Dogs.
50
Indian.

100
Man with his gun and dog in the woods by the side of a fire.
100 Indian, white man, woman and child in a snare.
BUCKSPORT BANK, Bucksport, Me.
Head of Washington.
100
C

1
ONE
1
CALAIS BANK, Calais, Me,
Male portrait; angel on left; cherub on right.
1
Female and fig. 1.

2
Farmer and sailor either side of shield
Saw mill; men seated on load of lumber drawn by two oxen.
Title of Bank.
2
Male portrait

3
Sailor and State Arms.
Ship yard scene in general.
Title of Bank.
THREE
3
Male portrait

☞ This Bank also uses the Perkins' stereotype plate which has the denomination printed in fine letters all over the face of the bill.

1
Female seated, in the act of crowning eagle with wreath; ship on left, and drover, drove of cattle, and sheep, and train of cars on right, in distance.
Head of Washington, figure 1.
CANAL BANK, Portland, Me.
1
Indian Princess.

Female seated with shield, eagle, etc., cars, cattle, and sheep in distance
2
Large fig. 2 across note. Washington at top
CANAL BANK Portland, Me. TWO DOLLARS
Head
2
Carpenter at work

Female crowning an eagle, ship in left, cattle, cars, etc. on right.
Male portrait in top of large 3 extending across face of bill.
3
CANAL BANK Portland, Me. THREE DOLLARS
Indian
3
Female portrait

5
Same as ones 5
CANAL BANK, Portland, Me.
5
Female Indian, seated with pole and cap, and shield.

10
Same as ones. X
CANAL BANK, Portland, Me.
10
Female partly nude with pen and tablet; cog wheel on left

20
Same as ones. 20
CANAL BANK, Portland, Me.
XX
Female with sheaf of grain under left arm.
20

50
Same as ones. 50
CANAL BANK. Portland. Me.
50
Female Portrait.
Med. Head.

100
Same as ones. 100
CANAL BANK, Portland, Me.
100
Female erect with sickle and sheaf of wheat

D
Same as ones. 500
CANAL BANK, Portland, Me.
500
Female figure erect, with flag; left hand on a warrior's shield.

☞ All denominations have on the back of the bill, a locomotive and one passenger car; three men and dog.

Block of stores.
1
Female and Merchandise; factory and shipping in background.
CASCO BANK, Portland, Me.
1
Sailor with quadrant, ships in background.

Block of stores.
2
Female and vegetables; river and village in background.
CASCO BANK. Portland, Me.
2
Female.

Block of stores.
THREE
3 Female seated on a bale; steamship and train of cars in background. 3
CASCO BANK. Portland, Me.
Female and Merchandise.
THREE

Boy's Head.
5
Landing of the pilgrims,
CASCO BANK. Portland, Me.
5
Girl's Head.

Three female figures and anchor. TEN	State Arms. Female, cycle, and sheaf of wheat. CASCO BANK, Portland, Me.	10 Portrait of Taylor.
Female with a rose. TWENTY	Family group at supper; Indians looking in at the door; dog barking at them CASCO BANK, Portland, Me. 20 20	20 Male portrait
Female portrait. 50	Signing treaty with the Pilgrims. CASCO BANK, Portland, Me. FIFTY	50 Male portrait
100	Marine view—large steamship; city in background. CASCO BANK, Portland, Me. HUNDRED	100 Male portrait
Female Portrait. 500	CASCO BANK, Portland, Me. Hunter with gun overlooking rock; female behind him. D D FIVE HUNDRED	500 Male portrait
M	Wharf scene—steamboats, men on dock, horses, drays, men at work; city in background. Male portrait. CASCO BANK, Portland, Me. 1000	1000 Sailor boy; two sailors in distance; ship seen in offing.
ONE Brig	Sailor reclining, anchor, capstan, cordage, &c; ship, brig and sloop in the distance, CITY BANK, Bath, Me.	1 ONE State Arms. ONE
2	Train of cars, factories in distance. CITY BANK, Bath, Me.	TWO Sailor on rail of ship, spy glass in hand
3 State Arms. 3	Ship and steamship in full sail; schooner in distance. CITY BANK, Bath, Me.	3 THREE 3
5	Ship-yard—Ships building. Shield dog, and safe; anchor on left; fact'ies in distance. CITY BANK, Bath, Me.	5 FIVE

Goddess of liberty, shield, eagle, &c.	10 Men seated, anvil, boxes; train of cars, hills, lake, buildings, &c. CITY BANK, Bath, Me.	10 Portrait of female.
	20 CITY BANK, Bath, Me. Sailor, two girls, anchor, cog-wheels, bbls, &c., tall chimney, hills and town, near shore of lake, light-house, &c.	20 Stream trees &c.; woman & child bathing.
50 Men load of hay, hills in distance.	CITY BANK, Bath, Me. Three females; on left town and hills, bridge; train of cars going out.	50 Ship and brig; city in distance.
Female erect holding oval portrait, in left hand a winged wand	100 CITY BANK Bath, Me. Signing declaration of independence.	100
ONE Female feeding fowls.	ONE on fig. 1. CITY BANK, Biddeford, Me. Cherub rolling silver dollar; cars and bridge in distance.	ONE on fig. 1 Female and figure 1.
TWO Female with flowers	Boot and shoe manufactory; men at work. CITY BANK, Biddeford, Me.	2 Santa Claus.
3 Washington	View of U. S. Capitol. CITY BANK, Biddeford, Me.	THREE on 3. Female seated by shield and fig. 3.
5 Portrait of a female.	CITY BANK, Biddeford, Me. Five cherubs and five silver dollars.	5 Sailor with quadrant; globe, bales, &c.
X State Arms. Sailor and farmer.	CITY BANK, Biddeford, Me. Nine cherubs, ten gold dollars, female, shield and cornucopia.	10 Portrait of a female.
20 Two children	Cattle, sheep, horse, dog and two men. CITY BANK, Biddeford, Me.	XX Female representing Agriculture.

Fountain 50	CITY BANK, Biddeford, Me. Three female representing Agriculture, Commerce and Manufactures; ship in distance.	50 Female churning.
C Female portrait.	CITY BANK, Biddeford, Me. Large spread eagle.	C Female portrait. C
	COBBOSSEECONTEE BANK, Gardiner, Me. This Bank uses the old Perkins Stereotype Plate, which has the denomination printed in fine letters all over the bill.	
1 Indian female seated, with shield, &c.	Vig. Farmer and sailor on either side of a shield on which is a deer and tree; on right, ships; on left, mill, &c. EASTERN BANK, Bangor, Me. Spread eagle.	1 Female seated with pen and tablet.
2 Female portrait.	Vig. Farmer and sailor on either side of a shield on which is a deer and tree; on right, ships; on left, mill, &c. EASTERN BANK, Bangor, Me. Spread Eagle.	2 Female portrait.
3 Mechanic seated with mallet and chisel in right and left hand.	Vig. Farmer and sailor on either side of a shield on which is a deer and tree; on right, ships; on left, mill, &c. EASTERN BANK. Bangor, Me. Spread eagle.	3 3
5 Spread eagle	Vig. Female leaning on anchor, merchandize, &c.; on right, sloop of war; on left, city, vessels, &c. EASTERN BANK. Bangor, Me. Horse.	5 Steamboat.
10 Portrait of Washington	Vig. Spread eagle, ships, &c. EASTERN BANK, Bangor, Me. Dog, key and safe.	10 Two females seated, one with scales and sword.
Female with sheaf of grain. TWENTY	Vig. Spread eagle on rocks; man-of-war on right, brig on left, EASTERN BANK, Bangor, Me. Female seated, ship, &c.	20
50 Medallion Head.	Female reclining, shield, cage, cornucopia, liberty, pole and cap, &c. EASTERN BANK. Bangor, Me. Agricultural implements.	50 Medallion head.

Left end	Centre	Right end
100 Female portrait.	Vig. Female seated; on right men loading wagon with hay; ship, steamboat, &c. EASTERN BANK Bangor, Me. Head of Indian.	100 Female Indian princess
1 Female Portrait. 1	Two farmers, one seated, apparently eating, the other smoking and holding a jug. FARMERS BANK, Bangor, Me.	1 Train of cars
ONE Female resting arm on fence. ONE	FARMERS' BANK. Bangor, Me. Has the denomination in small words and letters all over the middle part of the bill.	1 ONE 1
2 Ships, &c.	Man ploughing; village on right; on left steamboat in distance. FARMER'S BANK, Bangor, Me Bee-Hive	2 Female Portrait.
2 Man, horses, carts, buildings, etc. TWO	Title of Bank. Has the denomination same as ones.	2 TWO 2
3 Large figure 3, and three Cupids	Cattle and sheep, two cows standing in water. FARMER'S BANK, Bangor, Me. Agricultural Implements.	3 Female seated with flowers
FIVE Vessel; name Gold Hunter on sail. FIVE	Title of Bank. Has the denomination same as ones.	5 FIVE 5
5 Large figure 5, & female.	Drove of cattle and hogs, two men on horseback; train of cars, village &c., in background FARMER'S BANK, Bangor, Me. Locomotive.	5 Ship, steamer; lighthouse, &c., in distance.
TEN Vessel on stocks.	Title of Bank. Has the denomination	10 TEN

Left end	Centre	Right end
	FARMERS' BANK, Bangor, Me. Use Perkin's stereotype plate for 20s, 50s, 100s and 500s which have the denomination printed in fine letters all over the surface of the bill.	
20 Female with scales and sword; eagle, key & safe.	Female sitting with arms extended, scales in right hand, cap & pole in left; naked boy on one side and one partially draped on the other. FARMER'S BANK, Bangor, Me. Steamship.	20 Female with sheaf of wheat.
50 Female with sickle. 50	Two females seated with pieces of machinery, factories on right; ship in distance on the left. FARMER'S BANK, Bangor, Me. Engine & Tender.	50 Farmer gathering corn.
100 Sailor supporting a flag staff.	FARMER'S BANK Bangor, Me Female reclining with One Cupid Hundred scattering fruits over a city in foreground. Machines.	100 Portrait of female. 100
500 Female with bow & quiver surrounded by Coat of Arms of the different States.	FARMER'S BANK, Bangor, Me. Three females one seated the others reclining; train of cars & ship in the distance. Eagle.	500 500
	FREEMEN'S BANK, Augusta, Me. This Bank uses the old Perkins' Stereotype Plate, which has the denomination printed in fine letters all over the bill.	
ONE	Vig. Sailing vessels. 1 FRONTIER BANK, Eastport, Me.	ONE Female. ONE
2	Vig. Persons engaged with sheep; shrubbery and houses in the background; large figure "2" across the note and miniature view of four persons. FRONTIER BANK, Eastport, Me.	TWO Miniature view of female. TWO
	Vig. Farmers, farming implements, cattle, &c.; vig. on upper left corner. 3	Figure 3 and word Three. Miniature of Female.

Left end	Centre	Right end
X Indian with bow and arrow.	Vig. Steamboat, sail-vessels, &c. X FRONTIER BANK, Eastport, Me.	10 Female with sheaf of grain; forest in background.
20 Miniature view of female.	XX Vig. Spread eagle. XX FRONTIER BANK, Eastport, Me.	20 Shipping.
FIFTY Female standing erect. FIFTY	50 Vig. Man holding wild horse. 50 FRONTIER BANK. Eastport, Me.	Same as on opposite end.
Figure "100," with word "ONE HUNDRED" across. Male portrait.	Vig. Large covered wagon; horses, persons, &c.; shipping in background. FRONTIER BANK, Eastport, Me.	Figure "100," with word "ONE HUNDRED" across. Portrait of Columbus.
1	Female under sail; steamboat, &c. 1 GARDINER BANK, Gardiner, Me.	1 Man and sheep.
Cupid and female either side of shield on which is a res. Engine steamer, etc., in distance. 2	Circular die on which is ship on large figure 2 GARDINER BANK TWO DOLLARS Gardiner, Me.	2 Ship
3	Train of Cars, &c. 3 GARDINER BANK, Gardiner, Me	3 Female. THREE
	This Bank has also the Perkin's Stereotype Plate for all denominations except 500s.	
20	2 Female. 0	20 Female.

100 | Spread eagle; train of cars, canal, &c., in back ground. | 100
Vulcan | GARDINER BANK, Gardiner, Me. 100 | Female seated

Indians in canoe, trees and mountainous scenery in background. 500 | 500
500 | GARDINER BANK, Gardiner, Me. | Female holding scales.

---

1 | ONE DOLLAR 1 Female seated; ship in distance 1 | 1
Bale, ships, etc. | GEORGE'S BANK ONE DOLLAR | Agricultu'l implements
1 | Thomaston STATE OF MAINE | 1

Female seated; train of cars and canal in distance. | Large figure 1, and five male figures. | 1
1 | GEORGE'S BANK, Thomaston, Me. | Female and sheaf.

---

2 | TWO DOLLARS 2 Female seated beside shield on which is fig. 2 2 | 2
Officer on horse | GEORGE'S BANK TWO DOLLARS | Officer on horse
2 | Thomaston STATE OF MAINE | 2

Farmers washing sheep. | Large figure 2, and five male figures. | TWO
| | Female with wreath.
2 | GEORGE'S BANK, Thomaston, Me. | TWO

---

3 | THREE DOLLARS Female seated beside shield on which is fig. 3 3 | 3
Child's head. | GEORGE'S BANK THREE DOLLARS | Child's head
3 | Thomaston STATE OF MAINE | 3

Farmers and cattle; load of hay, &c. | 3 | The word three and figure 3.
| | Female with basket of flowers.
3 | GEORGE'S BANK, Thomaston, Me. | THREE

Female with rake and sickle, various emblems representing Commerce, Agriculture, Mechanic Arts &c. | F and Indian female. | 5
FI 5 VE | GEORGE'S BANK, Thomaston, Me. | Head of Washington

X | Steamboat and vessels. X | 10
Indian with bow. | GEORGE'S BANK, Thomaston, Me. | Female with sheaf of grain.

---

20 | 2 Female. 0 | 20
| GEORGE'S BANK, Thomaston, Me. | Female seated with horn of plenty, &c.
Minerva. | XX | 20

---

50 | Female with rake, and male with sledge. | 50
Female with spear. | GEORGE'S BANK, Thomaston, Me. | Cupid in sail boat.
| 50 | 50

---

100 | Spread eagle; train of cars and canal in distance. | 100
Male with sledge. | GEORGE'S BANK, Thomaston, Me. | Female with rake, &c.
| C 100 C |

GRANITE BANK. Augusta, Me. This Bank uses the old Perkin's Stereotype plate, which has the denomination printed in fine letters all over the bill.

---

1 | Ships under sail. | 1
Sailor, quadrant, capstan, etc. | INTERNATIONAL BANK, Portland, Me. |

---

2 | Female on bales of cotton; factory and farm in distance. | 2
| Title of Bank. | Cooper among barrels
Boy 's head | |

---

3 | Title of Bank. | 3
| Scene on sea-shore; sailor, anchor, boat, etc. | Eagle on shield.
State Arms. | |

---

5 | Railroad depot—cars leaving, etc. 5 | 5
| Title of Bank. | Five figures, male and female and large V.
5 | |

---

10 | Eagle. Sailor and mechanic seated, with State arms between; steamboat, wharf, factories. | X
Female, ship and pillar. | Title of Bank. |

Female head | INTERNATIONAL BANK, Portland, Me. | 20
20 | Man plowing with two horses; house, etc. | Female with flowers.

| Title of Bank. | 50
| Steamship and other vessels. |
FIFTY | | Girl's head.

| Three females and cupid in water. | 100
100 | Title of Bank. | Anchor, barrels, bales, etc.

D | INTERNATION'L BK Portland, Me. | 500
| Three females; shield; one crowning bust. |
Five Hun Dollars | dred Five | Hundred Dollars

Liberty with pole and cap resting on column on which is 1000. | M Washington | 1000
| INTERNATION'L BK Portland, Me. |

---

1 | Brig under sail. Spread eagle. Ship at anchor. | 1
General Taylor. | KENDUSKEAG BK. Bangor, Me, Bee Hive. | Female seated and supporting figure 1.

---

2 | Head of Harshall. Head of Clay. Ship under full sail. | 2
Female seated with pole and cap. | KENDUSKEAG BK. Bangor, Me. Horse. | Female seated.

---

3 | Female Dog & ir- Female portrait on chest portrait | 3
Female portrait. | KENDUSKEAG BK. Bangor, Me. Steamer. | Harrison.

FIVE | Head of Columbus. Figure in the air with horn of flowers. Portrait of Franklin | 5 FI 5 VE 5
Male and female. | KENDUSKEAG BK. Bangor, Me. Vessel. |
5 | |

---

10 | Female seated. Loading hay, two men, oxen &c. cart; in distance train of cars. 10 | TEN
Washington. | KENDUSKEAG BK. Bangor, Me. Eagle. | Female with sickle.

---

50 | KENDUSKEAG BK., Bangor, Me. Eagle and globe; female seated on right and Indian on left. | 50
Vulcan with sledge, anvil &c. | 50 |

Left end	Centre	Right end
100 Portrait of La Fayette. 100	100 KENDUSKEAG BK. Bangor, Me. Female seated, a child and sitting at her feet—plough, sheaf, &c. [illegible]	
Female figure holding scales of Justice. 1	Drove of cattle and sheep with man on horseback. LEWISTON FALLS BANK. Lewiston, Me.	1 Dairy maid churning.
TWO Cameos right	Vig. Female feeding an eagle; horn of plenty in foreground; ship in the distance. LEWISTON FALLS BANK. Lewiston, Me.	TWO Cupid, fig. 2, female erect supporting 2
3	View of Lewiston Falls on the Androscoggin river. LEWISTON FALLS BANK. Lewiston, Me.	3 Female and 3
5 Large V, with five male and female figures in and around it.	Vig. Ornamental figure 5, with five female figures around it; ship, steamer, locomotive, and factories in the distance. LEWISTON FALLS BANK. Lewiston, Me.	5 Large figure 5, with five male and female figures in and around it.
X	View of Lewiston Falls on the Androscoggin river. LEWISTON FALLS BANK. Lewiston, Me.	10 Cotton mill.
Fountain. XX	Vig. Spread eagle and shield; steam ship and building in distance. LEWISTON FALLS BANK. Lewiston, Me.	20 Head of Female.
Goddess of Liberty feeding an eagle. 50	Vig. Female resting on cotton bale, and linen wheel in foreground; manufacturing village in distance. LEWISTON FALLS BANK. Lewiston, Me.	50 Female, globe, shield, and Declaration of Independence.
Female worker at labor. 100	Vig. National capitol. LEWISTON FALLS BANK, Lewiston, Me.	100 Cupid and dolphin.
ONE 1	Farmer ploughing and farmer sowing; trees, &c. 1 LIME ROCK BANK, East Thomaston, Me.	1 Ship. ONE

Left end	Centre	Right end
TWO 2	Spread eagle on rock; train of cars on left in distance. 2 LIME ROCK BANK, East Thomaston, Me.	2 TWO Schooner.
THREE 3	Sailor, bales, casks, &c.; wharves, drays, &c., on right, and on left vessels, warehouses, &c. 3 LIME ROCK BANK, East Thomaston, Me. Medallion. Medallion	3 THREE Train of cars.
5 Ship on stocks, water and skiff. 5	Head of female. Lime shed and kilns; quarry on right, with casks and cooper, on left horse, man, vessel, &c. Head of child. LIME ROCK BANK, East Thomaston, Me.	5 Steamship. 5
5 Female seated; top sails of vessel in background.	State Arms. LIME ROCK BANK, East Thomaston, Me. Safe, dog, and key.	5 Female
TEN Steamer and ship. TEN	Farmer with team; house in distance. State Arms. Beehive and flowers. LIME ROCK BANK, East Thomaston, Me.	10 Farmer with rake and jug; load of grain, house, &c. 10
10 Justice with sword and scales; spread eagle on a safe.	Ship under full sail at sea. Large X, with ten dollars on both stems. LIME ROCK BANK, East Thomaston, Me.	Medallion head of female.
20 Female in partly nude state seated; safe, &c.	XX Eagle. XX LIME ROCK BANK, East Thomaston, Me.	20 Ship.
FIFTY Full length female, with wreath on head. FIFTY	50 Man and horse. 50 LIME ROCK BANK. East Thomaston. Me.	FIFTY Full length female. FIFTY
Same as on right. Bust of Male.	Wharf scene, wagon, men loading dray, vessels, &c. LIME ROCK BANK, East Thomaston, Me.	The words one hundred across figure 100. Male portrait.
Train of cars; horse on right. 1	LINCOLN BANK Bath, Me.	1 Man in his shirt sleeves, with tools at his feet.

Left end	Centre	Right end
Man ploughing with two horses; train of cars on the right. 2	Large figure 2 and a child. LINCOLN BANK, Bath, Me.	2 Female reclining.
Steamship; ships lying too. 3	LINCOLN BANK, Bath, Me.	3 Ship under full sail.
5	Schooner lying too; ship and brig. Large V, female and Cupid. LINCOLN BANK, Bath, Me.	5 Female with basket of flowers.
TEN Ship under full sail. TEN	Pilot boat, steamboat, shipping and a small boat with four men in it. LINCOLN BANK, Bath, Me.	10 Large X and a female.
XX Steamship.	Depot with engine and tender, man with wheelbarrow, steamboat at wharf, and also boat with two men. LINCOLN BANK, Bath, Me.	20 Ship under full sail.
50 Steamboat and pilot boat.	Farm house and out buildings, load of hay, two persons on top; man with rake in right hand, pail in left. LINCOLN BANK. Bath, Me.	L Female with sword in right hand.
100 Eagle. 100	C Neptune in car drawn by three horses 100 LINCOLN BANK. Bath, Me.	C Head of Washington. C
1	Female, cars, &c. 1 LONG REACH BANK Bath, Me.	1 Female.
2	Man washing sheep. 2 LONG REACH BANK, Bath, Me.	TWO Female. TWO
3	Scene in a farm yard. 3 LONG REACH BANK Bath, Me.	THREE Female with basket of flowers. THREE

F I V V E	FIVE Female with rake, grain, machinery, &c. Female Indian seated in V. LONG REACH BANK Bath, Me.	5 Washington

X	Signing Declaration of Independence. X LONG REACH BANK Bath, Me.	10 Cars, man, buildings, etc.

FIFTY Grain and fruit. 50	50 Three fem[illegible] anvil, ship, etc. LONG REACH B'K, Bath, Me.	FIFTY on 50 Man seated; anvil, hammer, etc.

C Boat at rocky landing; another in distance. C	Eagle on bale of goods; anchor, sheaf, horn of plenty, etc. 100 LONG REACH B'K, Bath, Maine.	100 Female with sickle in her hand. 10[illegible]

500 Old man with musket; boy with a gun.	500 Scene in Shipyard. LONG REACH B'K, Maine.	500 500

The word "one" and two cupids. Bust of a Female.	Shield—Indian seated on left and woodchopper on right. LUMBERMAN'S B'K, Old Town, Me. Dog.	1 Female seated with pole and cap.

TWO Bust of a Female.	Spread eagle; ships in the distance. 2 LUMBERMAN'S B'K, Old Town, Me. Agricultural implements.	TWO Sailor. Female seated.

3 Female erect surrounded with wreath with names of the States.	Neptune with sea-car, &c. LUMBERMAN'S B'K, Old Town, Me. Horn of Plenty, safe and key.	3 Large 3, sailor, mechanic, and farmer. THREE

FIVE Large figure 5, female seated, and portrait of Washington. FIVE	Milk-maid and cows. LUMBERMAN'S B'K, Old Town, Me. Horn of Plenty and anvil.	5 FIVE FIVE

Vulcan, with sledge and anvil; train of cars in distance. TEN	X LUMBERMAN'S B'K, Old Town, Me.	10 Man erect, with sickle and sheaf of wheat.

20 Female seated.	XX Spread Eagle. XX LUMBERMAN'S B'K, Old Town, Me.	20 Ship.

FIFTY. Female with wreath. FIFTY	50 Man and horse 50 LUMBERMAN'S B'K, Old Town, Me.	FIFTY. Female. FIFTY.

100 Eagle. 100	C Wild horses and chariot. 100 LUMBERMAN'S B'K, Old Town, Me.	C Washington. C

ONE Men catching cattle	1 Boy on horseback, horse, colt, sheep, cows, etc. MAINE BANK, Brunswick, Me.	1 1

TWO 2	Santa Claus in sleigh drawn by reindeers over roofs of houses. 2 MAINE BANK, Brunswick, Me.	TWO Cattle, hogs, sheep, etc.

Farmer drinking; woman and child; load of grain; farmers mowing; cars, crossing bridge, etc.	THREE MAINE BANK, Brunswick, Me. 3	3 DOLLARS Three on 3.

FIVE Franklin FIVE	MAINE BANK. FIVE 5 FIVE DOLLARS Brunswick, State of Maine.	5 Female seated on bale with quadrant, etc., vessels, etc. in distance.

Male portrait X	Ship yard scene; city in distance. MAINE BANK, Brunswick, Me.	10 Male portrait

20 Washington.	Female either side of anvil; building in distance. Title of Bank.	20 Sailor and farmer either side of shield on which is a deer and tree.

FIFTY Agricultural products. 50	50 Three females seated; eagle, shield, vessel, etc. Title of Bank.	Fifty on 50. Vulcan seated; cars, buildings, etc., in distance.

C Men and boats. 100	Eagle on bale; products, etc. 100 Title of Bank.	100 Female with sickle and sheaf. 100

ONE 1	Agricultural scene; farmer sowing; another in the distance harrowing. 1 MANUFACTURERS BANK, Saco, Me.	1 Ship. ONE

TWO 2	Spread eagle; iron castings, cannon balls, machinery, &c. 2 Title of Bank.	2 TWO Schooner rigged boat.

THREE 3	Sailor; hat in hand, reclining against bales; in the distance are vessels, warehouses, dray, horses &c 3 Title of Bank.	3 THREE Train of cars.

FIVE	Female resting upon her left knee, lifting veil from figure 5. Title of Bank,	5 Ship.

Female seated, holding rake in left hand and sickle in right, ships, buildings &c. in backgro'd.	Large V and Indian. Title of Bank.	5 Portrait of Washington.

10 X 10	Vig. Man with oxen. 10 Title of Bank.	TEN Female figure with cornucopia of fruits and flowers.

20 Female.	XX Eagle. XX Title of Bank.	20 Ship sailing.

FIFTY Female. FIFTY	50 Man and horse 50 Title of Bank.	FIFTY Female. FIFTY

Words one hundred and figures 100 Male portrait.	Vig. Market scene; shipping on left. Title of Bank.	Words one hundred, and figures 100. Male portrait.

Left	Centre	Right
Female seated, men loading hay in distance. 500	500 D Title of Bank.	500
1	Interior of an iron foundry; six men at work, pouring metal, &c. 1 MAN. and TRADERS BANK. Portland. Me.	Word ONE and fig. 1. Portrait of sailor.
1 Washington	Female. 1 Female. MAN. & TRADERS' BANK, Portland. Me.	1 Portrait.
ONE	Water scene, ships, &c. 1 MAN. & TRADERS' BANK, Portland. Me	ONE Female. ONE
2 2	Shield with bull's head thereon; on left female binding shoes; on right men dressing leather; safe, &c. Figure 2 and State Arms Title of Bank.	TWO Sailor seated on ship railing with spy glass
2 TWO 2	Water scene, ships, &c. 2 MAN. & TRADERS' BANK, Portland, Me.	TWO Female. TWO
2 Portrait.	[illegible] with cornucopia. 2 [illegible] with balances MAN. & TRADERS' BANK, Portland Me	2 Portrait
THREE	Female with hat in hand, man reaping and another carrying grain. 3 MAN. & TRADERS' BANK, Portland, Me.	THREE Ship. The word three and figure 3
THREE Figure 3 and portrait of Webster within.	MAN. and TRADERS' BANK. Portland, Me. Portrait of Washington; on either side female, on right train of cars, on left men at work, side steamer &c.	Word THREE and figure 3. Male portrait
3 Washington and his horse.	Portrait of Female. 3 Portrait of Female MAN. & TRADERS' BANK. Portland, Me.	3 Black-smith, anvil &c.

Left	Centre	Right
FIVE	Female, &c. V MAN. & TRADERS' BANK, Portland, Me	5 Ship.
Spread eagle. FIVE	Female with sceptre and horn of plenty, figure 5 and angel. MAN. & TRADERS' BANK, Portland, Me.	5 Female with hat and wreath in hands.
5 Female portrait.	MAN. & TRA. BANK. Portland, Me. Large letter V, and words FIVE DOLLARS	5 Portrait of Girl.
10 Female. TEN	MAN. & TRA. BANK. Portland, Me. Letter X, and word Ten, shipping on right; haycart trees, city and bridge on left.	10 Female. TEN
10 X 10	[illegible] 10 MAN. & TRADERS BANK, Portland. Me	TEN Female with horn of plenty, &c.
TEN	Blacksmith seated, sledge in right hand resting on anvil; block and wheel behind him. X MAN. & TRADERS' BANK, Portland. Me.	10 Farmer with sheaf of grain and sickle.
Steamship and other vessels; city in distance, factories on right XX	STATE OF MAINE MAN. & TRA. BANK Portland TWENTY	20 Female with grain in left hand, sickle in right
TWENTY Female seated.	XX Eagle. XX MAN. & TRADERS' BANK, Portland, Me.	20 Ship.
50 Washington	[illegible] MAINE 50 Steamship and other vessels MAN. & TRA. BANK FIFTY DOLLARS L Portland L Eagle	Sailor and mechanic; the former standing with flag, the latter seated with hammer in hand
FIFTY – Female. FIFTY	50 Man and horse. 50 MAN. & TRADERS' BANK, Portland, Me	FIFTY Female. FIFTY

Left	Centre	Right
100 Indian kneeling with bow in right hand	MAN. & TRA. BANK Train of cars running to the right, sailboat on right; factories in distance C	100 Sailor
The words one hundred and figures 100. Harrison.	Wharf scene, market wagon, drays, horses, men, vessels, &c. MAN. & TRADERS' BANK, Portland, Me.	Same as on left. Columbus.
500	Indian paddling in canoe; mountain, &c. 500 MAN. and TRADERS' BANK. Portland, Me D D	500 Female figure holding sword and scales.
1 Webster	Ships on the stocks. MARINE BANK Damariscotta, Me. Eagle.	1 Sailor.
2 Female	MARINE BANK Damariscotta. Me. Ship under full sail, and a small steamship.	2 Franklin.
3 Sailor with quadrant; small ship	Spread eagle; ship on right, and ship on left MARINE BANK Damariscotta. Me. Indian head.	3 Female with spy-glass
5 Washington.	John Adams Spread Eagle Jefferson MARINE BANK, Damariscotta. Me. Steamer.	5 Ship under sail
Indian and female; globe surmounted by an eagle between; State arms underneath. 10	Portrait of Jackson 10 MARINE BANK, Damariscotta, Me. Sloop.	Female. 10
20 Figure of Justice.	Female with extended arms; Cupid on either side. MARINE BANK, Damariscotta, Me. Steamship.	20 Female with sheaf of grain.
50 Female. 50	Two females seated; ship on right, and on left is rail cars and buildings MARINE BANK, Damariscotta, Me, Locomotive.	50 Boy gathering corn.

100
Sailor with American flag.
MARINE BANK,
Damariscotta, Me.
100
ONE Fe. HUNDRED male with Cupid.
Cog Wheels.
Female.

Female portrait.
1
MARKET BANK,
Cupid rolling silver dollar on railroad track; cars, steamboat and city in distance.
Bangor, Me.
Cow and calf.
1
Female Indian seated.

Female reclining with scales in right hand.
2
Two cupids and two silver dollars; cupids apparently in an engagement; train of cars, cattle, bulls, city, &c. in distance.
MARKET BANK,
Bangor, Me.
Two horses.
2
Bull's head.

THREE
Female seated, fruits, &c.
Three cupids and three silver dollars, all engaged at some art.
MARKET BANK,
Bangor, Me.
3
3

5
Cattle.
5
Five silver dollars and five cupids.
MARKET BANK,
Bangor, Me.
Man plowing with two horses;
5
Cattle; men seen on right.

Female feeding horse.
X
Two men, horse, dog and drove of cattle and sheep.
MARKET BANK,
Bangor, Me.
10
Boy's head.

Female portrait.
20
Drove of cattle and sheep; man on horseback.
MARKET BANK,
Bangor, Me.
20
Female churning.

50
State arms.
Female seated; barrels, bales, anchor, &c.; steamship on right, and ship on left.
MARKET BANK,
Bangor, Me.
50
Sailor with left hand on capstan; masts, blocks, &c.

Ornamental fountain.
C
Female reclining on safe [illegible] bales, cows, hay, stack, on right; train of cars, vessel, buildings, &c. on left.
MARKET BANK,
Bangor, Me.
100
State arms.

ONE
Female with sheaf.
ONE
State Arms, female and ship.
MECHANICS BANK,
Portland, Me.
Steamer.
1
Henry Clay.

2
Cupids.
Three Graces.
MECHANICS' BANK,
Portland, Me.
Plough and sheaf.
2
Female balancing scales.

THREE
Fame seated on a plate blowing trumpet.
Eagle, with steamers and ships in distance.
MECHANICS' BANK,
Portland, Me.
Dog, key and safe.
3
Girl playing a lute.

5
Female with trident.
5
Steamship.
MECHANICS' BANK,
Portland, Me.
Locomotive.
5
Female portrait.

10
Portrait of Washington.
Train of cars.
MECHANICS' BANK,
Portland, Me.
Eagle.
10
Female Indian, shield and liberty cap.

20 Cupids
Fame blowing trumpet; eagle and globe.
MECHANICS' BANK,
Portland, Me.
Steamship.
20
Roman female.

50
Sailor with flag.
Female Indian, eagle and flag.
MECHANICS' BANK,
Portland, Me.
Plough.
50
Portrait of female.

Eagle.
100
Female portrait.
MECHANICS' BANK,
Portland, Me.
Locomotive.
100
Sloop, &c.

Portrait of Franklin.
500
State Arms; two females, horse's head, &c.
MECHANICS' BANK,
Portland, Me.
500
Portrait of female.

ONE
Bust of male
ONE
Interior of a blacksmiths' shop; two men at work at [illegible] forge, &c.
MEDOMAK BANK,
Waldoboro, Me.
1
ONE
Female.
ONE

1
Female
Bull's head on shield; on right men dressing leather; on left female sewing shoes.
MEDOMAK BANK,
Waldoboro, Me.
Incorporated in 18.6.
ONE on 1.
Female.

1
Female seated; train of cars, sheep, and steam boat on right; on left canal, lock, &c.
Large 1, and five men.
MEDOMAK BANK,
Waldoboro, Me.
1
Female leaning head on her hand.

1
Male portrait.
Portrait of female; on left female and farming scene; on right female, bale, barrel, steamboat.
Title of Bank.
Incorporated in 18.6.
1
ONE
Female with a rake.

2
Female reaper.
Scene in an Iron Mill; men at work.
Title of Bank.
Incorporated in 1836.
2
Female with cornucopia.

2
Man and two boys; two sheep in water; drove on left, and buildings on right.
Large 2 and five men.
MEDOMAK BANK,
Waldoboro, Me.
TWO
Female seated.
TWO

TWO
Female.
2
2
Harvest scene; two men seated, one handing female drink; loading hay in background.
2
MEDOMAK BANK,
Waldoboro, Me.
TWO
Female.
2

Word Three and fig.
Girl.
Sailing scene—men, women and children on raft.
Title of Bank.
Incorporated in 1836.
3 on Dollars.
Female.

3
Man on horseback, cattle, dog, and man; load of hay entering barn, likewise three men; in distance city.
MEDOMAK BANK,
Waldoboro, Me.
3
Word three and figure 3.
Female erect with basket of flowers.
THREE

THREE
Farmer sharpening scythe.
Word Three, and figure 3.
3
Female seated, entwining wreath around eagles' neck; flowers, fruits, &c.
3
MEDOMAK BANK,
Waldoboro, Me.
THREE
Sailor with hat in hand horse and cart; ships, &c.
Word three, and figure 3.

Word five, letter V, and figure 5.
Female seated, right arm on shield; left hand pointing.
Train of cars; buildings, sloop, &c.
MEDOMAK BANK,
Waldoboro, Me.
Incorporated in 18.6.
5
Ship; steam boat on left.

FIVE
Portrait of Webster.
MEDOMAK BANK,
Waldoboro, Me.
Three females in clouds; one with quadrant; the middle one with sickle.
Incorporated in 18.6.
5
Female leaning on railing.

10 · Female portrait. · State arms on shield; Indian, squaw and papoose on right; female and three children on left, with globe, &c. · MEDOMAK BANK, Waldoboro', Me. · Same as fives. · 10 · Female portrait.

20 · Jenny Lind. · TWENTY · Steamship and ship; men in boat, view of New York City and Governor's Island. · MEDOMAK BANK, Waldoboro', Me. · Same as fives. · 20 · Female portrait.

50 · Female seated with sheaf and sickle; train of cars in distance on bridge. · State arms surmounted by an eagle; sailor and ship on right; Indian and hats on left. · MEDOMAK BANK, Waldoboro', Me. · 50 · Female portrait.

100 · Female with sheaf and sickle. · MEDOMAK BANK, Waldoboro', Me. · Female reclining, at her back eagle, city, train of cars, harvesting, &c., on left. · 100 · Incorporated in 1836.

Medallion head. · 1 · Winged female blowing a trumpet · Spread Eagle. · MERCANTILE BK. Bangor, Maine. · 1 · Sailor with spyglass in hand.

TWO · Female blowing trumpet, seated on globe, on which is fig 2 · 2 State Arms of Maine 2. · MERCANTILE B'K · TWO DOLLARS · Bangor, Me. · 2 · Ship. · 2

TWO · State Arms; farmer and sailor either side; ship, etc. · MERCANTILE B'K. Bangor, Maine. · Winged female, &c · 2 · Ship. · 2

3 · Head. · 3 · Eagle, &c. · MERCANTILE BK. Bangor. · 3 · Females; vessels, &c.

FIVE · 5 · State Arms; female either side; city, ship, &c. 5 · MERCANTILE B K, Bangor, Maine. · 5 · Indian squaw.

10 · Steamboat, vessels, &c · X · MERCANTILE B'K, Bangor, Maine. · 10 · Female.

20 · XX · 20 · 20 Female, vessels, goods, &c. 20 · MERCANTILE B'K, Bangor, Maine. · TWENTY

50 · Female, steamboat, &c. · FIFTY DOLLARS and 50 · MERCANTILE B'K, Bangor, Maine. · FIFTY

C · Washington. · C · 100 Man, vessel, &c. 100 · MERCANTILE B'K, Bangor, Maine. · ONE HUNDRED

500 · 500 · 500 · 500 500 · MERCANTILE B'K, Bangor, Maine. · 500 · D · 500

1 · Female, State arms, shipping and rail road. 1 · MERCHANTS' BK. Bangor, Me · ONE · Female supporting figure 1. · ONE

2 · Sailor, merchandise, and shipping. 2 · MERCHANTS' BK., Bangor, Me. · 2 · Portrait of female.

3 · Female, eagle and shield; factory and steamship in the distance. 3 · MERCHANTS' BK., Bangor, Me. · 3 · Sailor.

5 · Female and merchandise. · Large V, female and sheaf of wheat. · MERCHANTS' BK., Bangor, Me · Ship · FIVE · Indian female with bow and arrow

TEN · Farmer, dog and grain. · Female and X on right · MERCHANTS' BK., Bangor, Me. · 10 · Female.

20 · Female with book. · Large Eagle. · MERCHANT'S B'K. · TWENTY. · Bangor Maine. · 20 · Ship under full sail.

20 · Female figure, with spear and globe. · 2 Female. 0 · MERCHANTS' BK. Bangor, Me · XX · 20 · Female. · 20

50 · Female figure. · Male and female seated. · MERCHANTS' BK., Bangor, Me · 50 · 50 · Cupid in a sail-boat. · 50

100 · Vulcan the blacksmith. · Spread eagle standing on a tree; railroad and canal in background. · MERCHANTS' BK., Bangor Me. · 100 · 100 · Female seated.

Sailor seated and holding flag. · 1 · View of the Custom House, Portland. · MERCHANT'S BANK Portland, Me. · 1 · Ship under full sail.

1 · Train of cars crossing a bridge; mountains in the distance; boat on river and three figures in the foreground reclining. · MERCHANT'S BANK Portland, Me. · 1 · Female Portrait.

Figure with shield, pole and cap. · 2 · Spread Eagle; on right, man-of-war, and on left, a brig. · MERCHANT'S BANK Portland, Me. · Locomotive. · 2 · Female gathering flowers, &c.

Goddess of Liberty. · 2 · View of the Portland Custom House. · MERCHANT'S BANK Portland Me. · 2 · Washington and his horse.

3 · Large figure 3, and three Cupids. · Portrait of Daniel Webster; ship, steamship, &c. · MERCHANT'S BANK Portland, Me. · Agricultural Implements. · 3 · Cooper at work.

Portrait of female. · 5 · MERCHANT'S BANK Portland, Me. · View of the Portland Custom House. · FIVE · 5 · Female with basket.

Female reclining on bales of goods; ships, &c., in distance. · 10 · Portrait of female. · MERCHANT'S BANK Portland, Me. · Steamboat. · 10 · Train of cars.

Left end	Centre	Right end
20 Portrait of Fillmore.	Spread Eagle, houses, &c. MERCHANT'S BANK Portland, Me. Indian Head.	20 Portrait of Washington.
50 Female with scales.	MERCHANT'S BANK Portland, Me. Steamship, man-of-war, and brig.	50 Female leaning on a pedestal; harp at her feet.
C 100 C	MERCHANT'S BANK Portland, Me. Female figure holding shield, pole and cap; on right, Capitol at Washington	C 100 C
Agricultural scene; female seated pointing to teapots. 500	500 D MERCHANTS' BK. Portland, Me.	500
ONE Aerial figure and female reclining on the ground.	NEW CASTLE BK., New Castle, Me. ONE DOLLAR	1 Ship under full sail. Ship and steamboat in distance.
2 Eagle standing above the rising sun; female, anchor, &c.	NEW CASTLE BK., New Castle, Me. TWO DOLLARS.	2 Same as ones.
The word three and figure 3. Female seated with sword.	NEW CASTLE BK. New Castle, Me. THREE DOLLARS.	3 Three mechanics; man and two horses in background.
FIVE Five females, liberty cap, &c.	NEW CASTLE BK., New Castle, Me. 5 FIVE 5	FIVE
Letter X and words ten dollars. Female bathing	NEW CASTLE BK., New Castle, Me. Ship building, &c.; men at work.	10 Washington.
XX Signing the Declaration of Independence.	NEW CASTLE BK., New Castle, Me. TWENTY DOLLARS.	20 Washington.

Left end	Centre	Right end
50 Portrait of Jackson.	Ship under full sail; ship, steamer, schooner and boat at left; city on right. NEW CASTLE BK., New Castle, Me. Guinea hens.	50 Two sailors, flag, anchors, &c.
Goddess of Liberty, eagle, shield, pole and cap.	NEW CASTLE BK., New Castle, Me. Spread Eagle. 100	100 State Arms. Three Indians, four white men, globe, &c., house in background.
ONE Female seated. ONE	Cupid & Figure 1 — Cupid & Figure 1 Vig. Female seated, ship on right in distance NORTH BANK. Rockland, Me.	ONE Female. ONE
2	Female seated with Portrait of Washington and eagle; steamer ship &c., on right large building and train of cars on left. 2 NORTH BANK. Rockland, Me.	2 Figure of Justice.
3 Female with wreath and scales; eagle and shield.	Three silver dollars and three Cupids. NORTH BANK, Rockland, Me.	3 Female seated; globe, shield, and "Declaration of Independence"
5	Sailor and Indian with word FIVE between them; two females seated on either side of a frame, surmounted by an eagle; bust between Indian and female, steamer, ship and canal lock in distance. — Five at top of large figure 5 Title of Bank.	5 Female with pole and cap, and shield.
10	Female seated on rocks; three Cupids sporting with sea monster in water. — Large X & male Portrait. NORTH BANK, Rockland, Me.	X Female Portrait.
Farmer about to drink from jug. ONE	1 Corn husking scene in barn. NORTH BERWICK BANK, North Berwick, Me.	1 Female with sewing machine.
2 Female feeding fowls.	Title of Bank. 2 Female milking cow; one reclining; man, ladder, dog, house, etc., on right.	2 Male portrait.
5	Blacksmith shoeing horse; man at anvil — Eagle. 5 Title of Bank.	5 State Arms.

Left end	Centre	Right end
Female seated in chair. TEN	Title of Bank. Two females at work on looms.	10 Male portrait.
Female, with sheaf of wheat. 20	20 — Female portrait. NO. BERWICK BK., Maine.	20 Franklin.
FIFTY Flowers, grain, etc. 50	50 Three females, eagle and ship. NO. BERWICK B'K, Maine.	50 Vulcan.
C Boat, fisherman, rocks, etc. 100	Eagle on bale, flowers, and anchor. 100 NO. BERWICK B'K. Maine.	100 Female. 100
	NORTHERN BANK, Hallowell, Me. This Bank uses the old Perkin's Stereotype plate, which has the denomination printed in fine letters all over the bill.	
ONE	Blacksmith, anvil, and forge. 1 OAKLAND BANK, Gardiner, Me. ONE	ONE
TWO	2 Steamboat. 2 OAKLAND BANK, Gardiner, Me.	TWO
THREE	Interior of an iron foundry. 3 OAKLAND BANK. Gardiner, Me.	THREE
FIVE Mechanic, sailor, and two females; city and harbor in distance.	OAKLAND BANK, Gardiner, Me. 5	FIVE Farmer, two females, and a yoke of oxen.
X and Ten Girl with a sickle.	OAKLAND BANK, Gardiner, Me. Figures 10 across words Ten Dollars.	10 Female with horn of plenty.

Left	Centre	Right
XX Portrait of [illegible]	Figures 20 across words Twenty Dollars, and small figures 20 between words. OAKLAND BANK, Gardiner, Me. [illegible]	XX Sailor
Male, female, two children, and a lamb.	OAKLAND BANK, Gardiner, Me. 50	50 Sailors.
ONE HUNDRED Female with spear and shield	OAKLAND BANK, Gardiner, Me.	100 ONE HUNDRED
Word one, and figure 1.	Ship under full sail; ship, steam-boat and pilot-boat; city in distance. ONE OCEAN BANK, Kennebunk, Me.	1 Female with arm on American shield.
2	OCEAN BANK, Kennebunk, Me. Foundry; workman pouring out heated metal. TWO	2 Ship under full sail; steamboat in distance.
3	OCEAN BANK, Kennebunk, Me. Three persons in boat, one man rowing; female with spy-glass. Word three and figure 3.	3 Blacksmith with hammer sitting; buildings in background.
FIVE 5 FIVE	OCEAN BANK, Kennebunk, Me. State Arms. Ship yard; 2 vessels on stocks.	5 FI V VE 5
10 Tree; load of hay; train of cars on bridge with arches.	OCEAN BANK, Kennebunk, Me. Three females representing arts, agriculture and commerce.	10 Ships; city in background.
TWENTY	OCEAN BANK, Kennebunk, Me. Two male figures standing, one with quadrant; Two females sitting and holding tablet; one with dividers; spinning-wheel and anchor, sea, light-house, mountain and city in background.	TWENTY 20 TWENTY
FIFTY Five female figures, two sitting and three reclining; one with liberty cap and pole.	OCEAN BANK, Kennebunk, Me. L 50 L	50 Man with spy-glass; boy with quadrant.

Left	Centre	Right
Liberty, with cap and pole in left hand; right on Am. shield; eagle.	100 Three female figures, left one representing agriculture, with horn of plenty; middle one with wings, joining hands with first; reaching an apple to third, which has quadrant in one hand OCEAN BANK, Kennebunk, Me.	100
1 Blacksmith seated, implements around him.	Three females reclining and cupid ORONO BANK, Orono, Me.	1 Portrait of General Taylor.
2 Female with basket of flowers.	Female, horn of plenty, shield, eagle, colors, &c.; [illegible] and steam boat in the distance ORONO BANK, Orono, Me.	2 Portrait of Jackson.
3 Indian resting, his gun reclining.	State arms; ships in distance. ORONO BANK, Orono, Me.	3 Portrait of Henry Clay
5 Female seated.	Curved rail road track. Cars in the foreground and in the distance near bridge; also further in the distance, cars going out of sight. ORONO BANK, Orono, Me.	5 Man erect with whip in hand. House and steamer in distance.
10 Same as threes.	Heads of Washington and Franklin in frame; four cupids and X. ORONO BANK, Orono, Me. Steamboat.	10 Portrait of W. H. Seward.
Two winged females holding figures 20, two cupids.	Spread eagle and shield. ORONO BANK, Orono, Me	20 Female with sheaf of wheat.
50 Female in frame with sickle. 50	Two females seated; ship, factory buildings; train of cars crossing bridge. ORONO BANK, Orono, Me. Engine and tender.	50 Boy gathering corn.
100 Sailor seated with flag in hand.	Female and cupid over a city; water and vessels in the distance. ORONO BANK, Orono, Me. Cogwheel and cylinder.	100 Female Portrait. 100
Female and figure 1. One and 1.	Indian seated, holding fig. 1. PEJEPSCOT BANK, Brunswick, Me.	1 Female head

Left	Centre	Right
Two females carrying grain. 2	State Arms with females seated each side. PEJEPSCOT BANK, Brunswick, Me.	2 Female holding a flag with an Indian seated.
Factory. 3	Ships and steamer. PEJEPSCOT BANK, Brunswick, Me.	Three and 3 Head of Indian.
5 Washington.	Signing declaration of Independence. PEJEPSCOT BANK. Brunswick, Me.	5 Female head
X Head of Indian.	Capitol at Washington. PEJEPSCOT BANK. Brunswick, Me	10 Indian [illegible]
Female head XX	Capitol at Washington PEJEPSCOT BANK, Brunswick, Me.	20 Indian's [illegible]
50 Sailor standing with cap in hand.	Vessels and steamer. PEJEPSCOT BANK, Brunswick, Me.	50 Webster.
C Female seated beside a basket holding sheaf of grain.	Engine, Depot and cars. PEJEPSCOT BANK, Brunswick, Me.	100 100
500	Indian paddling canoe. 500 PEJEPSCOT BANK, Brunswick, Me. D D	500 Female holding scales.
Reaper. 1	Female reclining; milkmaids, cows, factories, shipping, locomotive, &c., in background. PEOPLES' BANK, Waterville, Me.	1 Female in kneeling posture.
Two females. 2	Female, merchandise and shipping. PEOPLES' BANK, Waterville, Me.	2 Female.

MAINE.	MAINE.	MAINE.
State Arms, reaper and sailor. 3 | Milkmaid and cows. PEOPLES' BANK, Waterville, Me. Loading hay | 3 Female sitting on a plow, with eagle and sheaf of wheat.	10 Male portrait | Milkmaid and cows. Title of Bank. | 10 Female.	Female feeding an eagle from a cup. 50 | Shipping and merchandise; female seated on a bale. ROCKLAND BANK. Rockland, Me. | 50 Ship; city in distance.
Female feeding an eagle from a cup. 5 | Indian sitting upon the ground, by the side of a slain deer. PEOPLES' BANK, Waterville, Me. | 5 Five female figures and figure 5.	Sailor, anchor, etc. FIFTY | Steamship. Title of Bank. | 50 Female holding a spy-glass.	100 | Female sitting on the ground; merchandise and shipping in the background. ROCKLAND BANK, Rockland, Me. | 100 Blacksmith, anvil and forge.
Farmer sharpening a scythe. 10 | Scene at a railroad station. PEOPLES' BANK, Waterville, Me. | X Female and ten gold dollars.	100 Female. | Title of Bank. Male. C Female. | 100 Portrait.	Female, cars, etc. 1 | 1 SAGADAHOCK BK., Bath, Me. | 1 Female.
20 Reaper and milkmaid. 20 | Cattle and sheep. PEOPLES' BANK, Waterville, Me. | 20 Indian woman.	ONE | Female sitting on the ground, supporting a figure 1; steamboat and train of cars in background. 1 ROCKLAND BANK, Rockland, Me. | 1 Portrait of a female.	Men washing sheep. 2 | 2 Title of Bank. | TWO Female. TWO
Female portrait. 50 | Three females representing Agriculture, Commerce and Manufactures. PEOPLES BANK, Waterville, Me. | 50 Webster.	TWO | Spread eagle, Capitol at Washington and steamship. 2 ROCKLAND BANK, Rockland, Me. | 2 Sail-boat.	Scene in a farm yard. 3 | 3 Title of Bank. | THREE Female with basket of flowers. THREE
Jefferson. 100 | Farming scene—men at lunch. PEOPLES BANK, Waterville, Me. | 100 Jackson.	Steamboat. 3 | 3 ROCKLAND BANK, Rockland, Me. | THREE Fountain. 3	5 Portrait of Washington. FIVE | View of City of Bath. Title of Bank. | 5 Indian. FIVE
Indian. 1 | Two ships and one steamship. RICHMOND BANK, Richmond, Me. | 1 Female.	FIVE | Scene in a ship-yard. Female and large V. ROCKLAND BANK, Rockland, Me. | 5 Indian girl	Eagle, shield, anchor, etc. FIVE | V Title of Bank. | 5 Girl.
2 Head of Washington. | Spread eagle. Title of Bank. Dog's head. | 2 Female.	TEN | Ships. X ROCKLAND BANK, Rockland, Me. | 10 Sailor.	10 Portrait of Washington. TEN | View of the City of Bath Title of Bank. | 10 Head of Indian.
3 Three persons supporting a globe. | Train of cars. Title of Bank | 3 Angel.	20 Female with spear. | 2 Female 0 ROCKLAND BANK, Rockland, Me. XX | 20 Female reclining. 20	Man and anvil, train of cars and village in background. TEN | X Title of Bank. | 10 Man holding a bundle of wheat.
5 Foul anchor. | Title of Bank. Sailor, FIVE ships DOLLARS and steamboats. | 5 Female.	Sailor hoisting a flag. | 20 Female reclining; eagle and globe; ships in background. 20 ROCKLAND BANK, Rockland, Me. | Goddess of Liberty.	FIFTY Female. FIFTY | 50 Male and horse. 50 Title of Bank. | FIFTY Female. FIFTY

ONE HUNDRED and figures 100. Portrait.	Covered wagon, shipping, etc. Title of Bank.	Same as on left side. Portrait.
Indian paddling canoe. 500	500 Title of Bank.	500 Female.
1 Female holding tablet and pencil.	Females working at looms. SANDY RIVER B'K, Farmington, Me. Eagle.	1 Portrait of Webster.
2 Male and female sitting.	Man standing against a fence with pipe in his mouth, another man lying on the ground. SANDY RIVER B'K Farmington, Me. Eagle.	2 Sailor with spyglass.
3 Female sitting and holding sheaf of grain.	Woman and cows in front cows, trees, &c., in background. SANDY RIVER B'K, Farmington, Me. Beehive.	3 Female portrait.
5 H. Clay and his dog.	Cattle grazing, sheep to left of cattle. SANDY RIVER B'K. Farmington, Me. State Arms.	5 Female portrait.
10 Female sitting leaning on a shield.	Vig. Same as 5's. SANDY RIVER B'K, Farmington, Me.	10 Currier at work on his leather.
20 Portrait of Pierce.	Men and women on a raft, buildings in left background, village on right, &c. SANDY RIVER B'K, Farmington, Me. Man and cow.	20 Portrait of Webster.
1 Head of Female.	Ship-yard — two ships on the stocks—City in distance. SEARSPORT BANK, Searsport, Me.	1 Ship under full sail.
2 Washington.	SEARSPORT BANK, Searsport Me. Steamship.	2 Female leaning on bale

THREE Sailor seated holding Am. flag.	3 Man on horse back, drove of cattle & sheep SEARSPORT BANK, Searsport, Me.	3 Female with spy-glass.
5 5	Spread eagle on rock; ship at right, and ship under sail on left. Head of Female. SEARSPORT BANK. Searsport, Me. Head of Indian	5 Bale of goods & anchor.
Group of 2 Females, the one above apparently supported by the others. TEN	Ship under sail; in distance steam-ship and sail-ship. SEARSPORT BANK, Searsport, Me.	10 Female with spear seated in car of Neptune.
1 Female leaning on a figure 1. 1	(Old Plate.) ONE Female horn of plenty, plow, schooners, &c. ONE SKOWHEGAN BANK Bloomfield, Me.	1 Eagle. 1
Female head. ONE 1	[New Plate.] SKOWHEGAN BANK Bloomfield, Me. Man ploughing with two horses.	1 Indian.
2 Female and eagle. 2	(Old Plate.) 2 Same as ones, old plate. 2 SKOWHEGAN BANK Bloomfield, Me.	2 Female with scales. 2
Two females. 2	[New Plate.] SKOWHEGAN BANK Bloomfield, Me. Haying scene.	2 Indian.
3 Eagle. 3	[Old Plate.] 3 Same as ones, old plate. 3 SKOWHEGAN BANK Bloomfield, Me.	3 Female. 3
Boy's head. 3	[New Plate.] SKOWHEGAN BANK Bloomfield, Me. Female with milk pail and cows.	3 Indian.
5 MAINE Female with horn of plenty. 5	[Old Plate.] SKOWHEGAN BANK Bloomfield, Me.	5 State arms. 5

5 Figure 5, and five females surrounding it.	[New Plate.] SKOWHEGAN BANK Bloomfield, Me. Female; on right steamer, and on left steamers and cars.	5 Indian holding an ear of corn and a letter V.
Female leaning on bale and sheaf of wheat, scales in her hand. 10	[New Plate.] SKOWHEGAN BANK Bloomfield, Me. State arms, with eagle on top and female on either side; in distance, on right train of cars, on left steamer.	10 Bust of female. TEN
	The old plate of 10s and 20s are the same in every particular as the old plate of 5s, except the denomination.	
FIFTY. Female. FIFTY	50 Man and horse. 50 SKOWHEGAN BANK Bloomfield, Me.	FIFTY Female. FIFTY
Words one hundred and figures 100. Portrait of Harrison.	Scene on a wharf—wagons, shipping, &c. SKOWHEGAN BANK Bloomfield, Me.	Same as on left. Portrait of Columbus.
ONE 1	Agricultural scene; farmer sowing; another in the distance harrowing. 1 SOUTH BERWICK BANK. South Berwick, Me.	1 Ship. ONE
1 Farmer sharpening scythe.	SOUTH BERWICK BANK. South Berwick, Me. Female seated, holding vase; vessels in the distance.	1 Blacksmith, forge, anvil &c.
2 Med. portrait of Franklin.	SOUTH BERWICK, BANK, South Berwick, Me. 2 Female seated, having a child in her lap; hogsheads, compass, quadrant. &c. 2	2 Med. head of female
TWO 2	Spread eagle; iron castings, cannon balls, machinery, &c. 2 SOUTH BERWICK BANK, South Berwick, Me.	2 TWO Schooner rigged boat.
THREE 3	Sailor; hat in hand, reclining against bales; in the distance are vessels, warehouses, dray, horses &c. 3 SOUTH BERWICK BANK, South Berwick, Me.	3 THREE Train of cars.

Left	Center	Right
Med. portrait of Lafayette. 3	Female figure seated; sickle in right hand; train of cars, ship and steamer in the distance SOUTH BERWICK BANK. South Berwick, Me.	3 Med. portrait of a female.
5 Blacksmith and anvil. FIVE	Vig. Figure of Mercury, sheaf of grain, anchor &c.; vessel in the distance. V SOUTH BERWICK BANK, South Berwick, Me.	5 Child kneeling. FIVE
Vig. Two females seated; vessels on their right; wagon on their left. 5	SOUTH BERWICK BANK, South Berwick, Me.	5 Med. of Washington.
X Indian and bow.	Steamer, sail-boat, &c. X SOUTH BERWICK BANK, South Berwick, Me.	10 Female figure; bonnet in right hand; sheaf of grain under left arm.
10 Portrait of Hancock. TEN	SOUTH BERWICK BANK, South Berwick, Me.	10 Spread eagle, shield, olive branch and arrows, ships approaching on either hand. TEN
Steamer. XX Train of cars.	Three female figures seated. 20 SOUTH BERWICK BANK. South Berwick, Me.	XX Milkmaid; pail in her right hand; cricket in her left hand.
20 Figure of Justice.	Female figure seated; arms extended; Liberty cap and staff in left hand; balance in right; a child on each side; fruit, bales, &c. SOUTH BERWICK BANK, South Berwick, Me.	20 Female with sheaf of grain on her back.
50 Bust of female, with sickle in her right hand; hat on her head. 50	Two females seated; factories, train of cars and ship in background. SOUTH BERWICK BANK, South Berwick, Me.	50 Boy gathering corn.
100 Sailor with flag and staff in right hand; left hand raised, holding his hat.	SOUTH BERWICK BANK, South Berwick, Me. Female and Cupid in the clouds.	100 Med. head of female. 100
ONE Portrait of Clay.	Cupid rolling silver dollar on railroad track; cars, steamboat and city in distance. STATE BANK, Augusta, Me.	1 Indian female seated.
2 Male portrait	Two cupids and two silver dollars; cupids apparently in an engagement; train of cars, cattle, hills, city, &c. in distance. STATE BANK, Augusta, Me.	2 Indian female erect with bow and spear.
Male portrait Figure 3 surrounded by sailor mechanic and farmer.	Three cupids and three silver dollars, all engaged at some art. STATE BANK, Augusta, Me.	3 Cupid astride a sea monster.
5 Male portrait	View of the Maine State House. STATE BANK, Augusta, Me.	5 Figure 5 surrounded by 5 females.
X Male portrait	Vig. Same as fives. STATE BANK, Augusta, Me.	10 State Arms Sailor on right, farmer on left.
Mercury ed between 2 and 0. XX	State Arms surmounted by an eagle; female on either side; on right in distance, train of cars and buildings; on left steamboat and vessels. Title of Bank.	20 Female reclining on cornucopia. TWENTY
Portrait of Webster. L	Train of cars leaving Depot, horses before carriage rearing; men, &c. STATE BANK. Augusta, Me.	50 Same as 10's
Portrait of Washington C	Spread eagle on shield; U. S. Capitol on right and steamship on left. STATE BANK, Augusta, Me.	100 Female seated; bales, &c., building in distance.
Indian princess. 500	Female reclining on safe; cattle and girls on right; wharf, vessels, bbls., bales, locomotive on right. STATE BANK, Augusta, Me.	500 Indian portrait.
1 Washington.	Female. 1 Female. THOMASTON BANK. Thomaston, Me.	1 Franklin.
1 Barrels, bales, ship, &c. 1	ONE DOLLAR 1 Female seated beside bales; ship on left. 1 THOMASTON BANK, Thomaston, Me.	1 Agricultural implements. 1
1 ONE	THOMASTON BANK Thomaston, Me. Head of Washington. DOLLAR ONE	1 DOLLAR
2 Webster.	Spread eagle. Title of Bank.	2 Small die with 2s on it
2 Male portrait.	Female. 2 Female. THOMASTON BANK, Thomaston, Me.	2 Male portrait.
2 Man on horse 2	2 Female seated with fig. 2. 2 THOMASTON BANK, Thomaston, Me.	2 Man on horse 2
3 Female portrait.	Shipping scene. Title of Bank.	3
3 Washington and his horse	Female. 3 Female. THOMASTON BANK, Thomaston, Me.	3 Vulcan with hammer.
Spread eagle on shield; ship and manufactories in distance. FIVE	Large V, female and child. THOMASTON BANK, Thomaston, Me.	5 Female with basket of flowers.
Vulcan seated, cars in distance. TEN	X THOMASTON BANK, Thomaston, Me.	10 Farmer seated.
20 Full length female figure with helmet and spear.	2 Female seated. 0 THOMASTON BANK, Thomaston, Me. XX	20 Female seated. 20
50	Vessel sailing on ocean THOMASTON BANK, Thomaston, Me.	50 Dog's head.

50 Male figure with spear in right hand.	Female seated with rake; male seated with scroll. THOMASTON BANK, Thomaston, Me. 50	50 Cupid in sail boat. 50
100	THOMASTON BANK, Thomaston, Me. Liberty with wreath, shield, etc.	100
100 Male figure seated.	Spread eagle on branch of a tree; train of cars, canal boats, bridge, &c. in distance. THOMASTON BANK, Thomaston, Me. 100	100 Female seated with rake.
	TICONIC BANK, Waterville, Me This Bank uses the old Perkins Stereotype Plate, which has the denomination printed in fine letters all over the bill.	
1 State Arms. ONE DOLLAR in part circle.	Eagle on an arch, three females sitting, ship on left, cars on right. TRADER'S BANK, Bangor, Me.	1 ONE
2	Spread eagle, State steamship on Arms. left, sail-ship on right. TRADER'S BANK. Bangor, Me. TWO	2 2
3 Maine Logging scene.	TRADER'S BANK, Bangor, Me. Portrait of Washington.	3 3
FIVE Maine Logging scene.	FIVE DOLLARS TRADER'S BANK, Bangor, Me. Male Portrait. 5	
X TEN	TRADER'S BANK, Bangor, Me. Three female figures sitting holding dividers, s[illegible] and sextant.	10 Ship under full sail, city and shipping in the distance.
State Arms, on the left two Indians and child, on the right female three children and globe. 20	Male Portrait. TRADER'S BANK, Bangor, Maine. TWENTY—curved,	20

Male Portrait. 50	State arms with eagle on top, Indian and tents on left, sailor on right. TRADER'S BANK, Bangor, Me. FIFTY	50
C on four strips of lathe work.	TRADER'S BANK, Bangor, Maine. Male portrait.	100 Two females seated; one erect, on left a temple.
1	Wood-choppers, cattle, and horse. 1 UNION BANK, Brunswick, Me.	1 Female with sickle.
2	Locomotive and train of cars. 2 UNION BANK, Brunswick, Me.	2 Portrait. 2
3	Three female figures; factories in back ground. 3 UNION BANK, Brunswick, Me.	3 Sailor boy.
5	Ship building. Large V, female, and sheaf of wheat. UNION BANK. Brunswick, Me	5 Ships.
TEN	Vulcan the blacksmith seated. X UNION BANK, Brunswick, Me.	10 Reaper.
10	Female seated with globe, distaff, quadrant, compass, etc.; ship and steamship in distance. X UNION BANK, Brunswick, Me.	X Indian seated.
20 Female.	2 Female. 0 UNION BANK, Brunswick, Me. XX	20 Female. 20
50 Female figure.	Male and female seated. UNION BANK, Brunswick, Me. 50	50 Cupid in a sail boat. 50

100 Vulcan the blacksmith.	Spread eagle standing upon a tree; railroad and canal in background. UNION BANK, Brunswick, Me. 100	100 Female seated.
Male portrait 1	Saw mills. 1 Saw mills, dam, lumber raft, &c. VEAZIE BANK, Bangor, Me.	1 Male portrait
Male portrait 2	Ship. 2 Ship. VEAZIE BANK. Bangor, Me.	2 Male portrait
Male portrait 3	Washington on horseback. 3 Washington on horseback. VEAZIE BANK, Bangor, Me.	3 Male portrait
Male portrait 5	Eagle on promontory; ship in distance. Letter V and Indian girl seated. Same as on left side. VEAZIE BANK, Bangor, Me.	5 Male portrait
Likeness of Gen. Jackson 10	Saw mills. X Saw mills, dam, &c. VEAZIE BANK, Bangor, Me.	10 Male portrait
20 Female sitting; right hand resting on book; open book on lap.	XX Vig. Spread eagle standing on rock. XX VEAZIE BANK, Bangor, Me.	20 Two ships, one in fore ground, one in distance.
FIFTY Full length figure of female in right hand wreath, and bunch of flowers in left. FIFTY	50 Vig. Man and horse; horse rearing. 50 VEAZIE BANK, Bangor, Me.	FIFTY Full length figure of female. FIFTY.
Words one hundred running across figures 100. Male portrait	Dray cart, into which men are rolling barrels, horses, shipping, &c. VEAZIE BANK, Bangor, Me.	Words one hundred running across figures 100. Male portrait
500	500 D Vig. Female sitting, sheaves of grain at her feet; load of grain and men reaping in distance. VEAZIE BANK, Bangor, Me.	500 C

Left	Center	Right
Group of statuary. 1000	THOUSAND Engine and cars. VEAZIE BANK, Bangor, Me.	1000 Ship 1000
ONE Ship; city in distance and other vessels.	1 Train of cars stopping at station. VILLAGE BANK, Bowdoinham, Me.	1 Wood cutter. ONE
2 Indians on cliff; city in distance.	Two oxen before load of hay, boy on top and another boy with fork. VILLAGE BANK, Bowdoinham, Me. Bee-hive.	2 Webster.
THREE Male portrait	Cattle and sheep. VILLAGE BANK, Bowdoinham, Me. Head.	3 State Arms. 3
V Male portrait	Ship. Washington. VILLAGE BANK. Bowdoinham, Me. Female bathing.	5 Eagle. FIVE
X TEN X	Spread eagle on globe with flags for every State surrounding it. VILLAGE BANK, Bowdoinham, Me. Ducks.	10 Washington
TWENTY Indian erect, with bow and quiver.	XX Wild horses. VILLAGE BANK, Bowdoinham, Me. Dog.	XX 20
FIFTY Steamship and schooner	L VILLAGE BANK, Bowdoinham, Me. Ship yard scene in general.	50 Cars, tunnel bridge, city, etc.
1 Indian seated on rock, gun beside him.	Two horses and a colt; farm house in distance. WALDOBORO BANK Waldoboro', Me. Beehive.	1 Spread eagle
TWO William Penn (full length) with scroll in hand	Indian seated on rock with gun in right hand; city, steamer, steamboat, &c., in distance. WALDOBORO BANK Waldoboro', Me. Spread eagle.	2 Vessel at sea TWO

Left	Center	Right
THREE	Man-of-war with sails set; in distance steamship and vessel, 3 WALDOBORO BANK Waldoboro', Me. State arms.	THREE
5 FIVE	Three females floating in water, supporting a cupid. 5 WALDOBORO BANK Waldoboro', Me. Head of sailor.	5 Female portrait.
10 Female portrait. TEN	WALDOBORO BANK Waldoboro', Me. X Spread eagle on rock at sea; ship on right and left.	10 TEN
Female seated with sword in right hand. TWENTY	Man with two horses (white and black); farm-house on right; train of cars, water, &c., on left. WALDOBORO BANK Waldoboro', Me. Steamboat.	20 Female seated about to look through spyglass; vessel in distance.
50 50	WALDOBORO BANK Waldoboro', Me. Ship yard; men at work, buildings in background. Dog, key, and safe.	50 Men sharpening scythe: steamboat in distance.
100 Henry Clay seated, dog by his side.	WALDOBORO BANK Waldoboro', Me. Female seated in a shell with trident; ships in background. Indian.	100 Female milking cow, cow lying down; girl on right
1 Bust of Washington.	Female. 1 Female. WATERVILLE B'K. Waterville, Me.	1 Bust of Franklin.
2 Bust of Columbus.	Female. 2 Female. WATERVILLE B'K, Waterville, Me.	2 Male portrait
3 Washington and home.	Female Bust. 3 Female Bust. WATERVILLE B'K, Waterville, Me.	3 Blacksmith hammer and anvil.
FIVE	Eagle with spread wings on American flag, steamer on left. Large V, cupid and female. WATERVILLE B'K, Waterville, Me.	5 Female with basket of flowers.

Left	Center	Right
TEN	Male figure seated on car with hammer on knee supported upright; buildings and cars in distance. X WATERVILLE B'K, Waterville, Me.	10 Full length portrait of man with sickle and bundle of wheat.
Steamship. XX Railroad cars and engine.	Group of three females Faith, Justice, Mercy; ship on right and eagle on left. 20 WATERVILLE B'K Waterville, Me.	XX Full length of female with milk-pail and stool
FIFTY Female full length with wreath in hand and on brow FIFTY	50 Man and horse. 50 WATERVILLE B'K, Waterville, Me.	FIFTY Full length female with sceptre in one hand and flowers in other. FIFTY
Words ONE HUNDRED and figures 100. Bust of Harrison.	Market, wagon, men rolling in casks; horse and wagon on right; ship on left. WATERVILLE B'K, Waterville, Me.	Words ONE HUNDRED and figures 100. Bust of Columbus.
	YORK BANK. Saco, Me. This Bank uses the old Perkins Stereotype Plate, which has the denomination printed in fine letters all over the bill.	
ONE Female figure.	AMOSKEAG BANK, Manchester, N. H. Vig. Indian reclining on frame, and motto "enterprise;" spread eagle, lake, mountains, and deer in background.	1 Portrait R. H. Ayer.
2 Portrait R. H. Ayer.	AMOSKEAG BANK, Manchester, N. H. Vig. Female on each side Coat of Arms, of New-Hampshire; steamboat, train of cars, &c., in background.	2 Two females
3 Male Portrait.	AMOSKEAG BANK, Manchester, N. H. Vig. Three females seated.	3 Small female figure reclining. Large figure 3, supported by three laborers.
5 Portrait R. H. Ayer	AMOSKEAG BANK, Manchester, N. H. Vig. Female seated; horn of plenty; books, owl, &c.; steamboat and merchandise on left; safe, harrow, rake, and train of cars on right.	5 Large figure 5, supported by 5 females
Female figure reclining holding scales. 10	AMOSKEAG BANK, Manchester, N. H. Vig. Female reclining on sofa; Pastoral scene on right; steam engine and merchandise on left; and commercial scene in background.	10 Portrait of Frank Pierce

20 Figure of Mercury between figures 20. AMOSKEAG BANK, Manchester, N. H. Harvest scene; railroad bridge; train of cars; church, &c., in background. 20 Portrait of Frank Pierce.	Female with spear, shield and helmet, and a book and globe at her feet. 50 Two men, boy and dog driving a flock of sheep across a stream, man in the foreground pushing a sheep into the stream. ASHUELOT BANK, Keene, N. H. Sheep, plough, rake, &c. 50 Female portrait.	Two children. C Female seated; sheep, etc. BANK OF LEBANON Lebanon, N. H. 100 100 Boys head.
Male Portrait. 50 Fig. Female seated; hat in lap, beside dog; cattle in background. AMOSKEAG BANK, Manchester, N. H. 50 Portrait of Frank Pierce	Male with arms extended, sitting between two cupids riding on the back of an eagle. C 100 ASHUELOT BANK, Keene, N. H. A man shearing sheep; factory in the background 100 Washington	100 One Hundred Man sitting; hand on sledge. Large eagle, wings stretched; railroad trains. BK., OF LEBANON, Lebanon, N. H. 100 100 One Hundred Female sitting; horn of plenty.
100 Male portrait 100 Female with wand; cupids and dolphin sporting. AMOSKEAG BANK, Manchester, N. H 100 Male portrait	1 Coat of Arms and two females. ONE Head of Franklin. Female, sheaf of wheat, sickle and plough. Head of Washington BK., OF LEBANON, Lebanon, N. H. Man sitting on a plow. 1 Female head	Female erect with emblems of liberty. ONE 1 Female seated on a rock; cupids playing with a dolphin. BANK OF NEW HAMPSHIRE, Portsmouth, N. H. 1 Portrait of female.
Mountainous native scene, Indian in canoe 500 500 AMOSKEAG BANK Manchester, N. H. 500 Female holding scales.	Female sitting with sickle. TWO Female head. BK., OF LEBANON, Lebanon, N. H. Dog's head. 2 Cow and hogs.	Figure of Justice. TWO 2 Agricultural scene; laborers seated, load of hay in distance. Title of Bank. 2 Female seated with sheaves and sickle.
1 A man sitting cutting a log, gold dollar, a hat, traveling wagon in distance. ASHUELOT BANK, Keene, N. H. 1 1 Female leaning on a fig. 1, sheaf at her feet.	Man sharpening scythe FIVE V Railroad train. V BK., OF LEBANON, Lebanon, N. H. Sheaf of wheat. 5 Female head	3 Artist with chisel and hammer. Two ships on the stocks; vessels in distance. Title of Bank. 3 Figure 3, sailor, farmer and mechanic.
TWO Female with spear, cap of liberty and scroll; shield at her feet. ASHUELOT BANK, Keene, N. H. 2 Milkmaid sitting with pail, cows; two gold dollars; man reclining with rake. 2 2	Blacksmith with sledge and anvil. TEN Female with horn of plenty between 1 and 0; male, key, female on right. BK., OF LEBANON, Lebanon, N. H. Deer. 10 Two females with sickle; sheaf of wheat, &c	5 Eagle. V Helmeted head. Female seated with shield. Helmeted head. Title of Bank. 5 Ship under sail. V
State arms. 3 ASHUELOT BANK, Keene, N. H. Farmer sitting with scythe, sailor sitting with spy glass, blacksmith sitting, and three gold dollars. 3 Female portrait.	20 Roman warrior, globe, &c. Female sitting, and large figure 20. BK., OF LEBANON, Lebanon, N. H. XX 20 Lady with horn of plenty; globe, &c. 20	5 Indian hunter overlooking deer; cabin and squaw in background. 5 BK OF NEW HAMPSHIRE, Portsmouth, N. H. Vessel 5 Female head
5 Large figure 5, with five images with scales, shield, spear, & cap of liberty. ASHUELOT BANK, Keene, N. H. Three cupids, five gold dollars; sportsman sitting on right, female Indian sitting on left. 5 Female portrait reading.	20 Female with tablets; child at her feet Boy, child, cattle, etc. Red word TWENTY on either side. BANK OF LEBANON Lebanon, N. H. 20 Female with flower.	10 Buchanan. Title of Bank. X Steamship sailing; men in boat. X X Am. shield.
Large X, with figures 10 across it. ASHUELOT BANK, Keene, N. H. Harvest scene; males, female, dog, &c.; female sitting with a basket. X Two females.	50 Roman warrior. Two figures seated; horn of plenty. BK., OF LEBANON, Lebanon, N. H. 50 50 Cupid in a sail-boat. 50	10 Head of male X TEN TEN X Brig and schooner sailing. X Title of Bank. Shield. TEN TEN TEN TEN 10 Head of male X
One figure with spear, shield, and helmet, and another with scales and sword. 20 Female in the clouds holding a shield; the American eagle flying with its back fastened to the shield. ASHUELOT BANK, Keene, N. H. Bull. 20 Two females, one with sword the other with sickle.	50 Boy Female either side of anvil; factories in distance. BANK OF LEBANON Lebanon, N. H. 50 Girl	Girl with sheafs on her head; loading grain in distance. 20 Title of Bank. Steamboat; lighthouse in background. 20 Female with flowers.

TWENTY Neptune seated; ship in distance. TWENTY	TWENTY TWENTY TWENTY Title of Bank. Shield. TWENTY TWENTY	TWENTY 20 Mercury in clouds. TWENTY

50 Washington	Storm on the coast; sailors in surf boat; ship in distress in distance. Title of Bank.	50 Spread eagle on shield.

50 Two helmeted heads. 50	50 Eagle and steamer in distance. 50 Title of Bank. Shield.	FIFTY

Reaper reclining by sheaves. HUNDRED.	One hundred One hundred Title of Bank.	100 Head of male 100

1 Portrait of Washington.	Female. 1 Female. BELKNAP CO. B'K. Meredith, N. H.	1 Portrait of Franklin.

ONE Sailor hoisting a flag.	ONE Female with sword and scales; ship on the stocks. BELKNAP CO. B'K. Meredith, N. H.	1 Indian girl with bow and spear.

TWO 2	Spread Eagle. 2 BELKNAP CO. B'K, Meredith, N. H.	2 TWO Sail-boats.

Female. 2	Wood choppers, cattle and horse. BELKNAP CO. B'K, Meredith, N. H.	2 Girl with sheaf of wheat.

3 Washington.	Female 3 Flower girl BELKNAP CO. B'K, Meredith, N. H.	3 Vulcan the blacksmith.

3 Female with flowers.	3 Harvest scene 3 BELKNAP CO. B'K, Meredith, N. H.	3 Females raking hay

Spread eagle FIVE	Large V, female and cupid. Title of Bank.	5 Flower girl

Female seated on a rock. V	Female reclining, Milkmaids, cows; locomotive and factories in background. Title of Bank.	5 Martha Washington

10 X 10	Cincinnatus standing by his plough. 10 Title of Bank.	TEN Female figure.

TEN Goddess of Liberty.	Capitol at Washington. Title o. Bank.	10 Washington

20 Female with spear.	2 Female. 0 Title of Bank 20	20 Female 20

FIFTY Female. FIFTY	50 Man and Horse. 50 Title of Bank.	FIFTY Female. FIFTY

50 Female.	Vulcan and a female. Title of Bank. 50	50 Cupid in a sail boat. 50

100 Vulcan the blacksmith.	Spread eagle standing on a tree; railroad and canal. Title of Bank. 100	100 Female with a rake.

ONE 1	CARROLL CO. BANK, Sandwich, N. H. Three female figures floating in the air nearly covering the face of the bill. ONE ONE	1 Portrait.

Female. Portrait of Z. Taylor.	2 Indian, squaw, and child; plough, sickle, and wheat. 2 CARROLL CO. BANK Sandwich, N. H.	Female. 2

3 Locomotive and train of cars. 3	Indian, squaw, and child; plough, sickle, and wheat. CARROLL CO. BANK, Sandwich, N. H.	THREE Portrait. THREE

V Dog and key.	5 Vig. same as 2s. 5 CARROLL CO. BANK. Sandwich, N. H.	V Portrait of female.

X Female.	10 Title of Bank. 10 Locomotive and train of cars.	X Female.

20 Portrait of Franklin.	CARROLL CO. BANK, Sandwich, N. H. Locomotive and train of cars.	20 Portrait.

50 50	CARROLL CO. BANK, Sandwich, N. H. Egyptian figure with wings seated beside globe, female, etc.	50 50

1 Medallion head with wreath around it.	Train of cars. CHESHIRE BANK, Keene, N. H. Ox.	1 Woman with plow, sheaf of wheat and cornucopia.

TWO Engine and cars. TWO	Ox-cart load of grain; man on horseback; agricultural implements; mill house in distance. CHESHIRE BANK, Keene, N. H. Fort and ship.	2 Fancy medallion head.

THREE 3 DOLLARS	Spread eagle on a branch; train of cars and canal boats and locks in distance. CHESHIRE BANK, Keene, N. H. Ploughing with horses.	3 Man shearing a sheep, woman standing by.

5 Eagle and shield, which bears the word five.	Medallion head. 5 Medallion head. CHESHIRE BANK, Keene N. H. Plow.	5 Woman with bow and arrow.

10 Head of Washington	Medallion head of Franklin. X Medallion head. CHESHIRE BANK, Keene, N. H. Ox.	10 Woman with cornucopia.

Left end	Centre	Right end
20 Roman soldier.	Female with one hand resting on 2 and the other on 0. CHESHIRE BANK. Keene, N. H. XX	20 Small female with corno copia, &c. 20
50 Roman soldier.	Male and female figures seated, with cornucopia between them. CHESHIRE BANK, Keene, N. H. 50	50 Cupid in a sail-boat. 50
FIFTY Grain and fruit. 50	50 Three females, shield and scales. CHESHIRE BANK, Keene, N. H.	50 on Fifty. Vulcan.
ONE	1 Three male figures; trees village, &c. 1 CHESHIRE CO. B'K, Keene, N. H.	ONE
TWO	CHESHIRE CO. B'K, Keene, N. H. TWO 2 Female feeding fowls.	TWO
FIVE DOLLARS FIVE DOLLARS	5 Anvil, plough, anchor, cogwheel, &c. CHESHIRE CO. B'K, Keene, N. H. Dog, key and safe.	5
Word ten, figure 10 and letter X. Ship on stocks.	CHESHIRE CO. B'K, Keene, N. H. Large X, and words ten dollars. Railing machine.	Word ten, figure 10 and letter X. Sailor at wheel.
XX Female gathering wheat.	CHESHIRE CO. B'K, Keene, N. H. Figure 20, across words twenty dollars.	20 Female with cornucopia.
Full length female with helmet, spear and shield. 50	\$50 Ship on stocks. 50 CHESHIRE CO. B'K, Keene, N. H. Fifty dollars.	Full length female. 50
Word one and figure 1.	Vig. Train of cars. 1 CITIZENS' BANK, Sanbornton, N. H.	1 Two females Indian grain, sickle, &c.

Left end	Centre	Right end
2 Female with quadrant, anchor at her side; eagle at top of shield on left.	Vig. Group of three females, with quadrant, chart, spy-glass, globe, liberty pole and cap. CITIZENS' BANK, Sanbornton, N. H.	2 Female with shield and balances.
3 Indian with tomahawk and bow.	Vig. Drove of wild horses. CITIZENS' BANK, Sanbornton, N. H	3 Squaw and pappoose.
FIVE	CITIZENS' BANK, Sanbornton, N. H. Vig. Drove of cattle, man plowing on left; farmers at work on right.	5 Two horses; cars on left.
TEN Female right hand resting on shield.	Puddling in an iron Mill. 10 CITIZENS' BANK, Sanbornton, N. H.	TEN Mechanic.
20 Two males and female with telescope in boat.	CITIZENS' BANK, Sanbornton, N. H. 20	20 Male, two females, dog and cattle.
L 50 Die	View of the U. S. Capitol CITIZENS' BANK, Sanbornton, N. H.	L 50 Die
100 Three females representing the Arts and Sciences.	CITIZENS' BANK, Sanbornton, N. H.	Female giving eagle drink. 100
1 Train of cars.	Ship on stocks. CITY BANK, Manchester, N. H. ONE	1
2 Female and eagle.	Blacksmith at forge. CITY BANK. Manchester, N. H. 2	TWO
3 Female.	Mechanic, forge, factorys, cars, &c. CITY BANK, Manchester, N. H. 3	3

Left end	Centre	Right end
FIVE Female.	Three mechanics. CITY BANK, Manchester, N. H.	FI 5 VE 5
Gen. Stark. TEN	X CITY BANK, Manchester, N. H.	10 Indian and two squaws, factorys in distance.
20	CITY BANK, Manchester, N. H. Three females.	20 F. Pierce.
L 50	CITY BANK. Manchester, N. H. Franklin.	50 Harvest scene, male and 2 females, cattle, dogs, &c.
C	Indian, squaw, and papoose on left of shield; female and three children with book and globe. CITY BANK. Manchester, N. H.	100 Washington.
D Suspension bridge, canal boats. 500	Safe, female, ship on stocks, grain, sheep, &c. CITY BANK, Manchester, N. H. Mermaid.	500 Two males and 1 female.
Female. 1	CLAREMONT BANK, Claremont, N. H. State Arms	1 Portrait of Webster.
2 Two cows. TWO	CLAREMONT BANK, Claremont, N. H. 2 Two females seated on each side of a frame on which is a vessel.	2
THREE Female seated on a bale.	CLAREMONT BANK, Claremont, N. H. 3 3 Portrait of Washington.	THREE Female seated on a bale.
5	Blacksmith shoeing horse; jackass tied to anvil, train of cars in background. Letter V and female. CLAREMONT BANK, Claremont, N. H. Wheels, bales, &c.	FIVE Figure Five surrounded by five females.

Left end	Centre	Right end
X	Female reclining on bale; city on left. Letter X and female. CLAREMONT BANK, Claremont, N. H.	10 Two females
20	Drove of Cattle XX CLAREMONT BANK, Claremont, N. H. Sheaf of wheat and farming implements.	20 Female holding sheaf and horn of plenty. TWENTY
Female with liberty cap. 50	Man ploughing with a span of horses; train of cars on right; house on left. Cupid and figures. 50. CLAREMONT BANK, Claremont, N. H.	FIFTY Female with horn of plenty.
100 Female representing commerce.	CLAREMONT BANK, Claremont, N. H. Man with a sledge on his shoulder, factory in distance, cars crossing bridge; three cows drinking at the river.	100 Goddess of Justice.
1 Indian on rock with gun.	Two females at work on machines. COCHECHO BANK, Dover, N. H. Building.	1 Mason at work.
1	Female seated train of cars and vessel on right, canal scene on left. 1 COCHECHO BANK, Dover, N. H.	1 Female resting arm on fence
2	Man forcing sheep in water, another man erect; boy driving flock; buildings on right. 2 Title of Bank.	TWO Female seated. TWO
Sailor seated on bale with flag. TWO	Female on either side of a frame surmounted by eagle, on which is seen plow, steamboat and buildings in distance. Title of Bank. Building.	2 Female with sheaf of wheat over shoulder.
3	Man on horseback; cows and men; load of hay entering barn. 3 COCHECHO BANK, Dover, N. H	Word three, and figure 3. Female with basket of flowers. THREE
3 Female seated, with sword and balances. THREE	Cattle and hogs; buildings in distance. COCHECHO BANK, Dover, N. H. Building.	3 Male portrait THREE

Left end	Centre	Right end
FIVE	Eagle on shield; city and ships in distance. Large V, female and Cupid. COCHECHO BANF, Dover, N. H.	5 Girl with basket of flowers or fruit.
5	Female seated representing agriculture; boats, village, &c., in distance. Male portrait. COCHECHO BANK, Dover, N. H.	5 Indian seated.
Female seated, at work on machine. 10	Ships, steamship, &c.; city on left. COCHECHO BANK, Dover, N. H.	10 Female portrait
TEN	Vulcan seated, with sledge and anvil; train of cars and buildings in distance. X COCHECHO BANK, Dover, N H.	10 Farmer with sheaf and sickle.
20 Female seated, with sword and scales; eagle standing on safe.	Three human figures; centre female with outstretched arms. COCHECHO BANK, Dover, N. H. Steamer.	20 Female with sheaf of wheat on shoulder.
50 Female with sickle 50	Two females seated; on right, ship; on left, factories and cars. COCHECHO BANK, Dover, N. H.	50 Boy gathering corn.
100 Sailor with flag, and swinging his hat	COCHECHO BANK, Dover, N. H. Female and cherub over town; cherub scattering flowers. Machinery.	100 Female portrait. 100
1	Stream of water and load of straw; mill in the distance. 1 CONNECTICUT RIVER BANK, Charlestown, N. H. Bundle of grain.	1 Justice with sword and scales.
2	Eagle on an old tree. 2 CONNECTICUT RIVER BANK, Charlestown, N. H. Ox.	2 Head of Washington
Man representing agriculture, surrounded by axe, sickle, plough, harrow with the motto "Enterprise." THREE	Head. 3 Head. CONNECTICUT RIVER BANK, Charlestown, N. H. Men shearing a sheep.	THREE Minerva with helmet and spear leaning on her shield.

Left end	Centre	Right end
5 Female seated, holding [illegible] State flag.	Female and eagle. CONNECTICUT RIVER BANK, Charlestown, N. H. Bundle of grain.	5 Bull.
10 Stream of water and load of straw; mill in the distance	Two females seated. CONNECTICUT RIVER BANK, Charlestown, N. H. Bull.	10 Eagle, bale, barrel and [illegible]
Female portrait. 20	Female seated on a rock; three cherubs sporting with dolphin in water. CONNECTICUT RIVER BANK, Charlestown, N. H.	20 Two females.
Female seated. 50	View of U. S. Capitol. 50 Title of Bank.	Justice
Soldier with sword. 100	Female seated on bale giving eagle drink, cornucopia and distaff at her feet; ship in distance. Title of Bank.	100 Female representing Agriculture.
1	Female seated; factories in distance; fig. 1 on right DERRY BANK, Derry, N. H. Machinery	1 Female with sheaf and basket of fruit.
Indian with bow and arrow. 2	Milkmaid and cattle, fig. 2 on left. DERRY BANK, Derry, N. H.	2 Female with sheaf.
3 Sea monsters Steamship	Three females, each leaning on a fig. 1; fig. 3 on left. DERRY BANK, Derry, N. H	3 Three male figures.
Hunter with gun and game. 5	Webster supported by figure of Fame and cupid; 5 on right. DERRY BANK, Derry, N. H.	5 [illegible]
TEN Justice and Minerva.	Woodcutter and oxen; figures 10 on left. DERRY BANK, Derry, N. H. Loading hay	X Beaver.

XX Female and bales.	Train of cars. DERRY BANK, Derry, N. H.	20 Female
Female and Agriculture. 50	50 Steamship. DERRY BANK. Derry, N. H Man plowing.	50 Two females
C Men, vessels, etc. 100	Eagle on bale; horn of plenty, grain, etc. 100 DERRY BANK, Derry, N. H.	100 Female with sheaf and sickle. 100
Female with sheaf of wheat. ONE	1 Ship on stocks DOVER BANK, Dover, N. H. 1	1 Sailor.
Female seated on bale of ... with sheaf of wheat, cars, factory in distance. TWO	2 Ship on stocks. DOVER BANK, Dover, N. H. 2	2 [illegible]
Female reclining, factories in distance. 3	3 Ship on stocks. DOVER BANK. Dover. N. H. Washington.	THREE Stone cutter
Washington	Ship on stocks and female either side 5 DOVER BANK, Dover N. H. Wheels.	5 Two females
TEN	Female illustrating industry. X Ship on stocks. DOVER BANK, Dover, N. H.	10 Blacksmith at his forge
20 Female.	XX Eagle. XX DOVER BANK, Dover, N. H.	20 Ship sailing.
FIFTY Female FIFTY	50 Man and horse. 50 DOVER BANK, Dover, N. H.	FIFTY Female. FIFTY

Word one hundred and figure 100. Male portrait.	Wharf scene—loading wagon, men, horses, shipping, &c. DOVER BANK, Dover, N. H.	Same as on left Male portrait.
ONE 1 Female seated with right arm resting on figure 1; owl, &c.	FARMINGTON BK. Farmington, N. H. Vig. Spread eagle; on left, steamship; on right, Capitol at Washington.	1 ONE Female seated, liberty pole and cap, shield, globe, &c.
Female reclining with scales in right hand. 2	Vig. Drove of cattle and sheep, two men, horse and dog. FARMINGTON BK., Farmington, N. H. Man ploughing.	2 Female erect, pole, cap and shield.
Mermaid holding horn out of which water is running. 3	Vig. Two men ploughing with horse and oxen; road, train of cars, horses, cows, &c., in distance is city on left, on right is a church, &c. FARMINGTON BK., Farmington, N. H.	3 Female portrait.
FIVE Female seated, pole and cap, shield, flowers, &c.	FARMINGTON BK., Farmington. N. H. 5	5 Blacksmiths at work, horses, men, &c.
TEN Indian princess.	FARMINGTON BK., Farmington. N. H. Vig. Female Indian seated with left arm uplifted; on left a deer, trees &c. Man loading hay.	X Horses. X
20 Man seated with gun, train of cars on right.	FARMINGTON BK., Farmington, N. H. Vig. Female on the back of an eagle, soaring in clouds.	20 Indian female reclining.
L Female seated, portrait of Washington; eagle, train of cars, &c.	FARMINGTON BK., Farmington, N. H.	50 Female portrait.
Female feeding an eagle from cup. 100	FARMINGTON BK., Farmington. N. H. Train of cars, depot, steamboat, &c. on right. Dog.	100 100
ONE Liberty and squaw	ONE on fig. 1. Indian, squaw and papoose seated; city in distance. FAR. & MECH. B'K, Rochester, N. H.	1 Female representing Agriculture.

Females laying. 2	Men at work in boot and shoe manufactory. FAR. & MECH. B'K, Rochester, N. H.	2 Two females.
3 Female, eagle, shield, and fig. 3.	Three cherubs and three silver dollars; mechanical and other implements. FAR. & MECH. B'K. Rochester, N. H.	THREE on 3. Female head.
Farmer with scythe. 5	5 Milkmaid milking cow; another cow on left. FAR. & MECH. B'K, Rochester, N. H.	5 Franklin.
TEN inverted Female feeding fowls.	X Cattle and sheep, dog, men and horse FAR. & MECH. B'K, Rochester, N. H.	10 Male portrait
TWENTY Officer with sword.	20 Female seated, locomotive and factory in distance FAR. & MECH. B'K, Rochester, N. H.	20 Male portrait
Two children 50	Farmer seated; others at work in distance. FAR. & MECH. B'K, Rochester, N. H.	50 Washington
Fountain. 100	Battle of Niagara. FAR. & MECH. B'K, Rochester, N. H.	100 Large building
1 Head of Washington	Female sitting. 1 Female sitting. FRANCESTOWN B'K Francestown, N. H.	1 Head of Franklin.
2 Head of Columbus.	Female 2 Female. FRANCESTOWN B'K Francestown, N. H.	2 Male portrait
3 Portrait of Washington	Female head. 3 Female head. FRANCESTOWN B'K Francestown, N. H.	3 Vulcan the blacksmith

Left	Centre	Right
Letter V with word ive running across it.	Female with sickle and rake, sheaf of grain; steam engine, store house, and shipping in the distance. V and Indian. FRANCESTOWN B'K Francestown, N. H.	5 Head of Washington
10 X 10	Pair of oxen and male standing by their side. 10 FRANCESTOWN B'K Francestown, N. H.	TEN Female with vase of flowers.
20 Female sitting.	XX Eagle. XX FRANCESTOWN B'K Francestown, N. H.	20 Ship, sails all set.
FIFTY Female. FIFTY	50 Man and horse. 50 FRANCESTOWN B'K Francestown, N. H.	FIFTY Female with vase of flowers. FIFTY
100 Eagle. 100	C Four horses abreast driven by Neptune. 100 FRANCESTOWN B'K Francestown, N. H.	C Head of Washington. C
Word one and figure 1. Bust of female	Harvest scene—farmers at lunch; female with child; men loading hay, and farm-house in distance. GRANITE STATE BK Exeter, N. H.	1 Female with pole and cap, seated on safe, right hand on figure 1.
2 Bust of female.	State arms surmounted by an eagle, female on either side. GRANITE STATE BK Exeter, N. H.	2 Two females erect, one with sickle and sheaf.
FIVE Letter V with three males and two females.	Milkmaid seated and two cows; three cows and farm house in distance. GRANITE STATE BK Exeter, N. H.	FIVE 5 and five females.
10 State Arms.	Drove of cattle and sheep; man on horseback GRANITE STATE BK Exeter, N. H.	10 Female seated with sheaf and cornucopia.
20 State arms.	Female seated with portrait of Washington, and with her left hand crowning eagle with a wreath; anchor, hogshead, &c.; in distance factory and steamboat. GRANITE STATE BK Exeter, N. H.	20 Female seated between 2 and 0.

Left	Centre	Right
50 Female holding wreath over eagle; in her left hand scales	Female seated holding in right hand emblems of wisdom; state arms on left also safe and coin; on right train of cars, bridge, and steamboat. GRANITE STATE BK Exeter, N. H.	50 50
100 State arms.	100 Female seated leaning on bales and looking at ships in distance; on her right train of cars, &c. GRANITE STATE BK Exeter, N. H.	100 100
500	Female seated among sheafs of grain, pointing to reapers and workmen loading grain. 500 D GRANITE STATE BK Exeter, N. H.	500
Female seated; at her feet is a figure 1. ONE	Female seated with agricultural implements and products; in distance is train of cars and canal-lock. GREAT FALLS BK., Somersworth, N. H. Female.	1 Female portrait
2 Female portrait	Female seated with mechanical implements around; train of cars, boat on stocks, and steamer in distance. Title of Bank. Dog's head.	2 Female portrait.
THREE Farmer with sheaf of grain and sickle. THREE	Two females seated. Title of Bank. Bell.	3 Female erect
Two females erect; one with sword and balances FIVE	Large figure 5 and female; 4 Cupids sporting around it. Title of Bank. Eagle and shield.	5 Two females seated—one with scales—shield between them FIVE
Female erect in clouds. 10	Female with key in left hand, is seated between 1 and 0; canal lock and train of cars in distance. Title of Bank. Agricultural implements.	10 Female portrait.
20 Female with spear; globe, behind her.	2 Female. 0 Title of Bank. XX	20 Female reclining. 20
50 Female with spear; pedestal.	Male and female seated. Title of Bank. 50	50 Cupid in a sail-boat. 50

Left	Centre	Right
100 Vulcan the blacksmith.	Spread eagle on branch of tree; train of cars, canal-boat, lock, etc. Title of Bank. 100	100 Female seated.
ONE 1	[Old Plate.] Vig. Farmer sowing seed. 1 INDIAN HEAD B'K, Nashville, N. H.	1 Ships. ONE
1 1	[New Plate.] INDIAN HEAD B'K, Nashua, N. H. Indians welcoming white man to shore.	1 Indian female and papoose.
TWO 2	[Old Plate.] Spread eagle on rock, train of cars on right. 2 INDIAN HEAD B'K, Nashville, N. H.	2 TWO Schooner and sloop.
TWO Indian Princess.	[New Plate.] INDIAN HEAD B'K. Nashua, N. H. Mechanic seated with sledge hammer, anvil, &c; train of cars and large building on left.	2 Female Portrait.
THREE 3	[Old Plate.] Sailor standing on wharf; ships, drays, &c. 3 INDIAN HEAD B'K, Nashville, N. H.	3 THREE. Train of cars.
3 Female seated.	[New Plate.] INDIAN HEAD B'K. Nashua, N. H. 3 Indian in canoe. 3	3 Figure 3, sailor, mechanic, and farmer.
Spread eagle; ships, &c., in distance. FIVE	[Old Plate.] Large letter V, and female and cupid. INDIAN HEAD B'K, Nashville, N. H.	5 Girl with basket of flowers.
5	[New Plate.] INDIAN HEAD B'K, Nashua N. H. Indian reclining on shield, on which is inscribed word "Enterprise;" eagle, deers, Indians in canoe, &c.	5 Figure 5, and five females surrounding it
TEN	[Old Plate.] Male seated with mechanical implements. X INDIAN HEAD B'K, Nashville, N. H.	10 Man with sheaf of grain.

10 | [New Plate.] INDIAN HEAD B'K, Nashua, N. H. | X
Female Indian seated. | Train of cars; depot, steamer, &c., on left. | Indian female seated.

20 | Female seated between figures 2 and 0. | 20
Female seated.
Full length figure of a female. | INDIAN HEAD B'K, Nashville, N. H. | 20

50 | Vig. Male and female seated; flowers, &c. | 50
Cupid in sail-boat.
Full length female; pedestal, &c. | INDIAN HEAD B'K, Nashville, N. H. | 50

100 | Spread eagle on branch of tree; train of cars on left, canal boat, &c., on right. | 100
Male seated with sledge hammer. | INDIAN HEAD B'K, Nashville, N. H. | Female seated with flowers.

Indians in canoe. 500 | 500
INDIAN HEAD B'K. Nashville, N. H.
500 | D D | Female holding scales.

Spread eagle and ship. | 1000 | 1000
INDIAN HEAD B'K, Nashville. N. H.
1000 | M M | Female.

1 | LAKE BANK. Wolfborough. N. H. | 1
Man seated with scythe. | Indian seated; deer; sailing vessel and steam-boat. | Female seated with pails

2 | Drover and cattle. | 2
Two females seated. | LAKE BANK. Wolfborough, N. H. | Male portrait

3 | Farmer ploughing with horses; buildings and cars in distance | 3
Man with grain cradle. | LAKE BANK, Wolfborough. N. H. | Female churning.

Large V, surrounded by five persons. | LAKE BANK. Wolfborough, N. H. | 5
Head of female.
5 | Steamboat. | 5

Portrait of female. | LAKE BANK. Wolfborough, N. H. | 10
Head of Frank Pierce
X | Ten gold dollars; nine cherubs; female seated. | 10

Female with balances and sheaf of wheat. | Shoe and boot manufacturers. | 20
XX | LAKE BANK, Wolfborough, N. H. | Portrait of Jackson.

Female seated. | Portrait of Washington. Cupid on right; winged female on left. | 50
50 | LAKE BANK. Wolfborough, N. H. | Portrait of Webster.

Portrait of Cass. | Harvest scene; haying; team hauling hay; female with child seated; pitcher, basket, &c. | 100
100 | LAKE BANK, Wolfborough, N. H. | Indian seated.

1 Winged female with trumpet and wreath. | LANGDON BANK, Dover, N. H. | 1
Another female figure reclining and eagle. | 1 Cupid rolling a silver dollar; village, train of cars, steamboat, in background.

Hunter resting on gun, game near him. | LANGDON BANK. Dover, N. H. | 2
Interior of shoe manufactory.
2 | Two horses. | Factory.

Man standing with sheaf of grain on left arm; female figure in sitting posture. | Three cupids and three silver dollars. | 3
LANGDON BANK. Dover, N. H. | Man resting on plow.
3 | Load of hay. | THREE

Goddess of Liberty with scroll and shield. | 5 LANGDON BANK, Dover, N. H. | 5
Winged female with wreath and trumpet. Portrait of Jackson. Cupid | Female with sheaf and sickle, plow and basket of fruit.

Portrait of female. | Female and nine cupids and ten gold dollars. | 10
TEN
X | LANGDON BANK, Dover, N. H. | Female, globe, and shield.

XX | Harvest scene. | 20
LANGDON BANK. Dover, N. H. | Sheaf of wheat.
Female portrait. | Cow and calf. | Female portrait.

Military officer, with left foot resting on gun carriage. | Goddess of Liberty, globe, eagle, ship, and steamboat. | 50
LANGDON BANK. Dover, N. H. | Portrait of Washington.
FIFTY | Plowing scene. | 50

100 | Winged female. Portrait of Webster. Cupid. | 100
Goddess of Liberty, shield, fruit, and grain. | LANGDON BANK, Dover, N. H. | Female portrait.

Female seated beside bales, etc., cars and vessels in the distance | Six men in top of large fig. 1 | 1
MANCHESTER B'K
ONE DOLLAR Manchester | Female with grain
1 | New Hampshire

ONE | Farmer sowing, two horses and man on right. 1 | 1
Ship.
1 | MANCHESTER BK., Manchester, N. H. | ONE

Farmer and boy driving sheep into the water | Three men in large figure 2 | TWO
MANCHESTER B'K | Female
TWO DOLLARS Manchester
2 | New Hampshire | TWO

TWO | Spread eagle, with wheels, cogwheels &c., on ground; on left train of cars in distance. 2 | 2
TWO
2 | MANCHESTER BK., Manchester, N. H. | Schooner and sloop.

Men, horses, cattle, etc. | Large 3 across note | 3 on THREE
MANCHESTER B'K | Female
THREE DOLLARS Manchester
3 | New Hampshire | THREE

THREE | Sailor standing by bales; vessels, wharf scene &c., on right; ships masts and building on left. 3 | 3
THREE
3 | MANCHESTER BK., Manchester, N. H. | Train of Cars.

Spread eagle on shield, ships and factories in distance | Female and child in large V | 5
MANCHESTER B'K
FIVE | FIVE DOLLARS Manchester | Child with basket of flowers
New Hampshire

FIVE | Female seated and in the act of raising drapery from off a figure 5. V | 5
MANCHESTER BK., Manchester, N. H. | Ship.

Left	Centre	Right
The word FIVE and letter V.	Female seated surrounded by mechanical and agricultural implements and products, on right vessels &c.; on left men, wagon, horses, building, &c. V and Female. MANCHESTER, BK., Manchester, N. H.	5 Head of Washington.
10 X 10	Male erect, behind him oxen. 10 MANCHESTER BK., Manchester, N. H.	TEN Female erect.
20 Female seated.	XX Eagle. XX MANCHESTER BK., Manchester, N. H.	20 Ship.
FIFTY Female. FIFTY	50 Man and Horse. 50 MANCHESTER BK., Manchester, N. H.	FIFTY Female. FIFTY
One Hundred and 100. Portrait.	Wharf scene, wagons, horses, shipping, &c. MANCHESTER BK. Manchester, N. H.	Same as left Portrait.
500	Indian paddling canoe. 500 MANCHESTER BK., Manchester, N. H. D D	500 Justice.
1 Female erect with shield and spear.	MECHANICKS' B'K, Concord, N. H. 1 View of a street with bank and other buildings.	1
ONE Portrait of Washington 1	Child's head. Interior of a blacksmith's shop. Child's head. MECHANICKS' B'K. Concord, N. H.	1 Portrait. ONE
TWO Ship building. 2	2 Interior of a blacksmith's shop. TWO MECHANICKS' B'K, Concord, N. H.	2 Female, eagle and bust of Washington TWO
2 Same as vig. of ones.	2 MECHANICKS' B'K. Concord, N. H. 2	Justice erect

Left	Centre	Right
THREE Female. 3	3 Interior of a blacksmith's shop. THREE MECHANICKS' B'K, Concord, N. H.	3 Female and ships. THREE
3 Wheels and bales. 3	MECHANICKS B'K, Concord, N. H, Same as ones.	3 Safe. 3
5 Pierce.	Same as ones. MECHANICKS' B'K, Concord, N. H.	5 Large fig. 5 surrounded by five females.
FIVE Portrait of Van Buren. 5	V Farmers, cattle and sheep. FIVE MECHANICKS' B'K, Concord, N. H.	5 Portrait of Jackson. FIVE
TEN Portrait of Jefferson. 10	X Farmer sowing seed. X MECHANICKS' B'K. Concord, N. H.	10 Portrait of Jackson. TEN
TEN Same as the X	MECHANICKS' B'K. Concord, N. H. vignette on ones.	10 Pierce. TEN
20 TWENTY Female portrait.	MECHANICKS' B'K, Concord, N. H. Same as ones.	20 DOLLARS Male portrait
20 Portrait of Franklin. TWENTY	Female in foreground; harvest scene in background. Canal and boat. MECHANICKS' B'K, Concord, N. H.	XX General Washington 20
FIFTY Agricultural products, etc. FIFTY	50 Three females seated; pole, cap, eagle, scales, ship, etc. MECHANICKS' BK., Concord, N. H.	FIFTY on 50. Vulcan seated by anvil.
FIFTY Female. FIFTY	50 Man and horse. 50 MECHANICKS' B'K, Concord, N. H.	FIFTY Female. FIFTY

Left	Centre	Right
Words One Hundred and figures 100. Portrait of Harrison.	Scene on a wharf. MECHANICKS' B'K, Concord, N. H.	Words One Hundred and figures 100. Portrait of Columbus.
1 Boy with fruit.	MECH. & TRA. B'K. Portsmouth, N. H. Red fig. 1. Vessel sailing. Cogwheel, spindles, etc.	1 1
1 Head of Washington.	Female 1 Female. MECHANICS' AND TRADERS' BANK, Portsmouth, N. H.	1 Head of Franklin.
2	Female with sheaf; man reaping, house, etc. in distance. Red 2. Title of Bank. 2 2	2 Old man, child and bust of Washington.
2 Head.	Female. 2 Female. MECHANICS' AND TRADERS' BANK, Portsmouth, N. H.	2 Head.
3 Washington, full length.	Female head and bust. 3 Female head and bust. MECHANICS' AND TRADERS' BANK, Portsmouth, N.H.	3 Vulcan, full length.
3 Red word THREE	Title of Bank. Female, sheep, farmhouse, etc. Red 3 Eagle.	3 Two children
Eagle resting on United States shield and an anchor. FIVE	A large V, with female figure and child. MECHANICS' AND TRADERS' BANK, Portsmouth, N. H.	5 Female figure and basket.
Male figure seated on machinery; cars at distance. TEN	X MECHANICS' AND TRADERS' BANK, Portsmouth, N. H.	10 Male figure with sheaf in hand.
20 Female figure seated.	XX Eagle. XX MECHANICS' AND TRADERS' BANK, Portsmouth, N. H.	20 Ship with sails partly furled.

FIFTY Female fig[illegible] FIFTY	50 Man and horse. 50 MECHANICS AND TRADERS' BANK, Portsmouth, N. H	FIFTY. Female [illegible] horn of plenty. FIFTY
Figures 100 and words one hundred. Head of Harrison.	Wagon with horses and goods; ship at a distance. MECHANICS' AND TRADERS' BANK. Portsmouth, N. H.	Figures 100 and words one hundred. Head and bust of male.
ONE Female portrait. ONE	1 Farming plowing with two horses. MERRIMACK CO. BK Concord, N. H. Bull.	1 Female portrait.
TWO Washington TWO	Deer, Indians in canoe, hills, trees, &c.; on a rock on left, the words "Penny Cook, 1723." MERRIMACK CO. BK Concord. N. H. Agricultural implements.	2 Indian female with bow.
5 Female erect with sword and scales.	Female soaring with eagle; shield, pole and cap, and horn of flowers. MERRIMACK CO. BK Concord, N. H. Deer.	5 Farmer with sheaf on his knee.
10 Female.	Female seated, with eagle; pole, cap and sheaf; shield on safe, &c. MERRIMACK CO. BK Concord. N. H. Agricultural implements.	10 Female on either side of a shield. 10
20 Female erect	Female seated on plow, with sickle, sheaf, &c.; on right, train of cars; on left, canal scene. 20 MERRIMACK CO. BK Concord, N. H Bull.	20 Figure with spear, shield and owl.
50 Female seated; sheaf, plow, &c., on her right.	Train of cars; two men in foreground. MERRIMACK CO. BK Concord, N. H. Agricultural implements and products.	50 Female seated, with spear and shield; ship on left.
100 Vulcan seated with sledge.	Spread eagle on branch of tree; cars and canal in background. MERRIMACK CO. BK Concord, N. H. 100	100 Female with rake.
1 Female operative drawing in.	River, falls, locks, ruins of old mills, island village and hills in the distance. MERRIMACK RIVER BANK Manchester, N. H.	1 Female portrait.

2 Two wheelwrights employed in mending farmers waggon.	Title of Bank. Vig. Same as ones.	2 Mill girl with shuttle, and shop boy with hammer and anvil. TWO
Three females on a cliff overlooking the ocean, one resting right hand on anchor; one with sheaf under her arm.	Title of Bank. Vig. Same as ones. 3	3
5 Indian overlooking the Falls.	Title of Bank. Female seated in large letter V with sheaf.	5 Portrait of female.
10 Mechanic with hammer and anvil.	Title of Bank. Bust of Washington, Continental soldiers, Indians, and figure of liberty.	10 Figure of Liberty.
20 The Genius of Manufactures and Mechanics.	Title of Bank Landing of Roger Williams among the friendly Indians.	20 Arms of the United States.
Design illustrating the tariff protecting American productions.	Title of Bank. American Eagle.	50 Dairy maid; farmhouse and village church.
100 Female resting on fabrics; village in distance.	MERRIMACK RIVER BANK, Manchester, N. H.	100 Train of cars and village; lake and scenery in distance.
1 Head of Washington.	Female. 1 Female. MONANDOCK BANK. East Jeffrey, N. H.	1 Head of Franklin.
2 Head.	Female. 2 Female. MONANDOCK BANK, East Jeffrey, N H.	2 Head.
3 Washington, full length.	Female head and bust. 3 Female head and bust. MONANDOCK BANK, East Jeffrey, N. H.	3 Vulcan, full length.

Spread eagle; city and vessels in distance. FIVE	Large V, female and Cupid. MONANDOCK BANK, East Jeffrey, N. H.	5 Portrait of a girl.
Vulcan seated; train of cars, &c., in distance. TEN	X MONANDOCK BANK, East Jeffrey, N. H.	10 Farmer with sheaf of wheat and sickle.
20 Female sitting, right hand upon a book.	XX Eagle. XX MONANDOCK BANK East Jeffrey, N H.	20 Ship under sail.
FIFTY Female. FIFTY	50 Man and horse. 50 MONANDOCK BANK, East Jeffrey, N. H.	FIFTY Female. FIFTY
Words one hundred running across figures 100. Male portrait	Dray cart, into which men are rolling barrels, horses, shipping, &c. MONANDOCK BK. East Jeffrey, N. H	Words one hundred running across figures 100. Male portrait
ONE Girl and dog. 1	1 An Indian with bow and arrows. ONE NASHUA BANK, Nashua. N. H.	1 Girl with rake. ONE
TWO Milkmaid with pail and stool.	Reapers. TWO NASHUA BANK, N. H.	2 Girl knitting. TWO
THREE Full length figure of Justice with scales and sword.	3 Rail road cars and workmen with pick and wheelbarrow. THREE NASHUA BANK, Nashua, N. H.	3 Washington standing by the side of horse. THREE
V 5	Eagle on limb of a tree, loaded canal boats, locomotive and cars in the distance, on right large V. NASHUA BANK, Nashua. N. H.	5 Portrait of girl with sprig in left hand.
TEN Head of Washington. 10	Female and Steamship Mercury. NASHUA BANK, Nashua. N. H	10 Head of Lafayette. X

Left	Centre	Right
20 Woman with spear, globe, &c.	2 Female seated. 0 NASHUA BANK, N. H. XX	20 Female seated. 20
50 Full length figure of female, pedestal, &c.	Male and female seated; flowers, &c. NASHUA BANK, N. H.	50 Cupid in small boat 50
100 Eagle C	Soldier, sailor, flag, fort, cannon, etc. NASHUA BANK. One Hundred Dollars	100 Daniel Webster
100 Male seated with sledge and hammer.	Spread eagle on branch of tree; train of cars on left, canal boat, &c., on right. NASHUA BANK. N. H.	100 Female seated, with flowers.
Spread eagle, shield, Capitol at Washington. 1	1 NEW IPSWICH B'K. New Ipswich, N. H. 1	1 Milkmaid seated with pail.
Farmer, man and sheep; mills in distance. 2	Heads of Hancock and Adams NEW IPSWICH B'K. New Ipswich, N. H.	TWO Woman with wreath. TWO
Man on horseback; another with scythe cattle. 3	NEW IPSWICH B'K. New Ipswich, N. H.	THR3EE Girl with flowers on shoulder. THREE
Washington. 3	Steamships and ship at sea. NEW IPSWICH BK., New Ipswich, N. H.	3 Webster.
Woman in the air holding shield, eagle beyond. 5	5 NEW IPSWICH B'K. New Ipswich, N. H.	5 State Arms.
Declaration of Independence; numerous heads. X	X NEW IPSWICH B'K, New Ipswich, N. H.	10 Locomotive, man with wheelbarrow

Left	Centre	Right
20 Woman with spear and globe.	2 Female sitting. 0 NEW IPSWICH B'K, New Ipswich, N. H. XX	20 20
50 Woman with helmet, pillar.	Woman and man seated, flowers between them. NEW IPSWICH B'K, New Ipswich, N. H. 50	50 Cupid in sail-boat. 50
100 Man seated hand on sword and scroll.	Eagle on branch of tree, cars and canal boat in distance. NEW IPSWICH B'K. New Ipswich. N. H. 100	100 Woman with flowers.
Indian in canoe. 500	500 NEW IPSWICH B'K, New Ipswich, N. H. D D	500 Woman with scales.
Ornamental work. Boy's head. ONE	1 Female seated on bale, with roll of cloth; factories, railroad, &c., on right; falls and village on left 1 NEW MARKET B'K. New Market, N. H.	Ornamental work. Girl's head. ONE
2 Male portrait	Farmers harvesting; male, female and child in front; man loading hay cart in background. Title of Bank. Mechanical implements.	Girl. 2 Female feeding chickens.
Cupid. 3	Female pouring water in trough; sheep drinking. NEW MARKET B'K. 3 N. H. 3	3 Old man, child, and bust of Washington.
5 Male portrait	Title of Bank. Declaration of Independence. Eagle.	5 Cass.
Ornamental work. 10	Portrait of Webster. Title of Bank. Farmer and drover bargaining for ox; barn yard scene. Horse.	10 Justice.
20 on ornamental work. Henry Clay	Two females with wings, and two Cupids entwined in figs. 20 in clouds. Figs 20 either side of vig. NEW MARKET B'K. N. H.	20 on ornamental work. Andrew Jackson.

Left	Centre	Right
Ornamental work. Female figure of Liberty; U. S. Capitol in distance.	50 Title of Bank. Large portrait of Washington.	50 Head of female.
Spread eagle, shield, etc. 100	Ship on stocks. Title of Bank.	100 Head of Indian female.
Eagle on shield. 1	PAWTUCKAWAY BANK. Epping, N. H. Flowers with shield and Indian, shield surmounted by an eagle; steamboat, rail cars, and factories in distance.	1 Indian squaw and papoose.
Female 2	PAWTUCKAWAY BANK, Epping, N. H. On right two female figures, one kneeling with a sickle in hand; portrait of Washington, milkmaid and cows on left.	2 TWO 2
State arms. 5	PAWTUCKAWAY BANK, Epping, N. H. Large V and word five.	5 Portrait.
Female portrait. 10	PAWTUCKAWAY BANK, Epping, N. H. Shield; on left Indians; on right women and children studying globe.	10 X 10
Portrait of Webster. XX	PAWTUCKAWAY BANK. Epping, N. H. Farming scene; sheaf of grain.	20 Two female figures.
Portrait of Cass. 50	PAWTUCKAWAY BANK. Epping, N. H. Female figure and iron chest; ship building, sheep &c., on right	50 Female holding globe in right hand, staff in left.
Cupid—a fountain of water. 1	PENNICHUCK B'K. Nashua, N. H. Indian female seated.	1 Portrait of Washington.
Female erect with glass in hand. TWO	State Arms and eagle; female on either side; cars, factories, steamboat and man plowing in distance PENNICHUCK B'K. Nashua, N. H. Man plowing with horse.	2 Portrait of Flores.

Sailor with flag.	Title of Bank. Three females seated with sickle, etc.	3
THREE	Load of hay.	Portrait of Clay.

Sailor, Indian, female, etc.	Large V. female within.	5
	PENNICHUCK B'K. Nashua, N. H.	
5	Mechanic seated.	Portrait of Cass.

Male portrait.	Female seated; cows, milkmaids, engine, ship, etc.	10
X	PENNICHUCK B'K. Nashua, N. H.	Female with liberty cap and declaration of Independence.

Indian portrait.	Female with liberty cap; portrait of Washington; factories and vessels.	20
XX	PENNICHUCK B'K. Nashua. N. H.	Dam and water fall.

Female with scales seated	Man seated with elbow resting on a column; two men &c, team of horses.	50
50	PENNICHUCK B'K. Nashua, N. H.	Portrait of Jackson.

Portrait of Webster.	Cattle, sheep and two men with horse and dog.	100
100	PENNICHUCK B'K. Nashua, N. H.	Hunter with dog, gun and game

ONE 1	PETERBOROUGH BANK, Peterborough, N. H.	1 ONE
Webster.	Spread Eagle and shield.	Washington.

TWO DOLLARS 2	Horses running, man on horseback in distance.	2 TWO DOLLARS
	PETERBOROUGH Peterborough, N. H.	

THREE	Men Loading Hay. 3 on Three.	THREE
	PETERBOROUGH BANK. Peterborough, N. H.	

FIVE	PETERBOROUGH BANK, Peterborough, N. H.	5
	Drove of sheep, and dogs, man on horseback, mill in distance. FIVE	Pierce.

Ship on stocks.	PETERBOROUGH BANK, Peterborough, N. H.	10
Word "Ten" letter "X," and figures "10."	Female and safe, cotton mill in distance.	Women drawing water, steamboat in distance.

20	PETERBOROUGH BANK, Peterborough, N. H.	XX
Three female figures.		Clay.

50	PETERBOROUGH BANK. Peterborough, N. H.	50
Signing Declaration of Independence.		Jackson

ONE	1 Man seated by basket of fruit and cradle; load of hay in distance.	1
Female feeding fowls.	PINE RIVER BANK, Ossipee, N. H. ONE ONE	Child's head.

Justice erect and Minerva seated.	Cattle, sheep and colt; boy on horse.	2
Two dollars.	PINE RIVER BANK, Ossipee, N. H. TWO TWO	Female with flowers.

3	3 Blacksmith shop; man shoeing horse; Jackass tied to anvil; cars in distance.	3
Man cutting down a tree	PINE RIVER BANK, Ossipee, N. H. THREE THREE	Boy's head.

Justice erect	Ox; house and oxen in distance.	5
FIVE	PINE RIVER BANK, Ossipee, N. H. FIVE FIVE	Female churning.

Reaper	Males and females, vines, etc.	10
X	PINE RIVER BANK, Ossipee, N. H. Ten Dollars Ten Dollars	Franklin.

	Female on either side of shield, surmounted by an eagle; steamboat in distance.	20
Indian on a cliff.		Male portrait
	PINE RIVER BANK, Ossipee, N. H. TWENTY TWENTY	20

FIFTY	Lion American shield; eagle at top surrounded by flags.	50
Washington	PINE RIVER BANK, Ossipee, N. H. FIFTY FIFTY	50

100	Female seated; letter C; factories and bridge in distance.	100
100	PINE RIVER BANK, Ossipee, N. H. ONE HUNDRED	D. Webster.

1	Ship on stocks. Winged female seated holding fig. 1. Vessel, men, bbls., &c.	1
Female with sickle.		Female.
1	PISCATAQUA EXCHANGE BANK, Portsmouth, N. H. Male Portrait.	1

Large figure 2; Portrait of Washington and ship on stocks within.	Farmer plowing with two horses; houses, and steamboat in distance.	Large figure 2, Portrait of Franklin and vessels within.
	PISCATAQUA EXCHANGE BANK. Portsmouth, N. H.	

3	Vessels in stocks, men at work, &c.; sloop and city in distance.	3
Sailor erect with quadrant.		Farmer whetting scythe.
THREE	PISCATAQUA EXCHANGE BANK, Portsmouth, N. H.	THREE

5	Male Portrait. Letter V, and female with sheaf within. Portrait of Washington.	5
Med. head.		Ship on Stocks.
5	PISCATAQUA EXCHANGE BANK. Portsmouth, N. H.	5

10	Med. Head of Franklin. Large letter X and portraits of 10 of the Presidents of the U. S. Med. Head.	10
Female seated, shield, &c.		Ship on Stocks.
10	PISCATAQUA EXCHANGE BANK, Portsmouth, N. H.	10

20	Portrait of Wm. Penn. Female seated with tub on knee; two cows; female milking &c. Portrait of Franklin.	20
Portrait of Washington.		Vessel on stocks.
20	Title of Bank. Spread Eagle.	20

100	Vessels. Two females seated; buildings on right, ship on left. Vessel on stocks.	100
Washington.		Male portrait
100	PISCATAQUA EXCHANGE BANK. Portsmouth, N. H. Agricultural Implements.	100

	Female seated; train of cars, sloop, and steamboat on right; on left canal, lock, &c. Large 1, and five men.	1
1	PITTSFIELD BANK, Pittsfield. N. H.	Female leaning head on her hand.

	Man and two boys; two sheep in water; drove on left, and buildings on right. Large 2 and five men.	TWO
		Female seated.
2	Title of Bank	TWO

3	Man on horseback, cattle, dog, and man; load of hay entering barn, likewise three men; in distance city. 3 Title of Bank.	Word three and figure 3. Female erect with basket of flowers. THREE
Spread eagle; city and vessels in distance. FIVE	Large V, female and Cupid. Title of Bank.	5 Portrait of a girl.
Vulcan seated; train of cars, &c., in distance. TEN	X Title of Bank	10 Farmer with sheaf of wheat and sickle.
20 Female with spear.	2 Female 0 Title of Bank XX	20 Female seated. 20
50 Female with spear.	Male and female seated. Title of Bank. 50	50 Cupid in boat. 50
100 Man with staff, anchor.	Vig. Spread eagle upon branch of tree; canal scene on right; train of cars crossing bridge on left. Title of Bank. 100	100 Female with rake, seated beside cornucopia.
ONE Figure of Justice, holding sword and balance.	Train of cars. ROCHESTER BANK, Rochester, N. H. Carding machine.	ONE Washington standing by his horse. ONE
2 Eagle and shield. 2	Three female figures. TWO ROCHESTER BANK. Rochester, N. H. Dog, key and chest.	2 Female; Goddess of Liberty, with shield and trident. 2
THREE Stone cutter 3	Female reclining; eagle; globe; ships in distance. ROCHESTER BANK. Rochester, N. H. Female and bee-hive.	THREE Blacksmith. 3
5 Franklin. 5	Drover on horse, with cattle and sheep. ROCHESTER BANK. Rochester, N. H. Deer.	5 Washington. 5
10 Female head. TEN	Female with key on right; chest on left. ROCHESTER BANK, Rochester, N. H.	10 Female head. TEN
20 Minerva; Goddess of wisdom, with spear and helmet; an owl and globe.	Female sitting with rake; between 2 and 0. ROCHESTER BANK, Rochester, N. H. XX	20 Female reclining 20
FIFTY. 50	50 Three females seated; eagle on left; sheep on right. ROCHESTER BANK, N. H.	FIFTY on 50 Blacksmith: anvil, cars in distance, &c.
C Fisherman and boat. 100	Eagle on bale; grain, flowers, &c. 100 ROCHESTER BANK, N. H.	100 Female; sickle and grain. 100
500	Indian paddling a canoe. 500 ROCHESTER BANK, Rochester, N. H.	500 Justice, with sword and scales.
1000	Eagle on cliff; sea and ship in distance. 1000 ROCHESTER BANK, Rochester, N. H.	1000 Indian female warrio with bow and arrow.
1 Portrait of John Jay.	View of the U. S. Capitol. ROCKINGHAM B'K, Portsmouth, N. H. American eagle.	1 Sea nymph.
TWO Steamship.	Portrait of Taylor. Portrait of Fillmore. ROCKINGHAM B'K, Portsmouth, N. H.	2 Brigantine.
3 Portrait of Henry Clay.	ROCKINGHAM B'K. Portsmouth, N. H. Portrait THREE of DOLLARS Daniel Webster.	3 Portrait of John C. Calhoun.
5 Sailor leaning on a capstan.	View of war ships, near the Navy Yard, Portsmouth, N. H. ROCKINGHAM B'K. Portsmouth, N. H.	5 Portrait of Mrs. Crittenden.
10 Portrait of girl.	View of a ship of the line, and merchant ship under sail. ROCKINGHAM B'K. Portsmouth, N. H.	10 Blacksmith at a forge.
Figure of a female representing Young America. 20	ROCKINGHAM B'K, Portsmouth, N. H. Portrait of Daniel Webster.	20 American eagle.
Sailor holding the American flag FIFTY.	Steamship of the Collins' line. ROCKINGHAM B'K. Portsmouth, N. H.	50 Figure of a female with horn of plenty, &c.
American eagle on a shield. 100	Portrait of Washington. ROCKINGHAM B'K. Portsmouth, N. H.	100
1 Commerce 1	ONE DOLLAR 1 Female reclining on bales, shipping on right 1 SALMON FALLS B'K ONE DOLLAR Rollinsford NEW HAMPSHIRE	1 Agriculture 1
1 Washington.	Female 1 Female SALMON FALLS BK., Rollingsford, N. H.	1 Franklin.
2 Officer on horse 2	TWO DOLLARS 2 Female seated, arm resting on fig. 2; cornucopia, etc 2 SALMON FALLS B'K TWO DOLLARS Rollinsford NEW HAMPSHIRE	2 Officer on horse 2
2 Columbus.	Female 2 Female SALMON FALLS BK., Rollingsford, N. H.	2 Portrait.
3 Child's head and wreath of flowers 3	THREE DOLLARS 3 Female seated, arm resting on figure 3 3 SALMON FALLS B'K THREE DOLLARS Rollinsford NEW HAMPSHIRE	3 Child's head and wreath of flowers 3
3 Washington and horse.	Female Portrait. 3 Female Portrait. SALMON FALLS BK., Rollinsford, N. H.	3 Vulcan at his forge.

Eagle on rock with wings extended. FIVE Large 5, Female and Cupid. SALMON FALLS BK., Rollingsford. N. H. 5 Female Portrait.	Female representing liberty, with eagle. XX Artist drawing plans; stone cutters and team in distance. Title of Bank. Bale and machinery. 20 Female head.	Fancy female head. 20 Farmers nooning. SOUHEGAN BANK, Milford, N. H. Loading hay 20 Fancy female head.
Vulcan the Blacksmith. TEN X SALMON FALLS BK. Rollingsford. N. H. 10 Reaper.	Blacksmith at anvil. 50 Mechanic in a sitting posture, leaning his arm upon a steam boiler; workmen in distance. Title of Bank. Safe. 50 Factory building.	Female figure of Justice. Boot making device; figure 50 on left. SOUHEGAN BANK, Milford, N. H. Shield, bales, etc 50 Fancy female head.
20 Female sitting. XX Eagle XX SALMON FALLS BK., Rollinsford. N. H. 20 Ship.	Female figure of Justice. 100 Female with shield, sheaf of wheat and horn of plenty. Title of Bank. Anvil, hammer and boiler. 100 Stone cutter at work.	Female reclining with tride t. 100 Arms of the Union; eagle, letter C on shield. SOUHEGAN BANK, Milford, N. H. Liberty. 100 Female representing Agriculture.
FIFTY Female standing. FIFTY 50 Man and Horse 50 SALMON FALLS BK., Rollinsford. N. H. FIFTY Female standing. FIFTY	Female figure representing agriculture; reapers in distance. 500 500 D Title of Bank. 500	Female reclining on bale with scales in right hand. 1 STATE CAPITAL BK. Concord, N. H. Female reclining with pole and cap; eagle and motto "E Pluribus Unum," on right; in distance on left, steamer and ship. 1 Female with sickle, leaning on ornamental figure 1.
ONE HUNDRED and figures 100. Portrait of Harrison, Loading baggage wagon, horses shipping at wharf. SALMON FALLS BK., Rollinsford. N. H. ONE HUNDRED and figures 100. Portrait	Laocoon and sons struggling with the serpent. 1000 THOUSAND Train of cars. Title of Bank. 1000 Vessels. 1000	2 STATE CAPITAL BK. Concord, N. H. Male at work on chart with compass; on right, three men, two horses and cart. TWO 2 Female sporting with a swan in water.
1 Farmers at lunch. 1 SOMMERSWORTH BANK, Sommersworth, N. H. Load of hay. 1 Sailor.	Female with American shield. 1 SOUHEGAN BANK, Milford, N. H. Blacksmith shoeing a horse. 1 Male portrait	THREE Female erect with pole, cap and scroll in hands; shield scales, &c. STATE CAPITAL BK. Concord, N. H. Milkmaid seated, with pail on lap; five cows on her left. 3 Female portrait.
2 Farmers at lunch; dog and sheaf of wheat. 2 Title of Bank. Blacksmith and anvil. 2 Sailor boy pulling oar	Indian female; arms of 20 States on the border. 2 State Arms surmounted by an eagle, female on either side. SOUHEGAN BANK, Milford, N. H. 2 Portrait of Washington	5 Female portrait. STATE CAPITAL BK. Concord, N. H. Five females, figure 5 between two of them, &c.; on left, vessels, &c.; on right building, locomotive and tender. 5 Figure 5 surrounded by five human figures.
3 Girls tending looms. 3 Title of Bank. Cattle. 3 Eagle. Train of cars	3 Farmer. SOUHEGAN BANK, Milford, N. H. Landscape. 3 Farmer's wife.	Female seated on rock, with pole and cap. 10 Indian female crowning bust with wreath; on right of bust, female with pole and cap, hhd., bale, ship, &c.; sheaf, fruit, &c., on left of Indian female STATE CAPITAL BK. Concord, N. H. X Man seated with rake; left arm resting on frame, on which is "Ten."
5 Man plowing with horses. 5 Title of Bank. Man plowing 5 Portrait of Washington.	Female with scales and sheaf of wheat. 5 Figure 5, surrounded by five females. SOUHEGAN BANK, Milford, N. H. 5 5 Figure 5, and five females.	XX XX STATE CAPITAL BK. Concord, N. H. Harvest scene; man, female and child; man with sickle—another sharpening scythe, and one reclining on ground; loading wagon on right. 20 Female barefooted, with sheaf of grain.
Portrait of a boy. X Drove of cattle. Title of Bank. TEN Horses. TEN X Man cradling wheat.	10 Female churning. Train of cars. SOUHEGAN BANK, Milford, N. H. X Female seated.	50 Blacksmith shoeing horse, colt present; anvil, &c.; steam engine. STATE CAPITAL BANK, Concord, N. H. FIFTY 50 Female feeding horse from apron.

Left	Centre	Right
100 Portrait of Frank Pierce	STATE CAPITAL BK. Concord. N. H. Farmer, wife and children in sitting posture; farm houses; load of grain, dog, &c. One Hundred	Large letter "C." Cupid astride of a sea mon ster.
1 Head of Washington.	Cows, woman milking, another woman seated. STRAFFORD BANK, Dover, N. H.	1 Female scales and Eagle
2 Head of Franklin.	Dog and safe. STRAFFORD BANK, Dover, N. H	2 Eagle.
3 Female bust	Female, plough, sheaf and sickle; cars in distance STRAFFORD BANK, Dover, N. H.	3 Med. head.
5 Indian female seated	STRAFFORD BANK, Dover, N. H. Fame with trumpet; globe and eagle. 5 5	5 Female lean ing on a column.
10 Head of Judge Marshall.	Female lean-ing on bale of goods; men load-ing hay. 10 STRAFFORD BANK. Dover, N. H.	TEN Female with a sheaf. 10
20 Locomotive & building.	Female with her arms extended; boy on each side. STRAFFORD BANK. Dover, N. H.	20 Female, sickle and sheaf
50 Female holding sickle. 50	Two females; sh'p, buildings and cars in the distance. STRAFFORD BANK. Dover, N. H.	50 Man stand-ing among corn.
100 Sailor with hat off, holding a flag	STRAFFORD BANK, Dover, N. H. Female and cherub in a cloud over city.	100 Ship. 100
500 Female.	STRAFFORD BANK, Dover, N. H. FIVE HUNDRED Three females; cars and vessel in the distance.	500 500
M Two females; ships, build-ings and cars in distance. 1000	STRAFFORD BANK, Dover, N. H. ONE THOUSAND	1000 1000
1 Milkmaid. ONE	Harvest scene. SUGAR RIVER B'K. Newport. N. H.	1 Locomotive.
2 Eagle on top of shield; female on right with quadrant.	2 Harvest scene; man on horse. SUGAR RIVER B'K, Newport. N. H.	2 Squaw and pappoose
THREE	SUGAR RIVER B'K. Newport, N. H. Commerce, Agriculture, and Manufacture.	3
FIVE	FIVE Sailor, mechanic, and farmer offering grain to Liberty; eagle on her right. SUGAR RIVER B'K, Newport, N. H.	5 Eagle and Liberty; shield and figure 5.
X Two men with rakes.	SUGAR RIVER B'K. Newport, N. H. Spread eagle and shield; on either side vessels.	10 Two females, one kneeling with sickle and grain.
Figure of Justice with shield.	20 Little girl; man plowing with oxen. SUGAR RIVER B'K, Newport. N. H.	20 Female, grain, and sickle.
Liberty with starry drapery and shield.	Three females. SUGAR RIVER B'K. Newport, N. H.	50
Female ... [illegible] eagle ... [illegible] 100	Shield with portrait of Washington, eagle at top; on either side Liberty, Truth, and Justice. SUGAR RIVER B'K. Newport, N. H.	100 Male head. 100
1 ONE	United states Capitol. Female head UNION BANK, Concord, N. H.	1 Female portrait
2 Male portrait TWO	UNION BANK, Concord, N. H. Medallion head on shield; Indian and two females on right; on left soldier.	2 Male portrait TWO
THREE 3 Wm. Penn.	Boys attempting to catch horse; dog, etc. UNION BANK. Concord, N. H.	3 Blacksmith and imple-ments.
5 Battle scene—female loa-ding gun; Old man gaz-ing at troops below.	Vessels at dock; cars, drays, &c. UNION BANK, Concord, N. H.	5 Male portrait
10 Washington	Launching of a steam-ship; city in background. UNION BANK, Concord. N. H.	10 Female feed-ing fowls.
20 Farmer, horse, dog, pigeons, etc.	Scene in blacksmith's shop; old man and boy hammering. Title of Bank.	20 Milkmaid, cow and calf.
50 Female seat-ed with sheaf and sickle.	Title of Bank, Cattle, sheep, stream, etc.	50 Webster.
C Man and boy mending carts.	Title of Bank. Female in clouds with eagle, pole, cap, shield, etc., 100 on left.	100 Female portrait.
ONE Ship build-ing scene. ONE	VALLEY BANK, Hillsborough. N. H. Boy, two horses, fe-male, etc. at trough.	1 Female portrait
TWO Female with flowers.	Female with eagle, and shield; steamer, etc. VALLEY BANK, Hillsborough, N. H.	2 Child's head.
3	White and black horse; cattle, trees, etc. VALLEY BANK, Hillsborough, N. H.	3 Two Indians

5 Farmer with scythe	5 Female portrait 5 VALLEY BANK, Hillsborough, N. H.	5 Female with smoking urn and flowers.

10 Youthful portrait	Boy and child on bank; cattle in stream. VALLEY BANK, Hillsborough, N. H. 10	10 Child's head.

Female with sword and shield. 20	Cattle, stream, etc. VALLEY BANK, Hillsborough, N. H.	20 Dog & safe.

100 THE 0	Female head. VALLEY BANK. Boy, child, cattle, sheep, etc. Hillsborough, N. H.	100 Youthful portrait.

ONE Medallion figure.	1 Two blacksmiths and anvil. 1 WARNER BANK, Warner, N. H.	ONE Figure of a Girl. ONE

TWO Lady's head resting on her hand, elbows on table. 2	2 Haying scene, Girl standing with rake handing cup of water to two men seated on the ground. 2 WARNER BANK, Warner, N. H.	TWO Lady with a sickle resting over her shoulder. 2

FIVE	Spread eagle standing on a shield. V, female and cupid. WARNER BANK, Warnor N. H.	5 Girl with Basket of Flowers in her hand.

TEN	Blacksmith seated, hammer in his hand, resting on an anvil, wheel by his side on the ground. X WARNER BANK, Warner, N. H.	10 Man tying up a bundle of grain, sickle in his hand.

20 Lady seated looking over shoulder.	XX Eagle. XX WARNER BANK, Warner, N. H.	20 Ship

FIFTY Female. FIFTY	50 Man leading a rearing horse. 50 WARNER BANK, Warnor, N. H.	FIFTY Female. FIFTY

ONE HUNDRED and figures 100. Male Portrait.	Wharf scene; men loading a covered team wagon, &c. WARNER BANK, Warner, N. H.	ONE HUNDRED and figures 100. Male Portrait.

ONE Female head. 1	Man on horseback with drove of cattle and sheep, &c. WEARE BANK, Hampton Falls, N. H.	1 Portrait of Gov. Baker. ONE

Portrait of Gov. Baker. 2	Man plowing with two horses. WEARE BANK, Hampton Falls, N. H. Loading hay.	2 Female with basket of fruits, sickle, sheaf of grain, sitting on a plough

Goddess of Liberty feeding eagle. 3	Husbandman sitting, with sheaf of grain and a cradling scythe lying near; mowing and loading grain in the background. WEARE BANK, Hampton Falls, N. H. Cow and calf.	3 Portrait of Gov. Baker.

FIVE Justice standing with sword and scales; Mars sitting with sword and shield, book and globe near.	Two trains of cars. WEARE BANK, Hampton Falls, N. H.	5 Portrait of Gov. Baker. FIVE

Boy standing with sheaf of grain under his arm, and farm girl sitting leaning on pail. X	Two men with horse and dog, among a drove of cattle part of them laying down. WEARE BANK, Hampton Falls, N. H.	10 Man sitting on plough. X

Man sharpening a cradling scythe 20	Ganymede and the eagle ship under sail in the distance; cornucopia lying in front. WEARE BANK, Hampton Falls N. H. Two horses	XX Portrait of Washington.

Portrait of Jefferson. 50	Ceres sitting by cornucopia; ship under sail in distance on left. WEARE BANK, Hampton Falls, N. H. Man ploughing with two horses.	50 Female churning.

1	Female seated; train of cars, sloop, and steam boat on right; on left canal, lock, &c. Large 1, and five men. WHITE MOUNTAIN BANK, Lancaster, N. H.	1 Female seated with head on her hand.

Two girls with sheafs. ONE	Cupid rolling silver dollar on track; cars, steamboat, city, etc., in distance. WHITE MOUNTAIN BANK, Lancaster, N. H.	1 Cattle, sheep, hogs, etc.

TWO Female and squaw.	2 Santa Claus in sleigh drawn by reindeers over roofs of houses. Title of Bank.	2 Cars; bridge, cars, etc, in distance.

2	Man and two boys; two sheep in water; drove on left, and buildings on right. Large 2 and five men. WHITE MOUNTAIN BANK, Lancaster, N. H.	TWO Female, seated. TWO

Three across 3. Female portrait.	Title of Bank. Man with scythe; loading hay on left.	THREE across fig. 3 Male portrait

3	Man on horseback, cattle, dog, and man; load of hay entering barn, likewise three men; in distance city. 3 WHITE MOUNTAIN BANK, Lancaster, N. H.	Word three and figure 3. Female erect with basket of flowers. THREE

Female giving eagle drink. 5	Female seated with spy-glass, shield and wheat; vessels, steamer, light-house, etc, in distance. Title of Bank.	5 Male portrait.

FIVE	Spread eagle on shield; city and ships in distance. Female, cupid, and letter V. WHITE MOUNTAIN BANK, Lancaster, N. H.	5 Little girl with flowers.

TEN	Vulcan seated, anvil, sledge, &c.; train of cars and buildings in distance. X WHITE MOUNTAIN BANK, Lancaster, N. H.	10 Farmer with sheaf on his knee.

20 Female.	XX Eagle. XX WHITE MOUNTAIN BANK, Lancaster, N. H.	20 Ship sailing.

FIFTY Female erect with wreath. FIFTY	50 Man and horse. 50 WHITE MOUNTAIN BANK. Lancaster, N. H.	FIFTY Female erect FIFTY.

Word one hundred and figure 100. Male portrait	Wharf scene—loading wagon, men, horses, shipping, &c. WHITE MOUNTAIN BANK, Lancaster. N. H.	Same as on left Male portrait.

ONE
Man ploughing with span of horses.
1
WINCHESTER B'K'
Winchester, N H
Female.
Female.

Blacksmith.
Female.
2
WINCHESTER B'K.
Winchester, N. H.
TWO
Reaper.

Man cradling grain.
Railroad cars.
3
WINCHESTER B'K.
Winchester, N. H.
THREE
Man and plow.
Cattle and swine.

Female.
Female reclining.
5
WINCHESTER B'K,
Winchester, N. H.
FIVE
Shearing sheep.
Group of females.

10
Female.
10
Female.
WINCHESTER B'K.
Winchester, N. H.
Female.
TEN
TEN

20
2 Female. 0
20
WINCHESTER B'K.
Winchester, N. H.
Female.
XX
20

50
Male and female.
50
Cupid in sailboat.
WINCHESTER B'K
Winchester, N. H.
Female.
50
50

100
Spread eagle on branch of tree; cars and canal boat in distance.
100
WINCHESTER B'K.
Winchester, N. H.
Male figure.
100
Female.

ONE
Vig. Ploughman ploughing with oxen and girl by his side.
ONE
State arms.
ASCUTNEY BANK.
Windsor, Vt.
Head of Washington.
ONE
Steam engine.
1

TWO
2 Vig. Blacksmith; rail road train in distance.
2
ASCUTNEY BANK,
Windsor, Vt.
State arms.
Head of Franklin.
Two
Wheelbarrow, plough and sheaf of grain.
TWO

THREE
Vig. Two horses and man crossing in front of mill and train; on left, fig. 3.
3
3
Medallion head.
ASCUTNEY BANK.
Windsor, Vt.
Female head.
State Arms.
Man's arm, with hammer and tools.
3

Head with five upon helmet.
5 Vig. Man on horseback, driving sheep, with dog; mill in distance; on left, fig. 5, with the word five on top.
ASCUTNEY BANK.
Windsor, Vt.
Head of J. Q. Adams
Eagle.

X
Signing of the Declaration of Independence.
Jefferson.
X
Franklin.
John Adams.
Title of Bank.
TEN
TEN

FIFTY
Man with gun and two Indians. Head and word "Fifty" on helmet, either side.
FIFTY
Female seated; steamboat and sloop in distance.
Female seated.
Title of Bank.
50
50

Female with spear supporting ornamental fig. 1.
1 Female seated with left arm on bale, spinning wheel on her right; city, bridge, &c. in distance.
1
BANK OF
BELLOWS FALLS.
ONE
Bellows Falls, Vt.
Cars

2
Train of cars; depot, steamboat &c. on left.
Cupid and fig. 2.
TWO
BANK OF
BELLOWS FALLS,
Bellows Falls, Vt.
Female seated on bale, horn of plenty at her feet.
Ox and a tree.

Large figure 5, in centre of which is portrait of Washington.
Female reclining on sheaf with sickle; in distance man loading wagon with sheafs and city.
5
BANK OF
BELLOWS FALLS,
Bellows Falls, Vt.
State arms.
Agricultural implements.

Large X with portrait of female and portrait of Franklin.
Man on horseback, drove of cattle and sheep.
10
BANK OF
BELLOWS FALLS,
Bellows Falls, Vt.
Female with sword and scales.

Female with horn of plenty, pole and cap.
BANK OF
BELLOWS FALLS.
Bellows Falls, Vt.
20
Sheaf.
20 Female seated with sickle, cows and house on left. 20
20
Cupid on back of reindeer.
20

50
Title of Bank.
50
State arms.
50 Male seated with pole, mechanical implements; ship on left. 50
Two men and cattle.
50
Spread eagle.
50

1
Vig. Train of cars and two horses.
ONE
Head of Washington.
BK OF BL'CK RIVER
Proctorsville, Vt
Female head
1
Fish.
ONE

TWO
Vig. Farmers home, two oxen, cart, and man loading hay.
2
Female holding scale and sword.
BK OF BL'CK RIVER
Proctorsville, Vt.
Female in sitting posture with staff.
TWO
Doves and bills.

THREE
Train of cars, female with sickle in hand, two Indians, Steamboat in distance.
3
Female seated on plow holding a sickle and sheaf of wheat.
BK OF BL'CK RIVER
Proctorsville, Vt.
Female head.
THREE
Female head.
3

FIVE
Man ploughing with two oxen and horse.
5
Head of B. Franklin.
BK OF BL'CK RIVER
Proctorsville, Vt.
Female head
FIVE
Eagle.
5

10
Female head.
Indian female and child.
10
Two females holding scales; Seal of State; Freedom and Unity.
Wharf scene with vessel in the ocean.
BK OF BL'CK RIVER
Proctorsville, Vt.
Engine.
TEN

TWENTY
20
Two Females, one with basket of fruit; XX between.
Male portrait.
BK OF BL'CK RIVER
Proctorsville, Vt.
TWENTY
Wheelbarrow and sheaf of grain.

BK OF BL'CK RIVER
Proctorsville, Vt.
50
Female erect holding staff with Flag of our Union; Eagle.
L Three females

1
ONE DOLLAR
1
Barrels, bales, ship, &c.
1 Female seated beside bales; ship on left. 1
Agricultural implements.
BK OF BRATTLEBORO,
Brattleboro, Vt.
1
1

1
Female. 1 Female.
1
BANK OF BRATTLEBORO,
Brattleboro, Vt.
Portrait of Washington.
Portrait of Franklin.

2
TWO DOLLARS
2
Washington on horseback
2 Female seated beside fig. 2; flowers, etc. 2
Washington on horseback
2
Title of Bank.
2

2 Male portrait	Female. 2 Female. BANK OF BRATTLE-BORO'. Brattleboro, Vt.	2 Male portrait

2 TWO 2	Female 2 Female BANK OF BRATTLE-BORO. Brattleboro. Vt.	TWO Female. TWO

3 Childs head. 3	THREE DOLLARS 3 Female seated beside fig. 3. 3 Title of Bank.	3 Childs head. 3

3 Washington and his horse	Female. 3 Female. BANK OF BRATTLE-BORO. Brattleboro, Vt.	3 Male figure

FIVE	Female. 5 BANK OF BRATTLE-BORO. Brattleboro, Vt.	5 Ship.

10 X 10	Man and [illegible]. 10 BANK OF BRATTLE-BORO, Brattleboro, Vt.	TEN Female.

X	Signing Declaration of Independence. X Title of Bank.	10 Cars, men, etc.

TEN	Blacksmith seated, sledge, anvil, etc. Title of Bank.	10 Farmer with sheaf and sickle.

20 Female.	XX Eagle. XX BANK OF BRATTLE-BORO, Brattleboro, Vt.	20 Ship.

FIFTY Female erect FIFTY	50 Man and horse. 50 BANK OF BRATTLE-BORO, Brattleboro Vt.	FIFTY Female erect [illegible]

Figures 100 and words one hundred Male portrait	Wharf scene, on a loading wagon; shipping, &c. BANK OF BRATTLE-BORO, Brattleboro, Vt.	Figures 100 and words one hundred Male portrait

ONE Female head. ONE	Milkmaid with pail and cows. BANK OF BURLINGTON, Burlington, Vt. Locomotive and tender.	1 Portrait of female. ONE

TWO Portrait of female. TWO	Two females in sitting posture, one with sickle and sheaf; steamboat and sail vessel in distance. BANK OF BURLINGTON. Burlington, Vt. State arms.	2 Female in sitting posture with sheaf and sickle. 2

THREE Goddess of liberty with shield and eagle on right. THREE	Drover on horseback, with cattle and sheep BANK OF BURLINGTON. Burlington. Vt. Safe, dog and key.	3 Female THREE

5 Portrait of female. FIVE	Side view of spread eagle on a branch; factory and cars in the distance. BANK OF BURLINGTON, Burlington, Vt. Carding machine	FIVE Female in sitting posture, right hand elevating liberty cap FIVE

TEN Train of cars on a curve approaching. TEN	Female sitting between 1 and 0; lake and steamer in the distance. BANK OF BURLINGTON, Burlington, Vt. Dog, key and safe.	TEN Young vulcan at the anvil. X

20 Sheaf of grain. 20	20 Female sitting holding sword in right hand, left resting on pillar, with lion reclining at her left. 20 BANK OF BURLINGTON, Burlington, Vt. Indian in canoe.	TWENTY

50 Ship. 50	50 Female sitting; right hand pointing to vessel; left around a pillar. 50 BANK OF BURLING-TON. Burlington, Vt. Spread eagle.	50 Ship. 50

100 Portrait of Hamilton. 100	100 Female sitting and feeding eagle from urn. 100 BANK OF BURLING-TON. Burlington, Vt. Steamboat.	100 Eagle. 100

ONE Female writing on desk, the desk representing a large figure 1 ONE	1 Man with [illegible] on his left shoulder, and cradle on his right arm, shoes dangling from the snaith, on the right in the distance a farm house and trees and a flock of sheep before it. 1 B'K OF CALEDONIA, Danville, Vt [illegible] eagle.	ONE

TWO Female with bundle of grain in her left hand raised over head forming top of figure 2, Cupid with sickle, &c., TWO	2 Man plowing with a span of horses; ship and steamboat on left and farm house on the right in the background. 2 Title of Bank. Sheaf of Grain and Agricultural Implements.	TWO

THREE Large figure 3 supported by a female and two Cupids. THREE	3 Two men on horseback with drove of cattle and sheep; a covered bridge and shop. 3 B'K OF CALEDONIA. Danville, Vt. Horse.	THREE

FIVE Commerce sitting on a bale of goods in a large V. 5	A large figure 5, supported by five winged Cupids 5 B'K OF CALEDONIA, Danville, Vt. Indian's Head.	FIVE

TEN Girl with sheaf of grain on her head, basket on her arm; boy sitting with boy in his lap dog team and load of grain TEN	X Mythological scene; the goddess Mercury descending from her car in the clouds with her attendants; X B'K OF CALEDONIA, Danville, Vt. Dove with a motto in its beak.	TEN DOLLARS

20 Man carrying grain; horse, dog, etc.	Cattle dealer selling cow to farmer. BK OF CALEDONIA, Danville, Vt. Boy on horseback.	20 Female portrait.

20 Female sitting, right hand upon a book	XX Eagle. XX BK OF CALEDONIA, Danville, Vt.	20 Ship under sail

FIFTY Female figure with wreath of flowers in right hand. FIFTY	50 Man and horse. 50 BK OF CALEDONIA. Danville, Vt. FIFTY DOLLARS	FIFTY Female figure standing, globe in her right hand, flowers at her right FIFTY

50 Man, woman and child. FIFTY	Landing of Roger Williams; Indians etc. BK. OF CALEDONIA. Danville, Vt.	50 Male portrait

100 Two farmers, woman and babe.	Female seated with bales, etc.; factories, dam and village in distance. Title of Bank.	100 Male portrait

Words One Hundred running across figures 100. Male portrait.	Dray cart, into which men are rolling barrels. horse, shipping, etc. BK OF CALEDONIA, Danville, Vt.	Words One Hundred running across figures 100. Male portrait.

ONE (First Plate.) 1
BANK OF LYNDON, Lyndon, Vt.
Eleven Indians in council; a chief addressing them.
Male Portrait. Ducks. Portrait of Webster.

ONE [Second Plate.] ONE
Large Spread Eagle.
BANK OF LYNDON, Lyndon, Vt.
ONE. Female bathing. Three females, anchor, sickle, sheaf of grain.

TWO. Three Indians in a canoe, one a female; hills, trees, &c. 2
Two females holding aloft sheaf of grain. BANK OF LYNDON, Lyndon, Vt. Dog. Male Portrait.

Word THREE and figure 3. Cattle Scene, 4 cattle, 1 standing 3 lying down, 3 sheep 1 standing 2 lying. 3
Man on horseback. BANK OF LYNDON, Lyndon, Vt. Little Girl standing her eyes with left hand.

V Wild horses running. 5
BANK OF LYNDON, Lyndon, Vt.
Train of cars. 5 5 Portrait of Jackson.

Large number of cattle and men entering and fording a river. BANK OF LYNDON, Lyndon, Vt. 10
10 Head of Washington. Man on horseback and boy on foot driving sheep.

XX Female and Indian seated on either side of view of sunrise, wigwams, ship and city in back ground. 20
Portrait of an Indian, bow in right hand, left hand over right shoulder drawing arrow from quiver. BANK OF LYNDON, Lyndon, Vt. Woodman chopping tree. Portrait of S. Houston.

50 3 cows lying down, 1 standing, 2 in background, 1 drinking. 50 FIFTY DOLLARS.
Spread Eagle. BANK OF LYNDON, Lyndon, Vt. Portrait of Webster.

C 2 male and 1 female Indians near wigwam watching and pointing to the approaching train. City, rail road bridge with cars on it, another train coming. 100
Indian seated with gun and dog, warming his hands at a fire on ground. BANK OF LYNDON, Lyndon, Vt. Ducks. Portrait of Clay.

1 1 Farmers and cattle. 1 1
Washington. BANK OF MIDDLEBURY, Middlebury, Vt. Head of a Horse.
1 1 1

2 TWO TWO 2
Farmers and cattle. Title of Bank. Three cherubs.
2 Harvest scene. 2

3 3 Female with her arm resting upon a wheel. 3 3
Male and female. Title of Bank. Farmers and cattle.
3 Female reclining. 3

5 5 Female, eagle and shield; ship in the distance. 5 Female leaning upon an urn, bearing the name of E. Allen and McDonald; also, winged female with a trumpet.
Farmers and cattle.
5 Title of Bank. 5

TEN 10 Vulcan the blacksmith and two females. 10 Child's face.
Ten Gold Dollars. Title of Bank. X
TEN Washington. Child's face.

20 Male and female; sheaf of wheat; canal and reapers in background. TWENTY
Washington.
20 Title of Bank. Female bust.

50 50 Officer mounted. 50 FIFTY
Female, eagle and scales; merchandise &c. Title of Bank.
50

100 Shepherd and sheep; village in the distance. 100
Title of Bank. Female with sheaf of wheat.
Female. 100

1 BK OF MONTPELIER Montpelier, Vt. 1
Female seated and two cows, one standing and the other lying down.
1 Steamboat. Female.

2 BK OF MONTPELIER Montpelier, Vt. 2
Female portrait. 2 Female.
Horse, train of cars in distance. TWO

Female and 3 3 Female head. 3
BK OF MONTPELIER Montpelier, Vt
THREE Female seated, bales, &c.

State capital. 5 5
BK OF MONTPELIER Montpelier, Vt.
5 Washington.

State capitol. TEN
BK OF MONTPELIER Montpelier, Vt
10 Female with sickle.

Female head. State Capitol. 20
BK OF MONTPELIER Montpelier, Vt.
20 Plough. Head of Pierce.

50 Two females; ship factories and railroad cars in distance. 50
Female. BK OF MONTPELIER Montpelier, Vt. Young man harvesting corn.
50

100 BK OF MONTPELIER Montpelier, Vt. 100
Sailor with flag in one hand and hat in the other. Female and cupid over a city. Female head.
100

BK OF NEWBURY, Wells River, Vt.
The 1s, 2s, 3s, 5s, and 10s, are a special stereotype plate with the words "Wells River," in fine letters throughout the upper part of the notes and the denomination in the same manner on lower half.

20 2 Female. 0 20
Female seated.
Female with spear. Title of Bank 20
XX

50 Male and female seated. 50
Cupid in boat.
Female with spear. Title of Bank. 50
50

100 Vig. Spread eagle upon branch of tree; canal scene on right; train of cars crossing bridge on left. 100
Man with sledge, anchor. Title of Bank. Female with rake, seated beside cornucopia.
100

1 BANK OF ORLEANS, Irasburg, Vt. 1
Nude female. 1 Ca.
1 Safe and dog 1

Left	Centre	Right
ONE Head of Washington. ONE	1 Blacksmith's shop. 1 BANK OF ORLEANS, Irasburg, Vt.	ONE Female. ONE
2 Man with sledge on his shoulder. 2	BANK OF ORLEANS. Irasburg, Vt. 2	2 Milkmaid and two cows. 2
TWO Female. 2	2 Family group. 2 BANK. OF ORLEANS, Irasburg, Vt.	TWO 2
3 Man with axe, oxen and cart. 3	BANK OF ORLEANS, Irasburg. Vt. 3 Man shearing sheep.	3 Two males, female and three children.
THREE Man with scythe. Word three and figure 3 across.	3 Female, eagle, anchor, &c. BANK OF ORLEANS, Irasburg. Vt. (There is imitations of this plate.)	THREE Sailor. Word three and figure 3 across.
5 Cattle. 5	BANK OF ORLEANS. Irasburg, Vt. Ox.	5 Workmen and boiler. 5
FIVE	Female V BANK OF ORLEANS, Irasburg, Vt.	Ship.
X	Signing the declaration of independence. X BANK OF ORLEANS, Irasburg, Vt.	10 Train of cars and man with wheel barrow.
X Agricultural scene — load of grain and man on horseback. X	BANK OF ORLEANS, Irasburg, Vt. X	X Two men and a woman in field. X
20 Female sitting, book in left hand, right hand on a box.	XX Eagle. XX BANK OF ORLEANS, Irasburg, Vt.	20 Ship, with buildings in the distance.

Left	Centre	Right
FIFTY Female with wreath of flowers on her head and in her hands. FIFTY	50 Man and horse. 50 BANK OF ORLEANS, Irasburg, Vt.	FIFTY Female with flowers in her left hand. FIFTY
100 Female with cornucopia. 100	100 100 BANK OF ORLEANS, Irasburg, Vt. 100 100	100 Waterfall and eagle. 100
Figures 100, with words one hundred across. Portrait of Harrison.	Covered wagon, wharf, ships, warehouses, truckmen, &c. BANK OF ORLEANS, Irasburg, Vt.	Same as on left end. Portrait of Columbus.
Female with pen, tablets, etc. ONE	1 1 BK of ORANGE CO., Chelsea, Vt. Old man with gun; female loading gun at his back.	Female with pole, cap, &c ONE
2 TWO Cupid.	Eagle. Title of Bank. Apotheosis of Washington; soldier on left; female and two Indians on right. Fig. 2 on right of vig.	2 Female, cow, calf, fowls, etc.
Female portrait. THREE	Title of Bank. Man and boy plowing with two horses.	3 Agricultural implements and products
Title of Bank. 5	Portrait of boy. Man with bag, horse, colt, mill etc.; boys on bridge.	5 Female feeding fowls.
10 Man, horse, dog, pigeons, etc.	Title of Bank. Scene in the Arctic Regions; men shoving boat; dog, icebergs, etc.	10 Blacksmith at forge.
20 bull.	Title of Bank. Large portrait of Washington; cupid either side at bottom	20 Two females one milking cows, etc.
50 Female, column, steamer, etc.	Title of Bank. Male, female, horses at trough, etc.	50 Male, female, child, etc.

Left	Centre	Right
C 100	Title of Bank. Man and woman either side of shield; girl, dog, oxen, etc.	100 Indian on horse.
ONE Farmer plowing. ONE	1 Two females seated, one with sickle; on right cows, on left a building with large steeple. 1 BK. OF POULTNEY, Poultney, Vt. Agricultural Implements.	ONE Female seated with tub at her feet. ONE
TWO Farmer barefooted with sheaf of wheat on left shoulder. TWO	2 Two females, one seated the other erect, the one erect has pail in her arms; on right outhouse and female milking cow; on right farm house and trees. 2 BK. OF POULTNEY, Poultney, Vt. Horse.	TWO Female erect with two pails at her feet. TWO
V Female seated within large letter V FIVE	5 Two females on either side of a frame, on which is tree, cow, &c., surmounted by head of reindeer. At bottom words "Vermont, Freedom and Unity." 5 BK. OF POULTNEY, Poultney, Vt. Dog's Head.	V Female seated within large figure 5 FIVE
State of X Head of Franklin.	(New Plate.) Vermont. Train of cars; Female village in portrait distance. BK OF POULTNEY. State Arms of Vermont.	10 Indian female seated; pole, cap, and shield.
20 Male with sledge on right shoulder; cog wheel, anvil, &c.	BK. OF POULTNEY, Poultney, Vt. Train of cars; village in distance. Dog's Head	20 Factory buildings, men, horse and wagon, &c.
ONE Indian with bow, spear, &c.	Agricultural scene, cattle, &c. Female seated with sickle. BANK of ROYALTON, Royalton, Vt.	The word ONE and figure 1. Man seated with agricultural implements and ONE on half shield.
Two females embracing each other. 2	Two farmers, one seated; female seated; load of hay in distance. BANK of ROYALTON Royalton, Vt.	2 Head of Jefferson.
Blacksmith and anvil. 3	Three females seated representing Agriculture, Manufactures and Commerce. BANK of ROYALTON Royalton, Vt.	3 Head of Henry Clay.
Large figure 5 and five females. 5	Head of Hon. Jacob Collamer BANK of ROYALTON Royalton, Vt.	5 Female seated with globe quadrant &c.

10	Boy pushing sheep into creek; man standing behind him; boy and dog driving sheep, &c.	10
Female seated, with sheaf of wheat.	B'K OF ROYALTON, Royalton, Vt.	Indian girl holding ear of corn in right hand and X in left.

Mercury seated between 2 and 0	Drover and drove of cattle and sheep.	20
XX	BANK of ROYALTON Royalton, Vt.	Female churning.

Female feeding a horse.	A farmer's family reclining in hay field; load of hay &c.	50
50	BANK of ROYALTON Royalton, Vt.	Head of Webster.

100	BANK of ROYALTON Royalton, Vt.	100
Head of Fillmore.	Female seated crowning an eagle with wreath; small head of Washington on left of vig.	Load of straw drawn by oxen; man on horseback.
100		

Cattle.	1 Vig. Farmers cutting grain. 1	ONE
	BANK OF RUTLAND, Rutland, Vt.	Female sitting, with rake, &c.
1	Eagle.	1

Male portrait	View of stone-yard.	1
Word one and figure 1.	BANK OF RUTLAND, Rutland, Vt.	Male portrait

Portrait of Washington.	Drover and cattle; boy in water; trees and house in distance.	2
2	BANK OF RUTLAND, Rutland Vt. Two dollars. Two dollars.	Portrait of Martha Washington.

Female churning.	Portrait of Hamilton. Portrait of Washington. Vig. Farmers sowing grain.	2
2	BANK OF RUTLAND, Rutland, Vt. Sheaf of wheat.	Farmer picking corn.

Female gathering wheat.	BANK OF RUTLAND, Rutland, Vt.	3
Word dollars and figure 3.	Blacksmith in shop.	Female with cornucopia.

Lafayette, full length; York Town monument.	5 Female sitting with eagle, &c. 5	V
	BANK OF RUTLAND, Rutland, Vt.	Sheep shearing.
V	Arm and hammer.	V

Stone cutter.	BK OF RUTLAND. Rutland, Vt.	5
5	5 Farmer sharpening scythe; agricultural scene in the distance. 5	Female portrait.
	FIVE Dog. FIVE	

10	Washington. Franklin. Female sitting with sickle and sheaf, cattle, &c.	10
Cattle, &c.	BANK OF RUTLAND, Rutland Vt.	Sheaf of corn, plow, &c.
10	Female and sheaf.	10

10	Spread eagle. BANK OF RUTLAND, Rutland, Vt.	10
Portrait of a General.	Tree and cow.	Portrait of a General

20	Title of Bank.	20
Farmer with scythe.	Marble quarries; oxen drawing load of marble.	Female with sheaf and scythe.

	20 Vig. Three female figures sitting. 20	20
Washington full length.	BANK OF RUTLAND, Rutland, Vt.	VERMONT
	Washington.	20

50	50 State arms and two females. 50	50
VERMONT	BANK OF RUTLAND, Rutland, Vt.	Female with scales, full length.
50	Washington.	50

50	Train of cars, etc. BANK OF RUTLAND Rutland, Vt.	50
Female portrait.	Dog's head.	Female portrait.

100	BANK OF RUTLAND, Rutland, Vt.	100
Indian beside dead deer.	C	Indian female seated and pointing

1	BK. OF VERGENNES Vergennes, Vt.	1
Portrait of Mcdonough	Agricultural scene—man ploughing, cattle, &c., spires in the distance.	ONE and 1.

2	BK. OF VERGENNES Vergennes, Vt.	2
Man on horseback, cattle drinking, farm-house, &c.	Eagle.	2

3	BK. OF VERGENNES Vergennes, Vt.	3
Hunting scene—dogs and birds.	Train of cars; horses frightened.	3

The word "five," letter "V," and figure "5."	BK. OF VERGENNES Vergennes, Vt.	V
Medallion head.	Man with rake on his shoulder, little girl running to meet him; female and boy rural scenery, &c.	
FIVE		5

X	Three females, one with cornucopia, one with wings, and the other with quadrant	10
X	BK. OF VERGENNES Vergennes, Vt.	

Portrait of Washington	BK. OF VERGENNES Vergennes, Vt.	XX
20	Steamship.	
XX		Horses and colt running

Three figures two seated; on left, factories, &c., on right, canal boat and lock.	L Man ploughing. L	50
	BK. OF VERGENNES Vergennes, Vt.	Female with ballances; eagle and shield; tiers of bills
50	Clasped hands.	50

100	100 Female seated with key in left hand. 100	Same as on left of 500.
Female soaring in clouds with scroll in left and; an eagle on left.	BK. OF VERGENNES Vergennes, Vt.	
100	Eagle.	100

	Cupid rolling silver dollar on railroad track, train of cars, and city in distance. Mechanical implements.	1
1	BANK OF WATERBURY, Waterbury, Vt.	Female, shield, and Declaration of Independence.

Goddess of Liberty, and eagle, drinking from cup.	BANK OF WATERBURY, Waterbury, Vt.	2
2	Two cupids, two silver dollars; train of cars, village, cows, &c., in distance.	Female Indian.

THREE	Farming scene; two males and female, dog, basket, &c.; in distance, men loading hay.	3
Female erect with pole and cap.	BANK OF WATERBURY, Waterbury, Vt.	Portrait of Washington.

FIVE	BANK OF WATERBURY, Waterbury, Vt.	5
A General erect with sword in hand.	Female reclining, with pole and cap eagle, globe &c., steamship, and ship on left.	

Left	Centre	Right
10 Spread eagle, U. S. Capitol on right; and steamer on left.	BANK OF WATERBURY, Waterbury, Vt.	X Farming implements and products.
TWENTY Female seated with pole and cap, flowers, &c.	Two men, horse, dog, and drove of cattle and sheep. BANK OF WATERBURY, Waterbury, Vt.	20 Male Portrait
50 50	BANK OF WATERBURY, Waterbury, Vt. Boy reclining with compass in right hand, engaged on chart; on right 3 men and 3 horses before cart.	50 Female erect with pole and cap, shield and scroll in right hand.
Female seated on rock. 100	BANK OF WATERBURY, Waterbury, Vt. Large public building, horses, carriages, &c., in front.	100 Train of cars
ONE Portrait of Washington. 1	Milkmaid sitting and cows. 1 BATTENKILL BANK Manchester, Vt.	1 Portrait of Lady Washington ONE
2 State arms. TWO	Stone cutters. 2 BATTENKILL BANK Manchester, Vt.	TWO Head of Franklin. TWO on Medallion head.
5 State arms. FIVE	Portrait of De Witt Clinton. 5 Portrait of Abby Hutchinson. BATTENKILL BANK Manchester, Vt.	5 Medallion head. 5
FIVE State arms FIVE	BATTENKILL BANK Manchester, Vt. Female Large V Female and man with sickle.	5 Medallion head,
10 State arms, TEN	Signing declaration of independence. Portrait of Washington and large X. BATTENKILL BANK Manchester, Vt.	X Female bust.
TWENTY State arms. TWENTY	20 Two men, with oxen, loading hay, and three men in background. BATTENKILL BANK Manchester, Vt. 20 Eagle. 20	20 Goddess of Liberty with eagle and shield.

Left	Centre	Right
50 State arms. 50	Man on horseback, and dog, driving sheep; mill in the distance. BATTENKILL BANK Manchester, Vt. 50 Female head. 50	50 Goddess of Liberty sitting; train of cars and buildings in distance. FIFTY
ONE Two females with sword, spear, and shield.	Wood chopper, one gold dollar; log cabin in background. BRADFORD BANK, Bradford, Vt.	1 Indian woman.
2 Winged female. Female and eagle.	Farmer boy and milkmaid; also cows; two gold dollars. BRADFORD BANK, Bradford, Vt.	2 Fountain.
Female giving eagle drink. 3	BRADFORD BANK, Bradford, Vt. Mechanic, sailor and farmer, with implements; three gold dollars.	3 Reaper encircled by Three
Farmer boy with sheaf of wheat, and milkmaid. 5	A hunter and Indian woman, and three cupids; five gold dollars. BRADFORD BANK, Bradford, Vt.	5 Portrait.
Two females. 10	Coat of arms surmounted; with female each side; steamboat and train of cars in distance. BRADFORD BANK, Bradford, Vt.	X Child and dolphin.
Female, XX	State arms, farmer and Indian. BRADFORD BANK, Bradford, Vt.	20 Agricultural imp. & pro'ts
50	Female reclining; milkmaids and cows; locomotive, shipping, factories in background. Wheels, bale, etc BRADFORD BANK, Bradford, Vt.	50 Portrait of Webster.
100 Female with scales.	State arms surmounted by an eagle, female on each side. BRADFORD BANK, Bradford, Vt.	100 Horses and load of hay.
1	Farming scene—haying and harvesting. 1 BRANDON BANK, Brandon, Vt. Wheels and shafts, representing the mechanic art.	1 Female with sickle in left hand and a head of grain in right hand ONE

Left	Centre	Right
TWO	Washing sheep. 2 BRANDON BANK. Brandon Vt. Bundle of grain, plough.	2 Blacksmith, hammer in hand; anvil.
3	Horses ploughing; house, steamboat and other vessels in the distance. 3 BRANDON BANK, Brandon, Vt. Train of cars.	3 Man chiseling marble, with mallet and chisel in hand.
FIVE	Farming scene—oxen ploughing, drove of cattle; cars moving in distance. 5 Seal of State. BRANDON BANK, Brandon, Vt. 5	5 Full length female with a flag. Three cherubs representing Agriculture, Mechanics, &c.
TEN	Farming scene—oxen and cart with load of grain; house in the distance. X BRANDON BANK, Brandon, Vt, Dog's head.	10 Two female figures erect.
20 Full figure of a female.	2 Female. 0 BRANDON BANK, Brandon, Vt. XX	20 Female reclining. 20
50 Male figure standing.	Female and male seated. BRANDON BANK, Brandon, Vt. 50	50 Cupid in a sail-boat. 50
Figures 100, and words one hundred, Male figure sitting.	Large spread eagle on a limb of a tree; cars, canal, and boats in distance. BRANDON BANK, Brandon, Vt. 100	Same as on left end. Female sitting
1 Head of Washington. ONE	Train of cars, COMMERCIAL B'K. Burlington, Vt. State Arms	1 Head of Female 1
TWO Head of Franklin TWO	Three females and eagle. COMMERCIAL B'K., Burlington, Vt. State Arms	TWO Girl with rake and boquet of flowers. TWO
THREE Eagle, ship, and female. THREE	Indian with spear and horse; cars in distance. COMMERCIAL B'K., Burlington, Vt. State Arms	3 Indian and female with sickle and sheaf of grain.

Left	Center	Right
5 Head. State Arms.	Vessels, steamboat and city. COMMERCIAL B'K., Burlington, Vt. Eagle.	5 Head of Washington. FIVE
Head. State Arms. TEN	TEN on Head. Declaration of Independence. COMMERCIAL B'K., Burlington, Vt. Blacksmith arm and anvil.	X TEN on Head. 10
TWENTY	COMMERCIAL B'K., Burlington, Vt. Mechanics, 2 females sitting, city at distance. Anchor, anvil, &c.	20 Farmer, two females, dog and oxen.
50 Head. FIFTY	State Arms and two horses; factory, cars and steamboat in background. COMMERCIAL B'K., Burlington, Vt.	50 Head of Female. FIFTY
100	COMMERCIAL B'K., Burlington, Vt. Three Females, anchor, sickle, &c.; train cars, vessels and city at distance. 100	100
1 Female erect left arm resting on bucket	EXCHANGE BANK, Springfield, Vt. Male Portrait. One dollar above.	1 Mechanic reclining holding hammer in right hand houses in background.
TWO 2 TWO Male Portrait TWO	EXCHANGE BANK, Springfield, Vt. Masons at work building house, man on ladder, with hod of bricks.	TWO 2 TWO Portrait of Gen. Jackson TWO
THREE 3	EXCHANGE BANK, Springfield, Vt. Picture of a Mechanic, hammer resting on his shoulder.	THREE 3
Figure 5 and medallion head. Portrait of Webster.	Portrait of Washington, on right two females, one seated the other standing, on left three females, one in center holds a sickle. EXCHANGE BANK, Springfield, Vt.	Figure 5 and medallion head. Male Portrait
10 Medallion head. Portrait of Franklin. Medallion Head.	Shield and letter X in center; on right woman children and globe, on left Indians. EXCHANGE BANK, Springfield, Vt. TEN TEN	Double Medallion head. 10 Portrait of Henry Clay. TEN on right Double Medallion head. X

Left	Center	Right
XX 20	EXCHANGE BANK, Springfield, Vt. Two horses, eagle overhead, tree, cow and sheaf of wheat in background, steamboat on right; cars and houses on left.	20
L 50	EXCHANGE BANK, Springfield, Vt. Large spread eagle resting on a limb of a tree: train of cars on right; house and small boat on left. 50	50
Female figure hovering over earth; steamboat, houses, cars, &c., beneath her.	Houses, stream of water, &c. FARMERS BANK Orwell, Vt. Farming scene—men gathering corn; large white 1 across	1
Two girls under shed; one churning the other making cheese; cattle, etc. on right.	2 Title of Bank. Man and girl gazing at boy playing with dog; farming scene on right. Large white 2 across.	2
3 Female beside table; blowing on horn.	FARMERS BANK Orwell, Vt. Load of hay, children, etc. Blacksmith's shop on right, large white 3 on face of vig. THREE DOLLARS	THREE on 3 Girl seated.
5 Eagle and serpent. 5	(First Plate.) V Vig. Female seated; V one arm resting on sheaf of grain; agricultural scene. FARMER'S BANK, Orwell, Vt. Man's head.	5 Female reclining against a monument V
FIVE Statue of Washington; cloak wrapped about him. FIVE	(Second Plate.) FARMER'S BANK, Orwell, Vt. 5 Vig. Two females, 5 V Canal boat about passing a lock.	FIVE Female erect FIVE
FIVE Female; sheaf of grain; sickle plough, rake, hoe, &c. V	(Third Plate.) V Neptune in chariot, pursuing an angel upon the sea; ship. fig. 5 on right FARMER'S BANK, Orwell, Vt. Horse head.	FIVE
TEN Franklin. TEN	FARMER'S BANK, X Orwell, Vt. Cottage scene; shearing a sheep, with family around. Eagle.	TEN Austin. 10
XX Eagle; Stars and Stripes. 20	FARMER'S BANK, Orwell, Vt. Sheaf of grain; plough and harrow. Horse.	20 Steam ferry-boat and canoe, with two men. 20

Left	Center	Right
FIFTY	50 FARMER'S BANK. 50 Orwell, Vt. Vig. Sheep, ships, and mountain in the distance; man making fence. Dog's head, safe, and key.	FIFTY
1 Mason at work	Female portrait in oval frame FAR. & MECH. B'K ONE DOLLAR Burlington, Vt. Beehive	1 ONE 1
Man and sheep. 1	(Old Plate) 1 Man and horse; cattle, sheep, &c. 1 FAR. & MECH. B'K, Burlington, Vt. Dog and safe.	Blacksmith seated. 1
Two dollars. Sheep. Two dollars.	2 Harvest scene; two full length figures and dog. 2 FAR. & MECH. BK., Burlington, Vt.	Two dollars. Cattle. Two dollars.
2 2	Train of cars; river and mountains in distance. FAR. & MECH. BK., Burlington, Vt. Steamer.	2 2
3 THREE 3	Female seated; fruit and grain lying around; vessels in distance. FAR. & MECH. BK., Burlington, Vt. Eagle.	3 THREE 3
THREE Milkmaid. 3	3 Blacksmith seated, with sledge-hammer; cars in distance. FAR. & MECH. BK., Burlington, Vt. Dog and safe.	THREE Reaper and dog. 3
5 Eagle.	Steamer and vessels. FAR. & MECH. BK., Burlington, Vt. Sheaf of wheat.	Head of female. 5
Female and child seated on a plough; reapers in distance. 10	10 FAR. & MECH. BK., Burlington, Vt. Eagle.	Steamboat and vessels. 10
20 Female.	Steamer and vessels. FAR. & MECH. BK., Burlington, Vt. Wheat.	Blacksmith. 20

Left	Centre	Right
FIFTY Female reaper.	Spread eagle. FAR. & MECH. BK., Burlington, Vt. Locomotive.	50
100 Portrait of Washington 100	Spread Eagle. FAR. & MECH. B'K. Burlington, Vt. Dog and safe.	100
ONE Female portrait.	Man sitting holding sledge; train of cars, factory, &c. in background. 1 FRANKLIN CO. B'K. St. Alban's Bay, Vt. Cog-wheel, bale, &c.	Female standing behind pillar. ONE
TWO Female and shield, spear in right hand, branch in left.	Female reclining on bale of goods; canal boat, train of cars, town, shipping, &c. in background. FRANKLIN CO. B'K, St. Alban's Bay, Vt. Safe.	2 Female sitting. TWO
FIVE Female Indian, bow, spear, &c. in right hand, quiver of arrows on back.	5 Female portrait, eagle, shield, &c.; steamer, sail vessel, train of cars, factory &c. in background FRANKLIN CO. B'K, St. Alban's Bay, Vt. Steamer.	FIVE Sailor, capstan, hogshead, &c.
10 Portrait of Franklin. 10	Steamboat; wharf buildings, sail vessels, &c. in background. FRANKLIN CO. B'K, St. Alban's Bay, Vt. Horn of plenty.	10 Locomotive and cars. 10
20 Locomotive. 20	Female, sheaves of grain, &c FRANKLIN CO. B'K, St. Alban's Bay, Vt. Sail vessel.	20 Steamship. 20
Shed, flowers on the roof; two women, one churning, one turning cheese, poultry and cattle, part in the water.	ONE Oxen, cart and hay; man lying, and man with fork on his shoulder. LAMOILLE CO. BK., Hyde Park, Vt.	1 Mechanics' arm.
TWO Woods, stream and Indian creeping with gun.	LAMOILLE CO. BK., Hyde Park, Vt. Woman, eagle, sword, &c. Ocean.	2 Two deers, one feeding; rocks, meadow, &c.
THREE	LAMOILLE CO. BK., Hyde Park, Vt. Cattle and sheep. Female bathing.	3 Lady with veil.

Left	Centre	Right
V Woman blowing horn, table and crockery, load hay in distance, span on load, man with rake, another with scythe sitting.	LAMOILLE CO. BK., Hyde Park, Vt. Wild horses running.	5
Santa Claus driving four reindeers. TEN	Female with hand over her eyes. LAMOILLE CO. BK., Hyde Park, Vt.	10 Village scene, coaches, load of hay, riding horseback, driving cattle, &c.
TWENTY 20 Three dogs.	Indian tent, squaw and two Indians houses, train of cars. Portrait of Webster. LAMOILLE CO. BK., Hyde Park, Vt. Dog	20 XX 20
L	LAMOILLE CO. BK., 50 Hyde Park, Vt. Two females, train of cars, ship, bundle of grain, &c. Head of Washington.	FIFTY. Two soldiers one seated with pipe.
100 Jackson.	LAMOILLE CO. BK., Hyde Park, Vt. Female seated, rooster, two cows, &c.; trees and shed	100 Clay.
Three females with anchor; party sitting; party standing. ONE	Train of cars; village in the distance. MERCHANT'S BK. Burlington, Vt. State arms.	1 Female with spy-glass, sitting beside a bale; ships in the distance.
Female head. 2	Female sitting by a bale; haying scene, and train of cars in the distance. MERCHANT'S BK., Burlington, Vt. State Arms.	2 Engine, depot, &c.
Portrait of McDonough. 3	Female seated with a basket containing ears of corn, melons, fruit, &c., by her side; lake, sails, village, mountains, &c., in the distance. MERCHANT'S BK., Burlington, Vt. State arms.	3 Female portrait.
Portrait of Madison. 5	[First Plate.] Three females with basket of fruit, trident and spear; ship in background. MERCHANT'S BK., Burlington, Vt. State Arms.	5 Sailor with spy glass.
FIVE Female with spear, shield and branch. FIVE	[Second Plate.] 5 Female with horn of plenty and trident, sitting beside her rale, and sheaf of grain; bridge, cars, village and ship in the distance. MERCHANT'S BK., Burlington, Vt. State Arms.	5 Portrait of Harrison.

Left	Centre	Right
TEN Female with spear, standing beside a globe.	10 Female, globe, book; factory in the background. MERCHANT'S BK., Burlington, Vt. State Arms.	10 Portrait of Franklin. TEN
20 Female seated with spear, standing beside a globe.	Female seated between figures 2 and 0. MERCHANT'S BK., Burlington, Vt. XX	20 Small figure of a female. 20
50 Female with spear and shield.	Male and female seated; horn of plenty. MERCHANT'S BK., Burlington, Vt. 50	50 Cupid in a sail-boat. 50
100 Male seated.	Eagle upon a branch; bridge, and train of cars passing over it. MERCHANT'S BK., Burlington, Vt C C 100	100 Female with rake, and horn of plenty.
1 Man with scythe.	MISSISQUOI BANK, Sheldon, Vt. Large spread eagle.	1 Female representing Agriculture.
1	Female seated; train of cars and vessel on right, canal scene on left. 1 MISSISQUOI BANK, Sheldon, Vt	1 Female resting arm on fence
Female portrait. 2	Female in clouds reclining on eagle. MISSISQUOI BANK, Sheldon, Vt.	2 Female portrait.
2	Man forcing sheep in water, another man erect; boy driving flock; buildings on right. 2 Title of Bank.	TWO Female seated. TWO
Indian head. 3	Female reclining on a chest; two females and cows on right; cars and ship on left. MISSISQUOI BANK, Sheldon, Vt.	3 Indian head.
3	Man on horseback; cows and men; load of hay entering barn. 3 Title of Bank.	Word three, and figure 3. Female with basket of flowers. TH 3REE

FIVE
Eagle on shield; city and ships in distance. Large V, female and Cupid.
Title of Bank.
5
Girl with basket of flowers or fruit.

TEN
Vulcan seated, anvil, sledge, &c.; train of cars and buildings in distance. X
Title of Bank.
10
Farmer with sheaf on his knee.

20
Female sitting, with book.
XX Eagle. XX
Title of Bank.
20
Ship under sail.

FIFTY
Female with wreath.
FIFTY
50 Man and Horse. 50
Title of Bank.
FIFTY
Full length female, Globe Bale, &c.
FIFTY

100
Eagle.
100
C Horses and Chariot, Female. 100
Title of Bank.
C
Washington.
C

Milkmaid, cows, etc.
1
MUTUAL BANK, Castleton, Vt.
Boy and two horses; house and train of cars in background.
1
Female with hen and chickens in her arms.

Two children
2
Title of Bank.
Two men and horse; city in distance
2
Two men, one husking corn, the other with basket on his shoulder.

Vulcan with anvil, sledge, wheel, etc.
FIVE
Title of Bank.
Bust of Washington and three female artists.
5
Cattle, cars, bridge, etc.

Washington.
10
Title of Bank.
Spread eagle on shield; city, ships, etc., in distance.
10
Castleton Seminary and grounds.

State Arms.
20
Title of Bank.
Cars passing under bridge; two laborers, etc.
Female bathing.
20
Bust of a Boy

1
Portrait of Frank Pierce
Farmer sitting; cows.
NORTHFIELD B'K, Northfield, Vt.
Beehive.
1
Train of cars

ONE
Treas. die.
Cupid and 1.
NORTHFIELD B'K., Northfield, Vt.
Four males, two females, child, dog; horses, load of grain and team in distance.
Boxes, bbls., &c.
1
Male portrait

2
Factory girl at work.
NORTHFIELD B'K. Northfield. Vt.
Blacksmith's shop, Blacksmith shoeing a horse.
2
Female head.

Treas. die.
Mechanic seated by a boiler; men at work on boiler in distance. Male portrait
NORTHFIELD BK, Northfield, Vt.
Agricultural Implements.
2
Cupid and 2

Treas. die.
3
Milkmaid seated with pail; cars in distance.
NORTHFIELD BK, Northfield, Vt.
Dog's head.
3
Male portrait

3
Horse market. Female head.
NORTHFIELD B'K. Northfield, Vt.
3
Dairy maid milking.

Treas. die.
5
NORTHFIELD BK., Northfield, Vt.
Five gold dollars, three Cupids, hunter and Indian; cars in distance.
Cog-wheels, etc.
5
Male portrait

5
Indian
Train of cars.
NORTHFIELD B'K. Northfield, Vt.
5
Female head

10
Female head.
Load of hay, train of cars and packet boat.
NORTHFIELD B'K. Northfield. Vt.
State Arms.
10
Vulcan.

TEN
Treas. die.
10
Train of cars; steamboat and houses in distance.
NORTHFIELD BK, Northfield, Vt.
Mechanics arm.
10
Male portrait

20
Henry Clay sitting, dog at his feet.
Cow and sheep, church in background.
NORTHFIELD B'K, Northfield, Vt.
20
Male portrait.

50
Vulcan, sledge on right shoulder, wheel in left hand.
NORTHFIELD B'K. Northfield, Vt.
Men on horseback, watering horse at trough; two boys and dogs.
50
Male portrait.

100
Vulcan.
NORTHFIELD B'K. Northfield, Vt.
Elliott preaching to the Indians.
100
Portrait of Gov. Paine.

ONE
PASSUMPSIC BANK, St. Johnsbury, Vt.
Cattle and sheep. 1
1
Blacksmith and anvil.

TWO
PASSUMPSIC BANK, St. Johnsbury, Vt.
Man with sledge on his shoulder; factory and cars in distance. 2
State arms.
2
Two females.

THREE
PASSUMPSIC BANK, St. Johnsbury, Vt.
Female with horn of plenty, barrels, &c.; ships, factories and train of cars. 3
Head of dog.
3
Head of Webster.

5
PASSUMPSIC BANK. St. Johnsbury, Vt.
Drove of cattle and sheep; man on horseback. 5
FIVE
Indian erect with bow and spear.

TEN
PASSUMPSIC BANK. St. Johnsbury, Vt.
Train of cars. X
Boy's head.
10
Female with pole and cap.

20
PASSUMPSIC BANK, St. Johnsbury, Vt.
Female seated on sheaf of grain; men loading grain in distance.
10
Female with scales and sword.

Eagle upon shield, bale and barrel, with anchor, sheaf of grain, &c.; falls and factory in distance.
50
PASSUMPSIC BANK, St. Johnsbury, Vt.
Imp. and products
50
Female with sheaf and sickle.

100 — PASSUMPSIC BANK, St. Johnsbury, Vt. 100. Female and eagle soaring in the air. Dog and safe. 100. Female with basket of flowers.

ONE — Two horses; farm-house in distance. 1 ONE. PEOPLES' BANK, Derby Line, Vt. Boy gathering corn. ONE.

1 — Female. 1 Female. 1. PEOPLE'S BANK, Derby Line, Vt. Portrait of Washington. Portrait of Franklin.

2 — Female with horn of plenty. 2 Female. 2. PEOPLE'S BANK, Derby Line, Vt. Male portrait. Male portrait.

2 — Man watering three horses; female feeding pigs; farm house in distance. 2. Title of Bank. Female picking fruit. Farmer with scythe.

3 — Child. 3 Child. 3. PEOPLE'S BANK, Derby Line, Vt. Washington standing by his horse. Blacksmith with hammer and anvil.

Eagle on shield with manufacturing village in distance. Large V with female with horn of plenty and a child. 5. PEOPLE'S BANK, Derby Line, Vt. FIVE. Child with basket.

5 — Drove of cattle and sheep. 5. Title of Bank. Washington. Train of cars.

10 — 10 Three farmers and female at lunch; horses, etc. X. Four small portraits of ex Presidents. Title of Bank. 10. Indian seated.

Blacksmith with hammer and anvil. X 10. PEOPLE'S BANK, Derby Line, Vt. TEN. Reaper with bundle of grain and sickle.

20 — 2 Female. 0 20. PEOPLES' BANK, Derby Line, Vt. Man with helmet and spear, globe under owl at his feet. XX. Female. 20.

50 — Vig. Female holding a cup sitting, man sitting, holding a scroll, foot resting on an anchor. 50. Man with helmet and spear standing beside a broken column. PEOPLE'S BANK, Derby Line, Vt. 50. Cupid in a sail boat. 50.

100 — Vig. Eagle on a branch of a tree, train of cars, locks and two canal boats. 100. Man sitting, holding a scroll, foot resting on an anchor. PEOPLE'S BANK, Derby Line, Vt. 100. Female sitting holding a rake.

1 — 1 Train of cars; moving blocks of marble, etc. 1. 1. RUTLAND CO. BANK. ONE DOLLAR. ONE 1 ONE. Rutland, Vt. Tree, cattle, grain, etc., in round die. Male portrait.

2 — 2 Man cutting marble in oval die. RUTLAND CO. BANK. Male portrait. Die TWO DOLLARS Die. Two Dollars. 2.

5 — RUTLAND CO. BANK. V and FIVE DOLLARS. 5. 5. Two children and cattle under tree, sheep in distance. Male portrait.

1 — ST. ALBANS' BANK, St. Albans, Vt. 1. View of Street, cattle and men, load of hay; town in distance. Vig. Selling Cattle.

2 — ST. ALBANS' BANK, St. Albans, Vt. 2. Sailor leaning on capstan, merchandise and anchor on right, ships masts on left. Vig. Catching Horse. Mechanic and tools.

3 — ST ALBANS' BANK, St. Albans, Vt. 3. Blacksmith's shop; men at work, smith shoeing horse. Squaw. Female and grain.

Three females on a rock with anchor spy-glass, &c. Three females and Cupid. 5. ST. ALBANS' BANK, St. Albans, Vt. FIVE. Eagle. Female.

10 — Train of cars; view of river and town; cars crossing bridge. 10. ST. ALBANS' BANK, St. Albans, Vt. Male portrait. Farming implements. Farmer gathering grain.

20 — Three females with wand, cornucopia, sword and balances; vessels on right. 20. ST. ALBANS' BANK, St. Albans, Vt. Female. Female artist; around her mechanical tools.

50 — ST. ALBANS' BANK, St. Albans, Vt. 50. Portrait of Washington. Female. Train of cars, village in background.

100 — U. S. Capitol at Washington. 100. ST. ALBANS' BANK, St. Albans, Vt. Soldiers with fife and drum. Portrait of Webster.

1 Female with cornucopia. 1. STARK BANK, Bennington, Vt. Goddess of Liberty with cap and shield and eagle. Head of Gen. Stark.

2 — Train of cars; city and mountains in distance. 2. STARK BANK, Bennington, Vt. Head of Abby Hutchinson. 2. Nymph bathing. Head of Gen. Stark.

FIVE 5 — Drover on horseback with dog, driving sheep; mill in distance. 5. STARK BANK, Bennington, Vt. Head of Gen. Stark. Wheelbarrow and sheaf. Head of Washington.

STARK BANK, Bennington, Vt. 10. Head of Gen. Stark. Winged female with cornucopia; female with quadrant. X. State arms and two females.

20 — Head of Gen. Stark supported by Liberty, Justice, and Truth; ship in background. 20. Female with sheaf, sickle, &c. STARK BANK, Bennington, Vt. Head of Webster.

Female seated. Signing the Declaration of Independence. 50. STARK BANK, Bennington, Vt. 50. Head of Gen. Stark.

Red 1. Cattle, load of hay.	STATE BANK, Montpelier, Vt. State House.	Red 1. State Arms.
Red 2. State Arms.	State House, separating the words "State Bank," and small female head on right	Red 2. Farmer gathering corn
Female portrait. Red 5.	State House. State Arms. Title of Bank.	Red 5. Female feeding fowls
1 Washington.	Female 1 Female UNION BANK, Swanton Falls, Vt.	1 Franklin.
1 Farmer with sickle and sheaf of grain; cars and canal-boat in distance.	Portrait of Washington. UNION BANK, Swanton Falls, Vt. Large figure 1, with words one dollar running across it,	1 Indian with bow sitting down; huts and canoe in distance.
2 Female sitting down with sword and scales; cars in distance.	Portrait of Franklin. UNION BANK, Swanton Falls, Vt. TWO 2 DOLLARS	2 Female sitting down with cap of liberty on a pole; church and houses in distance.
2 Portrait of Columbus.	Portrait of female with flowers. 2 Portrait of female with sword and scales. UNION BANK, Swanton Falls, Vt.	2 Male portrait.
3 Indian sitting down with bow; hut in distance.	UNION BANK, Swanton Falls, Vt. III 3	3 Sailor sitting on bale of goods; steamship in distance.
3 Washington standing beside his horse.	Portrait of female. 3 Portrait of girl. UNION BANK, Swanton Falls, Vt.	3 Man standing with sleigh.
FIVE	Female kneeling against a shield. V UNION BANK, Swanton Falls, Vt.	5 Ship.

Five on V. Drover on horseback with cattle and sheep. 5	Title of Bank. FIVE 5 DOLLARS	Five on V. 5
X Hunter and dog by fire.	Drove of wild horses. UNION BANK, Swanton Falls, Vt.	10 Girl.
X Indian with bow and arrows.	Steamboat and sail vessels; wharf and buildings in distance. X Title of Bank	10 Female with sheaf of grain under her arm, and hat in her hand.
Cattle and sheep; one of each standing the rest reclining. XX	Female portrait. UNION BANK, Swanton Falls, Vt.	20 Hunter drinking from a brook.
20 Female seated, book in left hand, right hand on a box.	XX Eagle. XX UNION BANK, Swanton Falls, Vt.	20 Ship, with buildings in the distance.
FIFTY Female with wreath of flowers on her head and in her hands FIFTY	50 Man and horse. 50 Title of Bank.	FIFTY Female with flowers in her left hand FIFTY
Fig. 100 with words one hundred across. Harrison.	Covered wagon, wharf, ships, warehouses, truckmen, &c Title of Bank.	Same as on left end. Columbus.
ONE State Arms. ONE	Cows; and man ploughing. VERMONT BANK. Montpelier, Vt.	1 Portrait of a lady. ONE
2 Head of Franklin. TWO	State Arms, surmounted with a stag's head; lady on left; man on right; fruit, &c., below. VERMONT BANK. Montpelier,	2 Head of Washington. TWO
THREE Locomotive and cars.	State Arms, with female; churn and pail on the right; man with plough and rake on the left. VERMONT BANK, Montpelier,	3 Female with bow and arrow.

5 Female with sheaf of wheat and sickle. FIVE	Agricultural scene; haymaker's and team; female seated on left; farmer's loading hay, on right. VERMONT BANK, Montpelier,	5 State Arms; female figure each side. FIVE
10 Lady's Portrait 10	Man ploughing; cattle grazing; cars passing under bridge; and in the distance, on left, village and train of cars. VERMONT BANK, Montpelier,	10 State Arms; female figure each side. TEN
20 Full length female, holding a spear; globe standing partly behind the female.	2 Female. 0 VERMONT BANK, Montpelier, XX	20 Female sitting; horn of plenty, and bales. 20
50 Full length female figure holding a spear in right hand; left hand rests on a shield.	Male and female seated. VERMONT BANK, Montpelier, 50	50 Cupid in a sail-boat. 50
100 Man sitting, holding a scroll.	Eagle on a tree; canal boat and cars in background. VERMONT BANK. Montpelier. 100 Vermont.	100 Female seated, holding a rake; fruit, &c.
Two females standing. 1	Cupid rolling silver dollar on railroad track, cars, city, &c. in distance. WEST RIVER B'K, Jamaica, Vt.	1 Female seated clasping figure 1 in her arms.
Two men bearing Goddess. 2	Two Cupids and two silver dollars; cars cattle, &c. in distance. WEST RIVER B'K, Jamaica, Vt. Cow and calf.	2 Female churning.
Female sitting holding scales; sheaf of grain. 3	Three cupids and three silver dollars. WEST RIVER B'K, Jamaica, Vt. Man ploughing.	3 State arms. THREE
Female head. V	Five cupids and five silver dollars. WEST RIVER B'K, Jamaica, Vt.	5 Sailor and Indian seated; five on shield between them.
X Goddess erect holding trumpet Female seated holding liberty cap; eagle, &c.	Goddess and cherub holding portrait of Washington between them. WEST RIVER B'K, Jamaica, Vt.	10 Stonecutter at work.

XX | Female seated by shield, sheaf, &c.; lighthouse and ships in distance. | 20
Female erect with shield and spear. | WEST RIVER BANK Jamaica, Vt. TWENTY | Female representing Agriculture.

Justice. | Female and eagle soaring. | 50
WEST RIVER BANK Jamaica, Vt.
FIFTY | FIFTY | Jackson.

State of Vermont
Boy watering horse in stream; dog, woods, etc. | 1 Male portrait 1 Bethel | 1
WHITE RIVER B'K
ONE | 1 ONE DOLLAR on ONE 1 | Tree, cow, and grain

Female representing Commerce. Man in top of 1. | 1
WHITE RIVER BK., Bethel, Vt. | Female with grain; fence, etc.
1

WHITE RIVER B'K
2 | TWO DOLLARS 2 on TWO 2 | 2
Soldiers, drummer-boy, etc | Bethel State of Vermont | Boy with bird's nest

---

Sheep washing scene. Man in top of 2 | TWO
WHITE RIVER B'K, Bethel, Vt. | Female with garland of flowers
2 | TWO

WHITE RIVER B'K
3 | Bethel Man with boy pointing THREE to bust THREE of Washington | 3
Female portrait | State of Vermont THREE DOLLARS | Boy's portrait

---

Man on horse; cattle, dog, load of hay, &c. 3 | 3
WHITE RIVER B'K. Bethel, Vt.
3 | Female with basket

---

5 | V Female with bird on her hand, leaning on column; flowers, etc. in background V | 5
WHITE RIVER B'K FIVE DOLLARS Bethel
Soldier loading gun | V

Spread eagle, on shield; village and ship in distance. | Large V, female and child. | 5
FIVE | WHITE RIVER BK., Bethel, Vt | Little girl with basket.

TEN on X | WHITE RIVER B'K TEN Scene in an encampment, officer reading dispatch, others writing, etc. TEN on X X | 10
Water fall | TEN DOLLARS Bethel | Indian girl

Vulcan the blacksmith seated, factory and building in distance. | X | 10
TEN | WHITE RIVER BK., Bethel, Vt. | Man tying up bundle of grain.

State of Vermont
TWENTY | Girl's head Bethel XX Girl's head | 20
Female writing on scroll, child at her feet | WHITE RIVER B'K TWENTY DOLLARS on TWENTY | Female with torch beside column
TWENTY

---

20 | XX Eagle XX | 20
Female seated. | WHITE RIVER BK., Bethel, Vt | Brig.

FIFTY | 50 Man and horse 50 | FIFTY
Female erect. | | Female erect.
FIFTY | WHITE RIVER BK., Bethel, Vt | FIFTY

The figures 100 with the words "one hundred" | Wharf scene, wagons, horses, men, vessels, &c. | Same as on the left.
Portrait of Harrison. | WHITE RIVER BK. Bethel Vt | Male Portrait.

ONE | WINDHAM COUNTY BANK, Brattleboro, Vt. | 1
Man and three horses at well; grain; sheep, houses, etc. 1 | Indian apparently asleep.

---

2 | Title of Bank. | 2
Farmer plowing. | Cattle; farming scenes, etc., in distance. | Female with sheaf and sickle.
TWO | 2

---

3 | WINDHAM COUNTY BANK, Brattleboro, Vt. THREE | 3
Indian head.
THREE | 3 Farmers operating with reaping machine.

---

5 | Title of Bank. | Five and 5.
Horse on either side of a shield, on which is an eagle, tree, cow, etc.; cars, building, etc. in distance
Indian head | 5

X | Title of Bank | 10
Three females and bust representing the Arts and Sciences.
10 | X

XX inverted. | Title of Bank. | 20 inverted.
TWENTY DOLLARS on dies.
Milkmaid and cows. | Two females on right of a shield, on it agricultural implements and products; cars, building, etc., in distance.

---

50 | Title of Bank. | 50
Mechanic erect with anvil and hammer; buildings in distance.
Milkmaid; cows and horse in the distance. | Liberty seated.

---

100 | Title of Bank. | 100
Female on either side of a beehive.
Washington | Martha Washington

ONE | One on 1. Cattle, sheep, and colt, boy on horse. | 1
Blacksmith with anvil; cars in distance. | WOODSTOCK BANK, Woodstock, Vt. | ONE

Two men carrying female on their shoulders. | Agricultural scene; man reaping, and female with sheaf in her arms. | 1
State Arms.
ONE | WOODSTOCK BANK. Woodstock. Vt. Female. | ONE

TWO | Two females seated with cornucopia; anvil between them; factory in distance. | 2
Two children. | WOODSTOCK BANK, Woodstock, Vt. | Female portrait.

---

2 Female seated on plow with sheaf and sickle; train of cars on right. 2 | Milkmaid erect.
Man with sheaf of grain on his knee. | WOODSTOCK BANK. Woodstock. Vt. Sheaf, plow, &c.

Female with scales, bale. | 3 Female reclining on cornucopia; ship in distance. | 3
WOODSTOCK BANK, Woodstock, Vt.
THREE | Three on 3.

Female with horn of plenty at her feet, figure 3 on shield. | Farm scene with drovers. | 3
THREE | WOODSTOCK BANK, Woodstock. Vt. Man plowing | Indian Queen

5 Portrait of Washington.	State Arms; on either side female and ea, ld. WOODSTOCK BANK. Woodstock, Vt. Sheaf, plow, &c.	5 Female Portrait.
10 Med. head and word TEN. Some cars	State Arms, on left female seated with pole and cap; on right eagle. WOODSTOCK BANK, Woodstock. Vt. Bull.	10 Male and female; male shearing sheep; mill in back ground.
Female erect and capstan. 20	Portrait of Washington surrounded by all the State Arms and implements of war. WOODSTOCK BANK, Woodstock, Vt. Bull.	20 Cupid in sail boat. 20
50 Female erect with spear and shield.	Female and eagle soaring in clouds with shield between them. WOODSTOCK BANK, Woodstock, Vt. Man plowing with two horses, Some dog's head	50 Female erect with hand on capstan.
Female 100	C Portrait of Washington surrounded by flags C WOODSTOCK BANK ONE HUNDRED	100 Cupid 100
Female.	Cherub reclining holding an American coin; cornucopia, box, barrels, &c. WOODSTOCK BANK, Woodstock, Vt. Bull.	Two males carrying a female. 100
1	Train of cars. 1 ABINGTON BANK. Abington, Mass. State Arms	1 Female ure an chorn'
2	Cattle, village and train of cars in the background. 2 ABINGTON BANK. Abington, Mass. Female, head.	2 State arms.
THREE	State arms with a female on either side Cupid and 3. ABINGTON BANK. Abington, Mass. Wheel, bale, etc	THREE Female. THREE
5	Female eagle and shield. V Female and sheaf of wheat. ABINGTON BANK. Abington, Mass. Wheels, bale, &c	FIVE Female and 5.

10	Female, eagle and safe. X ABINGTON BANK. Abington, Mass.	TEN Portrait of Adams.
20 Female	2 Female with rake 0 ABINGTON BANK, Abington, Mass. XX	20 Female 20
50 Female figure.	Male and female. ABINGTON BANK, Abbington, Mass. 50	50 Cupid in a sail boat. 50
100 Vulcan	Eagle, train of cars and canal. ABINGTON BANK, Abington, Mass. 100	100 Female.
Female giving eagle drink. 1	Cherub holding silver dollar; ship, cars, bridge and train of cars in distance. ADAMS BANK, North Adams, Mass.	1 Indian seated with fig. 1.
1 Portrait of Washington.	Female. 1 Female. ADAMS BANK, North Adams, Mass.	1 Portrait of Franklin.
ONE 1	Farmer sowing grain. 1 ADAMS BANK, North Adams, Mass.	1 Ship. ONE
2 Portrait of Columbus.	Female. 2 Female. ADAMS BANK, North Adams, Mass.	2 Portrait
Two females. 2	Two cherubs and two silver dollars; cars in distance. ADAMS BANK, North Adams, Mass.	2 Sailor and Indian on either side of TWO on shield.
TWO 2	Spread Eagle. 2 ADAMS BANK, North Adams, Mass.	2 Sail boats

3 Gen. Washington.	Portrait of female. 3 Portrait of female. ADAMS BANK. North Adams, Mass	3 Man with sledge.
THREE 3	Wharf and shipping. 3 on right ADAMS BANK. North Adams, Mass.	3 Train of cars
Girl stepping in water. FIVE	5 ADAMS BANK. FIVE DOLLARS. Two females; city in distance. North Adams.	5 Massachusetts. FiveDollars
Indian with bow. V	5 Vulcan and two female figures. 5 ADAMS BANK, North Adams, Mass.	V Train of cars V
Deer X TEN	ADAMS BANK. Female pouring water from urn. X TEN DOLLARS North Adams	10 Girl and dogs
10 Train of cars. 10	X Archimides. X ADAMS BANK. North Adams, Mass.	Female 10
20 Female with spear.	Female between figures 2 and 0. ADAMS BANK. North Adams. Mass. XX	20 Female 20
50 Female figure.	Male and female. ADAMS BANK. North Adams. Mass. 50	50 Cupid in a sail boat. 50
100 Vulcan with implements	Spread eagle, railroad and canal. ADAMS BANK, North Adams, Mass. 100	100 Female with rake.
Two males and female. ONE	Female supporting the figure 1. 1 AGAWAM BANK. Springfield, Mass. Deer	1 Portrait of a female.

2	Indian with figure 2, deer and canoe. AGAWAM BANK. Springfield, Mass. State Arms.	2 Reaper.
Two females. 3	3 AGAWAM BANK. Springfield, Mass. Cow	3 Portrait of a boy.
A party of Indians receiving a company of white men. 5	V and female. AGAWAM BANK. Springfield. Mass.	FIVE Female. 5
Female with sickle and sheaf of wheat. X	X AGAWAM BANK. Springfield Mass. Products and implements	10 Portrait of a girl.
20 Cupid in a sail boat. 20	Steamship. AGAWAM BANK. Springfield, Mass. Products and implements	20 Spread eagle and shield.
50 Indian girl with bow and arrows.	Female and eagle L on shield. AGAWAM BANK. Springfield, Mass. Cow	50 Female.
100 Female resting her hand upon a capstan.	Load of grain crossing a bridge. 100 AGAWAM BANK Springfield, Mass Dogs	100 Milk maid.
ONE Drove of cattle. ONE	(Old Plate.) 1 Train of cars. 1 AGRICULTURAL BANK, Pittsfield, Mass.	ONE
ONE on 1 Female instructing children.	(New Plate.) Farming scene. AGRICULTURAL BANK, Pittsfield. Mass.	1 Indian woman and child.
TWO	(Old Plate.) 2 Milk maids; vessels in the distance. AGRICULTURAL BANK. Pittsfield. Mass. State Arms.	2 Man ploughing with horses.

Two female figures.	(New Plate.) Farming scene; female in foreground. TWO in 2 on right AGRICULTURAL BANK. Pittsfield. Mass.	2 State arms.
Female with sickle and horn of plenty; ship in distance. Three on 3	AGRICULTURAL BK. Pittsfield. Mass. Vig. White and black horse facing each other, Indian on shield surmounted with eagle between them, at right of black horse a steamboat, on left of white horse canal boat, cars and manufacturing establishment.	3 Milk maid; cars and house in distance.
Female with sickle 3	State arms and 2 horses; factories, railroad and steamboat in distance. AGRICULTURAL BANK, Pittsfield, Mass.	3 Milk maid.
FIVE Man and agricultural implements. 5	5 View of Pittsfield. 5 AGRICULTURAL BANK. Pittsfield, Mass. State Arms	FIVE
FIVE Train of cars passing under a bridge.	Female reclining with her arm upon a chest; factories in background. AGRICULTURAL BK. Pittsfield, Mass.	5 Wood cutter.
10 X 10	Man and oxen. Large 10 at the right of Vig. AGRICULTURAL BANK. Pittsfield. Mass.	TEN Female figure.
10 Portrait of Webster.	Train of cars. AGRICULTURAL BK, Pittsfield, Mass.	Ten, X, 10. Hay makers.
20 Female.	XX Eagle. XX AGRICULTURAL BANK, Pittsfield, Mass.	20 Ship
TWENTY Farmer grinding scythe, stone being turned by negro. 20	XX AGRICULTURAL BANK, Massachusetts. TWENTY DOLLARS Pittsfield.	Horses drinking at trough; boy, women, &c. TWENTY. 20
Female figure holding plate, on which is written "Incorporated A. D. 1818."	FIFTY DOLLARS. 5 Agricultural implements. AGRICULTURAL BANK. FIFTY DOLLARS on FIFTY.	50 Dog on safe

1 Female with scales.	Train of cars. ANDOVER BANK Andover Mass. Eagle.	1 Portrait of Samuel Farrar.
TWO Female with the American flag.	Three female figures. ANDOVER BANK Andover, Mass. Indian head	2 Portrait of Samuel Farrar.
3 State arms.	Three female figures. ANDOVER BANK Andover, Mass, Cog-wheels, etc.	3 Portrait of Samuel Farrar.
Three female figures. FIVE	Spread eagle. ANDOVER BANK Andover, Mass. Girl's head.	5 Portrait of Samuel Farrar.
10 Portrait of Samuel Farrar.	Winged female blowing a trumpet. ANDOVER BANK Andover. Mass. Imp. and products	10 Female holding Scales
20 Portrait of Samuel Farrar.	Farming scene. ANDOVER BANK Andover, Mass	20 Female.
Female with sheaf of wheat. 50	Landing of Columbus ANDOVER BANK Andover. Mass.	50 Portrait of Female.
100	Female seated with eagle, shield, flags, etc. Female portrait. ANDOVER BANK, Andover, Mass.	100 Female portrait.
500 Indian princess.	Title of Bank. Three females; ship and cars in distance.	500 500
M 1000	Title of Bank. Two females seated; shipping and cars in distance.	1000 1000

Female figure beside column, with torch in hand
ONE
APPLETON BANK
1 Blacksmith seated, factory in background. 1
ONE DOLLAR
Lowell
Massachusetts
ONE on 1

ONE
Eagle with shield in talons; and ONE on shield.
Vig. Blacksmith blowing at forge, wheel behind him; anvil in front. 1
APPLETON BANK, Lowell, Mass.
1
Farmer with sickle and bundle of grain.

APPLETON BANK
Two women beside large machine
2 and Lowell
TWO DOLLARS
TWO
Massachusetts
2
Male portrait

2
Vig. Sheep washing scene. 2
APPLETON BANK, Lowell, Mass.
Cow and fence.
2
Locomotive and cars.

3
Landing of Europeans in America
APPLETON BANK
THREE DOLLARS on 3
Massachusetts
3
Blacksmith at work

3
Vig. Blacksmith's shop, man and horse, smith at anvil; dog at his feet, and boy at forge 3
APPLETON BANK, Lowell, Mass.
Dog
3
Male portrait.

5
Vig. A person driving horses in chariot, accompanied by train of people; an angel above horses. 5
APPLETON BANK. Lowell, Mass.
FIVE
Medallion head
5

X
Vig. Large house, train of cars; man with wheelbarrow; and steeple of church in distance. X
APPLETON BANK, Lowell, Mass.
TEN
Indian female.
TEN

20
Woman sitting, with left hand on an open book
XX Eagle XX
APPLETON BANK, Lowell, Mass.
20
Ship.

XX
Female with tablets; child at her feet.
APPLETON BANK, Lowell, Mass.
Title of Bank.
TWENTY
20
Boy and two horses at trough.

L
Washingt'n
APPLETON BANK. Lowell, Mass.
Title of Bank
50 DOLLS.
50
Martha Washingt'n

FIFTY
A woman with a wreath in her left hand.
FIFTY
50 Vig. A man with his right hand on the mane of a wild horse. 50
APPLETON BANK, Lowell, Mass.
FIFTY
A woman with a bunch of flowers in her left hand.
FIFTY

C
Female, cog wheels, etc.
APPLETON BANK Lowell, Mass.
Title of Bank
One Hundred Dollars
100
Female spinning wheel; factories, etc.

Same as right
Portrait of Harrison.
Vig. A wharf with a large covered waggon, into which two men are rolling a hogshead.
APPLETON BANK, Lowell, Mass.
One Hundred and 100.
Male portrait.

D
APPLETON BANK, Lowell, Mass.
Title of Bank.
Dog & safe.
500 DOLLS.
500
Eagle.

500
Vig. Woman sitting, pointing with her left hand to men reaping, and a man on horseback. 500 D
APPLETON BANK, Lowell, Mass.
500

Female.
ONE
View in Essex street, Salem.
ASIATIC BANK Salem Mass.
1
Elephants.
ONE

TWO
Elephants.
TWO
View in Essex street. Salem.
ASIATIC BANK Salem, Mass.
TWO
Female.
TWO

THREE
Female.
THREE
View in Essex street, Salem
ASIATIC BANK Salem, Mass.
3
Elephants.
THREE

Female.
FIVE
View in Essex street, Salem.
ASIATIC BANK. Salem, Mass.
V
Elephants.
FIVE

TEN
10 View in Essex street, Salem X
ASIATIC BANK Salem, Mass.
10
Female.

20
Man ploughing with Horses.
20
20 Party of milk maids.
ASIATIC BANK Salem, Mass.
20
Ship.
XX

20
Female.
XX Eagle XX
ASIATIC BANK Salem, Mass.
20
Ship

20
Female.
Female seated between fig. 2 and 0.
ASIATIC BANK, Salem, Mass.
XX
20
Female.
20

FIFTY
Female with wreath.
FIFTY
50 Man and horse. 50
ASIATIC BANK Salem, Mass.
FIFTY
Female.
FIFTY

50
Female figure.
Male and female.
ASIATIC BANK Salem Mass.
50
50
Cupid in sail boat.
50

Same as right
Portrait of Harrison.
Scene on a wharf.
ASIATIC BANK Salem, Mass.
One Hundred and 100.
Portrait of Columbus.

100
Vulcan
Spread Eagle train of cars and canal.
ASIATIC BANK Salem Mass.
100
100
Female.

500
Female seated pointing to reapers and load of hay. 500 D
Title of Bank.
500

Locomotive and serpents.
1000
THOUSAND
Title of Bank.
Cars and laborers
1000
Vessels.
1000

1 | ATLANTIC BANK, Boston, Mass. | 1
Portrait of Taylor enlarged | Spread eagle and ships above Title. | Female with spy glass.

1 | I Two sailors, anchor, rope, vessels, etc. | 1
ATLANTIC BANK, Boston, Mass.
State Arms | Female seated with spy glass; vessels, etc.

2 | Indian female, eagle, shield, steamer, etc. | 2 | TWO
Title of Bank.
Eagle, shield, etc. | Same as ones

2 | Steamship and other vessels. | TWO
Portrait of Taylor. | ATLANTIC BANK, Boston, Mass. | Female with spy glass.
TWO | TWO

Female seated with spy glass, vessels, etc. | Title of Bank. | 3
3 Sailor erect with spy-glass beside captain on vessel. 3
THREE | Female portrait.

Female with spy glass. | 3 Indian with gun and female with sickle. THREE between and eagle at top. | 3
ATLANTIC BANK, Boston, Mass.
3 | Sailor seated on a bale.

FIVE | Portrait of Taylor with Title on right. | FIVE
Male and female.
Winged female with trumpet. | V | 5

10 | Steamer and ships at sea | 10
Female seated with lamp, wheel, flowers, etc | ATLANTIC BANK TEN DOLLARS Boston | Female figure with scales and sword

Female. | Portrait of Taylor. | TEN
ATLANTIC BANK, Boston, Mass.
X | Female with spy glass.

20 | ATLANTIC BANK, Boston, Mass. | 20
20 Female reclining with quadrant, globe, etc. 20
Two females. | Pilot boat; vessels, etc

L | Title | Girl's head. | 50 on red die.
50 on red die. | Female erect with pen and tablets; child at her feet. | 50 on red die. | Man purchasing paper of news boy; bbls., steamer, etc.
FIFTY

100 | C Two children C | 100
ATLANTIC BANK, Boston, Mass.
Sailor, mechanic, vessels, etc. | Female

D | Title of Bank. | 500
Sailor, farmer, boy, dog, capstan, anchor, ocean view, etc.
Five Hundred | Five Hundred
500 | 500 | 500

1 ONE 1 | ONE Atlas supporting the globe on his shoulders. 1 | ONE DOLLAR
ATLAS BANK, Boston, Mass.

2 TWO 2 | TWO Vig. Same as ones. 2 | TWO DOLLARS
ATLAS BANK, Boston, Mass.

3 THREE 3 | THREE Vig. Same as ones. 3 | THREE DOLLARS
ATLAS BANK, Boston, Mass.

5 FIVE 5 | V Vig. Same as ones 5 | FIVE DOLLARS
ATLAS BANK, Boston, Mass.

10 TEN 10 | X Vig. Same as ones. | TEN DOLLARS
ATLAS BANK, Boston, Mass.

20 TWENTY 20 | XX Vig. Same as ones. 20 | TWENTY
ATLAS BANK, Boston, Mass.

50 FIFTY 50 | FIFTY Vig. Same as ones. 50 | FIFTY DOLLARS
ATLAS BANK, Boston, Mass.

100 | C Vig. Same as ones. 100 | ONE HUNDRED
100
ATLAS BANK, Boston, Mass.
100

This Bank also issues 500s and 1000s; they have the same vignette as all other denominations.

Vig. Locomotive and train of cars; village in the distance. | 1
1 | Drover and cattle.
1 | ATTLEBOROUGH BANK, Attleborough, Mass. | ONE

Vig. Farmer on horseback; load of hay entering barn; hay-makers, cattle, &c. 2 | 2
Female with bundle of grain and sickle.
2 | ATTLEBOROUGH BANK, Attleborough, Mass. | TWO

Female with grain under left arm; reapers, dwelling house and mill in the background. 3 | 3
Spread eagle.
3 | ATTLEBOROUGH BANK, Attleborough, Mass. | THREE

5 | Medallion head. Vig. Two females and cows other side surrounding the figure 5. | 5
Reaper sitting with a sickle in his hand. | Man harvesting corn.
5 | ATTLEBOROUGH BANK, Attleborough, Mass.

10 | Vig. Female and Eagle. | 10
ATTLEBOROUGH BANK, Attleborough, Mass.
Portrait of J. Q. Adams. | Man at work; house and bridge in background. | Farmer cradling grain.

20 | Vig. Two females sitting, plough and eagle between them; factory, man ploughing, steamboat and train of cars in the distance. | 20
Spread eagle. | Male portrait.
XX | ATTLEBOROUGH BANK, Attleborough, Mass. | XX
Dog.

50 | ATTLEBOROUGH BANK, Attleborough, Mass. | 50
Female bust. | Vig. Eagle bearing aloft person with arms extended; shrub under each arm. | Female sitting.
50 | State Arms. | 50

100 Vig. Male and female sitting; horn of plenty between. 100
ATTLEBOROUGH BANK, Attleborough, Mass.
Female sitting. | A deer. | Reaper with sickle and grain

1 ONE 1	View of Cattle fair hotel. B'K OF BRIGHTON, Brighton, Mass.	1 A bulls head. ONE
Milk Maid. 1	(Old Plate.) Cattle, sheep and hogs; scene in Brighton on a market day. B'K OF BRIGHTON, Brignton, Mass.	1 General Washington. ONE
TWO Female. 2	(Old Plate.) Cattle, sheep and hogs; a scene in Brighton on a market day. B'K OF BRIGHTON, Brighton, Mass.	2 TWO
2 TWO 2	(New Plate. View of cattle fair hotel. B'K OF BRIGHTON, Brighton, Mass.	TWO on 2. Yoke of oxen
3 Portrait. 3	(Old Plate.) Cattle, sheep and hogs; a scene in Brighton on a market day. B'K OF BRIGHTON, Brighton	3 Cattle. THREE
3 THREE 3	(New Plate.) View of Cattle fair hotel. B'K OF BRIGHTON, Brighton, Mass.	3 THREE Cattle.
5 Portrait of Franklin. 5	(Old Plate.) Cattle, sheep and hogs; scene in Brighton on a market day. B'K OF BRIGHTON, Brighton. Mass.	5 Female. V
5 V and FIVE 5	(New Plate.) View of Cattle fair hotel; B'K OF BRIGHTON, Brighton, N. Y.	FIVE, 5, V. Cattle and sheep.
10 Portrait of [illegible] 10	(Old Plate.) Cattle, sheep and hogs; a scene in Brighton on a market day. B'K OF BRIGHTON, Brighton, Mass.	10 Female; TEN
X Portrait of Webster. TEN	(New Plate.) View of cattle fair hotel. B'K OF BRIGHTON, Brighton. Mass.	10 Locomotive

TWENTY Female.	(Old Plate.) Cattle, sheep, and hogs; a scene in Brighton on a market day. B'K OF BRIGHTON, Brighton, Mass.	20 Train of cars. XX
XX Portrait of Washington.	(New Plate View of cattle fair hotel. B'K OF BRIGHTON, Brighton, Mass.	20 Female and shield.
Portrait of Washington. 50	Drove of cattle. B'K OF BRIGHTON, Brighton, Mass.	50 Locomotive.
Female with flowers. 50	B'K. OF BRIGHTON, Brighton, Mass. Boy running after horses; sheep, cattle, trees, etc.	50 View of a street and bank building.
100 Street and bank building.	B'K. OF BRIGHTON, Brighton, Mass. Drover and cattle, boy in water; trees and farm house in distance.	100 Men dressing leather.
Female. 100	Drove of cattle. B'K OF BRIGHTON, Brighton, Mass.	100 Portrait of Franklin.
Female erect with shield on which is figs. 500.	B'K. OF BRIGHTON, Brighton, Mass. State Arms; horse on either side with eagle at top. cars on right; building on left.	500 Large building
[illegible] Sailor, [illegible]	Schooners and sloops; men fishing; various vessels and lighthouse in distance. B'K OF CAPE ANN, Gloucester, Mass.	1 Boy with rabbits.
2	BANK OF CAPE ANN Gloucester, Mass. Vig. Same as ones.	2 Liberty, left arm on shield; train of cars and factory in distance.
Man with scythe in field; village in distance. 3	Two females; one feeding chickens; the other milking cow; cow, hay-stack, horse, &c. BANK OF CAPE ANN Gloucester, Mass.	3 Female.

5 Female with chickens.	Vig. Same as ones. B'K OF CAPE ANN, Gloucester, Mass.	Figure 5, word five on either side. Indian female, left hand resting on rock.
10 Female portrait.	Launching boat in sea, men in it apparently going to rescue passengers from ship that has stranded. B'K OF CAPE ANN, Gloucester. Mass.	X Shield in cornice work with motto, E Pluribus Unum.
Spread eagle on shield. 20	B'K OF CAPE ANN, Gloucester, Mass. Large Ship, steamship, and other ships in distance.	20 Sailor seated on rock with telescope.
50	Steamship; ships in distance Female with cornucopia and sheaf of wheat. B'K OF CAPE ANN, Gloucester, Mass.	50 Two males, one holding plan of pillar the other looking at it building a house.
100 Three female figures with pole and cap, and horn of plenty, &c.	B'K OF CAPE ANN, Gloucester, Mass.	C Indian seated on rock with bow.
1 Male portrait	Brig, merchant and man of war; light house on left, steamship in distance. B'K OF CAPE COD. Harwich, Mass. Codfish.	1 Female with spy glass seated on cask; ship in distance.
2 Sailor seated with stars and stripes; [illegible]	B'K OF CAPE COD. Harwich, Mass. Landing of Pilgrims at Provincetown. Codfish.	2 Portrait of Girl.
Portrait of female. 3	B'K OF CAPE COD. Harwich, Mass. Three sailors, one standing against wharf post, pipe in mouth, another standing at his right; third seated on anchor with spy-glass and pipe; casks, ships, &c. Codfish.	3 Portrait of Girl.
Portrait of a boy. 4 FOUR	B'K OF CAPE COD. Harwich, Mass. Signing Declaration of Independence. Codfish.	4 Female seated in sea shell, trident in hand; ships in distance.
5 Male portrait FIVE	B'K OF CAPE COD. Harwich, Mass. Vig. Signing the first constitution in the cabin of the May Flower in Cape Cod Harbor in 1620.	5 Male portrait

10 | Signing the first constitution on board the Mayflower, 1620; Indian princes on right, with bow and quiver. | 10
Sailor leaning on capstan; cask, bales and shipping
B'K OF CAPE COD. Harwich, Mass.
Codfish.
Portrait of J. Q. Adams
TEN

---

20 | B'K OF CAPE COD. Harwich, Mass. | 20
Vig. Scene on Marshfield farm; cattle and sheep grazing.
Portrait of Dan. Webster.

Portrait of female. | B'K OF CAPE COD. Harwich, Mass. | 50
Vig. Sailor standing against vessels rail; steamships and shipping in distance.
Codfish.
Anchor and chain; box, bales, cask; ships.
50

---

100 100
Sailor with flag; female with horn of plenty; bale, anchor, &c.
B'K. OF CAPE COD Harwich, Mass.
Portrait of Washington.
One Hundred.
Female figure of justice; ensign with stars, covering her lap.

ONE | | 1
BK OF COMMERCE, Boston, Mass.
State Arms. | Male portrait

---

1 | Train of cars. | 1
BK. OF COMMERCE, Boston, Mass.
Portrait. | Indian girl | Portrait.

---

2 | Spread eagle and shipping. | 2
BK. OF COMMERCE, Boston, Mass.
Portrait. | Ship | Female portrait

---

2 | | 2
BK OF COMMERCE, Boston, Mass.
Ship. | Male portrait

---

3 | Spread eagle with view of State street and Faneuil Hall. | 3
BK. OF COMMERCE, Boston. Mass.
Portrait. | Arms | Female figure.

THREE | | 3
BK OF COMMERCE, Boston, Mass.
Sailor, capstan, anchor, etc. | Male portrait

---

5 | Spread eagle with view of State street, and the Market House. | 5
BK. OF COMMERCE, Boston, Mass.
Male Portrait. | Scenery | Male Portrait

Steamship and sailing vessels. | 10
BK. OF COMMERCE, Boston, Mass.
Three female figures
TEN | Female, etc. | Male Portrait

Male Portrait. | View of the Boston Custom House. | 20
BK. OF COMMERCE, Boston, Mass.
20 | Vessels | Goddess of Liberty.

---

50 | Female with trumpet eagle globe, etc. | 50
BK. OF COMMERCE, Boston, Mass.
Sailor with flag. | Locomotive and tender | Washington

Male Portrait. | Three female figures vessels, etc. | 100
BK. OF COMMERCE, Boston, Mass.
C | Ship | Female portrait

Male portrait | Squaw reclining; shield, eagle and flags; steamship in distance. | 500
BK. OF COMMERCE, Boston, Mass.
D | Bee-hive | Female

Female reclining; shipping scene. | Male portrait | 1000
BK. OF COMMERCE, Boston, Mass.
1000 | Steamship

ONE | 1 Columbus. 1 | ONE
BANK OF THE METROPOLIS, Boston, Mass.
State Arms.

---

2 | Head of Franklin. | TWO
Title of Bank.
State Arms. | TWO TWO

THREE | State Arms. View of the State House, in Boston. 3 | THREE
Title of Bank

FIVE | Title of Bank. | 5
Signing the Declaration of Independence.
State Arms.

TEN | Large public building, horses, carriages, pedestrians, &c. | 10
Title of Bank.
State arms.

Red 20. | Title of Bank. | Red 20.
TWENTY | State Arms. | TWENTY
XX | | XX

Red 50. | Title of Bank. | Red 50.
Three sailors, one looking through telescope.
State Arms. | | Eagle.

Red C. | Title of Bank. | Red 100.
Anchor, bales, barrels, masts, etc.
State Arms. | | Girls' portrait.

Red 500 | Horse Eagle | Red 500.
Title of Bank.
Ocean scene; vessels, etc.
State Arms.

BANK OF MUTUAL REDEMPTION, Boston, Mass.

☞ This Bank uses the Perkins' stereotype plate; which has the denomination in fine print all over the face of the bill. They intend shortly to use a different plate.

State Arms of Mass. | MASSACHUSETTS | 5
FIVE DOLLARS
BK OF MUTUAL REDEMPTION.
FIVE across FIVE DOLLARS
5 | Boston, 5 Massachusetts. | State Arms of Mass.

Ship on stocks. | MASSACHUSETTS | 20
BK OF MUT. REDEMPTION
20 across TWENTY DOLLARS
20 | Boston, Massachusetts. | Ship on stocks.

Female seated and leaning on a bale; cars and canal; shipping in distance. | 1 | Female and 1
BK. OF NORTH AM., Boston, Mass.
1 | | ONE

Female recl ining on bale. Canal, cars, ships, &c. 1 | 1 | BANK OF NORTH AMERICA, Boston, Mass. | Indian female, trees, rocks, &c. | 1

Sailor and shipping. 2 | 2 | BK. OF NORTH AM., Boston, Mass. | State Arms. | 2

Sailor with spy glass in hand. Bale, barrels, and compass. Ships under sail. 2 | 2 | BANK OF NORTH AMERICA, Boston, Mass. | Goddess of liberty, shield, scales, &c. | 2

Two female figures and bust of Washington. 3 on right | 3 | BK. OF NORTH AM., Boston, Mass. | THREE | Female holding flag and 3 cupids

Two female figures and bust of Washington. 3 surrounded by small 3s. | THREE | BANK OF NORTH AMERICA, Boston, Mass. | Sailor aloft with spy-glass in left hand, right hand hold of stay. | 3

FIVE | Spread Eagle. Cupid either side holding fig. 5. | FIVE | BK. OF NORTH AM., Boston, Mass. | Female. | Female.

FIVE | Two females seated on bale of cotton. Factories; cotton fie'd, &c. | 5 | BANK OF NORTH AMERICA, Boston, Mass | Seal of the City of Boston. | Female.

Train of cars. 10 | TEN | BK. OF NORTH AM., Boston, Mass. | Squaw with bow and spear. | TEN | State Arms

Female with scroll, child at feet. | Female seated, resting on shield. Eagle, steamship, &c. | 10 | BANK OF NORTH AMERICA. Boston, Mass. | TEN | Eagle.

20 | Two female figures either side of shield | 20 | BK. OF NORTH AM., Boston, Mass. | Female. | Sailor.

20 | Two female figures either side of shield. | 20 | BANK OF NORTH AMERICA, Boston, Mass | Female seated on rock. | Goddess of liberty resting on shield.

Male and female. | 50 Female, eagle and shield. 50 | Sailor and female. | BK. OF NORTH AM., Boston, Mass.

100 | Steamship and vessels. | 100 | BK. OF NORTH AM., Boston, Mass. | Female. | Female.

500 | BK. OF NORTH AM., Boston, Mass. | 500 | FIVE HUNDRED | Female, eagle and shield. | Female, eagle and shield. | Squaw and papoose.

BK of the REPUBLIC | 1 | Settlers at their devotions. Indians entering the door. 1 1 | 1 | Mass. | Boston | Auditor's die | ONE DOLLAR | Eagle on rock.

2 | Title of Bank. | 2 | Fleet of fishing vessels at anchor, catching fish. | Auditors' die | Sailor, capstan, anchor

3 | Sailor on beach; anchor, boat, etc. | 3 | Auditors' die | Title of Bank. | THREE | Liberty with State Arms.

5 | Capitol at Washington. | 5 | Title of Bank | Ship, pilot boat and steam-tug. | Auditors' die

X | Shipping, wharves, etc. | 10 | Title of Bank. | Table with bust of Washington; old man and child. | Auditors' die

20 on edged die. | Female erect with sword and eagle on shield, etc.; building in distance, with part of Title above and on sides. Washington on left and Martha Washington on right. | 20 on edge-die. | State Arms. | Sailor seated, [illegible] hoisted cap. | TWENTY | 20 | 20

50 | Title of Bank. | 50 | Title of Bank. | State Arms. | 50 Dolls. | Two children

C with words "One Hundred Dollars" around it. | Title of Bank. | 100 | Title of Bank. | State Arms. | 100 Dolls. in red. | Franklin.

500 | Title of Bank. | 500 | Title of Bank. | State Arms. | 500 Dolls. in red. | Male portrait.

ONE | Ship. | Ship cutting in a whale. Vig. Eagle standing on shield, bundle of arrows in talons. | ONE | Female reclining on a fence, apron full of wheat | Vessel and lighthouse. | 1 1 | ONE | BARNSTABLE BK, Yarmouth, Mass. | ONE

2 | Eagle on cliff. | TWO | Eagle on cliff. | 2 | Sailor seated on bale of goods. | 2 2 | BARNSTABLE BK, Yarmouth, Mass. | Ship and stern of another. | TWO

3 | View of street with bank and other buildings. | THREE on 3. | Sailor standing by capstan, bbls., bales, &c. | BARNSTABLE B'K, Yarmouth, Mass. | Ship. | Male portrait.

FIVE | Vig train of cass; church on left; factory on right in distance. | 5 | Sailor one hand on anchor shipping seen in fore ground | V V | BARNSTABLE BK, Yarmouth, Mass. | Schooner discharging barrels into a flat boat. | FIVE | 5

10 | TEN Steamer, TEN etc. | 10 | Male portrait | X BARNSTABLE BANK X | TEN DOLLARS | Yarmouth. Mass. | Sailor at wheel | 10 | 10

20 | BARNSTABLE B'K, Yarmouth, Mass. | 20 | TWENTY | Same as above. | Liberty seated with globe and shield. | Male portrait

XX | Vig. Ship and brig in foreground, pilot boat on left, and one on extreme right; two ships in the distance, between ship and brig. | 20 | Sailor leaning against anchor stock smoking. Stern of vessel on left. | Steamboat, and ship behind | BARNSTABLE BK, Yarmouth, Mass. Anchor and fish gear | XX | 20

FIFTY | L L Vig. Female leaning on anchor by sea-side; ship in distance wrecked. BARNSTABLE BK, Yarmouth, Mass. Boats and two men | 50 50

50 Sailor boy's head. | Same as three. BARNSTABLE B'K, Yarmouth, Mass. Barrels | 50 Male portrait FIFTY

ONE HUNDRED | BARNSTABLE BK, Yarmouth, Mass. C C Vig. Female with grain on left, offering a part to a figure sitting on right with liberty pole and cap; ship in distance. Anchor and fish gear. | 100 Two ships and a part of another seen on right. 100

100 Male portrait | BARNSTABLE B'K, Yarmouth, Mass. Vig. Same as three. Ship. | 100 Female portrait.

ONE State Arms. | Vig. Female reclining on her left ship; on right houses, hills, &c. BAY STATE BANK, Lawrence, Mass. | 1 Indian with liberty cap, shield and quiver on back.

TWO State Arms. | Vig. Dog and safe; bags of specie, &c. BAY STATE BANK, Lawrence, Mass. | 2 TWO 2

THREE State Arms. | Vig. Mechanics at work, one with sledge upraised, and the other holding chisel; steam mill and other buildings in background. BAY STATE BANK, Lawrence, Mass. | 3 Medallion head.

FIVE State Arms. | Portrait BAY STATE BANK, Lawrence Mass. Vig. Commercial scene; boxes and men at work; horse and dray with a load of barrels; ferry boat crossing river; houses and hills in the background. | 5

10 Medallion head. | BAY STATE BANK, Lawrence, Mass. Vig. Carpenter at his bench, Satan behind him [illegible] head. | 10 State Arms.

20 Mechanic with sledge on his shoulder, anvil at his side. | BAY STATE BANK, Lawrence, Mass. State Arms. | 20 Indian with liberty cap, shield and quiver on his back.

FIFTY State Arms. | BAY STATE BANK, Lawrence, Mass. Vig. Horses and chariots; men holding horses, and one horse drinking; persons on the right | 50

100 State Arms. | BAY STATE BANK, Lawrence, Mass. Spread eagle. | 100

D | BAY STATE BANK, Lawrence, Mass. Vig. Female with shield, sitting on bale of goods; barrel on right, sheaf of wheat on left. 500 in dead letters. | 500 State Arms.

1 | 1 Child, dog, and cats; ship in distance. 1 BEDFORD COMMERCIAL B'K, New Bedford, Mass. | ONE

ONE Sailor hoisting flag. | Steamship and other vessels. BEDFORD COM BK, New Bedford, Mass. ONE Female. ONE | 1

2 Female with flowers. | Female seated with telescope by shield; ship in distance. Vig. 2 on right. Title of Bank. | Ship and other vessel TWO

2 | 2 Female and anchor, ship in the distance. 2 BEDFORD COMMERCIAL B'K, New Bedford. Mass. | TWO

THREE Female. | Spread eagle, capital at Washington and steamship. BEDFORD COMMERCIAL B'K, New Bedford, Mass. | 3

5 5 Indian sitting under a tree. FIVE | Spread eagle, canal and rail road BEDFORD COMMERCIAL B'K. New Bedford, Mass. Female | 5 FIVE

10 Medallion head 10 | X Spread eagle and ship X BEDFORD COMMERCIAL B'K, New Bedford. Mass. | TEN DOLLARS

20 Cupid. | (New Plate.) Ship and steamship. BEDFORD COMMERCIAL B'K, New Bedford, Mass. Wheels | 20

20 Portrait of Wm. Penn. 20 | (Old Plate.) 20 Female sitting on a bale, ship in distance. BEDFORD COMMERCIAL B'K, New Bedford, Mass. House | 20

FIFTY Female. FIFTY | Female, child and merchandise; ship in distance. BEDFORD COMMERCIAL B'K, New Bedford, Mass. Building | 50

100 Fancy piece. Steamship. | Ships, city in the distance. BEDFORD COMMERCIAL B'K, New Bedford, Mass. Justice | 100

Indian in canoe. 500 | 500 BEDFORD COMMERCIAL BANK, New Bedford, Mass. D D | 500 Justice.

Female erect with sickle and sheaf. | 1 1 1 BERKSHIRE BANK, South Adams, Mass. Boy, girl, cattle, sheep, trees, etc. | 1 Farmer cutting corn stalks.

Cupid with sheaf. Female with vase | 2 Title. 2 Two females at work on machine. 2 | Cupid with cornucopia. Mechanic at work at vice.

5 Girls head. | Title of Bank. White and black horse; cattle and trees. V 5 V | 5 Two children

10 Franklin in his study. | Title of Bank. Female with pen and tablets; child at her feet. TEN either side of vig. X X | 10 Female with globe.

1 | Female, train of cars and canal. BEVERLY BANK, Beverly, Mass. | 1 Female.

Female | BEVERLY BANK, Beverly, Mass. | 1
Cow, cupid. | Shipping. | Female.

2 | BEVERLY BANK, Beverly, Mass. | 2
2 | Female and eagle ships in distance. 2 | Two females.

Farmers washing sheep. | 2 | TWO
 | | Females.
2 | BEVERLY BANK, Beverly Mass. | TWO

Three female figures. | | 3
 | Portrait of Webster. |
3 | BEVERLY BANK, Beverly, Mass. | Shipping.

Farming scene. | | 3
 | | Female.
3 | BEVERLY BANK, Beverly, Mass. | THREE

FIVE | BEVERLY BANK Beverly, Mass. | 5
Sailor and flag. | Group of females factory and shipping. | Portrait of Washington.

Spread eagle. | V and female. | 5
FIVE | BEVERLY BANK. Beverly Mass. | Girl

Vulcan the the blacksmith. | X | 10
 | BEVERLY BANK, Beverly Mass. |
TEN | | Reaper.

10 | | X
 | | 10
Female merchandise and shipping. | BEVERLY BANK, Beverly, Mass. TEN | Cupid.

20 | XX Eagle XX | 20
Female. | BEVERLY BANK, Beverly, Mass. | Ship.

20 | Cows in brook: boy, girl, etc. | 20
 | BEVERLY BANK. TWENTY DOLLARS. |
Fowls. | Beverly, Mass. | Female with grain

Farmer seated on grain, sailor leaning on capstan; boy, dog, etc. | Beverly. 50 | 50
 | BEVERLY BANK. FIFTY DOLLARS. |
50 | Massachusetts. | Dog, safe, &c.

FIFTY | 50 Man and horse 50 | FIFTY
Female. | BEVERLY BANK. Beverly, Mass. | Female.
FIFTY | | FIFTY

100 | BEVERLY BANK. Beverly, Mass. | 100
 | C Washington. C |
Female beside State Arms, holding out wreath. | ONE HUNDRED DOLLARS. | Female reclining, globe, quadrant, &c.

Same as right. | Scene on a wharf. | One Hundred and 100.
 | BEVERLY BANK. Beverly, Mass. |
Harrison. | | Columbus.

1 | Ship yard scene—men at work, etc. | 1
 | BLACKSTONE BANK Boston, Mass. |
Vessels. | | Mechanic with sledge.

 | View of Haymarket Square. 1 on 1 on right | ONE
 | BLACKSTONE BANK Boston, Mass. | Indian female with bow and spear.
1 | |

 | Vig. Same as ones. 2 | 2
 | BLACKSTONE BANK Boston, Mass. |
TWO | | Sailor.

Two inverted. | Title of Bank. | 2
Sailor with female, vessels, etc., above him. | |
TWO | | Boy and rabbits.

 | Vig. Same as ones. 3 | 3
 | BLACKSTONE BANK Boston, Mass. |
3 | | Ship under full sail.

Washington. | Shoemakers at work; female attending to household duties in background. | 3
 | Title of Bank. |
3 | | Female, fig. 3

 | Vig. Same as ones. 5 | 5
 | BLACKSTONE BANK Boston, Mass. |
FIVE | | State Arms.

5 | Title of Bank. | 5
 | Large public building |
Female with flowers. | | Cooper at work on bbls

X | Title of Bank. | 10
 | State Arms, or Indian and lone star. |
Washington. | | Female with Ten on shield

 | Vig. Same as ones. Head of female on X on right. | 10
10 | BLACKSTONE BANK Boston, Mass. | Female.

20 | Vig. Same as ones. | 20
 | BLACKSTONE BANK Boston, Mass. |
Female, eagle and shield. | |

20 | Eagle, building and steamer. | 20
 | Title of Bank. |
Female with lore. | | Cars.

 | Vig. Same as ones. 50; Cupid with L on shield on right. | FIFTY
 | BLACKSTONE BANK Boston, Mass. |
50 | | Female.

50 | General railroad scene at depot. | 50
 | Title of Bank. |
Sailor, steamer, &c. | | Female portrait.

C | Female seated by side of shield, safe, etc.; steamer on right; cars and steamboat on left. | 100
 | Title of Bank. |
Female portrait. | |

Left	Centre	Right
Female. 100	Vig. Same as ones. BLACKSTONE BANK Boston, Mass.	100 Female.
500	Ocean scene. D Title of Bank.	500 Franklin.
1 Ox.	Horse Eagle BLACKSTONE BANK Uxbridge, Mass. 1 Female with sword & shield. 1	1 Girl's head.
1 Portrait of Washington.	Female. 1 Female. BLACKSTONE BANK Uxbridge, Mass.	1 Portrait of Franklin.
Female resting arm on ..., cars, ..., ... &c. 1	Large figure 1 with five heads in miniature view on it. BLACKSTONE B'K. Uxbridge, Mass.	1 Female with sheaf.
2 Portrait of Columbus.	Female. 2 Female. BLACKSTONE BANK Uxbridge, Mass.	2 Portrait.
Washing sheep; house in distance 2	Large figure 2, with five heads on it. BLACKSTONE B'K Uxbridge, Mass.	TWO Portrait of female. TWO
Two on 2 Two girls with sheafs.	BLACKSTONE BANK Uxbridge, Mass. Old man, child and bust of Washington. Words Two Dollars on 2 either side.	2 Female portrait.
Farming scene. 3	Large figure 3 across the bill. BLACKSTONE B'K. Uxbridge, Mass.	Fig. 3, word three. Female with basket of flowers. THREE
3 Washington	Female. 3 Female. BLACKSTONE BANK Uxbridge, Mass.	3 Vulcan the blacksmith.

Left	Centre	Right
3 Girl's head.	BLACKSTONE BANK Uxbridge, Mass. 3 Man oiling machinery. 3 3	3 Man at vice
Spread eagle. FIVE	V BLACKSTONE BANK Uxbridge, Mass.	5 Girl.
Five on 5. Male portrait	BLACKSTONE BANK Uxbridge, Mass. Female either side of anvil; buildings in distance.	5 Girl's head.
10 Girl's head. TEN	Train of cars. BLACKSTONE BANK Uxbr...g...a...	10 Male head.
Vulcan the blacksmith, train of cars, factories in the backgr'd TEN	X BLACKSTONE BANK Uxbridge, Mass.	10 Reaper.
20 Female.	XX Eagle. XX BLACKSTONE BANK Uxbridge, Mass.	20 Ship.
TWENTY 20 TWENTY	White and black horse; cattle, etc. Male head BLACKSTONE BANK Uxbridge, Mass.	20 Dog swimming with body of child
50 Female with name of Bank on scroll, child at her feet.	BLACKSTONE BANK Uxbridge, Mass. L Ma's portrait. L	50 Youthful portrait.
Same as r'ght Portrait.	Scene on a wharf. BLACKSTONE BANK Uxbridge, Mass.	One Hundred and 100. Portrait of Columbus.
Male portrait 100	BLACKSTONE BANK Uxbridge. Mass Three females reclining; vessel in distance. 100 C 100	100 Sailor boy; sailors, vessels, etc.

Left	Centre	Right
1 Female portrait.	View of a street with bank and other buildings. BLUEHILL BANK, Dorchester, Mass.	1 Cows.
ONE 1	Farmer sowing seed. 1 BLUE HILL BANK Dorchester, Mass	1 Ship. ONE
2 Portrait of a female.	Same as ones. BLUEHILL BANK, Dorchester, Mass. Flowers.	2 Female.
TWO 2	Spread eagle. 2 BLUE HILL BANK Dorchester, Mass.	2 TWO Sailboats.
3 Stone-cutter	Same as ones. BLUEHILL BANK, Dorchester, Mass.	3 Female.
THREE 3	Wharf and shipping. 3 BLUE HILL BANK Dorchester, Mass.	3 THREE Train of cars.
5 Liberty. FIVE	Same as ones. BLUEHILL BANK, Dorchester, Mass.	5 Female representing Agriculture.
FIVE	Spread eagle. Large V near the centre. BLUE HILL BANK Dorchester, Mass.	5 Girl.
X Farmer with scythe.	Same as ones. BLUEHILL BANK, Dorchester, Mass.	10 Two females.
TEN	Vulcan the blacksmith; train of cars and factories in the background. Large X near the centre BLUEHILL BANK Dorchester, Mass.	10 Reaper.

20 | 2 Female. 0 | 20
Female figure. BLUE HILL BANK Dorchester, Mass. 20

---

20 | Three men, dog in grist mill—corn grinding scene. | 20
Boy, dog, houses. BLUE HILL BANK, Dorchester, Mass. Two children.

---

50 | Boy on horse which is drinking from stream; dog, trees, etc. | 50
Man carrying leather. FIFTY BLUE HILL BANK, Dorchester, Mass. Dog & safe.

---

50 | Farming scene 50 | L
Steamboat and sail vessel. BLUE HILL BANK Dorchester, Mass. Female, sword and scales.

---

100 | Spread eagle, Railroad and canal. | 100
Vulcan the blacksmith. BLUE HILL BANK Dorchester, Mass. Female.

Man, two horses, and pig at pump; cattle and barn in background. C | 100
100 BLUE HILL BANK, Dorchester, Mass. C Female, spinning wheel; factories, etc.

D | BLUE HILL BANK, Dorchester, Mass. Wharf scene. | 500
Indian princess. Man at vice filing.

---

1 | 1 Shipping, etc. 1 | 1
Indian with bow. BOSTON BANK, Boston, Mass. Ship.
ONE ONE

---

2 | 2 Shipping, etc. 2 | 2
Mercury. BOSTON BANK, Boston, Mass. State Arms.
TWO TWO

---

3 | Large Vessels Large 3 in Boston harbor 3 | 3
Female with sword and shield. BOSTON BANK THREE DOLLARS Boston Massachusetts. Female with shield on which is figure 3

---

5 | 5 Shipping, etc. 5 | 5
Reapers. BOSTON BANK, Boston, Mass. Shipping.
FIVE FIVE

Female and X on shield X
BOSTON BANK, Boston, Mass.
10 10

---

20 | Deck of a ship; sailor at the wheel; 0 on right | TWENTY
BOSTON BANK, Boston, Mass.

50s and 100s, of the Perkins' Stereotype Plate, which has the denomination printed in fine letters all over the bill.

---

50 | Nautical scene in front of city. 50 either side. | 50
State Arms. BOSTON BANK, Boston, Mass. Female with view of town and motto

---

100 | C Nautical scene in front of city C | 100
Sailor with trumpet on vessel. BOSTON BANK, Boston, Mass. Beehive.

D | 500 | Shipping.
Sailor standing by capstan. BOSTON BANK, Boston, Mass. 500

M | 1000 | Shipping.
Female, eagle, wreath and scales. BOSTON BANK, Boston, Mass. 1000

Portrait of Washington; steamer and locomotive.
Same as right BOYLSTON BANK, Boston, Mass. Female on 1
ONE ONE

TWO | Vulcan. | TWO
Eagle on fig. 2. BOYLSTON BANK, Boston, Mass. Eagle on fig. 2.
TWO TWO

Steamship and sailing vessels. | THREE
Eagle on 3 BOYLSTON BANK, Boston, Mass. Indian and 3
THREE

V on Five | Eagle. | 5
BOYLSTON BANK, Boston, Mass.
Same as right Man, boy and sheep on V.

X | Portrait of Columbus. X Portrait of Washington. | 10
Farming scene. BOYLSTON BANK, Boston, Mass. Wharves, carmen and horses.

---

20 | XX Eagle. XX | 20
BOYLSTON BANK, Boston, Mass.
Female seated. Ship.

---

20 | TWENTY TWENTY BOYLSTON BANK, Boston, Mass. Female stepping into brook. Twenty on 20 Dollars on 20 | 20
Female portrait. Female portrait.

FIFTY Female. FIFTY | 50 Man and horse. 50 | FIFTY Female. FIFTY
BOYLSTON BANK, Boston, Mass.

BOYLSTON BANK, Boston. Massachusetts. State Arms | 50
Express wagon loading goods. FIFTY 50 Fifty Dollars. Female figure leaning against column, torch in hand.

Words one hundred and figs. 100. | Wharf scene—loading wagon, men, horses, shipping, &c. | Words one hundred and figures 100.
BOYLSTON BANK, Boston, Mass.
Male portrait. Male portrait.

---

100 | BOYLSTON BANK, Massachusetts. | C
Female figure leaning on column. Sailor & soldier, flags, fort, cannon, shot, &c. One Hundred Dollars. Female seated, with shield, on which is city of Boston.

D | Landing of the Pilgrims. Girl's head. | 500
D BOYLSTON BANK, Boston, Mass. Five Hundred Dollars. Female seated, with globe, book, &c.

Figs. 500. — Harvest scene; female seated pointing to rea-pers. 500 D — BOYLSTON BANK, Boylston, Mass. — 500

1 Female ONE — Street in Brighton; droves of cattle. BRIGHTON MARKET BANK. Brighton, Mass. — 1 Female and shield and fig. 1

Two female figures. 2 — Street in Brighton; droves of cattle. BRIGHTON MARKET BANK, Brighton, Mass. — 2 Sailor and Indian and TWO on shield.

3 Cattle. THREE — Same as above. BRIGHTON MARKET BANK Brighton, Mass. Man plowing — 3 Farmer sailor and black smith and fig. 3

5 Portrait of female 5 — Same as above. BRIGHTON MARKET BANK. Brighton, Mass. — 5 Female shield and globe.

Farmers washing sheep. X — Farming scene. BRIGHTON MARKET BANK, Brighton, Mass. Loading hay — 10 Train of cars.

Female, 20 — Farming scene BRIGHTON MARKET BANK. Brighton. Mass. Farmer cradling — 20 Cattle.

Female with a rake. 50 — BRIGHTON MARKET BANK, Brighton, Mass. Cattle. Imp. and products. — 50 Female and churn.

Female holding 50. FIFTY — Horse running; boys attempting to stop; dog, horses, houses, etc. BRIGHTON MARKET BANK, Brighton, Mass. — Female holding 50 FIFTY

C C — BRIGHTON MARKET BANK Brighton, Mass. Female reclining locomotive, factories, shipping and cattle in background, Two horses — 100 Portrait of Webster. 100

C 100 — Boy and horses at trough; female, pail, ducks, etc. Youthful portrait with cap. Title of Bank. — 100 Female, cow, calf, ducks, etc.

Boy's head. 500 — BRIGHTON MARKET BANK, Brighton, Mass. 500 — 500 Washington; female on left; Cupid on right.

1 Blacksmith, anvil, hammer, &c. — View of Taunton green. BRISTOL COUNTY BANK, Taunton, Mass. — 1 Female.

TWO Male and female. 2 — Iron workers; factory in background. BRISTOL COUNTY BANK, Taunton, Mass. Eagle — 2 Portrait of Filmore.

3 2 Cupids and fig 3 — View of Taunton green. BRISTOL COUNTY BANK. Taunton, Mass. Agricultural implements — 3 Portrait of Clay.

5 Female — Interior of an iron foundry. BRISTOL COUNTY BANK, Taunton, Mass. — 5 Train of car

10 Anchor and merchandise. — River, Railroad and train of cars. BRISTOL COUNTY BANK. Taunton, Mass. — 10 Portrait of Webster.

20 Soldier loading gun — Settlers at their devotions; table, dog, etc. Indians entering door. BRISTOL COUNTY BK Taunton, Mass. — 20 Two children.

50 State Arms. — BRISTOL COUNTY BK Taunton, Mass. Greetings of the Pilgrims at their landing in America. — 50 Female at work at sewing machine.

C Two children. — BRISTOL COUNTY BK Taunton, Mass. Cattle in stream; children on bank under tree. — 100 Female

Liberty giving eagle drink. 500 — D Party of males and females viewing Niagara Falls. BRISTOL COUNTY BK Taunton, Mass. — 500 D

1 — Machinery, etc. BROADWAY BANK, Boston, Mass. — 1 Indian female.

2 — BROADWAY BANK, Boston, Mass. Machinery, etc. — 2 Wheels, bale TWO

3 Female THREE — BROADWAY BANK, Boston, Mass. Machinery, etc. — 3

5 5 — BROADWAY BANK, Boston, Mass. Machinery, etc. — 5 Female and State Arms.

X Female and State Arms. — BROADWAY BANK, Boston, Mass. Machinery, etc — X X

20 XX — BROADWAY BANK, Boston, Mass. Machinery, locomotive, etc. — 20 Anchor, bales, barrels, etc

50 Bbls. and bales. FIFTY — BROADWAY BANK, Boston, Mass. Machinery, etc. — 50

C — BROADWAY BANK, Boston, Mass. Machinery, etc. — 100 Sailor seated on a bale.

500 Machinery, locomotive, etc. — Title of Bank. Female and swan. — 500

1 / Female resting her arm upon an urn, bearing the inscription of "Washington." / ONE | BUNKER HILL B'K. / 1 Bunker Hill Monument. 1 / Charlestown. Mass. | 1 / Gen. Washington / ONE

1 | BUNKER HILL BK., Charlestown, Mass. / Signing Declaration of Independence. Eagle. | 1 / Milkmaid, cow and calf.

Sailor and Indian either side of a red 2 on red shield surmounted by eagle. / 2 | Female, column, steamer, etc. / Title of Bank. | 2 / Girl's portrait.

2 / Female. / TWO | BUNKER HILL B'K. / 2 Bunker hill Monument. 2 / Charlestown, Mass. | 2 / Gen. Warren / TWO

3 / Gen. Warren / THREE | BUNKER HILL B'K. / 3 Bunker hill Monument. 3 / Charlestown, Mass. | 3 / Eagle and shield. / 3

3 / 3 | Title of Bank. / Launch of the Adriatic. | 3 / Eagle and shield.

V / Female portrait. | Landing of William Penn; whites and Indians. / Title of Bank. | 5 / Fowls.

FIVE / Female. | BUNKER HILL B'K. / Bunker hill Monument. / Charlestown Mass. | 5 / Gen. Warren. / FIVE

X / Gen. Warren / X | BUNKER HILL B'K. / Bunker hill Monument. / Charlestown Mass. | 10 / Female.

Female portrait / 10 | BUNKER HILL BK., Charlestown, Mass. / U. S. Capitol. | 10 / Female seated in a shell

20 / Anchor, etc. | BUNKER HILL BK. Charlestown, Mass. / Female, two Indians and old soldier gazing at portrait of Washington. 20 each side. | 20 / Jefferson.

20 / Female. | XX Eagle XX / BUNKER HILL B'K. / Charlestown, Mass. | 20 / Ship.

50 / Female head | Title of Bank. / Man with gun; female loading gun. | 50 / Adams.

FIFTY / Female. / FIFTY | 50 Man and horse. 50 / BUNKER HILL B'K. / Charlestown, Mass. | FIFTY / Female. / FIFTY

Same as right / Portrait of Harrison. | Scene on a wharf. / BUNKER HILL B'K. / Charlestown, Mass. | One Hundred and 100. / Portrait of Columbus.

C / Boy's portrait. | Angel blowing trumpet; eagle, globe, flags, etc. / Title of Bank. / C | 100 / Indian on shield.

D / Soldier and drum. | BUNKER HILL BK / Charleston, Mass. / Landing of the Pilgrims / 500 on Five Hundred. | 500 / Female portrait.

M / Washingt'n | Marine view. / BUNKER HILL BK / Charleston, Mass. / One Thousand. / 1000 | 1000 / Franklin

ONE / Man and boy driving sheep | Vig. Blacksmith shop; three men, horse, dog, &c 1 / CABOT BANK, Chicopee, Mass. | 1 / Man whet'ng scythe.

Men and boy, with sheep, etc. / 2 | Large 2 / CABOT BANK / TWO DOLLARS / Chicopee, Mass. | 2 / Female portrait

THREE / Man holding sheafs and sickle. / 3 | Eagle. 3 / CABOT BANK, Chicopee, Mass. | 3 / Indian seated in a shield.

FIVE / 5 | Vig. Cars, &c V / CABOT BANK, Chicopee, Mass. | FIVE / Blacksmith with hammer resting on figure 5. / FIVE

10 | Vig. Spread eagle, canal boats, and cars. X / CABOT BANK, Chicopee, Mass. | TEN / Cars. / TEN

20 / 20 / CAB | TWENTY DOLLARS / Portrait / OT BA / TWENTY DOLLARS / MASSACHUSETTS | 20 / 20 / NK / 20

20 / Female with chest and money bags. | XX Eagle. XX / CABOT BANK, Chicopee, Mass. | 20 / Ship.

50 / Statue of Justice with sword and scales | Fifty Dollars / Portrait of General McClellan / CABOT BAN / Fifty Dollars / 50 Fifty 50 | 50 / K / State Arms

FIFTY / Female with flowers. / FIFTY | 50 Man holding a horse. 50 / CABOT BANK, Chicopee, Mass. | FIFTY / Female with flowers. / FIFTY

C / Female with lamp, flowers, wheel, etc. | Massachusetts / CABOT Male portrait BANK / 100 100 / Chicopee / One Hundred Dollars | 100 / Soldier charging bayonet

The words one hundred with the figures 100 running across. / Male portrait. | Vig. Wharf scene; men loading waggon; ships, &c. / CABOT BANK, Chicopee, Mass. | The words one hundred with the figures 100 running across / Male portrait.

ONE / Blacksmith, engine; factory. | View of Bank and street in Cambridge, with pedestrians, horses, etc. / CAMBRIDGE BANK, Cambridge, Mass. | 1 / Boy.

MASS.	MASS.	MASS.
Female with scales, etc. 2 Vig. Same as above ones. Title of Bank. 2 Cattle; cars passing over bridge, etc.	3 Farmer, Sailor, and Mechanic, Female 3 gold dollars. CAMBRIDGE CITY BANK, Cambridgeport, Mass. 3 Farmer, Sailor, and Mechanic, and figure three.	Man plowing with horses. X 10 CAMBRIDGE MARKET BANK, Cambridge, Mass. TEN Female with scales.
3 Two females. Vig. Same as above ones. Title of Bank. 3 Female, globe, shield, pole and cap	5 Man with gun, Indian woman, 5 cupids and 5 gold dollars. Steamship CAMBRIDGE CITY BANK, Cambridgeport, Mass. 5 Group of Females, and figure five.	20 Cattle. Train of cars. CAMBRIDGE MARKET BANK, Cambridge, Mass. 20 Female.
5 Female portrait. Vig. Same as above ones. Title of Bank. 5 Franklin.	X X CAMBRIDGE CITY BANK. Cambridgeport, Mass. Train of cars. TEN TEN X Load of Grain.	50 Female figure. Cattle, houses in the distance. CAMBRIDGE MARKET BANK, Cambridge Mass. 50
TEN Washington. Vig. Same as ones. Title of Bank. 10 Blacksmith at forge, etc.	XX Man holding figs. 20. CAMBRIDGE CITY BANK. Cambridgeport, Mass. Female in foreground, R. R. and steamboat in background. Twenty Twenty 20	100 Cattle Spread eagle on shield; U. S. Capitol on right; steamship on right. CAMBRIDGE MARKET BANK, Cambridge, Mass. 100 100 Bull's head.
TWENTY Female feeding fowls. Vig. Same as ones. Title of Bank. 20 XX	50 Female. Spread eagle, capital at Washington and steamship in background. CAMBRIDGE CITY BANK. Cambridgeport, Mass. Fifty Fifty 50	D Five hundred. 500 [illegible]MBRIDGE MAR[illegible]ET BANK. [illegible] in woods, [illegible] sed drawn [illegible]oxen. [illegible]assachusetts. [illegible] 500 Five hundred. 500
50 50 Vig. Same as ones. Title of Bank. 50 Webster.	Female, spear and shield, Hundred CAMBRIDGE CITY BANK. Cambridgeport, Mass. Female, Eagle and globe shipping in the backgrounds. One Hundred 100 A hunter.	Female sitting with pen and scroll. ONE Vig. [illegible] and child; [illegible] sheaf, dog railroad [illegible]. CENTRAL BANK, Worcester, Mass. 1 Head of female.
100 Sailor, barrels, etc. C on 100. Vig. Same as ones. Title of Bank. 100 Female portrait	1 Bull's head. Figure 1 and cupid. Cows and sheep. CAMBRIDGE MARKET BANK. Cambridge Mass. ONE Female	Indian sitting on rock; waterfall. TWO Vig. Mechanic sitting with one hand resting on wheel; female standing; mechanical implements scattered around; ship on right. CENTRAL BANK, Worcester, Mass. 2 Female with sheaf on shoulder.
500 D 500 Street scene in Cambridge. CAMBRIDGE BANK. Cambridge, Mass. 500 500 500	TWO Female. Figure 2 and cupid Cows and sheep. CAMBRIDGE MARKET BANK, Cambridge, Mass. 2 Cattle and hogs.	Female with flowers in apron 3 CENTRAL BANK THREE DOLLARS State Arms of Mass. Indian on the u. Worcester female, grain and cars on right; plow, corn, fruit, etc. on left. 3 Female portrait
Female and fig. 1 1 CAMBRIDGE CITY BANK, Cambridgep't, Mass. Man chopping trees, cabin and waggon, one gold dollar. ONE 1	Female. THREE Man on horseback, cattle and sheep. CAMBRIDGE MARKET BANK, Cambridge, Mass. 3 Farmer, sailor, Mechanic and figure three.	Female with [illegible], holding figure 5. FIVE 5 CENTRAL B'K. 5 Worcester, Mass. Horse at full speed; train of cars in the distance. Female sitting on bale, holding the figure 5. FIVE
Female feeding an Eagle, from a Cup. 2 CAMBRIDGE CITY BANK. Cambridgeport, Mass. Farmer with rake, milk maid and cows, farm-house in back ground Two gold dollars. TWO TWO 2 Two Dollars Train of Cars.	Eagle. Female figure FIVE Man on horseback, cattle and sheep. CAMBRIDGE MARKET BANK, Cambridge, Mass. FIVE 5 Mass. Spread Eagle. FIVE	10 Vig. Three female figures, one on the left with horn of plenty; ship on the extreme right. Title of Bank. TEN Female with sickle and sheaf.

20 — CENTRAL BANK, Worcester, Mass. Winged figures supporting the figures 20 — 20

50 Small female head. — Vig. Cows standing in water, sheep on the bank lying down. CENTRAL BANK, Worcester, Mass. — 50 Head of Washington.

100 — Vig. Female with shield; capitol in the distance. Title of Bank. Horses at water trough. — 100 Head of Webster.

D — Vig. Female leaning on bale; ship on right. CENTRAL BANK, Worcester, Mass. — 500 Eagle and shield.

1 ONE — View of Harvard College. CHARLES RIVER BANK, Cambridge, Mass. — 1 Portrait of Judge Story. ONE

2 Genl. Washington. TWO — View of Harvard College. CHARLES RIVER BANK, Cambridge, Mass. — 2 Portrait of Judge Story. TWO

3 Female with sword and scales THREE — View of Harvard College and grounds CHARLES RIVER BK Cambridge, Mass. Grain, etc. — 3 Male portrait THREE

Female. FIVE — View of Harvard College CHARLES RIVER BANK. Cambridge, Mass. — 5 Portrait of Judge Story. FIVE

10 Portrait of Franklin. TEN — View of Harvard College. CHARLES RIVER. BANK. Cambridge, Mass. Male seated — 10 Portrait of Judge Story. TEN

20 Female. — Spread eagle; shipping and R. R., in background. CHARLES RIVER BANK. Cambridge, Mass. — TWENTY Female with sheaf of wheat. 20

Medallion head. 50 — State arms, female on either side, also spread eagle on the top. CHARLES RIVER BANK, Cambridge, Mass. — 50 Medallion head.

Female. 100 — CHARLES RIVER BANK. Cambridge, Mass. Horses, chariot and female figure. — 100

1 — Train of cars. Horse and 1. CHICOPEE BANK, Springfield, Mass. — 1 Spread Eagle ONE

2 Female seated, holding shield, on which are words 'Incorporated' etc. — Train of cars at depot. CHICOPEE BANK. TWO DOLLARS Springfield, Massachusetts. — 2 Female portrait

2 — Farmer, horses, & harrow & old Pynchon house. 2 CHICOPEE BANK, Springfield, Mass. — 2 Loading hay. TWO

Massachusetts
3 Indian girl and State Arms of Mass. — CHICOPEE BANK. THREE on 3 Large oval portrait of General Scott. THREE on 3 — 3 Female with torch beside column.

3 Medallion Head THREE — Vulcan the blacksmith. 3 CHICOPEE BANK, Springfield, Mass. — Three and 3. Gen. Washington.

5 Portrait of Washington. — Large V and reaper. CHICOPEE BANK, Springfield, Mass. — 5 Female. 5

X Female. TEN — Man ploughing with horses. CHICOPEE BANK, Springfield, Mass. — 10 State arms with female on either side. TEN

Goddess of liberty eagle & shield. — XX Signing the declaration of independence. CHICOPEE BANK, Springfield, Mass. 20 — 20 20

50 Medallion head. — Man on horse back, flock of sheep. CHICOPEE BANK, Springfield, Mass. 50 50 — 50 Medallion head.

100 Medallion head. 100 — Female reclining and horn of plenty. CHICOPEE BANK, Springfield, Mass. — 100 Medallion head.

State Arms. 500 — CHICOPEE BANK, Springfield, Mass. 500 — 500

Female figure and 1. ONE — Female supporting the figure 1. Railroad & Steamboat. CITIZENS BANK, Worcester, Mass. — 1 Blacksmith & anvil.

2 Portrait of Z. Taylor. — Farmer, dog & grain. CITIZENS BANK, Worcester, Mass. — 2 Cherub and dolphin. TWO

3 Sea monster. Steamship. — Man resting a sledge upon his shoulder, factories & stream of water in the background. CITIZENS BANK, Worcester, Mass. — 3 State arms.

FIVE — 5 Juno & Mercury, also a griffin standing upon a safe. 5 on right CITIZENS BANK, Worcester, Mass. Canal Locks — V Female with a rake. V

TEN — X Cupid. X CITIZENS BANK, Worcester, Mass. — Jupiter Juno and Mercury. 10

TWENTY — 20 Female & eagle, portrait of Washington. 20 CITIZENS BANK, Worcester, Mass. Cars — Jupiter. 20

Female warrior. 50 — L Train of cars. L CITIZENS BANK, Worcester, Mass. — 2 Female figures. 50

Left	Centre	Right
Indian shooting an arrow. 100	100 Neptune. 100 CITIZEN's BANK, Worcester Mass.	Statue of Washington. 100
1 Steamship.	View of Boston and the harbor. CITY BANK, Boston, Mass.	1 Ship under full sail.
2 Medallion.	Vig. Same as ones. CITY BANK, Boston, Mass.	2 Medallion.
3 Medallion. 3	Vig. Same as ones. CITY BANK, Boston, Mass.	3 Medallion.
5 Med head FIVE	Vig. Same as ones. CITY BANK, Boston, Mass. Indian on shield	5 Medallion.
TEN Word Ten on med. head.	Vig. Same as ones. CITY BANK, Boston, Mass.	10 Medallion.
	The 20s, 50s, 100s, and 500s, are of the Perkins' stereotype Plate, which has the denomination printed in fine letters all over the bill.	
Figure 1 with one running across it	View of Lynn Common. CITY B'K OF LYNN Mass.	ONE on 1 portrait.
2	View of Lynn Common. CITY B'K OF LYNN Mass	2 Sailor on shipboard.
3	CITY BANK, Lynn, Mass Yacht race; on the beach various males and females. 3	THREE on 3. Two females.

Left	Centre	Right
Female. 5	View of Lynn Common 5 CITY BANK 5 of Lynn, Mass.	V Ship. FIVE
FIVE 5 FIVE	View of Lynn Common. CITY B'K OF LYNN Mass.	5 The word "FIVE" with a large V running across. 5
10 State arms	View of Lynn Common. CITY B'K OF LYNN Mass.	10 X 10
20	CITY B'K OF LYNN Mass. State Arms. Female on each side	TWENTY 20 TWENTY
50	Train of cars. CITY B'K OF LYNN Mass.	50 Portrait of Webster.
C	CITY B'K OF LYNN Mass. Three cherubs, one turning a screw, one splitting a block with wedge, the other lifting rock with lever. C 100 C	100 Ship
1 View of a large building.	CITY BANK, Worcester, Mass Mechanic at work in machine shop.	Word one and figure 1 Same as above.
2 Same as on ones.	CITY BANK Worcester, Mass. Three farmers loading wheat, one on top of load another pitching up sheaf and the other holding horses. TWO	Word two and figure 2 2
3 Same as on ones.	Female reclining machine in centre of ring; sheep and sheaf of wheat on right, safe on left. CITY BANK Worcester, Mass.	3 Large figure 3
Word five and letter V	[illegible] men dressing leather and female sewing boots. CITY BANK Worcester, Mass.	V 5

Left	Centre	Right
X on 10 10	CITY BANK Worcester, Mass. City arms of Worcester	10 Building
XX 20	CITY BANK, Worcester, Mass. Three females.	20 City bank building.
50 50	CITY BANK, Worcester, Mass. Portrait of J. C. Calhoun.	50 City bank building.
100 C	CITY BANK, Worcester Mass. City Bank building.	100 Portrait of Webster. 100
D	Title of Bank. City Bank Building. Five Hundred Dollars.	500 Clay.
1 Washington. 1	COLUMBIAN BANK, Boston, Mass. 1 Two blacksmiths, anvil, &c. 1	1 Female. 1
Female bust. 1	COLUMBIAN BANK, Boston, Mass. Female; 1 either side.	1 Male Portrait
2 Female. 2	COLUMBIAN BANK, Boston, Mass. 2 Harvest scene. 2	2 Female. 2
Indian. 2	COLUMBIAN BANK, Boston, Mass. TWO Ships. DOLL'S	2 Male Portrait.
Female. THREE	3 3 COLUMBIAN BANK, Boston, Mass. 3 Portrait. 3	Female. THREE

3
COLUMBIAN BANK,
Boston, Mass.
3
Harvest scene.
3 Female, eagle, &c. 3
Sailor, coil of rope, &c.
3
3

Portrait.
Ship building.
COLUMBIAN BANK,
Boston, Mass.
5
5
Female in 5

5
COLUMBIAN BANK,
Boston, Mass.
5
Washington.
5 Female, Landing of Columbus; city in distance. 5
Male portrait
5
5

10
COLUMBIAN BANK,
Boston, Mass.
10
Portrait of Washington.
Ten, large X, Ten across the note.
Portrait of Columbus.
10
10

Three females with anchor.
Two females tending looms.
10
COLUMBIAN BANK,
Boston, Mass.
TEN
Male portrait

20
Spread eagle and ships.
20
COLUMBIAN BANK,
Boston, Mass.
Female.
Female.

50
Citizenship.
50
COLUMBIAN BANK,
Boston, Mass.
Female
50
Imp. and [illegible]

C
Female, eagle, shield and liberty cap.
100
COLUMBIAN BANK,
Boston, Mass.
Portrait of Washington.
Portrait of Columbus.

500
Landing of Columbus.
500
Man with cornucopia.
COLUMBIAN BANK,
Boston, Mass.
FIVE HUNDRED DOLLARS
500

1
COMMERCIAL BK.,
Salem, Mass.
1
Hunter killing buffalo.
State Arms.
Male portrait

1
Eagle and shipping. ONE
1
Female.
COMMERCIAL B'K.
Salem, Mass.
Female.
ONE
ONE

2
Female with cloth pointing to mills and road scene on right; on left village and falls.
2
Title of Bank.
Two Indians, city, etc.
Eagle.
Female with spy glass; vessel, etc.

TWO
2 Female, merchandise, and a ship in distance. 2
TWO
Ship.
COMMERCIAL B'K.
Salem, Mass.
Head of an Indian.
TWO
TWO

Two horses before load of hay, man on one, woman and child on top; boy, girl, dog, blacksmiths and shop.
3
3
Title of Bank.
Portrait of officer

3
THREE Indian THREE seated on a rock.
3
Male figure.
COMMERCIAL B'K.
Salem, Mass.
Ship.
THREE
THREE

FIVE
5 View of steamboat, schooner, men, bridge, etc. 5
FIVE
Justice.
COMMERCIAL BK.
Salem, Mass.
State Arms
FIVE
FIVE

5
Female. River, steamboat, ship and bridge. V
5
Cattle.
COMMERCIAL B'K.
Salem, Mass.
Cattle.
FIVE
FIVE

5
Two sailors and nautical instruments; vessels, steamer, etc.
5
Title of Bank.
Male head.
Female with globe, tablets, etc.

10
10 Whale ships. Large X, female and horn of plenty.
10
Ship.
COMMERCIAL B'K.
Salem, Mass.
Ship.
TEN
TEN

20
XX
20
(Old Plate.)
20 Female, merchandise, ship in distance. 20
COMMERCIAL B'K.
Salem, Mass.
TWENTY

20
(New Plate.)
2 Female. 0
20
Female, spear, and chain.
COMMERCIAL B'K.
Salem, Mass.
Female.
20

Female and eagle.
Word "TWENTY" across fig. 20.
Female
20
Title of Bank.
20
Franklin.

50
(New Plate.)
Male and female.
50
Female figure.
COMMERCIAL B'K.
Salem, Mass.
Cupid in a sail boat.
50

FIFTY
(Old Plate.)
50 Man and horse. 50
FIFTY
Female.
COMMERCIAL B'K.
Salem, Mass.
Female.
FIFTY
FIFTY

50
50 Man buying newspaper of boy; birds etc
50
COMMERCIAL BANK
Salem, Mass.
Sailor, captain, etc. on deck.
50
Cooper at work

100
(Old Plate.)
C Phœbus in the chariot of the sun, 100
C
Eagle.
COMMERCIAL B'K.
Salem, Mass.
Portrait of Washington
100
C

100
(New Plate.)
Spread eagle, railroad, and canal.
100
Vulcan the blacksmith.
COMMERCIAL B'K.
Salem, Mass.
Female.

C
Eagle on bale; agricultural products, etc.
100
100
Men and boats.
Title of Bank.
Female representing Agriculture.
100
100

100 inverted
100
COMMERCIAL BANK
Salem, Mass.
100
Female figure erect.
Large green C with small "C" at bottom.
Sailor, 2 farmers, vessels, etc.
100 inverted

Female seated pointing to reapers and load of hay.
500
D
500
Title of Bank.
500

Left	Centre	Right
Squaw in canoe. 500 D	COMMERCIAL BANK. Salem Mass. 500 D	500 Female figure of justice
	CONCORD BANK, Concord, Mass. This Bank uses the old Perkin's stereotype plate, which is the denomination printed in fine letters all over the bill.	
1 State Arms.	Man, two horses, and pig at pump; cattle and barn in distance. CONTINENTAL BK. Boston, Mass	1 Portrait of Continental soldier
2 State Arms.	CONTINENTAL BK. Boston, Mass. White and black horse, cattle, trees, etc	2 Washingt'n
3 State Arms	Scene in Arctic regions; white bear attacking sailors in boat. CONTINENTAL BK. Boston, Mass.	3 Continental soldier.
5 State Arms.	Men, sailor, boy, dog, vessels, fort, boats, etc. Fig 5 either side. CONTINENTAL BK, Boston, Mass.	5 Franklin.
10 State Arms.	CONTINENTAL BK. Boston, Mass. X Old man with gun; female loading gun. X	10 Soldier loading gun
Word Massachusetts across XX State Arms.	CONTINENTAL BK. Boston, Mass. Surrender of English General to Washington	20 Continental soldier with gun.
50 State Arms.	CONTINENTAL BK. Boston, Mass. Washington on horse; officers, tents, etc.	50 Male portrait
100 State Arms.	CONTINENTAL BK Boston, Mass. Figs. 100, Title & words One Hundred Dollars on green die.	100 Soldier with medallion head on shield

Left	Centre	Right
500 State Arms.	CONTINENTAL BK Boston, Mass. Female erect with sword and shield. 500 on green die.	500 Eagle
Farmer sowing seed. ONE	ONE Man on horseback, flock of sheep. CONWAY BANK. Conway, Mass. Ducks	1 Female.
2 Mechanic and sailor	CONWAY BANK. Conway, Mass. TWO DOLLARS.	TWO Two females supporting a sheaf of wheat.
3	Man driving a drove of cattle across a river. 3 CONWAY BANK, Conway, Mass	3 3 females and sheaf of wheat
V [illegible] with a [illegible] of cotton	CONWAY BANK. Conway, Mass Females weaving at factory looms.	5 Portrait.
TEN Indian.	Three Indians in a canoe. CONWAY BANK. Conway, Mass.	10 Portrait of a boy
XX Indian.	Santa Claus in a sleigh drawn by reindeers over the roofs of houses. CONWAY BANK. Conway, Mass	20 Fancy piece.
L Hunter warming himself; gun, dog, etc.	CONWAY BANK, Conway, Mass. Female in clouds with sword, scales, eagle, etc.	50 Female binding shoes; child.
C Portrait.	Men cutting timber in a forest CONWAY BANK. Conway, Mass	100 Rip Van Winkle smoking a pipe
1 Portrait.	Farmer eating dinner in the open field DANVERS BANK. Danvers, Mass.	1 Portrait.

Left	Centre	Right
2 Portrait.	Milk maid and cows. DANVERS BANK, Danvers, Mass.	2 Portrait.
3 Portrait.	Female resting upon a bale; manufacturing village in distance. DANVERS BANK, Danvers, Mass.	3 Portrait.
5 Portrait.	Farmer ploughing with horses. DANVERS BANK. Danvers, Mass	5 Portrait.
10 Portrait.	Spread eagle, capitol at Washington, and steamship in distance. DANVERS BANK. Danvers, Mass	10 Portrait.
20 Portrait.	TWENTY TWENTY Portrait surmounted by an eagle, female on either side. DANVERS BANK. Danvers, Mass.	20
Portrait. 50	DANVERS BANK, Danvers, Mass FIFTY State arms. DOLLARS.	50 Portrait.
100 Portrait.	100 Three female figures. 100 DANVERS BANK. Danvers, Mass.	100 Portrait.
1 Portrait of Fisher Ames. ONE	ONE Interior of a blacksmith shop. ONE DEDHAM BANK. Dedham, Mass.	1 Portrait of Washington. ONE
2 Portrait of Fisher Ames. TWO	TWO Spread eagle. TWO DEDHAM BANK. Dedham, Mass.	2 Portrait of Washington. TWO
3 Portrait of Fisher Ames. THREE	Female seated, farmers gathering grain. Factories and a machine. DEDHAM BANK. Dedham, Mass.	3 Portrait of Washington. THREE

5 Portrait of Fisher Ames. FIVE	Man on horseback, cars, and on foot. Train of Cattle. DEDHAM BANK. Dedham, Mass. Dog, key, safe	5 Portrait of Washington. FIVE
10 Portrait of Fisher Ames. TEN	Train of cars passing through a gap. Female with horn of plenty. DEDHAM BANK, Dedham, Mass. Dog, key, safe	10 Portrait of Washington. TEN
20	Vig. two females at loom; to the right is child's head either side of XX DEDHAM BANK, Dedham, Mass	20 Female and sewing machine.
20 Female and a chest.	XX Eagle XX DEDHAM BANK. Dedham, Mass	20 Ship.
FIFTY Female. FIFTY	50 Man and horses 50 DEDHAM BANK. Dedham, Mass.	FIFTY Female. FIFTY
50 Female with book.	DEDHAM BANK Dedham, Mass. Female, shield, eagle, vessel, etc.	50 Eagle
One Hundred and 100. Portrait of Harrison.	Scene on a wharf. DEDHAM BANK. Dedham, Mass.	Same as left. Portrait of Columbus.
C Female with tablets; child at her feet.	DEDHAM BANK, Dedham, Mass. Franklin.	100 Female with C on shield
D 500	DEDHAM BANK, Dedham, Mass. Two females, owl, building, steamer, etc. D	D 500 State Arms.
1 Interior of a blacksmith's shop. ONE	Spread eagle. 1 EAGLE BANK, Boston, Mass.	1 Man and horse. ONE

2 Flower girl. TWO	Spread Eagle. TWO EAGLE BANK, Boston, Mass.	2 TWO Female with sickle.
5	Spread Eagle. V, cupid either side. EAGLE BANK, Boston, Mass. Grain	FIVE Female.
X	Spread eagle, building, safe, dog and key. EAGLE BANK, Boston, Mass.	10 Female at well.
20	Spread eagle Cupid either side XX. EAGLE BANK, Boston, Mass	20 Female
L Steamboat. 50	Spread eagle; bust of female. EAGLE BANK, Boston, Mass.	50 Reapers. L
100 Female. 100	Spread eagle. EAGLE BANK, Boston. Mass.	100 Female. 100
	The 500s, are of the Perkins' Stereotype Plate, which has the denomination printed in fine letters all over the bill.	
1	Eliot preaching to the Indians. Portrait of Pierce ELIOT BANK, Boston, Mass. Female head	ONE Dog's head ONE
2	ELIOT BANK, Boston, Mass. Eliot preaching to the Indians. 2	TWO Sailors on board of a ship.
3 Boston Female.	Vig. Same as ones. ELIOT BANK, Boston, Mass.	3 Portrait of Webster.

FIVE Boston Indian.	Female head Vig. Same as ones. ELIOT BANK, Boston, Mass.	5 5
TEN Hunter seated by a fire in the woods	TEN X X Title of Bank.	TEN Hunter washing at a brook.
20	Ship under full sail. Portrait of Webster. ELIOT BANK, Boston, Mass.	20 Female with sickle and sheaf.
FIFTY Sailor and mechanic.	L Portrait of J. Q. Adams. 50 ELIOT BANK, Boston, Mass.	FIFTY Three females.
100 inverted Indian erect, with bow and arrow	Indians on cliff contemplating the progress of civilization. ELIOT BANK, Boston, Mass.	100 C
Indian with bow.	C Large Steamship. ELIOT BANK, Boston, Mass.	
D	Wreckers scene; ship wrecked in distance. ELIOT BANK, Boston, Mass.	500 D
Female sitting on the ground supporting the figure 1, train of cars and steamboat. 1	1 ESSEX BANK. Haverhill, Mass.	1 Female.
2	Two female figures, steamboat in the distance. 2 ESSEX BANK, Haverhill, Mass.	2 Female.
Train of cars. THREE	3 ESSEX BANK, Haverhill, Mass.	3 Blacksmith and sailor, and figure 3.

5	Two females and motto "Prosperity and liberty," factory, steamship and train of cars in the distance. 5 ESSEX BANK, Haverhill, Mass.	5 Group of females, and figure 5
TEN	Two females, bust and shield ship in the distance. X ESSEX BANK. Haverhill, Mass.	10 State arms
20 Anchor, bales, etc.	Ship, etc. ESSEX BANK, of Haverhill, Mass. Eagle.	20 Sailor boy, vessel, etc.
50 Three females.	ESSEX BANK, of Haverhill, Mass. Horse.	50 Female head.
100 Female with sewing machine.	ESSEX BANK. of Haverhill. Mass. Two horses, cattle, trees, etc.	100 Girl's head.
100 Vulcan the blacksmith.	Spread eagle, rail road and canal ESSEX BANK, Haverhill, Mass.	100 Female.
1	State Arms. 1 EXCHANGE BANK, Boston, Mass.	1 Girl.
2	Steamship. Female on 2 EXCHANGE BANK, Boston, Mass.	2 Female.
3 Eagle at the bottom. THREE	Steamship and sailing vessels. EXCHANGE BANK, Boston, Mass.	3 Sailor. THREE
5 Female.	Spread eagle. EXCHANGE BANK, Boston, Mass.	Female and cupid on V 5

10	Female figures, horses and chariot. X EXCHANGE BANK, Boston, Mass.	10 Steamship. TEN
Twenty on 20 Portrait of Columbus	Female with scales, shipping, locomotive and State Arms cupid, etc. EXCHANGE BANK, Boston, Mass.	Twenty on 20 Portrait of Washington.
FIFTY on 50	View of the Boston Custom House. 50 EXCHANGE BANK, Boston, Mass.	50 Franklin.
100	Female, canal, train of cars and shipping. EXCHANGE BANK, Boston, Mass.	Hundred on 100
500	Steamship and other vessels. EXCHANGE BANK, Boston, Mass. Dog's head.	500 Female.
	EXCHANGE BANK Boston, Mass. Female seated by horn of plenty and shield; ships, steamship, cars, bridge and city in distance.	1000 1000
1 Portrait. ONE	1 Female seated upon a rostrum with spear and shield, water, vessels, and mountains, in the background. 1 EXCHANGE BANK. Salem, Mass.	1 Female. 1
2 Female, spear and shield, TWO	2 Same Vig., as above. 2 EXCHANGE BANK. Salem, Mass.	TWO Female and ships. 2
3 Justice THREE	3 Same Vig., as above. 3 EXCHANGE BANK. Salem, Mass.	III Female and ship in distance. 3
5 Female. V	5 Same Vig. 5 EXCHANGE BANK Salem, Mass.	FIVE Female with scales and sword, 5

10 Portrait of Washington. TEN	Same Vig. EXCHANGE BANK. Salem, Mass.	TEN Portrait. 10
20 Female.	XX Eagle XX EXCHANGE BANK. Salem, Mass.	20 Ship
50 Male portrait.	EXCHANGE BANK. Fifty Dollars Massachusetts. Salem. 50	50 State Arms.
100 Man dressing leather.	Two females seated on bale, factories &c in distance. EXCHANGE BANK. Salem, Mass. One Hundred Dollars.	100 Two Children
Female head in large circular die. D D 500	EXCHANGE BANK. Dog on safe. Salem. Mass. Five Hundred Dollars.	D 500
Large figure across each end of bill with a figure on the body of it. ONE	Ships and steamboat. FAIRHAVEN BANK. Fairhaven, Mass.	Justice on a fig. 1. ONE
Large 2 and female bust. TWO	Whale fishing. FAIRHAVEN BANK. Fairhaven, Mass.	Same as left TWO
3 Sailor and captain.	Female and motto "enterprise." FAIRHAVEN BANK. Fairhaven, Mass. THREE THREE	3 Farmer, sailor and mechanic, and figure 3
5 Female 5	Eagle and shield. V FAIRHAVEN BANK. Fairhaven, Mass.	FIVE Medallion bust. 5
Female, grain, cars, rail road and canal in background. X	10 FAIRHAVEN BANK. Fairhaven, Mass.	TEN Medallion head. 10

20 2 Female. 0 20
FAIRHAVEN BANK.
Fairhaven, Mass.
Female with spear. Female. 20
XX

Female and eagle. TWENTY on 20. Female 20
FAIRHAVEN BANK
Fairhaven, Mass.
20 Franklin.

---

20 Female supporting shield on which is State Arms; nautical scene in distance. 20
FAIR HAVEN BANK
Fair Haven, Mass.
Female with basket, etc. Sailor.

FIFTY 50 Three females, eagle and shield 50
Title of Bank.
50 Mechanic and factory.

FIFTY DOLLARS
50 Medallion head Boy, child, cattle, sheep, etc. 50
FAIR HAVEN BANK
Fair Haven, Mass.
Boy, girl, child, horse, etc. Female feeding fowls.
L

---

50 Male and female. 50
Cupid in a sail boat.
FAIRHAVEN BANK
Fairhaven, Mass.
Female with spear. 50 50

C Eagle on bale. 100 100
Boats and men. Title of Bank. Female with sickle.
100 100

---

100 Spread eagle, R. R. and canal 100
FAIRHAVEN BANK.
Fairhaven, Mass
Vulcan the blacksmith. 100 Female.

C Sailor, farmer and boy; capstan, anchor and grain. 100
FAIR HAVEN BANK
Fair Haven, Mass.
100 Dog and safe.

Agricultural scene; female pointing to reapers. 500 D 500
500 Title of Bank.

---

1 Females weaving at factory rooms 1
FALL RIVER BANK
ONE DOLLAR
Fall River, Mass
Female seated in shell; ship on right Female portrait
Indian

---

2 Female leaning on a bale; ships in back ground. 2
Men, cattle and horses on a plank road. FALL RIVER BANK
Fall River Mass. Train of cars.
Steam boat

---

3 FALL RIVER BANK,
Fall River, Mass. 3
Anchor. Sailor, shipping in background. Portrait of female

---

5 FALL RIVER BANK.
Fall River, Mass. 5
Blacksmith anvil &c. Shipping. Portrait of Female.

---

10 Steamship. 10
FALL RIVER BANK.
Fall River, Mass.
Sailor. Female figure.

TWENTY. FALL RIVER BANK,
Fall River, Mass. 20
Male and female seated; two children and lamb. Word Twenty in a semi-circle, Dollars on fig. 20 on a die. Double med. head either side. Male portrait

---

Two girls in large circle. FALL RIVER B'K,
Fall River, Mass
Boy watering two horses at trough; female with pitcher and pail. 50
L Oval male portrait.

C Steamboat. 100
Title of Bank.
Girls' head. Male portrait

---

500 Title of Bank. 500
Three females; shipping, cars, etc., in distance.
Female. 500

M FALL RIVER BANK,
Fall River. Mass. 1000
Shipping and two females seated. ONE THOUSAND.
1000 1000

Female. 1 Female. 1
FALMOUTH BANK,
Falmouth, Mass.
Portrait of Washington. Portrait of Franklin.

---

1 FALMOUTH BANK,
Falmouth, Mass. 1
One on 1 Vessels on ocean, etc. One on 1
Sailor at wheel. 1 Female portrait

---

1 1 Female seated, bales, box, barrels, vessels, etc. 1 1
Box, bale, anchor, ship, etc. Agricultural implements, etc.
FALMOUTH BANK,
Falmouth. Mass.
1 1

---

2 2 Sailor on beach; anchor, boat, steamer, vessels, etc. 2 2
FALMOUTH BANK,
Falmouth, Mass.
Two females. Man with corn stalks

---

2 Female. 2 Female. 2
FALMOUTH BANK.
Falmouth, Mass.
Portrait of Columbus. Portrait.

---

2 2 Female seated with fig. 2 2 2
Man on horse. Title of Bank. Man on horse.
2 2

---

3 Female. 3 Female. 3
FALMOUTH BANK
Falmouth, Mass.
Genl. Washington. Vulcan the blacksmith.

---

3 3 Female and fig. 3 on shield. 3 3
Child's head. Title of Bank. Child's head.
3 3

Scene in Arctic regions; white bear attacking sailors in boat. Female portrait 3
FALMOUTH BANK,
Falmouth, Mass.
3 Indian princess.

Female with sword and scales. FIVE Female and cherubs. 5
FIVE FALMOUTH BANK,
Falmouth, Mass.
Ship Female.

10 | 1 Female, sheaf and boy. 0 | 10
Two female figures. | FALMOUTH BANK, Falmouth, Mass. | 2 females.

20 | Eagle and shield, factories and falls in back ground. | 20
Female. | FALMOUTH BANK, Falmouth, Mass. | Female.

50 | Bullock between man with axe, and hunter with gun. | 50
Female portrait. | Title of Bank | Portrait.
50

100 | C Shipping. C | 100
Female. | | Female.
100 | FALMOUTH BANK, Falmouth, Mass. | 100

100 | FALMOUTH BANK, Falmouth, Mass. | 100
Sailor, mechanic, vessels, etc. | Sailor, two farmers; agricultural and nautical scene. Green C either side. | Cooper at work.

1 | View of Faneuil Hall and other buildings. | 1
FANEUIL HALL BK. Boston, Mass.
Female and 1. | | Female with flag and cupid.

2 | Vig. Same as ones. | 2
FANEUIL HALL BK. Boston, Mass.
...uction | | Female.

3 | Vig. Same as ones. | 3
FANEUIL HALL BK. Boston, Mass.
Female | | Mechanic, sailor and farmer and fig. 3

Vig. Same as ones, with Cupid on V on right. | 5
FANEUIL HALL BK. Boston, Mass. | Two female figures and 5
5

View of Quincy Market. X | X
FANEUIL HALL BK. Boston, Mass. | Drove of cattle.
TEN

Ship. | Milkmaid and cows. | 20
FANEUIL HALL BK. Boston, Mass.
20 | | Female.

50 | Cows and sheep. | 50
FANEUIL HALL BK. Boston, Mass.
Female. | | State Arms.

100 | Farming scene. | 100
FANEUIL HALL BK. Boston, Mass.
Train of cars. | | Drove of cattle.

500 | Female reclining on bale with distaff in her hand; ships, city, canal, boats, and look, cars, &c., in distance. | 500
Washington and his horse. | FANEUIL HALL BK. Boston, Mass. 500 | 500

Train of cars. 1 | ONE Medallion head.
1 | FITCHBURG BANK, Fitchburg, Mass. | ONE

Spread eagle on branch of tree; cars, canal boat, etc. in distance. | Large ornamental 2 across note. | TWO Female with grain and sickle.
FITCHBURG BANK TWO DOLLARS Fitchburg, Mass.
2 | Pond and fence | TWO

Man on horse back, and drove of cattle. 3 | 3 Blacksmith, anvil and forge.
3 | FITCHBURG BANK, Fitchburg, Mass.

Female | Canal and inclined railway, buildings on each side. Train of cars. | 5 Portrait.
FIVE | FITCHBURG BANK, Fitchburg, Mass. | FIVE
Agricultural implements.

TEN | State arms. Wharf, shipping and merchandise. Sailor in fore-ground. | 10
Portrait, Mr. Van Buren. 10 | FITCHBURG BANK, Fitchburg, Mass. | Milk maid.

(1st. Plate.)
20 | XX Eagle. XX | 20
Female. | FITCHBURG BANK. Fitchburg, Mass. | Ship.

(2d. Plate.)
20 | 2 Female. 0 | 20 Female.
Female with spear and shield. | FITCHBURG BANK, Fitchburg, Mass. XX | 20

(New Plate.)
FITCHBURG BANK, Fitchburg, Mass. | 20
XX | Female seated on a bale, holding a sheaf of wheat. | Female.

FIFTY | 50 Man and horse. 50 | FIFTY
Female. | | Female.
FIFTY | FITCHBURG BANK, Fitchburg, Mass. | FIFTY

FIFTY | 50 Three females seated with liberty pole and cap, eagle shield &c; ship in distance. | Fifty on 50.
Grain, &c. | | Male seated with mechanical implements.
50 | FITCHBURG BANK, Fitchburg, Mass.

50 | FITCHBURG BANK, Fitchburg, Mass. | 50
Eagle on shield. | 50 Male Portrait. 50 | Dog and safe.

(Old Plate.)
100 | C Phaeton in the car of the Sun. 100 | C
Eagle. | | Portrait of Washington.
100 | FITCHBURG BANK, Fitchburg, Mass. | C

100 | FITCHBURG BANK, Fitchburg, Mass. | 100
Ox. woods, &c. | Male Portrait. | Small State Arms.

C | Spread eagle, grain &c. 100 | 100
Sailors and boat. | Title of Bank. | Female with sickle, grain.
100 | | 100

Same as right. | Scene on a wharf. | One hundred and 100.
Portrait of Harrison. | FITCHBURG BANK, Fitchburg, Mass. | Portrait of Columbus.

ONE | Cows, farmer ploughing and train of cars. | 1
Portrait of Webster. | FRAMINGHAM B'K Framingham, Mass. 1 | 2 females.

Left end	Centre	Right end
1 Female figure. 1	ONE Female ONE sitting on a bale with a horn of plenty. Shipping in background. FRAMINGHAM B'K, Framingham, Mass.	1 Eagle 1
Female with sickle and sheaf of wheat. Factory and train of cars TWO	2 Cattle and hogs. FRAMINGHAM B'K, Framingham, Mass. 2	2 Blacksmith, anvil and forge.
2 Female and eagle. 2	2 Female sitting on a bale with horn of plenty. Shipping in background. 2 FRAMINGHAM B'K Framingham, Mass.	2 Female figure. 2
3 Eagle standing upon a rock overlooking the sea. 3	3 Female sitting upon a bale with horn of plenty. Shipping in background. 3 FRAMINGHAM B'K Framingham, Mass.	3 Female figure. 3
3	Farming scene. 3 FRAMINGHAM B'K Framingham, Mass. Machinery and bale	3 Portrait of Washington
5	Farmers gathering corn. 5 FRAMINGHAM B'K Framingham, Mass.	FIVE 3 males and 2 female figures and a large V
	5s, 10s, 20s, 50s, and 100s old plate of Perkins stereotype.	
X	Milk maid and cows. [illegible] FRAMINGHAM B'K Framingham, Mass.	10 Female with flag, and 2 cherubs.
FIFTY Female. FIFTY	50 Man and horse. 50 FRAMINGHAM B'K Framingham, Mass.	FIFTY Female. FIFTY
ONE	Cattle, farmer ploughing, train of cars in the distance. 1 FRANKLIN Co. BANK. Greenfield, Mass. 1	1 Portrait of Washington.

Left end	Centre	Right end
Farmer ploughing, with horses; steamboat in the distance. TWO	2 FRANKLIN Co. BANK, Greenfield, Mass. 2	2 Portrait of Franklin.
Farmer, sailor and mechanic, 3 gold dollars. 3	FRANKLIN Co. BANK. Greenfield, Mass.	3 Portrait of Webster.
Farming scene. 5	5 FRANKLIN, Co. BANK, Greenfield, Mass. Imp. and products	FIVE Female. FIVE
Female, eagle and shield, portrait of Washington. TEN	X FRANKLIN Co. BANK. Greenfield, Mass.	10 2 females.
20 TWENTY Male portrait	FRANKLIN CO. B'K Greenfield, Mass.	20 Male portrait
50 Female with scroll on which is words "Fifty Dollars;" child at her feet.	FRANKLIN CO. B'K Greenfield, Mass. Male portrait. FIFTY DOLLARS.	50 FIFTY Dog & safe.
C State Arms.	FRANKLIN CO. B'K Greenfield, Mass. C Male portrait. C	100 Eagle.
ONE Sailing vessel 1	Battle of Bunker Hill. ONE on right. FREEMANS' BANK, Boston, Mass. Sloop, etc.	1 Female. ONE
TWO Girl. 2	Washington on horseback—ship builders. FREEMANS' BANK, Boston, Mass. Imp. and products	2 Franklin TWO
THREE Female. 3	Steamboat landing and sailing vessels. THREE FREEMANS' BANK Boston, Mass. Sloop	3 Washington and horse THREE

Left end	Centre	Right end
5 Wharf and shipping FIVE	View of Quincy Market. FREEMANS' BANK, Boston, Mass. Cow	5 Female.
TEN Interior of a blacksmith's shop. 10	X Ships TEN FREEMANS' BANK, Boston, Mass.	10 Male and female. TEN
XX Female. 20	Cows Female making hay. FREEMANS' BANK, Boston, Mass.	20 Ships. XX
FIFTY Female. FIFTY	50 Man and horse. 50 FREEMANS' BANK, Boston, Mass.	FIFTY Female FIFTY
50 City seal.	FREEMAN'S BANK, Boston, Mass.	50 Male Portrait
Words one hundred and figs. 100. Male portrait	Wharf scene—loading wagon, men, horses, shipping, &c. FREEMANS' BANK, Boston, Mass.	Words one hundred and figures 100. Male portrait
C Male Portrait.	FREEMAN'S BANK, Boston, Mass. FREEMAN'S BANK.	100 Arms of State.
D D Small State arms. D D	FREEMAN'S BANK, Boston, Mass. D Male Portrait. D FIVE HUNDRED.	500 Vessel under sail.
ONE 1 ONE	GLOBE BANK, Boston, Mass. The title of this Bank is repeated twice on the note—a special plate like Perkins', which has the denomination in fine letters all over the bill.	1 ONE 1
TWO 2 TWO	GLOBE BANK, Boston, Mass. Same as ones.	2 TWO 2

THREE 3 THREE	GLOBE BANK, Boston, Mass. Same as ones.	3 THREE 3
FIVE 5 FIVE	GLOBE BANK, Boston, Mass. Same as ones.	5 FIVE 5
TEN X TEN	GLOBE BANK, Boston, Mass. Same as ones.	10 TEN 10
FIFTY 50 FIFTY	GLOBE BANK, Boston, Mass. Same as ones.	50 FIFTY 50
C 100 C	GLOBE BANK, Boston, Mass. Same as ones.	100 C 100
	GLOBE BANK, Boston, Mass. 500s and 1000s, same as ones except in the denomination	
ONE	Wharfs and shipping ONE GLOUCESTER BANK Gloucester, Mass. Horses and dray	1 Sailing vessel. ONE
2 TWO 2	Wharfs and shipping. TWO GLOUCESTER BANK Gloucester, Mass. Ship, bbls., etc	2 Horse, cart, and barrels 2
THREE	Wharfs and shipping. GLOUCESTER BANK, Gloucester, Mass.	3 Ship.
FIVE	Wharfs and shipping. GLOUCESTER BANK Gloucester, Mass.	5 FIVE Horses and wagon. Merchandise.

TEN	Wharfs and shipping. GLOUCESTER BANK, Gloucester, Mass.	10 Sail boat. X
20 Eagle.	Wharfs and shipping. 20 GLOUCESTER BANK Gloucester, Mass.	XX Sail vessels 20.
50	Wharfs and shipping. 50 GLOUCESTER BANK, Gloucester, Mass.	50 Sailor, merchandise and shipping. FIFTY
100	Wharfs and shipping. GLOUCESTER BANK, Gloucester, Mass.	100 Sail vessels
ONE	Farmers and load of hay. Portrait. GRAFTON BANK, Grafton, Mass. Female bathing	1 Portrait of H. Clay.
TWO Portrait of Webster.	Female weaving at factory looms. GRAFTON BANK, Grafton, Mass. Dog	TWO Portrait.
Female blowing a horn, also farmers and load of hay.	GRAFTON BANK, Grafton, Mass. THREE	3 Portrait.
V Portrait.	(New Plate.) Scene in shoemaker's shop. GRAFTON BANK, Grafton. Mass.	5 Portrait.
V Interior of a shoemakers shop.	GRAFTON BANK, Grafton, Mass. Portrait V Portrait.	5 Female sewing book; child resting upon her lap.
X Portrait of W. Penn.	Wild horses running across a plain. GRAFTON BANK, Grafton, Mass.	10 Portrait.

XX Train of cars.	Female seated with bale, box, barrel, etc.; yacht and steamship in distance. GRAFTON BANK, Grafton, Mass.	20 Male portrait
Indian erect. FIFTY.	L Milkmaid and cows. GRAFTON BANK, Grafton. Mass.	50 Portrait.
50 Female in clouds with eagle, etc. 100	Male portrait. Title of Bank.	C Female binding shoes; child.
1 Male and female. ONE	1 Steamboat and sailing vessels. 1 GRAND BANK, Marblehead, Mass.	1 Female figure. ONE
2 Ship. 2	Female resting her arm upon fence; dog. 2 GRAND BANK, Marblehead, Mass.	2 Agricultural implements 2
Eagle FIVE	5 [illegible] figures 5 GRAND BANK, Marblehead, Mass.	Statue of Washington.
10 Sailor, his foot resting on a cannon. 10	X Ship. X GRAND BANK, Marblehead Mass.	10 Bee hive. 10
Female, eagle, etc 20	20 on TWENTY Female head GRAND BANK TWENTY DOLLARS Marblehead, Mass.	20 Portrait of Franklin
20 Female figure.	2 Female. 0 GRAND BANK, Marblehead, Mass. XX	20 Female. 20
Steamboat XX Train of cars.	3 female figures, eagle and shield. 20 GRAND BANK, Marblehead, Mass.	XX Milk maid.

Left end	Center	Right end
20 TWENTY. Sailor.	Steamship and other vessels at sea GRAND BANK. Marblehead, Mass. Twenty Dollars on Twenty.	20 TWENTY. Pilot-boat under full sail.
Massachusetts. 50	Marblehead. Ships, etc. 50 FIFTY GRAND BANK. Fifty Dollars. L	50 Male portrait.
1 on ONE Ship. ONE	Female with sanies, and motto, "Industry the means, plenty the result;" shipping and rail road in distance. ONE GRANITE BANK, Boston, Mass.	1 on ONE Bee hive. ONE
2 Ship. TWO	Vig. Same as ones. TWO GRANITE BANK, Boston, Mass.	2 Bee hive. TWO
3 Ship. THREE	Vig. Same as ones. THREE GRANITE BANK, Boston, Mass.	3 Bee hive. THREE
5 Ship. FIVE	Vig. Same as ones. FIVE, vessels 5 on right; 5, merchandise, etc., on left. GRANITE BANK, Boston, Mass.	5 Bee hive. FIVE
10 Ship. TEN	Vig. Same as ones. TEN, vessels, 10 on right; 10, merchandise etc., on left. GRANITE BANK, Boston, Mass.	10 Bee hive. TEN
20 Ship. TWENTY	Vig. Same as ones. TWENTY GRANITE BANK, Boston, Mass.	20 Bee hive. TWENTY
FIFTY Female. FIFTY	50 Men and horse. 50 GRANITE BANK, Boston, Mass.	FIFTY Female. FIFTY
100 Vulcan seated.	Spread eagle on branch of tree; cars and canal in distance. GRANITE BANK, Boston, Mass.	100 Female seated.

Left end	Center	Right end
Words one hundred and figs. 100. Portrait of Harrison.	Scene on a wharf. GRANITE BANK, Boston, Mass.	Same as on left. Portrait of Columbus.
ONE Large figure 1 with female on it.	Farmers driving sheep across a stream of water. GREENFIELD BANK Greenfield, Mass.	ONE Large figure 1 with female on it.
Factory and train of cars. 2	Large figure 2 with Indian. GREENFIELD BANK Greenfield, Mass.	2 Female with fruit basket upon her arm.
State arms. 3	Train of cars GREENFIELD BANK Greenfield, Mass.	THREE Portrait Z. Taylor THREE
FIVE Farmer sowing seed. 5	5 Cluster of buildings. 5 GREENFIELD BANK Greenfield, Mass.	FIVE Vulcan the blacksmith and fig. 5.
TEN Cattle. TEN	10 Cluster of buildings. 10 GREENFIELD BANK Greenfield, Mass.	X Female riding hay
Two females with grain, sickle, etc. 20	20 Dog swimming in water with child 20 Massachusetts GREENFIELD B'K TWENTY DOLLARS Greenfield	Indian girl beside rock 20
20 Female.	2 Female. 0 GREENFIELD BANK Greenfield, Mass XX	20 Female. 20
50 Female.	Male and female. GREENFIELD BANK Greenfield, Mass. 50	50 Cupid in a sail boat. 50
FIFTY Female with lamp, flowers, wheel, etc.	Fifty Dollars L Eagle, shield, etc. L GREENFIELD B'K FIFTY DOLLARS Greenfield. Mass	50 General McClellan

Left end	Center	Right end
Two children in large circular die 100	One Hundred Dollars State Arms GREENFIELD BANK One Hundred Dollars	C Blacksmith
100 Vulcan with implements.	Spread eagle on limb of tree; canal and railroad. GREENFIELD BK., Greenfield, Mass. 100	100 Female with rake
Youthful portrait with cap. 1	HADLEY FALLS BK., Holyoke, Mass. Hunter killing buffaloes. Dog.	1 Female portrait
1 Portrait of female.	Female sitting on a bale also two cherubs, shipping and train of cars in background. 1 HADLEY FALLS BANK, Holyoke, Mass.	1 Indian woman and child
2	American flag and shield surmounted by an eagle; at right is female instructing children; at left an Indian woman and child 2 on right. HADLEY FALLS BANK. Holyoke, Mass.	TWO 2 Anvil and hammer.
THREE Female feeding an eagle from a cup. THREE.	3 Three men 3 HADLEY FALLS BANK. Holyoke, Mass. Girl swimming.	3 Sailor and flag; shipping in background.
FIVE Female drawing water from a well. FIVE	5 Man at work at lathe. HADLEY FALLS BANK, Holyoke, Mass. FIVE	5
5 Portrait of two children	HADLEY FALLS BANK. Holyoke, Mass. 5 Husking scene; seven figures, dog, &c.	5 Male portrait.
5 Female beside column; steamer, etc.	Title of Bank. Men on horse, colt, dog, sheep; man on fence.	5 Boys' portrait.
Male portrait 5	Title of Bank. Steamship at sea. Indian boy's head.	5 Female portrait.

5 Boy and girl.	Title of Bank. Corn husking scene—males and females in barn. Female bathing.	5 Male portrait.
10 X	HADLEY FALLS BANK, Holyoke, Mass. View of Hadley Falls; mountains in background.	10 X
XX Female with scales and sword.	State arms and two horses, Factory, train of cars and steamboat. HADLEY FALLS BANK, Holyoke, Mass.	20 Female.
Indian princess seated; shield, &c. 50	HADLEY FALLS BK, Holyoke, Mass. Portrait of Daniel Webster; female each side; ships and farmer in distance. 50 Horse. 50	50 Blacksmith erect.
C River, train of cars crossing a bridge; city in distance.	HADLEY FALLS BANK Holyoke, Mass. Three female figures.	100 Ship; city in distance.
ONE Bust ONE	Eagle. 1 Eagle. HAMILTON BANK, Boston, Mass.	ONE Male Portrait. ONE
2 Male Portrait. TWO	Ship. 2 Ship. HAMILTON BANK, Boston, Mass.	2 Male Portrait TWO
THREE Male Portrait. THREE	Washington on his horse. 3 Washington on his horse. HAMILTON BANK, Boston, Mass.	THREE Male Portrait. THREE
	The 5s, 10s, 50s, and 100s, are of the Perkins' Stereotype Plate, which has the denomination printed in fine letters all over the bill.	
20 Male Portrait. XX	XX Portrait. XX HAMILTON BANK, Boston, Mass.	20 Male Portrait. XX

Figs. 500. Male portrait Figs. 500.	Female either side of Indian on shield. HAMILTON BANK, Boston, Mass.	Figs. 500. Female.
ONE Female with sickle and sheaf of wheat ONE	1 Hampden bank building, store and Hotel. 1 HAMPDEN BANK, Westfield, Mass.	ONE Farmers mowing. 1
Female erect with sword and scales. ONE	HAMPDEN BANK, Hampden, Mass. General view of street and buildings.	1 Franklin.
TWO Female with sheaf and sickle.	Title of Bank. Vig. Same as above ones.	2 Washington.
2 Female and sheaf of wheat.	2 Same vignette as above 2 HAMPDEN BANK, Westfield, Mass. Steamboat	2 Train of cars
THREE Female figure. THREE	3 Same as above 3 HAMPDEN BANK, Westfield, Mass. Ship	3 Men and sheep. THREE
5 Youthful portrait with cap.	Title of Bank. Vig. Same as above ones.	5 Female, portrait
FIVE Milk maid. FIVE	Same as above HAMPDEN BANK, Westfield, Mass.	FIVE Eagle and 5
TEN Portrait of Franklin. TEN	Same as above HAMPDEN BANK, Westfield, Mass.	10 Female with wreaths.
TWENTY	20 Street scene. HAMPDEN BANK, Westfield, Mass.	TWENTY on 20. Washington.

FIFTY Medallion Head. 50	Same vig. as the others. HAMPDEN BANK, Westfield, Mass.	50 Portrait. FIFTY
100	C View of buildings, country inn, pedestrians, etc. HAMPDEN BANK, Westfield, Mass. Dog, safe and building.	100 Female Red head.
1 Portrait of female. ONE	View of Ware village HAMPSHIRE MANUFACTURERS BANK Ware, Mass.	Cupids supporting the fig. 1 ONE
Large figure 2; Portrait of Washington, and Portrait of Franklin.	View of Ware village HAMPSHIRE MANUFACTURERS BANK Ware, Mass. Eagle	2 Indian girl with bow and arrows
3 Female.	View of Ware village, HAMPSHIRE MANUFACTURERS' BANK Ware, Mass. Clay	3 Cupids in large 3.
	5s 10s 20s 50s all of the Perkins Patent Stereotype steel plate,	
100 Eagle. 100	C Phoebus in the car of the sun. 100 HAMPSHIRE MANUFACTURERS BANK Ware, Mass.	C Portrait of Washington C
1 ONE State Arms	View of Harvard College; pedestrians, trees, etc. HARVARD BANK, Cambridge, Mass ONE 1 ONE	1 Male portrait.
TWO State Arms.	HARVARD BANK, Cambridge, Mass. Male portrait. 2 View of Harvard College, etc. Two Dollars	Fig. 2 with name of Bank either side.
5 State Arms.	HARVARD BANK, Cambridge, Mass. View of Harvard College, pedestrians, etc. FI5VE	5 Male portrait.

Left	Center	Right
10 State Arms.	HARVARD BANK. Cambridge, Mass X Male portrait X	10 Female with State Arms on shield.
20 State Arms.	View of Harvard College; pedestrians, etc. HARVARD BANK, Cambridge, Mass.	20 TWENTY 20
50 State Arms.	State Arms HARVARD BANK, Cambridge, Mass Male portrait	50 50
1 Children sailing boats in a tub. ONE	steamboat, sail vessels — Plough and sheaf of wheat HAVERHILL BANK Haverhill, Mass.	1 Blacksmith, anvil and forge. ONE
ONE Female with flowers in apron.	View of a street. HAVERHILL B'K. Haverhill, Mass.	Word one and figure 1. Portrait of Webster.
Hunter loading his gun; deer at his feet. TWO	Word Two and $ mark — View of a street. HAVERHILL B'K. Haverhill, Mass. Two Dollars Two Dollars	2 Female gathering wheat.
2 Indian with bow. TWO	Train of cars passing through a gap. — Female and shield. HAVERHILL BANK, Haverhill, Mass.	2 Vessel. TWO
3	View of a street. — Word three and figure 3. HAVERHILL B'K. Haverhill, Mass. Three Dols. Three Dols.	3 Female with cornucopia.
3 Ship building. THREE	Farmer sowing seed. — Cattle. HAVERHILL BANK, Haverhill, Mass.	3 Indian. THREE
FIVE Milk maid.	State arms. Farming scene State arms. HAVERHILL BANK, Haverhill, Mass.	5 Female. FIVE

Left	Center	Right
Man with child on his back; female, boy, dog, hen and chickens. FIVE	HAVERHILL B'K. Haverhill, Mass. View of a street. Five Dols. Five Dols.	5 Female binding shoes; box of shoes, etc.
Two men, horse, boy and negro holding bull by nose; cows, etc; barn, trees, etc, in back ground. Word Ten and letter X.	Word Ten and letter X. HAVERHILL BANK, Haverhill, Mass.	10 Female feeding fowls.
10 Female. TEN	TEN Cattle, man on horseback. TEN HAVERHILL, BANK Haverhill, Mass.	10 Female. 10
20 Female figure.	2 Female 0 HAVERHILL, BANK Haverhill, Mass.	20 Female. 20
XX General street view in village.	HAVERHILL BANK, Haverhill, Mass. TWENTY	20 Same as on left end.
50 General street view in village.	Title of Bank Words "Fifty Dollars" across red fig. 50.	50 Indian erect.
50. Female figure.	Male and female. HAVERHILL, BANK Haverhill, Mass.	50 Cupid in a sail... 50
100 Vulcan the blacksmith.	Spread eagle, R. R. and canal. HAVERHILL, BANK Haverhill, Mass.	100 Female.
500 Male figure with a stylus and tablet.	Washington. — Two females and beehive. HAVERHILL BANK Haverhill, Mass.	500 Martha Washington.
1 Indian erect and lone star.	Hunter on horseback catching wild bull. HIDE AND LEATHER BANK, Boston, Mass ONE	1 Sailor

Left	Center	Right
TWO	Indian on horse hunting buffaloes. — Boston Title of Bank. TWO	2 Head of bull.
3 Female with shield, cornucopia, &c	Fig. 3 on die; men dressing leather on right; female sewing shoes on left. Title of Bank. THREE	3
V 5	Scene in a leather manufactory; men dressing leather, etc. Title of Bank.	5 5
Men shaving leather. 10	HIDE & LEATHER BANK, BOSTON, State of Massachusetts Title of Bank again and X on red die.	10 Steamship.
XX Cattle.	Title of Bank. Title of Bank again and 20 on red die.	20 Old man, boy and dog.
50 Three men erect; vessels in distance.	Title of Bank.	50 Red letter L.
ONE HUNDRED	Title of Bank. Three females—two seated, one erect reading from book.	100
Female seated with book on lap. 500	Title of Bank.	500 Ship in red circular die.
Goddess of Liberty erect	Title of Bank. 1000 1000	1000 Cupids with grain between them.
ONE on 1 Sailor, quadrant, capstan; steamer.	Schooners, etc. HINGHAM BANK, Hingham, Mass.	1 Female portrait.

Left	Centre	Right
ONE	Steamboat and sail vessels. 1 HINGHAM. BANK Hingham, Mass.	ONE Indian girl with bow and arrows ONE
2	Title of Bank. Males, female, house, well, dog, horses at trough, etc.	2 Female portrait.
2 TWO 2	Ships 2 HINGHAM, BANK Hingham, Mass.	TWO Female drawing water from a well. TWO
3	Man haying, etc. Title of Bank.	THREE Milkmaid erect; boy pointing.
THREE	Reapers. 3 HINGHAM, BANK Hingham, Mass.	THREE Steamboat. 3
FIVE partly inverted. 5	Scene on sea shore. HINGHAM BANK, Hingham, Mass	5 Sailor boy rowing.
FIVE	Spread eagle shield and anchor, village and shipping in background. Large V and female within. HINGHAM, BANK Hingham, Mass.	5 Girl
Vulcan the blacksmith. TEN	X HINGHAM, BANK Hingham, Mass.	10 Reaper.
10 Machinist at work.	Steamboat. Title of Bank.	10 Railroad train.
20 Female.	XX Eagle. XX HINGHAM, BANK Hingham, Mass.	20 Ship.

Left	Centre	Right
20	Scene in Arctic regions—white bear attacking sailors in boat. 20 HINGHAM BANK, Hingham, Mass.	20 Franklin in his study.
50 Boy, dog, house.	HINGHAM BANK, Hingham, Mass. 50 Sailor, two farmers, vessel, etc. Dog's head.	50 50
Words One Hundred on die 100	HINGHAM BANK, Hingham, Mass. Vessel under full sail. C Barrels. C	100 Eagle.
ONE HUNDRED on die 100	HINGHAM BANK, Mass. C C Barrels and bales	100 Eagle.
100 across words One Hundred. Male portrait.	Wharf scene; loading wagons; ships, &c. HINGHAM BANK, Hingham, Mass.	Same as on left end. Male portrait.
ONE Portrait.	Milk maid and cows. HOLLISTON B'K Holliston, Mass.	1 Portrait of Clay.
TWO Portrait.	HOLLISTON BANK Holliston, Mass. Two females supporting a sheaf of wheat above their heads.	2 Female.
3 Portrait of Charles Sumner.	HOLLISTON BANK Holliston, Mass. Females weaving at factory looms	3 Boy
V Portrait.	HOLLISTON BANK Holliston, Mass. Train of cars.	V 5 V Portrait of Webster.
TEN Portrait of General Cass.	Spread Eagle. HOLLISTON BANK Holliston, Mass.	X Portrait.

Left	Centre	Right
20 Portrait of J. Q. Adams.	Train of cars and railroad station. HOLLISTON BANK Holliston, Mass.	20 Female and child
50 Portrait of Charles Sumner.	Cattle. HOLLISTON BANK Holliston, Mass.	50 Portrait of Washington.
C Farmer sowing seed.	Indians in a canoe. HOLLISTON BANK Holliston, Mass.	100 Portrait of Charles Sumner
1 Machinist & implements.	Man whittling stick beside horse, cow, sheep, boy on gate; boy in distance. HOLYOKE BANK, Northampton, Mass.	1 Buildings in background, bridge and buildings in foreground.
TWO Same as on right end of 1	Two females, spinning wheel; cattle scene on left; buildings on right. Title of Bank. Dog.	2 Female, cow, calf, ducks, etc.
5 Eagle	V View in street; buildings, church, etc. V Title of Bank.	5 Female portrait.
10 Clay.	X Settlers at their devotions; Indians entering door; dog. X Title of Bank.	Ten on X. Male portrait
20 Male portrait 20	HOLYOKE BANK. TWENTY 20 Twenty 20 Dollars 20 DOLLARS. Northampton, Massachusetts. Anvil.	20 Spread eagle on shield. TWENTY.
Female with liberty cap and pole.	20 Female sitting on the ground with horn of plenty HOLYOKE BANK Northampton, Mass. Eagle	XX Female figure flying in the air.
Female eagle and shield.	HOLYOKE BANK Northampton, Mass. 50 Three female figures. on med head Yacht and steamer	50

100 on med head | HOLYOKE BANK, Northampton, Mass. | 100 on med head
River, train of cars cross a bridge, city in distance. | Three females. 100 | Ships and city in the distance.

1 | HOPKINTON BANK, Hopkinton, Mass. | 1
Interior of a boot manufactory. 1 | Large figure 1 with words "ONE DOLLAR" running across. Dog's head. | Portrait of Lee Claflin.

2 | HOPKINTON BANK, Hopkinton, Mass. | 2
Interior of a boot manufactory. 2 | Large figure 2, with the words "TWO DOLLARS" running across. Dog's head | Portrait of J. P. Hale.

5 | HOPKINTON BANK, Hopkinton, Mass. | 5
Same as ones and twos. 5 | Large figure 5, with the words "FIVE DOLLARS" running across. Dog's head | Portrait of Lee Claflin.

X | HOPKINTON BANK, Hopkinton, Mass. | X
Same as ones twos and fives. 10 | Large X, with the words "TEN DOLLARS" running across. Dog's head | Portrait of J. P. Hale.

50 | HOPKINTON BANK, Hopkinton, Mass. | 50
Male head. | Boot makers at work.

C | HOPKINTON BANK, Hopkinton, Mass. | 100
Boot makers at work. | | Wheels, bale, etc.

1 | (Old Plate.) | ONE
Medallion head. 1 | 1 Indian woman and canoe. 1 HOUSATONIC B'K, Stockbridge, Mass. | Female. ONE

ONE | (New Plate.) | 1
Portrait of Taylor. ONE | Man with an axe and Indian with an ear of corn. Figure 1 each side. HOUSATONIC B'K, Stockbridge, Mass. Safe. | Stone cutter

TWO | (New Plate.) | 2
Farmer sharpening a scythe. | Two female figures and bust, ship in distance. fig. 2 each side. HOUSATONIC B'K, Stockbridge, Mass. Wheat, &c. | Female TWO

2 | (Old Plate.) | 2
Female. 2 | 2 Female, anchor, and spinning wheel, factories and train of cars in background. HOUSATONIC B'K, Stockbridge, Mass. | Medallion head.

FIVE DOLLARS | (Old Plate.) | Indian.
| 5 Female feeding an eagle from a cup. 5 HOUSATONIC B'K, Stockbridge, Mass. Drovers, cattle, &c. | 5

FIVE | 5 Man plowing with two horses. | 5
Blacksmith with sledge and anvil. | HOUSATONIC BANK, Stockbridge, Mass. Mechanics' arm. | Two children

10 | (Old Plate.) | TEN
Portrait of Washington. 10 | X Archimides raisin the world with a lever. X HOUSATONIC B'K, Stockbridge, Mass. Female with wheat | Portrait. TEN

Female and eagle. | (New Plate.) | 10
TEN | 10 Farmers and cattle. HOUSATONIC B'K, Stockbridge, Mass. Horses | Indian woman and X

Two female figures. | 20 Female sitting upon a rock also three cupids sporting with a dolphin in the water. | 20
| HOUSATONIC B'K, Stockbridge, Mass. | 2 Female 0

50 | Vig. Sailor and Indian on either side of a shield, shipping in distance; two females on either side of shield, surmounted by an eagle, canal boats and locks in distance. | Winged female with trumpet, another female at her feet with pole and cap; eagle and cornucopia
Portrait of female. | HOUSATONIC BANK, Stockbridge, Mass. Loading hay.

ONE | Drovers on horseback and cattle. | 1
Beehive. | HOWARD BANK, Boston, Mass. | Portrait of officer.

2 | Med. seal on shield surmounted by eagle; Continental soldier, cane. &c. etc., on right; female with pole and cap on left. | 2
Youthful portrait with cap. | Title of Bank. | Sailor and capstan.

3 | Title of Bank. | 3
THREE | Three females in clouds; vessels in distance. | Portrait of officer.

V | Sailor on beach with anchor, etc.; steamer and vessels in distance. | 5
Man dressing skins | Title of Bank. | Female with V on shield.

10 | Title of Bank. | 10
Female, column, steamer, etc. | | Portrait of officer.

Marine view; ship under sail. | HOWARD BANK, Boston, Mass. | 20
20 | | Male portrait.

50 | HOWARD BANK, Boston, Mass. | 50
Marine view, ships under sail, city in distance L | | Indian female on the ground.

100 | HOWARD BANK, Boston, Mass. | C
Steamship and ship under sail. | HUNDRED.

500 | HOWARD BANK, Boston, Mass. | 500
Female, globe, chart, ship, &c. 500 | | Female head.

1 | JOHN HANCOCK B'K, Springfield, Mass. | 1
| View of the U. S. armory at Springfield also spread eagle. | Portrait of female.

2 | JOHN HANCOCK B'K, Springfield, Mass. | 2
Portrait of female. | View of the U. S. Armory at Springfield also spread eagle. |

3 | JOHN HANCOCK B'K, Springfield, Mass. | 3
Females | Train of cars. | Female.

5 | JOHN HANCOCK B'K, Springfield, Mass. | 5
Female, eagle and shield, steamer in distance. | Portrait of J. Hancock. | Female and 5 on a shield.

MASS.

Left	Centre	Right
Female sickle and sheaf of wheat. TEN	10 Three female figures ships in the distance. JOHN HANCOCK B'K Springfield, Mass. Eagle	10 Female.
20 John Hancock. TWENTY	Female representing fame blowing trumpet; eagle globe, flag, &c. JOHN HANCOCK BK, Springfield, Mass.	20 State arms.
50 Female and factories.	Scene in a farm yard. JOHN HANCOCK B'K Springfield, Mass.	50 Female and shield.
Indian female with eagle globe, &c. 100	100 on large die. Title of Bank. Dog's head.	100 Farmer with scythe; cars, mill, etc., in distance.
ONE	Female sitting on the ground supporting the figure 1. 1 Portrait of Franklin. LAIGHTON BANK, Lynn, Mass. 1	1 Portrait of a boy.
2	Blacksmith shoeing a horse. 2 LAIGHTON BANK, Lynn, Mass. State Arms	2 Female.
3	Female and eagle. 3 Portrait of Washington. LAIGHTON BANK, Lynn, Mass.	THREE Indian woman and child.
5	State arms, female on each side. 5 LAIGHTON BANK, Lynn, Mass. Wheels, bales, etc.	5 Portrait of Webster.
TEN Female.	Farming scene. LAIGHTON BANK, Lynn, Mass Wheels bales, ect.	10 Portrait of Adams
20 Leather Dresser.	LAIGHTON BANK, Lynn, Mass. 20 Male Portrait. 20	20 Female at work on sewing machine.

MASS.

Left	Centre	Right
20 Female.	2 Female. 0 LAIGHTON BANK. Lynn, Mass. XX	20 Female. 20
50 Eagle on Shield.	LAIGHTON BANK. Lynn, Mass. Male portrait.	50 Child's head.
50 Female.	Male and female. LAIGHTON BANK, Lynn. Mass. 50	50 Cupid in a sailboat. 50
C Female seated on box, ship, schooner & goods.	LAIGHTON BANK, Lynn, Mass. Male portrait.	100 Sailor standing holding quadrant in left hand, right resting on capstan; ships & merchandise.
100 Male figure.	Spread eagle, railroad and canal. LAIGHTON BANK, Lynn, Mass. 100	100 Female.
D	LAIGHTON BANK, Lynn, Mass Small eagle. Male portrait. D Interior of shoemakers' shop; two men and one woman at work.	500
500	Queen pulling a cloor. 500 LAIGHTON BANK, Lynn, Mass.	500 Justice.
State arms. ONE	Milk maid and cows Cupid and 1 on right. LANCASTER BANK Lancaster, Mass.	ONE Female figure
Female. TWO	Female sitting upon the ground leaning upon a bale, factory, village in background. LANCASTER BANK Lancaster, Mass.	2 Indian woman and child.
3 Mass'ch'setts Figure of Justice with sword and scales	Man, boy, two horses, plow, etc. LANCASTER BANK THREE DOLLARS Lancaster	3 Carpenter at work

MASS.

Left	Centre	Right
FIVE	Female figure. V LANCASTER BANK Lancaster, Mass.	5 Ship.
FIVE Female sitting on a bale.	5 Cupid Cows, farmer ploughing also a train of cars. LANCASTER BANK Lancaster, Mass.	FIVE Indian girl with bow, spear and arrows
10 X 10	10 Man on ones. LANCASTER BANK Lancaster, Mass.	TEN Female figure.
10 Female figure.	Farming scene. LANCASTER BANK Lancaster, Mass.	TEN A bulls head.
20 Female.	XX Eagle. XX LANCASTER BANK Lancaster, Mass.	20 Ship.
20 Man and girl at well, man drinking.	LANCASTER BANK, Lancaster, Mass. XX Dog on safe. XX	20 Eagle.
FIFTY Female. FIFTY	50 Man and horse. 50 LANCASTER BANK Lancaster, Mass.	FIFTY Female. FIFTY
50 Small State arms.	LANCASTER BANK, Lancaster, Mass. Boy and child, seated under tree, cows and sheep.	50 Indian, woman, rock, &c.
Same as right Portrait of Harrison.	Scene on a wharf. LANCASTER BANK Lancaster, Mass.	One Hundred and 100. Portrait of Columbus
Female leaning on pillar, full length figure. 100	LANCASTER BANK, Lancaster, Mass. Goddess of liberty, holding wreath over small State arms.	100 Portrait of boy.

ONE Femal .	Railroad, and Cambridge bridge, train of cars, vessels, and East Cambridge in distance. LECHMERE BANK East Cambridge, Mass.	1 Portrait of Winchester.
2 Portrait of female.	LECHMERE BANK East Cambridge Mass. Same vig.	2 Portrait of Winchester.
3 Same Vig.	LECHMERE BANK East Cambridge, Mass.	3 Portrait of Winchester.
5	Same vig. Portrait of female. LECHMERE BANK East Cambridge Mass.	5 Portrait of Winchester
Female 10 TEN	LECHMERE BANK East Cambridge Mass Portrait of Winchester.	10 Female TEN
20 Sailor leaning upon a capstan.	LECHMERE BANK East Cambridge, Mass Blacksmith shoeing a horse	20 Portrait of Winchester.
50 State arms.	LECHMERE BANK East Cambridge Mass. Capitol at Washington, female and shield in fore ground.	50 Portrait of John Hancock.
100 Portrait of female.	Three female figures. LECHMERE BANK East Cambridge, Mass	100 Portrait of Winchester
D Portrait of Washington.	Vig. View of the Capitol at Washington. LECHMERE BANK East Cambridge, Mass. Eagle.	500 Male portrait
D Washington	U. S. Capitol. LECHMERE BANK, East Cambridge, Mass.	500 Male portrait

1 Washington	LEE BANK, Lee, Mass. 1 Girl with dove. 1	1 State Arms.
ONE Female. ONE	1 Female, also eagle and shield surrounded by the several state arms; ship in distance. 1 LEE BANK, Lee, Mass. State Arms	ONE Portrait of Washington ONE
2 Female portrait	LEE BANK, Lee, Mass. Three females and bust of Washington. TWO	TWO Large fig. 2 and 2 in top.
TWO Female, TWO	2 Female each side of figure 2 in centre; city in background. 2 LEE BANK, Lee, Mass. State Arms	Female figure, and large figure 2.
5 Blacksmith, anvil and forge FIVE	Male figure and anchor, shipping and a city in background. V LEE BANK, Lee, Mass.	5 FIVE
5 Female. 5	5 Female. 5 LEE BANK, Lee, Mass. State Arms	Cupid in a cloud, with a basket of flowers upon his head.
5 Female	5 LEE BANK, Lee, Mass.	5 Female
10 Figure of Justice with sword and scales, seated on box.	LEE BANK, Lee, Mass. Two female figures seated; owl, barrels, bust, globe, &c.; steamship on left; buildings on right.	10 Femalehead.
10 X 10	Man and yoke of oxen. 10 LEE BANK, Lee, Mass.	TEN Female.
10 Female.	(New Plate.) X LEE BANK, Lee, Mass. [illegible]	10 Squaw

XX Portrait of Indian female	Title of Bank. Female on either side of anvil; building in distance	20 Two children
20 Female.	XX Eagle. XX LEE BANK, Lee, Mass.	20 Ship.
FIFTY Female. FIFTY	50 Man and horse. 50 LEE BANK, Lee, Mass	FIFTY Female. FIFTY
Justice erect	50 Title of Bank. Three females representing Commerce, Manufacturers and Agriculture; vessel in distance.	50 FIFTY Male portrait
100 State Arms.	Title of Bank. Female resting on bale on which is letter C; city, etc., in distance on left	100 Male portrait
Female seated pointing to reaping scene. Figs. 500.	500 D LEE BANK, Lee, Mass.	500
1	State arms with female on each side, steamboat and train of cars in background. 1 LEICESTER BANK Leicester, Mass	1 Female.
TWO 2 Portrait of Fillmore.	Female with sword and scales also shipping and boy 2 LEICESTER BANK Leicester, Mass.	2 Portrait of Webster.
THREE 3 Clay.	Farmer and milkmaid. 3 LEICESTER BANK, Leicester, Mass.	3 Taylor.
5 Portrait of Washington.	Reindeer running across a plain bearing a female upon his back. Large V, female within LEICESTER BANK Leicester, Mass.	5 Female with a flag also three cherubs.

Left	Centre	Right
Large X; with figure 10 running across.	Female with horn of plenty and key sitting, figures 1 and 0. LEICESTER BANK Leicester, Mass.	X Female.
20 Female.	(Old Plate.) XX Eagle. XX LEICESTER BANK Leicester, Mass.	20 Ship.
20 Female.	(New Plate) 2 Female. 0 LEICESTER BANK Leicester. Mass. XX	20 Female. 20
20 TWENTY XX	Female, shield, eagle, hut, tree, &c. 20 LEICESTER BANK, Leicistar. Mass.	20 Female portrait
FIFTY Female figure. FIFTY	50 Vig. A wild horse 50 LEICESTER BANK. Leicester, Mass.	FIFTY Female figure. FIFTY
50 Figure of Liberty.	Vig. Two figures a male and female, the female holding a rake in one hand and in the other a handful of grain, male figure with a scroll in hand, his feet resting on an anchor, cog wheel, &c. LEICESTER BANK, Leicester. Mass.	Cupid in a boat. 50
50 Boy, dog, House.	Horses in field; brook, cows, &c. LEICESTER BANK, Leicester. Mass.	50 Female reclining with basket of fruit and flowers.
100 Male figure, cog wheel, &c.	Vig. Spread eagle on branch of tree; train of cars, canal boat, &c. LEICESTER BANK, Leicester, Mass.	100 Female with rake, fruit, &c.
One Hundred and 100. Portrait of Harrison.	Vig. Shipping, buggy, waggon and merchandise. LEICESTER BANK, Leicester, Mass.	Same as left. Portrait of Columbus.
Men loading express wagon. C	Small eagle. LEICESTER BANK. Leicester. Mass.	100 Female portrait.

Left	Centre	Right
Two females in water, [illegible], steamship. D	LEICESTER BANK. Eagle on rock. Leicester, Mass.	500
ONE Machinery	LOWELL BANK. 1 Men at work during freshet. 1 ONE DOLLAR Lowell.	ONE on 1 Massachusetts State Arms.
Female ONE	View of the city of Lowell. LOWELL BANK, Lowell, Mass Dog and safe.	Female. 1
TWO Man beside machinery	Female, State arms, etc. Lowell, Massachusetts 2 LOWELL BANK, TWO DOLLARS	2 Child's head.
TWO Female. 2	Same Vig. as ones. LOWELL BANK, Lowell, Mass Bales, bbls., etc.	TWO Female. 2
3 Fowl beside pump.	Man plowing, boy, two horses, etc. LOWELL BANK THREE DOLLARS Lowell.	3
THREE Female, 3 on THREE	Same Vig. as ones. LOWELL BANK, Lowell. Mass Men and horses	THREE Female 3 on THREE
	5s, 10s, all of the Perkins Stereotype Steel Plate	
20 State Arms	State of Mass. TWENTY. LOWELL BANK Twenty Dollars Lowell.	20 Girl beside spinning wheel.
20 Female.	XX Eagle. XX LOWELL BANK, Lowell, Mass	20 Ship.

Left	Centre	Right
50 Figure of Justice with sword and scales.	State of Mass FIFTY. LOWELL BANK. Fifty Dollars. Lowell.	50 Spread Eagle.
FIFTY Female. FIFTY	50 Man and horse. 50 LOWELL BANK, Lowell, Mass.	FIFTY Female. FIFTY
100 Mechanic beside Anvil.	State of Mass. ONE HUNDRED. LOWELL BANK, One Hundred. Lowell.	100 Dog and safe.
One Hundred and 100. Portrait of Harrison.	Scene on a wharf. LOWELL BANK. Lowell, Mass.	Same as left. Portrait of Columbus.
Female figure leaning against column with torch in hand. 500	State of Mass. 500 LOWELL BANK, Five Hundred. Lowell.	500 Eagle on rock.
Female seated pointing to reapers. 500	500 D LOWELL BANK, Lowell, Mass.	500
Two females, one kneeling.	1 Two females on right of shield, on which is farming utensils; factory in distance; on left, cars and bridge. LYNN MECHANICS' BANK, Lynn, Mass.	1 Female.
1 Portrait of Washington.	Female. 1 Female. LYNN MECHANICS' BANK, Lynn, Mass.	1 Portrait of Franklin.
Female with flowers. 2	State Arms with eagle at top; horse each side; cars, bridge, city and building in distance. Title of Bank.	2 Female with cornucopia.
2 Portrait of Columbus.	Female. 2 Female. LYNN MECHANICS' BANK, Lynn, Mass.	2 Portrait.

Left	Centre	Right
3 Gen. Washington.	Female. 3 Female. LYNN MECHANICS' BANK. Lynn, Mass.	3 Vulcan the blacksmith
3 Fremont.	Man watering three horses from trough by side of well; goat, bed and sheep; cattle and house in distance. Title of Bank.	3 Two cherubs soaring with distaff and sheaf.
5 Justice	Title of Bank. Three females sculpturing bust of Washington.	5 on FIVE. Female seated.
FIVE	Female. V LYNN MECHANICS' BANK, Lynn, Mass.	5 Ship.
X Five cupids, globe and anvil.	Title of Bank.	10 Five cherubs with rake and tablets.
10 X 10	Man, and yoke of oxen. 10 LYNN MECHANICS' BANK, Lynn, Mass.	TEN Female.
20 Female.	XX Eagle. XX LYNN MECHANICS' BANK, Lynn, Mass.	20 Ship.
XX Man dressing feather	LYNN MECHANICS' BANK, Lynn, Mass. Male portrait; female and children on right; Indian family on left.	20 Female portra[illegible]
L Female with dove.	Title of Bank. Hunter shooting deer; dog, water, trees, etc.	50 Indian seated.
FIFTY Female. FIFTY	50 Man and horse. 50 LYNN MECHANICS' BANK. Lynn, Mass.	FIFTY Female. FIFTY

Left	Centre	Right
100 Eagle. 100	C Phoebus in the chariot of the sun. 100 LYNN MECHANICS' BANK, Lynn, Mass.	C Portrait of Washington. C
Same as right Portrait of Harrison.	Scene on a wharf. LYNN MECHANICS' BANK, Lynn, Mass.	One Hundred and 100. Portrait of Columbus.
C Two medallion heads.	Title of Bank. Three females seated and one standing reading to others.	100 Two medallion heads.
500 D	LYNN MECH. BANK. Large spread eagle on shield, mortar, cannon, etc.; fort in distance Five Hundred Dollars.	500 D
500 Male seated with tablets.	Washington. Justice and Manufactures seated in alcove; beehive between them. Title of Bank. Machine.	500 Lady Washington.
Female. ONE	Male and female. 1 MACHINISTS' BANK Taunton, Mass. Man seated on plow	1 Female with scales.
TWO	Female, anvil, wheel &c.; ship building and train of cars in background. 2 MACHINISTS' BANK Taunton, Mass. Indian in canoe	2 Reaper.
THREE	Female with a pen in her right hand, her left resting on a globe. 3 MACHINISTS' BANK Taunton, Mass. Indian	3 2 females.
FIVE	Train of cars. Large V with female in the centre. MACHINISTS' BANK Taunton, Mass.	5 Female.
TEN	Spread eagle, railroad and canal. MACHINISTS' BANK Taunton, Mass.	10 Female.

Left	Centre	Right
20	MACHINISTS' BANK Taunton, Mass. Sailor by side of vessel with trumpet. Twenty on fig. 20 each side.	20
FIFTY Female with tablets; child at her feet. FIFTY	FIFTY DOLLARS L Cars, etc. L MACHINISTS' BANK Taunton, Mass.	50 Sailor, mechanic, vessels, etc.
50 Female figure.	Male and Female. MACHINISTS' BANK Taunton, Mass. 50	50 Cupid in a sailboat. 50
100 Female gazing out on ocean on which is steamer.	State Arms. MACHINISTS' BANK Taunton, Mass.	100
100 Female on rock gazing on wreck—anchor at her feet.	MACHINISTS BANK, Taunton, Mass. One Hundred Dollars on ONE HUNDRED.	100
500 D	MACHINISTS BANK. Taunton, Mass. Vignette, sailor seated on gun carriage, soldier resting on gun, flags, fort in distance, &c.	500 D
ONE Female.	Female sitting on the ground supporting the figure one. MAHAIWE BANK, Gt. Barrington, Mass. State Arms.	1 Cattle and hogs.
2 Female.	Man driving sheep across a brook. MAHAIWE BANK, Gt. Barrington, Mass. State Arms	2 Stone cutter
Female borne in the arms of 2 males. THREE	Train of cars. 3 MAHAIWE BANK, Gt. Barrington, N. Y. State Arms.	THREE Female figure. THREE
Two Indian women, one of them stepping from a precipice into ravine below	Five, V, 5 State Arms MAHAIWE BANK, Gt. Barrington, Mass.	5 Five female figures. and 5

Deer 10 Farmer seated upon plow	TEN X Surveying scene TEN X MAHAIWE BANK Great Barrington, Mass. State arms	10 Female with sheaf of grain

Deer. 10 Farmer sitting upon a plough.	TEN TEN Female sitting upon a bale with sickle and sheaf of wheat; train of cars and factory in background MAHAIWE BANK, Gt Barrington, Mass. State Arms.	10 Indian woman holding X

20 Two females with grain and sickle	Twenty Dollars XX State Arms XX MAHAIWE BANK TWENTY DOLLARS on TWENTY Massachusetts	20 Female with torch beside column

20 Female figure.	2 Female. 0 MAHAIWE BANK, Gt. Barrington, Mass. XX	20 Female. 20

L Mas'ch's'tts Three children with horse	Man, horse drinking at trough, cattle, hog, etc. in barnyard. MAHAIWE BANK FIFTY DOLLARS on FIFTY	50 Male portrait

50 Female figure.	Male and female. MAHAIWE BANK, Gt. Barrington Mass. 50	50 Cupid in a sailboat. 50

Female erect with pole and cap	1 MALDEN BANK, Malden, Mass. Farmer seated with cradle, etc.	1 Two children.

1 Female.	Train of cars. MALDEN BANK Malden, Mass. Arm and hammer	1 State arms

Indian girl with bow and spear. TWO	Man sitting upon the ground, anvil hammer &c., factory and train of cars in background. MALDEN BANK Malden Mass. Whole bale, eat,	2 Child and dolphin. TWO

Female. THREE	Farming Scene. MALDEN BANK Malden, Mass.	3 Female and cherubs

5 Portrait of female. FIVE	Female leaning upon a bale, factory village in background. MALDEN BANK Malden, Mass. State Arms	FIVE Portrait of Z Taylor. FIVE

10 Blacksmith anvil and forge.	1 Female key and horn of plenty. 0 MALDEN BANK Malden, Mass Cars.	10 Female.

20 Female.	Female, Eagle, and shield factory, and ships in background. MALDEN BANK Malden. Mass.	20 2 Female. 0

50 Female figure.	Male and Female. MALDEN BANK Malden, Mass. 50	50 Cupid in a sail boat. 50

100 Vulcan the Blacksmith.	Spread Eagle R. R. and Canal. MALDEN BANK Malden, Mass. 100	100 Female.

C Female.	MALDEN BANK, Malden, Mass. Boy, child, cattle, etc.	100 Girl's head.

1 Bales, ship, etc. 1	One Dollar 1 Female seated beside bales; ship in distance 1 MARBLEHEAD B'K ONE DOLLAR Marblehead Massachusetts	1 Agricult'r'l Implements 1

1 ONE Fowls, pump, etc.	1 Boy on horse, colt, female, trough, etc. MARBLEHEAD B'K Marblehead, Mass.	1 One on 1. 1

2 Man currying leather.	Shoemakers at work; female at domestic duties. MARBLEHEAD B'K Marblehead, Mass.	2 Female and sewing machine.

2 Washington on horse. 2	2 Female and fig. 2 2 MARBLEHEAD BK. Marblehead, Mass.	2 Washington on horse. 2

3 Head 3	Three Dollars 3 Female seated beside shield, on which is fig. 3 3 MARBLEHEAD B'K THREE DOLLARS Marblehead Massachusetts	3 Head 3

3 General Washington, and horse.	Female 3 Female MARBLEHEAD B'K Marblehead, Mass.	3 Vulcan the black smith.

Spread eagle FIVE	Large V; Female and Cupid. MARBLEHEAD B'K Marblehead, Mass.	5 Girl.

Five on 5 Locomotive	MARBLEHEAD B'K Marblehead, Mass. Sailor, vessels, etc.	5 Schooner under sail.

Washingt'n 10	MARBLEHEAD B'K Marblehead, Mass. Battle scene on ship-board.	10 Male portrait.

Vulcan the black smith. TEN	X MARBLEHEAD B'K Marblehead, Mass.	10 Reaper.

20 Female.	XX Eagle XX MARBLEHEAD B'K Marblehead, Mass.	20 Ship.

Two children. TWENTY	Twenty Twenty Man-of-war vessels, etc. MARBLEHEAD B'K Marblehead, Mass.	20 Indian princess

FIFTY Female with tablets; child at her feet. FIFTY	Man and two horses at pump; pig, cattle etc. MARBLEHEAD B'K Marblehead, Mass.	50 Female with dove.

FIFTY Female FIFTY	50 Man and horse. 50 MARBLEHEAD B'K Marblehead, Mass.	FIFTY Female. FIFTY

Left	Centre	Right
100 Franklin in his study.	MARBLEHEAD B'K Marblehead, Mass. Large C with small c at bottom.	100 Old man, child and bust of Washingt'n.
1	Shipping 1 MARINE BANK, New Bedford, Mass.	1 Female.
2	Shipping Female and 2. MARINE BANK, New Bedford, Mass.	2 Whale fishing.
Steamship and sail vessels. THREE 3	MARINE BANK, New Bedford, Mass. 3 THREE	3 Girl.
5 FIVE 5	V Eagle, anchor, merchandise, &c shipping in background. V MARINE BANK, New Bedford, Mass	5 FIVE 5
Wharf and shipping. 5	V MARINE BANK, New Bedford, Mass.	5 Sailor, merchandise and shipping. FIVE
X Indian with bow	Shipping and wharf MARINE BANK, New Bedford, Mass.	10 Female and sheaf of wheat.
Female, eagle and State Arms shipping and train of cars in background. TEN	X MARINE BANK, New Bedford, Mass.	10 Female.
20	Vig. Female, train of cars and canal in background. 20 MARINE BANK, New Bedford, Mass.	XX Portrait of Columbus.
50 FIFTY	Spread eagle, Railroad and canal 50 MARINE BANK, New Bedford, Mass.	50 Ship.

Left	Centre	Right
100 Portrait of Washington.	Ship and steamship. MARINE BANK, New Bedford, Mass.	100 Large C with female within it.
Shipping. 500	D MARINE BANK, New Bedford, Mass.	500 Sailor at helm.
Female, wheat, etc. 500	500 D MARINE BANK, New Bedford, Mass.	500
1 Sailor with bundle.	Scene in ship-yard—men at work. MARKET BANK, Boston, Mass.	1 Portrait.
Horse and cart. ONE Farming scene.	1 Indian on 1 1 MARKET BANK, Boston, Mass.	Man on horseback; cattle. ONE Horses and trucks with view of Quincy Market.
2 Basket of corn.	Forest scene—deer grazing MARKET BANK, Boston, Mass.	2 Male portrait.
Vase of flowers. 2	TWO 2 TWO MARKET BANK, Boston, Mass.	Ship. 2
3	Scene in harbor—steamboat, ships, &c. MARKET BANK, Boston, Mass.	3 Male portrait.
3 Indian seated on safe.	Two females either side of anvil. MARKET BANK, Boston, Mass.	3 3
3 Vase of flowers.	Bust of Washington. 3 Female. MARKET BANK, Boston, Mass	3 Vase of flowers.

Left	Centre	Right
Train of cars FIVE	Portrait of Lady Washington. 5 Portrait of Washington. MARKET BANK, Boston, Mass. Bull	5 Eagle and five on shield.
5 FIVE	Merchandise, shipping and Quincy Market V MARKET BANK, Boston, Mass.	5 Cows. FIVE
X	Ship under full sail. X MARKET BANK, Boston, Mass. Bull	10 Female Portrait. TEN
10 Female. TEN	X Merchandise, shipping and Quincy Market. X MARKET BANK, Boston, Mass.	10 Ship. TEN
20 Washington TWENTY	Spread eagle on branch of tree; cars and canal in distance. MARKET BANK, Boston, Mass. Steamship.	20 Male portrait TWENTY
50	Steamship. 50 MARKET BANK, Boston, Mass.	FIFTY Portrait of Columbus. FIFTY
100 Neptune. 100	Steamship. MARKET BANK, Boston, Mass.	100 Franklin. 100
500 Med. head. 500	Female seated with sheafs; boat and cars in distance. MARKET BANK, Boston, Mass.	500 Portrait of Washington.
1	MARTHA'S VINEYARD BANK, Edgartown, Mass. Shipping. Steamship.	1 Female, globe, and shield.
2	MARTHA'S VINEYARD BANK, Edgartown, Mass. Haymakers at the left, and females preparing dinner at the right; two trains of cars and a city in background.	2

Deer hanging on limb of tree; dog on ground.
Mechanic, sailor and farmer seated with implements; three gold dollars.
3
MARTHA'S VINEYARD BANK
Edgartown, Mass.
THREE
Female seated with fig. 3.

Sailor boy.
Hunter, Indian woman, three cupids, and five gold dollars.
5
MARTHA'S VINEYARD BANK,
Edgartown, Mass.
V
Female reclining; ship in distance.

Female.
Goddess of Plenty and cherubs, representing the gathering of the harvest.
10
MARTHA'S VINEYARD BANK.
Edgartown, Mass.
10
Ships.

Female.
Stonecutters and architect.
20
MARTHA'S VINEYARD BANK,
Edgartown, Mass.
XX
Sailor.

Sailor.
An Indian with bow and arrow; eagle flying; in the background is a lake; Indians in a canoe, wild deer, &c.
50
MARTHA'S VINEYARD BANK.
Edgartown, Mass
50
Two female figures.

C
State arms surmounted by an eagle; female on each side,
100
Spread eagle.
Female with sword and scales.
MARTHA'S VINEYARD BANK.
Edgartown, Mass.
100

1 on Med. head.
Indian sitting on the ground; mountains in distance.
ONE
MASSACHUSETTS BANK,
Boston, Mass.
Same as left
1 on med head

1
MASSACHUSETTS BANK.
Boston, Mass.
1
Massachusetts.
State arms; words "One Dollar" across fig. 1 each side.
ONE
ONE

TWO
Title of Bank.
TWO
2
2 State Arms. 2
2
TWO
TWO DOLLARS
MASS.
TWO

TWO
Ships.
MASS. BANK,
Boston, Mass.
TWO

V
State Arms.
5
Washington.
MASS. BANK,
Boston, Mass.
Male portrait
5
V

X
State Arms.
10
Washington
MASS. BANK,
Boston, Mass.
Male portrait
10
X

MASSACHUSETTS BANK
20 20
TWENTY State Arms. DOLL'S
MASS. BANK,
Boston, Mass.
20 20
TWENTY

MASSACHUSETTS BANK
50 Fifty Dollars 50
State Arms.
50
MASS. BANK,
Boston, Mass.
50 50
FIFTY DOLLARS.

MASSACHUSETTS BANK
100 100
ONE HUNDRED
State Arms.
MASS. BANK,
Boston, Mass.
100 100 100
ONE HUNDRED

FIVE HUNDRED
Five Hundred Dollars
Indian on shield, farming utensils around; ship in distance
MASS. BANK,
Boston, Mass.
500

MASSACHUSETTS BANK
1000
1000 1000
ONE THOUSAND
State Arms.
Title of Bank.
1000
1000
MASSACHUSETTS BANK

Large figure 1, in the centre of which is an Indian.
Vig. A large factory, and train of cars.
Large figure 1, in the centre of which is an Indian
ONE
MASSASOIT BANK,
Fall River, Mass.
ONE

2
Figure 2; spread eagle.
Steamboat. Bust of Indian. Locomotive.
MASSASOIT BANK,
Fall River, Mass.
2
Figure 2 and spread eagle.

3
MASSASOIT BANK,
Fall River, Mass.
3
Farmer with rake, etc.
Train of cars, harvesting scenes, etc.
Two females preparing dinner.

Indian, dog, and dead deer
V
Eagle.
5
5
MASSASOIT BANK,
Fall River, Mass.
FIVE

X
Female head
X
Female head.
10
Washington, and his horse
MASSASOIT BANK,
Fall River.
Indian springing bow.

Two Indians, and a steamboat.
20
XX
20
MASSASOIT BANK,
Fall River.
Female with basket on her head.

Massachusetts
Merman and maid in water; steamer, etc. in distance
Child's head
50
MASSASOIT BANK
FIFTY DOLLARS
50
Female portrait

FIFTY
Female figure.
50 Horse and groom. 50
FIFTY
Female figure.
MASSASOIT BANK,
Fall River.
FIFTY
FIFTY

C
MASSASOIT BANK
100
Two girls
One with sickle One Hundr'd and Hundr'd Dollars flowers. Dollars on Massachusetts on
Indian girl
C C
Eagle on rock

The figures 100, with the words one hundred across.
Vig. Baggage waggon, and men loading it.
The figures 100, with the words one hundred
Portrait.
MASSASOIT BANK,
Fall River.
Portrait.

Indian in a canoe.
500
500
MASSASOIT BANK,
Fall River.
500
Female with scales.

Female.
Steamship and sail vessels.
1
ONE
MATTAPAN BANK,
Dorchester, Mass.
Sailor.

Two Indian women, one stepping from a precipice into a ravine below.
Train of cars.
2
MATTAPAN BANK.
Dorchester, Mass.
Female.
TWO

Left	Centre	Right
3 Cattle.	Female seated with cornucopia, factories, bridge, canal and cars in distance MATTAPAN BANK, Dorchester, Mass.	3 Cattle.
3 Large figure 3 Mechanic, farmer and sailor.	Man sitting upon the ground, with a hammer upon his shoulder; train of cars and factory in the background. MATTAPAN BANK, Dorchester, Mass	3 Female.
Indian FIVE	Ships and steamship. MATTAPAN BANK, Dorchester, Mass. Wheels, bale, etc	5 Two female figures and 5.
10 Stone cutter.	Spread eagle, ship and Steamship. MATTAPAN BANK, Dorchester. Mass.	10 Indian woman.
20 Female figure.	2 Female. 0 MATTAPAN BANK, Dorchester, Mass. XX	20 Female. 20
20 Washingt'n	MATTAPAN BANK, Dorchester, Mass. Whites and Indians.	20 Girl's head
L 50	Female with shield—50, fifty on it; vessels, etc. 50 50 MATTAPAN BANK, Dorchester, Mass.	50 State Arms.
50 Female figure.	Male and female. MATTAPAN BANK. Dorchester, Mass. 50	50 Cupid in a sail boat. 50
100 Shipwright.	Three sailors, mast and ocean scene. C MATTAPAN BANK, Dorchester, Mass. C	100 Female feeding fowls.
100 Vulcan the blacksmith.	Spread eagle, railroad and canal MATTAPAN BANK. Dorchester. Mass. 100	100 Female

Left	Centre	Right
One on 1.	Ship building and city in distance. MAVERICK BANK, Boston, Mass.	1 Female.
2 TWO 2	MAVERICK BANK, Boston, Mass Ship building and city in distance.	2 Sailor.
3 Ibls., bales, cars, etc. 3	MAVERICK BANK, Boston, Mass. Ship building and city in distance. Three 3 Three	3
5 V	East Boston ferry landing. MAVERICK BANK, Boston, Mass.	5 Portrait of Webster.
10 X	East Boston Ferry Landing. MAVERICK BANK, Boston, Mass.	10 Sailor and Indian Ten on shield between.
XX	MAVERICK BANK, Boston, Mass. Winthrop block and street in East Boston.	20 Sailor.
50 FIFTY	MAVERICK BANK, Boston, Mass. Winthrop block and street in East Boston.	50 Ship and ship houses in Navy Yard.
100 Female. HUNDRED	Winthrop block and street in East Boston. MAVERICK BANK, Boston, Mass.	100 Female and ship.
Five hundred Washington 500	MAVERICK BANK, Boston, Mass. D Winthrop block and a street in East Boston.	500
1 Vulcan seated with anvil and hammer.	MECHANICS' BANK, Boston, Mass. Wood cutter; gold dollar; log hut and wagon in distance.	1 Ships.

Left	Centre	Right
Statue of Washington	Fishing vessels. Female MECHANICS' BANK, Boston, Mass.	1 ONE 1
2	TWO Interior of a blacksmith's shop. TWO MECHANICS' BANK, Boston, Mass.	2 Female portrait. 2
2 Blacksmith anvil and forge.	MECHANICS' BANK, Boston, Mass. Farmer boy with rake; milkmaid with pail; two gold dollars; farm house and cows in distance.	2 Locomotive.
THREE Washington and staff on Dorchester Heights. THREE	Ship building. Steamboat. MECHANICS' BANK, Boston, Mass.	3 Man on horseback; cattle. THREE
3 Female.	MECHANICS' BANK, Boston, Mass. Farmer with scythe, sailor with spy-glass, blacksmith, hammer and anvil; three gold dollars.	3 Stone cutter.
FIVE Female with pole and cap, shield at her feet.	MECHANICS' BANK, Boston, Mass. Indian female on left, hunter on right, three cupids in centre; five gold dollars; cars in distance.	5 Portrait of Webster.
FIVE	Washington and staff on Dorchester Heights; evacuation of Boston, 1776. MECHANICS' BANK, Boston, Mass.	5 Washington.
Wharf and shipping. 10	Steamboat landing and sail vessels Washington on horse on right. MECHANICS' BANK, Boston, Mass. [illegible] scene	10 Train of cars. TEN
XX Female with pail and stool.	Man on horseback, and man on foot; cattle, sheep and dogs. Cars MECHANICS' BANK, Boston, Mass.	20 Boy and girl sailing boat in tub.
MECHANICS BANK, Boston, Mass. Engine. 50	Sailor with telescope, &c. on yard-arm. FIFTY 50	50 DOLLARS

FIFTY — 50 Man and horse 50 — FIFTY
Female. — MECHANICS' BANK, Boston, Mass. — Female.
FIFTY — FIFTY

100 — MECHANICS BANK. Scene in Shipyard. One Hundred Dollars. Boston, Mass. — 100
Female seated with shield, on which is city of Boston. — Mechanic at work.

Words one hundred and figs. 100. — Scene on a wharf. MECHANICS' BANK, Boston, Mass. — Same as on left.
Portrait of Harrison. — Portrait of Columbus.

500 — Steamship and other vessels at sea. MECHANICS BANK Five Hundred Dollars. Boston, Massachusetts — 500
Mechanic beside column, on top of which is bust. — State Arms.

1 — Whale fishing. MECHANICS BANK New Bedford, Mass. Indian head — 1

2 — Sailor, merchandise, and ship in distance. MECHANICS BANK New Bedford. Mass. Cars — 2
Stone cutter. — Dog and safe.

3 — 3 Ships 3 MECHANICS' BANK, New Bedford, Mass. — 3
Two children — Sailor, barrel capstan, quadrant, etc.

5 — Whale fishing. MECHANICS BANK New Bedford, Mass. Three female figures — 5

10 — City, R. R. Station and train of cars. MECHANICS BANK New Bedford, Mass. Ship. — 10
Blacksmith anvil and forge. — Sailor with spy glass.

20 — 20 Child dog and safe. MECHANICS BANK New Bedford, Mass. Ship. — 20
Medallion — 20

50 — New Bedford City Hall. 50 MECHANICS BANK New Bedford. Mass. Head — 50
Medallion — 50

Indian in canoe. — 500 MECHANICS' BANK. New Bedford, Mass. D D — 500
500 — Justice

Train of cars and factory. — MECHANICKS B'K Newburyport. Mass. — 1
1 — Sailor at the wheel.

Shipping and ship building. — 2 and female head MECHANICKS B'K Newburyport, Mass. — 2
2 — Large figure 2 and eagle

Ships steamboat and landing. — MECHANICKS B'K Newburyport. Mass. — 3
3 — Blacksmith and forge.

Train of cars — Vful length MECHANICKS B'K Newburyport, Mass — 5
5 — Portrait of Franklin.

Ship and steamship. — MECHANICKS B'K Newburyport, Mass — 10
10 — Portrait of Washington.

20 — XX Eagle XX MECHANICKS B'K Newburyport, Mass. — 20
Female. — Ship.

20 — White bear attacking sailors in boat; Arctic regions scene. MECHANICKS' B'K Newburyport, Mass. — 20
TWENTY 20 — Female portrait.

50 — FIFTY DOLLARS. Two sailors, bales, anchor, vessels, etc. MECHANICKS' B'K Newburyport, Mass. 50 — 50
Two children. — Female blowing at flower

FIFTY — 50 Man and horse 50 — FIFTY
Female. — MECHANICKS B'K Newburyport, Mass. — Female.
FIFTY — FIFTY

100 — Cars. MECHANICKS' B'K Newburyport, Mass. Large green C. — 100
Vessels. — Sailor with telescope at side of vessel.

One Hundred and 100. — Scene on a wharf. MECHANICKS B'K Newburyport, Mass. — Same as left.
Portrait. — Portrait of Columbus.

1 — Blacksmith anvil and forge. MECHANICS BANK Worcester, Mass. Machine. — ONE and 1.
Portrait of Washington. — Female, eagle and shield.
ONE — ONE

TWO — Female Man on horse back; flock of sheep. Female MECHANICS BANK Worcester, Mass. 2 Arms 2 — 2
Portrait of Franklin. — Female.
TWO — TWO on med head

THREE — State arms surmounted by an eagle; three females MECHANICS BANK Worcester, Mass 3 Female 3 — 3
Portrait of John Adams. — Girl.
THREE — 3

5 — MECHANICS BANK Worcester, Mass. State Arms. Horn, Female sheaf of wheat, and sheep, ship in background 5 Eagle 5 — 5
Female sickle and sheaf of wheat. — Portrait of Webster.
5

Female, eagle and shield. — 10 Man and anvil, train of cars and village in background. MECHANICS BANK Worcester, Mass. X Arms X — 10
Portrait of Z. Taylor.

XX — MECHANICS BANK Worcester, Mass. Three female figures. Female. — 20
Portrait of J. Q. Adams.

Two females and two females. — 50 Farmer ploughing. MECHANICS BANK Worcester, Mass. — 50

Left	Centre	Right
100 Portrait. 100	State arms, Two horses, factories, and train of cars and steamboat MECHANICS BANK Worcester, Mass	100 Portrait. 100
D	MECHANICS' BANK, Worcester, Mass. Female seated with book and mechanical implements; factories on right and steamboat on left. Dog, key and safe.	500
1	Vessels, etc. 1 MERCANTILE BK Salem, Mass	1 Female, smoking urn and flowers. ONE
ONE 1	Farmer sowing seed. 1 MERCANTILE B'K. Salem, Mass	1 Ship. ONE
TWO 2	Spread eagle. 2 MERCANTILE B'K. Salem, Mass	2 TWO Sail boat.
Female with tablets, child at her feet. TWO	MERCANTILE BK Salem, Mass Three females reclining; vessels in distance.	2 Childs head
3 Child's head. 3	THREE DOLLARS. 3 Women and 3 MERCANTILE BANK THREE DOLLARS Salem, Massachusetts.	3 Child's head. 3
THREE 3	Sailor, wharf and shipping. 3 MERCANTILE B'K, Salem, Mass	3 THREE Train of cars
5 Sailor, and mechanic; vessels, etc	Female with shield, eagle, etc., steamer in distance. MERCANTILE BK Salem, Mass	5 FIVE Sailor, capstan, bbls. vessels, etc
The word five with large V across.	Female, also emblems of agriculture, commerce &c. Large V and Indian girl. MERCANTILE B'K. Salem, Mass	5 Portrait of Washington.

Left	Centre	Right
10 Pilot boat under full sail.	MERCANTILE B'K. Sailor seated with telescope, etc. TEN DOLLARS Salem, Mass	10 Female portrait.
TEN	Vulcan the blacksmith. X MERCANTILE B'K. Salem, Mass	10 Reaper.
20 Female.	XX Eagle. XX MERCANTILE B'K, Salem, Mass	20 Ship.
50 Figure of Justice with sword and scales.	Scene on dock; men rolling barrels from ship, etc. MERCANTILE B'K. Salem, Mass	50 Two Sailors.
FIFTY Female. FIFTY	50 Man and horse. 50 MERCANTILE B'K. Salem, Mass	FIFTY Female. FIFTY
C Female figure, with torch, &c.	Female seated; barrels, keys, coffee bags, &c. MERCANTILE B'K. Salem, Mass One Hundred Dollars.	100 State Arms. 100
Same as right. Portrait.	Horses, wagons, wharf and shipping. MERCANTILE B'K. Salem, Mass	One Hundred and 100. Portrait.
500	Female seated pointing to reapers and load of hay. 500 D MERCANTILE BK., Salem, Mass	500
Cupid on V. Female on safe with sword and scales.	View of Merchant's Bank and other buildings, street scene. MERCHANTS' BK., Boston Mass.	FIVE Fig. 5 on which is eagle, female and Washington. FIVE
5 Portrait of Franklin. V	View of the Merchants Bank and other buildings. V and cupid either side. MERCHANTS BANK, Boston, Mass. Cupid on V.	FIVE Female, eagle, Washington, on 5. FIVE

Left	Centre	Right
TEN Sailor leaning on capstan, with quadrant. TEN	Goddess of Liberty; female either side with shield. MERCHANT'S B'K. Ten Dollars Boston, Mass. TEN	10 Steamship at sea.
Medallion head. X	10 Boston Custom House. 10 MERCHANTS BANK, Boston, Mass. 10	TEN Female, with spear and shield. TEN
20 TWENTY. 20	MERCHANT'S B'K, Boston, Mass. United States Capitol. TWENTY.	20 Sailor boy raising his hat.
20 Female with flag. TWENTY	Ship of war and sail boats. MERCHANTS BANK, Boston, Mass Washington.	20 Spread eagle and shield. TWENTY
Female in kneeling position. 50	Female, sickle and sheaf of wheat; factory and Railroad in distance. MERCHANTS BANK, Boston, Mass Cornucopia, etc.	L Cupid in sail boat. 50
Female sickle and sheaf 100	Vig. Same as 50s. MERCHANTS BANK, Boston, Mass Steamer	C State Arms.
Figs. 500. Eagle. Figs. 500.	Sailor, vessels, horse, cart, men, buildings, etc. 500 Title of Bank.	Figs. 500. Ship. Figs. 500.
D 500 D Eagle D D	MERCHANTS' BANK Boston, Mass 500 on green die.	D 500
1000 Eagle	MERCHANTS' BANK Boston, Mass. Letter M and figs 1000 on green die.	1000 Female, child, sword pole & cap.
1000 Eagle. 1000	Vig. Same as 500s. Title of Bank.	1000 Female with figs. 1000. 1000

1	Female leaning upon a bale; stream of water, factories, railroad and shipping in background. 1 MERCHANTS BANK, Lowell, Mass.	1 Female.
TWO Ship. 2	Two females. 2 MERCHANTS BANK, Lowell, Mass.	2 Female and figure 2.
Female. 3	Large figure 3 and Three female figures; factory in background 3 on right. MERCHANTS BANK, Lowell, Mass.	3 Portrait.
5 Female and ship. 5	Female, ?red eagle; ship in distance 5 MERCHANTS BANK, Lowell, Mass.	5 Ship FIVE
10 Bales and barrels. TEN	Female, eagle and globe; ships in background. MERCHANTS BANK, Lowell, Mass.	10 Female.
20 XX	XX Portrait of female. XX MERCHANTS BANK, Lowell, Mass.	20 XX
50 Female.	Shipping; city in the background. MERCHANTS BANK. Lowell, Mass.	50 Portrait of Washington.
100 Portrait. C	Railroad depot, train of cars, wharfs, shipping, merchandise &c. MERCHANTS BANK. Lowell, Mass.	100 C
D State Arms.	MERCHANTS' BK. FIVE HUNDRED Dollars. Lowell, Mass.	500 Male portrait
D State Arms	MERCHANTS' BANK Lowell, Mass.	500 Justice seated on bale

ONE State Arms.	Male and female; train of cars and ship in background. MERCHANTS BANK, New Bedford, Mass. Locomotive	1 Female.
2 Female. TWO	Female sitting on bale; factory in background. MERCHANTS BANK, New Bedford, Mass Steamboat	2 Ship. TWO
3	Two females in foreground; shipping, train of cars in background. 3 on right. MERCHANTS BANK, New Bedford, Mass. Beehive	3 Portrait of female.
5 Female.	MERCHANTS BANK, New Bedford, Mass Female sitting on a bale; ships and light house in background. 5 each side. Wheat, &c.	5 Female.
10 State arms	(New Plate.) Female, child, dog, and safe. 10 MERCHANTS BANK New Bedford, Mass Eagle	TEN Female with sheaf of wheat. 10
TEN Ship building 10	(Old Plate.) 10 Interior of blacksmith shop. X MERCHANTS BANK, New Bedford, Mass.	10 Whale ship. TEN
20 Female.	(Old Plate.) XX Eagle XX MERCHANTS BANK, New Bedford, Mass. 20 State Arms 20	20 Ship.
TWENTY Female with sickle and sheaf of wheat.	(New Plate.) Eagle. Indian, female and public building. MERCHANTS BANK, New Bedford, Mass. Female and ship	20 Ship.
Portrait of female. 50	Three females, train of cars and ship in background. MERCHANTS BANK New Bedford, Mass. Building	50 Portrait of female.
100 Portrait of Washington. 100	Female sitting on a bale. MERCHANTS BANK, New Bedford, Mass. House	100 Female and anchor; city in the background.

500 Male and female. D	MERCHANTS BANK, New Bedford, Mass. State Arms; female on each side; eagle at top; steamboat on right; horses on left. Bank Building.	500 Female. 500
1 Ships. ONE	ONE Whale ships and a whale. 1 Female. MERCHANTS BANK, Newburyport, Mass.	1 Ship. ONE
TWO Train of cars. TWO	2 Ships. 2 MERCHANTS BANK, Newburyport, Mass.	2 Male figure 2
THREE Steamboat. THREE	Female Ship building. Sailor MERCHANTS BANK, Newburyport, Mass.	3 Ship. 3
Eagle. FIVE	Ship Washington and his troops crossing the Delaware. 5 MERCHANTS BANK, Newburyport, Mass.	Ships and merchandise FIVE
10 Surrender of Lord Cornwallis. TEN	Ship. Phœbus in the car of the Sun. Ship. MERCHANTS BANK, Newburyport, Mass.	10 Washington crossing the Delaware. TEN
TWENTY Female erect with sword and scales	Vig. rural scene, cows and sheep. 20 MERCHANTS' BK., Newburyport, Mass.	XX Female with sheaf of wheat.
FIFTY Male figure. 50	FIFTY Steam-boat; city in the distance. Female. MERCHANTS BANK, Newburyport, Mass	50 Bust. FIFTY
100 Statue of Washington.	Battle of Bunker Hill. Three female figures. MERCHANTS BANK, Newburyport, Mass.	100 Female.
ONE Sailor boy. ONE	MERCHANTS BANK. Salem, Mass. Has the title, denomination and place of issue in red letters—the words Merchants' Bank, Salem, and "One Dollar" all over the middle part of bill in fine letters.	1 ONE 1

Left	Centre	Right
TWO Vessel on stock. TWO	MERCHANTS BANK, Salem, Mass. Same as ones with denomination changed only.	2 TWO 2
FIVE Vessels. FIVE	MERCHANTS BANK, Salem, Mass. Same as ones with denomination changed only.	5 FIVE 5
TEN Vessels. TEN	MERCHANTS BANK, Salem, Mass. Same as ones with the denomination changed only	10 TEN 10
FIFTY Steamboat. FIFTY	MERCHANTS BANK, Salem, Mass. Same as ones with the denomination changed only.	50 FIFTY 50
100 Sailor and shipping. 100	MERCHANTS BANK, Salem, Mass. Same as ones with the denomination changed only.	100 C 100
	MERCHANTS BANK, Salem, Mass. The plates of the 500s, are of the general Plate of the N. E. Bank Note Co.	
ONE	Phœbus in the chariot of the Sun. Pier, safe and building. MERRIMACK B'K. Haverhill, Mass.	1 Female.
2 TWO 2	Female figure and cupid. TWO MERRIMACK BANK, Haverhill, Mass.	2 Ship building.
THREE	Horses, wagons, wharf and shipping. 3 MERRIMACK BANK, Haverhill, Mass.	Female.
5 FIVE Female.	Train of cars. MERRIMACK BANK, Haverhill, Mass.	5 Fancy piece
X Steamboat	Men on horseback, cattle and sheep. MERRIMACK BANK Haverhill, Mass.	10 Female. X
20 Female.	XX Eagle XX MERRIMACK BANK. Haverhill, Mass.	20 Ship.
Pilot boat tug and vessel. 20	Female seated with sickle, sheaf; farmhouse, etc. MERRIMACK BANK Haverhill, Mass.	20 Old man, white bust of Washington
Two children 50	50 Blacksmith at work on anvil. Title of Bank.	50 Female with sewing machine.
FIFTY Female. FIFTY	50 Man and horse. 50 MERRIMACK BANK, Haverhill, Mass.	FIFTY Female. FIFTY
100 Girl giving drink to boy	Grain and agricultural implements. MERRIMACK BANK One Hundred Dollars Haverhill, Massachusetts.	100 Eagle
One Hundred and 100. Portrait.	Horses, wagons, wharf, shipping, &c. MERRIMACK BANK. Haverhill, Mass.	Same as left Portrait
C Men and boats. 100	Eagle standing on bale of goods, etc. 100 MERRIMACK BANK. Haverhill, Mass.	100 Female with sickle, and bundle of grain.
Indian in a canoe. 500	500 MERRIMACK BANK. Haverhill, Mass.	500 Female holding balances in right hand
ONE Indian.	Indian. Indian woman and child in a canoe, the Indian throwing a harpoon at a fish. METACOMET BANK Fall River, Mass.	1 Portrait
TWO Portrait.	Steamboat and sail vessels. METACOMET BANK Fall River, Mass.	2 Indian.
3 Portrait.	Steamboat and sail vessels. METACOMET BANK. Fall River, Mass.	3 Indian in a canoe
V FIVE	METACOMET BANK Fall River, Mass. Same vig as one's.	5 Portrait.
10	10 Same vig as ones. METACOMET BANK Fall River, Mass.	X Portrait.
XX XX	Steamboat and sail vessels. METACOMET BANK Fall River, Mass.	20 Indian in a canoe
L 50	Same vig as ones. METACOMET BANK Fall River, Mass.	L Portrait
100	Steamboat "Bay State;" yachts and forts in distance. METACOMET BANK. Fall River, Mass.	C Indian in canoe spearing porpoise.
500 500	Indian, squaw and child in canoe; Indian is spearing porpoise. Title of Bank.	D Male portrait
1000	Vig. same as above 100s. Title of Bank.	Letter M in die and words "One Thousand" around. Indian
ONE Indian seated by tent.	Female seated; cars, factory and house in distance. 1 MILLBURY BANK, Millbury, Mass	1 Blacksmith with anvil.

ONE 1 Interior of blacksmiths shop. 1 ONE
Portrait of Washington.
MILLBURY BANK, Millbury, Mass.
Female.
ONE ONE

2 Females tending machines. 2
MILLBURY BANK, Millbury, Mass.
Catching wild bull.
Franklin.

(New Plate.)
Farmers driving sheep across a brook. 2 and 8 men TWO
2
Female.
MILLBURY BANK, Millbury, Mass.
TWO

(Old Plate.)
TWO 2 Farming scene. 2 TWO
Female.
Female.
2
MILLBURY BANK, Millbury, Mass.
2

3 Steamship at sea. THREE on 3.
MILLBURY BANK, Millbury, Mass.
Man sitting down ... tree.
3

Farming scene. 3 3
3
MILLBURY BANK, Millbury, Mass.
Female.
THREE

FIVE 5 Interior of a blacksmith's shop. V 5
Female crowning a bust of Washington Eagle.
MILLBURY BANK, Millbury, Mass.
Ship building.
5

TEN X Farming scene. 10 TEN
Washington and horse.
MILLBURY BANK, Millbury, Mass.
Portrait full length.
10
Canal Locks

20 20 Female holding scales; ship in background. 20
XX
MILLBURY BANK, Millbury, Mass.
TWENTY
20

50 FIFTY DOLLARS. 50
Female.
MILLBURY BANK, Millbury, Mass.
FIFTY
50

50 MILBURY BANK. 50
Fifty on L — Officer on horse-back receiving dispatches — Dollars on L
Milbury. Mass
50 50
General Scott.

100 Scene in farm yard; farmer, horse, pig, cows, sheep, ducks, &c 100
MILBURY BANK.
HUNDRED on One Hundred Dollars.
C
Daniel Webster

1 Vig. Interior of boot shop, with men at work. ONE on 1 on right 1
A female.
MILFORD BANK, Milford, Mass.
Washington on horseback
ONE
Locomotive and tender.

Vig. Same as ones. 2
Portrait of Henry Clay.
MILFORD BANK, Milford, Mass.
Portrait
Job waggon and two horses.

Dairy scene, maid milking, female looking on 3
Portrait of Jackson
MILFORD BANK Milford, Mass.
Large fig. 3 and three cupids

FIVE MILFORD BANK, Massachusetts. 5
Female with sheaf of wheat in large ornamental letter V
Male and Female.
Five Dollars
Daniel Webster.
FIVE

5 MILFORD BANK 5
Female seated in large figure 5
FIVE DOLLARS
Male portrait
Daniel Webster

X Vig. Large spread eagle. X 10
Portrait of female.
MILFORD BANK, Milford, Mass.
Male portrait
10
Job waggon and two horses.

20 Man, two horses, cars, farmhouse, etc. 20
MILFORD BANK
Mass'ch's'tts
Girls with chickens, etc.
TWENTY DOLLARS
Milford
Male portrait

20 Vig. Female, arms extended; cupids on either side. 20
Railroad depot and locomotive and tender.
MILFORD BANK, Milford, Mass.
Girl with a sickle in her hand and a sheaf of straw.
Ship and steamboat.

50 MILFORD BANK 50
50 Scene in shoe shop 50
FIFTY DOLLARS
Girl giving drink to boy
Milford
Girl with sewing machine

50 Vig. Two females sitting; ship on left, and houses on right. 50
Portrait of female.
MILFORD BANK, Milford, Mass.
Boy picking cotton.
50
Locomotive and tender.

Husking scene C Girls head C 100
MILFORD BANK
Mass'ch's'tts
One Hundred Dollars
100
Male portrait

100 MILFORD BANK, Milford, Mass. 100
Vig. Female and Cupid hovering over city.
Vessel under sail.
Sailor with flag.
100

500 MILFORD BANK, Milford, Mass. 500
Vig. Three females, and Railroad trains.
Portrait of Lincoln
Barrel and ship
Eagle
500

MILLERS' RIVER BANK, Athol, Mass. 1
Two females.
ONE DOLLAR
ONE
1

2 MILLERS' RIVER BANK, Athol, Mass. 2
Stream of water, bridge and train of cars.
TWO DOLLARS.
Indian woman and child.

3 MILLERS RIVER BK 3
Large THREE in half circle
Athol, Mass.
THREE across fig. 3 in circular die.
THREE
Man, woman, two children, sheep, grain, etc.
3

FIVE MILLERS' RIVER BANK, Athol, Mass. V
5
Blacksmith's shop.
FIVE DOLLARS.
FIVE

MILLERS, RIVER BANK, Athol, Mass. 10
10
Two females.
Portrait of Washington.

Left	Centre	Right
TWENTY Farmer, mechanic and sailor.	Female and eagle. Portrait of female. MILLERS' RIVER BANK. Athol, Mass.	20 Train of cars
FIFTY Group of females.	MILLERS' RIVER BANK, Athol, Mass. L	50 Spread eagle
ONE Full length female figure with sword.	MONSON BANK, A Monson, Mass. 1 Vig. Indian seated looking down upon a city; bow and arrows in hand 1	1 Female portrait.
ONE Girl with sheaf of grain on her head. ONE 1 ONE	Harvest field, farmers at work. B MONSON BANK. Monson, Mass. Vig. Female kneeling, holding shield, barrels and bales, cars and ship in back ground.	1 Locomotive horse, &c.
Female portrait. 2	Vig. Two men, one a farmer holding horse under a tree, factories several tall chimneys. MONSON BANK, Monson, Mass.	2 Shield, scroll E Pluribus Unum.
3 Male portrait	MONSON BANK, Monson, Mass. 3 Vig. Three figures, liberty pole and cap; cornucopia, anvil and hammer 3	3 Blacksmith making horse shoe.
5	MONSON BANK. A Monson, Mass. Vig. Train of cars.	FIVE 5 FIVE Female Indian standing
5 B Portrait of Washington	Vig. Locomotive and train of cars also second train going towards village in distance. MONSON BANK, Monson, Mass.	5 5
FIVE Farmer seated, sheaf of grain on either side, sickle in right hand.	MONSON BANK, Monson, Mass. 5 Vig. Two Females, one spinning. Train of cars in distance.	5
Vig. Train of oxen, horses in front Farmers loading wheat.	10 MONSON BANK, Monson, Mass. X X	X Justice leaning on shield, scroll at feet, vessel, cars and houses.

Left	Centre	Right
Full length female holding cornucopia. TWENTY	Vig. Two cows; mill, water, &c, in distance. MONSON BANK, Monson, Mass.	20 Male portrait
50 Medallion head. 50	MONSON BANK, Monson, Mass. Vig. Dogs chasing an elk.	50 Franklin.
1 Drummer boy and two soldiers seated.	Vig. Battle of Bunker Hill. Scene is the death of Warren. MONUMENT BANK, Charlestown, Mass. 1	1 Bunker Hill Monument.
2 Portrait of Warren.	MONUMENT BANK, Charlestown, Mass. Vig. Same as ones.	TWO Bunker Hill Monument.
THREE Bunker Hill Monument.	MONUMENT BANK, Charlestown. Mass. 3 Vig. Same as ones.	3
5 5	Vig. Same as ones MONUMENT BANK, Charlestown, Mass.	5 Bunker Hill Monument.
10 Two soldiers throwing up a breast work, officer giving orders	MONUMENT BANK, Charlestown. Mass. X Portrait of Washington. X	TEN Same as fives
L Bunker Hill Monument. FIFTY	MONUMENT BANK, Charlestown, Mass. 50 Surrender of Cornwallis at Yorktown.	50
C Bunker Hill Monument.	MONUMENT BANK, Charlestown, Mass. Spread eagle on shield; on the left is Charlestown with a view of the monument; on right schooners sailing. Rail cars in front.	100 Portrait of Webster.
FIVE HUNDRED	MONUMENT BANK, Charlestown, Mass. Vig. Two angels, one woman and little boy scattering gold coin on city below.	500 Bunker Hill Monument.

Left	Centre	Right
1 State Arms.	MOUNT VERNON BK Boston, Mass. Male portrait View of the home of Washington.	1 1
TWO State Arms. TWO	Man buying newspaper of boy; hhds, etc. Med head. MOUNT VERNON BK Boston, Mass. 2	2 Female seated with shield on which is view of city and motto.
3 State Arms.	Battle scene of the revolution. 3 MOUNT VERNON BK Boston, Mass.	3 Soldier loading gun
Five on 5 State Arms.	MOUNT VERNON BK Boston, Mass. View of the home of Washington. 5	5 Male portrait.
X State Arms.	Three men loading truck with bales. MOUNT VERNON BK Boston, Mass. 10	10 Old man, child, and bust of Washington.
20 State Arms.	MOUNT VERNON BK Boston, Mass. 20 TWENTY DOLLARS	20 Half length female
50 State Arms. FIFTY 50	Wharf scene in general. MOUNT VERNON BK Boston, Mass.	50 Half length female
100 State Arms.	C State Arms C MOUNT VERNON BK Boston, Mass.	100 Male portrait
500 State Arms.	MOUNT VERNON BK Boston, Mass. Female dressed in robes	500 Male portrait.
1 ONE Portrait of J. Q. Adams.	MOUNT WOLLASTON BANK, Quincy, Mass. Interior of a shoe makers shop.	1 Dog. ONE

2	MOUNT WOLLASTON BANK, Quin..., Mass.	TWO
Portrait of J. Q. Adams.	Stone cutters.	Church.
TWO		

3	Portrait of Chas F. Adams. Stone cutters.	3
3	MOUNT WOLLASTON BANK, Quincy, Mass.	3

V	View of the old mansion of J. Q. Adams.	5
Church.	MOUNT WOLLASTON BANK, Quincy, Mass.	Portrait of C. F. Adams

TEN	Sailing vessel.	X
Dog.	MOUNT WOLLASTON BANK, Quincy, Mass.	Church.
TEN		

XX	Horse. Female. Horse.	20
Hunter warming himself by a fire in the woods.	MOUNT WOLLASTON BANK, Quincy, Mass.	Portrait of J. Q. Adams

50	Train of cars.	50
Dog.	MOUNT WOLLASTON BANK, Quincy, Mass.	
L		Female.

C	Spread eagle and American flag.	100
	MOUNT WOLLASTON BANK, Quincy, Mass.	Indian

ONE	Wood cutter, gold dollar; house and wagon in distance	1
Sailor hoisting a flag.	NATIONAL BANK, Boston, Mass.	Female and flag.

Female.	Man with rake, female with pail; two gold dollars; house, barn and cows	2
2	NATIONAL BANK, Boston, Mass.	Sailor with spy glass.

3	Farmer with scythe, sailor with telescope and blacksmith with sledge, also three gold dollars.	3
Mermaid and merman.	NATIONAL BANK, Boston, Mass.	
Steamer.		Washington

FIVE	Three Cupids, five gold dollars, hunter and Indian female.	5
Liberty.	NATIONAL BANK, Boston, Mass.	Capitol at Washington.

	Capitol at Washington.	10
X	NATIONAL BANK, Boston, Mass.	Franklin.

Female giving eagle a drink.	View of building	20
XX	NATIONAL BANK, Boston, Mass.	Female feeding a horse.

Fountain.	Ship and two steamships	50
50	NATIONAL BANK, Boston, Mass.	Female bust.

100	Spread eagle and shield; Capitol at Washington on right; steamship on left	C
Female with spear and shield.	NATIONAL BANK, Boston, Mass.	Portrait.

	Female seated by shield; steamship, cars, bridge and city in distance.	500
D	NATIONAL BANK, Boston, Mass.	Female portrait.

	1000 on a shield, surmounted by eagle; female each side; steamboat and cars in distance.	1000
M	NATIONAL BANK, Boston, Mass.	Female with grain.

ONE	1 Street in Salem. 1	1
Interior of railroad depot.	NAUMKEAG BANK, Salem, Mass.	Indians.
ONE	Cars.	ONE

ONE	View of a street in Salem.	1
Indian and dead deer.	NAUMKEAG BANK, Salem, Mass.	Cars, passengers, etc.
ONE	Cars.	ONE

TWO	Street in Salem	2
Indians.	NAUMKEAG BANK, Salem, Mass.	Man sounding, and shipping.
2	Shipping scene.	TWO

THREE	3 Street in Salem. 3	3
Ships.	NAUMKEAG BANK, Salem, Mass.	Indian and female.
3	Vessels.	THREE

FIVE	Street view in Salem.	5
Indians.	Title of Bank.	FIVE
FIVE	Boats, men, etc.	Female. Massachusetts

V	5 Street in Salem.	5
Ships.	NAUMKEAG BANK, Salem, Mass.	Man with dog and gun
V	Vessels.	

5	NAUMKEAG BANK, Salem, Mass.	5
FIVE	Street in Salem.	FIVE
5	Anchor, etc.	5

Ship building.	Street in Salem.	10
Sampson destroying a lion.	NAUMKEAG BANK, Salem, Mass.	Train of cars.
	Anchor, &c.	10

Steamboat.	(Old Plate.)	XX
XX	Three female figures and eagle. 20	
Train of cars.	NAUMKEAG BANK, Salem, Mass.	Milk maid

20	(New Plate.) XX Eagle. XX	20
Female.	NAUMKEAG BANK, Salem, Mass.	Ship.

XX	Two females, anvil, building, etc.	20
Indian princess.	NAUMKEAG BANK, Salem, Mass.	Squaw.

FIFTY	Title of Bank.	50
Sailor with female, two sails, etc., above him.		Indian female; stream, bow, falls, etc.
FIFTY		

FIFTY	50 Man and horse. 50	FIFTY
Female.	NAUMKEAG BANK, Salem, Mass.	Female.
FIFTY		FIFTY

- 50 | Man with rake; load of hay, reapers, etc. 50 | L — Steamer and steamboat. | Title of Bank | Female with sword and scales.
- 100 NAUMKEAG BANK. Salem, Mass. 100 — Arm with scimetar. Mass State Arms | Indian, squaw, boy, and papoose on cliff viewing city, etc. | Load of grain.
- Same as right. Portrait. | Horses, wagons, and shipping. NAUMKEAG BANK. Salem, Mass. | One Hundred and 100. Portrait.
- 100 Eagle. 100 | C Phoebus in the chariot of the sun. 100 NAUMKEAG BANK. Salem, Mass. | C Portrait of Washington. C
- Sailor boy seated on spar, glass in hand 500 | NAUMKEAG BK, Salem. State Arms. Salem, Massachusetts. Five Hundred Dollars. | 500 D
- Spread eagle, shield, etc. Massachusetts. Washington. 1000 | NAUMKEAG BANK. One Thousand Dollars. 1000 | Female with torch, books, etc.
- ONE Bust. ONE | (Old Plate.) 1 Interior of a blacksmith's shop. 1 NEPONSET BANK. Canton, Mass. | ONE Female. ONE
- ONE Female figure. | (New Plate.) Farming scene. NEPONSET BANK, Canton, Mass. | 1 Spread eagle and shield. ONE
- Female figure. TWO | (New Plate.) Female, train of cars, and steamship in background. NEPONSET BANK. Canton, Mass. | 2 2 females.
- TWO Female. 2 | (Old Plate.) 2 Farming scene. 2 NEPONSET BANK, Canton, Mass. | TWO Female. 2

- 3 Female portrait. THREE | Cattle and sheep, man on horseback. NEPONSET BANK. Canton, Mass. | 3 Blacksmith, farmer and sailor. THREE
- FIVE Stone cutter. 5 | Viaduct of the Boston & Providence railroad. NEPONSET BANK. Canton, Mass. | 5 Indian. FIVE
- 10 Portrait of Washington. X | Viaduct of the Boston & Providence railroad. NEPONSET BANK, Canton, Mass. | 10 Portrait. TEN
- 20 Female. | XX Eagle. XX NEPONSET BANK. Canton, Mass. | 20 Ship.
- 20 Boy, girl, child, horse, etc. | NEPONSET BANK. Canton, Mass. TWENTY DOLLARS | 20 Two children.
- FIFTY Female. FIFTY | 50 Man and horse 50 NEPONSET BANK. Canton, Mass. | FIFTY Female. FIFTY
- 50 Girl with pitcher and basket. | NEPONSET BANK, Canton, Mass. Title of Bank L | 50 Dog & safe.
- C Child's head. | NEPONSET BANK, Canton, Mass. One Hundred Dollars. Title of Bank. | 100 State Arms.
- Same as right. Portrait. | Horses, wagons and shipping. NEPONSET BANK. Canton, Mass. | One Hundred and 100. Portrait.
- ONE Statue of Justice with sword and scales. MASSACHUSETTS | Female holding wreath over State Arms of Mass. NEW ENGLAND BK ONE DOLLAR | ONE on 1

- 1 on large 1. | Stone cutter. NEW ENGLAND BK. Boston, Mass. Eagle. | Same as left.
- Female with tablet; child at her feet. TWO | NEW ENGLAND BK. Female reclining; Boston beside map, on globe, compass, books, etc. 2 TWO DOLLARS. STATE OF MASS. | 2 Washington.
- 2 | Portrait of Washington and Franklin up large 2. NEW ENGLAND BK. Boston, Mass. | 2
- Title and locomotive on large 3. | Female with a roll of cloth; factories and steamboat in distance. Indian head. | 3 Ship.
- 5 FIVE DOLLARS | NEW ENGLAND BK. Bust of Washington; female on left; sailor on right. Boston | 5 FIVE DOLLARS
- 5 | Female seated on bale; city in distance. Fig. 5 running the entire length of the note. NEW ENGLAND BK. Boston, Mass. Female head. | 5
- TEN DOLLARS | Ten Dollars. Spread eagle on rock, overlooking the sea; ship in distance. NEW ENGLAND BK. Boston, Mass. | 10 Female with spear and shield.
- 20 TWENTY DOLLARS 20 | Twenty Dollars. Vig. same as tens. NEW ENGLAND BK. Boston, Mass. | 20 Female and 20 on shield.
- Indian in canoe. 50 | Fifty Dollars 50 NEW ENGLAND BK. Boston, Mass. | FIFTY
- 100 | ONE HUNDRED 100 Indian in a canoe; mountains in distance on upper left. NEW ENGLAND BK. Boston, Mass. | 100

Left	Centre	Right
Justice seated. 1000	Various vessels; city in distance. NEW ENGLAND BK. Boston, Mass. Locomotive.	1000 Portrait of Washington
1	Vig. The apostle "Elliot" attended by three others, with Bible in hand, preaching to seven Indians on a hill. Head of Franklin. 1 NEWTON BANK, Newton, Mass. Cog wheels resting on bale of cotton.	1 Head of J. Q. Adams. ONE
2	Vig. Same as ones. 2 NEWTON BANK, Newton. State Arms.	2 Head of Washington TWO
3	Vig. Same as ones. 3 NEWTON BANK, Newton Agricultural implements, and horn of plenty.	3 Female holding bow, arrows and quiver. THREE
5	Vig. Same as ones. on right med. head and 5. NEWTON BANK, Newton. Engine, tender, and car.	5 Cattle, sheep and swine. FIVE
10	Vig. Same as ones. X NEWTON BANK, Newton. Farmer sitting on plough.	10 Female Indian, left hand resting on an X
Female seated, holding horn of plenty; shield with the word TWENTY on it. 20	Vig. Same as ones. NEWTON BANK, Newton. Engine and cars.	20 State Arms.
50 Female holding spear in right hand.	Vig. Male and female figures seated with horn of plenty; rake, anchor, &c., representing Agriculture, Commerce, &c. NEWTON BANK, Newton. 50	50 Cupid in a sail boat; using an oar as a rudder 50
50 Whites treating with Indians	50 50 NEWTON BANK, Newton, Mass. Words fifty twice, Dollars and Massachusetts on green die. L	50 Male portrait

Left	Centre	Right
100 Male figure seated, representing Commerce, &c.	Vig. Eagle on a branch of tree over canal, on which are loaded boats; train of cars in backgr'nd NEWTON BANK, Newton. C 100 C	100 Female figures seated representing agriculture.
500	Vig. Female seated, sheaf at her feet; farmers reaping and loading grain in the distance. 500 D NEWTON BANK, Newton.	500
1 Female and 1.	(New Plate.) Female, electric machine and portrait of Franklin; Franklin drawing lightning from the clouds with a kite; telegraph, train of cars and State House in distance. NORTH BANK, Boston, Mass.	1 Female with sickle and fig 1
1 Female. 1	(Old Plate.) View of the State House and Boston Common. NORTH BANK, Boston, Mass.	1 Ship. 1
2 Ship. 2	Female. Three females. Vig. Same as old ones. NORTH BANK, Boston, Mass.	2 Ship. 2
TWO Female feeding an eagle from cup.	Vig. Same as new plate of ones. NORTH BANK, Boston, Mass.	2 Washington
3 Eagle and shield. THREE	Vig. Same as ones, new plate. NORTH BANK, Boston, Mass.	3 Female
3 Reapers. 3	Vig. Same as old ones with word three on either side. NORTH BANK, Boston, Mass.	3 3
5 Male portrait	Vig. Same as ones, new plate. NORTH BANK, Boston, Mass.	5 Five females and 5.

Left	Centre	Right
10 10	Ship. Female, spear and shield. Vig. Same as old ones. NORTH BANK, Boston, Mass.	10 Agricultural implements.
10 inverted Portrait of Fillmore.	Vig. Same as new ones. NORTH BANK, Boston, Mass.	10 inverted Sailor boy.
20 Female erect with eagle and shield.	Vig. Same as ones new plates. NORTH BANK, Boston, Mass.	20 Female portrait.
20 Female seated.	XX Eagle. XX NORTH BANK, Boston, Mass.	20 Ship.
Steamboat. XX Train of cars.	20 Three females; one with liberty cap; one with scales and the other with book; eagle and shield; ship in distance. NORTH BANK, Boston, Mass.	XX Milkmaid with pail and stool.
50 Female portrait.	Vig. Same as ones, new plate. NORTH BANK, Boston, Mass.	50 Female.
C Female with scales and sheaf.	Vig. Same as ones, new plate. NORTH BANK, Boston, Mass.	100 Female.
D inverted Sailor erect, leaning on capstan.	Vig. Same as ones, new plate. NORTH BANK, Boston, Mass.	500 inverted Female erect with cornucopia.
M Female seated with trident.	Vig. Same as ones, new plate. NORTH BANK, Boston, Mass.	1000 Female portrait. 1000

Female seated, barrel, the cars and vessel in distance. 1
Fig. 1 with six male heads in centre of it.
NORTHAMPTON BK, Northampton, Mass.
1
Female with grain.

ONE
Bust.
ONE
1 Interior of a blacksmith's shop. 1
NORTHAMPTON BK, Northampton, Mass.
ONE
Female.
ONE

1
Portrait of Washington.
Female. 1 Female.
NORTHAMPTON BK, Northampton, Mass.
1
Portrait of Franklin.

1
Same as right.
NORTHAMPTON BK, Northampton, Mass.
Female with words "Incorporated 1833," on tablets; child at her feet.
1
One, 1, and One Dollar on green die

2
Stone cutter
TWO
NORTHAMPTON BK Northampton, Mass.
Two Boy, child, Two on 2 cattle, sheep on 2 etc.
Horse.
2
Dog & safe.

Washing sheep.
2
Large 2; five men in small circular frame.
NORTHAMPTON BK Norhampton, Mass.
TWO
Female with wreath.
TWO

TWO
Female.
2
2 Farming scene 2
NORTHAMPTON BK, Northampton, Mass.
TWO
Female.
2

2
Portrait.
Female. 2 Female.
NORTHAMPTON BK, Northampton, Mass.
2
Portrait.

Farmer on horse; boy, team, load of hay, plough, &c.
3
Cattle; city, &c. in distance. 3
NORTHAMPTON BK Northampton, Mass.
3 across three.
Girl with flowers.
THREE

THREE
Man sharpening a scythe.
3
3 Female and eagle. 3
NORTHAMPTON BK, Northampton, Mass.
THREE
Sailor.
3

5
FIVE
5
V Spread eagle; shipping in background. V
NORTHAMPTON BK, Northampton, Mass.
5
FIVE
5

FIVE
Spread eagle and shield; village in distance.
Large V, female and cupid.
NORTHAMPTON BK, Northampton, Mass.
5
Girl.

5
Female seated, resting on wheel.
FIVE
5 Small State arms.
NORTHAMPT'N B'K, Northampton, Mass.
5

10
X
10
Man and oxen. 10
NORTHAMPTON BK, Northampton, Mass.
TEN
Female.

TEN
Vulcan the blacksmith; train of cars and factories in the background. X
NORTHAMPTON BK, Northampton, Mass.
10
Reaper.

NORTH AMPTON BANK, Northampton, Mass.
Old man, child, bust of Washington on table. Eagle.
10
Massachusetts.
10

20 XX Eagle. XX 20
NORTHAMPTON BK, Northampton, Mass.
Female.
Ship.

20
TWENTY
20
NORTHAMPTON BK Northampton, Mass.
20
TWENTY DOLLARS
20
TWENTY
20

FIFTY
Female.
FIFTY
50 Man and horse. 50
NORTHAMPTON BK, Northampton, Mass.
FIFTY
Female.
FIFTY

50
L
50
NORTHAMPTON BK Northampton, Mass.
50
FIFTY DOLLARS
50
L
50

Words One Hundred and fig. 100
NORTHAMPTON BK Northampton, Mass.
C One Hundred Dollars. C
100
C
100

Words one hundred and fig. 100.
Male portrait
Wharf Scene.
Title of Bank.
Words one hundred and fig 100.
Male portrait

1
NORTH BRIDGEWATER BANK, N. Bridgewater, Mass.
A street in N. Bridgewater.
Portrait.
1

A street in North Bridgewater.
Train of cars.
2
NORTH BRIDGEWATER BANK, N. Bridgewater, Mass.
Female
2
Portrait.

Female.
3
Street in North Bridgewater.
NORTH BRIDGEWATER BANK, N. Bridgewater, Mass.
Cow and calf
3
Portrait.

5
Portrait.
NORTH BRIDGEWATER BANK, N. Bridgewater, Mass.
A group of females; ships and factories in background.
FIVE
Group of females and large figure 5.

Title inverted
10
Train of cars.
NORTH BRIDGEWATER BANK, N. Bridgewater, Mass.
Loading hay
10
Female and X

Female with a basket of fruit and flowers.
XX
Female reclining; milk maids, cows, locomotive and factory in background.
NORTH BRIDGEWATER BANK, N. Bridgewater, Mass.
Man, horse, &c.
20
2 Female 0
TWENTY

Female.
50 50
NORTH BRIDGEWATER BANK, N. Bridgewater, Mass.
State arms, eagle and two females; steamboat and train of cars in the background.
Female.

Portrait of female.
100
View of the capitol at Washington.
NORTH BRIDGEWATER BANK, N. Bridgewater, Mass.
100
Blacksmith, anvil and forge.
100

1 | Train of cars. | 1
Portrait. | NORTHBOROUGH BANK Northborough, Mass. | Female seated on plough with sickle, &c.
ONE

2 | Female reclining, train of cars, factories, and shipping, milk maids and cows in background. | 2
Portrait. | NORTHBOROUGH BANK Northborough, Mass. | Interior of boot makers shop.
Man plowing

3 | Man pressing boxes in comb press; basket of boxes, etc | 3
Male portrait | NORTHBOROUGH BANK, Northborough, Mass | Farmer, sailor, blacksmith and [illegible]

5 | Portrait, a winged female with trumpet at the left of portrait and cupid at the right. | 5
Farmer with scythe. | NORTHBOROUGH BANK Northborough, Mass | Group of females, large figure &c.
Implements

10 | A female figure and nine cherubs. | X
Portrait. | NORTHBOROUGH BANK. Northborough, Mass | Female sitting and shield

XX | Female reclining also eagle on globe, ships in distance. | 20
Portrait of Washington. | NORTHBOROUGH BANK Northborough, Mass. | Castle.
Imp. and products

L | Drove of cattle and sheep, man on horseback. | 50
Male portrait | NORTHBOROUGH BANK, Northborough, Mass. | Female churning
Flowers.

100 | Blacksmith at work; boy and horse | 100
Portrait of Z. Taylor. | NORTHBOROUGH BANK, Northborough, Mass | Building.
HUNDRED | Oxen.

OCEAN BANK,
Newburyport, Mass.
This Bank uses Perkins' Patent Stereotype plate, which is the denomination printed in fine letters all over the bill.

1 | 1 Landing of the Pilgrims in 1620. 1 | 1
Female figure holding scales and sword | OLD COLONY BANK. Plymouth, Mass. | Portrait of Washington
ONE | | ONE

TWO | 2 Landing of the Pilgrims in 1620. 2 | 2
Female with scales and sword. | OLD COLONY BANK. Plymouth, Mass. | Female figure.
TWO | | TWO

3 | THREE Landing of the Pilgrims in 1620. 3 | THREE
Portrait of Washington. | OLD COLONY BANK. Plymouth, Mass.
3

States of Washington. | 5 Landing of the Pilgrims in 1620. 5 | Eagle standing upon a rock overlooking the sea.
| OLD COLONY BANK. Plymouth, Mass. | FIVE

Eagle standing upon a rock overlooking the sea. | 10 Landing of the Pilgrims in 1620. X | Female figure.
TEN | OLD COLONY BANK, Plymouth, Mass | TEN

20 | Landing of the Pilgrims in 1620. | 20
Indians. | OLD COLONY BANK. Plymouth, Mass. | Portrait of Washington
| | XX

Indians. | Landing of the Pilgrims in 1620. | 50
| OLD COLONY BANK. Plymouth, Mass. | Train of cars
| | FIFTY

100 | Landing of the Pilgrims in 1620. | 100
Reaper. | OLD COLONY BANK. Plymouth, Mass. | Female and eagle.

ONE | 1 Farming scene, ONE | 1
Eagle. | OXFORD BANK, Oxford, Mass. | Female figures
ONE | | 1

2 | Cattle and sheep, man on horseback. 2 | TWO
Female with scales and sword. | OXFORD BANK. Oxford, Mass. | General Washington.
2 | | 2

3 | THREE Surrender of Lord Cornwallis. 3 | THREE
Female. | OXFORD BANK, Oxford, Mass. | Agricultural implements.
3 | | 3

FIVE | V Battle of Bunker Hill. 5 | FIVE
Female. | OXFORD BANK. Oxford, Mass. | Portrait of Washington.
| | 5

States of Washington. | 10 Washington crossing the Delaware. 10 | TEN
| OXFORD BANK, Oxford, Mass. | Portrait.
| | X

20 | Three Indians mollising, city, etc. | 20
Two children and butterfly | OXFORD BANK, Oxford, Mass. | American shield.

Steamboat. | Three female figures and eagle. 20 | XX
XX | OXFORD BANK, Oxford. Mass. |
Train of cars. | | Milk maid.

50 | Farming scene. 50 | L
Steamboat and sail boat. | OXFORD BANK. Oxford, Mass. | Female with scales and sword.

50 | OXFORD BANK, | 50
State Arms. | Cows in brook; boy, girl, etc. Oxford, Mass. Fifty Dollars. | Woman with sewing machine.

Harvest scene
100 | Two horses startled at flash of lightning; cows in water on right. | C
Boy drinking from [illegible] girl, well etc | OXFORD BANK. One Hundred Dollars. | 100

100 | C Phaeton in the car of the sun. 100 | C
Eagle. | OXFORD BANK. Oxford, Mass. | Portrait of Washington
100 | | C

Ships and steamboats. | PACIFIC BANK Nantucket. Mass | ONE
| | Whale, fishing.
1 | | ONE

Whale fishing. | PACIFIC BANK Nantucket, Mass. | 2
2 | | Ship.

Ships. 3 PACIFIC BANK Nantucket, Mass. 3 Farmers and sheep.	X Three female figures. TEN Female, state arms and ships in background. PEMBERTON BANK Lawrence, Mass. 10 Blacksmith anvil &c.	Horses, chariot and a group of female figures. 10 PEOPLES BANK Roxbury, Mass. TEN Portrait of Washington TEN
5 Female. FIVE Neptune and three female figures. PACIFIC BANK Nantucket, Mass, 5 Sailor	20 Sailor leaning upon a capstan. Men and cattle. PEMBERTON BANK Lawrence, Mass. 20 Washington on horse back	20 Female. XX Eagle. XX PEOPLES BANK Roxbury, Mass. 20 Ship
10 Sea nymphs Steamship Spread eagle, ships in distance. PACIFIC BANK Nantucket, Mass. State Arms 10 Female. TEN	50 Portrait of Clay. PEMBERTON BANK Lawrence, Mass. Female and shield; capitol in distance. 50 Portrait of Female.	50 Soldier loading gun. PEOPLE'S BANK. Female seated; eagle, shield, etc. Fifty Dollars. Roxbury, Mass. 50 Male portrait.
20 Cupid in a sail boat. 20 Medallion. Neptune. Medallion. PACIFIC BANK Nantucket, Mass. 20 Female.	C Anchor, bale, etc. Female seated with shield, pole, cap, eagle, etc. PEMBERTON BANK, Lawrence, Mass. 100 Eagle	FIFTY Female. FIFTY 50 Man and horse. 50 PEOPLES BANK Roxbury, Mass. FIFTY Female. FIFTY
50 Medallion. 50 Medallion. Neptune. Medallion. female figure. PACIFIC BANK Nantucket, Mass. 50 Portrait of a girl. FIFTY	500 Dorchester Heights. Landing of the Pilgrims. Title of Bank. 500 Massach'sts D	C State Arms. Landing of the Pilgrims. PEOPLE'S BANK. Roxbury, Mass. One Hundred Dollars. 100 Benjamin Franklin
100 Ship building. 100 C Two females shipping in background. C PACIFIC BANK Nantucket, Mass. 100 Ships.	ONE Female. ONE Farming scene. PEOPLES BANK Roxbury, Mass. Large figure one, female within. ONE	One Hundred and 100 Portrait. Horses, wagons, shipping &c. PEOPLES BANK Roxbury, Mass. Same as left Portrait.
1 Portrait of female. ONE Stream of water R. R. train of cars. PEMBERTON BANK Lawrence, Mass. 1 Portrait of Webster. ONE	TWO Female. Train of cars. PEOPLES BANK Roxbury, Mass. TWO 2	D Washington Boy with two horses, cars, farm-house, &c. in distance. PEOPLE'S BANK. Roxbury, Mass. Five Hundred Dollars. 500 Eagle on rock.
2 Female. PEMBERTON BANK Lawrence, Mass. Female weaving at factory looms. 2 Portrait of Washington.	3 on THREE THREE on 3 THREE Eagle on branch of tree; cars, canal, etc. in distance. Large 3 PEOPLES BANK THREE DOLLARS Roxbury, Mass. 3 on THREE Washingt'n on horse. THREE	Farmer boy; horses drinking at trough; pig, fowl, cattle and house in back ground ONE on 1 MASSACHUSETTS State Arms of Mass. PITTSFIELD BANK ONE DOLLAR Pittsfield 1 Male portrait
3 Female Three female figures and cupid upon the water. PEMBERTON BANK Lawrence, Mass. 3 Portrait of Jackson. THREE	THREE Indian girl with bow and arrow. THREE Spread eagle R. R. and canal. PEOPLES BANK Roxbury, Mass. THREE General Washington. THREE	1 Stone cutters. PITTSFIELD BANK, Pittsfield, Mass. ONE Portrait.
FIVE White men in a boat and Indians on shore receiving them. PEMBERTON BANK Lawrence, Mass. 5 Portrait of Calhoun.	FIVE Female. Eagle and steamship. V PEOPLES BANK Roxbury, Mass. 5 Portrait.	TWO Portrait. Interior of a shoe makers shop PITTSFIELD BANK, Pittsfield, Mass. 2 2

Male Portrait.
PITTSFIELD BANK,
Pittsfield, Mass.
Two children.
TWO DOL-LARS. TWO DOL-LARS.
2 on TWO.
2
surrounded by 2's.
2
Male Portrait.

Male portrait
PITTSFIELD BANK,
Pittsfield, Mass.
Two females, spinning wheel, cattle scene on left; buildings on right.
5
Female bathing
5
5

FIVE
Spread eagle and flags bearing the name of each State in the Union.
V
PITTSFIELD BANK,
Pittsfield, Mass.
5
Portrait.

5
PITTSFIELD BANK,
Pittsfield, Mass.
Words "FIVE DOLLARS" on figure 5, and word FIVE.
Male Portrait.
5
Male Portrait.

X
Portrait. Steamship
PITTSFIELD BANK,
Pittsfield, Mass.
Indian.
X
TEN

X
Man cutting stick, horse, sheep, boy on gate, &c.
PITTSFIELD BANK,
Pittsfield, Mass.
Male Portrait.
10
Male Portrait.

20
Santa Claus in sleigh, drawn by reindeer over roofs of houses.
PITTSFIELD BANK,
Pittsfield, Mass.
Indian.
20
Portrait.

L
PITTSFIELD BANK,
Pittsfield, Mass.
Faust, Guttenberg and Schoeffer.
50
Portrait.

Three cupids raising figure 1 on pedestal on which is the word ONE
Landing of the Pilgrims, 1620
PLYMOUTH BANK
ONE DOLLAR
Plymouth
Steamboat
1
Large ship

2
Landing of the Pilgrims, 1620.
PLYMOUTH BANK,
Plymouth, Mass
Benjamin Franklin.
2
Two cupids in figure

5
Portrait of Washington.
FIVE
Landing of the pilgrims 1620.
PLYMOUTH BANK
Plymouth, Mass.
Indian
5
Female sickle and sheaf of wheat. in fig. 5.
FIVE

10
10
Landing of the pilgrims 1620.
X
PLYMOUTH BANK
Plymouth, Mass.
10
Female.

20
20
Landing of the Pilgrims, 1620.
XX
PLYMOUTH BANK,
Plymouth, Mass.
20
Twenty on Modallion. Head.

Female sickle and sheaf of wheat.
50
PLYMOUTH BANK
Plymouth, Mass.
Landing of the Pilgrims, 1620.
50

The figures 100 with the words One hundred running across.
Female; ship in distance
Landing of the pilgrims 1620
PLYMOUTH BANK
Plymouth, Mass
Eagle
100
100

ONE
Indian queen of Pocasset, crossing river on raft.
POCASSET BANK.
Figure 1 with one running across
1
Silver dollar

TWO on 2
Indian female
POCASSET BANK,
Fall River, Mass.
2 Cow, calf, sheep, stream, etc. 2
2
Two children

Figure 2, with two running across.
POCASSET BANK.
Vig. Same as ones.
Clasped hands.
2
Two silver dollars.

FIVE
Five silver dollars.
5
POCASSET BANK,
Vig. in centre of right end, same as ones.
State arms.
Figure 5 with five running across.
FIVE

10
Stonecutter at work; men hoisting in distance.
POCASSET BANK.
Vig. in lower right corner same as ones.
10

20
Indian queen on raft.
Twenty dollars.
20
Vig. Female soaring with sword in right hand; river scene, steamboat, &c.
POCASSET BANK,
State arms.
20

50
POCASSET BANK.
Vig. Scythe hanging to tree, female standing; man setting, dog lying down, water scene, steamboat, &c.
50
50
Indian queen on a raft.
50

100
Ship.
POCASSET BANK.
C Vig. Indian queen on raft; C on right.
100
Man whetting his scythe.

500
Ship of war under full sail; ship in distance.
POCASSET BANK,
D
Vig. Indian Queen on raft.
500

Vig. Indian Queen on raft
1000
POCASSET BANK.
M
1000
Indian seated smoking pipe, canoe on left, dog on right, squaw and wigwam.

ONE
View in the streets of Salisbury.
POWOW RIVER B'K,
Salisbury, Mass.
1
Farmers and sheep.

2
Interior of blacksmiths shop.
TWO
View in the streets of Salisbury.
POWOW RIVER B'K,
Salisbury, Mass.
2
Sail boats.
TWO

THREE
Female feeding poultry.
View of bank and stores; coach drawn by four horses passing
POWOW RIVER B'K,
Salisbury, Mass.
3
Andrew Jackson.

5
Indian.
FIVE
View of the town of Salisbury.
POWOW RIVER B'K,
Salisbury, Mass.
5
Farmers mowing.
FIVE

10
Justice guarding the Treasury
View of bank and stores; coach drawn by four horses passing.
POWOW RIV. B'K,
Salisbury, Mass.
10
Henry Clay

20 Girl's head.	POWOW RIVER B'K. Salisbury, Mass. 20 Dolls. in red.	20 View of bank stores, &c.
Ship at sea. 0	Female seated with grain, shield, &c. L POWOW RIVER B'K. Salisbury, Mass. Fifty Dollars.	50 Banking house
FIFTY Female. FIFTY	50 Man and horse. 50 POWOW RIVER B'K, Salisbury, Mass.	FIFTY Female. FIFTY
100 Female with sickle, dog, &c	POWOW RIVER B'K. C Female seated; factories in distance. C One Hundred Dollars. Massachusetts.	100 State Arms.
One Hundred and 100. Portrait.	Horses, waggons, shipping &c. POWOW RIVER B'K, Salisbury, Mass.	Same as left Portrait.
Train D	of Cars POWOW RIVER BANK Five Hundred Dollars Salisbury, Mass.	500
1	Two females, train of cars and steamboat in background. 1 PRESCOTT BANK. Lowell, Mass.	1 Female.
2	Man sitting on the ground with hammer on his shoulder; factory and train of cars in background. Cupid and figure 1. PRESCOTT BANK, Lowell, Mass.	TWO Female.
3	Farmers ploughing, man on horseback, train of cars running under a bridge. 3 PRESCOTT BANK, Lowell, Mass.	THREE Two females.
5	Female reclining; a stream of water and factories in background. 5 PRESCOTT BANK. Lowell, Mass.	FIVE Female. [illegible] shield.

5 with small 5's above and below it.	Figure of America erect, with wreath, shield, bundle of rods, &c. Interior of cotton factory, man, girl, boy, and machinery. PRESCOTT BANK, Lowell, Mass. FIVE DOLLARS.	5 In die with small 5's on it.
TEN	Female, eagle and shield, also portrait of Washington. X PRESCOTT BANK. Lowell, Mass.	10 State Arms.
Herd of [illegible] in forest [illegible] ground 10 On die with words TEN.	Waterfall [illegible] ground, trees, &c. PRESCOTT BANK. Lowell, Mass. TEN DOLLARS.	On die with words TEN. Head of Girl.
20 Female.	2 Female. 0 PRESCOTT BANK, Lowell, Mass. XX	20 Female. 20
20 Female portrait.	PRESCOTT BANK. Lowell, Mass. Female reclining with chart, dividers, quadrant, globe, etc.	20 Male head.
FIFTY Female with globe, etc.	PRESCOTT BANK, Lowell, Mass. FIFTY DOLLARS Title of Bank. FIFTY in red.	50 Male head.
50 Female.	Male and female. PRESCOTT BANK. Lowell, Mass. 50	50 Cupid in a sail boat. 50
100 Vulcan the blacksmith.	Spread eagle, railroad and canal. PRESCOTT BANK, Lowell, Mass. 100	100 Female.
C Male portrait.	PRESCOTT BANK, Lowell, Mass. Title of Bank. 100 DOLLS. in red.	100 Dog and safe.
500 D	PRESCOTT BANK. Lowell, Mass. Male portrait; D each side at bottom. FIVE HUNDRED	500 D

500	Female seated pointing to reapers and load of hay. 500 D PRESCOTT BANK. Lowell, Mass.	500
1 Man chopping down a tree. ONE	Ships. PROVINCETOWN BANK, Provincetown, Mass.	1 Girl.
2 Church.	Ships. PROVINCETOWN BANK, Provincetown, Mass.	2 TWO
3 Sailor erect and mechanic seated on bale of goods his hand resting on sledge hammer.	PROVINCETOWN BANK Provincetown, Mass. Ornamental figure 3	3 Vig. Large ship and small boats; in distance on right is a steamship, and ships on left.
Female and eagle. V	Portrait of Webster. PROVINCETOWN BANK, Provincetown, Mass.	FIVE Boy.
Female.	TEN Ships. PROVINCETOWN BANK, Provincetown, Mass.	10 X
XX Portrait of J. Q. Adams.	PROVINCETOWN BANK, Provincetown, Mass. Sailors on shore, throwing a rope with a mortar to a ship wrecked in the sea.	XX 20
L Portrait of female.	Female seated on a bale; steamship and sail vessels in the distance. PROVINCETOWN BANK, Provincetown, Mass.	50
C	Large Ship. PROVINCETOWN BANK, Provincetown, Mass. Large C in the middle of the bill printed in red.	100 Sailor leaning upon a capstan.
ON 1 E	Train of cars. 1 PYNCHON BANK, Springfield, Mass. 1	1 Head and shoulders of a man with hammer.

2 on TWO — Pynchon House — TWO
Female seated in large figure 2, farming scene in distance. 2
PYNCHON BANK TWO DOLLARS Springfield
TWO — Female with globe, pole and bird

3 — A bull's head. — THREE
Two horses and eagle; train of cars, factory and steamboat in background.
PYNCHON BANK, Springfield, Mass.
3 THREE

Large figure 5, female and shield. — FIVE
PYNCHON BANK, Springfield, Mass.
5 Three boys and ship. 5
5 — Old Pynchon House. — 5

X, 10, Ten — Old Pynchon House. — TEN
Man ploughing with yoke of oxen and horse.
PYNCHON BANK, Springfield, Mass. X
10 — Two females.

20 — Portrait of Webster.
Indian and plough, log cabin &c. 20 on right.
PYNCHON BANK. Springfield, Mass. XX
XX — Female.

Female.
50 Signing of the Declaration of Independence.
PYNCHON BANK. Springfield. Mass.
50 — Portrait of Washington

100 — Female.
PYNCHON BANK, Springfield, Mass
C Female leaning upon a chest; old Pynchon House in the distance.
100

1 — Head of John Adams — ONE
Vig. A scene in Quincy; horses, teams, stream of water, and sloops.
QUINCY STONE BK. Quincy, Mass.
1 — Head of John Hancock. — ONE

TWO — Head of John Hancock. — 2
Vig. Same as ones.
QUINCY STONE BK Quincy, Mass.
2 — Head of John Adams. — TWO

THREE — John Adams. — 3
Vig. Same as ones.
QUINCY STONE BK. Quincy, Mass.
3 — John Hancock. — THREE

5 — John Hancock. — FIVE
Vig. Same as ones.
QUINCY STONE BK. Quincy, Mass.
5 — John Adams. — FIVE

X — John Hancock. — TEN
Vig. Same as ones.
QUINCY STONE BK. Quincy, Mass.
10 — John Adams — TEN

20 — John Adams. — TWENTY
Vig. Same as ones.
QUINCY STONE BK. Quincy, Mass.
20 — John Hancock. — TWENTY

FIFTY — Female with wreath in hand. — FIFTY
50 Vig. Man and horse. 50
QUINCY STONE BK. Quincy, Mass.
FIFTY — Female with horn of plenty. — FIFTY

Stone quarry, oxen, wagon, men, railroad, &c.
50
L
QUINCY STONE B'K. Quincy. Mass.
50 — Male Portrait.

100 — Eagle. — 100
C Vig. Horses, car man with truck, &c. 100
QUINCY STONE BK. Quincy, Mass.
C — Head of Washington — C

Same as right. — Harrison
Scene on wharf.
QUINCY STONE BK., Quincy, Mass.
One Hundred and 100. — Columbus

C — State arms.
QUINCY STONE B'K. Quincy, Mass.
C Franklin in study. C
100 — Female Portrait.

500
Indian paddling in canoe. 500
Title of Bank.
D D
500 — Female with sword and scales.

500 — D
QUINCY STONE B'K, Quincy, Mass.
D Eagle. D
500 — D

1000
Spread eagle on promontory; ship in distance. 1000
QUINCY STONE B'K, Quincy, Mass.
1000 — Indian female with bow and arrows.

Head of female. — 1
Vig. Church, court-house, dwellings, trees, man on horseback, carriages, &c., which is a view of Main street, Worcester
QUINSIGAMOND BANK, Worcester, Mass.
1 — Portrait of male.

2 — Plank road scene.
Vig. Same as ones.
QUINSIGAMOND BANK, Worcester, Mass.
Female head.
2 — Horses in distance; railroad train &c.

Mason at work. — 3
Vig. Same as ones.
QUINSIGAMOND BANK, Worcester, Mass.
Eagle.
3 — Female with bundle of grain under her arm.

5
Vig. Same as ones. Male Portrait.
QUINSIGAMOND BANK, Worcester, Mass.
5 — Female with flowers.

Wm. Penn. — TEN
QUINSIGAMOND BK. Worcester, Mass.
Street in Worcester
10 — Indian seated.

10 — X — 10
Vig. Cincinnatus at his plough, oxen &c. 10
QUINSIGAMOND BANK, Worcester, Mass.
TEN — Full length female and horn of plenty.

State Arms. — 20
Vig. Female figure with wings, blowing trumpet; eagle with arrows, &c. in his talons.
QUINSIGAMOND BANK. Worcester, Mass.
20 — Portrait of J. Q. Adams

50 — Head of Washington.
QUINSIGAMOND BANK Worcester, Mass.
Vig. Two cows in water, one lying down; two sheep resting and one standing.
50

100 — Figure of justice with scales and sword.
Vig. House and cattle in distance; dairy maid, pail and two cows
QUINSIGAMOND BANK, Worcester, Mass.
100 — Head of Franklin.

500 — Three hares, balances, female, dog, basket, bottle, &c. — QUINSIGAMOND BANK, Worcester. — 500 — Medallion head of Washington.

1 — Female — 1 — Female seated inside shield, etc. ONE, cars and bridge in distance. 1 — RAILROAD BANK, ONE DOLLAR, Lowell, Massachusetts. — ONE

TWO — Archimedes — 2 — 2 Vig. same as $1 note. 2 — THE RAILROAD BK., Lowell, Mass. — TWO

3 — Vulcan. — 3 — THREE Female locomotive, buildings, etc. 3 — RAILROAD BANK, Lowell, Mass. — THREE

Male portrait — 5 — View of depot, cars, church, etc. — RAILROAD BANK, Lowell, Mass. — 5 — Five females surrounding fig. 5.

10 — X — View of buildings, pedestrians, etc. — Title of Bank. — X — Male portrait.

XX — 20 — RAILROAD BANK, Lowell, Mass. — Male portrait — 20 — Factory girl with wheel.

50 — Factories, etc. — Title of Bank. — 50 — Male portrait.

100 — Female seated holding spool of cotton; factories — Title of Bank. — Factories, etc. — 100 — Male portrait.

500 — 500 — Railroad depot, cars, church, etc. Male portrait — Title of Bank. — 500 — Indian chief erect on shield.

Two farmers, one tying up grain. — 1 — 1 Bee hive. — RANDOLPH BANK, Randolph, Mass. — 1 — Boots and shoes. — ONE

TWO — Boots and shoes. — 2 — 2 Vig. Drover on horseback, cattle dogs, &c.; cattle lying down — RANDOLPH BANK, Randolph, Mass. — Dog and safe. — 2 — Portrait of Franklin.

THREE — Portrait of Jefferson. — 3 — THREE Spr'd eagle. THREE — RANDOLPH BANK, Randolph, Mass. — Farmer's reaping. — 3 — Washington and his horse. — THREE

5 — Female child. — Vig. Three females, one with liberty pole and cap; Eagle on left of vig; and ship on right. V — RANDOLPH BANK, Randolph, Mass. — Dog and safe. — 5 — Boot and shoes. — FIVE

TEN — Female in the act of pouring water from a pitcher. — 10 Vig. Blacksmith shoeing horse, and man holding horse by the head. X — RANDOLPH BANK, Randolph, Mass. — Bundles of grain. — 10 — Boots and shoes.

20 — Minerva — 2 Female figure with rake. 0 — RANDOLPH BANK, Randolph, Mass. — XX — 20 — Female with horn of plenty; globe and trident. — 20

Female with ... and shield; Indian female at her feet — 20 Two shoemakers at work; female at household duties in background. — RANDOLPH BANK, Randolph, Mass. — 20 — Cattle, telegraph; cars on bridge

50 — Minerva. — Vig. State Arms. Male and female figure; horn of plenty between them; rake on females right, grain on left. — RANDOLPH BANK, Randolph, Mass. — 50 — 50 — Cupid afloat. — 50

FIFTY — Female representing Agriculture. — 50 — 50 Farmer seated with implements and products; load of hay, buildings, etc., in distance. 50 — Title of Bank. — 50 — Female portrait.

100 — Female portrait. — Two females seated; steamer, etc., in distance on left; buildings, monument, etc., on right. — Title of Bank — 100 — Train of cars bridge and cars in distance.

100 — Male sitting, with scroll in right hand. — Vig. Spread eagle on branch; canal boats and lock; railroad train in distance. — RANDOLPH BANK, Randolph, Mass. — 100 — 100 — Female sitting with rule in right hand, and grain in left, resting on horn of plenty.

Female figure; reapers; team laden with grain. — 500 — 500 D — RANDOLPH BANK, Randolph, Mass. — 500

1 — Man carrying leather. — 1 — REVERE BANK, Male portrait. Boston, Mass. — 1 — State Arms.

2 — Blacksmith's boy at forge. — Male portrait. Stonecutter and man with plan. — Title of Bank. — 2 — State Arms.

3 — Sailor boy, etc. — Title of Bank. — Male portraits. — 3 — State Arms.

5 — State Arms. — Steamship, tug, city, etc. — Title of Bank. — 5 — Male portrait.

10 — State Arms. — General scene in moulding shop: men, wheels, machinery, etc. — Title of Bank. — 10 — Male portrait.

20 — State Arms. — REVERE BANK, Boston, Mass. — 20 DOLLS. in red. — 20 — Male portrait.

50 — State Arms. — Title of Bank. — Male portrait. — L L — 50 — Mechanic, sailor, steamer vessels etc.

100 — State Arms. — Title of Bank. — Male portrait. C — 100 — Surveyors at work.

Left	Centre	Right
500 / State Arms	Title of Bank. Hogshead, bales, rope, masts, band, etc.; steamboat in distance.	500 / Male portrait
1	Oval die, through is seen a female, train of cars and city in distance; a female each side of the die, steamboat and train of cars in the background. ROCKLAND BANK, Roxbury, Mass.	1 / Farmer, plough and rake and ONE on half shield.
Portrait of female. / 2	Farmers and sheep. ROCKLAND BANK, Roxbury, Mass.	2 / Female and [illegible]
3	ROCKLAND BANK, Roxbury, Mass. Farmer with scythe, sailor with spy glass, [illegible] mechanic, anvil, hammer &c., also three gold dollars. THREE	3 / A dog's head
5 / Portrait. / FIVE	ROCKLAND BANK. Roxbury, Mass. A man with gun, Indian woman, three cupids and five gold dollars	5
X / Two females.	ROCKLAND BANK. Roxbury, Mass. Farming scene.	X / Portrait of Washington.
State Arms. / XX	Farmer ploughing, cattle and horses in pasture; city in distance. ROCKLAND BANK, Roxbury, Mass.	20 / Portrait.
50 / [illegible] and Cupid	ROCKLAND BANK. Roxbury, Mass. Ships, and city in the background.	50 / 50
C / Fountain.	ROCKLAND BANK, Roxbury, Mass. Farming scene, men women and children.	100 / Portrait of Jefferson.
D / Female and horse.	ROCKLAND BANK, Roxbury, Mass. Female reclining, eagle, globe; ship and steamship in distance. 500	500 / 500

Left	Centre	Right
ONE / 1	Vig. Wood scene, man sowing grain; ox team. 1 ROCKPORT BANK, Rockport, Mass.	1 / Full rigged ship. / ONE
Blacksmith, sledge and anvil. / 1	Team of oxen, stone quarry, &c. ROCKPORT BANK, Rockport, Mass. Man plowing.	1 / Stone cutter
Sailor and capstan; masts, bbls and bales. / 2	Same as ones. ROCKPORT BANK, Rockport, Mass. Loading wagon.	2 / Two females.
TWO / 2	Vig. Spread eagle, cannon balls, cog wheels; train of cars. 2 ROCKPORT BANK, Rockport, Mass.	2 / TWO / Schooner and sloop in a storm.
THREE / 3	Vig. Sailor, bales of goods, shipping; houses, horse, dray, &c. 3 ROCKPORT BANK, Rockport, Mass.	3 / THREE / Train of cars.
THREE / Knickerbocker.	Same as ones. ROCKPORT BANK, Rockport, Mass. Eagle.	3 / Female reaper
Man with cradle. / 5	Same as ones. ROCKPORT BANK, Rockport, Mass.	5 / Female.
FIVE	Vig. Eagle standing on shield and anchor; town in distance; foundries, &c. Female and child in large figure five. ROCKPORT BANK, Rockport, Mass.	FIVE / Girl holding basket.
Soldier with sword. / TEN	Same as ones. ROCKPORT BANK, Rockport, Mass.	10 / Female portrait.
TEN	Vig. Man sitting holding sledge; train of cars crossing bridge. X ROCKPORT BANK, Rockport, Mass.	10 / Man holding sickle and sheaf of grain

Left	Centre	Right
20 / Female sitting, book in her lap.	XX Eagle XX ROCKPORT BANK, Rockport, Mass.	20 / Full rigged ship.
Female. / XX	Same as ones. ROCKPORT BANK, Rockport, Mass. Cow and calf	20 / Male portrait
Female. / 50	Same as ones. ROCKPORT BANK, Rockport, Mass. Shield.	50 / Male portrait
FIFTY / Female.	50 Vig. Man training horse. 50 ROCKPORT BANK, Rockport, Mass.	FIFTY / Female. / FIFTY
Male portrait / 100	Same as ones. ROCKPORT BANK, Rockport, Mass. Dog's head.	100 / Webster
The figures 100, with the words one hundred across. / Portrait of Harrison.	Vig. Loading covered waggons with merchandise. ROCKPORT BANK, Rockport, Mass.	The figures 100, with the words one hundred across. / Fancy portrait.
ONE	Female seated on the ground; factory village in the distance 1 on right. ROLLSTONE BANK, Fitchburg, Mass. Wheels, bale, etc	1 / Female and 2 cherubs.
2	Female riding upon the back of a reindeer. 2 ROLLSTONE BANK, Fitchburg, Mass. Cars	TWO / Two females
3	Milk maid and cows. 3 ROLLSTONE BANK, Fitchburg, Mass.	3 / Portrait of female. / THREE
5	Train of cars. Female in large V. ROLLSTONE BANK, Fitchburg, Mass. State Arms	5 / Females, chest and horn of plenty and 5.

10 TEN
Female with sickle, farmers gathering grain in the background. X
ROLLSTONE BANK, Fitchburg, Mass
Female head
Female figure.

20 Female.
2 Female. 0
ROLLSTONE BANK, Fitchburg, Mass.
XX
20 Female. 20

50 Female.
Male and female.
ROLLSTONE BANK, Fitchburg. Mass
50
50 Cupid in a sail boat. 50

100 Vulcan the blacksmith.
Spread eagle, railroad and canal.
ROLLSTONE BANK, Fitchburg. Mass
100
100 Female.

100 ROLLSTONE BANK, Fitchburg. Mass. 100
Female with tablets, chest at her feet.
C Male portrait. C
Female, child, pole and cap.

ONE
Three females floating in water supporting cupid.
SAFETY FUND BK, Boston, Mass.
1 State Arms.

2 Female erect beside pedestal; steamer in distance.
Scene in the Arctic Regions; men shoving boat; dog, icebergs, etc.
Title of Bank.
2 State Arms.

THREE on 3.
Scene in Printing office, Faust, Guttenberg and Schoeffer. Eagle
Title of Bank.
3 State Arms 3

State Arms. 5
Title of Bank.
Apotheosis of Washington; soldier on left; female and two Indians on right. Red V each side.
5 Dog, key and safe.

10 Franklin at work at printing case
State Arms Two females, owl, buildings, steamer, etc.
Title of Bank.
Eagle.
10 Sailor with anchor.

20 State Arms.
Three females, safe, etc.
SAFETY FUND BK., Boston, Mass.
20 City

50 Boy and rabbits.
Female on left of view of city, boats, shipbuilding, etc.; 50 on stone and Indian in canoe on right; steamboat in distance.
SAFETY FUND BK., Boston, Mass.
50 State Arms.

C State Arms.
Title of Bank.
Four females on globe.
One Hundred Dollars.
100 Male portrait.

500 Female seated on bale; globe, steamboat, etc.
SAFETY FUND BK Boston, Mass.
Auditors Die.
Five Hundred Dollars
500 Old man, child and bust of Washington on table.

1 Three female figures. 1
Machinery and factories. Ship. Beehive.
SALEM BANK, Salem. Mass.
1 Portrait of Washington 1

2 Masts, carbbls., fruit, &c. 2
TWO
Shipping. Female figure. Farming scene.
SALEM BANK, Salem, Mass.
2 Female crowning a bust of Washington. 2

THREE
Female sitting on the ground, also anchor and bale; ship in distance. 3 Female, anchor, merchandise and ships.
SALEM BANK, Salem, Mass.
3 Portrait of Washington 3

5 Female. 5
5 Female figure and ship. 5
FIVE
SALEM BANK. Salem, Mass.
5 Female and sickle, 5

Statue of Liberty leaning on column on which is letter X
Zouaves charging
SALEM BANK
TEN
Salem, Mass.
10 DOLLARS

10 Portrait of female. TEN
1 Female with key and horn of plenty. 0
SALEM BANK, Salem, Mass.
TWENTY
10 Portrait of female. TEN

10 X 10
(Old Plate.)
Man and oxen. 10
SALEM BANK, Salem. Mass
TEN Female

20 Female.
2 Female. 0
SALEM BANK, Salem, Mass.
XX
20 Female. 20

Ships at sea
Massachusetts
SALEM BANK'
FIFTY DOLLARS
Salem
50
50 Dog's head

50 Female figure
Male and female.
SALEM BANK, Salem, Mass.
50
50 Cupid in a sail boat. 50

FIFTY Grain, fruit, &c. 50
50 Three female fig's, ship, eagle, etc.
SALEM BANK, Salem, Mass.
Fifty on 50 Vulcan seated with implements.

Female portrait 100
Massachusetts
Salem
SALEM BANK
One Hun'd Dol's
Cars passing over bridge, cattle in water, etc.
100

100 Vulcan the blacksmith.
Spread eagle, railroad and canal.
SALEM BANK. Salem, Mass.
100
100 Female.

Letter C. Men and boats. 100
Spread eagle on bale; products, etc. 100
SALEM BANK, Salem, Mass.
100 Female. 100

500
Indian paddling canoe. 500 in red across light 500.
Title of Bank.
D
500

ONE View of Merchants' Row 1
Indian seated on a rock; ship in distance.
SHAWMUT BANK, Boston, Mass.
1 View of Boston from the harbor.
ONE

Left end	Centre	Right end
2 Same as ones TWO	Vig. Same as ones. SHAWMUT BANK, Boston, Mass. Men in boat, etc.	2 Same as ones TWO
THREE Same as ones on right end THREE	Vig. Same as ones. SHAWMUT BANK, Boston, Mass. Eagle	3 View of Merchants' Row
5 View of Boston from the harbor. FIVE	Vig. Same as ones. SHAWMUT BANK, Boston, Mass. Anchor, etc	5 Same as 2s.
10 Same as fives 10	Vig. Same as ones. SHAWMUT BANK, Boston, Mass. 10	10 Same as fives 10
View of Merchants' Row XX	Vig. Same as ones. SHAWMUT BANK, Boston, Mass.	20 View of Boston from the harbor. 20
50 Same as 20s. 50	Vig. Same as ones. SHAWMUT BANK, Boston, Mass.	50 Same as 20s. 50
C View of Boston from the harbor. C	Vig. Same as ones. SHAWMUT BANK, Boston, Mass.	100 View of Merchants' Row. 100
FIVE HUNDRED	Spread eagle, shield, etc. SHAWMUT BANK, Boston, Mass	Figs. 500. Male portrait Figs. 500.
1000	Spread eagle shield and motto "E Pluribus Unum," etc. Title of Bank.	1000 Washington 1000
Female erect by fig. 1. ONE on 1.	View of Shelburne Falls. SHELBURNE FALLS BANK, Shelburne Falls, Mass.	1 Female churning.

Left end	Centre	Right end
2 Farmer with scythe.	Farmers mowing; others loading wagon in distance Title of Bank.	2 Female representing Agriculture.
3 Blacksmith; anvil.	View of Shelburne Falls. 3 Title of Bank.	Liberty.
5 Washington	Mechanic seated with hammer; cars, factory, bridge and cattle in distance. Title of Bank.	5 Female with grain.
X	Female seated before shield, Two men reclining on chest; milkmaid and cows in distance on right; cars and ships on left. Title of Bank.	10 Female with shield, cornucopia and anirea
50 Female with flowers.	View of Shelburne Falls. Title of Bank.	50 Male portrait
100 Female portrait.	Three females representing Agriculture, Commerce and Manufactures. Title of Bank.	100 Franklin.
1 Man dressing leather. ONE	Shoe and Leather Dealers Store, horses, wagon, wharf and shipping. SHOE & LEATHER DEALERS' BANK, Boston, Mass.	1 Interior of shoemaker's shop. ONE
2 Interior of a shoemaker's shop. TWO	Vig. Same as ones. Title of Bank.	2 Morocco dressing TWO
3 Cows THREE	Vig. Same as ones. Title of Bank.	3 Interior of a shoemaker's shop. THREE
5 Morocco dressing	Vig. Same as ones Title of Bank.	5 Justice.

Left end	Centre	Right end
10 Washington and his horse TEN	Vig. Same as ones. Title of Bank.	10 Shipping. TEN
XX Indian with bow. 20	Vig. Same as ones. Title of Bank.	20 Eagle. XX
FIFTY Washington 50	Vig. Same as ones. Title of Bank. Some have fig. 50 on vig.	50 Franklin FIFTY
Words one hundred and figs. 100. Male portrait	Wharf scene—loading wagon, men, horses, shipping, &c. Title of Bank.	Words one hundred and figures 100. Male portrait
100 Justice seated.	Shoe and Leather Dealers store; horses, wagon, men wharf and shipping SHOE & LEATHER DEALERS BANK, Boston, Mass.	100 Female portrait.
500	Same as 100s. Title of Bank.	500 Cows
1	Vig. A man ploughing with two horses, and another sowing, two or three baskets in the fore ground; cars in the distance. 1 SOUTHBRIDGE BK, Southbridge, Mass.	1 Spread Eagle. ONE
2	Vig. A large building; train of cars, man with wheelbarrow, and church in the distance. 2 SOUTHBRIDGE BK. Southbridge, Mass.	2 Man pitching hay
3	Vig. Train of cars, church and village at the left in the distance; and a building with cupola. 3 SOUTHBRIDGE BK, Southbridge, Mass.	3 Female with a basket in her hands
5 Female with torch beside column	V Large country house V SOUTHBRIDGE B'K FIVE DOLLARS Southbridge	5 General Geo. B. McClellan

FIVE
(Old Plate.)
FIVE Two female figures and eagle; train of cars and ship in background. FIVE
SOUTHBRIDGE B'K. Southbridge, Mass.
5 Portrait. FIVE

FIVE
Vig. Female sitting; a hand spinning wheel on the right of the scene, factory buildings, in the distance. 5
SOUTHBRIDGE BK,
Female head
5 Bust of a female FIVE

Sailor and female either side of pedestal on which is bust of Washington
MASSACHUSETTS 10 ON Southbridge
SOUTHBRIDGE BK
10
TEN DOLLARS
10 Girl beside bank

10 Portrait. 10
(Old Plate.)
X Spread eagle. X
SOUTHBRIDGE B'K, Southbridge, Mass.
10 Female.

TEN
Vig. A female sitting between the digits 1 & 0, holding key in her left hand a cornucopia at her right hand. X
SOUTHBRIDGE BK, Southbridge, Mass.
Shield.
10 General Taylor. TEN

20 Female sitting.
XX Eagle XX
SOUTHBRIDGE BK, Southbridge, Mass.
20 Ship

20 Female with flowers.
SOUTHBRIDGE B'K Southbridge, Mass.
Female seated; sheep, etc.
20 Boy

50 Female and anchor; steamboat in distance. 50
FIFTY DOLLARS 50
SOUTHBRIDGE B'K. Southbridge, Mass.
FIFTY

FIFTY Large female figure wreath in right hand FIFTY
50 50
Vig. A man holding a horse which is apparently trying to break away.
SOUTHBRIDGE BK, Southbridge Mass.
FIFTY Female standing, her left elbow resting on a column. FIFTY

50 Two females.
SOUTHBRIDGE B'K Southbridge, Mass.
Cattle scene; drovers, farmers, etc.
L
50 50

THE 100
SOUTHBRIDGE B'K Southbridge, Mass.
Female at work on looms. C
100
100 Female, spinning wheel, factories, etc.

Words one hundred across the figure 100. Bust of Gen. Harrison.
Market waggon man and team.
SOUTHBRIDGE BK, Southbridge, Mass.
Words one hundred across the figure 100. Bust of Kosciusko

500
Vig. Agricultural scene, female among sheaves, men in the distance reaping. 500 and D on right.
SOUTHBRIDGE BK, Southbridge, Mass.
500

Female and fig. 1. 1
Cupid rolling a silver dollar upon a Railroad track, train of cars and village in the distance.
SOUTH READING BK South Reading, Mass
1 Portrait.

Female. 2
Two cherubs and two silver dollars, train of cars and cattle in the background.
SOUTH READING BK South Reading, Mass.
2 Portrait.

3 Portrait.
Three cherubs and three silver dollars.
SOUTH READING B'K South Reading. Mass
3 Blacksmith anvil and forge.

5 Portrait. 5
Five cherubs and five silver dollars.
SOUTH READING BK South Reading, Mass.
5 Female and fig. 5

Farmer with basket of fruit and a cradle 10
Portrait.
SOUTH READING BK South Reading, Mass.
X Female and anchor.

XX Female.
Female reclining, locomotive and factory, milk maids and cows in background.
SOUTH READING BK South Reading, Mass
20 Portrait.

Girl with sheaf of grain. 50
Female sitting on a rock, and cupids sporting with a dolphin in the water.
SOUTH READING BK South Reading, Mass
50 Portrait.

Female, feeding an eagle from a cup. 100
Capitol at Washington.
SOUTH READING BK South Reading, Mass
100 Portrait.

ONE The arm of a man holding a hammer.
Factory.
SPICKET FALLS B'K. Methuen, Mass.
1 Portrait of Webster.

TWO
Factory. Portrait of J. Q. Adams.
SPICKET FALLS B'K, Methuen, Mass.
2 2

3 3
Train of cars and railroad station.
SPICKET FALLS B'K. Methuen, Mass.
3 Blacksmith.

5 Female sewing.
Interior of a shoemakers shop.
SPICKET FALLS B'K. Methuen, Mass.
V Dog

TEN Indian.
Farmers, and horse and sled gathering grain.
SPICKET FALLS B'K, Methuen, Mass.
X X

XX A hunter warming himself by a fire.
20
SPICKET FALLS B'K. Methuen, Mass.
20 Portrait of Lewis Cass

50
Cattle.
SPICKET FALLS B'K. Methuen, Mass.
50 Female with sickle and sheaf of wheat.

100
Santa Claus in sleigh drawn over roofs of houses by a reindeer.
SPICKET FALLS B'K. Methuen, Mass.
C Santa Claus sitting at a fire place.

1 Cattle. ONE
Man and dog in a forest.
SPRINGFIELD B'K Springfield, Mass.
Vessel.
1 Portrait of Jenny Lind

Female. TWO	Man and dog in a forest. SPRINGFIELD B'K Springfield, Mass. Safe and boxes.	TWO 2 Hay makers.
	The Springfield Bank uses the old sterotype plate for all other denominations.	
1 Ship.	Winged female with scales and sword and fig. 1. STATE BANK, Boston, Mass. Steamer	1 State Arms.
2 State Arms.	Female and child, bale and bhds; steamboat on right, and vessels on left. STATE BANK, Boston, Mass. Machinery	2 Cupids and 2.
3 Cupids and 3	Spread eagle and ships. STATE BANK, Boston, Mass. Steamer	3 State Arms.
Female. 5	Female portrait. 5 Female portrait. STATE BANK, Boston, Mass.	5 State Arms.
10 Portrait of Washington.	State Arms; female and factories on right; female and shipping on left. X on right. STATE BANK, Boston, Mass.	10 State Arms.
20 State Arms.	Two females; shipping railroad and canal. STATE BANK, Boston, Mass. Dog's head	20 Med. head.
State Arms 50	Three females. STATE BANK, Boston, Mass. Horse	50 Sailor with telescope.
State Arms. 100	Female seated on a bale, ships and lighthouse in distance. STATE BANK, Boston, Mass.	100 Two females, eagle and globe.

500 Med. head. 500	STATE BANK, Boston, Mass. Female seated representing Commerce; ship and rainbow in distance. Steamship.	500 State Arms. 500
Justice seated. 1000	Spread eagle on limb of tree; ships in distance. STATE BANK, Boston, Mass. Ships	1000 State Arms.
1 Washington and his horse	Female portrait. 1 Female portrait. SUFFOLK BANK, Boston, Mass.	ONE Eagle. ONE
TWO Washington and his horse TWO	2 2 2 SUFFOLK BANK, Boston, Mass.	TWO Female. TWO
Female.	THREE 3 THREE SUFFOLK BANK, Boston, Mass.	3 Dog, safe and building. 3
5 Two females V	Winged female with trumpet. On right portrait of Columbus. On left portrait of Washington. SUFFOLK BANK, Boston, Mass. Eagle	5 State Arms. V
Washington	10 Female, eagle and shield. SUFFOLK BANK, Boston, Mass. Building	10 Boat.
XX Female portrait. XX	Female on rock, cupids and dolphin sporting in water. SUFFOLK BANK, Boston, Mass. TWENTY TWENTY	20 Dog's head. XX
50 Female with sword and shield.	FIFTY DOLLARS SUFFOLK BANK, Boston, Mass. Fifty in block letters across face. L	50 Eagle. FIFTY
100 100 100	One Hundred Dollars SUFFOLK BANK, Boston, Mass. Words One Hundred in large block letters across face. C	100 100 100

500 Female with pole and cap and view of Boston.	500 SUFFOLK BANK, Boston, Mass. Five large block letter D's across face. D	500 Female and Indian with bow and shield
1000 Justice	One Thousand Dollars SUFFOLK BANK, Boston, Mass. 1000 M	1000 Letter M and words One Thousand Dollars. 100
Girl's head. 1	Train of cars at depot. One Dollar. TAUNTON BANK. Taunton, Mass	1 Female head.
1 Reaper. ONE	Reaper gathering grain. 1 Shipping. TAUNTON BANK. Taunton, Mass	1 Vulcan the blacksmith.
Goddess of Liberty, with wreath and Am shield, on which is figure 2	Men and two horses in oval die TAUNTON BANK TWO DOLLARS Taunton	2 Female portrait
TWO Indian 2	Eagle. 2 Washington on horseback. TAUNTON BANK. Taunton, Mass	2 Train of cars
3 on ornamental die. Female portrait	Three children in circular die, reading book. TAUNTON BANK, Taunton, Mass THREE DOLLARS.	3 on ornamental die. Male portrait.
Female with grain; reapers on left, farm-house on right. THREE	Large 3 TAUNTON BANK THREE DOLLARS Taunton Mass	3 Male figure
Ornamental die, on which is name of bank 8 times & one large and eight smaller 5s.	View of Factory; train of cars, etc. 5 in ornamental die FIVE DOLLARS. TAUNTON BANK. Taunton, Mass.	Ornamental die on which is name of bank 8 times & one large and eight smaller 5s.
5	Female seated; railroad and canal in background. V TAUNTON BANK. Taunton, Mass	FIVE Five and Eagle FIVE

Dog's head | Farmers at work with machines | 10 | TAUNTON BANK | TEN DOLLARS | Taunton Massachusetts | 10 | Female portrait

10 | State Arms, also a train of cars crossing a bridge. X | 10 | TAUNTON BANK. Taunton, Mass. | Reaper.

Sailor with bundle on shoulder | Massachusetts | Vessels at sea | 20 | TAUNTON BANK | TWENTY DOLLARS | Taunton, Mass. | 20 | Male portrait

20 | 2 Female 0 | 20 | TAUNTON BANK. Taunton, Mass. | Female. | Female figure. | XX | 20

Massachusetts | Scene at mill | Farmer seated on fence, scythe in hand | 50 | TAUNTON BANK | FIFTY DOLLARS | Taunton | 50 | Male portrait

50 | Male and female. | 50 | TAUNTON BANK. Taunton, Mass. | Cupid in a sail boat. | Female figure. | 50 | 50

Statue of Liberty leaning on column on which is figures | Taunton | State Arms of Mass. | 100 | TAUNTON BANK | One Hundred | Massachusetts | 100 | Male portraits

One Hundred and 100. | Horses, waggons, shipping &c. | Same as left | TAUNTON BANK. Taunton, Mass. | Portrait. | Portrait.

Large eagle spread on rock | Massachusetts Five Hundred Dollars | 500 | TAUNTON BANK | Taunton | 500 | Male portrait

ONE and 1 | TOWNSEND BANK, Townsend, Mass. | 1 | Merchandise. | Cupid rolling a silver dollar upon the railroad track, train of cars and city in distance, | Two females. | 1 | Farmer cradling

2 | Two cupids and two silver dollars. | 2 | TOWNSEND BANK, Townsend, Mass. | Two females and eagle. | Female and large figure 2.

3 | TOWNSEND BANK, Townsend, Mass. | 3 | Portrait. | Three cupids and three silver dollars. | Female reading. | 3 | Mechanic seated

Female feeding an eagle from a cup. | Five cupids and five silver dollars, | 5 | TOWNSEND BANK. Townsend, Mass. | Group of females and large figure 5 | 5

10 | TOWNSEND BANK, Townsend, Mass. | X | Farming scene | Female. | X

TWENTY | TOWNSEND BANK. Townsend. Mass. | 20 | Indian woman with bow and spear. | Indian sitting on the ground beside a slain deer. | Farmer-boy and XX on half shield.

50 | Capitol at Washington. | 50 | TOWNSEND BANK. Townsend, Mass | Female feeding a horse. | Female.

C | TOWNSEND BANK | 100 | Townsends, Mass. | Vig. Blacksmith shoeing a horse. | Female, arm resting on a tub. | Farming scene; load of grain, tree &c.

1 | Wharf and shipping; view of Boston in distance. 1 on right. | 1 | Ship building | TRADERS' BANK, Boston, Mass. | Male and female. | ONE | ONE

2 | Vig. Same as ones. 2 | 2 | Boy and girl sailing boats in a tub. | TRADERS' BANK, Boston, Mass. | Girl. | TWO | TWO

3 | Vig. Same as ones. 3 | 3 | Interior of a blacksmith's shop. | TRADERS' BANK, Boston, Mass. | Female in a forest | THREE | THREE

FIVE | Vig. Same as ones. 5 | 5 | TRADERS' BANK, Boston, Mass. | Portrait of Webster. | Justice. | FIVE

TEN | Vig. Same as ones. X | 10 | TRADERS' BANK, Boston, Mass. | Female. | Female. | TEN

20 | Vig. Same as ones. | 20 | Female. | TRADERS' BANK, Boston, Mass. | Justice | XX | XX

Vig. Same as ones. 50 | 50 | TRADERS' BANK, Boston, Mass. | Covered waggon and merchandise. | 50

Vig. Same as ones. | ONE HUND | Hundred on 100 | TRADERS' BANK, Boston, Mass. | 100 | Washington

Vig. Same as ones 500 | 500 | TRADERS' BANK, Boston, Mass. | Eagle and shield. | 500

Female with a spear and shield, holding a pillar in the form of a figure one | 1 | Vig. View of Chelsea ferry boat going into slip. | ONE | TRADESMAN'S BK. Chelsea, Mass. | State Arms

Vig. Same as ones. | 2 | 2 | TWO | TRADESMAN'S BK. Chelsea, Mass. | Figure of Justice.

Vig. Same as ones. | 3 | 3 | THREE | TRADESMAN'S BK. Chelsea, Mass. | Blacksmith and anvil.

Figure 5 formed by an eagle and horn of plenty; likeness of Washington in the scroll or finials. | Same as ones. | 5 | TRADESMAN'S BK. Chelsea, Mass. | FIVE | Portrait of Gen. Taylor.

Left end	Centre	Right end
TEN	Vig. Same as ones. X TRADESMAN'S BK. Chelsea, Mass.	10 Female with horn of plenty, in right hand, left hand on an elbor.
20 Indian girl with bow and arrows.	Vig. Same as ones. TRADESMAN'S BK. Chelsea, Mass. TWENTY Machinery.	20 Female with 2 in right hand, and on her knee and 0 under her left.
50 Female in the act of stepping into the water, an urn in her left hand.	Vig. Same as ones. TRADESMAN'S BK. Chelsea, Mass. FIFTY	50 Female holding a flag; three children representing Agriculture &c. all floating in the air.
100 Sailor and ship in the distance.	Vig. Same as ones, TRADESMAN'S BK. Chelsea, Mass. 100	100 Figure of a Stone cutter
500 Ship on stocks. 500	Vig. Same as ones. TRADESMAN'S BK. Chelsea, Mass. 500 State Arms	500 Steamboat. 500
ONE Liberty. ONE	Neptune; on right, Boston in 1852; on left Boston in 1630. TREMONT BANK, Boston, Mass.	1 Female
1 ONE 1	View of Street. TREMONT BANK, Boston, Mass.	Word one, fig. 1 and $ mark. Male portrait
2	View of a street. 2 TREMONT BANK, Boston, Mass.	Word two and fig. 2 and II. Two females
Female surrounded by the names of the States. TWO	Vig. Same as first ones. TREMONT BANK, Boston, Mass.	2 Two females
3 THREE 3	3 View of a street. TREMONT BANK, Boston, Mass.	Word three and fig. 3 and III. Three females

Left end	Centre	Right end
3 Female seated on a barrel.	Vig. Same as first ones. TREMONT BANK, Boston, Mass.	3 Blacksmith, sailor and farmer.
	All other notes of the Tremont Bank are of the Perkins' Stereotype Plate, which has the denomination printed in fine letters all over the bill.	
1 Portrait of Fillmore.	State Arms; female and cars on right; female and steamboat on left. UNION BANK, Boston, Mass.	Female and 1. ONE
TWO Indian female with bow and spear	Female seated, leaning on bale; railroad, ships and city in distance. UNION BANK, Boston, Mass.	2 Gen. Taylor.
3 Female	Spread eagle and ships. UNION BANK, Boston, Mass.	3 Webster
5 Washington	Three females. Figure 5 running the entire length of the bill. UNION BANK, Boston, Mass.	5
10 10	Sailor with flag; ships. Letter X running the entire length of the bill. UNION BANK, Boston, Mass.	10 10
XX State Arms	20 Female and eagle. 20 UNION BANK, Boston, Mass. Hercules	XX Portrait. XX
50 Indian female with bow and arrow	State Arms with female on each side. UNION BANK, Boston, Mass. Clasped hands	50 Portrait of J. Q. Adams.
100 State Arms.	Portrait of Washington surrounded by arms of the States. UNION BANK, Boston, Mass. Hercules	100 Cupid in a sail boat. 100

Left end	Centre	Right end
500 D	Two female figures with spear, wand, etc., ship and building in distance UNION B'K. Boston Five Hundred Dollars Boston	500 D
ONE	State Arms supported by two females. 1 Head of Franklin UNION BANK, Haverhill, Mass. Eagle	1 Female. ONE
TWO	Farming scene; female and four males reclining; load of hay. 2 UNION BANK, Haverhill, Mass. Clasped hands	2 Boy.
THREE	Female with horn of plenty; ships on left in distance; on right manufacturing scene. 3 UNION BANK, Haverhill, Mass. Wheels, bale, etc	3 Squaw and child.
5	Two females supporting an oval, with head of female enclosed; eagle on top; head of Washington on right hand corner, enclosed in large fig. 5. 5 UNION BANK. Haverhill, Mass. Imp. and products.	5
TEN	Horse clearing scene. Female on X. UNION BANK, Haverhill, Mass. State arms	10 Female and three children.
20 Female with helmet and spear.	2 Female. 0 UNION BANK, Haverhill, Mass. XX	20 Female, globe and horn of plenty. 20
Man holding fig. 20. 20	Female reclining on cornucopia with distaff; ship in distance. UNION BANK, Haverhill, Mass.	20 Sea monster. Steamship
50 Female.	Male and female. UNION BANK, Haverhill, Mass. 50	50 Cupid in boat 50
Cherub and dolphin. 50	Squaw seated; deer and hills in distance. UNION BANK, Haverhill. Mass.	50 Justice seated.

100 | Facie on limb of tree; cars and canal scene in distance. | 100
UNION BANK,
Haverhill, Mass.
Male seated | 100 | Female seated.

State Arms. | Indian reclining; deer. | 100
UNION BANK,
Haverhill, Mass.
100 | Female representing Agriculture.

Agricultural scene; female prominent. | 500 D | 500
UNION BANK,
Haverhill, Mass.
500

Laocoon and serpents. | THOUSAND | 1000
Cars
Ship.
Title of Bank.
1000 | 1000

(Old Plate.)
ONE | 1 Interior of a blacksmith's shop. 1 | ONE
Bust of Washington. | Female.
UNION BANK OF WEYMOUTH AND BRAINTREE,
Weymouth, Mass.
ONE | ONE

(New Plate.)
1 | ONE
Female with sickle and sheaf of wheat; reapers and farm house in background.
UNION BANK OF WEYMOUTH AND BRAINTREE,
Weymouth, Mass.
Portrait of Washington. | Train of cars. | 1

(Old Plate.)
TWO | 2 Farming scene. 2 | TWO
Female. | Female.
UNION BANK OF WEYMOUTH AND BRAINTREE,
Weymouth, Mass.
2 | 2

(New Plate.)
TWO | 2
UNION BANK OF WEYMOUTH AND BRAINTREE.
Weymouth, Mass.
Portrait of Z. Taylor.
TWO | Spread eagle and several flags bearing the names of the States.

(Old Plate.)
THREE | 3 Female and eagle. 3 | THREE
Farmer sharpening his scythe. | Sailor.
UNION BANK OF WEYMOUTH AND BRAINTREE,
Weymouth, Mass.
3 | 3

(New Plate.)
I I I | 3
UNION BANK OF WEYMOUTH AND BRAINTREE,
Weymouth, Mass.
3 | Two females, train of cars and ship in background. | Portrait of J. Q. Adams.

(Old Plate.)
5 | V Eagle and shipping. V | 5
FIVE | FIVE
UNION BANK OF WEYMOUTH AND BRAINTREE,
Weymouth, Mass.
5 | 5

(New Plate.)
FIVE | V
UNION BANK OF WEYMOUTH AND BRAINTREE.
Weymouth, Mass.
Webster
V | A street in Weymouth. | V

(Old Plate.)
10 | Man and oxen. 10 | TEN
X
UNION BANK OF WEYMOUTH AND BRAINTREE,
Weymouth, Mass.
Female.
10

(New Plate.)
TEN | X
UNION BANK OF WEYMOUTH AND BRAINTREE.
Weymouth, Mass.
Portrait of Washington.
A street in Weymouth.

(Old Plate.)
20 | XX Eagle. XX | 20
UNION BANK OF WEYMOUTH AND BRAINTREE,
Weymouth, Mass.
Female. | Ship.

(New Plate.)
XX | 20
UNION BANK OF WEYMOUTH AND BRAINTREE,
Weymouth, Mass.
Portrait of Franklin. | A street in Weymouth.

FIFTY | 50 Man and horse. 50 | FIFTY
Female. | Female.
UNION BANK OF WEYMOUTH AND BRAINTREE,
Weymouth, Mass.
FIFTY | FIFTY

100 across One Hundred. | Horses, wagons, shipping &c. | 100 across One Hundred.
UNION BANK OF WEYMOUTH AND BRAINTREE,
Weymouth, Mass.
Portrait. | Portrait.

Female seated pointing to reapers. | 500 D | 500
UNION BANK OF WEYMOUTH AND BRAINTREE,
Weymouth, Mass.
500

Laocoon and sons strangled by serpent. | Train of cars. | 1000
THOUSAND.
Title of Bank.
Female.
1000 | 1000

1 | Cattle and hogs; village in the background. 1 | ONE
VILLAGE BANK,
North Danvers, Mass.
Female.

2 | 2 | Female.
VILLAGE BANK,
North Danvers, Mass.
Ships and steamship. | TWO

3 | Train of cars. | 3
VILLAGE BANK,
North Danvers, Mass.
Portrait of Fillmore. | Female.

Female and sickle. | 5 | 5
VILLAGE BANK,
Danvers, Mass.
FIVE | Female and wheel, train of cars and steamship in background. | Female.

Female with sheaf of wheat. | Cattle and sheep, man on horseback. | 10
VILLAGE BANK,
North Danvers, Mass.
X | Washington on horseback.

20 | Female figure and two cherubs. | 20
VILLAGE BANK,
North Danvers, Mass.
Female, eagle, chest, &c. | Female.

20 | VILLAGE BANK,
Danvers, Mass. | 20
Female holding grain in right hand. | Figures 20, XX, and the word Twenty. | Man plowing with two horses.

50 | Two females; factories and ship in background. | 50
Female with sickle. | VILLAGE BANK,
North Danvers, Mass.
50 | Farmer gathering corn.

50 | VILLAGE BANK,
Danvers, Mass. | 50
FIFTY
Horses and portion of wall, man, etc. | Male portrait.

100 | VILLAGE BANK,
Danvers, Mass. | 100
1 0 0
C
Female portrait. | Two mechanics erect.

100 — VILLAGE BANK, North Danvers, Mass. — 100. Female and cupid floating in the air, over a city. Portrait of female. Sailor and flag. 100.

D — VILLAGE BANK, Danvers, Mass. — 500. Three females, two seated, one erect with open book. Round red die on which is figs. 500 and words Five Hundred. Female holding cornucopia and flowers.

WALTHAM BANK, Waltham, Mass. — 1. Sailor hoisting a flag. Female reclining, locomotive and factories, millstream and cows in background. Cupid. 1.

3 — WALTHAM BANK, Waltham, Mass. — 2. A mechanic [illegible] stone cutting. Females raking hay. Farmer, rake and plough.

3 — WALTHAM BANK, Waltham, Mass. — 3. Female reclining on bales; barrels; factory in distance. Farmer with scythe. Mechanic, sailor and farmer with fig. 3.

Female. — WALTHAM BANK, Waltham Mass. — 5. Men, women and children; [illegible] scene. 5. Female.

10 — WALTHAM BANK, Waltham, Mass. — 10. Indian; river, canoe, deer in background. Female. Female.

20 — TWENTY. Boy TWENTY. watering two horses at trough; woman, &c. — 20. Two females with sickle, grain, &c. WALTHAM BANK. Twenty Dollars. Waltham, Mass. Female beside spinning wheel.

20 — 2 Female 0 — 20. WALTHAM BANK, Waltham, Mass. XX. Female. Female figure. 20.

Factories, &c. — Two females seated on bale. FIFTY State Arms. — 50. WALTHAM BANK. Fifty Dollars. 50. Mechanic at work.

50 — Male and female. WALTHAM BANK, Waltham, Mass. 50 — 50. Cupid in a sailboat. Female. 50.

100 — WALTHAM BANK. C Two children at foot of tree; cows, sheep, &c. C. Waltham. One Hundred Dollars. Massachusetts. — 100. Sailor, mechanic, ships, machinery, &c. Public Building.

100 — Spread eagle, railroad and canal. WALTHAM BANK. Waltham, Mass. 100 — 100. Vulcan the Blacksmith. Female.

D — WALTHAM BANK, Massachusetts. Sailor and soldier, flag, fort, cannon, shot, &c. Five Hundred. — 500. Five Hundred Dollars. Five Hundred Dollars.

1 — Brick layers. 1 — 1. Indian with bow and hatchet. WAMESIT BANK Lowell, Mass. Stone cutter.

TWO, U, S — Carpenter at work. 2 — 2. Indians. WAMESIT BANK Lowell, Mass. Female bathing. Man sitting on the ground, factories in background.

3 — Indian [illegible] a cliff overlooking a city. Large figure 3 with State Arms top—Title across 3. — 3. THREE. Hay makers.

FIVE — Large V with five at top, Man with sickle and sheaf of wheat, at bottom. — 5. Train of cars passing under a bridge. WAMESIT BANK Lowell, Mass. Cattle, train of cars in distance.

TEN — 10 TEN. Two males and two females, city in background. WAMESIT BANK Lowell, Mass. TEN. A male and two females, [illegible] yoke of oxen.

Male, female, two children and a dog. State arms. 20 — Female. WAMESIT BANK Lowell, Mass. TWENTY. 20.

FIFTY DOLLARS 50 Four female figures so arranged as to extend across the entire length of the bill. — 50. WAMESIT BANK Lowell, Mass. Female bathing.

100 — WAMESIT BANK, Lowell, Mass. — 100. Two men loading wagon with sheafs; man holding horses. ONE HUNDRED. Female bathing. Squaw and female.

D — WAMESIT BANK, Lowell, Mass. Female erect with shield and spear. Three females in clouds with quadrant, sickle, compass and cornucopia. 500.

ONE — Indian reclining; deer behind him; gold dollar. — 1. Female erect with fig. 1. WAMSUTTA BANK, Fall River, Mass. Indian head.

2 — Male and female seated, two gold dollars; cattle, trees and house in distance. — 2. Female representing Agriculture. WAMSUTTA BANK, Fall River, Mass. Squaw seated.

3 — Mechanic, sailor and farmer seated with implements and three gold dollars. — THREE. Female portrait. WAMSUTTA BANK, Fall River, Mass. Liberty and a squaw.

V — Five gold dollars, three cherubs, hunter and Indian, cars in distance. — 5. Farmer with scythe. WAMSUTTA BANK, Fall River, Mass. Female portrait.

10 — Nine cherubs, ten gold dollars, female, cornucopia, shield, &c.; cars and steamboat in distance. — X. WAMSUTTA BANK, Fall River, Mass. Indian head. Mechanic. Cherub and dolphin.

FIFTY — Indian, squaw and papoose seated; city in distance. — 50. Female with shield and spear. WAMSUTTA BANK, Fall River, Mass. Female portrait.

Deer and dog. — Female seated on rock; three cherubs sporting in water with dolphin. — 100. HUNDR'D. WAMSUTTA BANK, Fall River, Mass. Indian head.

1 | Female Railroad and shipping. 1 | 1
WAREHAM BANK Wareham, Mass. | Female.

1 | View of Tremont Iron Works, buildings, horse and chaise, cars, &c. | 1
WAREHAM BANK, Wareham, Mass.
Man and machinery. | ONE DOLLAR. | Male Portrait.

2 | Farm, ox and sheep. 2 | TWO
WAREHAM BANK Wareham, Mass. | Female.
2 | TWO

Boy whittling under tree, child lying down, cows, sheep, &c. | WAREHAM B'K. Wareh'm. Mass. | TWO on 2
Eagle poised on rock.
2 | TWO DOLLARS. | Male Portrait.

3 | Farming scene. 3 | 3
Female.
WAREHAM BANK Wareham, Mass.
3 | T HREE

Spread eagle and shield; village in distance. | Large V; female and cupid with it. | 5
FIVE | WAREHAM BANK Wareham, Mass. | Girl

V WARE'H'M BK. V Small State arms. V | 5
5 | Wareham, Mass.
Sailor aloft with spy glass in hand, other hand on stay.
5 | Male Portrait.

Signing of the Declaration of Independence. X | 10
WAREHAM BANK Wareham, Mass. | Train of cars.
X

Vulcan the blacksmith. X | 10
TEN | WAREHAM BANK Wareham, Mass. | Reaper.

TEN | Small arms of State. | 10
WAREHAM B'K, Wareham, Mass.
Female, anchor, steamship, and light-house | TEN. Male Portrait. | TEN

20 | XX Eagle. XX | 20
WAREHAM BANK Wareham, Mass.
Female. | Ship.

View of Tremont Nail Works. | WAREHAM B'K. Wareham, Mass. | 20
20 | Male Portrait

FIFTY | 50 Man and horse. 50 | FIFTY
Female | WAREHAM BANK Wareham, Mass. | Female.
FIFTY | FIFTY

FIFTY DOLLARS. | WAREHAM BANK. Wareham, Mass. | 50
State arms.
50 | Male Portrait. | Interior of an Iron Foundry.
FIFTY DOLLARS on FIFTY.

One Hundred and 100. | Horse, waggons, shipping, &c. | Same as left
Portrait. | WAREHAM BANK Wareham, Mass. | Portrait.

View of Tremont Iron Works. | C
WAREHAM B'K, Male Portrait.
Wareham, Mass.
100 | ONE HUNDRED DOLLARS. | Dog and safe.

Portrait | 1
WARREN BANK, Danvers, Mass.
1 | Large portrait. ONE | Female

Portrait. | 2
WARREN BANK, Danvers, Mass.
2 | Large portrait. TWO | Female and fig. 2

Female | 3
WARREN BANK, Danvers, Mass.
3 | Large Portrait. | Indian, woman.

5 | 5
WARREN BANK, Danvers, Mass.
Two females. | Large portrait. | Portrait.

10 | 10
WARREN BANK, Danvers, Mass.
Indian, woman. | Large Portrait. | Female.

XX inverted | WARREN BANK, South Danvers, Mass. | 20
Justice. | Large portrait of George Peabody red 20 each side. | Milkmaid churning.

FIFTY | Title of Bank. | FIFTY
Goddess of Liberty with cap, pole, shield and scroll.
Peasant girl. | Same as above 20s.

100 | Title of Bank. | 100
Same as above 20s.
Farmer and dog. | Female portrait.

500 | WARREN BANK | 500
So. Danvers | Large oval male portrait
Five Hundred Dollars | Five Hundred
MASSACHUSETTS

1 | Spread eagle; capitol at Washington on right; steamboat on left. | Merchandise
WASHINGTON B'K, Boston, Mass. | 1
Washington. | Train of cars

ONE | 1 Indian in a canoe. 1 | ONE
Washington and his horse | WASHINGTON B'K, Boston, Mass. | Bust of Washington.
ONE | ONE

1 | Washington reading paper; man writing on drum head; horse, negro, cannon, men, etc. | 1
WASHINGTON BK., Boston, Mass.
Drummer and soldiers. | Portrait with frilled cap.

Cupid and 2. | Title of Bank. | 2 and Cupid
Washington on frame; female, soldier, Indians, TWO either side.
2 | 2

2 | View of the State House. | 2
WASHINGTON B'K, Boston, Mass.
Portrait of Washington. | State Arms.

Left end	Centre	Right end
TWO TWO	2 Shipping. 2 WASHINGTON B'K., Boston, Mass.	TWO Washington and his horse TWO
3	Washington on horse; officer submitting plans; other officers, cannon, horses, etc. Title of Bank.	3 Washington.
Female THREE	Large steamships and sail vessels. WASHINGTON B'K., Boston, Mass. Washington	3 Sailor.
5 Washington and his horse	View of the State House. WASHINGTON B'K., Boston, Mass.	5 Female.
TEN Washington and his horse	Train of cars. WASHINGTON B'K., Boston, Mass. State Arms	10 Steamship TEN
TWENTY Squaw with bow and spear.	XX Spread eagle and shield; Capitol at Washington on right; steamship on left. WASHINGTON B'K., Boston, Mass. Washington	20
50 Washington.	Female seated, leaning on a bale; ships on right; railroad and canal on left. WASHINGTON B'K., Boston, Mass. Shell	50 50
100 Washington and his horse	100 Sailor seated on the ground. WASHINGTON B'K., Boston, Mass.	100 100
Bunker Hill Monument. ONE	WEBSTER BANK, Boston, Mass. Portrait of Webster. ONE DOLLAR	1
Bunker Hill Monument. TWO	WEBSTER BANK, Boston, Mass. Portrait of Webster. TWO DOLLARS	2
Bunker Hill Monument. THREE	WEBSTER BANK, Boston, Mass. Portrait of Webster. 3 DOLLARS	3
Bunker Hill Monument. FIVE	WEBSTER BANK, Boston, Mass. Portrait of Webster. FIVE DOLLARS	5
5	WEBSTER BANK, Boston, Mass. 5 Full length figure of Webster. 5	5
Bunker Hill Monument. X on left TEN	WEBSTER BANK, Boston, Mass. Portrait of Webster. TEN DOLLARS	10 X
XX Twenty on XX	WEBSTER BANK, Boston, Mass. Portrait of Webster. TWENTY DOLLARS	20 View of Faneuil Hall.
50 FIFTY	WEBSTER BANK, Boston, Mass. Portrait of Webster. FIFTY DOLLARS	50 View of Faneuil Hall.
100 100	WEBSTER BANK, Boston, Mass. Portrait of Webster. ONE HUNDRED DOLLA'S	C View of Faneuil Hall.
500 500	WEBSTER BANK, Boston, Mass. Portrait of Webster.	500 View of Faneuil Hall.
M 1000	WEBSTER BANK, Boston, Mass. Portrait of Webster.	1000 View of Faneuil Hall.
ONE Portrait of Z. Taylor. 1	Indian sitting on a rock, also plough and log cabin. 1 WESTFIELD BANK Westfield, Mass. Female.	1 ONE on Medallion head. ONE
2 State arms. TWO	Two females; farming scene in background. 2 WESTFIELD BANK Westfield, Mass. Fish.	TWO Indians. TWO
THREE Dogs. THREE	WESTFIELD BANK Westfield, Mass. Three men. Dog, key and safe.	3 Female teaching children. THREE
Two males and three females.	FIVE Westfield Green. WESTFIELD BANK Westfield, Mass.	5
10 Train of cars and vessel.	Westfield Green. WESTFIELD BANK Westfield, Mass. Locomotive	X Medallion head. 10
TWENTY Female drawing water at a well.	Westfield Green. WESTFIELD BANK Westfield, Mass. Load of hay.	20 on med head Blacksmith shop.
50 Cattle.	WESTFIELD BANK Westfield, Mass. Westfield Green.	50 Female on whip machine.
1 1	WOBURN BANK Woburn, Mass. Female reclining, train of cars, milk maids and cars in background. Wheels, bale, etc.	1 Child and Dolphin.
Farmer, milk maid and cows 2	Train of cars. WOBURN BANK Woburn, Mass.	2 Females raking hay.
Female eagle, and ships. 3	WOBURN BANK Woburn, Mass.	3 Cupid and figure 3.
Female feeding an eagle from a cup. 5	WOBURN BANK Woburn, Mass. FIVE	5 Five females and fig. 5.

TEN Female. WOBURN BANK Woburn, Mass. Train of cars. TEN 10 Horses and load of hay.	L 501 Shepherd boy and sheep. WORCESTER BANK, Worcester, Mass. 50 Female.	X Squaw. WORCESTER CO. BK Blackstone, Mass. Three females representing Agriculture, Commerce and Manufactures. 10 Cupid and dolphin
20 Portrait of Washington. WOBURN BANK Woburn, Mass. Spread eagle, Capitol at Washington and steamship in background. 20 TWENTY	100 Female, sickle and sheaf of wheat. Vig. Winged female with a trumpet, also globe and eagle. WORCESTER BANK, Worcester, Mass. C Female. C	TEN Vulcan the blacksmith. X WORCESTER CO. B'K Blackstone, Mass. 10 Reaper.
50 WOBURN BANK Woburn, Mass. Two females, factories steamship and train of cars in background. 50 Female, vessel, etc. FIFTY	500 Med. head Spread eagle on shield, cars, city, vessels, &c., in distance. WORCESTER BANK, Worcester, Mass. D D Med. head.	20 Female. 2 Female 0 WORCESTER CO. B'K Blackstone, Mass. XX 20 Female. 20
100 State Arms WOBURN BANK Woburn, Mass. 100 Capitol at Washington. 100	1 Portrait of Webster. (New Plate.) Man sitting on the ground, anvil, hammer &c, Factories and train of cars in background. WORCESTER CO. B'K Blackstone, Mass. 1 Indian woman.	20 Girl's head. WORCESTER CO BK Mass. Three 20s and words Twenty Dollars on green die 20 Cattle, telegraph, bridge, cars etc
1 Female. Large figure 1 with portrait of Washington. WORCESTER BANK, Worcester, Mass. 1 Carpenter at his bench.	Female, Railroad and canal 1 (Old Plate.) 1 WORCESTER CO B'K Blackstone, Mass 1 Female.	50 Two children. WORCESTER CO. BK Mass. Green die with fig. 50, words Fifty, Fifty Dollars and Massachusetts on it. 50 Clay.
2 Farmer sharpening a scythe. Portrait of Washington, and large figure 2. WORCESTER BANK, Worcester, Mass. 2 Dog and safe.	2 Female. (New Plate.) WORCESTER CO. B'K Blackstone, Mass. Two females, and bust of Washington, ship in distance 2 Portrait of Washington.	50 Female. Male and female. WORCESTER CO. B'K Blackstone, Mass. 50 50 Cupid [illegible] boat. 50
3 Portrait. Large figure 3 and portrait. WORCESTER BANK, Worcester, Mass. 3 Female.	2 Farmers and sheep; stream of water. 2 WORCESTER CO. B'K Blackstone, Mass. TWO Female. TWO	C Franklin. WORCESTER CO. BK Mass. Green die with fig. 100, words One Hundred Dollars and Massachusetts on it. 100 Dog & safe.
5 Female Indian. Portrait of female. 5 Portrait of female. WORCESTER BANK, Worcester, Mass. 5 Female.	3 Farming scene 3 WORCESTER CO. B'K Blackstone, Mass. 3 Female. THREE	100 Vulcan the black smith. Spread eagle, Railroad and canal. WORCESTER CO. B'K Blackstone, Mass. 100 100 Female.
10 Blacksmith. Female, farmers loading hay; train of cars. WORCESTER BANK, Worcester, Mass. 10 10 [illegible]	5 Train of cars. (New Plate.) WORCESTER CO. B'K Blackstone, Mass. Female reclining, train of cars, shipping, milk maids and cars in background. 5 Arms.	C Man fishing. 100 Eagle on bale of goods, &c. 100 WORCESTER CO. BK. Blackstone, Mass. 100 Female with sickle and grain. 100
Female with sheaf of wheat. 20 Indian and female. WORCESTER BANK, Worcester, Mass. 20 Farmer sowing seed	FIVE (Old Plate.) Spread eagle and shield. Large V; Female and cupid. WORCESTER CO. B'K Blackstone, Mass. 5 Girl.	1 Soldiers, boy beating drum. Man shoeing horse, man sitting on log and man standing. WRENTHAM BANK, Wrentham, Mass. 1 Two children

2 on TWO Pynchon House TWO	Female seated in large figure 2, farming scene in distance. Mass. 2 PYNCHON BANK TWO DOLLARS Springfield	TWO Female with globe, pole and bird
3 A bull's head. THREE	Two horses and eagle; train of cars, factory and steamboat in background. PYNCHON BANK, Springfield, Mass.	3 THREE
Large figure 5, female and shield. FIVE	PYNCHON BANK, Springfield, Mass. 5 Three boys and ship. 5	5 Old Pynchon House. 5
X, 10, Ten Old Pynchon House. TEN	Man ploughing with yoke of oxen and horse. PYNCHON BANK, Springfield, Mass. X	10 Two females.
20 Portrait of Webster.	Indian and plough, log cabin &c. 20 on right. PYNCHON BANK. Springfield, Mass. XX	XX Female.
Female.	50 Signing of the Declaration of Independence, PYNCHON BANK. Springfield. Mass.	50 Portrait of Washington.
100 Female.	PYNCHON BANK, Springfield, Mass C Female leaning upon a chest; old Pynchon House in the distance.	100
1 Head of John Adams. ONE	Vig. A scene in Quincy; horses, teams, stream of water, and sloops. QUINCY STONE BK. Quincy, Mass.	1 Head of John Hancock. ONE
TWO Head of John Hancock. 2	Vig. Same as ones. QUINCY STONE BK Quincy, Mass.	2 Head of John Adams. TWO
THREE John Adams. 3	Vig Same as ones. QUINCY STONE BK. Quincy, Mass.	3 John Hancock. THREE

5 John Hancock. FIVE	Vig. Same as ones. QUINCY STONE BK. Quincy, Mass.	5 John Adams. FIVE
X John Hancock. TEN	Vig. Same as ones. QUINCY STONE BK. Quincy, Mass.	10 John Adams. TEN
20 John Adams. TWENTY	Vig. Same as ones. QUINCY STONE BK. Quincy, Mass.	20 John Hancock. TWENTY
FIFTY Female with wreath in hand. FIFTY	50 Vig. Man and horse. 50 QUINCY STONE BK. Quincy, Mass.	FIFTY Female with horn of plenty. FIFTY
Stone quarry, oxen, wagon, men, railroad, &c. 50	L QUINCY STONE B'K, Quincy, Mass.	50 Male Portrait.
100 Eagle. 100	C Vig. Horses, one man with truck, &c 100 QUINCY STONE BK. Quincy, Mass.	C Head of Washington C
Same as right. Harrison.	Scene on wharf. QUINCY STONE BK., Quincy, Mass.	One Hundred and 100. Columbus
C State arms.	QUINCY STONE B'K, Quincy, Mass. C Franklin in study. C	100 Female Portrait.
500	Indian paddling in canoe. 500 Title of Bank. D D	500 Female with sword and scales.
500 D	QUINCY STONE B'K, Quincy, Mass. D Eagle. D	500 D

1000	Spread eagle on promontory; ship in distance. 1000 QUINCY STONE B'K, Quincy. Mass.	1000 Indian female with bow and arrows.
Head of female. 1	Vig. Church, court-houses, dwellings, trees, men on horseback, carriages, &c., which is a view of Main street, Worcester QUINSIGAMOND BANK, Worcester, Mass	1 Portrait of male.
2 Plank road scene.	Vig Same as ones QUINSIGAMOND BANK, Worcester, Mass Female head.	2 Houses in distance; railroad train &c.
Mason at work. 3	Vig. Same as ones, QUINSIGAMOND BANK, Worcester, Mass. Eagle.	3 Female with bundle of grain under her arm.
5	Vig Same as ones. Male Portrait. QUINSIGAMOND BANK, Worcester, Mass.	5 Female with flowers.
Wm. Penn. TEN	QUINSIGAMOND BK Worcester, Mass. Street in Worcester	10 Indian seated.
10 X 10	Vig. Cincinnatus at his plough, oxen &c. 10 QUINSIGAMOND BANK, Worcester, Mass.	TEN Full length female and horn of plenty.
State Arms. 20	Vig. Female figure with wings, blowing trumpet; eagle with arrows, &c. in his talons. QUINSIGAMOND BANK. Worcester, Mass.	20 Portrait of J. Q. Adams.
50 Head of Washington.	QUINSIGAMOND BANK Worcester, Mass. Vig. Two cows in water, one lying down; two sheep reclining and one standing.	50
100 Figure of Justice with scales and sword.	Vig. House and cattle in distance; dairy maid, pail and two cows QUINSIGAMOND BANK, Worcester, Mass.	100 Head of Franklin.

Left	Centre	Right
500 Three horses, balances, female, dog, basket, bottle, &c.	QUINSIGAMOND BANK, Worcester.	500 Medallion head of Washington.
1 Female 1	Female seated beside shield, etc ONE cars and bridge in distance 1 RAILROAD BANK ONE DOLLAR Lowell Massachusetts	ONE
TWO Archimedes 2	2 Vig. same as $1 note 2 THE RAILROAD BK, Lowell, Mass.	TWO
3 Vulcan. 3	THREE Female locomotive, buildings, etc. 3 RAILROAD BANK, Lowell, Mass.	THREE
Male portrait 5	View of depot, cars, church, etc. RAILROAD BANK, Lowell. Mass.	5 Five females surrounding fig. 5.
10 X	View of buildings, pedestrians, etc. Title of Bank.	X Male portrait
XX 20	RAILROAD BANK, Lowell, Mass. Male portrait	20 Factory girl with wheel.
50	Factories, etc. Title of Bank.	50 Male portrait
100 Female seated holding spool of cotton; factories	Title of Bank. Factories, etc.	100 Male portrait.
500 500	Railroad depot, cars, church, etc. Male portrait Title of Bank.	500 Indian chief erect on shield.

Left	Centre	Right
Two farmers, one tying up grain. 1	1 Beehive. RANDOLPH BANK, Randolph, Mass.	1 Boots and shoes. ONE
TWO Boots and shoes. 2	2 Vig. Drover on horseback, cattle dogs, &c.; cattle lying down RANDOLPH BANK, Randolph, Mass. Dog and safe.	2 Portrait of Franklin.
THREE Portrait of Jefferson. 3	THREE Spr'd eagle. THREE RANDOLPH BANK, Randolph, Mass. Farmer's reaping.	3 Washington, and his horse. THREE
5 Female child.	Vig. Three females, one with liberty pole and cap; Eagle on left of vig; and ship on right. V RANDOLPH BANK, Randolph, Mass. Dog and safe.	5 Boots and shoes. FIVE
TEN Female in the act of pouring water from a pitcher.	10 Vig. Blacksmith shoeing horse, and man holding horse by the head. X RANDOLPH BANK, Randolph, Mass. Bundles of grain.	10 Boots and shoes.
20 Minerva	2 Female figure with rake. 0 RANDOLPH BANK, Randolph, Mass. XX	20 Female with horn of plenty; globe and trident. 20
Female with flag and shield; Indian female at her feet	20 Two shoemakers at work; female at household duties in background. RANDOLPH BANK, Randolph, Mass.	20 Cattle, telegraph; cars on bridge
50 Minerva.	Vig. State Arms. Male and female figure; horn of plenty between them; rake on females right, grain on left. RANDOLPH BANK, Randolph, Mass. 50	50 Cupid afloat. 50
FIFTY Female representing Agriculture. 50	50 Farmer seated with implements and products; load of hay, buildings, etc., in distance. 50 Title of Bank.	50 Female portrait.
100 Female portrait.	Two females seated; steamer, etc., in distance on left; buildings, monument, etc., on right. Title of Bank	100 Train of cars bridge and cars in distance.

Left	Centre	Right
100 Male sitting, with scroll in right hand.	Vig. Spread eagle on branch; canal boats and lock; railroad train in distance. RANDOLPH BANK, Randolph, Mass. 100	100 Female sitting with rule in right hand, and grain in left, resting on horn of plenty.
Female figure; reapers; team laden with grain. 500	500 D RANDOLPH BANK, Randolph, Mass.	500
1 Man carrying leather.	1 REVERE BANK, Male portrait. Boston, Mass.	1 State Arms.
2 Blacksmiths boy at forge.	Male portrait. Stonecutter and man with plan. Title of Bank.	2 State Arms.
3 Sailor boy, etc.	Title of Bank. Male portrait.	3 State Arms.
5 State Arms.	Steamship, tug, city, etc. Title of Bank.	5 Male portrait
10 State Arms.	General scene in moulding shop; men, wheels, machinery, etc. Title of Bank.	10 Male portrait
20 State Arms.	REVERE BANK, Boston, Mass. 20 DOLLS. in red.	20 Male portrait
50 State Arms.	Title of Bank. Male portrait. L L	50 Mechanic, sailor, etc. and [illegible]
100 State Arms.	Title of Bank. Male portrait. C	100 Surveyors at work.

500 State Arms.	Title of Bank. Hogshead, bales, rope, masts, land, etc.; steamboat in distance.	500 Male portrait
1	Oval die, through is seen a female, train of cars and city in distance; a female each side of the die, steamboat and train of cars in the background. ROCKLAND BANK, Roxbury, Mass.	1 Farmer, plough and rake and ONE on half shield.
Portrait of female. 2	Farmers and sheep. ROCKLAND BANK, Roxbury, Mass.	2 Female and 1 2
3	ROCKLAND BANK, Roxbury, Mass. Farmer with scythe, sailor with spy glass, and mechanic, anvil, hammer &c., also three gold dollars. THREE	3 A dog's head
5 Portrait. FIVE	ROCKLAND BANK, Roxbury, Mass. A man with gun, Indian woman, three cupids and five gold dollars.	5
X Two females.	ROCKLAND BANK, Roxbury, Mass. Farming scene.	X Portrait of Washington.
State Arms. XX	Farmer ploughing, cattle and horses in pasture; city in distance. ROCKLAND BANK, Roxbury, Mass.	20 Portrait.
50 . and Cupid	ROCKLAND BANK, Roxbury, Mass. Ships, and city in the background.	50 50
C Fountain.	ROCKLAND BANK, Roxbury, Mass. Farming scene, men women and children.	100 Portrait of Jefferson.
D Female and horse.	ROCKLAND BANK, Roxbury, Mass. 500 Female reclining, eagle, globe; ship and steamship in distance.	500 500

ONE 1	Vig. Wood scene, man sowing grain; ox team. 1 FOCKPORT DANK, Rockport, Mass.	1 Full rigged ship. ONE
Blacksmith, sledge and anvil. 1	Team of oxen, stone quarry, &c. ROCKPORT BANK, Rockport, Mass. Man plowing.	1 Stone cutter.
Sailor and capstan; masts, bbls and bales. 2	Same as ones. ROCKPORT BANK, Rockport, Mass. Loading wagon.	2 Two females.
TWO 2	Vig. Spread eagle, cannon balls; cog wheels; train of cars. 2 ROCKPORT BANK, Rockpcrt, Mass.	2 TWO Schooner and sloop in a storm.
THREE 3	Vig. Sailor, bales of goods, shipping; houses, horse, dray, &c. 3 ROCKPORT BANK, Rockport, Mass.	3 THREE Train of cars.
THREE Knickerbocker.	Same as ones. ROCKPORT BANK, Rockport, Mass. Eagle.	3 Female reaper
Man with cradle. 5	Same as ones. ROCKPORT BANK, Rockport, Mass.	5 Female.
FIVE	Vig. Eagle standing on shield and anchor; town in distance; foundries, &c. Female and child in large figure five. ROCKPORT BANK, Rockport, Mass.	FIVE Girl holding basket.
Soldier with sword. TEN	Same as ones. ROCKPORT BANK, Rockport, Mass.	10 Female portrait.
TEN	Vig. Man sitting holding sledge; train of cars crossing bridge. X ROCKPORT BANK, Rockport, Mass.	10 Man holding sickle and sheaf of grain

20 Female sitting, book in her lap.	XX Eagle. XX ROCKPORT BANK, Rockport, Mass.	20 Full rigged ship.
Female. XX	Same as ones. ROCKPORT BANK, Rockport, Mass. Cow and calf	20 Male portrait
Franklin. 50	Same as ones. ROCKPORT BANK, Rockport, Mass. Shield.	50 Male portrait
FIFTY Female.	50 Vig. Man training horse. 50 ROCKPORT BANK, Rockport, Mass.	FIFTY Female. FIFTY
Male portrait 100	Same as ones. ROCKPORT BANK, Rockport, Mass. Dog's head.	100 Webster
The figures 100, with the words one hundred across. Portrait of Harrison.	Vig. Loading covered waggons with merchandise. ROCKPORT BANK, Rockport, Mass.	The figures 100, with the words one hundred across. Fancy portrait.
ONE	Female seated on the ground; factory village in the distance 1 on right. ROLLSTONE BANK, Fitchburg, Mass. Wheels, bale, etc	1 Female and 3 cherubs.
2	Female riding upon the back of a reindeer. 2 ROLLSTONE BANK, Fitchburg, Mass. Cars	TWO Two females
3	Milk maid and cows. 3 ROLLSTONE BANK, Fitchburg, Mass.	3 Portrait of female. THREE
5	Train of cars. Female in large V. ROLLSTONE BANK, Fitchburg, Mass. State Arms	5 Female, chest and horn of plenty and 5.

TEN
Female with sickle, farmers gathering grain in the background. X
10
ROLLSTONE BANK, Fitchburg, Mass
Female figure.
Female head

20
Female.
2 Female. 0
ROLLSTONE BANK. Fitchburg, Mass.
XX
20
Female.
20

50
Female.
Male and female.
ROLLSTONE BANK, Fitchburg, Mass
50
50
Cupid in a sail boat.
50

100
Vulcan the blacksmith.
Spread eagle, railroad and canal.
ROLLSTONE BANK, Fitchburg, Mass
100
100
Female.

100
Female with ta[illegible] [illegible] at [illegible]
ROLLSTONE BANK, Fitchburg, Mass.
C Male portrait. C
100
Female, child, pole and cap.

ONE
Three females floating in water supporting cupid.
SAFETY FUND BK, Boston, Mass.
1
State Arms.

2
Female erect beside pedestal; steamer in distance.
Scene in the Arctic Regions; men shoving boat; dog, icebergs, etc.
Title of Bank.
2
State Arms.

THREE on 3.
Scene in Printing office, Faust, Gutenberg and Schoeffer. Eagle
Title of Bank.
3
State Arms
3

State Arms.
5
Title of Bank.
Apotheosis of Washington; soldier on left; female and two Indians on right. Red V each side.
5
Dog, key and safe.

10
Franklin at work at printing case
State Arms. Two females, owl, buildings, steamer, etc.
Title of Bank
Eagle.
10
Sailor with anchor.

20
State Arms.
Three females, safe, etc.
SAFETY FUND BK., Boston, Mass.
20
Clay

50
Boy and rabbits.
Female on left of view of city, boats, shipbuilding, etc.; 50 on stone and Indian in canoe on right; steamboat in distance.
SAFETY FUND BK., Boston, Mass.
50
State Arms.

C
State Arms.
Title of Bank.
Four females on globe.
One Hundred Dollars.
100
Male portrait

500
Female seated on bale; globe, steamboat, etc.
SAFETY FUND BK Boston, Mass
Auditors Die.
Five Hundred Dollars.
500
Old man, child and bust of Washington on table.

1
Three female figures.
1
Machinery and factories. Ship. Beehive.
SALEM BANK. Salem. Mass.
1
Portrait of Washington.
1

2
Masts, carrots, fruit, &c.
2
TWO
Shipping. Female figure. Farming scene.
SALEM BANK, Salem, Mass.
2
Female crowning a bust of Washington.
2

THREE
Female sitting on the ground, also anchor and bale; ship in distance. 3 Female, anchor, merchandise and ships.
SALEM BANK. Salem, Mass.
3
Portrait of Washington.
3

5
Female.
5
5 Female figure and ship. 5
FIVE
SALEM BANK. Salem, Mass.
5
Female and sickle.
5

Statue of Liberty leaning on column on which is letter X
Zouaves charging
SALEM BANK
TEN
Salem, Mass.
10
DOLLARS

10
Portrait of female.
TEN
1 Female with key and horn of plenty. 0
SALEM BANK. Salem, Mass.
[illegible]
10
Portrait of female.
TEN

10
X
10
(Old Plate.)
Man and oxen. 10
SALEM BANK, Salem. Mass.
TEN
Female

20
Female.
2 Female. 0
SALEM BANK, Salem, Mass.
XX
20
Female.
20

Ships at sea
50
Massachusetts
SALEM BANK
FIFTY DOLLARS
Salem
50
Dog's head

50
Female figure
Male and female.
SALEM BANK, Salem, Mass.
50
50
Cupid in a sail boat.
50

FIFTY
Grain, fruit, &c.
50
50 Three female fig's, ship, eagle, etc.
SALEM BANK, Salem, Mass.
Fifty on 50.
Vulcan seated with implements.

Female portrait
100
Massachusetts
Salem
SALEM BANK
One Hun'd Dol's
Cars passing over bridge, cattle in water, etc.
100

100
Vulcan the blacksmith.
Spread eagle, railroad and canal.
SALEM BANK, Salem, Mass.
100
100
Female.

Letter C.
Men and boats.
100
Spread eagle on bale; products, etc. 100
SALEM BANK, Salem, Mass.
100
Female.
100

500
Indian paddling canoe. 500 in red across light 500.
Title of Bank.
D
500

ONE
View of Merchants' Row
1
Indian seated on a rock; ship in distance.
SHAWMUT BANK, Boston, Mass.
[illegible]
1
View of Boston from harbor.
ONE

Left end	Centre	Right end
2 Same as ones TWO	Vig. Same as ones. SHAWMUT BANK, Boston, Mass. Men in boat, etc.	2 Same as ones TWO
THREE Same as ones on right end THREE	Vig. Same as ones. SHAWMUT BANK, Boston, Mass. Eagle	3 View of Merchants' Row
5 View of Boston from the harbor. FIVE	Vig. Same as ones. SHAWMUT BANK, Boston, Mass Anchor, etc	5 Same as 3s.
10 Same as fives 10	Vig. Same as ones. SHAWMUT BANK, Boston, Mass. 10	10 Same as fives 10
View of Merchants' Row XX	Vig. Same as ones. SHAWMUT BANK, Boston, Mass.	20 View of Boston from the harbor. 20
50 Same as 20s. 50	Vig. Same as ones. SHAWMUT BANK, Boston, Mass.	50 Same as 20s 50
C View of Boston from the harbor. C	Vig. Same as ones. SHAWMUT BANK, Boston, Mass.	100 View of Merchants' Row. 100
FIVE HUNDRED	Spread eagle, shield, etc. SHAWMUT BANK, Boston, Mass	Figs. 500. Male portrait Figs 500.
1000	Spread eagle shield and motto "E Pluribus Unum, etc. Title of Bank.	1000 Washington. 1000
Female erect by fig. 1. ONE on 1.	View of Shelburne Falls. SHELBURNE FALLS BANK, Shelburne Falls, Mass.	1 Female churning.

Left end	Centre	Right end
2 Farmer with scythe.	Farmers nooning; others loading wagon in distance Title of Bank.	2 Female representing Agriculture.
3 Blacksmith; anvil.	View of Shelburne Falls. 3 Title of Bank.	Liberty.
5 Washington	Mechanic seated with hammer; cars, factory, bridge and cattle in distance. Title of Bank.	5 Female with grain.
X	Female seated before shield, reclining on chest; milkmaid and cows in distance on right; cars and ships on left. Two men Title of Bank.	10 Female with shield, cornucopia and knives.
50 Female with flowers.	View of Shelburne Falls. Title of Bank.	50 Male portrait
100 Female portrait.	Three females representing Agriculture, Commerce and Manufactures. Title of Bank.	100 Franklin.
1 Men dressing leather. ONE	Shoe and Leather Dealers Store, horses, wagon, wharf and shipping. SHOE & LEATHER DEALERS' BANK, Boston, Mass.	1 Interior of shoemaker's shop. ONE
2 Interior of a shoemaker's shop. TWO	Vig. Same as ones. Title of Bank.	2 Morocco dressing TWO
3 Cows THREE	Vig. Same as ones. Title of Bank.	3 Interior of a shoemaker's shop. THREE
5 Morocco dressing	Vig. Same as ones Title of Bank.	5 Justice.

Left end	Centre	Right end
10 Washington and his horse TEN	Vig. Same as ones. Title of Bank.	10 Shipping. TEN
XX Indian with bow. 20	Vig. Same as ones. Title of Bank.	20 Eagle. XX
FIFTY Washington 50	Vig. Same as ones. Title of Bank. Some have fig. 50 on v'g.	50 Franklin. FIFTY
Words one hundred and figs. 100. Male portrait	Wharf scene—loading wagon, men, horses, shipping, &c. Title of Bank.	Words one hundred and figures 100. Male portrait
100 Justice seated.	Shoe and Leather Dealers' store; horses, wagon, men, wharf and shipping SHOE & LEATHER DEALERS BANK, Boston, Mass.	100 Female portrait.
500	Same as 100s. Title of Bank.	500 Cows
1	Vig. A man ploughing with two horses, and another sowing, two or three baskets, in the fore ground; cars in the distance. 1 SOUTHBRIDGE BK, Southbridge, Mass.	1 Spread Eagle. ONE
2	Vig. A large building; train of cars, man with wheelbarrow, and church in the distance. 2 SOUTHBRIDGE BK, Southbridge, Mass.	2 Man pitching hay
3	Vig. Train of cars, church and village at the left in the distance; and a building with cupola. 3 SOUTHBRIDGE BK, Southbridge, Mass.	3 Female with a basket in her hands
5 Female with torch beside column	V Large country house V SOUTHBRIDGE B'K FIVE DOLLARS Southbridge	5 General Geo. B. McClellan

FIVE
(Old Plate.)
FIVE Two female figures and eagle; train of cars and ship in background. FIVE
SOUTHBRIDGE B'K.
Southbridge, Mass.
5
Portrait.
FIVE

FIVE
Vig. Female sitting; a hand spinning wheel on the right of the scene, factory buildings; in the distance.
5
SOUTHBRIDGE BK,
Female head
5
Bust of a female
FIVE

Sailor and female either side of pedestal on which is bust of Washington
10
MASSACHUSETTS
10
on
Southbridge
SOUTHBRIDGE BK
TEN DOLLARS
10
Girl beside bank

10
Portrait.
10
(Old Plate.)
X Spread eagle. X
SOUTHBRIDGE B'K,
Southbridge, Mass.
10
Female.

TEN
Vig. A female sitting between the digits 1 & 0, holding key in her left hand a cornucopia at her right hand.
X
SOUTHBRIDGE BK,
Southbridge, Mass.
Shield.
10
General Taylor.
TEN

20
Female sitting.
XX Eagle XX
SOUTHBRIDGE BK,
Southbridge, Mass.
20
Ship

20
Female with flowers.
SOUTHBRIDGE B'K
Southbridge, Mass.
Female seated; sheep, etc.
20
Boy

50
Female and anchor; steamboat in distance.
50
FIFTY DOLLARS
50
SOUTHBRIDGE B'K.
Southbridge, Mass.
FIFTY

FIFTY
Large female figure wreath in right hand
FIFTY
50 50
Vig. A man holding a horse which is apparently trying to break away.
SOUTHBRIDGE BK,
Southbridge Mass.
FIFTY
Female standing, her left elbow resting on a column.
FIFTY

50
Two females.
SOUTHBRIDGE B'K
Southbridge, Mass.
Cattle scene; drovers, farmers, etc.
L
50
50

THE
100
SOUTHBRIDGE B'K
Southbridge, Mass.
Female at work on looms.
C
100
100
Female, spinning wheel, factories, etc.

Words one hundred across the figure 100.
Bust of Gen. Harrison.
Market waggon man and team.
SOUTHBRIDGE BK,
Southbridge, Mass.
Words one hundred across the figure 100.
Bust of Kosciusko

500
Vig. Agricultural scene, female among sheaves, men in the distance reaping. 500 and D on right.
SOUTHBRIDGE BK,
Southbridge, Mass.
500

Female and fig. 1.
1
Cupid rolling a silver dollar upon a Railroad track, train of cars and village in the distance.
SOUTH READING BK
South Reading, Mass
1
Portrait.

Female.
2
Two cherubs and two silver dollars, train of cars and cattle in the background.
SOUTH READING BK
South Reading, Mass.
2
Portrait.

3
Portrait.
Three cherubs and three silver dollars.
SOUTH READING B'K
South Reading. Mass
3
Blacksmith anvil and forge.

5
Portrait,
5
Five cherubs and five silver dollars.
SOUTH READING BK
South Reading, Mass.
5
Female and fig. 5

Farmer with basket of fruit and a cradle.
10
Portrait.
SOUTH READING BK
South Reading, Mass.
X
Female and anchor.

XX
Female.
Female reclining, locomotive and factory, milk maids and cows in background.
SOUTH READING BK
South Reading, Mass
20
Portrait.

Girl with sheaf of grain.
50
Female sitting on a rock, and cupids sporting with a dolphin in the water.
SOUTH READING BK
South Reading, Mass
50
Portrait.

Female feeding an eagle from a cup.
100
Capitol at Washington.
SOUTH READING BK
South Reading, Mass
100
Portrait.

ONE
The arm of a man holding a hammer.
Factory.
SPICKET FALLS B'K,
Methuen, Mass.
1
Portrait of Webster.

TWO
Factory. Portrait of J. Q. Adams.
SPICKET FALLS B'K,
Methuen, Mass.
2
2

3
3
Train of cars and railroad station.
SPICKET FALLS B'K,
Methuen, Mass.
3
Blacksmith.

5
Female sewing.
Interior of a shoemakers shop.
SPICKET FALLS B'K,
Methuen, Mass.
V
Dog

TEN
Indian.
Farmers, and horse and sled gathering grain.
SPICKET FALLS B'K,
Methuen, Mass.
X
X

XX
A hunter warming himself by a fire.
20
SPICKET FALLS B'K,
Methuen, Mass.
20
Portrait of Lewis Cass.

50
Cattle.
SPICKET FALLS B'K,
Methuen, Mass.
50
Female with sickle and sheaf of wheat.

100
Santa Claus in sleigh drawn over roofs of houses by a reindeer.
SPICKET FALLS B'K.
Methuen, Mass.
C
Santa Claus sitting at a fire place.

1
Cattle.
ONE
Man and dog in a forest.
SPRINGFIELD B'K
Springfield, Mass.
Vessel.
1
Portrait of Jenny Lind

Left	Centre	Right
Female. TWO	Man and dog in a forest. SPRINGFIELD B'K Springfield, Mass. Bales and boxes.	TWO 2 Hay makers.
	The Springfield Bank uses the old stereotype plate for all other denominations.	
1 Ship.	Winged female with scales and sword and fig. 1. STATE BANK, Boston, Mass. Steamer	1 State Arms.
2 State Arms.	Female and child, bale and hhds.; steamboat on right, and vessels on left. STATE BANK, Boston, Mass. Machinery	2 Cupids and 2
3 Cupids and 3	Spread eagle and ships. STATE BANK, Boston, Mass. Steamer	3 State Arms.
Female. 5	Female portrait. 5 Female portrait. STATE BANK, Boston, Mass.	5 State Arms.
10 Portrait of Washington.	State Arms; female and factories on right; female and shipping on left. X on right. STATE BANK, Boston, Mass.	10 State Arms.
20 State Arms.	Two females; shipping railroad and canal. STATE BANK, Boston, Mass. Dog's head	20 Med. head.
State Arms 50	Three females. STATE BANK, Boston, Mass. Horse	50 Sailor with telescope.
State Arms. 100	Female seated on a bale, ships and lighthouse in distance. STATE BANK, Boston, Mass.	100 Two females, eagle and globe.

Left	Centre	Right
500 Med. head. 500	STATE BANK, Boston, Mass. Female seated representing Commerce; ship and rainbow in distance. Steamship.	500 State Arms. 500
Justice seated. 1000	Spread eagle on limb of tree; ships in distance. STATE BANK, Boston, Mass. Ships	1000 State Arms.
1 Washington and his horse	Female portrait. 1 Female portrait. SUFFOLK BANK, Boston, Mass.	ONE Eagle. ONE
TWO Washington and his horse TWO	2 2 2 SUFFOLK BANK, Boston, Mass.	TWO Female. TWO
Female.	THREE 3 THREE SUFFOLK BANK, Boston, Mass.	3 Dog, safe and building. 3
5 Two females. V	Winged female with trumpet. On right portrait of Columbus. On left portrait of Washington. SUFFOLK BANK, Boston, Mass. Eagle	5 State Arms V
Washington	10 Female, eagle and shield. SUFFOLK BANK, Boston, Mass. Building	10 Bust.
XX Female portrait XX	Female on rock, cupids and dolphin sporting in water. SUFFOLK BANK, Boston, Mass. TWENTY TWENTY	20 Dog's head. XX
50 Female with sword and shield.	FIFTY DOLLARS. SUFFOLK BANK, Boston, Mass. Fifty in block letters across face. L	50 Eagle. FIFTY
100 100 100	One Hundred Dollars SUFFOLK BANK, Boston, Mass. Words One Hundred in large block letters across face. C	100 100 100

Left	Centre	Right
500 Female with pole and cap and view of Boston.	500 SUFFOLK BANK, Boston, Mass. Five large block letter D's across face. D	500 Female and Indian with bow and shield
1000 Justice.	One Thousand Dollars SUFFOLK BANK, Boston, Mass. 1000 M	1000 Letter M and words One Thousand Dollars. 100
Girl's head. 1	Train of cars at depot. One Dollar. TAUNTON BANK, Taunton, Mass.	1 Female head.
1 Reaper. ONE	Reaper gathering grain. 1 Shipping. TAUNTON BANK, Taunton, Mass.	1 Vulcan the blacksmith.
Goddess of Liberty with wreath and Am shield, on which is figure 2	Man and two horses in oval die TAUNTON BANK TWO DOLLARS Taunton	2 Female portrait
TWO Indian 2	Eagle. 2 Washington on horseback. TAUNTON BANK, Taunton, Mass.	2 Train of cars
3 on ornamental die. Female portrait	Three children in circular die, reading book. TAUNTON BANK, Taunton, Mass. THREE DOLLARS.	3 on ornamental die. Male portrait.
Female with grain; reapers on left, farm-house on right. THREE	Large 3 TAUNTON BANK THREE DOLLARS Taunton Mass.	3 Male figure
Ornamental die, on which is name of bank 8 times & one large and eight smaller 5s.	View of Factory; train of cars, etc. 5 in ornamental die. FIVE DOLLARS. TAUNTON BANK, Taunton, Mass.	Ornamental die on which is name of bank 8 times & one large and eight smaller 5s.
5	Female seated; railroad and canal in background. V TAUNTON BANK, Taunton, Mass.	FIVE Five and Eagle FIVE

Dog's head 10	Farmers at work with machines TAUNTON BANK TEN DOLLARS Taunton Massachusetts	10 Female portrait

10	State Arms, also a train of cars crossing a bridge. X TAUNTON BANK. Taunton, Mass.	10 Sleeper.

Sailor with bundle on shoulder 20	Massachusetts Vessels at sea TAUNTON BANK TWENTY DOLLARS Taunton, Mass.	20 Male portrait

20 Female figure.	2 Female. 0 TAUNTON BANK. Taunton, Mass. XX	20 Female. 20

Scene at mill TAUNTO 50	Massachusetts Farmer seated on fence, scythe in hand N BANK FIFTY DOLLARS Taunton	50 Male portrait

50 Female figure. B	Male and female. TAUNTON BANK, Taunton, Mass. 50	50 Cupid in a sail boat. 50

Statue of Liberty leaning on column on which is figures 100	Taunton State Arms of Mass. TAUNTON BANK One Hundred Massachusetts	100 Male portrait

One Hundred and 100, Portrait.	Horses, wagons, shipping &c. TAUNTON BANK. Taunton, Mass.	Same as left Portrait.

D Large eagle 500	spread on rock Massachusetts Five Hundred Dollars TAUNTON BANK Taunton	500 Male portrait

ONE and 1 Merchandise. 1	TOWNSEND BANK, Townsend, Mass. Cupid rolling a silver dollar upon the railroad track, train of cars and city in distance, Farmer cradling	1 Two females.

2 Two females and eagle.	Two cupids and two silver dollars. TOWNSEND BANK, Townsend, Mass.	2 Female and large figure 2.

3 Portrait. 3	TOWNSEND BANK, Townsend, Mass. Three cupids and three silver dollars. Mechanic seated	3 Female reading.

Female feeding an eagle from a cup. 5	Five cupids and five silver dollars, TOWNSEND BANK. Townsend, Mass.	5 Group of females and large figure 5

10 X	TOWNSEND BANK, Townsend, Mass. Farming scene.	X Female.

TWENTY Indian woman with bow and spear.	TOWNSEND BANK. Townsend. Mass. Indian sitting on the ground beside a slain deer.	20 Farmer-boy and XX on half shield.

50 Female.	Capitol at Washington. TOWNSEND BANK. Townsend, Mass	50 Female feeding a horse

C Female, arm resting on a tub.	TOWNSEND BANK Townsends, Mass Vig. Blacksmith shoeing a horse.	100 Farming scene; load of grain, tree &c.

1 Ship building ONE	Wharf and shipping; view of Boston in distance. 1 on right. TRADERS' BANK, Boston, Mass.	1 Male and female. ONE

2 Boy and girl sailing boats in a tub. TWO	Vig. Same as ones. 2 TRADERS' BANK, Boston, Mass.	2 Girl. TWO

3 Interior of a blacksmith's shop. THREE.	Vig. Same as ones. 3 TRADERS' BANK, Boston, Mass.	3 Female in a forest THREE

FIVE Justice	Vig. Same as ones. 5 TRADERS' BANK, Boston, Mass.	5 Portrait of Webster. FIVE

TEN Female.	Vig. Same as ones. X TRADERS' BANK, Boston, Mass.	10 Female. TEN

20 Female. XX	Vig. Same as ones. TRADERS' BANK, Boston, Mass.	20 Justice XX

50	Vig. Same as ones. 50 TRADERS' BANK, Boston, Mass.	50 Covered wagon and merchandise.

Vig. Same as ones. 100	ONE HUND TRADERS' BANK, Boston, Mass.	Hundred on 100 Washington

500	Vig. Same as ones 500 TRADERS' BANK, Boston, Mass.	500 Eagle and shield.

Female with a spear and shield, holding a pillar in the form of a figure one ONE	Vig. View of Chelsea ferry boat going into slip. TRADESMAN'S BK. Chelsea, Mass.	1 State Arms

TWO	Vig. Same as ones. 2 TRADESMAN'S BK. Chelsea, Mass.	2 Figure of Justice.

THREE	Vig. Same as ones. 3 TRADESMAN'S BK. Chelsea, Mass.	3 Blacksmith and anvil.

Figure 5 formed by an eagle and horn of plenty; likeness of Washington in the scroll or finish.	Same as ones. TRADESMAN'S BK. Chelsea, Mass. FIVE	5 Portrait of Gen. Taylor.

TEN
Vig. Same as ones.
X
TRADESMAN'S BK.
Chelsea, Mass.
10
Female with horn of plenty, in right hand, left hand on an chor.

20
Indian girl with bow and and arrows.
Vig. Same as ones.
TRADESMAN'S BK.
Chelsea, Mass.
TWENTY
Machinery.
20
Female with 2 in right hand, and on her knee and 0 under her left.

50
Female in the act of stepping into the water, an urn in her left hand.
Vig. Same as ones.
TRADESMAN'S BK.
Chelsea, Mass.
FIFTY
50
Female holding a flag; three children representing Agriculture &c. all floating in the air.

100
Sailor and ship in the distance.
Vig. Same as ones,
TRADESMAN'S BK.
Chelsea, Mass.
100
100
Figure of a Stone cutter

500
Ship on stocks.
500
Vig. Same as ones.
TRADESMAN'S BK.
Chelsea, Mass.
500
State Arms
500
Steamboat.
500

ONE
Liberty.
ONE
Neptune; on right Boston in 1851; on left Boston in 1630.
TREMONT BANK,
Boston, Mass.
1
Female

1
ONE
1
View of Street.
TREMONT BANK,
Boston, Mass.
Word one, fig 1 and 6 mark.
Male portrait

2
View of a street. 2
TREMONT BANK,
Boston, Mass.
Word two and fig 2 and II.
Two females

Female surrounded by the names of the States.
TWO
Vig. Same as first ones.
TREMONT BANK,
Boston, Mass.
2
Two females

3
THREE
3
3 View of a street.
TREMONT BANK,
Boston, Mass.
Word three and fig. 3 and III.
Three females

3
Female seated on a barrel.
Vig. Same as first ones.
TREMONT BANK,
Boston, Mass.
3
Blacksmith, sailor and farmer.

All other notes of the Tremont Bank are of the Perkins' Stereotype Plate, which has the denomination printed in fine letters all over the bill.

1
Portrait of Fillmore.
State Arms; female and cars on right; female and steamboat on left.
UNION BANK,
Boston, Mass.
Female and 1.
ONE

TWO
Indian female with bow and spear.
Female seated, leaning on bale; railroad, ships and city in distance.
UNION BANK,
Boston, Mass.
2
Gen. Taylor.

3
Female
Spread eagle and ships.
UNION BANK,
Boston, Mass.
3
Webster

5
Washington
Three females. Figure 5 running the entire length of the bill.
UNION BANK,
Boston, Mass.
5

10
10
Sailor with flag; ships. Letter X running the entire length of the bill.
UNION BANK,
Boston, Mass.
10
10

XX
State Arms.
20 Female and eagle. 20
UNION BANK,
Boston, Mass.
Steamer
XX
Portrait.
XX

50
Indian female with bow and arrow.
State Arms with female on each side.
UNION BANK,
Boston, Mass.
Clasped hands
50
Portrait of J. Q. Adams.

100
State Arms.
Portrait of Washington surrounded by arms of the States.
UNION BANK,
Boston, Mass.
Steamer
100
Cupid in a sail boat.
100

500
D
Two female figures with spear, wand, etc., ship and building in distance
UNION B'K. Boston
Five Hundred Dollars
Boston
500
D

ONE
State Arms supported by two females. 1 Head of Franklin
UNION BANK,
Haverhill, Mass.
Eagle
1
Female.
ONE

TWO
Farming scene; female and four males recumbent; load of hay. 2
UNION BANK,
Haverhill, Mass.
Clasped hands
2
Boy.

THREE
Female with horn of plenty; ships on left in distance; on right manufacturing scene. 3
UNION BANK,
Haverhill, Mass.
Wheels, bale, etc
3
Squaw and child.

5
Two females supporting an oval, with head of female enclosed; eagle on top; head of Washington on right hand corner, enclosed in large fig. 5. 5
UNION BANK,
Haverhill, Mass.
Imp. and produce.
5

TEN
Horse chasing scene. Female on X.
UNION BANK,
Haverhill, Mass.
State arms ?
10
Female and three children.

20
Female with helmet and spear.
2 Female. 0
UNION BANK,
Haverhill, Mass.
XX
20
Female, globe and horn of plenty.
20

Man holding fig. 20.
20
Female reclining on cornucopia with distaff; ship in distance.
UNION BANK,
Haverhill, Mass.
20
Sea monsters
Steamship

50
Female.
Male and female.
UNION BANK,
Haverhill, Mass.
50
50
Cupid in boat
50

Cherub and dolphin.
50
Squaw seated; deer and hills in distance.
UNION BANK,
Haverhill, Mass.
50
Justice seated.

100 — Eagle on limb of tree; cars and canal scene in distance. — 100
UNION BANK, Haverhill, Mass.
Male seated. — 100 — Female seated.

State Arms. — Indian reclining; deer. — 100
UNION BANK, Haverhill, Mass.
100 — Female representing Agriculture.

Agricultural scene; female prominent.
500 — D — 500
UNION BANK, Haverhill, Mass.
500

Laocoon and serpents. — THOUSAND — Farm. — 1000
Ship.
Title of Bank.
1000 — 1000

(Old Plate.)
ONE — 1 Interior of a blacksmith's shop. 1 — ONE
Head of Washington. — Female.
UNION BANK OF WEYMOUTH AND BRAINTREE, Weymouth, Mass.
ONE — ONE

1 — (New Plate.) — ONE
Female with sickle and sheaf of wheat; reapers and farm house in background.
UNION BANK OF WEYMOUTH AND BRAINTREE, Weymouth, Mass.
Portrait of Washington. — Train of cars. — 1

(Old Plate.)
TWO — 2 Farming scene. 2 — TWO
Female. — Female.
UNION BANK OF WEYMOUTH AND BRAINTREE, Weymouth, Mass.
2 — 2

(New Plate.)
TWO — 2
UNION BANK OF WEYMOUTH AND BRAINTREE. Weymouth, Mass.
TWO — Spread eagle and several flags bearing the names of the States. — Portrait of Z. Taylor.

(Old Plate.)
THREE — 3 Female and eagle. 3 — THREE
Farmer sharpening his scythe. — Sailor.
UNION BANK OF WEYMOUTH AND BRAINTREE, Weymouth, Mass.
3 — 3

(New Plate.)
III — 3
UNION BANK OF WEYMOUTH AND BRAINTREE, Weymouth, Mass.
3 — Two females, train of cars and ship in background. — Portrait of J. Q. Adams.

(Old Plate.)
5 — V Eagle and shipping. V — 5
FIVE — FIVE
UNION BANK OF WEYMOUTH AND BRAINTREE, Weymouth, Mass.
5 — 5

(New Plate.)
FIVE — V
UNION BANK OF WEYMOUTH AND BRAINTREE. Weymouth, Mass.
Webster.
V — A street in Weymouth. — V

(Old Plate.)
10 — Man and oxen. 10 — TEN
X
UNION BANK OF WEYMOUTH AND BRAINTREE, Weymouth, Mass.
Female.
10

(New Plate.)
TEN — X
UNION BANK OF WEYMOUTH AND BRAINTREE. Weymouth, Mass.
Portrait of Washington.
A street in Weymouth.

(Old Plate.)
20 — XX Eagle. XX — 20
UNION BANK OF WEYMOUTH AND BRAINTREE, Weymouth. Mass.
Female. — Ship.

(New Plate.)
XX — 20
UNION BANK OF WEYMOUTH AND BRAINTREE, Weymouth, Mass.
Portrait of Jackson. — A street in Weymouth.

FIFTY — 50 Man and horse. 50 — FIFTY
Female. — Female.
UNION BANK OF WEYMOUTH AND BRAINTREE, Weymouth. Mass.
FIFTY — FIFTY

100 across One Hundred. — Horses, wagons, shipping &c. — 100 across One Hundred.
UNION BANK OF WEYMOUTH AND BRAINTREE, Weymouth, Mass.
Portrait. — Portrait.

Female seated pointing to reapers.
500 — D — 500
UNION BANK OF WEYMOUTH AND BRAINTREE, Weymouth, Mass.
500

Laocoon and sons strangled by serpents. — Train of cars. — 1000
THOUSAND.
Female.
Title of Bank.
1000 — 1000

Cattle and hogs; village in the background. — 1 — ONE
VILLAGE BANK, North Danvers, Mass.
1 — Female.

2 — 2 — Female.
VILLAGE BANK, North Danvers, Mass.
Ships and steamship. — TWO

3 — Train of cars. — 3
VILLAGE BANK, North Danvers, Mass.
Portrait of Fillmore. — Female.

Female and sickle. — 5 — 5
VILLAGE BANK, Danvers, Mass.
FIVE — Female and wheel, train of cars and steamship in background. — Female.

Female with sheaf of wheat. — Cattle and sheep, man on horseback. — 10
VILLAGE BANK. North Danvers, Mass.
X — Washington on horseback.

20 — Female figure and two cherubs. — 20
VILLAGE BANK, North Danvers, Mass.
Female, eagle, shield, &c. — Female.

20 — VILLAGE BANK, Danvers, Mass. — 20
Female holding grain in right hand. — Figures 20, XX, and the word Twenty. — Man plowing with two horses.

50 — Two females; factories and ship in background. — 50
Female with sickle. — VILLAGE BANK. North Danvers, Mass. — Farmer gathering corn.
50

50 — VILLAGE BANK, Danvers, Mass. — 50
FIFTY
Horses and goats at well, man, etc. — Male portrait.

100 — VILLAGE BANK, Danvers, Mass. — 100
100
C
Female portrait. — Two mechanics erect.

Left	Center	Right
100 Sailor and flag.	VILLAGE BANK, North Danvers, Mass. Female and cupid floating in the air, over a city.	100 Portrait of female. 100
D Three females, two seated, one erect with open book.	VILLAGE BANK, Danvers, Mass. Round red disc on which is figs. 500 and words Five Hundred.	500 Female holding cornucopia and flowers.
Sailor hoisting a flag	WALTHAM BANK, Waltham, Mass. Female reclining, locomotive and factories, milkmaid and cows in background.	1 Cupid. 1
2 Females raking hay.	WALTHAM BANK, Waltham, Mass. A mechanic dragging a stone cutting	2 Farmer, rake and plough.
3 Farmer with scythe.	WALTHAM BANK, Waltham, Mass. Female reclining on bales; barrels; factory in distance.	3 Mechanic, sailor and farmer with fig. 3.
Female. 5	WALTHAM BANK, Waltham Mass. Men, women and children; farming scene.	5 Female.
10 Female.	WALTHAM BANK, Waltham, Mass. Indian; river, canoe, deer in background.	10 Female.
20 Two females with sickle, grain, &c.	TWENTY. Boy TWENTY. watering two horses at trough, woman, &c. WALTHAM BANK. Twenty Dollars Waltham, Mass	20 Female beside spinning Wheel.
20 Female figure.	2 Female 0 WALTHAM BAN. Waltham, Mass. XX	20 Female 20
Factories, &c. 50	Two females seated on bale. FIFTY State Arms. WALTHAM BANK. Fifty Dollars	50 Mechanic at work.

Left	Center	Right
50 Female.	Male and female. WALTHAM BANK, Waltham, Mass. 50	50 Cupid in a sailboat. 50
100 Sailor, mechanic, ships, machinery, &c.	WALTHAM BANK. C Two children at foot of tree; cows, sheep, &c. C Waltham. One Hundred Dollars Massachusetts.	100 Public Building.
100 Vulcan the Blacksmith.	Spread eagle, railroad and canal. WALTHAM BANK. Waltham, Mass. 100	100 Female.
D Five Hundred Dollars.	WALTHAM BANK, Massachusetts. Sailor and soldier, flag, fort, cannon, shot, &c. Five Hundred.	500 Five Hundred Dollars.
1 Indian with bow and hatchet.	Brick layer. 1 WAMESIT BANK Lowell, Mass.	1 Stone cutter.
TWO, II, 2 Indians.	Carpenter at work. 2 WAMESIT BANK Lowell, Mass. Female bathing	2 Man sitting on the ground, factories in back ground
3 Indian upon a cliff over looking a city. THREE	Large figure 3 with State Arms top—Title across 3.	3 Boy umbers
FIVE Train of cars passing under a bridge	Large V with five at top, Man with sickle and sheaf of wheat, at bottom. WAMESIT BANK Lowell, Mass.	5 Cattle, train of cars in distance.
TEN Two males and two females, city in background.	10 WAMESIT BANK Lowell, Mass. TEN	TEN A male and two females, sitting on bale of wool
20	Male, female, two children and a dog. State arms 20 WAMESIT BANK Lowell, Mass.	Female. TWENTY

Left	Center	Right
FIFTY	DOLLARS 50 Four female figures so arranged as to extend across the entire length of the bill. WAMESIT BANK Lowell, Mass. Female bathing	50
100 Two men loading wagon with abrafs; man holding horse.	WAMESIT BANK, Lowell, Mass. ONE HUNDRED Female bathing	100 Squaw and female.
D	WAMESIT BANK, Lowell, Mass. Three females in clouds with quadrant, sickle, compass and cornucopia.	Female erect with shield and spear. 500
ONE Female erect with fig. 1.	Indian reclining; deer behind him; gold dollar. WAMSUTTA BANK, Fall River, Mass.	1 Indian head.
2 Female representing Agriculture.	Male and female seated, two gold dollars; cattle, trees and house in distance. WAMSUTTA BANK, Fall River, Mass.	2 Squaw seated
3 Female portrait.	Mechanic, sailor and farmer seated with implements and three gold dollars. WAMSUTTA BANK, Fall River, Mass.	THREE Liberty and a squaw.
V Farmer with scythe.	Five gold dollars, three cherubs, hunter and Indian; cars in distance. WAMSUTTA BANK, Fall River, Mass.	5 Female portrait
10 Indian head.	Nine cherubs, ten gold dollars, female, cornucopia, shield, &c; cars and steamboat in distance. WAMSUTTA BANK, Fall River, Mass. Mechanic.	X Cherub and dolphin.
FIFTY Female with shield and spear.	Indian, squaw and papoose seated; city in distance. WAMSUTTA BANK, Fall River, Mass.	50 Female portrait.
Deer and dog HUNDR'D	Female seated on rock; three cherubs sporting in water with dolphin. WAMSUTTA BANK, Fall River, Mass.	100 Indian head.

1 — Female Railroad and shipping. 1 — 1 — WAREHAM BANK Wareham, Mass. — 1 — Female.

1 — View of Tremont Iron Works, buildings, horse and chaise, cars, &c. — 1 — WAREHAM BANK, Wareham, Mass. — Man and machinery. — ONE DOLLAR. — Male Portrait.

2 — Farm, sea and sheep. 2 — TWO — WAREHAM BANK Wareham, Mass. — Female. — 2 — TWO

Boy whittling under tree, child lying down, cows, sheep, &c. — WAREHAM B'K., Wareh'm, Mass. — TWO on 2 — Eagle poised on rock. — 2 — TWO DOLLARS. — Male Portrait.

3 — Farming scene. 3 — 3 — Female. — WAREHAM BANK Wareham, Mass. — 3 — THREE

FIVE — Spread eagle and shield; village in distance. — Large V; female and cupid with-in. — 5 — WAREHAM BANK Wareham, Mass. — Girl.

V WAREHAM BK. V Small State arms. V — 5 — Wareham, Mass. — 5 — Sailor aloft with spy glass in hand, other h and on stay. — 5 — Male Portrait.

X — Signing of the Declaration of Independence. X — 10 — WAREHAM BANK Wareham, Mass. — Train of cars.

TEN — Vulcan the blacksmith. X — 10 — WAREHAM BANK Wareham, Mass. — Reaper.

TEN — Small arms of State. — 10 — WAREHAM B'K, Wareham, Mass. — Female, anchor, steamship, and light-house. — TEN. — Male Portrait. — TEN

20 — XX Eagle. XX — 20 — WAREHAM BANK Wareham, Mass. — Female. — Ship.

View of Tremont Nail Works. — WAREHAM B'K. Wareham, Ms. — 20 — 20 — Male Portrait.

FIFTY — 50 Man and horse. 50 — FIFTY — Female — WAREHAM BANK Wareham, Mass. — Female. — FIFTY — FIFTY

FIFTY DOLLARS. WAREHAM BANK. Wareham, Mass. — 50 — State arms — 50 — Male Portrait. — Interior of an Iron Foundry. — FIFTY DOLLARS on FIFTY.

One Hundred and 100. — Horses, waggons, shipping, &c. — Same as left — Portrait. — WAREHAM BANK Wareham, Mass — Portrait.

View of Tremont Iron Works. — C — WAREHAM B'K, Wareham, Mass. — Male Portrait. — 100 — ONE HUNDRED DOLLARS. — Dog and safe.

Portrait — 1 — WARREN BANK, Danvers, Mass. — Large portrait. — 1 — ONE — Female

Portrait. — 2 — WARREN BANK, Danvers, Mass. — Large portrait. — 2 — TWO — Female and fig. 2

Female. — 3 — WARREN BANK, Danvers, Mass. — 3 — Large Portrait. — Indian woman.

5 — 5 — WARREN BANK, Danvers, Mass. — Two females. — Large portrait. — Portrait.

10 — WARREN BANK, Danvers, Mass. — 10 — Indian woman. — Large Portrait. — Female.

XX inverted — WARREN BANK, South Danvers, Mass. — 20 — Justice. — Large portrait of George Peabody red 20 each side. — Milkmaid churning.

FIFTY — Title of Bank. — FIFTY — Peasant girl. — Same as above 20s. — Goddess of Liberty with cap, pole, shield and scroll.

100 — Title of Bank. — 100 — Farmer and dog. — Same as above 20s. — Female portrait.

500 — WARREN BANK — 500 — So. Danvers — Large oval male portrait — Five Hundred Dollars — Five Hundred — MASSACHUSETTS

1 — Spread eagle; capital at Washington on right; steamboat on left. — Merchandise — 1 — WASHINGTON B'K., Boston, Mass. — Washington. — Train of cars

ONE — 1 Indian in a canoe. 1 — ONE — Washington and his horse — WASHINGTON B'K., Boston, Mass. — Bust of Washington. — ONE — ONE

1 — Washington reading paper; man writing on drum head; horse, negro, cannon, men, etc. — 1 — Drummer and soldiers. — WASHINGTON BK., Boston, Mass. — Portrait with frilled cap.

Cupid and 2. — Title of Bank. — 2 and Cupid — Washington on frame; female, soldier, Indians, TWO either side. — 2 — 2

2 — View of the State House. — 2 — WASHINGTON B'K., Boston, Mass. — Portrait of Washington. — State Arms.

TWO TWO	2 Shipping. 2 WASHINGTON B'K, Boston, Mass.	TWO Washington and his horse TWO
3	Washington on horse; officer submitting plans; other officers, cannon, horses, etc. Title of Bank.	3 Washington.
Female THREE	Large steamships and sail vessels. WASHINGTON B'K, Boston, Mass. Washington	3 Sailor.
5 Washington and his horse.	View of the State House. WASHINGTON B'K., Boston, Mass.	5 Female.
TEN Washington and his horse	Train of cars. WASHINGTON B'K, Boston, Mass. State Arms	10 Steamship TEN
TWENTY Squaw with bow and spear.	XX Spread eagle and shield; Capitol at Washington on right; steamship on left. WASHINGTON B'K, Boston, Mass. Washington	20
50 Washington.	Female seated, leaning on a bale; ships on right; railroad and canal on left. WASHINGTON B'K, Boston, Mass. Shell	50 50
100 Washington and his horse	100 Sailor seated on the ground. WASHINGTON B'K, Boston, Mass.	100 100
Bunker Hill Monument. ONE	WEBSTER BANK, Boston, Mass. Portrait of Webster. ONE DOLLAR	1
Bunker Hill Monument. TWO	WEBSTER BANK, Boston, Mass. Portrait of Webster. TWO DOLLARS	2

Bunker Hill Monument. THREE	WEBSTER BANK, Boston, Mass. Portrait of Webster. 3 DOLLARS	3
Bunker Hill Monument. FIVE	WEBSTER BANK, Boston, Mass. Portrait of Webster. FIVE DOLLARS	5
5	WEBSTER BANK, Boston, Mass. 5 Full length figure of Webster. 5	5
Bunker Hill Monument. X on left TEN	WEBSTER BANK, Boston, Mass. Portrait of Webster. TEN DOLLARS	10 X
XX Twenty on XX	WEBSTER BANK, Boston, Mass. Portrait of Webster. TWENTY DOLLARS	20 View of Faneuil Hall.
50 FIFTY	WEBSTER BANK, Boston, Mass. Portrait of Webster. FIFTY DOLLARS	50 View of Faneuil Hall.
100 100	WEBSTER BANK, Boston, Mass. Portrait of Webster. ONE HUNDRED DOLLARS	C View of Faneuil Hall.
500 500	WEBSTER BANK, Boston, Mass. Portrait of Webster.	500 View of Faneuil Hall.
M 1000	WEBSTER BANK. Boston, Mass. Portrait of Webster.	1000 View of Faneuil Hall.
ONE Portrait of Z. Taylor. 1	Indian sitting on a rock, also plough and log cabin. 1 WESTFIELD BANK Westfield, Mass. Female.	1 ONE on Medallion head. ONE

2 State arms. TWO	Two females; farming scene in background. 2 WESTFIELD BANK Westfield, Mass. Fish.	TWO Indians. TWO
THREE Dogs. THREE	WESTFIELD BANK Westfield, Mass. Three men. Dog, key and safe.	3 Female teaching children. THREE
Two males and three females.	FIVE Westfield Green. WESTFIELD BANK Westfield, Mass.	5
10 Train of cars and vessel.	Westfield Green. WESTFIELD BANK Westfield, Mass. Locomotive	X Medallion head. 10
TWENTY Female drawing water at a well	Westfield Green. WESTFIELD BANK Westfield, Mass. Load of hay.	20 on med head Blacksmith shop.
50 Cattle.	WESTFIELD BANK Westfield, Mass. Westfield Green.	50 Female on whip machine.
1 1	WOBURN BANK Woburn, Mass. Female reclining, train of cars, mill, public and cars in background. Wheels, bale, etc.	1 Child and Dolphin.
Farmer, milk maid and cows 2	Train of cars. WOBURN BANK Woburn, Mass.	2 Females raking hay.
Female, eagle, and ships. 3	WOBURN BANK Woburn, Mass.	3 Cupid and figure 3.
Female feeding an eagle from a cup. 5	WOBURN BANK Woburn, Mass. FIVE	5 Five females and fig. 5.

TEN — WOBURN BANK, Woburn, Mass. — 10
Female. Train of cars. Horses and load of hay.
TEN

20 — Portrait of Washington. — 20
WOBURN BANK, Woburn, Mass.
Spread eagle, Capitol at Washington and steamship in background.
TWENTY

50 — WOBURN BANK, Woburn, Mass. — 50
Two females, factories, steamship and train of cars in background. Female, vessel, etc.
FIFTY

100 — WOBURN BANK, Woburn, Mass. — 100
State Arms. 100 Capitol at Washington.

1 — Large figure 1 with portrait of Washington. — 1
WORCESTER BANK, Worcester, Mass.
Female. Carpenter at his bench.

2 — Portrait of Washington, and large figure 2. — 2
Farmer sharpening a scythe. WORCESTER BANK, Worcester, Mass. Dog and safe.

3 — Large figure 3 and portrait. — 3
WORCESTER BANK, Worcester, Mass.
Portrait. Female.

5 — Portrait of female. 5 Portrait of female. — 5
WORCESTER BANK, Worcester, Mass.
Female Indian. Female.

10 — Female, farmers loading hay; train of cars. — 10
WORCESTER BANK, Worcester, Mass.
Blacksmith. Stonecutter.
10

Female with sheaf of wheat. — Indian and female. — 20
WORCESTER BANK, Worcester, Mass.
20 Farmer sowing seed.

L — Shepherd boy and sheep. — 50
WORCESTER BANK, Worcester, Mass.
50 Female.

100 — Winged female with a trumpet, also globe and eagle. — C
Female, sickle and sheaf of wheat. WORCESTER BANK, Worcester, Mass. Female.
C

500 — Spread eagle on shield, cars, city, vessels, &c., in distance. — D
WORCESTER BANK, Worcester, Mass.
Med. head. D Med. head.

1 — (New Plate.) Man sitting on the ground, anvil, hammer &c. Factories and train of cars in background. — 1
Portrait of Webster. WORCESTER CO. B'K, Blackstone, Mass. Indian woman.

Female, Railroad and canal. — (Old Plate.) 1 — 1
WORCESTER CO. B'K, Blackstone, Mass.
1 Female.

2 — (New Plate.) WORCESTER CO. B'K, Blackstone, Mass. — 2
Two females, and bust of Washington, ship in distance.
Female. Portrait of Washington.

Farmers and sheep; stream of water. 2 — TWO
Female.
2 WORCESTER CO. B'K, Blackstone, Mass. TWO

Farming scene 3 — 3
Female.
3 WORCESTER CO. B'K, Blackstone, Mass. THREE

5 — (New Plate.) WORCESTER CO. B'K, Blackstone, Mass. — 5
Female reclining, train of cars, shipping, mills maids and cars in background.
Train of cars. Arms.

(Old Plate.) — 5
Spread eagle and shield. Large V; Female and cupid.
FIVE WORCESTER CO. B'K, Blackstone, Mass. Girl.

X — WORCESTER CO. BK, Blackstone, Mass. — 10
Three females representing Agriculture, Commerce and Manufactures.
Squaw. Cupid and dolphin.

Vulcan the blacksmith. X — 10
WORCESTER CO. B'K, Blackstone, Mass. Reaper.
TEN

20 — 2 Female. 0 — 20
Female. WORCESTER CO. B'K, Blackstone, Mass. Female.
XX 20

20 — WORCESTER CO BK, Mass. — 20
Three 20s and words Twenty Dollars on green die.
Girl's head. Cattle, telegraph, bridge, cars, etc.

50 — WORCESTER CO. BK, Mass. — 50
Green die with fig. 50, words Fifty, Fifty Dollars and Massachusetts on it.
Two children. Clay.

50 — Male and female — 50
WORCESTER CO. B'K, Blackstone, Mass. Cupid in a boat.
Female. 50 50

C — WORCESTER CO BK, Mass. — 100
Green die with fig. 100, words One Hundred Dollars and Massachusetts on it.
Franklin. Dog & safe.

100 — Spread eagle, Railroad and canal. — 100
WORCESTER CO. B'K, Blackstone, Mass.
Vulcan the blacksmith. 100 Female.

C — Eagle on bale of goods, &c. 100 — 100
Men fishing. WORCESTER CO. BK, Blackstone, Mass. Female with sickle and grain.
100 100

1 — Man shoeing horse; man sitting on log and man standing. — 1
WRENTHAM BANK, Wrentham, Mass.
Soldiers, boy beating drum. Two children.

MASS.

Left	Centre	Right
1	Female, train of cars and canal in background. 1 WRENTHAM BANK Wrentham, Mass.	1 Female.
2 Female resting on pillar.	Man loading hay on cart with oxen. WRENTHAM BANK. Wrentham, Mass.	2 Portrait of Webster.
2	Farmer and sheep, stream of water. 2 WRENTHAM BANK Wrentham, Mass.	TWO Female. TWO
Blacksmith at forge. THREE	WRENTHAM BANK, Wrentham, Mass. Female seated holding urn; ship, stove, goods, etc.	3 Boy, child and sheep. THREE
3	Farming scene. 3 WRENTHAM BANK Wrentham, Mass.	3 Female. THREE
FIVE	(Old Plate.) Female. 5 WRENTHAM BANK Wrentham, Mass.	5 Ship.
Large V with five running across.	Female with sickle rake &c, shipping in background. Large V with Indian girl. WRENTHAM BANK Wrentham, Mass.	5 Portrait of Washington.
5 Female seated, dogs, etc.	Two horses in field. WRENTHAM BANK. Wrentham, Mass.	5 Portrait.
10 X 10	(Old Plate.) Man and .... 10 WRENTHAM BANK Wrentham, Mass.	TEN Female.
X	Signing of the declaration of independence. X WRENTHAM BANK Wrentham, Mass.	10 Train of cars

R. ISLAND.

Left	Centre	Right
10 Continental soldier; small State arms	Female seated holding cloth; factories, steam boat, &c. WRENTHAM BANK, Wrentham, Mass.	10 Old man seated; child bust of Washington on table.
20 Female.	XX ... XX WRENTHAM BANK Wrentham, Mass.	20 Ship.
20 Two men at work on wagon.	Small eagle WRENTHAM BANK, Wrentham, Mass.	20 Female feeding horse, hens chickens & ducks.
50 Steamboat and sail-vessel.	Farming scene. 50 WRENTHAM BANK Wrentham, Mass.	L ...ale.
WRENTHAM BANK, Wrentham, Mass. 50 Female seated, arm resting on shield; eagle and steamboat. 50		50 Gen. Scott
One Hundred and 100. Portrait.	Horses, wagons, shipping &c. WRENTHAM BANK Wrentham, Mass.	Same as left Portrait.
100 Female Portrait.	Man cutting stick, horse, cow, sheep, boy on fence. WRENTHAM BANK. Wrentham, Mass	100 Female Portrait.
1 Female erect holding tablet upon pillar with left arm, pen in right hand.	[New Plate.] Female seated resting arm upon shield and quiver; view of niagara falls upon left; trees in background upon right. AMERICAN BANK, Providence, R. I.	1 Male portrait
1 Men in boat, sloops in distance 1	[Old Plate.] 1 Female seated beside steam engine factory with water-wheel in distance on left. 1 Title of Bank. State Arms.	1 Steamboats upon river. 1
2 Spread eagle grasping arrows and shield in talons. 2	[Old Plate.] 2 Three females seated representing commerce, agriculture, &c. 2 AMERICAN BANK. Providence, R. I. State Arms.	Same as on left.

R. ISLAND.

Left	Centre	Right
Male portrait 2	[New Plate.] View upon East River, large steamer sailing to right of note, ships, sloop, mail steamboat, &c. AMERICAN BANK. Providence, R. I.	2 Female seated resting right arm upon shield.
3 3	AMERICAN BANK. Providence, R. I. Scene in a factory, females at work with machines, &c. 3	3 Male portrait
3 Portrait of Washington. 3	Portrait of female. Vig. Indian in canoe, padding past high rocks; forest scenery around. Portrait of male. AMERICAN BANK. Providence, R. I. State Arms.	3 Male portrait 3
5 Male portrait	Vig. Nautical view; large steamship in foreground; sailing vessels on either side. AMERICAN BANK. Providence, R. I. Spread Eagle.	5 Female seated in large ornamental figure. 5
FIVE Hunting wild cattle.	AMERICAN BANK. Providence, R. I. Female seated by fig. 5; ships in distance.	5 Farmer feeding hogs.
Portrait of girl	AMERICAN BANK Providence, R. I. Large Spread Eagle Extending across bill	5 Female portrait
5 Portrait of Washington. 5	5 Vig. Washington crossing the Delaware. 5 AMERICAN BANK, Providence, R. I State Arms.	5 Portrait of Franklin. FIVE
5 Two girls carrying sheafs.	Five silver dollars and five cherubs, AMERICAN BANK, Providence, R. I.	5 Female portrait.
Male portrait 10	AMERICAN BANK, Providence, R. I. X Vig. State Arms; on right, resting right arm upon it female with liberty pole and cap; steamship in distance on left; female seated with sickle in right hand; locomotive, &c., in distance.	10
10 Bird head. 10	TEN Vig. Locomotive and train of cars; forest scenery in background. TEN AMERICAN BANK. Providence, R. I. State Arms.	10 Bird. head. 10

20 — Indian on ground, dead deer, scenery &c.
AMERICAN BANK, Providence, R. I.
Female on eagle soaring in clouds.
Red 20.
20 — Squaw seated.

---

50 — Female seated; cornucopia in left hand. — 50
Steam-boat. Vig. Head of Washington in circular shield, surmounted by eagle on half globe; female on either side; vessels in distance. Steam-boat.
AMERICAN BANK. Providence, R. I.
State Arms.
50 — Same as left end. — 50

---

100 — Female erect holding balances in right hand; sword in left. — 100
100 Vig. Two females; one with wings, wreath and book seated on right; the other standing with sword and scales; sun breaking through dark clouds over their heads. 100
AMERICAN BANK, Providence, R. I.
State Arms.
100 — Same as left end. — 100

---

500 — Male portrait.
Vig. Indian girl seated upon ground; on left shield, spread eagle upon globe, drum, flags liberty pole and cap, battle axe, &c.; on right ship in distance.
Title of Bank.
State arms.
500 — D

1000
Vig. Spread eagle upon shield. Male portrait.
AMERICAN BANK. Providence, R. I.
State arms.
1000 — M

American shield in which is figure 1. Spanish dollar.
Vig. State arms on either side, male figure; locomotive and cars on left; Indian huts and canal on right.
AQUIDNECK BANK, Newport, R. I.
Old stone mill.
1 — Female sitting upon figure 1.

---

2 — Express wagon. — 2
AQUIDNECK BANK, Newport, R. I.
Death of King Phillip.
Old Stone Mill.
2 — Spanish and American Dollar.

FIVE — Two Spanish and three American dollars.
AQUIDNECK BANK. Newport, R. I.
Vig. Steamboat ferry, and view of the city of Newport on left.
Old stone mill.
5 — Cars, Indians and ornamental figures.

---

10 — State arms on either side of a female.
AQUIDNECK BANK. Newport, R. I.
Letter X and figures 10 across; on left lighthouse; on right sailor with spy-glass; man in boat.
10 — Indian looking at the sea on which a vessel is dimly seen.

---

20 — Female child. — 20
AQUIDNECK BANK, Newport, R. I.
Old mill; Indian squaw and papoose in a canoe.
20 — Female. — 20

50
Large steamship. Portrait of Webster.
AQUIDNECK BANK, Newport, R. I.
State arms.
50 — Ship under sail.

C — Two females and shield; steamship on right.
ONE HUNDRED
100 Head of Columbus. 100
Old mill.
AQUIDNECK BANK, Newport, R. I.
C

ONE
1 View of Arcade city of Providence. 1
ARCADE BANK. Providence, R. I.
State Arms.
Beehive. Portrait of Female. American shield.

TWO
2 Same as Ones. 2
ARCADE BANK, Providence, R. I.
State Arms.
Beehive. Female seated with liberty pole and cap. Shield.

THREE
3 Same as Ones. 3
ARCADE BANK, Providence, R. I.
State Arms.
Female with sickle, sheaf of grain, &c. THREE

Female with her right hand resting on desk, and her left holding a pen.
5 Vig. Same as ones. 5
ARCADE BANK, Providence, R. I.
State arms.
Eagle on Bush.

Male portrait — 10 — Male portrait
10 Vig. Same as ones. 10
ARCADE BANK. Providence, R. I.
State arms.
Male portrait — TEN — Male portrait

XX — Female. — XX
Vig. Three females seated, with beehive on the right, and sheaf of grain on the left. 20
ARCADE BANK, Providence, R. I.
Die.
20 — Drover and cattle. — 20.

Full length male figure.
50 Vig. Figures, globe, ship, scroll, &c.
ARCADE BANK, Providence, R. I.
State arms.
50 — Male portrait. — 50

---

100 — Portrait. — 100
100 Vig. Man on horseback. 100
ARCADE BANK, Providence, R. I.
State arms.
100 — Portrait. — 100

500
Vig. Indian paddling a canoe. 500
ARCADE BANK, Providence, R. I.
500 — Female with a sword and scales.

1000
Vig. Eagle standing upon a rock overlooking the sea, upon which a ship is dimly seen. 1000
ARCADE BANK, Providence, R. I.
1000 — Indian girl seated upon a rock, with bow and arrows.

ONE — Male seated, pitcher by his side.
Indian seated with bow; plough, sickle, sheaf, hut, trees, &c. on left.
ASHAWAY BANK. Ashaway, R. I.
1 — Female portrait.

2
Two horses (white and black); train of cars on left.
ASHAWAY BANK, Ashaway, R. I.
2 — Two males erect, and a female seated.

Two females, one erect with spear, and the other kneeling with sprig of wheat in right hand.
Word Dollars and figure 3. Two females seated, one with sickle; bbl., bales, and vessels in distance on right.
ASHAWAY BANK. Ashaway, R. I.
3 — Two men with fork and rake, and dog; two males in background coming forward.

Webster. — 5
Man on horseback, drove of cattle, boy in water, man with whip; house in background.
ASHAWAY BANK, Ashaway, R. I.
5 — Squaw and papoose; forest scene in background.

Portrait of Indian. — X
ASHAWAY BANK. Ashaway, R. I.
Female reclining on a box gazing at miniature view of city; sheep on right.
10 — Female drawing water from a well; steamboat in distance.

FIFTY — Head of Liberty surmounted by stars. — 50
ASHAWAY BANK, Ashaway, R. I.
50
50 — 50

ONE — Two females erect, one with sickle and sheaf. — ONE
Steamship, sail vessels &c.; man in boat sailing toward steamship.
ATLANTIC BANK, Providence, R. I.
Female Head
1 — Spread eagle on shield. — ONE

ONE — Two females. — ONE
Steamer and other vessels.
ATLANTIC BANK, Providence, R. I.
Girls' head.
1 — Eagle on rock in ocean. — ONE

Left	Centre	Right
2 TWO Small figure with cornucopia.	ATLANTIC BANK, Providence, R. I. Female seated with left arm resting on shield; on her right, sheaf of wheat, fruit, and cars crossing viaduct in distance; on left ship and steamboat. Head of Female.	2 TWO Small figure with cornucopia.
2 TWO Cupid.	Title of Bank. Female and State Arms; vessels; cars, etc., in distance. Girls' head.	2 TWO Cupid.
Large V with word FIVE running across it. Two figures seated. 5	ATLANTIC BANK, Providence, R. I. Steamship and three vessels, largest of which is in the foreground. Female Head	FIVE Sailor seated among bales; ship in distance. 5
10 Large X with figures 10 upon it; light house on right, two sailors, one with spyglass other in boat	ATLANTIC BANK, Providence, R. I. Large ship under full sail. Female Head	10 Female erect standing on rock, ship below under sail.
Female seated with sword in right hand, balances in left. 50 FIFTY	Female seated with sheaf and sickle; sailor with spy glass and quadrant on right; Artisan with hammer in hands on left. ATLANTIC BANK, Providence, R. I. Female seated.	50 Sailor erect
Female seated; locomotive, steamship and vessel in distance. 100 Sailor seated bales, &c.	ATLANTIC BANK. Providence, R. I. Sailor in circular shield, on either side small figure. Female Head	100 Female erect holding sheaf on her head with right hand, sickle in left.
1 Ornamental Fountain.	Cupid rolling silver dollar; locomotive and city in distance on right. ATLAS BANK, Providence, R. I. Goddess of liberty.	1 Santa claus with bag of toys on back
Hunter leaning upon rifle. 2	ATLAS BANK. Providence, R. I. Female seated, dog and pail beside her on right; cattle on left.	2 Female with sheaf of grain.
3 Indian girl seated.	Female floating on water; cupids on left and sea monster. ATLAS BANK. Providence, R. I.	3 Cupid astride of sea monster.
FIVE Female erect with spear and shield, Gto .'at feet	Locomotive and cars; Depot on left. ATLAS BANK, Providence, R. I. Dog's Head.	5 Portrait of Female. 5

Left	Centre	Right
Sailor leaning upon capstan, spy glass in hand. 10	Artisan seated beside machinery; factories on right in distance. ATLAS BANK. Providence, R. I. Loading Hay.	10 Female seated on anchor ship in distance.
Sailor boy in attitude of rowing. 20	State Arms surmounted by eagle; female with sword and scales on right female with spear and cornucopia on left, locomotive on right in distance; steamboat on left. Title of Bank.	20 Goddess of liberty with pole cap and shield beside globe.
Female with spear and shield. 50	ATLAS BANK. Providence, R. I. Female with sword and scales reclining upon shield, view upon it; Cupid soaring on right.	50 Indian girl seated upon ground forest scenery in distance.
Female portrait. 100	Vig. Female resting arm upon shield; safe, sheaf, plough, and cars in distance on right; large steamship on left. ATLAS BANK, Providence, R. I.	100 Atlas prying up globe.
1 Male portrait	Vig. Female seated between two pillars; shield, spread eagle, cars crossing bridge on right; anchor, &c.; city in the distance on left. BANK OF AMERICA, Providence, R. I.	1 Female bearing sheaf on shoulder.
2 Female holding tablet on pillar.	Vig. Female reclining upon bales; ships on right; vessel on left. BK., OF AMERICA. Providence, R. I	2 TWO Male portrait
3 Female seated, holding sword and scales.	Vig. Portrait of Indian girl in ornamental shield, surrounded by drums &c. BK., OF AMERICA. Providence, R. I. Spread eagle between sig.	3 Ship under full sail.
Goddess of Liberty with wreath and shield. FIVE	5 Male portrait. BANK OF AMERICA FIVE DOLLARS Providence	5 Anchor on rock
5	Vig. Spread eagle upon shield, looking to left. Portrait of Washington BK., OF AMERICA, Providence, R. I. Steamship.	5 State Arms.
10	BK., OF AMERICA, Providence, R. I. Vig. Female seated, holding American shield; Liberty pole and cap laying across lap; United States Capitol in background.	10

Left	Centre	Right
20 Locomotive, &c.	Vig. Female seated, holding scales in right hand; pole and liberty cap in left; small figure on either side. BK., OF AMERICA, Providence, R. I. Steamship.	20 Female with sickle and grain.
50 Portrait of female with sickle. 50	Vig. Two females seated; factories and cars crossing bridge on right; ship in distance, on left. BK., OF AMERICA. Providence, R. I. Locomotive.	50 Boy holding ears of corn in either hand.
100 Full length sailor; American flag in right arm; cap in left hand.	BK., OF AMERICA, Providence, R. I. Vig. Female and Cupid soaring in air, above city. Cog-wheel, &c.	100 Large ship under full sail. 100
ONE 1	1 Vig. Indian seated upon ground, bow in right hand 1 BANK OF BRISTOL, Bristol, R. I,	RHODE ISLAND.
II 2	2 Vig. Same as one 2 BANK OF BRISTOL, Bristol, R. I.	RHODE ISLAND
3 III	3 Same as ones. 3 BANK OF BRISTOL, Bristol, R. I.	RHODE ISLAND.
V 5	5 Same as ones. 5 BANK OF BRISTOL, Bristol, R. I.	RHODE ISLAND.
X 10	10 Same as ones. 10 BANK OF BRISTOL. Bristol, R. I.	RHODE ISLAND
XX 20	20 Same as ones 20 BANK OF BRISTOL. Bristol. R. I.	RHODE ISLAND.
30 XXX	30 Same as ones. 30 BANK OF BRISTOL. Bristol. R. I.	RHODE ISLAND.

Left	Centre	Right
50 50	50 Same as above. L BANK OF BRISTOL. Bristol, R. I.	RHODE ISLAND.
1 Sailor erect on ship's deck, holding spyglass	Vig. Female seated reclining on bale; ship on right; factories in distance on left. B'K OF COMMERCE. Providence, R. I.	1 Female erect holding tablet in left arm, pen in left hand.
Indian seated upon rock, rifle resting upon right leg. 2	B'K OF COMMERCE, Providence, R. I. 2 Vig. Large ship under sail at sea, another large vessel following her; schooner on left. 2	2 Female with sheaf of grain under right arm.
3 Female seated, holding sickle in right hand; bundle of grain in left.	Vig. Spread eagle upon shield, overlooking sea, upon which ship is dimly seen. BK., OF COMMERCE, Providence, R. I.	3 Indian seated, holding gun in right hand.
FIVE Large steamship in foreground; vessels on either side, in distance.	Vig. Portrait of Henry Clay. BK., OF COMMERCE, Providence, R. I. Ornamental star.	5 Female seated, holding cornucopia.
10	Vig. A number of vessels upon water opposite a city. B'K OF COMMERCE, Providence, R. I.	TEN Female seated holding scales in left hand, sword in right.
50 Small cupid with cornucopia under left arm.	Vig. Female seated, resting left arm upon cogwheel; ship on right; cars leaving station on left. BK OF COMMERCE. Providence, R. I. State arms.	50 Small figure holding sheaf under right arm.
100	BK. OF COMMERCE, Providence, R. I. Vig. Female leaning upon anchor, resting against bale; brig and steamboat on right; city, with vessels laying at wharfs.	100
D	Vig. Female seated, with either hands resting on pillar; spread eagle, locomotive, and train crossing viaduct, on right; town and vessels upon water, in distance on left. Portrait of Washington BK., OF COMMERCE, Providence, R. I.	500
	BK., OF COMMERCE, Providence, R. I. Vig. Large steamship in foreground; ships on either side. 1000	1000

Left	Centre	Right
1 Female with scales, sword etc.	Female seated with cloth; bale, factory, etc. BANK OF KENT, Coventry, R. I.	1 Anchor and word 'Hope'
ONE	Inside of a weaving room; females and looms. 1 on left. 1 BANK OF KENT, Coventry, R. I.	ONE Male Portrait ONE
2	Man driving cows; factory and village. 2 BANK OF KENT, Coventry R. I. State arms	TWO Head of Franklin. TWO
2 Female with dove.	Two females seated; buildings in distance. Title of Bank.	2 Mechanic at work at vise
5	White and black horse; cattle, stream, etc. 5 Title of Bank.	5 Female, spinning wheel, factory.
5	Forest and factory standing back. 5 BANK OF KENT. Coventry' R. I. State arms.	FIVE Head of Washington FIVE
10 X 10	Yoke of oxen and man. 10 BANK OF KENT, Coventry, R. I. State arms.	TEN Female erect
20 Female seated	XX Eagle. XX BANK OF KENT, Coventry, R. I.	20 Ship, &c.
FIFTY Female erect FIFTY	50 Man and horse. 50 BANK OF KENT. Coventry, R. I.	FIFTY Female erect FIFTY
100 Eagle 100	C Horses and men in a chariot, in the clouds. 100 BANK OF KENT, Coventry, R. I.	C Head of Washington. C

Left	Centre	Right
Indian erect with bow and arrow. ONE	1 View of railway station; two boats upon the water before it steamer. 1 B'K OF N. AMERICA. Providence, R. I. Dog's Head.	Medal. Head with word ONE across
1 Female seated blowing trumpet	Goddess of liberty seated on globe; eagle on her right and small figure with cornucopia on her left. B'K OF N. AMERICA, Providence, R. I. Female and anchor.	1 Male portrait
2 Female seated on globe; eagle on the right and a small figure with cornucopia on left.	Male portrait BANK OF NORTH AMERICA, Providence, R. I.	2
TWO	B'K OF N. AMERICA, Providence, R. I. 2 Goddess of liberty leaning upon shield TWO Dog's Head.	2 Word TWO upon Medal Head.
3	Indian princess surrounded by flags, drums, etc. 3 BANK OF NORTH AMERICA, Providence, R. I.	THREE Farmer with sickle and sheaf. THREE
FIVE Female seated; pole, cap, &c.	Fig. 5 with word five running across it. Vig. Sailor in boat; city in extreme distance. B'K OF N. AMERICA. Providence, R. I. Steamship.	5 Portrait of Franklin.
TEN Female seated with battle axe in left hand, pole with liberty cap in right.	B'K OF N. AMERICA, Providence, R. I. 10 Vig. Three male figures, 10 representing commerce, agriculture and mechanics; ship on their left in distance; locomotive and town on their right. Clasped hands.	
50 Indian female seated with bow and arrows.	B'K OF N. AMERICA, Providence, R. I. State arms. 50	50 Female seated.
100 Small figure holding cornucopia. 100	B'K OF N. AMERICA, Providence, R. I. Vig. Spread eagle upon shield; sailing vessels on right, steamship on left.	100 Small figure holding cornucopia. 100
500 Spread eagle on shield. 500	Vig. Goddess of liberty seated, with her left hand on shield. D B'K OF N. AMERICA, Providence, R. I. Anchor in shield.	500 Figure erect with left hand on shield, at whose feet is a female with globe and compass.

Left end	Centre	Right end
Female soaring in the air, olive branch in left hand, sword in right. 1000	B'K OF N. AMERICA, Providence, R. I. Vig. Portion of the globe showing the continent of North America, and extending in a half circle across the face of the note.	Female soaring in the air, strewing flowers with right hand, cornucopia in her left. 1000
ONE State arms, upon which is mounted an eagle. ONE	1 Vig. View of water and large ship; also smaller vessels, row-boats, &c. 1 BANK OF RHODE ISLAND, Newport, R. I. Head of female.	ONE Bust of Commodore Perry. 1
2 Man seated; on right public buildings; on left scrolls of paper. TWO	2 Vig. Female seated with wand in right hand; building on right, and holding key in left hand. 2 B'K OF R. ISLAND, Newport, R. I. Steamboat.	2 Female seated near safe; eagle on left; also small portrait of Washington. TWO
Female reclining on anchor, looking over the sea. 3	3 Catching Buffaloes. 3 B'K OF R. ISLAND, Newport, R. I. Head of Female.	3 Launching a vessel. 3
FIVE Female seated with eagle on her lap. 5	5 Man seated with mechanical tools &c., ship on left. 5 B'K OF R. ISLAND, Newport, R. I. Head of Lion.	FIVE View of city in distance. Male raising the world. 5
TEN Female seated with wand in left hand, looking up to male figure. 10	10 Vig. Ship. 10 B'K OF R. ISLAND, Newport, R. I. State Arms.	TEN Old Stone Mill. X
XX Washington.	Military officers and warlike implements. BANK OF RHODE ISLAND, Newport, R. I.	20 Clay
XXX Justice seated	Landing of the Pilgrims. Title of Bank.	30 Male portrait
L Washington.	Military officers and warlike implements. Title of Bank.	50 Franklin.
FIFTY	State Arms. B'K OF R. ISLAND, Newport, R. I. 50	50 I

Left end	Centre	Right end
C Male portrait	View of a battle. Title of Bank.	100 Male portrait
100 DOLLARS	State Arms. B'K OF R. ISLAND, Newport, R. I. 100	100 Letter C.
1 Anchor beside rock	BLACKSTONE CANAL BK 1 Girl and boy driving cattle through gate ONE DOLLAR Providence	1 General Burnside
1 Washingt'n 1	1 Female blowing trumpet; banner, globe, eagle, etc. 1 BLACKSTONE CANAL BK ONE DOLLAR Providence State Arms	1 Male bust erect 1
2 Blacksmith	BLACKSTONE CANAL BK Large steamer TWO DOLLARS Providence	2 Female
2 Male portrait.	Vig. Female seated upon bale, figure at her feet; locomotive, canal, &c. in distance on right of vig.; ships, town, &c. on left. BLACKSTONE CANAL BANK, Providence, R. I. State arms	2 Indian girl seated with shield, pole and liberty cap.
5 Female seated, olive branch in left hand, spear in right.	Vig. State arms, female figure on either side, schooner, locomotive and cars in distance on right; bales, barrels, steamboat and ship on left. BLACKSTONE CANAL BANK, Providence, R. I. Bale and cogwheels.	5 Female seated, spindle in right hand wand in left
10 Female portrait.	Vig. Mechanic seated, sledge hammer resting on his left shoulder; factories, &c., on right. 10 BLACKSTONE CANAL BANK. ProvidenCe, R. I. State arms.	TEN Indian erect with bow and spear in her right hand.
50 FIFTY 50	RHODE ISLAND 50 Female seated arm resting on bale; vessels in background BLACKSTONE CANAL FIFTY DOLLARS Providence Steamer	50 BNK
100 HUNDRED 100	100 Vig. Female 100 seated beside anchor, hogshead, &c., with horn of plenty. BLACKSTONE CANAL BANK. Providence, R. I. Steamship.	ONE HUNDRED

Left end	Centre	Right end
D Mason at work, level in his hand	Vig. View of the Capitol at Washington. BLACKSTONE CAN'L BANK, Providence, R. I.	500 Locomotive
M Two large ships under full sail.	Vig. Large steamship under full sail at sea; ships on either side. BLACKSTONE CAN'L BANK. Providence, R. I.	1000 Anchor, bales, bbls., &c.; ship in background.
Male portrait 1	BUTCHERS & DROVERS' BANK, Providence, R. I. Drove of cattle, hogs, &c.; two men on horseback; cars crossing viaduct in distance.	1 Female portrait.
2 Male portrait TWO	Title of Bank. Drove of oxen and sheep; man on horseback; trees, etc., in distance.	2 Female portrait. TWO
Small figure 5	Vig. Three females floating through water, supporting Cupid. BUTCHERS' & DROVERS' BANK, Providence, R. I. Ox.	5 Male portrait
10 Drovers, cattle, hay, &c.	Vig. Two females seated on either side of state arms, steamship on the right, locomotive and cars on the left. Title of Bank. Beehive.	10 Portrait of Andrew Jackson.
50	Vig. Female reclining on bale of goods. Portrait of Henry Clay. BUTCHERS' & DROVERS' BANK. Providence, R. I.	50 Anchor on a bale of goods.
Indian looking in distance. 100	Vig. Steamship and other vessels. BUTCHERS' & DROVERS' BANK. Providence, R. I.	100 Male portrait
1 Indian reclining, looking over rock.	Vig. Dog, safe and keys; bags of money. CENTREVILLE BK., Warwick, R. I. Shield and anchor.	1 Farmer erect, with sheaf of wheat, and scythe. Shoes hanging on handle of scythe.
2 Female seated, with sceptre and sword.	Vig. Large eagle and shield CENTREVILLE BK., Warwick, R. I. Wheel and rollers.	2 Female with spy-glass; ships on left, in distance.

Left	Centre	Right
3 Female reclining, with sickle in left hand, she holds grain.	Vig. Female, shield, anchor, sheaf of wheat, plough, &c.; female holds sickle in left hand; cars and bridge on right. CENTREVILLE BK., Warwick, R. I.	3 Indian reclining.
5 Male Portrait.	CENTREVILLE BK., Warwick, R. I. Vig. Horse, boys, and dog; the boys are trying to catch the horse; one boy is laying on ground.	5 Male Portrait.
10 Male Portrait.	CENTREVILLE BK., Warwick, R. I. Vig. Blacksmith shoeing a horse; two man on left, one seated on log; wagon and wheel on right.	10 Male Portrait.
50 Male portrait	CENTREVILLE BK., Warwick, R. I. Men gathering and loading cart with corn; colt, etc.	50 Male portrait
100 Male portrait	Title of Bank. Horses in fields.	100 Male portrait
1 Washington.	Female. 1 Female. CITIZENS BANK, Cumberland, R. I.	1 Male.
1 ONE	CITIZENS' BANK, Woonsocket, R. I. Female seated with wheat in her hand; town in the distance.	1 ONE
2 Male.	Female. 2 Female. CITIZENS BANK, Cumberland, R. I.	2 Male.
2 Eagle.	Two females. CITIZENS BANB, Woonsocket, R. I.	2 Bull's head. TWO
3 Washington and horse.	Female. 3 Female. CITIZENS BANK, Cumberland, R. I.	3 Blacksmith with sledge.

Left	Centre	Right
3 Train of cars. 3	CITIZENS BANK, Woonsocket, R. I. Three females.	3 Cabin. THREE
Eagle. FIVE	V CITIZENS BANK, Cumberland, R. I.	5 Female with basket of flowers.
Two males and two females.	5 Anchor. 5 CITIZENS BANK, Woonsocket, R. I.	Female and eagle. FIVE
10 Female. TEN	1 Female. 0 CITIZENS BANK, Woonsocket, R. I.	10 Female. TEN
20 Female with spear.	2 Female. 0 CITIZENS BANK, Woonsocket, R. I. XX	20 Female 20
50 Female with spear.	Male and female seated. CITIZENS BANK, Woonsocket, R. I. 50	50 Cupid in boat. 50
100 Man with sledge, anchor	Vig. Spread eagle upon branch of tree; canal scene on right; train of cars crossing bridge on left. CITIZENS BANK, Woonsocket, R. I. 100	100 Female with rake, seated beside cornucopia.
1 Female seated on bale; ship in distance. 1	Female seated with left arm on shield; pole and cap, eagle, coin, &c. CITIZENS' UNION BANK, Scituate, R. I. Head of female.	1 Female seated with sickle and sheaf on right shoulder. ONE and fig. 1.
2 Sailor with flag, female at his feet.	Clay. Ancient Puritans around table. CITIZENS' UNION BANK, Scituate, R. I.	2 Male and female seated.
TWO 2	Spread eagle; iron castings, cannon balls, machinery, &c. 2 Title of Bank.	2 TWO Schooner rigged boat.

Left	Centre	Right
3 Same as 1's.	Fame in clouds blowing trumpet; eagle, globe, &c. CITIZENS' UNION BANK, Scituate, R. I.	3 Three Cupids and fig. 3.
5 Female seated with sheaf of grain.	Figure 5, and five females; ship on right; building on left. CITIZENS' UNION BANK, Scituate, R. I. Agricultural implements.	5 Indian Princess.
10 Washington. 10	William Tell and boy on right; man on horseback surrounded by six others. X X CITIZENS' UNION BANK, Scituate. State Arms.	10 Military officer on horse back. 10
20 Spread eagle 20	20 Washington on horseback, receiving gift from a female supporting pole and cap of liberty. 20 Title of Bank. Dog, &c.	20 Lafayette. 20
FIFTY	L Agricultural scene, buildings, load of hay, laborers with rakes, forks, &c. L Title of Bank. Engine and car.	50 Man and cattle. 50
100 Female; steeple, man and a pair of horses in distance. 100	C Steamboat filled with passengers ship and sloop on left. C Title of Bank. Ornamental star.	100 Three females seated.
1	CITY BANK, Providence, R. I. Female with shield and eagle; steamer, etc. Schooner etc.	1 Girl's head.
ONE Female portrait. ONE	1 Vig. Spread eagle upon limb, cars crossing canal on left, canal scene on right. 1 CITY BANK, Providence, R. I. Steamship.	ONE Farmer shearing sheep, woman standing behind him. ONE
Female standing erect in large ornamental figure 2.	2 Vig. Scene upon the ocean; capturing whale in foreground, boat and ship in background. 2 CITY BANK, Providence, R. I.	TWO Cupid in sail boat. TWO
Female with sickle; dog's head. 2	CITY BANK, Providence, R. I. Boy, child, cattle, etc.	2 Building.

R. ISLAND.	R. ISLAND.	R. ISLAND.
Sailor, mechanic, vessels, etc. THREE CITY BANK, Providence, R.I. 3 Mechanic and boilers. 3 3 Dog & safe.	500 Indian paddling canoe; forest in background. CITY BANK, Providence, R.I. D D 500 Female with sword and scales.	Two females; city in distance. 10 TEN DOLLARS. RHODE X ISLAND X on State arms of R. I. COMMERCIAL BANK TEN DOLLARS Bristol. 10 Female with spear, seated on cannon.
5 Portrait of female with sheaf in hand. 5 5 Vig. Female with shield, eagle, &c., seated in ornamental V, covering centre of note. 5 CITY BANK, Providence, R. I. FIVE Female seated with staff and cap in left hand. V	Washingt'n 1000 CITY BANK, Providence, R.I. Female with cornucopia; vessel, etc. 1000 M	Vulcan seated; train of cars, &c., in distance. TEN X Title of Bank. 10 Farmer with sheaf of wheat and sickle.
Pilot boat, and other vessels. 5 CITY BANK, Providence, R.I. Sailor with trumpet on vessel. 5 Female and V on shield.	1000 CITY BANK, Providence, R.I. Spread eagle on rock; vessel in distance. 1000 Indian female seated.	20 Female sitting, with book. XX Eagle. XX Title of Bank. 20 Ship under sail.
10 10 CITY BANK, Providence, R.I. Sailor and farmer either side of anchor on shield. 10 Child's head.	RHODE ISLAND ONE on 1 Sailor 1 Scene at wharf 1 COMMERCIAL BANK ONE DOLLAR Bristol. 1 Female portrait	FIFTY Female. FIFTY 50 Man and horse. 50 Title of Bank. FIFTY Female FIFTY
10 Female seated with grain in left hand. X Vig. Ships, steamboat and other vessels. X CITY BANK, Providence, R. I. Ship under sail. 10 Female with shield and scales in right hand, barrels in rear. X	ONE 1 Agricultural scene; farmer sowing; another in the distance harrowing. 1 COMMERCIAL BANK Bristol, R. I. 1 Ship. ONE	100 Small spread eagle. 100 C Vig. Man in chariot 100 with four horses abreast driving through air, clouds beneath. Title of Bank. Letter C. Portrait of Washington. Letter C.
L 50 CITY BANK, Providence, R.I. L Sailor, two farmers, etc L 50 State Arms.	2 R Island Dog's head TWO Sailor reclining on dock TWO COMMERCIAL BANK TWO DOLLARS Bristol 2 Two sailors	ONE Farmers boy with ears of corn in left hand holding cornstalk in right. ONE 1 Deck of ship with sailor at wheel steering. 1 COMMERCIAL B'K, Providence, R. I. ONE Portrait of Indian female with bow in hand, quiver on back. ONE
50 Female with left hand resting upon shield, right arm upon the neck of eagle. FIFTY CITY BANK. Providence. R. I. Vig. Large steamship under full sail 50 Female seated, sickle in right hand, horn of plenty in left, sheaf, boxes, &c. FIFTY	TWO Male in grain field. TWO 2 Naval engagement; ships of war; men in boat, &c. 2 Title of Bank. Anchor and word "hope" on shield. 2 Male portrait	1 Storm at sea; steamship, vessels, etc. COMMERCIAL BANK Providence, R.I. Bales. 1
100 Male portrait 100 Vig. Ship building; ship on stocks; ship at wharf on right; sloop under sail in distance on left. CITY BANK, Providence, R. I. Cornucopia, anchor, hand, &c. 100 Portrait of female holding dish of fruit. 100	THREE 3 Sailor; bale in hand, reclining against bales; in the distance are vessels, warehouses, dray, horses &c. 3 Title of Bank. 3 THREE Train of cars.	2 Two Dollars COMMERCIAL BANK Providence, R.I. Harbor scene—steamship, steamboats, vessels, etc. Barrels. 2 Two Dollars
C 100 CITY BANK, Providence, R.I. C Female with sheaf and shield; vessels in distance C 100 Eagle.	5 Goddess of Justice. RHODE ISLAND. COMMERCIAL BANK 5 General Burnside 5 FIVE Five Dollars. FIVE 5 Female with glass; large 5 at her back.	2 Male portrait COMMERCIAL B'K, Providence, R. I. Man-of-War and other vessels. 2 Commercial scene, sailor with quadrant, right hand on capstan.
Franklin. 500 CITY BANK, Providence, R.I. Indians receiving whites in boat 500 D	Spread eagle; city and vessels in distance. FIVE Large V, female and Cupid. Title of Bank. 5 Portrait of a girl.	THREE Female with basket of grapes in right hand. THREE 3 Two females sitting, at right orange tree, team and waggon in distance; on left bale of goods, ship and steamer in distance. COMMERCIAL B'K, Providence, R. I. THREE Sailor on deck of ship with telescope; ship in distance. THREE

5 Female seated holding roll of cloth in left hand, machinery on right. 5
Vig. Steamboat Boston. 5 Three medallions in frame with words "Five Dollars" running across.
Title of Bank.
Cupid mounted on Stag.
FIVE

5 Male portrait
COMMERCIAL B'K, Providence, R. I.
Commercial scene group of three sailors; one seated with spyglass.
5 [illegible] Head

10 Blacksmith's boy beside anvil
State arms of Rhode Island; female either side, vessels and buildings in distance
COMMERCIAL B'K
TEN DOLLARS
Providence
10 Male portrait

10 Ship under full sail. 10
Female seated left arm resting on vase; in right hand pitcher pouring water in basin; spread eagle on left.
COMMERCIAL B'K, Providence, R. I.
Anchors, barrels, and ship in distance.
10 Shield with view of mill on left; female with pole and cap on right; Indian with rifle. X

20 Female erect with pole and cap, shield with view of mill on right. 20
20 Neptune in car drawn by sea horses; on right ship in distance. 20
COMMERCIAL B'K, Providence, R. I.
Indian in canoe.
20 Female seated with sword and balances, resting with left arm on column. 20

50 Female with cornucopia on right hand resting left arm resting on shield with view of house. 50
Title of Bank.
Shield; view of machinery on shield, eagle surmounting; on right female with sword and balances, on left female with spear and helmet, bridge and ship in distance. 50 FIFTY
FIFTY

Female erect with hands supporting anchor on right. 100
100 Shield with eagle holding small shield in talons on large shield; on left female seated with pole and cap; ship in distance, on right cog wheel, anvil, &c. 100
Title of Bank.
Female reclining.
Female erect holding anchor on right 100

Full length statue of Washington. 500
500 500
COMMERCIAL B'K, Providence, R. I.
Female supporting shield in right hand, pole and cap in right, on left spread eagle, all resting on globe.
Spread swan feeding young swans.
Full length figure of female, left arm resting on column in right hand scroll. 500

1 Anchor, bales, &c.,
Locomotive and train of cars; another train crossing bridge, water vessel &c., in background
CONTINENTAL B'K, Providence. R. I.
Spread eagle.
1 Portrait of Female.

2
Same as Ones.
Portrait of Webster.
CONTINENTAL B'K, Providence, R. I.
Sheaf and Plow.
2 Spread eagle and shield.

Three females upon rock, one erect with hand on anchor, stock. THREE
CONTINENTAL B'K. Providence, R. I.
Child seated upon the shoulder of a man, at whom woman behind is gazing.
3 3
3 Female seated, leaning on bale; ship in background.

5 Indian with gun, seated upon rock.
Surrender of Lord Cornwallis.
CONTINENTAL B'K, Providence, R. I.
Sheaf and Plow.
5 Portrait of Washington.

Male portrait Medal Head.
CONTINENTAL B'K, Providence, R. I.
10 Goddess of liberty with eagle and globe.
X
10 Male portrait

20 Female seated with spool factory in background.
Ornamental figures 20, with winged females on either side, two small figures in the middle of large 2 & 0.
CONTINENTAL B'K. Providence, R. I.
20 Female seated in shell with trident.

50 Ship under sail.
Female seated leaning on bale, barrels, &c; ship on right, factory in distance on left.
CONTINENTAL B'K, Providence, R. I.
50 Portrait of Fillmore.

100 Female portrait.
Vig. Spread eagle on rock, large ship on either side.
CONTINENTAL B'K, Providence, R. I.
100 Female erect holding tablet on pillar, cogwheels, &c. around.

500 Portrait of Henry Clay.
Vig. Steamship under full sail, ships on either side.
CONTINENTAL B'K, Providence, R. I.
500 Sailor on ship's deck, with spy-glass in hand.

1 Female seated upon bale of goods with spool of yarn factories in the background.
Three females seated, one is one lower than other two, ships in the distance on the right.
COVENTRY BANK, Anthony Village, R. I.
State Arms.
1 Washington on horseback

Three females on a cliff overlooking the ocean, one resting right hand upon anchor, one with sheaf of wheat under her arm. TWO
Female seated resting one arm upon the State Arms of R. I. an ocean scene with ships in the background.
Title of Bank.
Mechanic Emblems.
2 Medal head of Franklin.

5 Male Figure resting one arm upon a short column pain-ters pallet, &c., at her feet.
Female seated on a safe, child playing with a dog at her feet; cars with ship in the distance at the right agricultural emblems on the left.
Title of Bank.
Sheaf of wheat, plow, &c.
5 Female figure resting right arm on shield pole with cap of liberty in her hand, bunch of arrows at her back.

5 Female seated with pen, pencil, harp, &c.
Eagle and shield.
COVENTRY BANK, Anthony Village, R. I.
5 Indian princess.

10 Male seated.
Female seated with agricultural implements at her left; Female in Medallion; on right, blacksmith shop in background on right.
Title of Bank.
Dog beside a Safe.
10 Three females erect

20 Train of cars entering a city, seen in the background.
Female seated with extended arms, scales in one hand, pole with cap of liberty in the other child upon each side.
Title of Bank.
Steamship.
20 Female with sheaf of wheat and sickle in her hand.

50 Female Portrait. 50
Two female figures seated: view of factories; cars and ship in the background.
Title of Bank.
Locomotive.
50 Men picking cotton in a field.

100 Sailor with American flag.
Title of Bank.
Female with child scattering flowers over a city.
Mechanic emblems.
100 Ship under sail. 100

1 Portrait of Washington
Female 1 Female
CRANSTON BANK. Cranston, R. I.
1 Portrait of Franklin.

TWO Two Indians reclining, one smoking, falls in background. TWO
2 Three females, two erect and one seated, plow, &c., ship on stocks, &c. 2
CRANSTON BANK. Cranston, R. I.
Cattle.
TWO Washington TWO

THREE
Farmer in field of wheat. Spread eagle, shield, &c. 3
CRANSTON BANK. Cranston, R. I.
Old fashioned cars and locomotive.
THREE Portrait of Female. 3

5 Franklin.
Female Three females seated; Cupid vessel on right, eagle on left.
CRANSTON BANK. Cranston, R. I.
River scene, &c.
5 Washington and his horse

X Indian in act of shooting with bow.
Steamboat, vessel, &c., buildings on right. X
CRANSTON BANK. Cranston, R. I.
10 Female with hat and sheaf.

20 XX Eagle. XX 20
CRANSTON BANK, Cranston, R. I.
Female seated with book on lap. — Ship

FIFTY 50 Man and horse. 50 FIFTY
CRANSTON BANK, Cranston, R. I.
Female. FIFTY — Female erect. FIFTY

Words ONE HUNDRED and figures 100. — Wheat scene, loading wagon with bbls. rum, horses, shipping, &c. — Same as on left.
CRANSTON BANK, Cranston, R. I.
Portrait of Harrison. — Male portrait

ONE — Vessels, &c. 1 — ONE
CUMBERLAND B'K, Cumberland, R. I.
Female Indian. ONE

2 TWO 2 — Vessels, &c., 2 — TWO
CUMBERLAND B'K, Cumberland, R. I.
Female with rope in hand. TWO

THREE — Farmers reaping, on right female with hat in hand and sheaf under arm. 3 — THREE
CUMBERLAND B'K, Cumberland, R. I.
Steamboat with masts. Word THREE and fig. 3.

FIVE — Female raising drapery from a 5 on shield. V — 5
CUMBERLAND B'K. Cumberland, R. I.
Vessel.

10 X 10 — Man, men and plow. 10 — TEN
CUMBERLAND B'K, Cumberland, R. I.
Female erect with horn of flowers in left hand.

20 — XX Eagle. XX — 20
CUMBERLAND B'K, Cumberland, R. I.
TWENTY — Ship.

FIFTY 50 Man and horse. 50 FIFTY
CUMBERLAND BK, Cumberland, R. I.
Female erect. FIFTY — Female. FIFTY

All other denominations are of the General Plate of the New England Bank Note Co.

ONE — EAGLE BANK, Bristol, R. I. — 1
Vig. Indian chief squaw, and child upon back, gazing below them from rock. Eagle.
Female seated, eagle beside her on shield.

Goddess of liberty erect with pole and cap in right hand, shield — Spread Eagle. — Vig. Female reclining upon cornucopia. — 2
EAGLE BANK, Bristol, R. I.
2 — Female swimming. — Female soaring in air, holding ornamental figure.

Goddess of liberty erect with pole and cap in right hand; shield eagle — 5 Vig. Farmer driving drove of sheep, mill in distance. — FIVE
EAGLE BANK, Bristol, R. I.
Indian erect resting hand on tomahawk.

50 — 50
Female erect leaning on a rock, cornucopia. 50
EAGLE BANK, Bristol, R. I.
FIFTY

C — 100 Vig. figure 100 pouring water from vessel; ship on right. — ONE HUNDRED
Portrait of Washington. C
EAGLE BANK, Bristol, R. I.

Spread eagle — 1 Portrait of female harp on right; book, scroll and globe on left. 1
EAGLE BANK, Providence, R. I.
State Arms. — Portrait of Washington.

1 — EAGLE BANK, Providence, R. I. — ONE
Machinist, bust of Watts, machinery, &c
Eagle on rock.
1 1 — Two children.

TWO — 2 Portrait of female, resting left arm, on pail; agricultural implements around. 2 — TWO
Locomotive and cars crossing bridge. TWO
EAGLE BANK, Providence R. I.
State Arms. — Steamboat. TWO

Full length figure of America. — 2 EAGLE BANK, Providence, R. I. — 2
Eagle on rock.
2 — 2

Spread eagle on limb of tree — 3 Two females seated; safe and ship on right; steamer in distance on left. 3
EAGLE BANK, Providence, R. I.
State Arms. — Portrait of Female.

FIVE — 5 Female seated on small globe spread eagle by her side on left. V — RHODE ISLAND
EAGLE BANK, Providence, R. I.
Anchor.

5 5 — Title of Bank — 5 5
Vig. Large V. in centre of note; on right female seated, bales, barrel, &c. at her back; river and sloop in background before her; on left man reclining, two men seated on casks, dray, with man and two horses, in background on his right.
Female seated.

FIVE — EAGLE BANK, Providence, R. I. — 5
Female resting on wheel. 5 Portrait of Abe Lincoln. 5 — Eagle on rock.

TEN — 10 Vig. Neptune in car, drawn by two horses. X — RHODE ISLAND
EAGLE BANK, Providence, R. I.
Anchor.

X X — Title of Bank. — X X
Vig. Large X in centre of note; on right goddess of Liberty reclining, eagle behind her, globe, ship, and steam-ship on her left; on left of X female seated on bale, resting on hogshead; anchor, bale, and ship on her left; steamship in distance on her right.
Dog.

RHODE I. — 20 Vig. Ship sailing, 20 shore, on which is anchor upright, and motto in scroll, "In God we hope. — TWENTY
Title of Bank.
Anchor.

RHODE ISLAND — 50 Vig. Sh[illegible] sea 50 of [illegible]; ship sailing ahead of her. — FIFTY
Title of Bank.
Anchor on shield.

RHODE ISLAND — 100 Vig. Spread 100 eagle upon anchor leaning against rock, overlooking sea, on which ship is seen; upon the rock is a scroll and motto; "In God we hope." — ONE HUNDRED
Title of Bank.
Anchor upon shield.

1 — View of Elmwood Village. — ONE
Head of Webster. ONE
ELMWOOD BANK, Cranston, R. I.
Elm Tree. — Large figure 1 with male supporting it

2 — View of Elmwood village. Head of Frank Pierce. II. Female supporting large figure 2. ELMWOOD BANK, Cranston, R. I. Elm Tree. 2

FIVE — Figure representing a man eating, woman talking and dog watching; high bluff of land water in distance. 5 View of Elmwood village. ELMWOOD BANK, Cranston, R. I. Elm Tree. 5 Figure of Justice with scales. FIVE

TEN — Female supporting large X. 10. ELMWOOD BANK, Cranston, R. I. View of Elmwood Village. Elm Tree. 10 Letter X covered with vines, female with pail and cow.

50 — Female Head. ELMWOOD BANK, Cranston, R. I. View of Elmwood Village. 50. Figures 50 supported by three men representing agriculture, manufacture and commerce.

100 — Ornamental letter C surrounding sheaf and head of female. ELMWOOD BANK, Cranston, R. I. Two females with scythe and shield. Tree. 100 View of village. 100

1 — Locomotive and cars. ONE. Vig. Group of females, representing toiling scene. Steamboat. EXCHANGE BANK, Providence, R. I. State arms. 1 Female bailing. ONE

ONE — Female supporting ornamental fig. 1. ONE. Male portrait with cupid on either side. EXCHANGE BANK, Providence, R. I. State arms. ONE Vig. Boy, sheep, dog, basket, &c.; cars crossing bridge. 1

2 — Vessel and steamboat on river opposite town. Vig. Female seated holding key in right hand, receiving cornucopia from winged figure on right; rafe and griffin on left. TWO. EXCHANGE BANK, Providence, R. I. State arms. 2 Female with state arms on right, scales on left. TWO

2 — Portrait of Daniel Webster. Male portrait. Vig. Two figures: mechanic, milk and anvil; ship on right; cars on left. EXCHANGE BANK, Providence, R. I. State arms. 2 TWO

Female seated on bales, with cornucopia; 5 at her feet. FIVE. EXCHANGE BANK, Providence, R. I. Large V; female seated, sheaf, etc. 5 Female portrait.

10 — Vig. Human figure with sickle in right hand; plough, rake, &c. on right; sheaf of grain on left. 10. EXCHANGE BANK, Providence, R. I. State arms. 10 Two male figures supporting female with wreath of flowers. 10

Female soaring in air, with ear of corn in left hand. FIFTY. 50 Male portrait. 50 EXCHANGE BANK, Providence, R. I. State arms. Female soaring in air, sickle in right hand, grain in left. FIFTY

100 — Cupid. C. EXCHANGE BANK, Providence, R. I. Vig. New York Crystal Palace. State arms. 100 Cupid. Mal portrait.

Sailor sitting upon bale of goods with spy glass; ship in [illegible]. 500. EXCHANGE BANK, Providence, R. I. Vig. Male portrait with cupid on either side. State arms. 500 D. Female with sword in right hand, scales in left, cars on left.

M. Steamship Humboldt. Male Portrait. EXCHANGE BANK, Providence, R. I. State Arms. 1000 Sailor throwing the lead.

ONE — Ships on the ocean. 1. Figure 1 and eagle; in left Indian seated; on right, sailor seated, holding quadrant; in distance ship. EXETER BANK, Exeter, R. I. Female with sickle and sheaf. ONE Female seated; left arm resting on State Arms. 1

TWO — Female seated, right arm resting above figure 2. 2. 2 Cupid holding figure 2 in front of a block of stone. 2 EXETER BANK, Exeter, R. I. Eagle and small urn. Female erect, left arm resting on stone pillar. TWO

3 — Portrait of Washington. 3. 3 Female giving cattle drink. 3 EXETER BANK, Exeter, R. I. 3. 3 Portrait of De Witt Clinton.

FIVE — Female seated, holding eagle. V. 5 Female seated, with sickle; cows standing, and farm-house in distance. 5 EXETER BANK, Exeter, R. I. Indian in canoe. FIVE

10 — Female erect and State Arms. 10. TEN Agricultural implements; beehive, cornucopia, tree, sheaf of wheat, linen wheel, &c. TEN. EXETER BANK, Exeter, R. I. Cupid on the back of a deer. 10

1 — Man on horseback, boy standing with left hand over cow, three other cows standing around on left of man, dog houses in distance. Large figure 1, view of sea monster standing on rock on right. FALL RIVER UNION BANK, Tiverton, R. I. Steamboat and vessel. ONE Full length figure of Indian with bow and arrow. 1

2 — Train of Cars; Depot and men on right; on left pier steamship, sail vessels, &c. Large figure 2, with portrait of female on right. Title of Bank. 2 Washington standing beside horse, battle in distance. TWO

FIVE — Vig. Indian in canoe; sloops and other sail vessels in distance; on right; on left, house, trees, &c.; large letter V, extending across bill. FALL RIVER UNION BANK, Tiverton, R. I. [illegible] 5 Female figure holding shield in hands, on which is figure 5.

X — Vig. Blacksmith sitting on bolster, blowing bellows; forge, anvil, and bench with tools at right; wheel on left, large ornamental X extending across bill. Title of Bank. TEN Large portrait of Washington. TEN

20 — Female sitting; right hand resting on chest; open book on lap. XX Vig. Spread eagle standing on rock. XX FALL RIVER UNION BANK, Tiverton, R. I. 20 Two ships, one in foreground, one in distance.

FIFTY — Full length figure of female in right hand wreath, and bunch of flowers in left. FIFTY. 50 Vig. Man and horse; horse rearing. 50 FALL RIVER UNION BANK, Tiverton, R. I. FIFTY Full length figure of female. FIFTY

Words one hundred running across figures 100. Male portrait. Dray cart, into which men are rolling barrels, horses, shipping, &c. FALL RIVER UNION BANK, Tiverton, R. I. Words one hundred running across figures 100. Male portrait.

500 — Vig. Female sitting, sheaves of grain at her feet; load of grain and men reaping in distance. 500 D. FALL RIVER UNION BANK, Tiverton, R. I. 500

1 — Female seated, steamer in the distance. Large figure 1 and portrait of five men. FRANKLIN BANK, Chepachet, R. I. 1 Female with sheaf of wheat.

ONE — Vessels. 1 FRANKLIN BANK, Chepachet, R. I. ONE Female. ONE

Left end	Centre	Right end
2	Agricultural scene. Large 2, and portraits of five men. FRANKLIN BANK, Chepachet, R. I.	TWO Female. TWO
2 TWO 2	Vessels. 2 FRANKLIN BANK, Chepachet, R. I.	TWO Female. TWO
THREE	Agricultural Scene. 3 FRANKLIN BANK, Chepachet, R. I.	Word THREE and fig. 3. Female. THREE
THREE	Man with sickle cutting grain; on right female with sheaf of wheat. 3 FRANKLIN BANK, Chepachet, R. I.	THREE Steamer. Word THREE and fig. 3.
FIVE	Eagle on shield and anchor; V, female and child buildings, vessels, &c. FRANKLIN BANK, Chepachet, R. I.	5 Girl with basket of flowers.
FIVE	Female. 5 FRANKLIN BANK, Chepachet, R. I.	5 Female.
X Indian with a bow.	Steamer and sailing vessels. X FRANKLIN BANK, Chepachet, R. I.	10 Female holding bonnet, and sheaf of wheat.
Vulcan seated, anvil, &c. around him; a distance buildings, train of cars. TEN	X FRANKLIN BANK, Chepachet, R. I.	10 Farmer with sheaf on his knee.
10 X 10	Oxen and man erect. 10 FRANKLIN BANK, Chepachet, R. I.	TEN Female.
20 Female seated, with ... on lap.	XX Eagle. XX FRANKLIN BANK, Chepachet, R. I.	20 Ship
Steamer. XX Female.	Figure of a female seated with spear and balances; eagle on left. 20 FRANKLIN BANK, Chepachet, R. I.	XX Female.
FIFTY Female. FIFTY	50 Man and horse. 50 FRANKLIN BANK, Chepachet, R. I.	FIFTY Female. FIFTY
50 Vessels.	Agricultural scene. 50 FRANKLIN BANK, Chepachet, R. I.	L Female.
100 Eagle. 100	C Ferries. 100 FRANKLIN BANK, Chepachet, R. I.	C Washington C
Words One Hundred, and figures 100. Portrait of Harrison.	Wharf scene; men loading wagon with bbls.; horses, drays, men, shipping, &c. FRANKLIN BANK, Chepachet, R. I.	Same as on left. Male portrait
1 [illegible] 1	1 1 Spread eagle ... [illegible] FREEMAN'S BANK, Bristol, R. I. ONE	1 ONE 1
2 [illegible] 2	2 2 Same as ones. Title of Bank. TWO	2 TWO 2
3 [illegible] 3	3 3 Same as ones. Title of Bank. THREE	3 THREE 3
FIVE	Spread eagle on shield; city and ships in distance. Female, cupid and letter V. Title of Bank.	5 Little girl with ... [illegible]
Male figure seated on machinery; cars at distance. TEN	X Title of Bank.	10 Male figure with sheaf in hand.
FIFTY 50 Female figure standing globe in her right hand, flowers at her right. FIFTY	Man and horse. 50 Title of Bank.	FIFTY Female figure with wreath of flowers in right hand. FIFTY
Words one hundred, and figures 100. Male portrait	Vig. Wharf scene; loading wagon ..., horses, shipping, &c. Title of Bank.	Words one hundred, and figures 100. Male portrait
1 Ornamental work and cupid with horn of plenty.	GLOBE BANK, Providence, R. I. Male supporting the world on shoulders on which is four females, representing the nations; female reclining on left; and male representing time on right, cars and steam ship in distance.	1 Same as left
2 Same as ones	GLOBE BANK, Providence, R. I. Same as ones.	2 Same as ones
3 Same as ones	GLOBE BANK, Providence, R. I. Same as ones.	3 Same as ones
FIVE	Five Globe Dollars with three females around it, and male at bottom. GLOBE BANK, Providence, R. I. Shield.	Word five and figure 5 5 Word five and figure 5
Female seated on rock with trident. FIVE	Nautical scene—ships, man of war, steamship, &c. GLOBE BANK, Providence, R. I. 5	5
FIVE	GLOBE BANK, Three females around globe, ... bottom. Providence, R. I. Anchor on shield.	Five on 5. 5 Five on 5
TEN	Title of Bank. Same as above fives. Anchor on shield.	X 10 X
X 10 X	Ten Vig. Dollars Same as fives. GLOBE BANK, Providence, R. I. Shield.	TEN

10 — Sailor with hand on capstan; bbls., ships' masts, &c., behind. | Female reclining on bale with wand; city and vessels on right; cars, canal boat, lock, &c., on left. GLOBE BANK Providence, R. I. | 10

50 — Female erect with spear and shield. | Male and female seated. GLOBE BANK, Providence, R. I. 50 | 50 — Cupid in sail boat. 50

FIFTY DOLLARS — Large fig. 50 surrounded by numerous small 50s. | Female resting with quadrant, globe, etc. GLOBE BANK, Providence, R. I. 50 | Same as left end.

100 — Vulcan seated with sledge. | Spread eagle on limb of tree; train of cars on left, and canal scene on right. GLOBE BANK, Providence, R. I. 100 | 100 — Female seated with rake.

One Hundred across 100. Male portrait | Wharf scene—men, horses, wagons, carts, etc. GLOBE BANK, Providence, R. I. | Same as on left end.

100 — Anchor, bales, etc. | State Arms; female either side. GLOBE BANK, Providence, R. I. | 100 — Female

500 — Washingt'n | GLOBE BANK, Providence, R. I. Two females seated on bale; factories in distance. | 500 — Female, spinning wheel; factories, etc.

Female fig. seated, holding bank notes in right hand. 1 | GLOBE BANK Smithfield, R. I. View of a public building. | 1 — Male portrait

THE GLOBE BANK. The word TWO in extreme corner and partly lengthwise. | Ocean scene—steamships and sail vessels. | 2 — Female with bunch of flowers and grass in left hand.

Female seated, with liberty pole and cap in left hand. 3 | GLOBE BANK Smithfield, R. I. Group of hay makers, with female and children sitting and laying on ground; load of hay, with horses in background. | 3 3

Water spouting from fountain. 5 | Two steamships and sail vessel. GLOBE BANK Smithfield, R. I. | 5 — Female portrait.

Two females standing. 10 | GLOBE BANK Smithfield, R. I. TEN Landscape scene; load of unthrashed wheat. TEN | 10 — Female figure standing, ear of corn in right hand, and letter X in left.

20 | GLOBE BANK Smithfield, R. I. Globe with Neptune seated in a shell; steamer and sail vessel in background. | XX — Squaw

50 | GLOBE BANK Smithfield, R. I. Globe with Heathen God, and two cherubs astride an eagle. L | 50 — Portrait of Webster.

C | GLOBE BANK Smithfield, R. I. Harbor and shipping. C | 100 — Female with a bundle of wheat.

Wild scenery [illegible] 500 D | 500 GLOBE BANK Smithfield, R. I. D | 500 — Female with balances and sword.

Spread eagle standing on rock near water; sail vessel under full sail. 1000 M | 1000 GLOBE BANK Smithfield, R. I. M | 1000 — Indian female, with bow and arrow.

One Dollar — 1 — Barrels, bales, ship, cornucopia, etc. 1 | 1 Female seated, bales, grain, etc. ship in distance. 1 GRANITE BANK ONE DOLLAR Pascoag Rhode Island | 1 — Agricultural implements. 1

1 — Head of Washingt'n | Female 1 Female. GRANITE BANK, Pascoag, R. I. | 1 — Head of Franklin.

2 — Head. | Female 2 Female. GRANITE BANK, Pascoag, R. I. | 2 — Head.

3 — Washingt'n full length. | Female head and bust. 3 Female head and bust. GRANITE BANK, Pascoag, R. I. | 3 — Vulcan full length.

Eagle resting on United States shield and an anchor. FIVE | Large V, with female figure and child. GRANITE BANK, Pascoag, R. I. | 5 — Female figure and basket.

Male figure seated on machinery; cars in distance. TEN | X GRANITE BANK, Pascoag, R. I. | 10 — Male figure with sheaf in hand.

20 — Female with spear. | 2 Female 0 GRANITE BANK, Pascoag, R. I. XX | 20 — Female seated. 20

50 — Female with spear. | Male and female seated. GRANITE BANK, Pascoag, R. I. 50 | 50 — Cupid in boat. 50

100 — Man with sledge, anchor. | Vig. Spread eagle upon branch of tree; canal scene on right; train of cars crossing bridge on left. GRANITE BANK, Pascoag, R. I. 100 | 100 — Female with rake, seated beside cornucopia.

1 — ONE on fig. 1 | GREENWICH BANK East Greenwich, R. I. Sailor reclining with implements; ships in distance. 1 Stockholders, etc. 1 | 1 — Train of cars

2 — TWO DOLLARS | Man, female, boy, girl, dog, hen and chickens. Two females on right is female instructing children; on left is Indian, squaw and papoose. GREENWICH BANK East Greenwich, R. I. Red 2. Red 2 | 2 — Squaw and female.

5, V & FIVE. State Arms. FIVE | Signing Declaration of Independence. Washington GREENWICH BANK East Greenwich, R. I. Red 5. Arm. Red 5 | 5 on ord. head. Male portrait

X — Liberty, eagle and shield. | GREENWICH BANK East Greenwich, R. I. View of buildings, trees and park. Stockholders, etc. | 10 — Female portrait.

Female with veil. XX	Title of Bank. Train of cars coming from under arch; two laborers. Stockholders, etc.	20 Man plowing with two horses.
50 Sailor, mechanic, two females, city, lighthouse, chimney, hills etc.	50 Title of Bank. State Arms.	Fifty inverted. Plow boy, two females, drg. oxen, sheaf, &c
1 Two cattle one standing other lying down. ONE	GROCERS' AND PRODUCERS' BANK, Providence, R. I. Vig. Two females seated, one on right holding bale of goods upon her lap; factories in distance behind her; steamboat in extreme distance on left.	1 Female on either side of state arms.
2 Blacksmith leaning over anvil. TWO	GROCERS' AND PRODUCERS' BANK. Providence, R. I. Female seated in large ornamental 2.	2 Portrait of little girl. TWO
5 male.	State Arms; Indian seated upon right, farmer with sickle upon left; canoe upon river on right; cars in distance on left Title of Bank.	Figure 5 with word FIVE. Portrait of Sailor,
10 Large X with 10 on it, glass on right light house on left.	GROCERS' AND PRODUCERS' BANK. Providence, R. I. State Arms, eagle upon globe surmounting it; female on either side.	10 Large ship at sea.
50	Title of Bank. Two females seated; one on left supporting shield with sheaf upon its face; one on right holding wand in left hand; portrait of Franklin on right; steamboat vessel &c., on right in distance, wagon crossing bridge cars &c., on left in distance.	50 State Arms 50
100	Female seated supporting shield, with arm and hammer upon it; cars, steamship, &c., on right. GROCERS' AND PRODUCERS' BANK, Providence, R I	100 Boy with basket seated among sheep; cars in distance upon left. 100
D Small Cupid holding cornucopia. 500	Title of Bank Large steamboat sailing past city in background. 500	Farmer erect sharpening scythe, cars bridge in distance. 500
ONE 1	Farmer sowing. 1 HIGH STREET B'K, Providence, R. I.	1 Ship. ONE
1 Portrait of Washington.	Female. 1 Female. HIGH STREET B'K. Providence, R. I.	1 Portrait of Franklin.
1 Clay.	HIGH STREET BK. Providence, R. I. Washington reading despatches; man writing resting on drum; horse, cannon, soldiers, &c.	1 Eagle on Shield.
TWO 2	Eagle on a rock. 2 HIGH STREET B'K, Providence, R. I.	2 TWO Vessels.
2 Female, bales, horn of plenty, etc.	Title of Bank. Cows in brook; children on bank; tree, etc.	2 Franklin.
2 Male portrait	Female. 2 Female. HIGH STREET B'K, Providence, R. I.	2 Male portrait.
3 Blacksmith at work	HIGH STREET BK. Providence, R.I. Washington	3 Man dressing leather.
THREE 3	Sailor with hat in hand; bales of merchandise, shipping, &c. 3 HIGH STREET B'K, Providence, R. I.	3 THREE Train of cars.
3 Washington and Lafayette	Female 3 Female HIGH STREET B'K, Providence. R. I	3 Male figure.
FIVE	Eagle on shield and anchor; buildings, vessels, &c V, female and child. HIGH STREET B'K, Providence, R. I	5 Girl with basket of flowers.
FIVE	Female. 5 HIGH STREET B'K, Providence, R. I.	5 Ship.
TEN	Vulcan seated; factory and cars in distance. X HIGH STREET B'K, Providence, R. I.	10 Farmer with sheaf on his knee.
10 X 10	Man and oxen. 10 HIGH STREET B'K, Providence, R. I.	TEN Female.
20 Female.	XX Eagle. XX HIGH STREET B'K, Providence, R. I.	20 Ship.
Female erect with wand, eagle, etc. 20	20 Female portrait. HIGH STREET BK., Providence, R. I.	20 Franklin.
FIFTY Agricultural products. 50	50 Three females seated; vessel on left. HIGH STREET BK., Providence, R. I.	Word FIFTY and fig. 50. Vulcan seated with anvil, hammer, etc.; cars on left.
FIFTY Female erect FIFTY	50 Man and horse. 50 HIGH STREET B'K. Providence, R. I.	FIFTY Female erect FIFTY
Figures 100 and words one hundred Male portrait	Wharf scene, men loading wagon; shipping, &c HIGH STREET B'K Providence, R. I.	Figures 100 and words one hundred Male portrait
Male portrait 1	Two trains of cars, another crossing bridge in distance. HOPE BANK, Warren, R. I.	1 Female portrait
ONE	Vig. Scene upon water; sailing vessels &c. 1 HOPE BANK, Warren, R. I.	ONE Indian girl erect with bow and arrows. ONE
Male portrait 2	Two cherubs with swords and two silver dollars; cars, bills and steamboat in distance. HOPE BANK, Warren, R. I.	2 Female portrait.

Left	Centre	Right
2 TWO 2	Vig. Ships sailing upon water, &c. 2 HOPE BANK, Warren, R. I.	TWO Female drawing water from a well. TWO
THREE	Vig. Farmers reaping grain; female with sheaf under left arm, on right. 3 HOPE BANK, Warren, R. I.	THREE Steamboat. THREE with figure 3 across it.
3 Male portrait THREE	Milkmaid milking cow, another lying down. HOPE BANK, Warren, R. I.	3 Female portrait
Soldier with sword. FIVE	Male and female portrait. 5 HOPE BANK, Warren, R. I.	Justice erect FIVE
FIVE	Vig. Female raising drapery from shield, upon which is figure 5. V HOPE BANK. Warren, R. I.	5 Ship at sea with signals flying.
Five with V running across it.	Vig. Female with rake in left hand, sickle in right; ship, canons, &c. on right; men, team, &c. on left. V and Indian queen HOPE BANK, Warren, R. I.	5 Portrait of Washington
Female portrait X	Bales and barrels. Female seated representing Commerce; ship in distance. HOPE BANK, Warren, R. I.	10 Indian princess.
10 X 10	Pair of oxen with a man standing by an ancient plow. 10 HOPE BANK. Warren, R. I.	TEN Female erect holding cornucopia in left hand, barometer in right.
50 Vessel and steamboat sailing.	Vig. Farming scene, loading waggon with grain, man with rake in right hand on right. 50 HOPE BANK, Warren, R. I.	L Female kneeling with sword and scales.
50 Female erect with resting upon shield on pillar	Vig. Male and female seated, cornucopia between them. HOPE BANK, Warren, R. I. 50	50 Cupid in a sailboat. 50

Left	Centre	Right
100 Male portrait.	HOPE BANK. Vessels at sea. One Hundred Dollars.	100 Two children.
100 Spread Eagle. 100	C Vig. Mercury in car with torch, drawn by four horses. 100 HOPE BANK, Warren, R. I.	C Portrait of Washington. C
100 Vulcan seated, hammer and scroll.	Vig. Spread eagle upon branch of tree; canal scene on right; train of cars crossing bridge on left. HOPE BANK. Warren, R. I. 100	100 Female with rake, seated beside cornucopia.
1 Drummer, two men seated.	JACKSON BANK, Providence, R. I. 1 Large Portrait Gen. Jackson. 1	1 Blacksmith erect beside anvil.
2 View on battle field, throwing up entrenchments.	JACKSON BANK, Providence, R. I. 2 Same as ones. 2	2 Soldier erect holding flag beside canon.
5 Scene upon prairie, Indians hunting buffalo.	JACKSON BANK. Providence, R. I. Vig. Small portrait of Jackson	5 Country scene, two children, one in foreground, man felling tree on right of them.
X Portrait of Gen. Taylor.	Vig. Jackson and staff on horseback overlooking battle field of New Orleans JACKSON BANK, Providence, R. I. Spread eagle.	10 Portrait of Gen Scott.
C C	Vig. View of Harbor of N. Y. ships and steamships sailing off city. JACKSON BANK, Providence, R. I. State Arms.	100 Portrait of President Jackson.
1 State arms. 1	1 Vig. Landing of the Pilgrims. 1 LANDHOLDERS B'K. Kingston, R. I. State arms.	Female figure on large figure 1.
TWO Head of Washington. TWO	2 Female figure. 2 Figure of Justice. 2 LANDHOLDERS B'K, Kingston, R. I. State arms.	2 Female sitting, sheaf of wheat &c. 2

Left	Centre	Right
3 Female head 3	3 Vig. Train of cars; houses in back ground 3 LANDHOLDERS B'K, Kingston, R. I. State arms.	THREE Boat. 3
V on FIVE	Female seated with agricultural implements; factories, shipping, etc. Indian girl in V. LANDHOLDERS' BANK, Kingston, R. I.	5 Washington.
10 X 10	Pair of oxen with a man standing by an ancient plow. 10 LANDHOLDERS B'K. Kingston, R. I.	TEN Female figure with cornucopia of fruits and flowers.
Mercury with wand and eagle. 20	Twenty on 20 Female portrait. LANDHOLDERS B'K. Kingston, R. I.	20 Benjamin Franklin
FIFTY Grain, fruit flowers, etc 50	50 Three females seated with pole, cap, scales book, eagle, ship. Title of Bank.	Fifty on 50 Blacksmith seated with implements
C Men and boats. 100	Eagle on bale. 100 Title of Bank.	100 Female with sickle. 100
1 Hunter with rifle in hand, dog beside him.	LIBERTY BANK, Providence, R. I. 1 Vig. Large horse running in foreground; boys trying to stop him, one with cap in hand on right; factory in distance; one boy fallen down, one running, on left; dog and horses in distance. 1	1 Portrait of child.
2 TWO 2	LIBERTY BANK, Providence, R. I. Female erect with sword and shield. Horses alarmed at light plug, cars in distance TWO TWO	2 Portrait of female.
2 Female portrait.	LIBERTY BANK, Providence, R. I. Vig. Drover buying cattle of farmer; sheep and two men on left.	2
5 Full length sailor looking to right of note.	LIBERTY BANK, Providence, R. I. 5 Vig. Landing of Roger Williams on Slate Rock. 5	5 Female portrait.

10 Anchor leaning upon bales; ship in background.	Vig. Goddess of Liberty with pole and cap, shield; spread eagle on left. Portrait of Indian girl with bow and quiver LIBERTY BANK, Providence, R. I. Spread eagle.	10 Portrait of Washington. TEN
50 le portrait	Vig. Spread eagle upon shield, scroll in beak, "E pluribus unum" upon it; vessels on right; cars and city in distance on left. LIBERTY BANK, Providence, R. I. Spread eagle.	50 Indian seated resting right hand upon shield, with pole and cap, quiver on her shoulder.
100	Vig. Surrender of Lord Cornwallis to George Washington. LIBERTY BANK, Providence, R. I.	100 Spread eagle upon shield looking to left of note.
1 Two sailors [illegible] ing ONE	LIME ROCK BANK, Providence, R. I. Sailor and Indian either side of State Arms surmounted by eagle.	1 Male portrait
2 Old man with gun; female loading gun.	Girl's head. TITLE Red 2. Man and boy plowing with two horses.	2
Three females erect supporting figure 3.	Vig. sailor seated among bales, with spy glass in his left hand; ship in distance on left of vig. Title of Bank.	3 Wild horse upon the prairie fleeing from locomotive.
5 5	Vig. Mechanic seated on ground, surrounded with wheel, tools, &c.; boy making in distance. 5 Title of Bank. Dog's head.	FIVE Goddess of Liberty erect FIVE
X 10	Vig. Female seated upon ground, corn, fruit, &c.; vessels upon stream in distance on left. Title of Bank. Spread eagle.	10 Mason at work, level in his hand
20 Female erect; spear in left hand, small globe at her feet.	Vig. Female seated between ornamental figures 2 and 0. Title of Bank. XX	20 Female seated; cornucopia, etc. 20
50	Steamship sailing out of harbor, steamboat, sail vessels, etc. LIME ROCK BANK, Providence, R. I.	50 Female portrait

Female portrait	Title of Bank. Marine view; man-of-war and other vessels under sail.	100
1	Female seated with rod on left of shield on which is Hope and anchor; train of cars on right, buildings on left. 1 MANUFACTURERS' BANK, Providence, R. I.	ONE Female Portrait.
2	Same as 1's. 2 MANUFACTURERS' BANK, Providence, R. I.	TWO Female Portrait.
2 Portrait of a girl	Fig. 2 on shield; eagle on right and female with pole, cap, bales, etc. on left. TWO MANUFACTURERS' BANK, Providence, R. I.	2 Female portrait.
3 Female erect with hand on capstan.	THREE Female reclining with pole and cap in left hand; right arm resting on bbls; cornucopia, &c.; steamboat on left; Sheep on right. Title of Bank.	3 Female erect holding aloft scales; sword in left hand.
5 Male seated in an arm chair. FIVE	FIVE Female seated with pen in right hand and left resting on globe, &c., building, locomotive and tender on left; vessel on right. Title of Bank.	5 Female with spear; globe and owl at her feet.
10	View of bridge, coach and four crossing it; buildings in background; canal scene in front. X MANUFACTURERS' BANK, Providence, R. I.	TEN Female reclining on cogwheel; pedestal or column in rear. 10
TWENTY	Female seated with arm around column, pointing to sloop on water, behind her sheaf, rake, &c. XX MANUFACTURERS' BANK, Providence, R. I.	20 View of bridge, &c., same as vig. 10's. XX
50	Canal boat loaded with bales of cotton; factory and other buildings in distance; waterfalls; schooner, sloop, &c. FIFTY MANUFACTURERS' BANK, Providence, R. I.	50 Male with tablet, reclining on screw wheel, &c.
100 Female. 100	Vig. Same as 50's. MANUFACTURERS' BANK, Providence, R. I.	100 Vulcan with sledge; right arm pointing.

500	Female seated pointing to farming scene. 500 D MANUFACTURERS' BANK, Providence, R. I.	500
Laocoon statue; serpents around human figures. 1000	THOUSAND Train of cars. MANUFACTURERS' BANK, Providence, R. I.	1000 Vessels. 1000
ONE Sailor with flag.	Shipping: navy yard in background. MARINE BANK, Providence, R. I.	1 Anchor and bales.
Sailor with flag and female figure of Agriculture.	2 Whaling scene MARINE BANK, Providence, R. I.	2 Female with glass looking seaward.
Three females representing Agriculture, Commerce and Manufactures.	Steamship; city in distance. MARINE BANK, Providence, R. I.	3 Female figure of Commerce.
5 Sailor leaning on capstan.	Launch of the Adriatic MARINE BANK, Providence, R. I.	5 Head of Falcon. FIVE
RHODE ISLAND 10 X	MARINE BANK, Providence, R. I. Female, anchor and word "Hope" in a frame; on right, female, vessels, etc.; on left female and view of Niagara Falls. TEN DOLLARS	10 RHODE ISLAND X
50 Fancy female head	Steamboat landing and railroad depot; city view, etc. MARINE BANK, Providence, R. I.	50 Eagle on a shield.
100 Sailor leaning on capstan.	Fame blowing trumpet; eagle, globe, etc. MARINE BANK, Providence, R. I.	100 Washington
Mechanic, anvil, cogwheel, sledge, &c. ONE	Vig. Spread eagle American shield, &c. MECHANICS' BANK, Providence, R. I. State arms.	1 Male portrait

Left end	Centre	Right end
ONE	1 Two Eagles with State Arms in centre. 1 MECHANICS' BANK, Providence, R. I.	ONE
2 Male portrait	Female resting upon State Arms, schooner in distance on right, and buildings on left. Title of Bank Blacksmith's Arm.	2 Male portrait
TWO	2 Two Eagles with State Arms in centre. 2 MECHANICS' BANK, Providence, R. I.	TWO
FIVE	5 Woman, eagle resting on Globe on left. 5 MECHANICS' BANK, Providence, R. I. Cogwheel.	FIVE
FIVE	5 Two Eagles with State Arms in centre. 5 MECHANICS' BANK, Providence, R. I.	FIVE
10 Mechanics Arm and sledge.	Two females with State Arms between them, with eagle resting upon State Arms. Title of Bank.	10 Portrait of Washington.
20 Male portrait	Mechanic with tools and pieces of machinery. MECHANICS' BANK, Providence, R. I. State Arms.	20 Portrait of Franklin.
FIFTY Female with wreath. FIFTY	50 Man and Horse. 50 MECHANICS' BANK, Providence, R. I.	FIFTY Full length female, Globe, Rule, &c. FIFTY
Words one hundred and figures 100 Male portrait.	Vig. Market scene; shipping on left. MECHANICS' BK., Providence, R. I.	Words one hundred, and figures 100. Male portrait.
Female seated, with farmer at work in distance. 500	500 D MECHANICS' BK., Providence, R. I.	500

Left end	Centre	Right end
1000	THOUSAND Vig. In upper left corner of note, which is incomplete—a classical name, MECHANICS' BK., Providence, R. I.	1000 Locomotive and cars. Ship. 1000
1 Female seated resting her arm on shield.	MECH'S & MAN. BK., Providence, R. I. Vig. Santa Claus in sleigh drawn by deers.	1 Female leaning on ornamental figure 1, sickle in her right hand
ONE Female erect writing in book resting on ornamental figure 1. ONE	1 Vig. Two females, one kneeling, the other standing; bales, ship, and steamer on right; fruit, tree, wagon, &c., on left. MECH'S & MAN. BK., Providence, R. I.	ONE Female erect with sickle beside ornamental fig. 1. ONE
Female figure either side of large fig. 2 2	MECHANICS & MANUFACTURERS BANK TWO DOLLARS Providence, R. I.	2 Female with grain, etc.
TWO Female portrait in circular die TWO	2 Vig. Female with compass and book; cogwheel and anvil on right; plough, yoke, screw, hammer, &c., on left. MECH'S & MAN. BK., Providence, R. I.	2 Female seated, child beside her, cornucopia at her feet. 2
Portrait of Webster. 3	MECH'S & MAN. BK., Providence, R. I. 3 Vig. Figure 3 resting on book; two females reclining, one with arm on book on right; one female seated on left with wand in hand; factory in distance behind her.	3 3
5	Vig. Figure 5, Justice standing behind it holding scales; on either side of the 5 are two female figures; locomotive and factory on right of vig.; ships, bales, &c., on left. Title of Bank. Dog's head.	5 Head of boy
5 Female seated in large V. FIVE	5 Vig. Large 5 with five figures around it. 5 MECH'S & MAN. BK., Providence, R. I.	5 Female with sheaf of grain seated in large figure 5. FIVE
X Bales, cogwheels, &c. X	MECH'S & MAN. BK., Providence, R. I. Vig. Large Indian with bow, arrow, and quiver, reclining upon shield; three deers, woods, and water, on his right; deer, Indians in canoe, and soaring eagle on his left.	10 Female portrait.
10 Farmer sowing grain. TEN	Vig. Jupiter erect, with anchor, shield, sheaf, bags, bales and barrels; ship and steamer in distance, on right; coaches, factory, &c., on left. On right of vig., divided by a small space, is a scene on canal. MECH. & MAN. BK., Providence, R. I.	10 Ship and other vessels sailing by a light-house. TEN

Left end	Centre	Right end
XX Portrait of female.	MECH. & MAN. BK., Providence, R. I. Vig. Female kneeling beside globe; quadrant, compass, paper, &c., before her; sailing vessel and steamship on her right.	20 Bales, anchor, &c.
Steamer. XX Locomotive and cars.	Vig. Three females representing liberty, justice and learning; ship on right; eagle on left. 20 MECH. & MAN. BK., Providence, R. I.	XX Female erect, with roll under right arm; stool in left hand.
50 50	MECH. & MAN. BK., Providence, R. I. Vig. Scene in a boiler yard; men working on boilers in background; in foreground, man seated with tools in his hands, leaning on piece of steamer's pipe.	50 Female portrait.
50 Steamer and schooner.	Vig. Harvesting scene; loading wagon with hay; farm-house in view. 50 MECH. & MAN. BK., Providence, R. I.	L Female kneeling, with sword and balance
100 Ornamental fountain.	MECH. & MAN. BK., Providence, R. I. Vig. Female seated with pole and liberty cap; eagle behind her; globe, ship, and steamship on left.	100 100
100 Spread eagle. 100	C Vig. Four horses drawing chariot through the air, in which is [illegible] figure with torch. 100 MECH. & MAN. BK., Providence, R. I.	C Portrait of Washington C
500	Vig. Indian paddling canoe, forests in the background. MECH. & MAN. BK., Providence, R. I. D D	500 Female with sword and scales.
1000	MEC. AND MANUFACTURERS' B'K, Providence, R. I. Spread eagle upon a rock, overlooking the sea, on which a ship is dimly seen.	1000 Indian maiden seated.
1 Portrait of female.	MERCANTILE BANK Providence, R. I. Figure of sailor; ships in distance.	1 Female figure.
2 Figure of mechanic.	MERCANTILE BANK Providence, R. I. Train of cars, male and female figures.	2

3 — Scene in blacksmith's shop; man shoeing horse, &c. — 3
Female figure. MERCANTILE BANK Providence, R. I. Male figure.

5 — Steamship, sailing vessels, &c. — 5
Sailor leaning on capstan. MERCANTILE BANK Providence, R. I. Female reaper with bundle of grain.

Rural scene—cows; church in the distance. — 10
10 — MERCANTILE BANK Providence, R. I. — Portrait of female.

20 — Ships, &c., sailing — 20
Anchor, boxes, barrels, &c. MERCANTILE BANK Providence, R. I. Train of cars, village in the distance.

50 — MERCANTILE BANK Providence, R. I. — 50
Jupiter (God of Thunder) in his chariot. Man with arms full of corn stalks.

Portrait of Columbus. MERCANTILE BANK Providence, R. I. — 100
Head of Franklin; on either side cupid. Head of Washington; on either side cupid.
100

500 — MERCANTILE BANK Providence. R. I. — 500
Figures of mechanic and sailor, bale of goods; ship in distance.
Portrait of Webster. Portrait of Washington.

1 RHODE ISLAND 1 — 1 One Dollar. 1 — 1 ONE 1
MERCHANTS' BK., Newport, R. I.
1

1 View of paper mill and eagle. — Cupid supporting figure 1.
MERCHANTS' BK., Newport, R. I.

1 — Female reclining and supporting figure 1; train of cars on right; steamboat on left. — 1
Sailor and capstan. MERCHANTS' BK., Newport, R. I. Female seated on safe, pole, Liberty cap and figure 1.

2 View of a stone mill.
MERCHANTS' BK., Newport, R. I.

2 RHODE ISLAND 2 — Two Dollars. 2 — TWO
MERCHANTS' BK., Newport, R. I.
2

TWO — Farmers washing sheep. — 2
Indian with bow and arrow. MERCHANTS' BK., Newport, R. I. Two females.

3 RHODE ISLAND 3 — 3 Three Dollars. 3 — THREE
MERCHANTS' BK., Newport, R. I.
3

3 — Three male figures, and three gold dollars; scythe and sheaf of grain on left; ship and factory on right. — 3
Female with anchor. MERCHANTS' BK., Newport, R. I. Female giving eagle drink.

V RHODE ISLAND V — 5 Five dollars. V — FIVE
MERCHANTS' BANK Newport, R. I.
V

RHODE ISLAND — 5 5 View of State House. — FIVE
MERCHANTS' BANK Newport, R. I.

5 — Female reclining with wand in right hand; steamship on right, and locomotive and bridge on left. — 5
Female portrait. MERCHANTS' BANK Newport, R. I. Group of female supporting figure 5.
FIVE

X RHODE ISLAND X — 10 Words ten dollars. X — TEN
MERCHANTS' BANK Newport, R. I.
X

10 — Female with spear reclining on state arms, sheaf of grain, safe, plow, and rake; cars in distance on right; steamship on left. — 10
Tritons supporting cornucopia. MERCHANTS' BANK Newport, R. I. Spread eagle.
Steamship. TEN

TWENTY — MERCHANTS' BANK Newport, R. I. — Squaw and female.
TWENTY
Two Indians. Twenty Twenty 20

50 — View of steamship and ship. — 50
Four females, globe, &c. MERCHANTS' BANK Newport, R. I. Locomotive.

RHODE ISLAND — 50 Title of Bank. 50 — FIFTY
Med. head of Com. Perry.

Train of cars. — Female portrait.
MERCHANTS' BANK Newport, R. I.
100 Ship. 100

1 — Large ship at sea under sail; ship in distance on left. — 1
Portrait of Franklin. MERCHANTS' B'K, Providence, R. I. Sailor, erect holding spy glass in left hand, hat in right.
ONE State Arms.

1 On die with words ONE. — Ocean view, ships, &c. — 1 On die with words ONE.
MERCHANTS' B'K, Providence, R. I.
Bust of Female with han'k'rchief on her head. ONE DOLLAR on ornamental die. Female, plough, barrels, &c.

2 — Spread Eagle on limb of tree; cars crossing bridge over canal on left; canal scene on right. — 2
Portrait of Washington. MERCHANTS' B'K, Providence, R. I. Female erect representing Justice with scales and sword.
TWO State Arms.

2 On die with words TWO. — MERCHANTS' B'K, Providence, R. I. — 2 On die with words TWO.
Shipping.
Bust of Female in green die. Bust of Female in green die.
TWO DOLLARS.

Vulcan erect sledge over right shoulder; left hand on cog wheel. — Indian and female seated; miniature view of city between them, over which is globe with spread eagle upon it. — 3
3 Title of Bank. Portrait of Indian female holding bow in right hand.

Three females upon bales, one erect with hand upon anchor stock. — Vig. A number of ships opposite a city. — 5
MERCHANTS' B'K, Providence, R. I.
FIVE Portrait of female.

Left	Centre	Right
Sailor standing erect holding aloft a flag; at his feet a female reclines against a cornucopia, bale, anchor, &c.	Vig. Female seated resting left arm on shield, representing state arms; ship and steamship on right; ships in extreme distance on left. MERCHANTS' B'K, Providence, R. I.	10 Indian female seated, holding shield, liberty pole and cap with right hand.
Female supporting 50, holding sickle in right hand. 50	50 Portrait of Henry Clay. 50 MERCHANTS BANK, Providence, R. I. State arms.	Female seated supporting 50. 50
ONE HUNDRED	100 Female seated 100 ships on right; schooner in extreme distance on left. MERCHANTS' B'K, Providence, R. I. Ship.	ONE HUNDRED
500	Vig. Large ship under full sail in the foreground; sailing vessel on right; steamship and vessel in extreme distance, on left. Portrait of Franklin MERCHANT'S BK., Providence, R. I.	500
1000	MERCHANT'S BK., Providence, R. I. Vig. Female seated, with right arm resting on cog wheel; steamship on right; locomotive and depot on left. 1000	ONE THOUSAND
ONE 1	Farmer plowing with two horses; man sowing, train of cars in background. 1 NARRAGANSETT BK. Wickford, R. I.	1 Indian erect with bow and spear.
2	Female on right of a shield on which is an chor, cupid on left, and ships; on right in background train of cars. 2 Title of Bank.	2 Same as one.
Medallion head. 3	Spread Eagle on shield; buildings and vessels in distance. 3 Title of Bank.	THREE Same as ones
FIVE	5 Letter V on shield; Indian seated on right, with gun in hand; female on left erect, with spear. 5 Title of Bank. Hope, anchor and shield.	FIVE
10	10 Female seated holding eagle and twig; vessels in distance. X Title of Bank. Head of Indian.	TEN Full length Female.

Left	Centre	Right
TWENTY	20 Two females seated with wand, cornucopia, &c., on left, wharf scene, vessels, bbls., &c., on right, steamboat; sails of a vessel seen at their back. 20 Title of Bank. Clasped hands	XX Steamboat 20
FIFTY	L Female seated receiving horn of plenty from two floating figures; train of cars, bbls, &c. on right; on left, griffin on safe, vessels, &c. L Title of Bank. Train of cars.	50 Steamboat. 50
ONE on 1 Henry Clay	RHODE ISLAND. NATIONAL BANK, Providence. 1 on ONE DOLLAR America crushing Secession. 1 on ONE DOLLAR	ONE on 1 Eagle on rock
1 Henry Clay	RHODE ISLAND 1 Spread eagle on shield; ocean on right, town on left. 1 NATIONAL BANK ONE DOLLAR Providence	1 Washingt'n
1 Female reclining on ornamental pillar.	Spread eagle, overlooking sea; ships on right, and ships on left. NATIONAL BANK. Providence, R. I. State Arms.	1 Female Indian with shield, liberty pole, cap, &c.
1 Female gathering flowers	Vig. Spread eagle with ships on right and left. NATIONAL BANK, Providence, R. I. State Arms.	1 Sailor with spy glass.
ONE Spread eagle, American shield, &c. 1	NATIONAL BANK Providence R. I. Vig. Naval engagement. State Arms.	1 Spread eagle. American shield, &c. ONE
2 Goddess of Justice	RHODE ISLAND. NATIONAL BANK, Providence. 2 on TWO DOLLARS Washington on horse, two officers, etc. 2 on TWO DOLLARS	2 Eagle on rock
2 Spread eagle overlooking sea, with ships on left.	Vig. Large ship, with vessel on right; steamship on left in distance. NATIONAL BANK Providence, R. I. State arms.	2 Spread eagle, American shield; ship on right.
Male portrait	NATIONAL BANK, Providence, R. I. 2 Vig. Female and safe on left; locomotive and safe on right. 2 Dog, safe and key.	Portrait of Franklin.

Left	Centre	Right
2 Female seated on safe with sword and scales.	NATIONAL BANK, Providence, R. I. 2 Three officers; one on horse, cannon, etc. 2	2 Eagle and shield.
2 Spread eagle, shield, &c.	NATIONAL BANK, Providence, R. I. Vig. Two females; ships on right; also, female with wand in right hand; American shield and public buildings on left.	2 Spread eagle and shield.
THREE Sailor on shipboard. DOLLARS.	NATIONAL BANK, Providence. 3 Man, boy, bust of Washington, etc. 3 THREE DOLLARS.	3 Camp scene
THREE	3 Vig. Large spread eagle, 3 on a rock, overlooking the sea. NATIONAL BANK, Providence, R. I. State Arms.	THREE
5 Soldier charging bayonet	NATIONAL BANK Spread eagle on shield, etc.; rock and fort in distance FIVE DOLLARS Providence	5 Female with glass; large 5 at her back
FIVE	5 Vig. Large spread eagle 5 on a rock, overlooking the sea. NATIONAL BANK, Providence, R. I. State Arms.	FIVE
5 Indian upon rock, with bow in left hand.	5 Vig. Steamboat and sail. 5 boat on right; ship and row-boat on left. NATIONAL BANK, Providence, R. I.	Indian with left hand holding on tree, overlooking precipice. 5
Large spread eagle on rock X TEN DOLLARS	State of R. I. TEN DOLLARS NATIONAL BANK Providence	10 Female portrait
10 Male portrait	(New Plate.) Vig. Large spread eagle standing on anchor; cog-wheel and vessels on right; vessels on left. NATIONAL BANK, Providence, R. I. State Arms.	10 Portrait of Washington
Soldier with flag, beside cannon FIFTY	STATE OF R. ISLAND. L Portrait L NATIONAL BANK FIFTY Providence	50

Soldier erect with flag in right hand. FIFTY | Male Portrait. NATIONAL BANK. Providence, R. I. | 50

Figure of Liberty with pole, cap, and shield. U.S Capitol in background 100 | STATE OF R. ISLAND Portrait of Washington NATIONAL BANK ONE HUNDRED Providence | 100

100 | Female seated holding shield; U. S. Capital in distance. Washington. NATIONAL BANK, Providence, R. I. | 100

500 Justice. | NATIONAL BANK. Providence, R. I. Spread Eagle on shield—Letter D on each side of vig. | 500 Goddess of Liberty.

Female, shield, liberty pole and cap, starry drapery across her lap; U. S. Capitol in rear. 1000 | Portrait of Washington. NATIONAL BANK. Providence, R. I. | 1000

1 Head of Washington. | Female. 1 Female. NEW ENGLAND COMMERCIAL BANK Newport, R. I. | 1 Head of Franklin.

2 Head. | Female 2 Female Title of Bank | 2 Head.

3 Washington full length. | Female head and bust. 3 Female head and bust. Title of Bank. | 3 Vulcan, full length.

Eagle resting on United States shield and an anchor. FIVE | A large V, with female figure and child. Title of Bank. | 5 Female figure and basket.

Male figure seated on machinery; cars at distance. TEN | X Title of Bank. | 10 Male figure with sheaf in hand.

FIFTY Female figure standing globe in her right hand, flowers at her right. FIFTY | 50 Man and horse. 50 Title of Bank | FIFTY Female figure with wreath of flowers in right hand. FIFTY

Figures 100 and words one hundred. Head of Harrison. | Wagon with horses and goods; ship at a distance. Title of Bank. | Figures 100 and words one hundred. Head and bust of male

ONE | 1 Two farmers seated at lunch; female pouring drink; dog, man reaping, etc. on left. 1 N. E. PACIFIC B'K ONE DOLLAR No. Providence, R. I. State Arms | 1 Figure of Justice with sword and scales

TWO | 2 Female seated on left of frame; representing Agriculture and Manufacture; train of cars and steamboat. 2 N. E. PACIFIC BANK N. Providence, R. I. State arms. | 2 Indian female with bow, &c. 2

THREE | 3 Male and females, six in all, cows, &c.; house on left; vessels on right 3 N. E. PACIFIC BANK N. Providence, R. I. State arms. | 3 Female portrait. 3

FIVE | Spread eagle on shield; buildings and vessels in distance. V, female, and cupid. N. E. PACIFIC BANK N. Providence, R. I. | 5 Girl with basket of flowers.

TEN | Vulcan seated with sledge, anvil, &c.; cars, buildings, &c. in distance. X N. E. PACIFIC BANK N. Providence, R. I. | 10 Man with sheaf on his knee.

Female and eagle 20 | 20 Female N. E. PACIFIC B'K Pawtucket, R. I TWENTY | 20 Franklin

20 Female with spear. | 2 Female. 0 N. E. PACIFIC BANK N. Providence, R. I. XX | 20 Female seated. 20

FIFTY Wheat FIFTY | N. E. PACIFIC B'K 50 | 50 Vulcan and machinery

50 Female erect with spear and shield. | Male and female seated. N. E. PACIFIC BANK N. Providence, R. I. 50 | 50 Cupid in a sail boat. 50

C Boats and men 100 | Eagle 100 N. E. PACIFIC B'K | 100 Female 100

100 Vulcan seated with sledge. | Spread eagle on limb of tree; canal scene on right; train of cars on left. N. E. PACIFIC BANK N. Providence, R. I. 100 | 100 Female seated with rake

Female seated pointing to farming scene. 500 | 500 D N. E. PACIFIC BANK N. Providence, R. I. | 500

ONE Med. head. ONE | 1 Vig. View of factory, river, &c.; female Indian and canoe; small deer on right. 1 NEWPORT BANK, Newport, R. I. State arms. | 1 1

TWO Med. head. TWO | 2 Vig. 2; on either side a female, one with liberty pole and cap, the other with sword and balances; railroad cars and bridge and view of view of city in distance. 2 Title of Bank State arms. | 2 2

5 Med. head with fire across it. V | Vig. Steamship and other vessels. NEWPORT BANK, Newport, R. I. State arms | FIVE View of Ocean House Newport. FIVE

10 Med. head. TEN | Vig. Large spread eagle upon shield; United States Capitol on right; steamship, &c., on left. NEWPORT BANK. Newport. R. I. State arms. | Deer, &c. 10 Buffalo

50 Med. head. 50 | Vig. View of sea and rising sun, vessels, &c.; cupid on right; female with sword and balances on left. NEWPORT BANK, Newport, R. I. State arms. | FIFTY Female in ornamental figure, with shield in left hand, and spear in right hand. 50

100 Med. head. 100 | View of city in distance, shipping, &c. NEWPORT BANK, Newport, R. I. State arms. | 100 Spread eagle 100

ONE | State Arms on either side, female one with scales and the other with shield. 1 | Female reclining on State Arms; Neptune in chariot drawn by sea monsters. EXCHANGE BANK, Newport, R. I. | 1 Two figures one holding wand. 1

TWO Female seated; ship on left. TWO | 2 Female with wand; ship in distance on left. 2 EXCHANGE BANK, Newport, R. I. | Indian with bow and arrow. TWO

Female seated, one looking at sea with eagle seated upon her lap. 3 | 3 Vig. Steamboat. 3 EXCHANGE BANK, Newport, R. I. | THREE Female erect with balances, eagle on left and miniature portrait of Washington. 3

FIVE Female, sheaf of wheat and sickle. 5 | 5 Female, eagle and miniature of Washington. 5 EXCHANGE BANK, Newport, R. I. | FIVE Flying female with wand. 5

10 Cupid with scroll figure 10 engraved. 10 | Ships. Bust of Com. Perry. Female sitting, on right State Arms upon which is engraved an eagle and shield; ship &c., on left. Title of Bank. | X Female State Arms on right upon which is mounted an eagle. 10

TWENTY | XX Neptune and female riding in sea car. XX EXCHANGE BANK, Newport, R. I | 20 Cupid and basket of flowers. 20

50 Eagle feeding her young. 50 | Female seated with wand in right hand. Same as on left. Indian and native American seated, between them the arms of one of the States, upon which is mounted an eagle. Title of Bank. | 50 Eagle feeding her young. 50

1 | Vig. Two Indians on horseback, train of cars in distance. American silver dollar. NIANTIC BANK, Westerly, R. I. 1 | 1 Portrait of Webster. ONE

Figure 2 with word two across it. Female seated holding ornamental figure 2. | Vig. Drover and cattle. NIANTIC BANK, Westerly, R. I. Clasped hands. | 2 Farmer sharpening scythe.

Ship under full sail. Figure 3 with word three running across it. | Vig. Two females seated, canal boat and factory on right; bales, steamboat and sloop on left. NIANTIC BANK, Westerly, R. I. State arms. | III Large fig. 3 in centre of which is lighthouse, female seated in the 3.

V Indian queen seated with bow and arrows. | Vig. Indians and squaw in a canoe. NIANTIC BANK, Westerly, R. I. Moonlight scene. | 5 Farmer carrying basket of corn.

10 Ornamental X with figs. 10 and lighthouse on its left; sailor with glass in hand on right. | NIANTIC BANK, Westerly, R. I. Vig. Goddess of liberty and Justice reclining on right of shield; spread eagle; ship in distance on left. Dog. | 10 Female erect, light house above her.

Figures 50 upheld by three full length figures representing commerce, agriculture and mechanics. | NIANTIC BANK, Westerly, R. I. L Vig. Portrait of Henry Clay. L FIFTY | 50 Indian hunter upon brink of precipice looking down upon ship at sea.

ONE Mercury. | Female and State Arms; ships, etc., in distance. NORTHERN BANK, Providence, R. I. | 1 Female with sheaf, cow and sickle

TWO Female figure of Mechanics and the Fine Arts. | Spread eagle on shield. NORTHERN BANK, Providence, R. I. | 2 Farmer carrying stalks.

THREE Justice. | Steamship and other vessels. NORTHERN BANK, Providence, R. I. | 3 Female feeding fowls.

FIVE V Dr. Kane and party in the Arctic Regions. | NORTHERN BANK, Providence, R. I. | 5 Milkmaid, cow and calf.

X Hen and chickens. | NORTHERN BANK, Providence, R. I. Puritans at prayer surprised by Indians. | 10

50 Beaver. | Nooning—farmer, two horses, etc. NORTHERN BANK, Providence, R. I. | 50 Dog and game.

100 Deer. | A party of surveyors. NORTHERN BANK, Providence, R. I. | 100 Men building railroad.

500 Bull. | Horses at trough, and girl filling bucket. NORTHERN BANK, Providence, R. I. | 500 Indian.

1000 Indian on horseback. | Signing the first Constitution on board the May-flower. NORTHERN BANK, Providence, R. I. | 1000 Dog and chest.

ONE Schooner. ONE | 1 Female seated representing Agriculture and Commerce; train of cars, steamboats, &c., in distance. 1 NORTH KINGSTON BANK, Wickford, R. I. Spread Eagle, &c. | ONE Female. ONE

TWO Vessels, &c. TWO | 2 Two females seated; wharf scene and vessel on left; steamboat on right, and ship at the females back. 2 NORTH KINGSTON BANK, Wickford, R. I. Arm, hammer, &c. | TWO Female seated with shield on which is anchor. TWO

THREE Vessels, and men in row boats. 3 | 3 Male and female in car drawn by two sea horses; ships and steamboat in distance. 3 NORTH KINGSTON BANK, Wickford, R. I. Schooner. | THREE Female seated with scroll, book, eagle and portrait Washington. 3

5 Train of cars | Sea god and goddess in chariot drawn by sea horses and attended by followers. NORTH KINGSTON BANK, Wickford, R. I. State Arms. | 5 Cattle

10 Female with scales, eagle, etc. 10 | X Female seated by shield on which is eagle, etc. 10 Title of Bank. Head of lion. | TEN Ten coins lapped. TEN

50 Pelican and its young. 50 | Indian; eagle on shield; female figure on right. Female with wand etc., on either side of vignette. Title of Bank. Steamboat. | 50 Pelican and its young. 50

100 Female with torch, eagle, Washington, &c. 100 | 100 Washington. 100 Title of Bank. Eagle. | 100 Vessels. 100

ONE Female leaning on altar. ONE | 1 Indian erect with gun, dog, and body of a deer; Indian and forest scene on left. 1 NORTH PROVIDENCE BANK, N. Providence, R. I. Female portrait. | ONE Female holding key and eagle. ONE

Left end	Centre	Right end
Female with sheaf and sickle. 2	Three females seated; eagle on left, vessel on right. 2 N. PROVIDENCE BK. N. Providence, R. I. Cars.	TWO Canal scene; buildings in distance. TWO
FIVE	5 A naval engagement, men in row-boat, &c. 5 N. PROVIDENCE BK. N. Providence, R. I. Beaver.	5 Waterfall, building, &c. 5
10 and X across. Female seated, at her side word ten; ship in distance.	Steamer, vessels, row-boat, buildings, hills, &c. N. PROVIDENCE BK. N. Providence, R. I. Hope, shield, and anchor.	X Female seated with sickle, surrounded by grain.
20 XX 20	20 Female seated with scales, sheaf, bbls., bales, &c.; on left men plowing; on right ship. 20 N. PROVIDENCE BK. N. Providence, R. I.	TWENEY
50 Female erect, steamboat in distance. 50	FIFTY DOLLARS 50 N. PROVIDENCE BK. N. Providence, R. I.	FIFTY
Words one hundred and figures 100. Portrait of Harrison.	Wharf scene, loading wagon with bbls., men, horses, shipping, &c. N. PROVIDENCE BK. N. Providence, R. I.	Same as on left. Male portrait.
500	Indian paddling in a canoe 500 N. PROVIDENCE BK N. Providence, R. I. D D	500 Female with scales and sword.
1000	Spread eagle on promontory; ship on ocean in distance. 1000 N. PROVIDENCE BK N. Providence, R. I.	1000 Indian female with bow and arrows.
1	Vig. State arms; Indian on left, man with axe in left hand on right. 1 PAWTUXET BANK, Providence, R. I. Plough and sheaf.	1 Bull's head.
2	Vig. Spread eagle behind shield, female on left, holding portrait of Washington, staff and cap; cars in distance; steamship in distance on right. 2 Title of Bank. State arms.	TWO Large ship under sail at sea; vessel on either side.

Left end	Centre	Right end
THREE Farmer erect with sheaf under left arm, female with pail at his feet. 3	Vig. Ornamental figure 3, medallion head on either side. PAWTUXET BANK. Providence, R. I. State arms.	3 Portrait of Indian girl with bow and arrow in hands.
Steamboat and three sailing vessels; city in distance. FIVE	Vig. Female with sheaf of grain seated in large ornamental V. PAWTUXET BANK, Providence, R. I. State arms.	5 Sailor erect, leaning upon binnacle, spy-glass in left hand.
10 Head of girl with long hair. TEN	Female seated between ornamental I and O. PAWTUXET BANK, Providence, R. I.	10 Female head TEN
10 X 10	Yoke of oxen, male figure erect beside them. Large ornamental 10. PAWTUXET BANK, Providence, R. I.	TEN Female erect holding horn of plenty in left hand, spade in right.
20 Female seated, book on her lap, left hand resting upon it.	XX Spread eagle XX standing upon rock. PAWTUXET BANK, Providence, R. I.	20 Large sized ship under sail.
50 Female erect resting left arm upon shield, spear in right hand.	Vulcan seated beside female holding rake on left; cornucopia between them. PAWTUXET BANK. Providence, R. I. 50	50 Cupid in sailboat. 50
100 Vulcan seated with sledge in left hand.	Spread eagle upon limb of tree; cars on left crossing canal, canal scene on right. PAWTUXET BANK, Providence, R. I. 100	100 Female seated with rake in right hand, grain in left.
Washington. 1	State Arms with females. PEOPLES BANK, N. Providence, R. I.	1 ONE Female with sickle, wheat, &c.
Med. head. TWO 2	Two females, wheat, sickles &c.; ship in background. PEOPLES BANK, N. Providence, R. I.	2 Female, eagle and shield.
5 Eagle and female.	Three females. PEOPLES BANK. N. Providence, R. I. The denomination across the bill in red letters.	5 Locomotive.

Left end	Centre	Right end
X F. Pierce. 10	State Arms. PEOPLES BANK, N. Providence, R. I.	10 Telegraph wires, cattle, &c.
20 Female with spear.	2 Female. 0 PEOPLES BANK, N. Providence, R. I. XX	20 20
50 Female with spear, &c.	Female figure with rake. Male figure with scroll in right hand. PEOPLES BANK, N. Providence, R. I. 50	50 Cupid in sailboat. 50
100 Male figure with scroll and staff.	Eagle on branch of tree, train of cars and canal in distance. PEOPLES BANK, N. Providence, R. I. 100	100 Female, rake, &c.
Indian in canoe. 500	5 0 0 PEOPLES BANK. N. Providence, R. I. D D	500 Female, scales, sword, &c.
Eagle, ship in background. 1000	1 0 0 0 PEOPLES BANK, N. Providence, R. I. M M	1000 Female Indian with bow & arrow.
1	Two females sitting by Seat of Arms; steam engine, &c. PEOPLES' EXCHANGE BANK, Wakefield, R. I. ONE	1
2	Three male figures, cart and horse, farming scene. 2 on right. PEOPLES' EXCHANGE BANK, Wakefield, R. I. TWO	2 2 Female
3	Three male figures sitting, farming scene. fig. 3 on right. PEOPLES' EXCHANGE BANK, Wakefield, R. I. THREE	3 Three men & 3
5	Female sitting; steamboat, rail car, steamer, &c. PEOPLES' EXCHANGE BANK, Wakefield, R. I. FIVE	5 5 females & 5

10 — Female figure with pail and cows, &c. PEOPLE'S EXCHANGE BANK, Wakefield, R. I. — 10 TEN

20 — Four figures, load of hay, team and farming implements. PEOPLES' EXCHANGE BANK, Wakefield, R. I. TWENTY TWENTY — 20 Female figure standing

50 — Agricultural Cattle scene, team, cattle, railway, cars, &c. PEOPLES' EXCHANGE BANK, Wakefield, R. I. TWENTY — 50 Bull Stock.

100 Fig. of Male with bag of dollars. — Three men washing sheep, village, &c. PEOPLES' EXCHANGE BANK, Wakefield, R. I. — 100 Girls with a rose making hay.

1 Female seated; cars in distance. — Vig. Spread eagle upon rock, overlooking sea; large ship on either side. 1 PHENIX BANK, Providence, R. I. Phenix. — 1 Female seated; spy-glass in hands.

2 — Vig. Three females, one on right with sword; one on left with cornucopia; ships in distance on right. 2 PHENIX BANK, Providence, R. I. Phenix. — 2 Vulcan with sledge on right shoulder.

3 Female seated, with pen and scroll. — Vig. Female reclining on bale; ships on right, under sail. 3 PHENIX BANK, Providence, R. I. Phenix — 3 Portrait of Henry Clay.

FIVE Female with sheaf of grain in left arm. 5 — Vig. Spread eagle upon shield. 5 PHENIX BANK, Providence, R. I. Phenix. — 5 Goddess of Liberty, with shield, liberty pole and cap.

X Portrait of Washington 10 — 10 Vig. Female seated; liberty pole and cap on her lap; her right hand upon shield; her left upon cornucopia; spread eagle on right. PHENIX BANK, Providence, R. I. Phenix. — 10 Female seated, reclining on bale.

20 — State Arms, female with sickle on right; and cars crossing bridge; plow, corn, grain, scenery, &c., on left. Title of Bank. Steamboat — 20 Portrait of Fillmore.

50 Portrait of Gen. Taylor. FIFTY — Female seated, arm resting on bale; farm scene, loading hay, locomotive and cars in distance on right. Title of Bank. Locomotive and Tender. — 50 Female bearing sheaf of grain.

C — Female leaning upon anchor, resting against bale, of Franklin. schooner and stm. boat in distance on right; city with ships at wharfs in distance on left. Title of Bank. Spread eagle — 100 Portrait

D Large ship under sail at sea. — PHENIX BANK, Providence, R. I. Figures 500 on Circular shield. Head of Female. — Sailor seated on bale, spy-glass in right hand. 500

1 Portrait of Washington. 1 — Female with sheaf of wheat; right hand uplifted, with stems of wheat thereon; plow, female, locomotive, &c. PHENIX BANK, Westerly, R. I. Phenix with spread wings — 1 Squaw 1

2 Portrait of J. Q. Adams. 2 — Steamship, with a sail vessel before and aft. PHENIX BANK, Westerly, R. I. Phenix with spread wings. — 2 Female with paper and dividers. 2

3 Female. — Female figure and Indian chief; the former holding stems of grain in one hand, and sickle in the other; both reclining against a globe, on which stands a spread eagle. PHENIX BANK, Westerly, R. I. Phenix with spread wings — 3 Portrait.

5 Portrait of Henry Clay. 5 — Male and female figure with machinery; ship on right, and locomotive and train on left. PHENIX BANK, Westerly, R. I. Phenix with spread wings — 5 Female head. V.

10 Indian Princess with implements of war. — Spread eagle holding the American flag in its talons. PHENIX BANK, Westerly, R. I. Phenix with spread wings — 10 Female in a sitting posture, holding scales over eagle, one of whose wings are extended over American flag.

20 TWENTY — Female in a sitting posture, with one arm thrown over an eagle, which stands on a segment of the globe, labelled "America." PHENIX BANK, Westerly, R. I. Phenix with spread wings — 20

Female with sheaf of grain, whose feet rest on the figures below. 50 — Three females in a group; one holding scales; ships on the right. PHENIX BANK, Westerly, R. I. Phenix with spread wings — 50

1 ONE — PHENIX VILLAGE BANK, Phenix, R. I. View of bridge, water falls, houses and trees. Male portrait ONE — 1 1 ONE

2 TWO — Title of Bank. Vig. Same as ones. — 2 2 2

3 THREE — Title of Bank. Vig. Same as ones. — 3 THREE 3 THREE

FIVE — 5 Title of Bank. Man tending large machinery. 5 — 5 Male portrait

X TEN — Men at work in an Iron Mill. X Title of Bank. — 10, X and Ten Male portrait

60 on red die — Title of Bank. View of factories, cars, water, hills, etc. — 60 on red die

100 and C on red die. — Title of Bank. Male portrait — 100 and C on red die.

Shield, female, starry drapery, liberty pole and cap. — Eagle. Indian viewing the improvement of the white man. 1 PRODUCERS' BANK, Woonsocket, R. I. Female bathing. — 1 Mechanic's arm, anvil and hammer.

TWO Franklin. TWO — Liberty, justice and truth; eagle at top of shield; bridge and cars on right; ship on left. PRODUCERS' BANK, Woonsocket, R. I. Dog, safe and key. — TWO Female with rake. TWO

3 Washington. — PRODUCERS' BANK, Woonsocket, R. I. Two horses and train of cars. Farming implements. — 3 Female.

5 — Locomotive. — FIVE
Horses on either side of shield; eagle at top; steamboat on right; factories, canal scene and cars crossing bridge, on left.
PRODUCERS' BANK, Woonsocket, R. I.
5 — Fenn of cattle.

X — Female. — 10
Female seated between figures 10; farming scene on either side. Letter X on shield.
PRODUCERS' BANK Woonsocket, R. I.
Machinery.
10 — Two female Indians with sickle, bow, and arrows.

Female with liberty pole and cap. — TWENTY
20 Man ploughing with oxen; little girl on right.
PRODUCERS' BANK. Woonsocket, R. I
20 — Female, grain, and sickle.

Female with wand; right hand holds med. head, which rests on pillar.
50 Spread eagle on American shield
PRODUCERS' BANK. Woonsocket, R. I.
50 — Washington.

100 — Man seated instructing a little child.
PRODUCERS' BANK. Woonsocket, R. I.
C
100 — Med. head. — 100

500 — Artist at work.
Washington. Two females on either side of a beehive.
PRODUCERS' BANK, Woonsocket, R. I.
Machinery.
500 — Portrait of Mrs. Washington

ONE — 1 — ONE
Vig. Man seated on rock; ship under full sail on right.
PROVIDENCE BANK Providence, R. I
State arms.
1 — State arms; Indian on left; female on right. — 1

1 — Female sitting on bale of goods, with distaff in left hand.
Vig. State arms supported by female reclining on ground, with left arm resting on bale of goods; factory and cars on right in distance, on left steamers and ships in distance.
PROVIDENCE BANK Providence, R I
ONE — Female seated, holding roll of goods.

Full length figure of female standing in large ornamental 2 which reaches from bottom to top of bill.
Vig. State arms, with female seated on left holding liberty pole and cap; ship in distance; cogwheel and anvil on right.
PROVIDENCE BANK Providence. R I.
State Arms.
TWO — 2 — TWO

Large ornamental figure 2 with female seated within, wall behind her.
PROVIDENCE BANK Providence. R I.
Vig. same as second description of ones.
2 — Female seated on bale of goods, holding figure 2 in right hand, cornucopia in left; bridge and water in distance.

III — 3 — III
Vig. Female and state arms.
PROVIDENCE BANK Providence, R. I.
3
Full length figure of female in ornamental fig. 3.

3 — Female seated on bale of goods with figure 3 in right hand; cornucopia in left; bridge and water in distance.
PROVIDENCE BANK Providence, R. I.
Vig. same as second description of ones.
THREE — Lighthouse and rocks seen through large ornamental 3; female seated reclining on rocks in front of 3.

5 — Female with horn of plenty. — FIVE
Vig. Ornamental figure 5, supported by female on right; cupid and sickle; cupid in centre of five; female on left with sword and balances; cupid with cornucopia. 5
Title of Bank.
State Arms.
FIVE — Female erect with sword and balance — FIVE

FIVE — Large ornamental V; female seen through V; females on right and left; factory in distance. — 5
PROVIDENCE BANK Providence, R. I.
Vig. Female seated on bale of goods holding state arms, bridge and train of cars in distance; on left steamer and ship in distance.
FIVE — Shield surmounted by two cupids; in centre of shield figure 5 and V.

10 — Indian female with bow in hand, quiver on back. — TEN
Vig. Cupid holding $10 gold piece; chest, money and keg on right; on left horn of plenty, barrels, &c.
PROVIDENCE B'K, Providence, R. I.
State Arms.
TEN — Female erect with helmet on head, spear in hand; left arm resting on shield, which rests on column. — TEN

X X — Female seated on rock writing, child with wreath at feet.
PROVIDENCE B'K, Providence, R. I.
Words ten dollars on word ten and fig. 10.
10 — State Arms.

10
PROVIDENCE BANK Providence, R. I.
Vig. same as five above, with words "ten dollars" on right and left of vignette.
10
10

TWENTY — Female resting on pillar with torch in hand, foot resting on mortar.
PROVIDENCE B'K, Providence, R. I.
Words twenty dollars on word twenty and figure 20.
20 — Female head.

Female seated resting on shield, key in left hand, cornucopia on right. — 20 — Spread eagle
XX Vig. Female with right arm resting on stone column, in left hand bunch of wheat; on left packages of goods, sheep, and rocks in distance on right. XX
Title of Bank.
Spread eagle.
Female seated, pole and cap; ship in distance on left. — 20 — Spread eagle

FIFTY
Vig. State arms surmounted by wreath; female on right with spear and shield, helmet on head; bridge and cars in distance; female on left with pole and cap, bales of goods.
PROVIDENCE BANK Providence, R. I.
50 — State arms; Indian with bow on left; female on right. — 50

ONE HUNDRED
Vig. Same as fifty.
PROVIDENCE BANK Providence, R. I.
100 — Same as fifty — 100

D — Medallion head with figures 500 running across.
Vig. Female holding keys, &c., in right hand, with cherubs, all floating in clouds, over-guarding a city.
PROVIDENCE BANK Providence, R. I.
500
500 — Med. head with figures 500 running across. — 500

1000
Vig. Same as 500s.
PROVIDENCE BANK Providence, R. I.
1000
Large letter M with one thousand running across. — Med. head with figures 1000 running across.

1 — barrel, bales, ship, etc. — 1
ONE DOLLAR
1 Female seated; ship in distance 1
RAIL ROAD BANK
ONE DOLLAR
Woonsocket
Rhode Island
1 — Agric'l'tur'l implem'ts etc. — 1

ONE — 1
Farmer sowing grain and man and horses harrowing. 1
RAIL ROAD BANK,
1 — Ship. — ONE

TWO — 2
Spread eagle on a bale, gears, &c., cars and man plowing in distance. 2
RAIL ROAD BANK,
2 — TWO — Schooner and sloop.

THREE — 3
Wharf scene with Sailor, bales boxes shipping, storehouses, &c. 3
RAIL ROAD BANK
3 — THREE — Train of cars

Large V and word FIVE.
Wharf scene with female sitting among agricultural implements and merchandise holding sickle and rake. Large V and figure with bow and arrow.
RAIL ROAD BANK, Woonsocket, R. I.
5 — Portrait of Washington

10 — X — 10
(First Plate.)
Oxen, man, &c 10
RAIL ROAD BANK, [illegible]
TEN — Female with cornucopia in left hand

X
(Second Plate.)
Signing the declaration of Independence. X
RAIL ROAD BANK, Woonsocket, R. I.
10 — Train of cars building with steeple.

Left	Centre	Right
20 Female seated with book on lap	XX Eagle. XX RAIL ROAD BANK,	20 Ship.
FIFTY. Female holding flowers in one hand and a wreath in the other. FIFTY	50 Man and horse. 50 RAIL ROAD BANK,	FIFTY Female with a Barometer in one hand and flowers in the other. FIFTY
ONE HUNDRED and figures 100. Portrait of Harrison.	Wharf scene with men putting barrels into a large covered wagon, shipping, &c., in distance. RAIL ROAD BANK,	ONE HUNDRD and figures 100. Male Portrait
Water and trees and an Indian in a canoe. 500	500 RAIL ROAD BANK, Woonsocket, R. I.	500 Female holding scales and sword.
1 Blacksmith with sleigh.	Man watering three horses from trough by side of well; goat, kid and sheep; cattle, trees and house in distance. RICHMOND BANK, Alton, R. I. Stockholders, etc.	1 Jenny Lind.
2 Female erect, and another kneeling.	Shield containing a sheaf and agricultural implement; two females on right; cars, &c., on left. RICHMOND BANK, Alton. R. I. Stockholders, &c.	2 Two cherubs soaring, with distaff and sheaf.
3 Arm, hammer, anvil, etc.	RICHMOND BANK, Alton, R. I. Spread eagle on State Arms, horse either side; steamer on right; factories and cars on left. Stockholders, etc.	3 Two men erect, female seated; factories, etc.
5 5 in red. Rolling machine.	Three females, one in centre with wings; one on right has quadrant; the other cornucopia. RICHMOND BANK, Alton, R. I. V in red.	5 5 in red. Stockholders etc.
10 Clay.	Title of Bank. Scene in an iron mill—five men at work. X, Stockholders, etc., on right of vig.	10 Female feeding fowls.
Female child in ornamental die.	1 Ships and sea scene. R. I. UNION BANK, Newport, R. I. Clasping hands.	1

Left	Centre	Right
Wharf scene.	2 Portrait of Gen. Green. R. I. UNION BANK, Newport. R. I. Clasped hands.	2
Indian with bow and arrow, horse on right and dog on left	5 Vig. Winged female cupid and anchor. R. I. UNION BANK, Newport. R. I. Clasped hands.	5
10 X 10	[Old Plate.] Vig. Man with oxen. 10 R. I UNION BANK, Newport. R. I.	TEN Female figure with cornucopia of fruits and flowers
TEN	Vulcan seated, anvil, sledge, &c.; train of cars and buildings in distance. X R. I. UNION BANK, Newport, R. I.	10 Farmer with sheaf on his knee.
20 Female.	XX Eagle. XX R. I. UNION BANK, Newport, R. I.	20 Ship sailing
FIFTY Female with wreath. FIFTY	50 Men and Horse. 50 R. I. UNION BANK, Newport, R. I.	FIFTY Full length female, Globe, Rule, &c. FIFTY
Words one hundred and figures 100 Male portrait.	Vig. Market scene; shipping on left. R. I. UNION BANK, Newport, R. I.	Words one hundred, and figures 100. Male portrait.
Portrait of female. Spread eagle. Portrait of Indian female.	1 Portrait of female with trident in left hand; quadrant, anchor, bale, &c., on right; antique vase, painter's pallet, &c. on left. 1 ROGER WILLIAMS BANK, Providence, R. I.	Portrait of female with cornucopia. Spread eagle on limb. Portrait of Indian with bow and arrows.
THE ROGER WILLIAMS BANK Female portrait	Spread eagle on shield ONE DOLLAR Providence, R. I.	1 Female portrait
2 Words Two Dollars on red die.	Title of Bank. Three females in clouds; one crowning bust.	2 Words Two Dollars on red die.

Left	Centre	Right
Portrait of two females. Male portrait. Portrait of farmer with sickle.	2 Vig. Portrait of female with left arm resting on pail; scythe, rake, and pitcher on right; plow, sheaf of grain, &c. on left. 2 Title of Bank.	Portrait of three females Portrait of Washington. Portrait of young girl seated.
Male portrait.	5 Vig. Female reclining, with right hand upon anchor, overlooking sea on which is dimly seen a ship. 5 Title of Bank. Spread eagle.	State die.
Three females erect, supporting shield.	Vig. Shepherd boy reclining watching sheep; village in distance. 5 Title of Bank. 5 5 Spread eagle.	FIVE Female erect with sickle in right hand.
Male portrait.	10 Vig. Neptune seated with trident. 10 Title of Bank.	Spread eagle upon limb of a tree.
Female seated holding up fig. 10. 10	Title of Bank. Vig. Mercury seated upon clouds; bag in outstretched left hand.	Female seated holding up figure 10. 10
20	Vig. State arms, on right of which is farmer seated on sheaf of grain, with sickle in hand; in distance behind him man on horse and man driving swine; on left of vig. female seated; steamer in distance. Title of Bank. Female seated.	20 Portrait of female.
50 Female seated in shell with trident; ship on either side.	Title of Bank. Indian.	50 Sailor standing erect; ship on either side.
100 Two ships under sail one after the other, schooner in distance.	Vig. Female portrait. Title of Bank.	100 Indian seated upon rock, gun in right hand.
D Medallion head.	Vig. Female seated holding roll of goods and stick with left hand; bale, barrels, cogwheels and church in extreme distance on right; steam boat and factories on left. Title of Bank.	500 Medallion head.
Female erect holding sickle in her right hand. 1000	Large steamship under sail at sea; three sailing vessels on right; two left. Title of Bank	Female representing Justice. 1000

Left	Centre	Right
1 Minerva with shield, spear, sprig and laurel.	View of Pawtucket falls SLATER BANK, N. Providence, R. I. State Arms.	1 Male portrait
TWO Female holding figure 2.	View of Pawtucket falls. SLATER BANK, N. Providence, R. I State arms.	2 Male portrait.
V	View of Pawtucket falls. Male portrait. SLATER BANK, N. Providence, R. I. State arms.	5 Female with roll of cloth.
10 Male portrait.	SLATER BANK, N. Providence. R. I. View of Pawtucket falls State arms.	10 X
50 Cupid Mechanic.	SLATER BANK, N. Providence, R. I Lovers at the well. State Arms.	50 Cupid. Portrait of Slater
Letter C. Portrait of Slater.	Liberty and Eagle. SLATER BANK, N Providence, R. I. State Arms.	100 Female Manufacturer.
500 Portrait.	Fame, etc., Female blowing trumpet SLATER BANK, N. Providence, R. I State Arms.	500 Mechanic.
ONE Washington. 1	Milkmaid seated, cows, &c. 1 SMITHFIELD EXCHANGE BANK, Greenville, R. I.	1 Portrait of elderly female. ONE
2 State arms. TWO	Stone cutters at work, &c. 2 SMITHFIELD EXCHANGE BANK Greenville, R. I.	TWO Franklin. Med. head and word two
5 State arms. FIVE	Portrait of Gen. Taylor. Large figure 5 and word five at top. Female portrait SMITHFIELD EXCHANGE BANK. Greenville, R. I.	5 Med. head 5

Left	Centre	Right
X	Signing Declaration of Independence. X SMITHFIELD EXCHANGE BANK. Greenville, R. I.	10 Train of cars, man with wheelbarrow
20 Female with book on lap.	XX Eagle. XX SMITHFIELD EXCHANGE BANK. Greenville, R. I.	20 Ship.
FIFTY Female erect FIFTY	50 Man and horse. 50 SMITHFIELD EXCHANGE BANK. Greenville, R. I.	FIFTY Female erect FIFTY
Figures 100 and words one hundred across. Portrait of Harrison.	Wharf scene, &c. SMITHFIELD EXCHANGE BANK, Greenville, R. I.	Same as on left. Male portrait.
ONE	Sea view with shipping, &c. 1 SMITHFIELD UNION BANK, Woonsocket. R. I.	ONE Female Indian with bow & arrow. ONE
2 TWO 2	Vessels, &c. 2 Title of Bank.	TWO Female drawing water. TWO
THREE	Female with hat in right hand and sheaf in left; farmer reaping, with man behind him with grain in his arms. 3 Title of Bank.	THREE Steamship. TH 3 REE
FIVE	Female lifting drapery from a shield on which is figure 5. V Title of Bank.	5 Vessel.
Large V and word FIVE.	Wharf scene with female sitting among agricultural implements and merchandise holding sickle and rake. Large V and figure with bow and arrow. Title of Bank	5 Portrait of Washington.
Vulcan with anvil, hammer, &c. TEN	X Title of Bank.	10 Female with sickle and grain.

Left	Centre	Right
20 Female sitting; right hand resting on book; open book on lap.	XX Eagle. XX Title of Bank.	20 Ship
FIFTY Female erect with wreath of flowers in right hand, and flowers in left. FIFTY	50 Man and horse. 50 Title of Bank.	FIFTY Female erect holding cornucopia in left hand, barometer in right. FIFTY
Figures 100 and words one hundred. Head of Harrison.	Wagon with horses and goods; ship at a distance. Title of Bank.	Figures 100 and words one hundred. Head and bust of male.
1 Ship. 1	Indian female seated, with left arm pointing; a deer, trees &c. in distance. SOWAMSET BANK, Warren, R. I. Vessel.	1 Indian reclining supporting figure 1.
TWO Train of cars Steamship. TWO	Wild horses. SOWAMSET BANK, Warren, R. I.	2 Human figure holding ear of corn and figure 2.
Vessels, &c. THREE	Indians trading with white men. SOWAMSET BANK, Warren, R. I. Loading hay.	3 Indian princess with bow and arrow.
V	Large view of steamship, ships, &c. SOWAMSET BANK. Warren, R. I.	FI 5 VE Figure 5, represented by female, eagle, portrait of Washington FIVE
Sailor boy in act of rowing. 10	Female soaring in air with eagle. SOWAMSET BANK, Warren, R. I. Vessel on stocks.	X Female portrait gazing intently.
50 Man with rake, fork, canteen, and dog.	SOWAMSET BANK, Warren, R. I. Train of cars, load of hay, men, &c.; city, hills, &c. in distance.	50 Two females, one with dinner horn; table, dishes, &c.; chickens, &c.
Female with scroll, pole, and cap; shield, pedestal, &c. 100	Scene—Whale fishing in Arctic regions. SOWAMSET BANK. Warren, R. I.	100 Sailor with left hand on capstan; bbls., bales, ships' masts, &c.

STATE BANK. Providence, R. I. | 1
Vig. Female seated, resting upon state arms; ship; steamship on right; vessels in distance on left. | View of house and trees.
Dog, safe, and key.

Locomotive. Female and cars. portrait. | 2
STATE BANK, Providence, R. I. | View of house and trees.
State arms.

STATE BANK. Providence. R. I. | 3
Vig. Female resting upon State Arms, with steamships and ship on right; ships on left. | Female portrait.
Eagle.

Vig. Female resting upon State Arms, with steamship and ship on right; ships on left. | 5
STATE BANK, Providence, R. I. | Portrait of Washington.
Locomotive;

10 Vig. Female resting upon State Arms, with steamship and ship on right; ships on left. | 10
STATE BANK. Providence, R. I. | View of house and trees.

10 Female resting on State Arms; ship and steamship on right; ships on left. | 10
STATE BANK, Providence, R. I. | View of house and trees.

20 Vig. Cupid, dog, female seated upon a safe, with vessel and locomotive on the right; sheaf of wheat and plow on left. | 20
STATE BANK, Providence, R. I. | View of house and trees.
State Arms.

STATE BANK. Providence, R. I. | 50
Vig. Female resting upon state arms; steamship on right; ship on left. | Female portrait.

Vig. Spread eagle, American shield, &c. | 100
STATE BANK. Providence, R. I. | Female portrait.
State Arms.

STATE BANK, Providence, R. I. | 500
Vig. Female seated; on her left, female seated, with sheaf of grain; and on her right, railroad in extreme distance; man with spade. | 500
Eagle.

M | STATE BANK, Providence, R. I. | 1000
Vig. Female seated upon bale; figure kneeling at her feet; cars crossing bridge; canal scene on right; ship and town on left. | ONE THOUSAND
1000 | | 1000

| Female seated; train of cars on right; man on horseback, and canal scene on left. | Group of male figures. In large 1.
1 | TRADERS' BANK. Newport, R. I. | Female and sheaf of wheat.

1 | 1 Farmers implements; city on right, and cars on left. | ONE
Cupid, flowers, &c. | | Man erect, with axe in right hand, and sickle in left; sheaf, plow, &c.
1 | TRADERS' BANK, Newport, R. I. | ONE

| Vig. Farmers washing sheep; 4 men 2 on right. | TWO
| | Female sitting, holding wreath of flowers.
2 | TRADERS' BANK, Newport, R. I. | TWO

2 | Vig. Ships on sea | TWO
TWO
2 | TRADERS' BANK, Newport, R. I. | TWO

3 | 3 Vig. Female sitting; building, safe, horn of plenty, &c., on right; man plowing with horses and sheaf of grain on left. | 3
Med. head.
3 | TRADERS' BANK, Newport, R. I. | Female bathing.

THREE | Vig. Female sitting; in right hand sickle; in left rake; sheaf of grain and vessels on right; locomotive and building on left. | THREE Word Three and figure 3.
Beehive. | | Farmers gathering grain.
THREE | TRADERS' BANK, Newport, R. I. | Word Three, and figure 3.

| Vig. Female sitting; sickle in right hand, holding rake in left; vessels, sheaf of grain, on right; building, &c., in background, on left. | Large letter V in which is sitting an Indian female. | 5
FI V VE | TRADERS' BANK, Newport, R. I. | Portrait of Washington.

FIVE | Vig. Female kneeling, with arms extended. | 5
| TRADERS' BANK, Newport, R. I. | Vessel.

X | Vig. Scene on river; steamboat, vessels, &c. | 10
Indian with bow and arrow. | TRADERS' BANK, Newport, R. I. | Female, sheaf of grain; and in her right hand, hat.

10 | Vig. Man and oxen. 10 | TEN
X
10 | TRADERS' BANK. Newport, R. I. | Full length female.

20 | XX Eagle. XX | 20
Female sitting. | TRADERS' BANK. Newport, R. I. | Ship, &c.

FIFTY | 50 Man and horse. 50 | FIFTY
Female erect with wreath of flowers in right hand, and flowers in left. | | Female, globe, anchor, &c.; elbow resting on ornamental pillar.
FIFTY | TRADERS' BANK, Newport, R. I. | FIFTY

Words one hundred, and figures 100. | Vig. Wharf scene; loading wagon; men, horses, shipping, &c. | Words one hundred, and figures 100.
Male portrait | TRADERS' BANK. Newport, R. I. | Male portrait

ONE | Three females one seated receiving cornucopia; Griffin standing upon safe on left; schooner, &c., locomotive and train in distance on right | ONE
Scene upon wharf, ship, steamboat, &c. | | Female seated with staff and liberty cap, ship on left.
ONE | TRADERS' BANK, Providence, R. I. | ONE
Clasped hands.

1 | Female reclining supporting ornamental figure 1. 1 | ONE
Portrait of Female. | TRADERS' BANK, Providence, R. I. | Sailor erect gazing down upon female seated at his feet.
Deer.

St. George fighting the dragon. | 2 Neptune seated in his car, drawn by two sea horses, winged figure with cornucopia soaring above. | 2
2 | TRADERS' BANK, Providence, R. I. | Hercules combatting with many headed dragon.
Cupid on Horse.

TWO | 2 Female reclining upon State Arms, spread eagle upon right, bales &c., on left. | 2
Farmer erect with sheaf of grain and rake, female with pail seated at his feet. | TRADERS' BANK, Providence, R. I. | Sailor erect leaning upon binnacle spy glass in his left hand.
2 | Ox.

THREE | 3 Vessel under full sail; lighthouse and steamer in distance. | 3
Female, anchor, lighthouse, vessel, etc. | TRADERS' BANK, Providence, R. I. | Two children with fruit.

3 | Indian chief, Vig. Two Indians watching buckle water-fall in background, forest scene around. | 3
Drovers and cattle | TRADERS' BANK, Providence, R. I. | Washington with his hat in hand, on white horse.
3 | Large goblet

V — Ship launching. — V
5 Vig. Sheaf of grain and agricultural implements in foreground; locomotive and bridge in distance on left; waterfall and city on right. 5
TRADERS' BANK. Providence, R. I.
Steamboat.
V — Female seated among bales, &c. — V

V — Female portrait.
Sailor reclining; anchor, boat, etc.; steamship in distance.
Title of Bank.
5 — Eagle.

Ten Dollars. — Vulcan seated beside anvil, figure beside and behind him. — 10
X Vig. Mammoth ox standing looking to left of note. X
TRADERS' BANK, Providence, R. I.
Spread eagle.
TEN — Drover and cattle. — 10

XX — Ship upon the stocks.
Vig. Scene upon a wharf, men loading dray, before which is two horses.
TRADERS' BANK. Providence, R. I.
Locomotive.
20 — Indian erect extending hand to female seated on left. — XX

FIFTY
Vig. Same as 20s.
TRADERS' BANK. Providence, R. I.
Cattle standing in water.
50 — Scene in a shoemaker's shop, two men at work. — 50

ONE HUNDRED
TRADERS' BANK, Providence, R. I.
Vig. Female erect holding wreath and wand in right hand; bag in left; her right foot upon a small globe, C each side.
100 — Samson overcoming the lion. — 100

Female seated, holding scales in left hand; sword in right. — 1
Vig. Female reclining upon bale; ships on right; schooner on left.
UNION BANK, Providence, R. I.
State Arms.
1 — Female seated, holding spy-glass; ship on left.

TWO — Female seated upon rocks; pail at her feet. — TWO
Vig. Three females reclining; one on right, with sword and scales; one on left, with cornucopia; ships in distance on right.
UNION BANK. Providence, R. I.
State Arms.
2 — Ship under sail. — TWO

Three females upon rock; one erect with left hand upon anchor stock.
Vig. Large ship sailing at sea, off light-house; vessel in distance on left.
UNION BANK, Providence, R. I.
State Arms.
3 — Portrait of Washington.

Female holding sheaf of grain in left arm. — 5
Vig. Female seated upon plough, with left arm on sheaf with sickle; bunch of grain in right hand; cars crossing viaduct on right; bridge on left.
UNION BANK, Providence, R. I.
State Arms.
5 — Steamboat.

X — Portrait of Franklin. — 10
Vig. Large steamship in foreground; sailing vessels on either side.
UNION BANK, Providence, R. I.
State Arms.
10 — Female seated, resting left arm on scroll on pillar; pen in right hand.

50 L 50
50 Female reclining upon tablet with 50 upon it; ship on stocks upon left, woods in distance on right. 50
UNION BANK, Providence, R. I.
L Rhode Island. L

100 C 100
100 State Arms in shield; barrels and factories in distance on right; bales, boat with two men in it, and ships on left 100
C C
UNION BANK, Providence, R. I.
100
C Rhode Island. C

500 D 500
500 Ships upon water opposite a city; light house upon left. 500
UNION BANK, Providence, R. I
D D
State Arms.
500 Rhode Island 500

1 — Female with liberty cap; emblem of Liberty.
Vig. Cupid holding silver dollar; churches and steamboat in the distance.
VILLAGE BANK, Smithfield, R. I.
1 — Female figure, emblem of com. and manufacturers.

2 — Farmer with a cradle, seated on sheaves of grain.
Vig. Two silver dollars; two boys (nude;) mountain and train of cars in background.
VILLAGE BANK, Smithfield, R. I
2 — Female in round miniature

THREE — Standing female figure, with a spear and emblems of the arts.
Vig. Three silver dollars, and three Cupid's.
VILLAGE BANK. Smithfield, R. I.
3 — Bust of a sailor, with part of an oar in his hand.

5 — Letter V., with 5 persons around it.
Vig. Five silver dollars, and five Cupid's.
VILLAGE BANK. Smithfield, R. I.
5 — Head of a female and a horse.

Standing female, with flowers and frags in her hand. — TEN
Vig. Railroad cars depot; shipping and wharf scene.
VILLAGE BANK, Smithfield, R. I.
X — Indian female in sitting posture.

20 — Female seated, with a book.
XX Eagle. XX
VILLAGE BANK, Smithfield, R. I.
20 — Ship.

FIFTY — Female standing, with wreaths and flowers. — FIFTY
50 Men and horse. 50
VILLAGE BANK, Smithfield, R. I.
FIFTY — Female standing. — FIFTY

Figures 100, and words ONE HUNDRED across — Portrait.
Shipping, baggage, wagon, &c.
VILLAGE BANK. Smithfield, R. I.
Figures 100, and words ONE HUNDRED across — Portrait.

ONE — Cattle. — 1
[Old Plate.]
1 WAKEFIELD BANK. 1
Wakefield, R. I.
Indian in a canoe.
Bird feeding her 4 young in a nest.
1 — ONE — ONE — ONE — ONE — 1

ONE
[New Plate.]
Schooner, large Sloop, steamboat, and ship. 1
WAKEFIELD BANK. Wakefield, R. I
ONE — Female Indian with bow and arrow. — ONE

ONE on fig. 1 — ONE — ONE on 1.
Two females with cornucopia; anvil between them; factory in distance
WAKEFIELD BK., Wakefield, R. I.
ONE ONE
1 — Portrait of a female.

2 — TWO — 2
[New Plate.]
Ships and schooner. 2
WAKEFIELD BANK, Wakefield, R. I.
TWO — Female drawing water at a spring with pail and rope — TWO

TWO — Men reaping; furnace, factory and canal locks in background — TWO
[Old Plate.]
Portrait of Washington. 2
WAKEFIELD BANK. Wakefield, R. I.
TWO — Ship at sea — 2

2 — Shearing sheep
WAKEFIELD BANK Wakefield, R. I.
Two females seated; house and steamship in distance
TWO DOLLARS
2 — Washing sheep

Rail road engine and cars. — 3 — Schooner and ship in the distance.
[Old Plate.]
3 Dairywoman churning. 3
WAKEFIELD BANK, Wakefield, R. I.
THREE — Cattle. — 3

THREE
Girl with bonnet in right hand and sheaf of grain in left; on left men reaping. 3
WAKEFIELD BANK, Wakefield, R. I.
THREE — Steamboat. — Word THREE and figure 3.

5 Mechanic with vice, anvil and tools; female figure and emblems of commerce. V	[Old Plate.] WAKEFIELD BANK, Wakefield, R. I. Archimedes lifting the world. FIVE	5 Female sitting with cattle on her right and sheaf on her left. FIVE
Word FIVE and large letter V.	[New Plate.] Female sitting, emblems of manufactures, commerce, and agriculture; factory and locomotive on left. V WAKEFIELD BANK, Wakefield, R. I.	5 Portrait of Washington.
Indian with a drawn bow and arrow. 10	[Old Plate.] X Jupiter with his car and horses. X WAKEFIELD BANK, Wakefield, R. I. Female with a sheaf of wheat.	10 Farmer with his scythe in his field. TEN
X	[New Plate.] Signing the declaration of Indepence. X WAKEFIELD BANK, Wakefield, R. I. TEN	10 Railroad cars.
20 Farmer plowing with pair of horses, 20	20 Milkmaids with pails, and laborers, some standing and others sitting 20 WAKEFIELD BANK, Wakefield, R. I.	Small ship. XX
50 Female Portrait. 50	Woodman with axe, and hunter with gun, seated on either side of a frame on which is a bull; on right in distance ships' masts and sails. 50 WAKEFIELD BANK, Wakefield, R. I.	
100 Man sitting.	[New Plate.] Eagle on branch of tree; cars, canal boats, &c., in background. WAKEFIELD BANK, Wakefield, R. I. C ONE HUNDRED C 100	100 Female sitting.
100 Female figure reclining with a cap of liberty in right hand. 100	C Ships, &c. C WAKEFIELD BANK, Wakefield, R. I. 100 100	100 Justice with scales. 100
ONE Goddess of liberty erect, shield beside her.	WARREN BANK, Warren, R. I. Indian reclining upon shield, bow and arrows in hand; eagle soaring on left. ONE ONE	1 Female portrait.
2	WARREN BANK, Warren, R. I. Goddess of liberty seated, holding wreath over spread eagle on shield on right; pole, cap and portrait of Washington in right hand. TWO	2 Ornamental fountain

3 Mercury in air, with cornucopia and bag of coin. THREE	WARREN BANK, Warren, R. I. Vig. Goddess of liberty with wreath and scales; spread eagle upon shield.	3 Female seated with cornucopia, &c THREE
5 5	WARREN BANK, Warren, R. I. Vig. Ship building, ship on stocks, &c, vessels at wharf. FIVE Cars FIVE	5 Cupid astride of dragon.
FIVE	Female holding drapery over shield on which is a 5. V WARREN BANK, Warren, R. I.	5 Ship.
10	Vig. Farming scene: loading hay in distance; farmers reclining in foreground WARREN BANK, Warren, R. I. TEN Wheels, etc TEN	X Man horses. TEN
20 Female figure seated.	XX Eagle. XX Title of Bank.	20 Ship with sails partly furled.
XX inverted Justice on safe.	WARREN BANK, Male portrait; 20 and word Twenty on red die on left; 20 and word Dollars on red die on right Warren, R. I.	20 Female churning.
FIFTY Female erect with wreath. FIFTY	50 Man and horse. 50 WARREN BANK, Warren, R. I.	FIFTY Female erect FIFTY.
FIFTY Girl with sheaf.	Title of Bank. Male portrait. Fifty and 50 on red die on left; Dollars, and 50 on red die on right.	FIFTY Female with pole, cap, scroll, etc.
100 Farmer with rake, fork, keg, dog, etc	Title of Bank. Male portrait. C and One Hundred on red die on left; C and Dollars on red die on right.	100 Portrait of female.
ONE	1 Vig. Portrait of Washington; bales, locomotive and ships on right; scene on wharf, men and dray and steamboat on left. 1 WASHINGTON B'K, Westerly, R. I. Arm and hammer.	Med. head. ONE

TWO	2 Vig. Same as ones. 2 WASHINGTON B'K, Westerly, R. I. Arm and hammer.	Med. head. TWO
THREE Female seated, eagle on her lap, grain in right hand. 3	3 Vig. Portrait of Washington, locomotive, bales, barrels, and sloop. 3 WASHINGTON B'K, Westerly, R. I. Spread eagle.	THREE Female seated with grain and sickle. 3
FIVE	5 Vig. Same as threes. 5 WASHINGTON B'K, Westerly, R. I. Spread eagle.	FIVE Female erect, hand upon shield, with balances. V
X Goddess of liberty, hand upon state arms, pole and cap. 10	10 Vig. Same as 5s. 10 WASHINGTON B'K, Westerly, R. I. Cupid upon deer.	Female erect, scroll in right hand. X
TWENTY	XX Vig. Same as 5s. XX WASHINGTON B'K, Westerly, R. I. Spread eagle.	20 Mercury soaring in air. 20
FIFTY	L Vig. Same as 5s. L WASHINGTON B'K, Westerly, R. I. Female seated, with sickle, &c.	50 Portrait of Franklin. 50
ONE HUNDRED	C Vig. Same as 5s. C WASHINGTON B'K, Westerly, R. I. Ship under sail.	100 Justice with sword and scales. 100
1 Farmer, dray, horse, pigeons, etc.	WASHINGTON CO. BANK, Carolina Mills, R. I. Washington	1 Female feeding fowls.
2 Two mechanics at work on frame of cart.	Man seated; two horses; male portrait on each side of vig. Title of Bank.	2 Washington
3 Farmers at lunch.	Title of Bank. Female portrait.	3 Blacksmiths at work.

Left	Centre	Right
5 Soldiers erecting breast work.	Title of Bank. Soldier, shield with hand on it; female, two Indians etc.	5 Female; cow, heifer, ducks, etc.
10 Female seated with pole, cap and shield; buildings in distance.	Indians apparently frightened at white man; men in distance on right. Title of Bank.	10
50 Blacksmith's apprentice.	Cattle WASHINGTON CO. BANK, Carolina Mills, R. I.	50 Train of cars
1 Male portrait.	WESTMINSTER B'K, Providence. R. I. Vig. Country scene; one man seated on left, one standing on right.	1 Beehive.
2 Male portrait	WESTMINSTER B'K. Providence. R. I. 2 Vig. Two females seated; town in distance on right. 2	2 Female portrait.
5 Male portrait	Vig. View of city of Providence; cars leaving railway station; water in background. WESTMINSTER B'K, Providence, R. I.	5 Male portrait
TEN Large steamship, vessels on either side.	Vig. Two male portraits. WESTMINSTER B'K. Providence, R. I.	10 Brig sailing.
20	Vig. Farming scene; farmer on horse drinking out of trough; two figures on right; sheep on left. Female portrait. WESTMINSTER B'K. Providence. R. I.	20 Male portrait.
50 Male portrait.	WESTMINSTER B'K, Providence, R. I Male portrait. Vig. Female seated holding spy glass; ship in distance on left. Male portrait.	50 Female portrait.
100	WESTMINSTER B'K, Providence R. I. Vig. A number of horses running in a field.	100 Male portrait.

Left	Centre	Right
FIVE HUNDRED	WESTMINSTER B'K, Providence, R. I. Vig. Eagle surmounting a globe; Indian seated with rifle on left; female seated with sickle and grain on right. Male portrait.	500 Male and female seated in foreground; two figures in background, one with a sickle, the other sharpening scythe.
RHODE Female erect with basket upon arm. ISLAND.	Vig. Indian paddling in a canoe. WEYBOSSET BANK, Providence. R. I. State arms.	1 ONE
1 Female portrait.	WEYBOSSET BANK, Providence. R. I. Vig. Meeting of the pilgrims with the Indians. Head of Indian.	1 Male portrait.
2 TWO	WEYBOSSET BANK, Providence, R. I. Vig. Sailor seated upon bale, holding flag in right hand; ships on either side. Spread eagle	TWO State arms.
2 Female portrait.	WEYBOSSET BANK, Providence, R. I. Vig. Elliott preaching to the Indians.	2 Male portrait
RHODE ISLAND.	Vig. Female seated raising lid of chest with right hand. WEYBOSSET BANK, Providence. R. I. Spread eagle.	Star with fig. 2 upon it. Star with fig. 2 upon it.
5 Female erect beside State Arms.	Scene upon the prairie; Indians hunting buffalo. WEYBOSSET BANK, Providence, R. I.	5 Male portrait
5 Female leaning with shield, pole, and liberty cap.	Portrait of Washington. Vig. Ship under full sail. Portrait of Madison. WEYBOSSET BANK, Providence. R. I. State arms.	5 Female seated resting arm upon scroll upon pillar.
Spread eagle upon rock overlooking the sea. TEN	10 10 WEYBOSSET BANK, Providence. R. I. Vig. Cornucopia, wand with wings on it, barrel, &c.; ship in distance on left.	Washington full length.
X Portrait of Harrison. 10	Female portrait. Vig. Dog and safe; bag of coin. Female portrait. WEYBOSSET BANK, Providence, R. I. Spread eagle.	10 Portrait of Henry Clay. X

Left	Centre	Right
FIFTY	50 Vig. Female standing erect resting left hand on shield; anchor on right; ship on left. WEYBOSSET BANK. Providence, R. I. L	50 State arms. 50
Spread eagle upon rock. 100	100 WEYBOSSET BANK, Providence, R. I. Vig. Female reclining on state arms.	100 Male portrait 100
500	Vig. Female reclining upon bales; ships on right; vessel on left. Portrait of Millard Fillmore. WEYBOSSET BANK, Providence, R. I. Female Indian head.	500
1 Female seated beside anvil, holding sledge in right hand.	Vig. Indian seated upon rocks, rifle in right hand; steamboat upon water and city in distance on right. WHAT CHEER B'K, Providence. R. I. Sheaf and plough.	1 Female portrait.
2 Female holding tablet upon pillar with left arm, pen in right hand.	Vig. Three horses running loose in a field; farm house on left in distance. WHAT CHEER B'K Providence, R. I. Spread eagle.	2 Female portrait.
Female portrait. 5	Vig. State arms, eagle surmounting it, female with sword and scales on right, female with cap and staff on left; ship in distance on right; steamboat on left. Title of Bank. Steamboat.	5 Indian seated with gun in right hand.
10 Portrait of D. Webster.	Vig. Cattle, one lying down, two standing in water; sheep on left. WHAT CHEER B'K, Providence. R. I. Indian head.	10 Anchor, bales, ship, &c.
FIFTY Female in clouds holding bag in left hand, wand in right.	Vig. Three females floating upon water; cupid in centre with wings extended. WHAT CHEER B'K, Providence, R. I.	50 Portrait of H. Clay.
100 Henry Clay seated with his dog beside him.	Vig. Female seated between two pillars, eagle and shield at her feet; in distance on right cars crossing bridge; town and ships on left in distance. WHAT CHEER B'K, Providence, R. I.	100 Female seated holding spy-glass; ship on left.
1 Blacksmiths' boy at forge.	View of Falls, village, factories, etc. WOONSOCKET FALLS BANK, Woonsocket. R. I.	1 Portrait of female.

R. ISLAND.

ONE 1	Agricultural scene; farmer sowing; another in the distance harrowing. 1 WOONSOCKET BK, Cumbarland, B, I,	1 Ship. ONE
2 Henry Clay	WOONSOCKET FALLS BANK, R. I. View of the falls; road and village in distance.	2 Female portrait.
TWO 2	Spread eagle; iron castings, cannon balls, machinery, &c. 2 WOONSOCKET B'K, Cumberland. R. I.	2 TWO Schooner rigged boat.
THREE 3	Sailor; hat in hand, reclining against bales; in the distance are vessels, warehouses, dray, boxes &c. 3 WOONSOCKET B'K, Cumberland, R. I.	3 THREE Train of cars.
5 Two males and female.	WOONSOCKET FALLS BANK, Woonsocket, R I. View of Village and Falls.	5
Eagle resting on United States shield and an anchor. FIVE	A large V, with female figure and child. WOONSOCKET B'K, Cumberland, R. I.	5 Female figure and basket.
10 Girl.	WOONSOCKET FALLS BANK, R. I. View of the falls; road and village in distance.	10 Female feeding fowls.
Male figure seated on machinery; cars at distance. TEN	X WOONSOCKET B'K, Cumberland, R. I.	10 Male figure with sheaf in hand.
20 Female figure seated.	XX Eagle. XX WOONSOCKET B'K. Cumberland, R. I.	20 Ship with sails partly furled.
Female 20	View of Village and Falls. WOONSOCKET FALLS BANK, Woonsocket, R.I	20 Washingt'n

CONN.

50	View of Village and Falls. Female WOONSOCKET, FALLS BANK. Woonsocket, R.I.	50 Portrait of boy.
FIFTY Female figure standing globe in her right hand, flowers at her right. FIFTY	50 Man and horse. 50 WOONSOCKET B.K, Cumberland, R. I. FIFTY DOLLARS	FIFTY Female figure with wreath of flowers in right hand. FIFTY
Figures 100 and words one hundred. Head of Harrison.	Wagon with horses and goods; ship at a distance. WOONSOCKET B'K, Cumberland, R. I.	Figures 100 and words one hundred. Head and bust of male.
100	WOONSOCKET FALLS BANK Woonsocket, R.I. View of Village and Falls. State Arms.	100 Female with sheaf of wheat.
1 Sailor leaning against capstan	1 Female seated beside grain, pointing to ship and volcano in distance 1 ÆTNA BANK ONE DOLLAR ONE 1 ONE Hartford Connecticut	ONE on 1 Female portrait
ONE across figure 1. Sailor with quadrant gazing to seaward; steamer in distance.	1 Female, with arm resting on bundle of grain, pointing to Mt. Ætna in distance; ship, &c., on left of her. 1 THE AETNA BANK, Hartford, Conn.	ONE across figure 1. ONE ONE across figure 1.
TWO Vessels. TWO	2 Vig. Same as ones. AETNA BANK, Hartford, Conn.	2 City Arms; deer, water, trees, etc. TWO
3 Two girls carrying grain.	AETNA BANK, Hartford, Conn. 3 Vig. Same as ones. 3	3 Agricultural implements and products THREE across fig. 3.
FIVE	AETNA BANK, Hartford, Conn. V and words Five Dollars. Vig. same as ones. 5	5 CONNECTICUT FIVE
10 inverted. Train of cars. 10 inverted.	Vig. Same as ones with green X each side. AETNA BANK, Hartford, Conn.	10 City Arms, deer, water, trees, etc.

CONN.

FIFTY Female with sheaf and sickle.	50 Vessel under sail; lighthouse, vessels, etc. AETNA BANK. Hartford, Conn.	50 Portrait of female.
100 Shield and motto.	Title of Bank. 100 C 100	100 Female portrait.
Female portrait. 1	Angel blowing a trumpet; eagle globe, flag, &c. ANSONIA BANK, Ansonia, Conn. Sheaf, plow, &c.	1 Male portrait.
Statue of Liberty. 2	Eagle, shield, &c. ANSONIA BANK. Ansonia, Conn. Beehive.	2 Male portrait.
3	Farmer seated, with scythe; man loading hay; bridge in distance. ANSONIA BANK. Ansonia, Conn.	3 Female with tablet, cog wheel, &c.
5 Male portrait.	Five men working in foundry. ANSONIA BANK. Ansonia, Conn.	5 Male portrait.
10	Cars, steamboat, vessels, &c. ANSONIA BANK. Ansonia Conn.	10 Indian reclining.
Male head. 20	ANSONIA BANK. Ansonia, Conn. Female, steamship, vessels, &c.	20 Female.
Female with liberty cap, flag, &c.; U. S. Capitol. 50	50 ANSONIA BANK, Ansonia, Conn.	50 Indian squaw.
100 Female with sickle, &c.	Male head. ANSONIA BANK, Ansonia, Conn.	100 Females, ships, tools, factory, cars, &c.

1 — B'K OF COMMERCE, New London, Ct. — 1
Female seated with mechanical tools, &c.; building on right.
Vig. Ship carpenter at work; view of city. Ship on stocks.
Boy's head

2 — Vig. View of ocean, upon which is a large ship and other vessels. — 2
B'K OF COMMERCE, New London, Ct.
Female portrait.
Locomotive and tender.
Two Cupids and 2.

3 — Vig. Girl seated, by her side basket of corn; also view of village and river — 3
B'K OF COMMERCE, New London, Ct.
Cooper at his work.
View of church.

Train of cars; another train crossing bridge in distance. — 5
BK OF COMMERCE, New London, Conn.
5
Eagle.
Female.

10 — Vig. Whaling scene. — 10
BK OF COMMERCE, New London, Conn.
Cooper at work.
Female seated, ship on left.

Same as on right end of ones.
B'K OF COMMERCE, New London, Ct — 50
Vig. Female seated in ornamental die, vases, &c. on left; bale of goods, anchor, wand, quadrant, &c. on right.
Sailor, in left hand quadrant, right hand resting on capstan; ship on right; steamship on left.
50

Female seated, globe on her right, upon which is an eagle, with American flag across its wing.
Female portrait.
B'K OF COMMERCE, New London, Ct.
100 — 100
Steamboat.
Anchor, bales, etc.

Deer
Masons at work.
1 ONE — 1
B'K OF HARTFORD COUNTY, Hartford, Ct.
1
Female, anchor, &c.

ONE — Bk of HARTFORD Co. Hartford, Conn. — 1
Spread eagle and flag
Words "One Dollar" across ONE on die.
ONE
Female portrait

2 2 — Bk of HARTFORD Co. Hartford, Conn. — 2
Statue of female.
Words "Two Dollars" across Two on die.
2 2
Waterfalls, Indians, etc.

Two cherubs
Interior of a machine shop; mechanics at work.
Ornamental Die with word TWO and fig. 2.
B'K OF HARTFORD COUNTY, Hartford, Ct.
TWO — 2
Locomotive and Cars.

3 — Three Male Figures. Two females on right.
B'K OF HARTFORD COUNTY, Hartford Ct. — 3
View of Rail Road Depot and Cars passing through.
Eagle.

Cars passing through a tunnel.
Female portrait.
B'K OF HARTFORD CO., Hartford, Ct. — 5
FIVE
Female bathing

Female — 10
B'K OF HARTFORD CO., Hartford, Ct.
X
Two females seated, one looking up to man; dog on right, cattle on left.
TEN

B'K OF HARTFORD CO., Hartford, Ct. — 20
20 — Vie. U. S. Capitol
TWENTY

50 — View of New York harbor with steamship and ship. — 50
THE — BK. OF HARTFORD — COUNTY
Hartford, Ct.
Die work. — Die work.

100 — Spread eagle; ship, steamship and steamboat in distance. — 100
THE — BK. OF HARTFORD — COUNTY
Hartford, Ct.
C — $100

1 — State die.
Vig. Harvest scene.
BANK OF LITCHFIELD CO., New Milford, Ct. — 1
Female, arm resting on pillar; farm house and cattle on right.
Dog & safe. ONE Geese.

Connecticut — New Milford
2 on TWO — B K of LITCHFIELD COUNTY
Cattle in road; cars passing over bridge; telegraph, etc.
Female portrait.
Loading grain on cart. — 2
TWO DOLLARS

Two and figure 2.
Title of Bank.
Vig. Farmers loading grain.
View of cattle, telegraph and rail road.
State die. — 2

3 — Vig. Men plowing with horses and cattle.
State die.
Female, quadrant and anchor, eagle on shield.
Title of Bank. — 3
THREE

5 — Train of cars. State die.
Title of Bank. — 5
FIVE

X — Title of Bank. — 10
TEN State die.
State arms; two females, and factories in distance.

XX — Title of Bank. — 20
Vig. Three females; one with harp and two engraving on tablet.
$20
State die.

XX — BK. OF LITCHFIELD COUNTY, New Milford, Conn. — 20
20 on two stripes of lathe work.
Three females seated with pen, tablet, book, harp, etc.
State Arms.

1 — BANK OF NEW ENGLAND, East Haddam, Conn. — ONE
Female.
Bust of male.
View Goodspeed's landing
ONE — ONE

2 — BANK OF NEW ENGLAND, East Haddam, Conn. — TWO
View Goodspeed's landing.
Male portrait
2

BANK OF NEW ENGLAND, East Haddam, Conn. — 3
Steamboat Granite State.
3 — 3
THREE

5 — BANK OF NEW ENGLAND, East Haddam, Conn. — FIVE
Ship building. Female
5

X — View of Goodspeed's Landing. — 10
Male portrait on right.
BANK OF NEW ENGLAND, East Haddam, Conn.
TEN

20 | View of Goodspeed's Landing. BANK OF NEW ENG-LAND, East Haddam, Conn. | 20 Head of D. Webster. | 20

1 Female with sewing machine. | BK OF NORWALK, Norwalk, Conn. Blacksmith's shop. Male portrait | 1

TWO Scene in a blacksmith shop | Milkmaid seated, cows, &c. B'K OF NORWALK, Norwalk, Conn. | 2 Male portrait

3 | Sailors on shore; one looking through telescope; ships, men, etc., in distance. Male portrait. BK OF NORWALK, Norwalk, Conn. | 3 Sheep

5 Blacksmith shop. | Male portrait. Two females, shield, &c; ships, houses, etc., in distance. BK OF NORWALK, Norwalk, Conn. | 5 5

B'K OF NORWALK. TEN Female standing beside pillar. Steamship and vessels. | 10 Male portrait

Male portrait 20 | B'K OF NORWALK. Indian. Female seated beside eagle, shield, &c. Sailor. | 20 20

50 Male portrait | BK. OF NORWALK, Norwalk, Conn. Male and female harvesters resting; cow, calf, etc. | 50 Female portrait.

ONE on 1 Farmer with scythe | State of Conn. View of the city of Bridgeport BRIDGEPORT BANK ONE DOLLAR Bridgeport Bee-hive | ONE on 1 Female portrait

ONE Farmer at work. | Vig. View of the city of Bridgeport. BRIDGEPORT B'K, Bridgeport, Ct. Beehive. | 1 Female portrait.

TWO Female holding American flag. | Vig. Same as Ones. BRIDGEPORT B'K, Bridgeport, Ct. Eagle. | 2 Female artist

Two females. THREE | 3 Female reclining, globe, chart, &c. 3 BRIDGEPORT B'K, Bridgeport, Conn. Eagle. | 3 Dog and safe.

3 Female Indian. | Vig. Female reclining on bale; goods, ships on right and left. BRIDGEPORT B'K, Bridgeport, Ct. Locomotive and tender. | 3 Portrait of Daniel Webster.

5 Portrait of Clay 5 | BRIDGEPORT B'K, Bridgeport, Ct. Vig. Same as ones. Female head. | 5 Male portrait. 5

TEN Washington on horseback. | BRIDGEPORT B'K, Bridgeport, Ct. Female portrait. Vig. Large spread eagle. Female portrait. Steamship. | 10 View of church.

20 Locomotive and cars. XX | Med. head on which is twenty. Vig. Med. head on which figure is twenty. ... BRIDGEPORT B'K, Bridgeport, Ct. Steamboat. | 20 Sculptor. XX

50 Female seated. | BRIDGEPORT BK., Bridgeport, Ct. Vig. View of the City of Bridgeport. FIFTY. | 50 Figure soaring in air.

100 Portrait. 100 | Female seated, mechanical tools, &c. Med. head on which is fig. 100. BRIDGEPORT B'K, Bridgeport. Ct. Locomotive and tender. | 100 City of Bridgeport. 100

1 Sailor leaning on capstan. | BRIDGEPORT CITY BANK, Conn. ONE 1 DOLL 1 AR Vig. Portrait of Washington. | 1 Female

2 Large ships, steamers, etc. 2 | Bridgeport TWO BRIDGEPORT CITY BANK TWO DOLLARS 2 Connecticut | 2 Woman working at sewing machine.

2 Female | Vig. View of Ocean on which is two large ships; steamship between other vessels in distance. BRIDGEPORT CITY BANK, Conn. | 2 Portrait of Calhoun.

5 Female seated at sewing machine. | BRIDGEPORT CITY BANK. Catching horses; three boys, one on the ground, one by horse's side, and one hat in hand; some have 5 on either side. Bridgeport, Conn. | 5 Daniel Webster.

Large manufactory. 10 | 1 Female portrait. 0 BRIDGEPORT CITY BANK, Bridgeport, Conn. | 10 Female with sewing machine.

Two horses; farmer feeding hogs. 10 | Female portrait. BRIDGEPORT CITY BANK, Conn | 10 Female portrait.

XX Female with wheat. | BRIDGEPORT CITY BANK, Conn. Large ornamental die with figure 20 engraved, also the words twenty dollars running across it. | Ornamental die with twenty at top also figure 20.

Female with vase, flowers 50 | BRIDGEPORT CITY BANK, Conn. Ornamental Die on which is figure 50 and the word FIFTY DOLLARS across it. | 50 Female, eagle, shield.

Four cupids supporting figure 1. ONE | Vig. Horses; cars on the left. CENTRAL BANK, Middletown, Ct. | 1 Female.

Eagle and shield. 2 | CENTRAL BANK, Middletown, Ct. Vig. Train of cars. | 2 Male portrait

3 Female and basket of flowers. | Vig. Farmer seated; farming scene and bridge on right; buildings on left. CENTRAL BANK, Middletown, Ct. | 3 Female artist; anvil and hammer on left.

4 FOUR 4 | CENTRAL BANK Middletown, Ct. Vig. Female with triton riding on sea in shell; on either side ship. | 4 FOUR 4

Left	Center	Right
Three females on a rock; anchor, spyglass, &c. FIVE	Large ship; vessel on right; steamship on left. CENTRAL BANK, Middletown, Ct.	5 Male portrait
Washington. X	Females seated; eagle at top of globe, flag across eagles neck. CENTRAL BANK, Middletown, Ct.	TEN Female, sword and balance.
Indian with gun looking over precipice. 25	Female seated on bale of goods; steamship on right; mechanical implements, depot and cars on left. CENTRAL BANK, Middletown, Ct. Female Head.	25 Washington on horseback.
Female with grain. 50	Ship Carpenters at work. CENTRAL BANK, Middletown, Ct.	50 Portrait of Franklin.
Figure 1 and word ONE. 1	CHARTER OAK B'K. Hartford Ct. 1 Soldiers under a large oak tree. 1 ONE	1 Figure 1 and word ONE. ONE
2 TWO 2	CHARTER OAK B'K. Hartford Ct. 2 Vig. Same as Ones. 2	2 Locomotive and Train Cars.
Charter Oak 3	Hartford Connecticut THREE DOLLARS CHARTER OAK B'K.	3 THREE over 3
FIVE Soldiers under a large oak tree.	CHARTER OAK B'K. Hartford. Ct. FIVE in Ornamental Die.	5 5
X Same as fives.	CHARTER OAK B'K, Hartford, Ct. Ornamental Die in which is figures 10, letter X, and word TEN. X each side.	10 X
1 Male Portrait.	CITIZENS' BANK, Waterbury, Ct. Male Portrait, train of cars on right; factories on left.	1 Male Portrait.

Left	Center	Right
2 Female.	CITIZENS' BANK, Waterbury, Ct. Portrait of Aaron Benedict; cars on right; factories on left.	2 Female, olive branch in left hand.
3 Drove of cattle, load of hay.	CITIZENS BANK, Waterbury, Conn. Interior of a Blacksmith shop.	3 Farmer carrying corn.
5 Bee Hive	CITIZENS' BANK, Waterbury, Ct. Portrait of J. M. L. Scovill; cars on right; factories on left. 5 on each side.	5 Bale of goods, machinery, &c.
10 Farming scene—male and female with child seated, man standing against tree.	CITIZENS BANK, Waterbury, Conn. X	10 Blacksmith standing by his anvil.
20 Cupid and cornucopia.	CITIZENS' BANK, Waterbury, Conn. Female feeding fowls. 20 Farmer horse dog, etc	20 Cupid on sheaf.
C Henry Clay and his dog.	CITIZENS BANK, Waterbury, Conn. Landing of the pilgrims.	100 Female portrait.
ONE ONE ONE	Two horses alarmed at lightning. CITY BANK OF HARTFORD Conn	1 [illegible] two horses and trough.
ONE Railroad bridge, cars and vessel ONE	Vig. View of Public building in Hartford, CITY BANK. Hartford, Ct.	1 ONE Female seated, eagle and shield on right.
2 Man dressing leather.	Mowing scene. Title of Bank.	2 Men gathering corn
TWO Two men, carrying implements on their shoulders, dog at their side.	Vig Same as ones. Med. head TWO across. CITY BANK, Hartford. Ct.	2 Female in figure 2 with sword and balances. TWO

Left	Center	Right
THREE Two females and city in distance.	CITY BANK, Hartford, Ct. Vig. Shield, group of Indians on left; group of females on right, globe, &c. Eagle	3 Female.
3 State Arms.	Tree on shield; Indian one side, sailor on the other. Title of Bank.	3 Deer.
5 Female, sheaf of wheat and sickle.	Female seated; deer on a shield; sheep on right. CITY BANK, Hartford, Ct. Dog's head.	5 Female seated, locomotive, factory and cars on left. FIVE
10	Female with pole and cap, shield on right. Vig. Farmers loading grain. CITY BANK, Hartford, Ct.	10 Female, Indian and squaw.
20 Cattle. TWENTY	Vig. Female reclining on rock; canal locks, rail road and city in distance. CITY BANK, Hartford, Ct.	20 Med. head. XX
50 Med. head. FIFTY	Med. head. 50 on it. Vig. Man on either side of a shield, ship above it. CITY BANK, Hartford, Ct.	50 Two females—Indians one with sickle and grain the other with bow & arrow
Female giving eagle drink C	Vig. horse on either side of shield, eagle at top, bridge, train of cars and factory on left. CITY BANK, Hartford, Ct.	100 Med. head. 100
1 Male portrait 1	Vig Public park in New Haven. 1 1 CITY BANK, New Haven. Ct. 1 Eagle. 1	1 Female Indian. 1
TWO	2 Vig Same as ones. CITY BANK, New Haven. Ct. Farming implements	2 Portrait of General Taylor.
THREE	3 Vig. Same as ones. 3 CITY BANK, New Haven. Ct. Locomotive and tender.	3 Three females supporting figure 3.

5 Shield, &c. FIVE	Large steamship; towboats in foreground; vessels, city, &c., in distance. CITY BANK OF NEW HAVEN. Eagle.	5 Male portrait FIVE

X Webster. 10	Four cupids, letter X, medallion head of Franklin and Washington blended together. CITY BANK OF NEW HAVEN. Bee-hive	10 Fillmore. 10

10 X	[Old Plate.] Vig. Same as ones. CITY BANK, New Haven, Ct Females head.	10 X

20 Portrait of H. Clay. XX	Vig. Same as Ones. CITY BANK, New Haven, Ct Indian.	20 Portrait of Gen. Taylor. XX

50 Female. 50	Vig. Same as Ones. CITY BANK, New Haven, Ct Female Indian.	50 Medallion Head, the word Fifty engraved at top.

100 Portrait of Washington.	CITY BANK, New Haven, Ct. Vig. Same as Ones.	100 Male Portrait

ONE Farmer, female, boy, girl, dog, chickens, &c.	CLINTON BANK, Clinton, Conn. Train of cars; sloop, hills, trees, etc.	1 Female with sword, book, and scales.

Connecticut Female erect with medal. head on shield.	2 Farmer plowing with oxen; milkmaid, etc. CLINTON BANK, Clinton, Conn.	2 Female seated with sickle and sheaf.

3 THREE	CLINTON BANK, Clinton, Conn. Yacht race; males, females, etc., on beach.	3 Sailor

FIVE	5 Female and boy; girl and dog; man entering gate with rake. CLINTON BANK, Clinton, Conn.	5 DeWitt Clinton.

TEN TEN	Farmer gathering grain; on right men reaping; on left man on horse talking to farmer. CLINTON BANK, Clinton, Conn.	10 Portrait of Boy.

1 Washingt'n	CONNECTICUT B'K Bridgeport, Conn. 1 Female seated with coffee bags, bbls., kegs, vessels, etc. 1	1 State Arms.

Portrait of of Washington Female, sickle and grain. Male portrait.	CONNECTICUT B'K, Bridgeport, Conn. 1 Vig. Female supporting figure 1. 1	1 Female with arms extended.

2	[First Plate.] View of wharf, steamboat, large ship and other vessels. CONNECTICUT B'K, Bridgeport, Conn. State arms.	2 Male portrait.

TWO Female seated on globe, holding liberty pole and blowing trumpet.	[Second Plate.] Vig. Two females seated; factories on the right, ship on left; cog-wheel, anvil and vice between them. 2 CONNECTICUT B'K, Bridgeport, Ct.	TWO Two females, Eagle at top of a shield. TWO

Two children.	Wharf scene—unloading boats; men, horses, etc. CONNECTICUT B'K Bridgeport, Conn.	2 Boy's portrait

Anchor, bales, bbls., etc. 3	Three on 3 Man buying paper of newsboy, hhds. etc CONNECTICUT B'K Bridgeport, Conn.	3 Indian female.

3	Locomotive and cars. Large figure 3 CONNECTICUT B'K. Bridgeport, Ct. State arms.	3 Female.

5 Washington on his horse.	Three females, ship in distance. CONNECTICUT B'K, Bridgeport, Conn. Shield, etc.	5 Liberty.

5 Farmer at work. 5	CONNECTICUT B'K. Bridgeport. Ct. Vig. Female with grain in ornamental V.	5 Female Portrait. FIVE

Two females supporting letter X.	X Vig. view of ship yard; ship carpenter at work. X CONNECTICUT B'K. Bridgeport, Ct.	10 Female portrait. TEN

Washington and his horse. 20	Vig. Group of three females; ship on right. CONNECTICUT B'K. Bridgeport, Ct. State arms.	20 Female and shield, liberty pole and cap.

Female with sword and ballances. FIFTY	CONNECTICUT B'K. Bridgeport, Ct. Female seated, before her is winged figure holding wand; on right is Neptune in his car drawn by sea serpents. State arms.	50 50

Two females, farming implements on left, ship on right.	CONNECTICUT B'K, Bridgeport. Ct. Eagle holding shield on which is figures 100.	Three cupids 100

I named. head Portrait of Washington.	Vig. Man on horse, drove of sheep; mill on left. Fig. 1 on shield. CONN. RIVER BANKING CO. Hartford, Ct. Eagle.	ONE Full length female. ONE

2 Portrait of Washington. 2	Vig. Head of Franklin in ornamental die, on either side a female; steamboat and ships on right; farming scene on left. Title of Bank	2 Female seated in fig. 2, railroad cars, and factory on left.

3 Portrait of Franklin. 3	Vig. View of ocean, steamship and other vessels. Title of Bank. Barrels, bales and goods.	THREE Female erect with spear in right hand. THREE

5 5	Portrait of Gen. Taylor, with title of bank above and below it. Two females soaring in air	5

TEN	Portrait of Washington, with title of bank above and below it. Indian group looking over precipice; view of city and river below. Locomotive and tender.	Letter X on American shield.

L L	50 Vig. Female seated with wand, right hand resting on shield; steamboat on left; anchor on right. 50 Title of Bank.	L L

Left	Centre	Right
C C	100 100 Vig. Three females, two seated, one standing holding spear in her hand. Title of Bank.	C C
1 Female with hands up raised holding sickle. ONE	[First Plate.] Male portrait. Reapers at work. DANBURY BANK, Danbury, Conn. Farming implements.	1 Female and basket of flowers.
ONE Large monument.	[Second Plate.] DANBULY BANK, Danbury, Conn. Three figures, Farmer, Mechanic and Sailor representing industry.	1 Male portrait
Man resting on safe. 2	[First Plate.] DANBURY BANK, Danbury, Conn. 2 2 Male portrait.	TWO Large monument.
2 Female with arms extended. 2	[Second Plate.] Vig. Farmers at lunch; Horses on right. DANBURY BANK, Danbury, Conn. Horse.	2 Farmer gathering corn.
3 Three cupids in figure 3	Vig. Drove of cattle and sheep; mill in background vessel in distance. DANBURY BANK, Danbury, Conn. Farming tools.	3 Female in figure 3.
5 Female.	[First Plate.] Vig. Female seated liberty pole across her lap, eagle and shield on right. DANBURY BANK, Danbury, Conn. Bank building.	5 Med. head.
Male portrait FIVE American shield.	[Second Plate.] DANBURY BANK, Danbury, Conn. U. S. Capitol. 5 Female.	5 5
10 Portrait of Washington.	Vig. Farming scene—farmers at work. DANBURY BANK, Danbury, Conn. Bank building.	10 Female.
20 Female seated with sword and balances 20	20 Vig. Three females with wand sickle and grain; ship and American shield on right; cars on left. DANBURY BANK, Danbury, Conn. Eagle.	20

Left	Centre	Right
50 Med. head.	DANBURY BANK, Danbury, Conn. Female blowing trumpet; globe and eagle on right; flags on left.	50 S. A. head.
ONE ONE Washington.	Word and figure 1. Map of Conn. 1 on which is seen words New Haven, Hartford, Norwich, Deep River, and L. I. Sound; globe and ship on left, factory, on right. DEEP RIVER BANK, Deep River, Ct.	ONE
Head. TWO Head.	2 Same as ones. 2 DEEP RIVER BANK, Deep River, Ct. 2	TWO
Three heads or portraits on this end.	3 Same as ones. 3 DEEP RIVER BANK, Deep River, Ct. 3	THREE
Same as 3s.	5 Same as ones 5 DEEP RIVER BANK Deep River, Ct. 5	Head FIVE Head.
TEN Map same as on ones. TEN	10 Eagle. 10 DEEP RIVER BANK, Deep River, Ct. 10	TEN Female figure of Minerva. TEN
XX Elephant. TWENTY	Map—same as ones. 20 DEEP RIVER BANK, Deep River, Ct. 20	Figure of Justice. TWENTY
1 Female Indian with bow and arrows.	Female blowing trumpet; eagle on right; flags on left. EAST HADDAM B'K, East Haddam, Ct. Farming implements.	1 Female artist at work.
ONE Blacksmith with sleigh.	1 Female seated; ship on left; lighthouse, etc, on right. EAST HADDAM BK, East Haddam, Conn.	1 Cars passing over and cattle under arch.
TWO Female and child, flag, liberty pole and cap.	Vig. Squaw with horn of plenty at her feet, flags, safe, shield, eagle at top of globe; steamship on right; cars and factory on left. EAST HADDAM B'K, East Haddam, Ct. Cogwheels, &c.	2 Ship. TWO

Left	Centre	Right
2 Buchanan.	EAST HADDAM BK, East Haddam, Conn. Two females on either side of anvil; buildings on right.	2 Female portrait.
3 Female with sword and balances.	Portrait of Washington. Male portrait. Vig. Female seated among merchandise; vessels on right. EAST HADDAM B'K, East Haddam, Ct. Beehive.	3 Female, sickle and grain. THREE
THREE Female feeding owls.	3 Inside of factory; females weaving. EAST HADDAM BK, East Haddam, Conn.	3 THREE Farmer shearing sheep.
5 Female. 5	Vig. Large spread eagle. EAST HADDAM B'K, East Haddam, Ct. Steamboat	5 Female with sword and balances; shield, safe, eagle, &c.
V Girls' head.	EAST HADDAM BK, East Haddam, Conn. View of ship yard; men at work, etc. V V	5 Sailor boy, shield, barrels, etc.
X Washington. 10	EAST HADDAM B'K, East Haddam, Ct. 10 Vig. Female seated; factories and cars on left. Steamship & merchandise.	X Male portrait 10
XX Male portrait. XX	XX XX Vig. Female seated; ship on right. EAST HADDAM B'K, East Haddam, Ct. Vessels, &c.	20 Washington. 20
Female with some branches on head load of hay and village in distance. ONE	ELM CITY BANK, New Haven, Conn. Portrait of Washington.	1 Boy with rabbits.
2 Female with chickens.	ELM CITY BANK, New Haven, Ct.	2 Three men by side of a small boat, partly finished; ship on stocks.
3 Three females with liberty pole and ship, &c.	Three male figures, blacksmith, sailor and farmer; interior of blacksmith shop; horse, anvil and man. ELM CITY BANK, New Haven, Ct.	3 3

5 Eagle on shield.	View of steamboat Elm City; vessels in distance. ELM CITY BANK, New Haven, Ct. Sailing vessels.	5 Female.

10 Mower drinking from jug; scythe, fence and field.	Two sailors, one standing; the other seated on box; wharf scene; steamship in distance. ELM CITY BANK, New Haven, Ct.	10 Portrait of female.

20 Portrait of Columbus	Large ship, steamships; ships in distance. ELM CITY BANK, New Haven, Ct.	20 Boy with globe and compass.

Three females representing liberty, justice, and agriculture; field &c	ELM CITY BANK, New Haven, Ct. L 50 L	50 Portrait of Franklin.

100	ELM CITY BANK New Haven. Ct. Mechanics and farmer; horse, trees, &c.; factories in distance in lower left corner of note. C on right.	100 Female Indian, left hand on rock.

ONE Medal. Head. ONE	[First Plate.] EXCHANGE BANK, Hartford, Ct. Two females, view of river; steamboat and sail vessel on left, locomotive and cars on right; medal. head with word ONE on either side.	ONE Full Length Female. ONE

ONE Small male fig., anvil and hammer. 1	[Second Plate.] Rail Road Depot, cars passing through. EXCHANGE BANK, Hartford, Ct. Barrels, &c.	ONE DOLLAR

TWO Indian reclining on shield. TWO	[First Plate.] Med. Head, with word TWO across Med. Head, with word TWO across A female on either side of a shield. EXCHANGE BANK, Hartford, Ct.	Medallion Head with word TWO across.

Full length female, right hand resting on shield. TWO	[Second Plate.] 2 Locomotive and Cars. EXCHANGE BANK, Hartford, Ct.	2 Female with pole and cap on right Eagle standing on shield

THREE Locomotive and cars. THREE	Female seated with pole and cap, before her two youthful artists; shipping on left; cars on right. EXCHANGE BANK, Hartford, Ct.	3 Two farmers farming implements on their shoulders, farm house on right.

Female with starry drapery holding pole and cap; eagle and American shield on right.	5 View of public buildings in Hartford. EXCHANGE BANK, Hartford, Ct. Locomotive and tender.	5

Full length female with spear. TEN	X Vig. Three females, eagle, &c.; bridge, locomotive and cars on right; ship on left. EXCHANGE BANK, Hartford, Ct. Steamship.	X Female with pole and cap resting on shield.

20 View of city, bridge, railroad and cars.	EXCHANGE BANK, Hartford, Ct. Vig. Three female figures; sickle, anchor and quadrant. XX	20 Large ship, view of city and shipping.

50 Man under large tree; church on right; building on left. FIFTY	EXCHANGE BANK, Hartford, Ct. Vig. River scene; view of city in distance. Eagle.	FIFTY 50

100 Sculptor.	Vig. Group of female figures, eagle between them; waterfalls in background. EXCHANGE BANK, Hartford, Ct. Head of female.	100 Spread eagle, shield, &c. 100

ONE Washington. ONE	Vig. Banking house. FAIRFIELD CO. BK. Norwalk, Ct.	Figure 1 on shield.

ONE Male portrait	FAIRFIELD CO. BK, Norwalk, Conn. View of buildings, etc—a general street view.	1 1

TWO Male portrait. TWO	2 Milkmaid seated with cattle. FAIRFIELD CO. BK. Norwalk, Ct.	2

TWO Blacksmith	Female with two calves; cars, canal scene, cows, etc., in distance on left. Title of Bank.	2 Male portrait

THREE Female. THREE	View of sea, on which is two ships; Light house on right. FAIRFIELD CO. BK. Norwalk, Ct.	3

THREE Male portrait	Large fig. 3 on which is Title of Bank, words "Three Dollars," etc.	3 Female soaring in clouds with quadrant.

Statue of Justice with sword and shield FIVE	V Vessels at sea V FAIRFIELD CO. B'K FIVE DOLLARS Nor 5 walk	5 5

Female with sword and balances. FIVE	Vig. Steamship and other vessels. FAIRFIELD CO. BK. Norwalk, Ct.	5

Female with shield, liberty pole and cap.	10 Female with cornucopia. FAIRFIELD CO. BK. Norwalk, Ct.	10

TWENTY Female Indian with bow & arrow	Vig. Train of cars; wharf, steamboat and depot in the background. FAIRFIELD CO. BK. Norwalk, Ct.	XX Female between 2 & 0.

50 Male portrait FIFTY	Drove of cattle. FAIRFIELD CO BK. Norwalk, Ct.	50 Male portrait

Med. head and figure 100.	Two horses alarmed at cars, two men. FAIRFIELD CO BK. Norwalk, Ct	Same as the other end.

1 Female and ONE on ornamental die 1	Bridgeport portrait DOLLAR large Females tending looms FARMER'S BANK ONE DOLLAR on 1 Connecticut	1 ONE

ONE ONE	FARMERS' BANK, Bridgeport, Conn. Female portrait on large die; words "one dollar. Two females tending looms.	1 ONE

Four Cupids holding figure 1 1.	Vig. Mechanic seated; by his side mechanical tools; farmers at work, on left. FARMER'S BANK, Bridgeport, Ct. Locomotive and tender.	1 Male portrait.

Left	Center	Right
2 Washington	FARMERS' BANK, Bridgeport, Conn. Milkmaid and boy.	2 Female with rose.
Female; sheaf of wheat 2	Vig. Female seated; on right, farmers at work; and locomotive and cars in distance. FARMER'S BANK, Bridgeport, Ct. Steamship.	2 Male portrait.
3 Female portrait	FARMERS BANK 3 Two blacksmiths, female on with grain, etc. 3 on THREE DOLLARS Bridgeport	3 Dog's head
3 Male portrait.	Vig. Horses and hogs; one horse drinking out of trough; female on left, feeding hogs; farm houses in background. FARMER'S BANK, Bridgeport, Ct. Locomotive and tender.	3 Female with wreath of flowers.
FIVE	FARMERS' BANK, Bridgeport, Conn. Vigs. in lower right and left corners. Blacksmiths' shop, man, shoeing horse, etc.; farmer, wife and boy at lunch &c.	5
5 Male portrait.	Mechanic and large letter V; also, mechanical tools. FARMER'S BANK, Bridgeport, Ct. Eagle.	5 Female with sword and balances.
X Female portrait. 10	Three females seated; ship on right. FARMER'S BANK, Bridgeport, Ct. Sheaf of wheat, plow, &c.	10 Male portrait.
Female with compass 20	Vig. Group of figures, supporting figure 20. FARMER'S BANK, Bridgeport, Ct. Dog's head.	20 Male portrait.
Male portrait. 50	Vig. Female Indian seated; steamship on right; flags, shield, eagle, etc., locomotive and cars, on left. FARMER'S BANK, Bridgeport, Ct. Locomotive and tender.	50 Female holding American flag.
100 Portrait of Washington. 100	FARMERS' BANK, Bridgeport, Ct. Vig. Sailor standing erect holding American flag.	100 Male portrait 100

Left	Center	Right
1 Milkmaid and cattle.	FAR. & MECH. BK., Hartford, Conn. Vig. Blacksmith, arm and hammer.	1 Spread eagle
Full length female, with pole and cap.	1 Vig. Milkmaid seated, with cattle. FAR. & MECH. BK., Hartford, Ct.	ONE Cupid, anvil and hammer ONE
Full length female with grain and sickle.	Shield; Indian on right; female with sickle on left. FAR. & MECH. B'K., Hartford, Conn.	2 Female, with sheaf and sickle.
3 Ship under full sail.	Farmer and blacksmith on either side of shield; cars on right; view of farm on left. FAR. & MECH. B'K., Hartford, Conn.	3 Female
Female erect, with pole and cap; shield with figure 3 on left.	Eagle with wings extended. FAR. & MECH. BK., Hartford, Ct.	Two females; one reclining, the other soaring in air between them, is figure 3.
5 Sculptor or engraver. V	Med. head, five across. Med. head, five across. Vig. Interior of a blacksmith's shop. FAR. & MECH. BK., Hartford, Ct.	V Cattle. 5
10 Farmer seated; by his side sickle, rake, etc. X	Female clasping book, mechanical implements, steamboat in distance. Med head and ten on either side. FAR. & MECH. B'K., Hartford, Conn.	X 10 on med. head. 10
TWENTY	20 Group of 3 male figures. FARMERS AND MECHANICS BANK, Hartford, Ct.	20 Two females, one with sickle and grain.
Full length female with wand in her left hand, shield in right on which is engraved medal head.	Family group, woman seated, by her side a little boy, man coming towards him with rake on his shoulder in front of him is a little girl, by her side is dog in attitude of barking. Figures 50 at left of vig. Title of Bank. Barrels, bales, &c.	50
100 Mechanical implements. 100	Bank Building. FAR. AND MEC. BK., Hartford, Ct., Horse.	100

Left	Center	Right
1 Girl	CONNECTICUT Ships at sea HARTFORD BANK ONE DOLLAR Hartford	1 Male portrait
1 ONE Female portrait.	HARTFORD BANK, Hartford, Ct. Vig. Two females and eagle; portrait of Washington, ship on left.	1 Portrait of Jenny Lind.
1 Med head. 1	Med. head; one across. Figuring the Declaration of Independence. Med. head; one across. HARTFORD BANK, Hartford, Conn. Female and anchor.	1 Med head 1
2 Male portrait.	Connecticut Canal, cars, bridge, men, boat, lock, etc. HARTFORD BANK TWO DOLLARS Hartford	2 Female with barrel and sickle
2 Med. head. 2	Med. head; two across. View of river, steamboat and ship; city on right. Med. head; two across. HARTFORD BANK, Hartford, Ct. Dog's head.	2 Med. head. 2
TWO Female portrait. TWO	2 Vig. Sailor reclining, nautical implements, &c.; view of sea and three vessels. HARTFORD BANK, Hartford, Ct.	2 Female seated in fig. 2; factory and locomotive on left. TWO
3 Male portrait	HARTFORD BANK Three children in circular die reading book THREE DOLLARS Hartford Conn	3 State Arms
THREE Two females seated, above them sailor and mechanic; view of city and mountain in distance.	HARTFORD BANK, Hartford, Ct. Vig. Anchor, anvil, and sheaves.	3 Male Two females, cattle, dog, &c.
Female, liberty pole, and cap. Figure 4	4 Vig. Ships storming a fort. 4 HARTFORD BANK, Hartford, Ct. Dog, safe, and boy.	Female with sword Figure 4
5 Squaw and papoose.	View of the Deaf and Dumb Asylum. HARTFORD BANK, Hartford, Conn.	5 Male head.

FIVE
Med. head; five across.
Vig. Sailor erect, with flag; view of harbor and shipping
Med. head; five across.
HARTFORD BANK,
Hartford, Ct.
Eagle.
5
5 on med. head.
5

TEN
Med. head, and fig. 10 on it.
Vig. Railroad and train of cars.
Med. head, and fig. 10 on it.
HARTFORD BANK,
Hartford Ct.
Mechanics, arm and anvil.
TEN
Steamboat and row-boat.
TEN

10
Male portrait
Steamboat "Granite State;" hills and raft.
HARTFORD BANK,
Hartford, Conn.
10
Female.

XX
XX
20 Vig. Female 20 seated, with figure 20 on right; vessel on left.
HARTFORD BANK,
Hartford, Ct.
20
20

XX
Female with cornucopia.
HARTFORD BANK,
Hartford, Conn.
Vig. Same as first.
20
Male portrait

L
L
50 Vig. Female 50 seated; view of canal in distance.
HARTFORD BANK,
Hartford, Ct.
L
L

Female with flowers.
50
Title of Bank.
Shield on which is a deer; eagle at top, horse on either side; bridge and city in distance on right; building on left.
50
Indian.

C
C
HARTFORD BANK,
Hartford. Ct.
100 Vig. Female 100 seated on rock; wood scene.
C
C

100
View of U. S. Capitol.
C
HARTFORD BANK,
Hartford, Conn.
100.
Liberty surrounded by stars.

1
1
Milkmaid beside cattle; farmhouse in distance.
HATTERS BANK
ONE DOLLAR
Bethel, Conn.
ONE
Female figure.

ONE
ONE
Three females binding hats; hatter on left pressing hats.
HATTERS' BANK,
Bethel, Ct.
ONE
Milkmaid pail on her head, farmhouse on right, cattle on left.

TWO
Female binding hats.
Two horse team, hay on one horse, man attaching team to plow.
HATTERS' BANK,
Bethel, Ct.
2
Mechanics and mechanical implements; sledge on his back.

2
Indian head
2
HATTERS' BANK,
Bethel, Conn.
Scene in stable—two horses and colt.
2
Female binding hats.

3
Cattle
HATTERS BANK
Two men weighing load of hay
THREE DOLLARS
Bethel
3
3

3
Portrait of Washington.
Two females, Cornucopia between them; one seated with pole and cap; view of river and vessel, bridge, locomotive and cars on right.
HATTERS' BANK,
Bethel, Ct.
3
Man pressing hats.

5
5
HATTERS' BANK,
Bethel, Conn.
Female portrait with train of cars and view of river on right; steamboat, factories and men on left.
5
5

FIVE and fig. 5.
FIVE
FIVE
Train of cars; telegraph and bridge.
HATTERS' BANK,
Bethel Ct.
FIVE
Man pressing hats.

TEN
TEN
X
Large spread eagle on globe; flags with the names of different States on either side.
HATTERS' BANK,
Bethel, Ct.
X
Portrait of Webster.

20
Two men with guns.
XX Portrait of Washington. XX
Horses on right, cattle on left.
HATTERS' BANK,
Bethel, Ct.
X X
20
Two soldiers, one seated with gun and pipe, the other standing holding gun.

50
Eagle and figures 50.
Drove of cattle and sheep.
HATTERS' BANK,
Bethel, Ct.
50
Male portrait

1
Figure of Mercury with bag of money.
HOME BANK,
Meriden, Conn.
Drover and farmer bargaining for ox.
1
Female figure.

2
Wheelwright and apprentice.
Female figure of manufacture.
HOME BANK,
Meriden, Conn.
2
Genius of America.

3
Indian looking over rock.
HOME BANK,
Meriden, Conn.
Arm and hand with hammer.
3
Female feeding chickens.

5
Justice with scales.
HOME BANK,
Meriden, Conn.
Apotheosis of Washington.
5
Beehive.

10
Female holding up counter.
TEN
HOME BANK,
Meriden, Conn.
Train of cars.
Female head.
10
Female figure.

Word twenty and three dies above on which is Title and figs. 20.
Machinist at work; vice, etc.
Spread eagle on shield.
HOME BANK,
Meriden, Conn.
20
Beehives.

Female portrait
50
Man plowing with two horses.
HOME BANK,
Meriden, Conn.
50
Horse's head

100
Washington
ONE HUNDRED
ONE HUNDRED DOLLARS
Title of Bank
ONE HUNDRED
100
Webster.

1
State die.
[First plate.]
HULBURT BANK,
West Winsted, Ct.
1 Large ornamented 1 die, with One Dollar, running across it.
1
Male portrait

Wild horses
ONE
[Second Plate.]
Girl
HULBURT BANK,
West Winsted, Ct.
1
Male portrait

TWO
Female standing beside table blowing dinnerhorn, men on load of hay on right
West Winsted
2 Female portrait
HURLBUT BANK
TWO DOLLARS
TWO
Lewis Cass

3
Male portrait
Vig. Shield and Indian on right, with tomahawk; Female on left, with wand; steamboat, vessel, and city in distance, on left.
HULBURT BANK,
West Winsted, Ct.
Female bathing.
3
Male portrait

Drove of cattle.
V
State die.
HULBURT BANK.
West Winstad, Ct.
Geese.
5
Spread eagle
Ox.

X
Male portrait
HULBURT BANK.
West Winsted. Ct.
Vig Group of Indians, view of city and cars crossing bridge, and also cars passing through tunnel.
TEN
10
State die.

20
Man on horseback.
HURLBUT BANK,
West Winsted, Conn.
Female holding pole and cap in left hand, and frame with 20 on it in right.
XX
Soldier with musket.

ONE
View of town.
ONE
Male Portrait Vig. Puddling in an iron mill Male Portrait
IRON BANK,
Falls Village, Conn.
Locomotive and cars.
ONE
Mechanic's arm.
ONE

2
TWO
Locomotive and cars.
2 Vig. View of falls; and town. 2
IRON BANK,
Falls Village, Conn.
Cog wheel
2
Female, sword, and balances.

3
Farmer with scythe.
Two milkmaids seated, one milking cow, and one with pail on her lap; farm house on right; vessels on left.
IRON BANK,
Falls Village, Conn.
Bee hive.
3
Mechanic at work.

5
Man at work in iron foundry.
View of Falls and village.
IRON BANK,
Falls Village, Conn.
Building and trees.
5
Male portrait

5
Man forging iron.
Two men tending furnace.
IRON BANK.
Falls Village, Conn.
5
Franklin.

5
Mechanic at work.
Puddling in an iron mill.
IRON BANK,
Falls Village, Conn.
Building and trees.
5
Portrait of Franklin.

10
Portrait of Washington.
Vig. Puddling in an iron mill.
Male portrait Male portrait
IRON BANK,
Falls Village, Conn.
Steamboat.
10
Male portrait

Male Portrait
20
View of Falls Village.
IRON BANK,
Falls Village, Ct.
Beehive.
20
View of factories, etc.

Female portrait.
Connecticut
1
JEWETT CITY BANK
1 Locomotive and cars 1
ONE DOLLAR.
ONE on 1
Ducks, etc.

1
Portrait of Gen. Taylor.
ONE
Man on horseback; dog, flock of sheep, grist mill, &c.
JEWETT CITY B'K.
Jewett City. Conn
Chartered June, 1, 1831.
1
Cars
ONE

ONE
1
Female with scales, eagle and portrait of Washington.
ONE
Female seated holding eagle with olive leaf; horn of plenty at her feet; ships in distance.
JEWETT CITY B'K.
Jewett City, Conn.
Sheaf, plow, rake, &c.
1
Female resting on anchor; ship in distance.

Dog's head.
Connecticut
2
Two Dollars 2 Female with grain, machinery, etc.
JEWETT CITY BANK
TWO DOLLARS
2
Female portrait

TWO
Female, scales, eagle, rod, portrait of Washington, &c.
TWO
2 Female, anchor, and hope; cars in distance on right; on left spinning wheel, factory, &c. 2
JEWETT CITY B'K.
Jewett City, Conn.
House, cattle, plow, trees, &c.
Female reclining on anchor.

2
Portrait of Washington.
TWO
Signing the Declaration of Independence.
JEWETT CITY B'K,
Jewett City, Conn.
Spread Eagle.
2
Portrait of Martha Washington.
TWO

Female, scales, eagle, horn of plenty, casks &c.
3 Two females and one male; horn of plenty, cars, ship, safe, &c.
JEWETT CITY B'K,
Jewett City, Conn.
Agricultural Implements.
3

CONNECTICUT.
Girl feeding calf
FIVE
JEWETT CITY BANK
5 Child with beads. 5
FIVE DOLLARS.
5
Eagle on shield

5
Female, scales, eagle, horn of plenty, casks &c.
FIVE
Two females, horn of plenty, goods, shipping, steamboat, &c.
JEWETT CITY B'K.
Jewett City, Conn.
Dog, safe, &c.
5
Female, scales, &c.
FIVE

5
Female with scales and rod; eagle and portrait of Washington.
FIVE
Figure 5; two females, Cupid with scales, eagle &c., surrounding the figure.
JEWETT CITY B'K,
Jewett City, Conn.
5
Two Heads
5

10
CONNECTICUT.
Children with horse.
Cattle in water, children on bank, etc.
JEWETT CITY BANK
TEN DOLLARS
Jewett City.
10
Female portrait

XX
Three children seated.
JEWETT CITY B'K,
Jewett City, Conn.
View of manufacturing village.
TWENTY
20
Washington on horseback

Female erect resting right arm on anchor; ship in distance.
FIFTY
50 State arms; on left female 50 erect with horn of plenty at her feet; on right female erect with key in right hand, and "charter 1831" on left.
Title of Bank.
Female seated on rock.
FIFTY

1
Washingt'n
ONE
State of Connecticut.
View of river and town.
MANUFACTURERS BANK,
Birmingham.
Locomotive.
1
Ship.
ONE

2
Male portrait.
TWO
View of town and river.
MANUFACTURERS BANK.
Birmingham.
TWO
Mechanic's arm & tools
2
Train of cars, village in background.
TWO

THREE 3 THREE
Male portrait.
THREE.
State of Connecticut
View of town and river.
MANUFACTURERS BANK,
Birmingham.
THREE.
Steamboat.
3
Agriculture female, grain, and sickle.
THREE.

5
Female.
FIVE
State of Connecticut.
Man plowing, with horse and oxen.
MANUFACTURERS BANK,
Birmingham.
FIVE
Spread Eagle.
5
Blacksmith at work.
FIVE

10 | Connecticut. Liberty, Justice, and Truth, on either side of shield; eagle on top of shield. | 10
Female and cornucopia. | MANUFACTURERS BANK, Birmingham. | Mechanic's arm, anvil, hammer, &c.
TEN X TEN X TEN

TWENTY | State of Connecticut. Indian and female on either side of shield. MANUFACTURERS BANK, Birmingham. TWENTY. | 20
Mechanic seated, factories on left.

50 | State of Connecticut. Three female figures; Agriculture, Liberty, and Art. MANUFACTURERS BANK. Birmingham. | 50
Three dogs barking at birds. | | Female reaping.

C | State of Connecticut. Wild horses. MANUFACTURERS BANK, Birmingham. | 100
Little girl and dog. | | Machinery; female at work.
C 100 C

1 | 1 Vig. Female seated; ships on right. 1 | 1
Portrait of Franklin. | MECHANICS' BANK, New Haven, Ct. | Portrait of Washington.
1 | Banking house. | 1

2 | Vig. same as ones. | 2
2 | MECHANICS' BANK, New Haven, Ct. Banking house. | Mechanic and mechanical implements.

3 | 3 Vig. Female seated on bale of goods, vessel on either side. | 3
Female with triton. | MECHANICS' BANK, New Haven, Ct. | Female
3 | Banking house. | 3

5 | MECHANICS BANK, New Haven, Conn. | 5
Mechanic's arm. | Female seated; eagle on globe, flag across his back, &c. | Ship.
V | Bank building. | 5

5 | Group of five Am. Presidents in letter V, two flags, and eagle at top | 5
Mechanic's arm | MECHANIC'S BANK New Haven, Conn. | Ship
V | | V

10 | Sailor seated holding flag; ship on left. | X
Female Indian. | MECHANICS' BANK, New Haven, Ct. | Female seated with sword and balances, safe and shield.
10 | Mechanic's Arm.

| Three females overlooking precipice, one holding sword and balance. | 20
20 | MECHANICS' BANK, New Haven, Ct. Banking House. | Female.

Artist at work, building on right. | 50 | Male figure, the word Franklin engraved on pillar.
50 | MECHANICS' BANK, New Haven, Ct. Male Portrait | State Arms.

Female Erect with sword and balances. | State Arms. 100 100 | Female feeding an eagle.
100 | MECHANICS' BANK, New Haven, Ct. Portrait of Washington. | 100

ONE on 1 | MERCANTILE B'K 1 Steamships, etc. 1 | 1
Figure of Justice with sword and scales | ONE DOLLAR Hartford, Conn. | State Arms

Figure 1, and one running across. | MERCANTILE BK., Hartford, Ct. | 1
Female portrait. | Vig. Female seated; safe, sheep &c. | Sailor seated; spy-glass in left hand.

2 | MERCANTILE B'K Tug towing TWO large DOLLARS ship | 2
Anchor, bales, etc. | Hartford, Conn. 2 | Sailor seated

TWO DOLLARS | MERCANTILE BK., Hartford, Ct. 2 | 2
View of ocean; steamship and other vessels. 2

Steamer bales, car | Connecticut at dock, 3 Dog on safe
3 | MERCANTILE B'K THREE DOLLARS Hartford | 3
Female seated supporting shield

3 | Vig. Shield and figure 3; eagle at top of shield; on either side, a horse; steamboat on right; canal, bridge, cars and factories on left. 3 | THREE
Female portrait. | MERCANTILE BK., Hartford, Ct.

Loading wagons; horses. | Express men, etc. V FIVE | Connecticut Female head | 5
5 | MERCANTILE B'K FIVE DOLLARS Hartford | Female with [illegible]

| 5 Three females seated, with cornucopia, sickle, and quadrant. | 5
FIVE | MERCANTILE BK., Hartford, Ct. | Sailor.

10 | Train of cars leaving depot; ships, steamboats, etc. in distance. | 10
Sailor, female and boy looking towards the sea | MERCANTILE B'K TWO DOLLARS Hartford | Ship on ways

10 X 10 | Indian head, 10 and X. MERCANTILE BK., Hartford, Ct. | TEN
Two female Indians; one seated with sickle and grain; the other with bow and arrow.

XX | MERCANTILE B'K. Hartford, Ct. Sailor at wheel. | 20
Female gathering wheat. | | Female with flowers in her apron.

Female with cornucopia. | MERCANTILE B'K. Hartford, Ct. Male Portrait. FIFTY | 50
50 | | Ship.

Figures 100 and $ mark. | MERCANTILE BK. Hartford, Ct. | 100
Large red letter C. | Large die with figures 100, and words one hundred dollars. | Large red letter C.

Full length female with pole and cap, starry drapery across her shoulder | 1 Floating female with cornucopia. | 1
MERCHANTS' BANK. New Haven, Ct. | Female.

TWO | View of Ocean; steamship and other vessels. | 2
Female hunting in air. | MERCHANT BANK, New Haven, Ct | Female feeding an Eagle.
TWO | Female Bathing.

3 | Vig. Three females with quadrant, liberty pole and cap, grain, &c. | 3
Two male figures. THREE | MERCHANTS' B'K. New Haven, Ct. Shells | Male portrait.

| View of public square in New Haven. 5 | FIVE
5 | MERCHANTS' B'K. Now Haven, Ct. Barrels, bales, goods, &c. | Sailor and mechanic, sailor with flag, mechanic seated, anchor and [illegible]

TEN Train of cars. TEN	Vig. Public square in New Haven. MERCHANTS B'K, New Haven, Ct. Female bathing.	10 Sailor.
20 XX	Vig. Three females; building in background. MERCHANTS' B'K, New Haven, Ct. Eagle.	20 XX
L and Fifty	MERCHANTS B'K, New Haven, Ct. Floating female. Vig. Group of Indians overlooking precipice; view of city below. Female.	50 female floating
C Ship	MERCHANTS' B'K, New Haven, Ct. Vig. Sailor reclining, quadrant in left hand, coil of rope, capstan, &c on right; river, ships, &c. on left. Eagle	100 Male portrait.
ONE Female and balances, state arms, eagle, &c. ONE	1 Vig. Female with wand in right hand; ship on left. 1 MERCHANTS' B'K, Norwich, Ct.	1 Female seated with pole and cap; ship on left. 1
Female erect with spear in left hand; right hand resting on shield, on which is figure 2. TWO	2 Vig. Female seated; state arms, anvil and cogwheel on right; ship on left. 2 MERCHANTS' B'K, Norwich, Ct.	Female head with wreath 2 Female head.
3 Agricultural machine. 3	MERCHANTS' B'K., Norwich, Conn. Whaling scene. Three on 3 on left; dollars on 3 on right.	THREE DOLLARS
FIVE Portrait of Washington. FIVE	[First Plate.] 5 Vig. Whaling scene. 5 MERCHANTS' B'K, Norwich, Ct.	Female soaring in air with wand in right hand. 5
5 Male portrait FIVE	[Second Plate.] Vig. Locomotive and train of cars MERCHANTS' B'K, Norwich, Ct.	5 Sailor seated with spy-glass, steamboat on left.
TEN Portrait of Washington. TEN	[First Plate.] 10 Vig. Whaling scene. 10 MERCHANTS' B'K, Norwich, Ct.	Female erect with spear; state arms on right. 10

10 Male portrait.	(Second Plate.) Vig. Whaling scene. MERCHANTS' B'K, Norwich, Ct.	10 Male portrait. X
20 Ship. 20	XX Two women, cattle, &c., in circular die. XX MERCHANTS BANK, Norwich, Conn.	20 Machinery 20
Two winged figures and urn. Portrait of General Harrison.	L Vig. Man seated with horn of plenty, safe, bags and scales on right; ship, bale of goods, &c. on left L MERCHANTS' B'K. Norwich, Ct. Sail vessel.	50 Launching a ship. 50
A collection of vessels.	C Vig. Female seated, eagle on her lap; ships on left. C MERCHANTS' B'K. Norwich, Ct. Steamboat.	100 Shearing sheep. 100
1 Goat and kids.	Female holding flowers. Large 1 to left. MER. & MANUFA'RS BANK Hartford, Conn.	1
Sailor with bundle, steamer. TWO	Large 2 with Title of Bank to the right.	2 Dog's head.
FIVE inverted. Sailor seated on bales; in stern, vessel and steamer above him. Green 5 and word Five.	MERCHANTS' AND Green lined V and machinery. MANUFACT'S B'K., Hartford, Conn.	5 Female gazing at stars.
X State Arms sailor, bbls., etc.	MERCHANTS' 10 AND Two females seated; owl, bust, globe, etc; steamship, etc., on left; buildings monument, &c., on right. MANUFACT'S B'K. Hartford, Conn.	10 Two children with fruit and butterfly
20 Connecticut Female seated on safe with sword and scales.	THE MERCHANTS' Female either side of anvil; one on left has cornucopia of flowers; factories, etc.; in distance on right. AND MANUFACTUR'S BK	20 Hartford, City Arms—deer, tree, water, &c.
FIFTY DOLLARS	MER. & MAN. BANK, Hartford, Conn. 50 50 Male portrait.	FIFTY DOLLARS

100 Female on rock gazing at ocean on which is steamer, etc.	Title of Bank. Green C. Male portrait	100 C
1 ONE Portrait of John Hancock.	MERIDEN BANK, Meriden, Conn. Farmer ploughing with oxen and horse. Elephant.	1 Train of cars.
ONE Portrait of Lafayette. ONE	Blacksmith seated, anvil, &c.; factories in distance MERIDEN BANK, Meriden, Conn. Locomotive.	1 Two Indians, one holding spear.
TWO Portrait of Franklin.	Group of persons separated by a shield; child with hand on globe, &c. MERIDEN BANK, Meriden, Conn. Blacksmith's arms, anvil, &c.	2 Female portrait.
3 Indians viewing factories, &c. THREE	Train of cars MERIDEN BANK, Meriden, Conn. Horse.	3 Blacksmith with hammer resting on anvil, &c.
5 Washington. 5	Female holding sickle and sheaf of grain; village in the distance. MERIDEN BANK, Meriden, Conn. Arm, anvil, &c.	5 Goddess of Liberty.
Goddess of Liberty.	10 Female, sickle, sheaf of grain; village in distance. MERIDEN BANK, Meriden, Conn. Eagle.	TEN Youth hammering an anvil. 10
20 XX 20	20 Female 20 seated on bales, leaning against cask, sheaf of grain at her feet; vessels in the distance. MERIDEN BANK Meriden, Conn.	TWENTY
50 Female leaning on rock, boat steam-boat in distance. 50	50 MERIDEN BANK Meriden, Conn.	FIFTY
C Washington. C	100 100 Man pouring water; bales &c.; vessel in distance. MERIDEN BANK Meriden, Conn.	ONE HUNDRED

Left end	Centre	Right end
1 Male portrait ONE	Stone Quarry; view of city and cars crossing bridge. MIDDLESEX CO. B'K Middletown, Ct. Machinery.	1 Female.
Female, liberty pole and shield; starry drapery across her shoulder.	TWO Male portrait with female each side; steamboat and vessel on right; farmers at work on left. 2 2 MIDDLESEX CO. B.K, Middletown, Conn. Mechanics arm.	TWO Two Indians with spear and arrows. TWO
3 Portrait of Franklin. 3	Signing the Declaration of Independence. Spread Eagle on shield. MIDDLESEX CO. B'K, Middletown, Ct. 3 3 Goods, &c.	Fig. 3 on American shield. Female pole and cap eagle at top of shield.
5 Washington. 5	Milkmaid seated with cattle. 5 MIDDLESEX CO. B'K, Middletown, Ct. Female Bathing.	FIVE Female. FIVE
10 Vessel, train cars crossing bridge. TEN	Two Horses and train cars. 10 MIDDLESEX CO. B'K. Middletown, Ct. Steamship.	TEN Large ship. TEN
20 20	20 20 Vig. Female giving eagle drink. MIDDLESEX CO. B'K, Middletown, Ct.	TWENTY
50 50	50 50 Vig. Spread eagle. MIDDLESEX CO B'K Middletown, Ct.	FIFTY
ONE	1 Dog and safe. 1 MIDDLETOWN B'K. Middletown, Ct. Ship.	ONE
TWO Some have red ends with white 2	2 Milkmaid and cows 2 MIDDLETOWN B'K TWO DOLLARS Middletown, Conn. Cog wheels, etc.	Some have red ends with white 2 TWO
THREE	3 Three females seated; one with Mercury's wand, and leaning on shield. 3 MIDDLETOWN B'K. Middletown, Ct. State arms.	THREE

Left end	Centre	Right end
5 FIVE 5	5 Female resting on anchor and bale of goods; schooner and steamboat on right; city and shipping on left. 5 MIDDLETOWN B'K. Middletown, Ct. Agricultural implements.	5 Portrait of H. Clay. V
10 TEN 10	10 Female, agricultural products and implements around her; on left canal boat and lock; on right cars and bridge. 10 MIDDLETOWN B'K. Middletown, Ct. Locomotive.	10 Washington 10
TWENTY	20 Two winged figures and two cupids upholding large 20. MIDDLETOWN B'K, Middletown, Ct. Steamship.	20 TWENTY 20
50 FIFTY 50	50 Female seated upholding large 50; safe, casks, cornucopia, &c.; two ships on left. MIDDLETOWN B'K, Middletown, Ct. Spread eagle.	FIFTY.
100 HUNDRED 100	C Sailor with spyglass, compass leaning against bales, hhds. in rear; ship and steamer on left. MIDDLETOWN B'K, Middletown, Ct. Horse.	ONE HUNDRED
ONE Ship. ONE	MYSTIC BANK, Mystic, Conn. 1 1 Vig. Indian in canoe going over rapids. Locomotive and tender.	Male figure erect. ONE
2 Female, sickle and grain; figure 2 on left. TWO	2 Vig. female seated with wand; ship on left; State Arms on right 2 MYSTIC BANK, Mystic, Conn. State Arms.	Female warrior with spear, right hand resting on shield on which is figure 2. TWO
THREE Female and mechanical tools. 3	3 Beehive. 3 Vig. Indian and native American on either side of a shield, eagle at top of shield; ship on right. MYSTIC BANK, Mystic, Conn. Female grain and sickle.	3
5 Female with rake. 5	V Vig. Female with balances representing Industry. 5 MYSTIC BANK, Mystic, Conn.	FIVE
10 Launching a ship. 10	X Vig. Female with grain, leaning on pillar vessel on right. X MYSTIC BANK, Mistic, Conn. Canal lock, &c.	10

Left end	Centre	Right end
TWENTY	MYSTIC BANK, Mystic, Conn. Vig. Archimedes raising the world. XX	Indian with bow & arrow. 20
1 Portrait of Washington.	View of ship-yard. MYSTIC RIVER B'K, Conn.	1 Groton. Girls head.
2 Groton.	MYSTIC RIVER B'K. Conn. Female feeding swine, three horses drinking, and man.	2 Portrait of Cass.
3 Groton. Portrait of Clay.	MYSTIC RIVER B'K. Conn. Ships, &c.; city in distance.	3 Portrait
Female portrait 5	MYSTIC RIVER B'K. Conn. Ships.	5 Groton. Portrait of Webster.
Female sheaf of wheat. X	10 10 MYSTIC RIVER B'K Conn. Portrait of Fillmore.	Female with sheaf of wheat. X
20	Whaling scene. Indian Queen. MYSTIC RIVER B'K, Conn.	20 Cooper and barrel.
50	MYSTIC RIVER B'K, Conn. Female reclining on a bale of goods, city and ship in distance. Eagle.	50 Groton. Female head.
C	Female reclining on a bale; portrait of Franklin on right, ships in distance. MYSTIC RIVER B'K, Conn. Dog and Safe.	100
Dog's head. 1	NEW BRITAIN B'K New Britain, Conn. Blacksmith's shop—man at vice; anvil, hammer, etc. 1	1 Beehive.

Left end	Centre	Right end
2 Barn-yard, fowls, etc.	Farm horse; farmers resting; man playing with child, horse, dog, fowls, etc. NEW BRITAIN B'K New Britain, Conn.	2 Man, girl, machinery, etc.
3	Mill, boy on horse, men, child, dog, fowls, etc; female crossing bridge on right 3 NEW BRITAIN B'K New Britain, Conn.	3 Female holding flowers
5	Cars crossing bridge, cattle in stream drinking; trees, fence, etc. Male portrait NEW BRITAIN B'K New Britain, Conn.	5 Head of horse.
Female with pole and cap leaning on column, flowers at her feet.	X Spread eagle and shield. NEW BRITAIN B'K New Britain, Conn.	Ten inverted. 10
1 First Sabbath.	[First Plate] Female seated; Female. ship on right. NEW HAVEN B'K. New Haven, Ct. Bee-hive.	1 Sailor at work.
1 First Sabbath.	[Second Plate.] Vig. Council of Indians. NEW HAVEN B'K, New Haven, Ct.	1 Beehive.
ONE First Sabbath.	Wharf scene— Female. men, horses, boxes, bbls., carts, ship, steamship and other vessels. NEW HAVEN B'K, New Haven, Conn. Bee hive.	ONE 1
Female and sheaf of wheat. 2	Vig. Two females seated; cars and canal scene on right; ships on left. NEW HAVEN BK., New Haven, Ct. Beehive.	2 First Sabbath.
Female entwined in fig. 2. Female.	Two females and shield; steamship in distance. NEW HAVEN BANK New Haven, Conn. Bee-hive.	2 First sabbath.
3 First Sabbath.	Vig. Large ship. NEW HAVEN BK., New Haven, Ct.	3 Female Indian.

Left end	Centre	Right end
3 Female head. First sabbath.	NEW HAVEN BANK New Haven, Conn. Mechanic, sailor and farmer with implements. Beehive.	THREE 3,
5 Female seated on globe; arm is extended, holding sickle and grain. FIVE	[First Plate.] Cupid Cupid and grain. Female reclining on bale of goods; ship on either side. NEW HAVEN BK., New Haven, Ct. Beehive	5 First Sabbath.
Drover selling cattle. Beehive.	[Second Plate.] Female portrait. NEW HAVEN BK., New Haven, Ct.	5 First Sabbath.
FIVE Large 5: cars crossing bridge; two Indians and water falls. FIVE	Two males and a female representing Agriculture, Commerce, &c.; steamboat, train of cars and city in distance. NEW HAVEN BANK New Haven, Ct. Beehive.	Letter V, and three females. The first Sabbath preaching.
10 Female artist at work.	[First Plate.] Vig. Female and mechanic representing trade and industry; ship on right; bridge, locomotive and cars on left. NEW HAVEN BK., New Haven, Ct. Beehive.	10 First Sabbath.
Beehive. 10	[Second Plate.] NEW HAVEN BK., New Haven, Ct. Vig. Three figures; blacksmith shoeing horse. Ships	10 First Sabbath.
Female portrait. Large X, word ten in centre. Female, cow, &c.	Vessels at sea. NEW HAVEN BANK. New Haven, Conn. Bee-hive	10 First Sabbath
First Sabbath. 20	Vig. City, depot, and cars. NEW HAVEN BK., New Haven, Ct. Beehive.	20 Female.
First Sabbath. XX	Female resting on shield; steamer, ship, cars, bridge, &c., in distance. NEW HAVEN BANK. Bee-hive.	20 Female.
FIFTY Female erect holding flag and spear.	NEW HAVEN B'K, New Haven, Ct. Vig. Female and child; steamboat on right; vessels on left. 50 50 Beehive.	50 First Sabbath.

Left end	Centre	Right end
100 First Sabbath.	NEW HAVEN B'K. New Haven, Ct. Female and Indian on either side of globe, eagle at top; female holding grain, Indian gun, letter C between them. Beehive,	100 Mechanic and tools, sledge on his shoulder.
Fig. 1 on American shield. River, steamboat, row boat and city in distance,	N. H. CO. BANK. New Haven, Ct. View of sea, ship and other vessels. 1 1 Dog, Safe and Key.	Female erect with spear.
TWO Sailor leaning on Capstain, spy-glass in hand TWO	N. H. CO. BANK, New Haven, Ct. View of River; two ships, steamboat and smaller vessels. 2 2 Dog, Safe and Key.	Medal Head and figure 2 Ship.
3 Female grain and sickle. THREE	N. H. CO. BANK. New Haven, Ct. Farming scene, man on horse. 3 3 Dog, Safe and Key.	THREE Milkmaid.
5 Mechanic at work.	N. H. CO. BANK, New Haven, Ct. Large spread Eagle on limb of tree, ships on right, steamboats and vessels on left. 5 Dog, key, safe 5	5 Female Portrait.
X Bull's Head TEN	[First Plate. N. H. CO. BANK, New Haven, Ct. Cattle, Man Plowing with oxen and horse; man at work. Dog, key and safe,	Medal. Head and fig. 10. Male Portrait
10 Sailor seated; bale of goods, &c.	N. H. CO., BANK. New Haven, Ct. Vig. Female seated on chest; small child and dog on right; plough and sheaf of grain, shield, &c., on left. Eagle.	10 Portrait.
XX 20	N. H. CO., BANK. New Haven, Ct. Vig. State Arms; American group on right; Indian, squaw and papoose on left. Dog, safe and key.	XX 20
50 View of city and cars crossing bridge; load of hay on left.	N. H. CO., BANK, New Haven, Ct. Vig. Three females with sickle, quadrant, and cornucopia. Dog, safe and key.	50 View of river and ship; city in distance.
Group of figures; two females seated, spinning wheel by their side; sailor and mechanic above them; city in distance.	N. H. CO., BANK, New Haven, Ct. C The vig. extends on both ends and across lower margin of note. C Anchor and mechanics' implements; oxen.	Three figures Two females seated; one with sickle; man standing with pitchfork in right hand dog on right

Left end	Centre	Right end
Female erect with grain in right hand, and sickle in left. ONE	(1s and 2s are alike.) Med. head and fig. 1. Vig. View of sea upon which is two ships; light-house in distance on right. Med. head and fig. 1. NEW LONDON B'K, New London, Ct.	ONE DOLLAR.
FIVE Female; eagle on right, scales, barrels, &c., on left. 5	5 Vig. Indian and native American seated between the arms of one of the States, upon which is standing an eagle; also ship on right. 5 NEW LONDON B'K, New London, Ct.	5 Beehive. 5
X CONNECTICUT. X	10 Vig. View of harvest field and reaper sitting under a tree. 10 NEW LONDON B'K. New London. Ct.	10 10
XX XX	20 Vig. Farmer preparing for work; sail vessel on left. 20 NEW LONDON B'K, New London. Ct.	20 20
1	NORFOLK BANK, Norfolk, Conn. Drove of cattle, horses and sheep; trees, barn, fence and boy in distance.	1 1 ONE
2	NORFOLK BANK, Norfolk, Conn. Drove of cattle, drover on horseback, boy in water; trees and farmhouse in distance.	2 2 TWO
3 Man dressing leather.	NORFOLK BANK, Norfolk, Conn. Two horses frightened at train of cars.	3 3 3
5, V & FIVE. Six men at work in an iron mill.	NORFOLK BANK, Norfolk, Conn.	5 5 5
5	State arms; eagle at top; two females, cars and trees on right; female and ship on left. NORFOLK BANK, Norfolk, Conn.	FIVE FIVE 5
TEN on X. TEN	Female with cornucopia. Female with wings. NORFOLK BANK, Norfolk, Conn.	10 Female with quadrant.

Left end	Centre	Right end
XX 20	NORFOLK BANK, Norfolk, Conn. State Arms with eagle at top and horse each side; cars, bridge and city in distance, on right and a building on left.	20
L FIFTY	NORFOLK BANK Norfolk, Conn. Portrait of Washington.	50 Male, two females, dog, cattle and sheaves
ONE Female, shield, eagle, liberty pole and cap. ONE	1 Female seated; farming implements, &c.; bridge, locomotive and cars on right. 1 NORWICH BANK, Norwich, Ct. Barrels, Bales, &c.	ONE Female drawing water from a well; steamboat on left.
Female. ONE Female.	View of Norwich Bank Building; female pole and cap on right; vessel on left. NORWICH BANK, Norwich, Ct. Eagle.	Female. ONE Female.
2 Two Cupids in Ornamental fig. 2.	Spread Eagle on limb of tree; vessels on right; steamboat on left; NORWICH BANK, Norwich, Ct. Bank Building.	2 Two figures in Ornamental fig. 2.
TWO Female seated in Ornamental fig. 2, sword in left hand, Balances in right.	NORWICH BANK, Norwich, Ct. Three females, between them the Arms of one of the States, eagle at top of shield. Eagle.	Fig. 2 on American shield. Female seated in Ornamental fig. 2; City on left.
CONNECTICUT	Figure 4. Figure 4. Group of females seated, Grain, sickle, &c.; one resting arm on chest, key in her right hand; eagle on left, building on right; vessels in distance. NORWICH BANK, Norwich, Ct.	Figure 4. Figure 4.
5	Five females supporting figure 5; vessels on right. NORWICH BANK, Norwich, Ct. Bank Building.	5
FIVE Sailor with glass; anchor at his feet. FIVE	NORWICH BANK, Norwich, Conn. Three cherubs one with flag; grain, rake, etc., on right; sheep on left; vessels in distance. Female bathing.	5 Eagle on shield. FIVE
X CONNECTICUT X	X Vig. River, on which is sail-boat; also, man on horse. X NORWICH BANK, Norwich, Ct. Female, grain and sickle.	10 10

Left end	Centre	Right end
XX CONNECTICUT XX	20 Vig. Female seated, left hand extended; under it is engraved figure 20; vessel on left. 20 NORWICH BANK, Norwich, Ct. Steamboat.	20 20
CONNECTICUT	L Vig. An ox. L NORWICH BANK, Norwich, Ct. Steamboat.	50 50
Washington and C.	Vig. Signing the "Declaration of Independence." NORWICH BANK, Norwich. Ct. Eagle.	100 Female.
D 500	NORWICH BANK, Norwich, Ct. Group of females on right; Indian, squaw and child on left; between them the Arms of one of the States.	500 Portrait of Daniel Webster.
1 1	OCEAN BANK, Stonington, Conn. 1 Locomotive and cars. Steamboat.	1 Female seated holding spy-glass; ship on left.
Sailor seated upon bale of goods with American flag on left, anchor on right. TWO	Steam ship and other vessels OCEAN BANK, Stonington, Conn. State Arms.	2 Female Portrait.
Group of three females supporting figure 3.	3 Ships. 3 OCEAN BANK, Stonington, Conn. Steam ship.	3 Sailor, spy glass &c.; vessel on right.
5 Locomotive and cars. FIVE	OCEAN BANK, Stonington, Conn. V V Female seated resting upon State Arms of Connecticut, steam ship and ship on right also vessels on left.	5 Female Portrait.
Sailor seated by his right foot is a coil of rope, flag on left, also hat raised aloft in left hand. TEN	Large spread eagle on American shield, &c. OCEAN BANK, Stonington, Conn Locomotive and Tender.	10 Large ship.
Female reclining sheaf of grain on left and in right hand sickle. XX	20 OCEAN BANK, 20 Stonington, Conn. View of sea, large ship; light house on right in distance; sail vessel in distance on left.	Female sitting upon barrel with wand in left hand, ship on right. XX

Three females on a rock; spy glass, anchor &c.
100

View of city of New York and Brooklyn with shipping.
OCEAN BANK,
Stonington, Conn.
Eagle.

100
Female reclining on bale of goods; ships on right, also ... on left.

ONE
Mechanic &c

1 Indian looking down upon city.
PAHQUIOQUE BANK
Danbury, Conn.

1
Female

Female, Indian, farming scene in distance.
2

PAHQUIOQUE BANK
Danbury, Conn
2 Vig. Two oxen; farm house on right.
Indian's head.

2
Eagle.

Child and chickens.
3

PAHQUIOQUE B'K,
Danbury, Ct.
Drover and cattle.

3

5
FIVE
Female

PAHQUIOQUE BANK
Danbury, Conn.
5 Vig. Wild horses. 5

FIVE 5 FIVE
Female Indian.

TEN
Three cupids, anvil, hammer, grain, plough, &c.

PAHQUIOQUE B'K,
Danbury, Ct.
Child with rabbits.
TEN

10
Franklin.

XX
Word twenty and two XX.

PAHQUIOQUE B'K,
Danbury, Conn.
State Arms with female on either side
TWENTY

20
Word dollars and two XX.

On this end is figure 50, (sunk), word fifty, and letter L.

PAHQUIOQUE B'K.
Danbury, Conn.
State Arms, horse on either side and eagle at top; on right train of cars and city; on left building

On this end is figure 50 word dollars and letter L.

ONE
Two Indians erect.
ONE

Vig. Female reclining on horn of plenty. Portrait of Washington.
PAWCATUCK BANK.
Pawcatuck, Ct.
Bales and barrels.

1
Two females one erect; the other kneeling with grain.

TWO
Portrait of Gen. Taylor.
TWO

Vig. State Arms; eagle surmounting it; two females on right, seated; Goddess of Liberty on left.
PAWCATUCK BANK,
Pawcatuck, Ct.
Weaving loom.

2
Female with sickle and sheaf.
2

THREE
Female seated feeding eagle.
THREE

Vig. State arms; female and three children on right; Indian squaw and papoose on left.
PAWCATUCK BANK.
Pawcatuck, Ct.

3
Farmer with rake, dog, &c.; town background.

FOUR
Stonecutter at work.

Vig. Planing machine, man standing beside it.
PAWCATUCK BANK.
Pawcatuck, Ct.

4
Girl reaping; farmhouse in background.

FIVE 5 FIVE

Vig. Indian, squaw, and child on precipice overlooking city. Portrait of two females.
PAWCATUCK BANK.
Pawcatuck, Ct.
Female swimming.

5
Goddess of Liberty; eagle upon shield behind her

10
Locomotive crossing bridge, city in distance.

PAWCATUCK BANK,
Pawcatuck, Ct.
Vig. Three females representing Commerce, Agriculture, and Science.
Hand and hammer.

10
Ships sailing in front of city.

Female erect resting upon column, right hand upon shield.
TWENTY

PAWCATUCK BANK,
Pawcatuck, Ct.
Vig. Blacksmith seated, anvil, &c.; city in background. On left of vignette is 20 with words twenty dollars across it.

20
XX

50
Portrait of John Adams.

PAWCATUCK BANK,
Pawcatuck, Ct.
Vig. Winged female seated on clouds, female soaring on either side.
Steamship.

50

ONE
Farmers loading wagon

PEQUONNOCK B'K.,
Bridgeport, Ct.

ONE
One male and two female Indians over-looking precipice city in distance
ONE

2

PEQUONNOCK B'K.,
Bridgeport. Ct.
Mechanics at work, view of shipyard. 2

2
Two female Indians, one seated the other erect.

Portrait of P. T. Barnum
3

PEQUONNOCK B'K.,
Bridgeport. Ct.
Vig. Country seat of P. T. Barnum.
3 3

3
Portrait of Jenny Lind

5
Portrait of Barnum.

Same as three.
PEQUONNOCK B'K.,
Bridgeport, Ct.
V V

5
Portrait of Jenny Lind

Female gathering wheat.
X

PEQUONNOCK B'K.,
Bridgeport, Ct
Vig. Shield, on either side sailor and Indian; eagle at top of shield.

10
Female with flowers.

20
Two Indians, canoe, &c.

Vig. Harvest scene.
PEQUONNOCK B'K.,
Bridgeport, Ct
XX

20
Two females seated, balances, shield &c.

FIFTY
Mechanic, sailor and 2 females; city on right.

PEQUONNOCK B'K.,
Bridgeport, Ct.
Harvest scene, man erect, dog by his side two females seated one holding sickle; also oxen grain &c., Indian with bow and arrow, in shield on right.

50

100
Two Indians with bow and arrow.

Vig. Sailor seated amid Nautical instruments; view of sea and ships on left.
PEQUONNOCK B'K.,
Bridgeport, Ct.

100
C

1
Portrait of Washington.
ONE

1 Vig. Female seated on barrel; cars on left. 1
PHENIX BANK,
Hartford, Ct.
Locomotive and cars.

Full length female.
ONE

ONE
Full length female, hand resting on shield.

[New Plate.]
1 ONE 1
PHENIX BANK,
Hartford, Ct.
Safe.

ONE
Blacksmith at work.

2
Portrait of Washington
TWO

Vig. Two females seated, one holding sickle; grain on left; ship on right. 2
PHENIX BANK.
Hartford, Ct.
Steam propeller.

TWO
Sculptor at work.
TWO

2
Male portrait

PHENIX BANK,
Hartford, Ct.
TWO

2
Head of sailor.

3
Portrait of Gen. Taylor.
THREE

Vig. Group of mechanics; ship building on left, vessels on right.
PHENIX BANK.
Hartford, Ct.
Mechanic's arm and anvil.

3
Female.
THREE

Male portrait.

Group of figures drawing a chariot. 5 on left. 5
PHENIX BANK,
Hartford, Ct.
State Arms.

Female and sword.
FIVE

Left	Centre	Right
5 V 5	PHENIX BANK, Hartford, Ct. Vig. Three females seated; one with sickle, the other with quadrant. FIVE	5 V 5
5 Five across V 5	PHENIX BANK, Hartford, Conn. View of a river and steamboat; town in distance.	FIVE 5 FIVE
10 Portrait of Washington. 10	Female seated, letter X on shield. Female seated with horn of plenty, letter X on shield. PHENIX BANK, Hartford, Ct. Female seated; view of ocean; ship on right; goods and ships on left.	10 Female with pole and cap. 10
10 X 10	PHENIX BANK, Hartford, Ct. Vig. Locomotive and train of cars.	10 X 10
TWENTY DOLLARS	Two females seated with grain and sickle. 20 on either side of vig., and also on each side of title. PHENIX BANK, Hartford, Conn. 20	CONNECTICUT
TWENTY DOLLARS	20 Vig. Two females seated, one with grain. 20 20 20 PHENIX BANK, Hartford, Ct. 20	CONNECTICUT
FIFTY DOLLARS	50 Vig Female seated, with wand in right hand; river vessels and houses on left; barrels, &c., on right. 50 50 50 PHENIX BANK, Hartford, Ct. L	CONNECTICUT
FIFTY DOLLARS	50 Female seated representing Commerce; boxes, bbls, etc. 50 50 Title of Bank. 50 L	CONNECTICUT
ONE HUNDRED	Female seated holding letter C; ship in distance—C and 100 on each side. 100 Title of Bank. 100 C	CONNECTICUT
ONE HUNDRED	100 Vig. Female seated overlooking sea, on which is ship. C 100 100 PHENIX BANK, Hartford, Ct. C	CONNECTICUT

Left	Centre	Right
1 Female seated on bale of goods, with arms extended. 1	View of City Rail Road Depot and Train of Cars. QUINEBAUG BANK, Norwich, Ct. Cogwheel.	1 Medallion Head.
2 Two Cupids in fig. 2.	Female Indian reclining, bow and arrows by her side; steamboat on left. QUINEBAUG BANK, Norwich, Ct. Locomotive and Tender,	2 Female seated, child by her, male holding sickle.
3 Female sheaf of wheat and sickle.	Two females seated: locomotive and cars on right, buildings and vessels on left. QUINEBAUG BANK, Norwich, Ct. Cogwheel.	3 Three figures in fig. 3.
5	Spread Eagle, grain mechanical implements, &c., by his side; ships on right; sheep on left. QUINEBAUG BANK, Norwich, Ct. Female.	5
TEN Female, sword, and balances. TEN	10 Female soaring in air. QUINEBAUG BANK, Norwich, Ct. Eagle.	10
20 Indian. 20	XX Representation of raising the Globe. XX QUINEBAUG BANK, Norwich, Ct.	TWENTY
50 50	QUINEBAUG BANK, Norwich, Ct. Female, American shield, eagle, liberty pole and cap.	50 Male Portrait 50
100 Female with grain, leaning. 100	QUINEBAUG BANK, Norwich, Ct. ONE HUNDRED	100 Male Portrait 100
1 Male portrait.	QUINNIPIACK BK., New Haven, Ct. Vig. Indian, squaw and pappoose in a canoe.	1 Sailor, capstan, etc. ONE
Male portrait. 2	QUINNIPIACK BK., New Haven. Ct. Vig. Same as ones.	2 Two Cupids in large 2.

Left	Centre	Right
Portrait of Webster. Three cupids in figure 3.	QUINNIPIACK BK., New Haven, Ct. Vig. Same as ones.	3 Beehive, etc. THREE
5 Anchor, bales, goods, etc.	Vig. Same as ones. QUINNIPIACK B'K, New Haven, Conn.	5 Female.
10	Vig. Same as ones. Male portrait. QUINNIPIACK B'K. New Haven, Ct.	10 Male and female. TEN
20 Mechanic, anvil, and cogwheel.	QUINNIPIACK B'K, New Haven Ct. Vig. same as ones.	20 Female in a shell.
50 Ship.	QUINNIPIACK B'K. New Haven, Ct. Vig. same as ones.	50 Female and mechanical implements.
100	Vig. same as ones. QUINNIPIACK B'K, New Haven. Ct.	100 Vessel.
1 ONE 1	Two Looms, girls weaving. ROCKVILLE BANK, Rockville, Conn. Female bathing.	1 Portrait of Webster.
2 Man on horseback.	Agricultural scene; cat tle grazing. ROCKVILLE BANK, Rockville, Conn. Ducks.	2 Male portrait
THREE on 3 Indian girl at door of wigwam	Agricultural scene, milkmaid with pail; two cows, etc. 3 ROCKVILLE BANK Rockville, Conn. THREE DOLLARS Dog	THREE Three females with grain, sickle, anchor, etc
FIVE	ROCKVILLE BANK, Rockville, Conn. 5 Load of hay; boy sleeping on top; boy walking by side of oxen. 5 Ducks.	5 Female head.

X | ROCKVILLE BANK, Rockville, Conn. State Arms. | 10
Iron foundry | | Girl.

XX | ROCKVILLE BANK, Rockville, Conn. Figures 20, two XX's and words twenty dollars. | 20
Sheep shearing. | | Boy's head.

1 | SAUGATUCK BANK, Westport, Conn. 1 Drove of sheep, boy on right. 1 | ONE
Dogs head. | | State Die.

1 | SAUGATUCK BANK, 1 Drove of sheep, boy on right. 1 Connecticut. | ONE
Westport. ONE | | Man sowing; man ploughing in distance.

2 | SAUGATUCK BANK, Westport, Conn. 2 Boy asleep on load of hay drawn by two oxen; boy walking with pitchfork in hand. 2 | TWO
Train of cars. | | Village scene

2 | SAUGATUCK BANK, Westport, Conn. 2 2 State Die | TWO
Train of cars | | Village scene

THREE on 3 | SAUGATUCK BANK 3 Two children, cows, sheep, etc, under tree. 3 THREE DOLLARS Westport, Conn. | 3
Female seated. | | Daniel Webster THREE

3 | View of Westport village. SAUGATUCK BANK, Westport, Conn. | 3
Female | | Portrait of Daniel Webster.

V | Scene in blacksmith shop, man shoeing horse. SAUGATUCK BANK FIVE DOLLARS Westport, Conn. | 5
Indian with bow and arrow | | Female head

V | Interior of a Blacksmith shop, man shoeing horse. SAUGATUCK BANK, Westport, Conn | 5
Indian with bow and arrow. | | State Die.

TEN | 10 Shoemaker shop, men at work and female binding shoes. 10 SAUGATUCK BANK, Westport, Conn. | X
Indian. | | Jackson

Ship; other vessels and city in background. 50 | Female with sheaf and sickle SAUGATUCK BANK, Westport, Conn. | 50
| | Henry Clay.

100 | 100 Ship; other vessels and lighthouse in distance. SAUGATUCK BANK, Westport, Conn. | 100
Sailor and blacksmith, each with implements of profession. | | Sailor leaning on capstan with quadrant in hand.

ONE | Eagle, ships, &c. SAYBROOK BANK, Essex, Ct. ONE Bust of female. | 1
View of Essex and the Conn River at Essex. ONE | | Female, ships, bales of goods, &c. 1

2 | Train of cars, three females, ship, &c. 2 SAYBROOK BANK, Essex, Ct. Agricultural implements, &c. | TWO
Ship building 2 | | View of Essex and Conn. River at Essex. TWO

THREE | Female, bale, hhd., ship, &c. 3 SAYBROOK BANK, Essex, Ct. Beehive. | THREE

| Female, bale of goods, shipping, &c. 5 SAYBROOK BANK, Essex, Ct. Steamboat, | 5
5 | | Female with pallet, &c.

10 | Man, woman, bales, train of cars, anvil, nautical instruments, shipping, &c. X SAYBROOK BANK, Essex, Ct. Fish. | 10
Indian, liberty cap, shield, &c. | | Female bust.

20 | Two females, bale, train of cars, steamboat, state arms, and horn of plenty. SAYBROOK BANK, Essex, Ct. Elephant. | 20
Washington on horseback | | Female resting on bale, shipping, &c

1 | SHETUCKET BANK, Norwich, Ct. Vig. Three figures, man, woman, and child. | 1
Female. | | Filler

2 | Vig. Milkmaid seated with cattle; farmhouse and trees in background. SHETUCKET BANK, Norwich, Ct. | 2
Female and flowers. | | State die.

3 | Title of Bank Vig. Farmers resting from work. Eagle. | 3
Load of hay, drover, and cattle; view of street, buildings, &c., in distance. | | Female

Female reclining, sailor holding flag; bale goods, anchor, &c. by his side. FIVE | Vig. View of ocean, steamship and other vessels. SHETUCKET BANK. Norwich, Ct. | 5
| | Child.

10 | Vig. Horses, farm house and cottages. SHETUCKET BANK, Norwich, Ct. | 10
Mason at work; building on left. | | State die.

50 | SHETUCKET BANK, Norwich, Conn. Signing the Declaration of Independence. | 50
Cass. | | Webster.

C | United states Capitol. SHETUCKET BANK, Norwich, Conn. | 100
C | | Female head

1 | State Arms; eagle at top; two females on right; one on left with pole and cap. SOUTHPORT BANK, Southport, Conn. | 1
Washington | | Martha Washington

Two and figure 2. | Vig. Three male figures; view of city on right. SOUTHPORT BANK. Southport. Ct. | 2
Large ship and shipping in distance. | | Female Indian and child.

THREE | Vig. Group of Indians, looking down upon a city. Train of cars. SOUTHPORT BANK. Southport. Ct. | 3
THREE | | Two farmers and dog; two men and farm-house in background.

5 | Vig. Female reclining on sheaf; State Arms on right. SOUTHPORT BANK, SouthpOrt. Ct. | 5
Head quarters of Gen. Washington, at Newburgh FIVE | | Portrait of Jenny Lind

10 — Vig. View of ocean; steamship and other vessels. X — 10
SOUTHPORT BANK, Southport, Ct.
10 — Eagle. — X, 10, Ten.

50 — Vig. Female seated with grain; cars crossing bridge on right; farming implements and canal scene on left. — 50
Female with shield, liberty pole, and cap. — SOUTHPORT BANK, Southport, Ct. — Mechanic and mechanical tools, sailor holding flag.

C — Title of Bank. Vig. Three females holding quadrant, sickle, and compass, cornucopia between them. — 100
View of cars crossing bridge; city in distance; load of hay on left — 100 — View of river and ship; city in distance.

1 — STAFFORD BANK, Stafford Springs, Conn. — 1
Washington. — Two females beside loom. — Female head.

1 — STAFFORD BANK, Stafford Springs, Ct. — 1
Washington. — Man talking to a stone cutter, masons at work in background. Female. — Fig. 1 and word ONE.

1 — Drovers and cattle. — 1
Child and rabbits. — STAFFORD BANK, Stafford Springs, Ct. — Locomotive.

Farmer with scythe, village in distance. — STAFFORD BANK, Stafford Springs, Ct. — 2
TWO — Drove Wild horses. — Child holding hen and chicken.

3 — STAFFORD BANK, Stafford Springs, Ct. — 3
3 Three Cupids anvil, hammer, grain, globe, compass and square. 3
Female. — Portrait of Franklin.

Female with grain on her head in the background. — Dog chasing deer; harvesting — 5
5 — STAFFORD B'K, Stafford Springs, Conn. — FIVE — FIVE

Farm yard scene. — STAFFORD BANK, Stafford Springs, Ct. — 5
5 — FIVE — Female. — Female.

5 — 5 STAFFORD B'K, 5 Stafford Springs, Ct. Female on either side of portrait of Webster representing Commerce and agriculture. — 5
FIVE — FIVE

TEN — STAFFORD BANK, Stafford Springs, Ct. — 10
Farmer sickle and grain. — Man and horse.
10 — X Spread eagle on shield, cornucopia on left; view of ocean and ships. X — X

Three females representing Liberty, Justice and Agriculture. — STAFFORD BANK, Stafford, Conn. — 20
TWENTY DOLLARS — Indian seated.
20 20

50 — STAFFORD BANK, Stafford, Conn. — 50
Farmer in act of drinking from jug. — FIFTY DOLLARS — FIFTY — Lathe die. — Two females, ship on ocean

Female and shield, liberty pole and cap; starry drapery across her lap. — 1 Vig. Bank building; carriage, &c.; lady and gentleman on horseback. — 1
STAMFORD BANK, Stamford, Ct. — Goods, &c. — Female.

TWO — Vig. Group of figures on either side of shield. — 2
Female. — STAMFORD BANK, Stamford, Ct. — Females head. — Female, sheaf of wheat and sickle.
TWO — 2

THREE — Female portrait. Female portrait. — 3
Portrait of Washington. — Vig. River on which is row boat; train of cars crossing bridge. — Female.
THREE — STAMFORD BANK, Stamford, Ct. Eagle. — THREE

5 — Steamer, ship, yachts, etc. — 5
STAMFORD BANK, Stamford, Conn.
Female portrait. — Webster.

5 — Vig. Three females with cornucopia, wand, sword and balances, overlooking precipice. — 5
Female. — STAMFORD BANK, Stamford, Ct. — Female Indian liberty pole and shield.
FIVE — Farming Implements.

TEN — Sailor seated on anchor, two others erect; ship in distance. — 10
Male, female and child — STAMFORD BANK, Stamford, Conn. — CONNECTICUT — Clay.

10 — Vig. Female Indian seated, horn of plenty at her side, flags, safe, shield, &c.; eagle on globe; train of cars on left; steamboat on right. — 10
Male portrait. — STAMFORD BANK, Stamford, Ct. Eagle. — Female.

20 — Cattle, sheep, stream. — 20
STAMFORD BANK, Stamford, Conn.
Female portrait — Fillmore.

XX — Female seated, elbow on State Arms; steamship and vessel on right; farming implements on left. 20 on either side of vig. — 20
Washington — Cattle and sheep.
XX — Title of Bank. — Horse's head. — 20

50 — Depot, steamboat landing, wharf, buildings and shipping. — 50
Title of Bank.
Male portrait. — Female portrait.

50 — L Vig. Indian female reclining; sailor pointing to ship in distance. L — 50
Two females with rakes. — STAMFORD BANK, Stamford, Ct. Eagle. — Male portrait.
50 — 50

100 — Launch of the Adriatic; river, ship-yard, city, etc. — 100
Title of Bank.
Female portrait. — Male portrait.

ONE — Vig. Man ploughing with two horses; river and steamboat on left. — 1
Blacksmith seated on a boiler. — STATE BANK, Hartford, Ct. — State arms. — Female seated; factories in background.
ONE

1 — Vig. View of Trinity College, Hartford. — 1
Female resting on ornamental pillar; mechanical tools, &c. around her. — STATE BANK, Hartford, Ct. — Female and sheaf of grain.

TWO — Vig. Same as second plate of ones. — 2
Female Indian with bow and arrows, liberty pole and cap; hands resting on shield. — STATE BANK, Hartford Ct. State Arms. — Female with basket of flowers.

TWO — 2 Female and sailor seated, female with sickle and grain, sailor holding Quadrant. — 2
Female seated on chest holding sword and balances. — STATE BANK, Hartford, Ct. State Arms. — Farmer and Basket of Corn.
Locomotive and Tender.

THREE Female seated; American shield, &c.	Same as 2d Plate of Ones. STATE BANK, Hartford, Ct	3 State Arms. THREE
3 Female, anvil and hammer.	Two females, one holding sword and scales; the other reclining with pole and cap; Eagle and State Arms on left; ship in distance. STATE BANK, Hartford, Ct. Horn of Plenty, bales, &c.	3 Male figure holding cornucopia.
5	Female on either side of State Arms; Locomotive and cars on left; steamship on left. Female Portrait. STATE BANK, Hartford, Ct. Sail Vessel.	5 Female in ornamental figure 5.
5 Sailor seated on bales of goods; Quadrant in right hand. FIVE	State Arms; female on right; flags on left. STATE BANK, Hartford, Ct. Horn of Plenty, Bales &c.	5 Female seated; mechan. tools, &c. FIVE
10 Sailor resting on bale of goods; hat in right hand, Quadrant in left; ship on right	Female resting her left arm on bale of goods, wand in right hand; vessel on left; Locomotive and cars on right. STATE BANK, Hartford, Ct. State Arms.	10 Female seated with sickle and grain.
TWENTY Female resting her arm on barrel, wand in right hand, vessel on right. XX	20 View of Park and Public Building. 20 STATE BANK, Hartford, Ct. State Arms.	TWENTY Blacksmith, anvil and hammer. XX
50 Female seated, factories in back ground.	Locomotive and Train of cars. 50 STATE BANK, Hartford, Ct. State Arms.	FIFTY Female, sword and balances. 50
100 Female seated with anvil and hammer.	Vig. Large spread eagle on American shield. STATE BANK, Hartford, Ct. State arms.	100 Male figure holding cornucopia. 100
ONE 1 ONE	1 Fort, ships, &c. 1 STONINGTON B'K, Stonington, Ct. Figure 1 and word One.	Small figure 1. Small figure 1.
Male portrait ONE	Sailor seated with nautical implements; vessels in distance. STONINGTON BK, Stonington, Conn.	1 Vessels.

TWO	Whaling scene. Male portrait. Title of Bank.	2 Sailor at helm.
TWO 2 TWO	2 Catching seals; ships in distance on left. 2 STONINGTON B'K, Stonington, Ct. 2	2 2
3 CONNECTICUT 3	(First Plate.) 3 Whaling scene, ship on right; men in small boat on left. 3 STONINGTON B'K, Stonington Ct. 3	3 THREE 3
Figures, anvil, sledge &c. 3	(Second Plate.) 3 Locomotive and Train Cars. 3 STONINGTON B'K, Stonington, Ct. Steam Boat.	Female reclining wand in right hand key in left; building on right. Sail vessel. 3
3 Male portrait	Steamboat "Plymouth Rock," and other vessels. Title of Bank.	3 Sailor with glass.
4 Female with Liberty pole and cap, also State Arms on right. 4	4 View of Ocean with large ship; ship in distance on right, sail vessel in extreme distance on left. 4 STONINGTON B'K. Stonington, Ct.	FOUR Vessel. FOUR
Chariot in which is seated a female: American shield, &c., in right hand Liberty pole and cap, representation of Neptune and car.	(New Plate.) STONINGTON B'K, Stonington, Ct. 5 Large ornamental letter V in which is a female; Eagle, Liberty Pole and cap on left; Globe at her feet.	5
5 Male Portrait 5	(Old Plate.) 5 Chariot drawn by two horses in which is seated a female 5 STONINGTON B'K, Stonington, Ct. Locomotive and cars.	FIVE DOLLARS
10	(New Plate.) Whaling scene. STONINGTON B'K, Stonington, Ct. X	10
10 Sheaf of Wheat. 10	(Old Plate.) STONINGTON B'K, Stonington, Ct. Neptune and chariot drawn by sea horses. Locomotive and cars.	TEN

20 Portrait of Washington. 20	STONINGTON B'K. XX Chariot in which is seated a female holding key in left hand drawn by lions. XX Locomotive and cars.	TWENTY
50	50 STONINGTON B'K, 50 View of ocean upon which is a large ship, also vessel in distance on right; sail vessel in extreme distance on left.	FIFTY
ONE Female supporting figure 1. ONE	(First Plate.) 1 Vig. Female seated; mechanical tools on right; farming implements on left. THAMES BANK. Norwich, Ct. Female head.	1 Female head
1 Man resting on safe; factories in background.	(Second Plate.) Vig. Drove of cattle; two men on horseback; one man sitting by a tree; public house on left, THAMES BANK, Norwich, Ct. Man and horse.	1 Man on horse
Farmer in act of drinking from mug. ONE	THAMES BANK, Norwich, Conn. Circular die enclosing female head—"One" over it—"Dollar" beneath.	1 Goddess of Liberty.
2	Vig. Female overlooking sea, on which is seen ships; anchor at her side; light-house on right. fig. 2 on right. THAMES BANK, Norwich, Ct. Female Indian.	TWO View of ocean, steamship and ships; female in ornamental figure 2. TWO
TWO Gleaner with sheaf and sickle.	THAMES BANK, Norwich, Conn Henry Clay.	2 State Arms.
3 Three females soaring in clouds	THAMES BANK, Norwich, Conn. Milkmaid seated holding stool in left hand; shading her eyes with right; boy beside; cows, etc.	3 Eagle on shield.
THREE Three cupids in large figure 3. THREE	3 Vig. Two females on either side of a shield, one with liberty pole and cap, and one with grain; steamboat on right; bridge, locomotive, and train of cars on left. 3 THAMES BANK, Norwich, Ct. Indian, bow, and arrows.	THREE Three figures in large figure 3. THREE
5 Female Indian seated with tomahawk. FIVE	5 Vig. Five cupids in ornamental figure 5. 5 THAMES BANK, Norwich, Ct. Female head.	5 Female seated in letter V; wand in right hand; bale of goods on right. FIVE

Left	Center	Right
5 Male portrait	Vig. Two figures, sailor and farmer; farmer with sickle, grain, &c.; sailor with spyglass, capstan, and anchor at his feet; sheep on left. THAMES BANK, Norwich, Ct	5 Female Indian.
V Female. V	Ship. Vig. Female seated, emptying water out of pitcher; liberty pole and cap on left. FIVE THAMES BANK. Norwich, Ct. Cupid. Mech's arm	Five dollars running across three circular dies.
X Male head. X	Vig. View of Mad. Bee-Greenwich head. hive. Falls in Connecticut. THAMES BANK. Norwich, Ct. Machinery.	X TEN X
10 Portrait of D. Webster.	Vig. View of ocean in storm and boat putting off. THAMES BANK. Norwich, Ct	10 Two females, one seated with spyglass and one standing.
XX Male portrait XX	Vig. Three females seated; beehive, farming implements, &c. THAMES BANK, Norwich, Ct TWENTY	20 Male portrait 20
FIFTY Franklin FIFTY	FIFTY DOLLARS 50 Two children. 50 THAMES BANK, Norwich, Conn	50 State Arms.
100 Male portrait 100	100 Vig. Female on either side of a shield holding balances and spear, eagle at top of shield; ships on right; bridge on left. 100 on right. THAMES BANK, Norwich, Ct C	100 Group of cupids in circular die. 100
1 Round die. 1	1 Female seated on the ground; eagle and shield; ship in distance. 1 THOMPSON BANK, Thompson, Conn	ONE Female figure. ONE
TWO Female holding an eagle. TWO	THOMPSON BANK. Thompson, Conn. 2 2 Female with sickle and sheaf of wheat, also cows Bird	2 Female holding scales. TWO
THREE Female with scales; merchandise. 3	3 Female feeding an eagle from a cup. 3 THOMPSON BANK, Thompson, Conn	THREE Female, sickle, and sheaf of wheat. 3

Left	Center	Right
FIVE	5 Female and wheel. V THOMPSON BANK. Thompson, Conn. Fema	FIVE
10	10 Two female figures and eagle; ship and canal in background. 10 THOMPSON BANK, Thompson, Conn	X Female. 10
TWENTY	20 Female and lion; steamboat in distance. XX THOMPSON BANK, Thompson, Conn Cupid astride deer.	20 Female. XX
50 Female and anchor; steamboat in distance. 50	FIFTY DOLLARS 50 THOMPSON BANK, Thompson, Conn	FIFTY
C Portrait of Washington. C	100 Neptune, merchandise; ship in distance. 100 THOMPSON BANK, Thompson, Conn	ONE HUNDRED
ONE Female supporting a figure 1. ONE	1 Female seated on a bale; factories in background. 1 TOLLAND CO. BANK, Tolland, Conn	ONE Portrait of Washington. ONE
TWO A cooper at work. TWO	2 Harvest scene. 2 Title of Bank.	TWO Female with grain, and child with sickle. TWO
THREE Female figure and cherubs in fig. 3 THREE	3 Farmer boy, with cradle and sheaf of wheat; house in background. 3 Title of Bank. Female head.	THREE Interior of a blacksmith shop. THREE
5 Female supporting the above figure. V	Five female figures and figure 5. Title of Bank. Machinery.	5 Farmer boy
10 Female with sickle and sheaf.	Two females; factories in background. Title of Bank.	10 Indian girl.

Left	Center	Right
XX Cherubs XX	TOLLAND CO. BANK 20 Male figure upon globe seat. TWENTY tering TWENTY corn	XX Head of Franklin XX
50 Female figur.	Male and female Title of Bank.	50 Cupid in a sail boat. 50
1 Female head. ONE	TRADESMENS' B'K, New Haven, Conn. Battle scene. ONE ONE	1 View of Bank building.
2 Cows and dairy maids.	TRADESMENS' B'K, New Haven, Conn. Blacksmith and anvil; farmer, horse and dog.	2 Sailor and shipping.
3 Landing of R. Williams.	TRADESMENS' B'K. New Haven, Conn. THREE 3 DOLLARS 3	3 Female and bale of goods; factories in the distance
5	Railroad, steamboat and wharf scene. TRADESMENS' B'K, New Haven, Conn.	5 View of Bank building.
10 Battle field.	Farmers resting at noon; two horses attached to plough, feeding. TRADESMENS' B'K, New Haven, Conn.	10 View of Bank building
20 TWENTY	TRADESMENS' BK. Three blacksmiths with with forge and implements. New Haven, Conn	20 DOLLARS
Indian with gun overlooking precipice. 1	UNCAS BANK, Norwich, Ct Vig. Cotton factories and two females at work.	1 State die.
Indian erect with bow, arrow, and tomahawk. TWO	Vig. Three females and cupid bathing. UNCAS BANK. Norwich, Ct Horse.	2 State die.

Left	Center	Right
3	Vig. Indian with gun overlooking river. State die. UNCAS BANK, Norwich, Ct. Steamboat.	THREE Full length female
5	Vig. Three cattle in water, one reposing; sheep on left. State die UNCAS BANK, Norwich, Ct.	5 Female Indian. FIVE
Three females on rock; anvil, grain, &c., between them. TEN	Vig. Spread eagle on American shield. UNCAS BANK, Norwich, Ct. Indian head.	10 State die.
50 Female with chickens.	UNCAS BANK, Norwich, Conn. Indian seated resting his head on right hand.	50 Child and rabbits.
100 C	UNCAS BANK, Norwich, Conn. State Arms, female on either side	100 C
ONE Small boy, anvil and hammer. ONE	Vig. Whaling scene. UNION BANK, New London, Conn. Arm, hammer and anvil.	ONE
TWO Female, shield, Liberty pole, cap and eagle. TWO	Vig. Milkmaid, seated with cattle. UNION BANK, New London, Conn. Steamboat.	TWO
THREE Same as Two's. THREE	Vig. Milkmaid; one cow standing, and one reposing in front of her. UNION BANK, New London, Conn.	THREE
FIVE Large ship. FIVE	Vig. Farmer's loading hay. UNION BANK, New London, Conn. Machinery.	FIVE
TEN Male portrait. TEN	Vig. View of river, upon which is large ship, steamboat and other vessels. UNION BANK, New London, Ct.	TEN

Left	Center	Right
20 Male portrait. TWENTY	Vig. Stone cutter's at work. UNION BANK, New London, Ct.	20
50 Male portrait. FIFTY	Vig. Ship carpenter; ship building on left; ships and view of city on right. UNION BANK, New London, Ct.	50
100 Portrait of Washington. 100	Vig. Group of three male figures. UNION BANK, New London, Ct.	100
1 Two females, one with sword and balances, one with shield and spear. C	Vig. Female on either side of state arms. WATERBURY BANK Waterbury, Ct. Goods, cog-wheels, &c.	1 Two females erect, with wand, sickle, and grain.
2 Female.	Vig. Female and eagle, liberty pole and cap, shield, horn of plenty, &c. WATERBURY BANK Waterbury, Ct. Farming implements.	2 Male portrait
3 Mechanic and anvil.	Title of Bank. Vig. Female seated, one foot resting on globe, left hand resting on shield, which stands upright on a safe, arm around eagle's neck, right hand holding pole and cap, cornucopia at her feet; farming scene on left; factories and cars on right. Cornucopia, bale, etc.	3 Mechanic at work.
5 Three figures—females scattering flowers.	Vig. Female and spread eagle; steamship in distance on right; miniature portrait of Washington; factories, bridge, and cars on left. WATERBURY BANK Waterbury, Ct. State arms.	5 Female with wand and sickle; man in full armor and 5.
10 Female, sword, and balances.	Female seated between figures 10, key in left hand; cornucopia, safe, bridge, railroad cars on left; grain on right. Title of Bank. Dog's head, and collar marked Fidelity.	10 Female, hand resting on capstan, &c.
20 Female 20	Female seated between figures 20, rake in right hand. WATERBURY BANK Waterbury, Ct. Imp. and products	20 Female 20
100 Portrait of Washington.	Vig Female seated; bridge, locomotive, and cars on right; canal scene on left. WATERBURY BANK Waterbury, Ct. Bale of goods, cogwheel, &c.	100 Female.

Left	Center	Right
1 Groton monument. 1	1 Vig. Whaling scene. 1 WHALING BANK, New London, Ct. Ship, barrel, anchor, &c.	1 Female seated, wand in right hand key in left. 1
TWO Hunter, gun in right hand dog at his feet. TWO	2 Vig. same as ones. 2 WHALING BANK, New London, Ct. Steamboat.	TWO Female, sheaf of wheat, sickle, plow, rake, &c. TWO
THREE	3 Vig. same as ones. 3 WHALING BANK. New London, Ct. Blacksmith's arm and hammer.	3 Female; on right state arms, on which is eagle standing, on left scales, barrels, &c. 3
FIVE 5	WHALING BANK. New London, Ct Vig. same as ones. Three circular dies with words five dollars running across Indian in canoe.	5 Female giving eagle drink. V
TEN Female seated, eagle on her lap, in right hand sprig of flowers. 10	TEN Vig same as TEN ones. WHALING BANK. New London, Ct. Cupid seated on reindeer.	TEN Female resting on stone pillar, upon which is engraved letter X. X
20	XX Female seated giving eagle drink. 20 WHALING BANK, New London, Ct. Ship.	TWENTY
FIFTY	WHALING BANK, New London Ct. L Vig. same as ones. L Indian and canoe.	50 Female seated, sheaf of wheat on right, on left scroll on which is engraved figures 50. 50
100	Vig. same as ones. 100 WHALING BANK, New London, Ct. Indian and canoe.	100 Male portrait 100
1 Indian female figure.	Agricultural scene. WINDHAM BANK. Windham, Conn.	1 Froggs.
2 Head of Washington. 2	WINDHAM BANK Windham, Conn. Large figure 2, Indian male with gun on left, white female with sheaf of wheat on right.	2 Froggs.

CONN.

3	Manufacturing scene; state arms, cotton, and wheat. Female head.	3
Med. head.	WINDHAM BANK, Windham, Conn.	
THREE		Froggs.

5	WINDHAM BANK, Windham. Conn.	5
Train of cars	Large V, with female figure and wheat inside, and female head on either side.	
FIVE		Froggs.

X	WINDHAM BANK, Windham. Conn.	10
TEN	Two females; state arms, steamboat, railroad.	
10	X	Froggs.

ONE	Two cows with no horns; one standing, the other laying down; mill on right.	1
Mechanic erect, with arms folded; buildings in distance.	WINDHAM CO., BK., Brooklyn. Conn. Agricultural implements.	Female Portrait.

Little girl, with sheaf of grain on head; harvesting scene in distance.	2 Farmer, sailor, and blacksmith, apparently talking; horse and man on right.	2
2	WINDHAM CO., BK., Brooklyn. Conn.	Female with pole and cap; word Liberty, at her feet; buildings and train of cars on left.

3	Loading hay, two horses and four men; house in distance.	3
		THREE
Male portrait.	WINDHAM CO., BK., Brooklyn. Conn.	3

FIVE 5 FIVE	Title of Bank Two men; one with no hat, horse and buildings in background.	5
Head of Washington.		FIVE

10	View of the Capitol at Washington.	10
Two females.		
TEN	WINDHAM CO., BK., Brooklyn. Conn.	Female portrait.

20	Train of cars, hills, &c.; a train of cars, city and bridge in distance.	20
Med. Head.	WINDHAM CO., BK. Brooklyn. Conn.	
20	Two men; one with spade.	Female with flowers.

50	Male and female seated.	50
Female erect, with helmet and shield.	WINDHAM CO., BK., Brooklyn. Conn. 50	Cupid in a sail-boat. 50

N. Y. CITY.

100	Large eagle on a tree; with canal and boats, and railroad with cars, in background.	100
Male figure sitting.	WINDHAM CO., BK., Brooklyn, Conn. C C 100	Female figure with rake, sitting; load of hay in the distance.

ONE on 1	ONE ONE WINSTED BANK 1 Cupid either side of portrait of boy 1	1
Girl giving drink to boy	ONE DOLLAR on DOLLAR Winsted, Conn.	Male portrait

2	2 Children under tree; cows in brook, etc.	2
Male portrait.	WINSTED BANK TWO DOLLARS on TWO 2 TWO	Two children

Portrait of boy	Cupid, etc. 3 Childs' head	3
THREE	WINSTED BANK Connecticut THREE DOLLARS on 3	Male portrait

5	WINSTED BANK FIVE on V — Men, horses, etc. — FIVE on V	5
Abraham Lincoln	FIVE DOLLARS on FIVE 5 FIVE	Male portrait

TEN	WINSTED BANK 10 Child and dog 10	TEN
Male portrait	TEN DOLLARS	Male portrait
TEN	Connecticut	TEN

20 Twenty	Scene near blacksmith's shop; mending wheel barrow; female with grain, etc.	Twenty 20
TWENTY Male portrait	WINSTED BANK	Gen. McClellan TWENTY
20 XX	TWENTY DOLLARS on TWENTY	20 20

1	Vig. Steamship under way, vessels in distance.	1
Male portrait	AM. EX. BANK, New York. Locomotive.	Compt's die.

Male portrait	Vig. A farmer buying cattle of drover; cattle on right, sheep on left.	2
2	AM. EX BANK, New York. Steamboat.	Compt's die.

3	AM. EX BANK. New York.	3
Male portrait	Vig. Drove of horses, fences, trees, etc., in background. Eagle.	Compt's die.

N. Y. CITY.

5	AM. EX. BANK, N. Y. City.	5
Eagle.	Five Dollars, FIVE and figure 5 on green die.	Compt's die.

5	V 5 and three females; shipping, cars, etc., in distance. V	5
Female, safe, eagle, snakes, etc.		Med. head.
FIVE	AMERICAN EX. BK. New York City. Eagle.	FIVE

10	Female on either side of shield; shipping, city, canal scene, etc.	10
Same as fives	AMERICAN EX. BK New York City.	Two females, eagle, cornucopia and motto "Excelsior."
TEN	Eagle.	TEN

TWENTY	20 Female seated; scientific apparatus; in distance steamship. 20	Die.
Same as fives		XX
TWENTY	AMERICAN EX. BK., New York City. Eagle.	Die.

FIFTY	Two Indians and white man. FIFTY on med. head on each side.	FIFTY
Female seated; steamboat.	AMERICAN EX. BK., New York City.	Female seated; screw-press; buildings in distance.
50	Capitol.	50

HUNDRED	100 on med. head. Female on either side of shield, eagle at top; cars, shipping, etc. 100 on med head	ONE HUNDRED
Female.		
100	AMERICAN EX. BK., New York City. Capitol	

500	500 Cars; steam-vessels in distance.	500
Same as fives		
500	AMERICAN EX. BK., New York City. Eagle.	

1000	Steamship and other vessels; houses, etc. Figs. 1000 on each side.	ONE THOUSAND
Same as fives		
1000	AMERICAN EX. BK., New York City.	

1	Spread eagle; ship on either side.	1
Male portrait.	ATLANTIC BANK, New York City.	Compt's die

2	Steamship and other vessels.	2
Compt's die.	ATLANTIC BANK, New York City.	Male portrait

Large steam-ship and other vessels | Male portrait | ATLANTIC BANK, New York City. | 3 | THREE | Compt's die.

5 | Three females and Cupid in water. | ATLANTIC BANK, New York City. | 5 | Compt's die. | Fire Engine. | Henry Clay.

10 | Steamship and other vessels. | ATLANTIC BANK, New York City. | 10 | Anchor, bales, &c. | Secured, etc. | Compt's die.

20 | ATLANTIC BANK, New York City. | 20 | Sailor erect; vessels in distance. | Portrait of Webster. | Compt's die.

50 | ATLANTIC BANK, New York City. | 50 | Female with pole, cap, eagle, &c. | Male portrait | Compt's die.

C | Vessels, view of city, &c. | ATLANTIC BANK, New York City. | 100 | Male portrait | Compt's die.

5 | FIVE Goddess of FIVE Liberty, eagle, shield, &c. | 5 | Large white V on red ground work | BANK OF AMERICA, New York City. | Large white 5 on red ground work | Compt's die.

5 | 5 Two females and two spread eagles. 5 | 5 FIVE 5 | Compt's die. | B'K. OF AMERICA, New York City. | 5

X | TEN Goddess of TEN Liberty, eagle, shield, &c | 10 | Red end with white X across the end. | BANK OF AMERICA New York City. | White X across red end. | Compt's die.

X | Vig. Same as fives. | 10 | Compt's die. | B'K. OF AMERICA, New York City. | TEN | X

Compt's die. | B'K OF AMERICA, New York City. | 20 | Vig. Spread eagle; cars on left; vessels on right. | XX

50 | B'K OF AMERICA, New York City. | 50 | Eagle. | Compt's die.

100 | B'K. OF AMERICA, New York City. | 100 | Compt's die. | Eagle. | 100

500 | 500 Spread eagle. | Compt's die. | B'K. OF AMERICA, New York City. | 500

Female portrait. | 1000 Eagle. 1000 | Compt's die. | B'K. OF AMERICA, New York City. | Female portrait.

One and fig. 1 across. | BANK OF THE COMMONWEALTH, New York City. | One and fig. 1 across. | Female seated with eagle, shield, etc. | Large die on which is words "one dollar" and Compt's die. | Sailor at wheel.

Large die with TWO repeated | Some bills have red ends with white 2 | Man plowing TWO DOLLARS | BANK OF THE COMMONWEALTH N. Y. City | Compt's die | Some bills have red ends with white 2 | Large die with TWO repeated | TWO | TWO

Bank of the | Large die with female portrait, words three dollars, and Compt's die at bottom. | Commonw'th | Die with fig. 3, and word three. | Same as on left.

Milkmaids and cows; in distance on right, canal scene; on left house. | Figure 5, and two trains of cars. | BANK OF THE COMMONWEALTH, New York City. | Figure 5 full length of the note; view of city at top, and wharf scene and shipping at bottom. | Compt's die.

TEN | The arms of each State of the Union in miniature scale, completely surrounding the whole note. | BANK OF THE COMMONWEALTH, New York City. | Compt's die. | TEN | 10 | 10

Compt's die. | Steamship, sail vessels, view of city, etc. | 50 | Sailor leaning on capstan. | BANK OF THE COMMONWEALTH, New York City. | Blacksmith, anvil, forge, etc.

100 | BANK OF THE COMMONWEALTH, New York City. | 100 | View of New York harbor and city life scenery generally. | Male portrait | Compt's die. | Male portrait

500 | Compt's die. | BANK OF THE COMMONWEALTH, N. Y. City. | 500 | 500 | 500

1 | Horse. Eagle. B'K OF NEW YORK, N. Y. City. | 1 | 1 Female with tablets; child at her feet. 1 | Compt's die. | ONE on 1.

1 | Bee hive surrounded by flowers. Large red fig. 1 across face of bill. | 1 | BK. OF NEW YORK, New York City. | Compt's die | Eagle. | 1

2 | Bee hive surrounded by flowers. Red fig. 2 across face of bill. | 2 | BK. OF NEW YORK, New York City. | Compt's die. | Female head.

2 | Title of Bank. | 2 | TWO on 2. | Female with sword and shield. | TWO on 2. | Compt's die. | TWO on 2.

Compt's die. | Bee hive surrounded by flowers. | 3 | BK. OF NEW YORK, New York City. | 3 | Head of Indian.

Compt's die. | Female with quadrant, scroll, compass and globe. | THREE on 3. | Title of Bank. | 3 | Three Green dies with fig. 3 on each. | 3

Female portrait. | View of N. Y. harbor, shipping, etc. Word Five in red letters across face of bill. | 5 | BK. OF NEW YORK, New York City. | 5 | Compt's die.

Sailor with flag; female reclining at his feet; anchor, bale, &c.	10 Shipping. Word Ten in red letters across face of bill. BK. OF NEW YORK, New York City.	10 Compt's die.
20 Compt's die. 20	Male portrait. Eagle on rock; shipping. Word Twenty in red letters across face of bill. BK. OF NEW YORK, New York City.	20
50 Compt's die. 50	Winged female seated on flags; globe, eagle, etc. Word Fifty in red letters across face of bill. BK. OF NEW YORK, New York City. Secured, etc.	50
C Compt's die.	Female seated on bales, pointing with wand to shipping in distance; lighthouse on left of note. BK. OF NEW YORK, New York City. Secured, etc.	100 Male portrait
Shipping. 300	Compt's die. BK. OF NEW YORK, New York City.	300 Portrait of J. Q. Adams.
400 Male portrait	Spread eagle on rock; shipping. BK. OF NEW YORK, New York City.	400 Compt's die.
500 Med. head of Washington.	Two females seated on either side of a frame, surmounted by an eagle, in which is a view of coun-ries, and word "Excelsior;" shipping in distance. BK. OF NEW YORK, New York City.	500 Compt's die.
ONE THOUSAND	View of New York harbor, with shipping, city, &c. BK. OF NEW YORK, New York City.	1000 Compt's die.
ONE Compt's die. ONE	1 Neptune and female in a shell, drawn by two horses on the sea. 1 BANK OF THE NEW YORK DRY DOCK CO. New York City. Ship.	ONE
2 Compt's die 2	2 Female with safe and key, bird perched on safe, female in background. 2 Title of Bank. Ship.	TWO Female with sheaf in her hand. TWO

3 Compt's die. 3	3 Goddess of Liberty with pole and cap, flag around her, leaning on a shield; money flowing from the base of the shield. 3 Title of Bank. Ship.	THREE Female with sheaf. 3
5 Compt's die 5	5 Neptune in a sea car drawn by two horses, raising his arms towards a winged female. 5 Title of Bank. Ship.	FIVE Franklin. 5
10 Compt's die. 10	X Vig. Same as fives. X Title of Bank running around the vig. Ship.	Female with pole leaning on an anchor 10
20 Compt's die 20	XX Vig. Same as fives, with title running around it. XX Red figures 20. Ship.	Female with scroll in her hand. 20
50 Compt's die	Female seated with sheaf and sickle; steamboat in distance. 50 Title of Bank.	Sailor with coil of rope on his shoulder looking at female sitting with hand raised.
100 Compt's die.	Female seated with pole, cap and key, eagle, safe etc. Title of Bank.	100 Female, horn of plenty, etc.
1 Compt's die. ONE	Spread eagle; steamer and buildings in distance. BK. OF NORTH AM., New York City. Sheaf, plow, etc.	1 Female with ear of corn and fig. 1.
Compt's die. Indian princess.	2 Vig. Same as ones. BK. OF NORTH AM., New York City. City Arms.	TWO Two females. TWO
THREE Compt's die. THREE	3 Vig. Same as ones. BK. OF NORTH AM., New York City. Cog-wheel, etc.	3 Two males bearing aloft a female.
Compt's die. Indian with bow, arrow and belt.	5 Vig. Same as ones. BK. OF NORTH AM., New York City. Steamboat.	FIVE Squaw and papoose.

Compt's die. 10 Steamship.	Vig. Same as ones. 10 BK. OF NORTH AM., New York City. Arms.	TEN Helmeted female with spear and shield. TEN
Compt's die. 10 Steamer.	TEN Washington. X BK. OF NORTH AM., New York City. Arms.	TEN Helmeted female with spear and shield. TEN
20 Female seated with spear and shield.	Compt's die. Vig. Same as ones. BK. OF NORTH AM., New York City. Machinery.	XX Female with vase of flowers, etc.
50 Female with flag and balances; buildings in distance. FIFTY	Compt's die. Vig. Same as ones. BK. OF NORTH AM., New York City. Steamship.	50 Female with spear and shield.
100 Helmeted female with spear and globe.	Compt's die. Vig. Same as ones. BK. OF NORTH AM., New York City. Merchandise.	100 Female arm
500 Compt's die. 500	Vig. Same as ones. BK. OF NORTH AM., New York City. Safe.	500 Female with flag, and three cupids in clouds.
1000 Female, eagle, wreath, shield, etc.	Compt's die. Vig. Same as ones. BK. OF NORTH AM., New York City. Arms.	1000
ONE Eagle and shield Compt's die	1 View of the U. S. Capitol 1 BK of the REPUBLIC ONE DOLLAR New York City Arms	ONE Eagle Female with liberty cap, pole, & shield enclosed in oval wreath
TWO Female with shield, etc in oval frame, on which are the names of all the States. Compt's die	2 Female either side of shield, on which is eagle; cars, factory, barrels, etc. in distance. BK of the REPUBLIC TWO DOLLARS New York Safe	2 Female erect with spear and shield.
Sailor with spy-glass 3	BK of the REPUBLIC, New York City. 3 Ship under full sail; steamboat on left. 3 Compt's die.	3 Female with eagle and shield.

Left	Centre	Right
5 Compt's die.	BK of the REPUBLIC, New York City. V View of shipping. V Female and anchor.	5 Sailor with flag in left hand, and hat in right.
10 Compt's die.	Shipping and view of city on right in distance. BK of the REPUBLIC, New York City. Building.	10 Eagle on a shield.
20 Compt's die.	View of steamship and other vessels. BK of the REPUBLIC, New York City. Dog, key and safe.	20 Agricultural implements.
FIFTY Compt's die. 50	Eagle on limb of tree; cars and canal scene in distance. BK of the REPUBLIC, New York City. Shield.	50 Female leaning on a column; two females in background.
100 Compt's die. 100	Two females and bust of Washington on shield in centre; shipping, etc. 100 BK of the REPUBLIC, New York City. Shield.	Merchandise Female portrait. Train of cars.
Steamboat, schooner, buildings, men, etc. ONE Compt's die.	1 Two females, shield, surmounted by an eagle; cars; shipping, etc. 1 BK OF THE STATE OF NEW YORK, New York City.	Spanish dollar.
II Compt's die TWO	Vig. Same as ones. 2 Title of Bank.	Two spanish dollars lapped.
Two spanish dollars and one American lapped.	3 Vig. Same as ones. Title of Bank.	III Compt's die. THREE
5 Compt's die. 5	5 Two females; steamboat and sail vessels in distance. 5 BK. OF THE STATE, New York City. Eagle and shield.	FIVE Female representing Justice. FIVE
10 Compt's die. 10	X Vig. Same as fives. X BK. OF THE STATE, New York City. Canal Lock.	10 Cupid. X

Left	Centre	Right
20 Compt's die 20	20 Vig. Same as fives. 20 BK. OF THE STATE, New York City. Eagle on view of rising sun.	XX Justice. TWENTY
50 Compt's die. 50	L Vig. Same as fives. L BK. OF THE STATE, New York City. Eagle, &c.	50 Steamboat and sail vessels. 50
100 Compt's die. 100	C Vig. Same as fives. C BK. OF THE STATE, New York City. Eagle, &c.	100 Sail Vessel. 100
500	500 Vig. Same as fives. BK. OF THE STATE, New York City. Eagle, sunrise, etc.	Die. Compt's die. Die.
1000	Vig. Same as fives. 1000 BK. OF THE STATE, New York City. Eagle, sunrise, etc.	Die. Compt's die Die.
ONE Building, street, &c. Compt's die.	1 Spread eagle; steamer, ships, etc. BROADWAY BANK, New York City. Implements	ONE Female and fig. 1.
TWO Building, street, etc. Compt's die.	2 Female, shield, eagle, portrait of Washington; cars, vessels and buildings in distance. BROADWAY BANK, New York City. Arm.	2 Female seated; building, etc.
THREE Building, street, etc. Compt's die.	3 Two females seated, ship between; on left steamboat and ship; on right in distance, cars, schooner, etc. BROADWAY BANK, New York City. Sheaf, plow, &c.	3 Mechanic in frame; cars in distance.
5 5 Compt's die	Female seated on either side of shield, surmounted by eagle, cars, steamboat, in background. BROADWAY BANK New York Cogwheel, etc.	5 Figure of Justice with sword and scales.
Compt's die. Female seated with spear and head on shield.	10 Female reclining on merchandise; on left, cars, canal scene; on right ships and city. BROADWAY BANK, New York City. Safe.	10

Left	Centre	Right
Two females representing Liberty and Justice. Compt's die.	20 Female seated with sheaf; cars and canal scene in distance. BROADWAY BANK, New York City. Boxes, bbls., bales, etc	20 Female seated between a 2 and 0.
50 Compt's die. FIFTY	Female with pole, cap and shield. 50 BROADWAY BANK, New York City. State Arms.	FIFTY Winged female seated.
100 Compt's die. 100	Vessels and view of city. BROADWAY BANK, New York City. Steamship.	100 Female erect with right hand on capstan.
1 with ONE running across it. Telegraph, roads and cows	BULLS HEAD BANK, New York City. Vig. Bull's head with title of Bank running around it. 1, one running across it. 1, one running across it.	1 with ONE running across it. Compt's die.
2 Compt's die.	Vig. Same as Ones. BULL'S HEAD BANK New York City. 2 with Two running across it. 2 with word dollars running across it.	2 TWO 2
3 Compt's die. THREE	Vig. Same as ones. BULL'S HEAD BANK New York City. 3 3	3 THREE 3
5 Bull's head V	Rosa Bonheur's Horse fair BULL'S HEAD B'K FIVE DOLLARS N. Y. City	5 5 Compt's die 5 V
5 Compt's Die.	Bull. BULL'S HEAD BANK New York City. Man buying newspaper of boy; hhds., etc.	5 Bull's head. FIVE
10 Bull's head. 10	Vig. Agricultural scene; oxen in foreground. BULL'S HEAD BANK New York City.	10 with TEN running across it. Compt's die.
XX Compt's die.	BULL'S HEAD BANK New York City. Vig. Mill, drove of sheep and man on horseback in foreground.	20 Bull's head. 20

50 Bull's head.	BULL'S HEAD BANK New York City. Vig. Two horses. State Arms.	50

ONE HUNDRED. Bull's head. Compt's die.	ONE HUNDRED DOLLARS. BULL'S HEAD BANK New York City.	100

1 Compt's die. 1	BUTCHERS' & DROVERS' BANK, New York City. 1 Drovers and cattle in a frame. 1	ONE DOLLAR

2 Compt's die 2	2 Vig. Same as 1s. 2 Title of Bank.	2 Female 2

3 Compt's die 3	3 Vig. Same as ones. 3 Title of Bank.	3 Female bathing 3

5 Compt's die. 5	5 Two females with ornamental figure 5; two cupids on either side. 5 BUTCHERS' AND DROVERS' BANK. New York City. Wheat, plough, spade.	5 Cattle. 5

5 Compt's die. 5	5 Cattle and sheep. 5 Title of Bank. Die.	5 Four females 5

10 Compt's die. 10	Cattle and sheep lying on the ground. 10 Title of Bank.	TEN

20 Compt's die. 20	20 Vig. Same as tens. 20 Title of Bank. Ship.	TWENTY Female bust TWENTY

50 Compt's die. 50	50 Female with sheaf; cars and factory in distance. 50 Title of Bank. Ship.	50 FIFTY Drovers and cattle. DOLLARS 50

100 Compt's die 100	C Two females leaning on a view of drovers and cattle. C Title of Bank. Ship.	Female erect with sheaf and sickle. 100

ONE Compt's die. ONE	1 Firemen, fire engine, buildings, etc. CHATHAM BANK, New York City. Male portrait	1 Secured, &c. ONE

2 Compt's die. TWO	Female seated surrounded by mechanical implements. CHATHAM BANK, New York City. Male portrait	2 Secured, &c. TWO

Sailor seated on Compt's die; vessel below	3 Female seated on left of City Arms. 3 CHATHAM BANK, New York City. Male portrait	Ship. 3

Sailor erect, leaning on bale. Compt's die.	5 Steamship and other vessels. CHATHAM BANK, New York City. Male portrait	Large 5, cars, bridge, falls, indians, etc 5

10 Compt's die. 10	Female seated on left of shield, sheafs of grain; cars and bridge in distance. CHATHAM BANK, New York City. Male portrait	10 City Arms. 10

Female seated on Compt's die TWENTY	20 Sailor and female seated; steamer on left in distance; on right farming scene. CHATHAM BANK, New York City. Male portrait	20 Secured, etc. Female seated.

50 Compt's die. 50	Two females on right of shield; eagle and vessel on left. CHATHAM BANK, New York City. Male portrait	50 Steamboat FIFTY

100 Compt's die.	Spread eagle. CHATHAM BANK, New York City. Male portrait	100 Female with sledge.

500 Compt's die	Portrait of Washington, with flags and cannon on each side. CHATHAM BANK, New York City. Male portrait	500 City Arms. 500

Large figure of Mercury with bag of coin and wand. 1000	Portrait of Washington. CHATHAM BANK, New York City. Compt's die.	Female with sickle and sheaf. 1000

1 Compt's die	CHEMICAL BANK, One Female figure leaning against column, torch in hand. Dollar across 1 1 City of New York.	1 Dog on safe.

ONE Two sailors and females.	Compt's die. Vig. Forest scene; dogs in pursuit of game. CHEMICAL BANK, New York City.	1

2 Compt's die. TWO	CHEMICAL BANK, New York City. Vig. Same as ones.	2 Two females one kneeling.

TWO Compt's die. TWO	Two females and sheaf; ship in the distance, Medallion head and 2 on either side CHEMICAL BANK, New York City.	Female bust. Male portrait Female bust

5 Red figure 5.	CHEMICAL BANK, New York City. Female. Word five and fig. 5. Female. Compt's die.	5 Red fig. 5.

Female with pole and cap.	5 Female reclining with cornucopia. CHEMICAL BANK, New York City.	5 Compt's die

TEN Compt's die TEN	X Spread eagle CHEMICAL BANK, New York City.	X Female with shield, eagle, pole and cap.

TEN	X on 10 Female seated with torch, eagle, portrait of Washington, &c. X on 10 CHEMICAL BANK, New York City. Chemists laboratory.	X Compt's die. X

TWENTY	XX on 20 Eagle and shield. XX on 20 CHEMICAL BANK, New York City. Chemical laboratory.	XX Compt's die XX

TWENTY Compt's die.	20 Two females, shield, cars, etc.; ship in distance. CHEMICAL BANK, New York City.	TWENTY Washington.
Compt's die, fig. 50 on either side. Female seated with fig. 50.	CHEMICAL BANK, New York City. Secured, &c.	50
100	Female with shield. C CHEMICAL BANK, New York City.	100 Compt's die 100
D	Compt's die. 500 CHEMICAL BANK, New York City. Three females; building in background.	500
M	CHEMICAL BANK, New York City. Figures 1000 and words one thousand across. Compt's die	1000
1 Compt's die. ONE	Drover and cattle. CITIZENS BANK, New York City. City Arms.	1 Female portrait ONE
TWO Compt's die. TWO	Farmer with basket of corn; farmers gathering corn, cars in distance. CITIZENS BANK, New York City. Bales, boxes, etc.	2 Two females
3 Compt's die	Farmer reclining on sheafs, with pitcher, dog, basket, &c. CITIZENS BANK, New York City. Cog wheel, box, &c.	3 Med. Head. THREE
5 Compt's die. V	Blacksmith reclining on anvil, hammer in his hand; factory, cars, &c., in distance. CITIZENS BANK, New York City. Cog wheel, bales, &c.	5 Med. head and word five. FIVE
10 Compt's die.	Sailor with glass in hand, reclining on bales, etc.; shipping in distance. CITIZENS BANK, New York City. City Arms.	10 Med. head. TEN
20 Compt's die. XX	Washington. Female with cap, shield, grain, etc. Franklin. CITIZENS BANK, New York City. Female.	20 Female between 2 and 0.
50 Med. head.	Compt's die. Female with globe, chart, quadrant, book, ink-stand, pen, &c.; cars, shipping, factory, etc., in distance. CITIZENS BANK, New York City. Anchor, bale, &c.	50 Two females.
100 Med. head. 100	Compt's die. Female with eagle, shield, safe, cap, harrow, sheaf, etc. CITIZENS BANK, New York City. Dog, key and safe.	100 Female with fruit leaning on anchor
Compt's die. ONE Male portrait	1 Indian princess, fig. 1, shield, water fall and rainbow. 1 CONTINENTAL BK., New York City. City Arms.	ONE Female erect; ship in distance.
Compt's die. TWO Male portrait	2 Female seated on either side of a fig 2. 2 CONTINENTAL BK., New York City. City Arms.	TWO Spread eagle Male portrait
Compt's die. 3 Male portrait	Three females and fig. 3; buildings in distance. 3 CONTINENTAL BK., New York City. View of reservior.	Male portrait THREE Male portrait
Male portrait 5 Male portrait	Compt's die. Five females and fig. 5; shipping, cars and buildings in distance. 5 CONTINENTAL BK., New York City. Eagle.	Male portrait Male portrait Male portrait
10 Continental dies.	Compt's die. Signing Declaration of Independence CONTINENTAL BK., New York City.	10 Female with pole, cap, shield and Declaration of Independence.
TWENTY Two females representing Liberty and Justice.	Compt's die. Male portrait 20 CONTINENTAL BK., New York City.	Winged female erect; female seated with pole, cap, eagle and cornucopia.
FIFTY Male portrait Compt's die.	50 Steamer at sea. CONTINENTAL BK., New York City. Shield.	50 Sailor with quadrant, globe, etc.
100 Compt's die. 100	Female on either side of a shield, surmounted by an eagle; steamboat, vessels, cars and buildings in distance. CONTINENTAL BK., New York City. Cornucopia and anvil.	100 Male portrait 100
Female erect; an eagle in act of drinking from urn. 500	500 Compt's die. CONTINENTAL BK., New York City.	500 Male portrait
1000 Washington and other military officers. Compt's die.	Vig. The Globe. CONTINENTAL BK., New York City.	1000 Head of Washington.
1 Compt's die.	CORN EX. BANK, New York City. Two male figures; sheafs; house and ship in distance ONE	1 ONE
2 Farmer and mechanic seated, bundle of grain; coil of rope, etc., ocean in distance	New York CORN EXCH. BANK Compt's die	2 TWO DOLLARS 2
3	Vig. Same as ones. CORN EX. BANK, New York City. THREE	THREE Compt's die 3
FIVE Compt's die.	CORN EX. BANK, New York City. Female with pole, cap, eagle, etc.	5
TEN	NEW YORK Two men, grain, beehive, etc. CORN EXCHANGE BANK TEN DOLLARS	10 Compt's die
10 TEN	CORN EX. BANK, New York City. Vig. Same as fives.	10 Compt's die.
Compt's die. 50	Male portrait CORN EX. BANK, New York City.	50 Four females representing Agriculture, Merchandise etc.

Left end	Centre	Right end
Compt's die. C	CORN EX. BANK. New York City. Vig. Four females, representing Agriculture, Merchandise, etc.	100 Male portrait
1 Compt's die. 1	Farmer and child at lunch boy playing with dog, &c EAST RIVER BANK, New York City.	ONE Some have portrait of girl; others sailor at capstan on this end.
1 Compt's die. 1	View of buildings in course of erection; laborers, horse, truck, &c. EAST RIVER BANK, New York City.	ONE Sailor leaning on capstan with quadrant in hand.
TWO Female sewing on a cap.	Train of cars passing a railroad station; ladies on platform. EAST RIVER BANK, New York City.	2 Compt's die. TWO
3 Female portrait.	EAST RIVER BANK, New York City. Faust, Guttenberg and Schoeffer, chests, wheels, books, etc.	3 III Compt's die.
5 FIVE	View of ship yard, three ships on ways; factory to left; men at work, &c. EAST RIVER BANK, New York City.	V Compt's die. V
5 FIVE	Two females reclining; factory on right; sheep and cattle on left. EAST RIVER BANK New York City.	V Compt's die. V
TEN Dogs head.	Compt's die. Two blacksmiths in shop; one shoeing horse, the other blowing forge. EAST RIVER BANK, New York City.	X
20 Sailor with spy glass, quadrant and compass.	Compt's die. Steamboat, wharf, etc. EAST RIVER BANK, New York City.	XX
50 Compt's die.	Steamship. Portrait of Franklin. EAST RIVER BANK, New York City.	50 Female portrait. L

Left end	Centre	Right end
C	Sailor seated on ground with quadrant, telescope, compass, &c., boxes, bbls.; shipping in distance. Compt's die. EAST RIVER BANK, New York City.	100 Arm and hammer.
Steamboat	1 FULTON BANK 1 Bust of Fulton, mechanic seated on right, cars and steamship in distance. ONE DOLLAR New York	ONE One Dollar Sailor erect, vessel in distance. One Dollar ONE
Steamboat.	2 Vig. Same as ones. FULTON BANK, New York City.	2 Female with sheaf and sickle. TWO
Compt's die. Male portrait THREE	Bust of Fulton; mechanic seated on right; cars and steamship in distance. FULTON BANK. New-York City.	3 Steamboat.
Steamboat.	5 Vig. Same as ones. FULTON BANK, New York City. Eagle.	5 Female with trident. 5
Steamboat.	10 Vig. Same as ones. FULTON BANK, New York City.	X Boy in cornfield.
Steamboat.	50 Vig. Same as ones. FULTON BANK, New York City. Female and ship.	50
Steamboat.	100 Title of Bank. Vig. Same as ones. Sheaf and plow.	100
ONE Compt's die. ONE	1 Winged female with sword and scales, holding fig. 1. 1 GREENWICH BANK, New York City.	ONE Female with flowers. ONE
2 Compt's die.	Ship carpenter at work, with axe lying beside him; ship in background. GREENWICH BANK, New York City.	2 Two Cupids holding an ornamental figure 2.

Left end	Centre	Right end
3 Compt's die.	Three females representing Agriculture, Manufactures and Commerce. GREENWICH BANK, New York City.	THREE Three Cupids supporting a fig. 3. THREE
FIVE Full length female figure	Compt's die. Figure of Justice. FIVE GREENWICH BANK, New York City. Steamboat.	FIVE DOLLARS
10 Washington. 10	Compt's die. Eagle on City Arms. TEN GREENWICH BANK, New York City.	X Male portrait X
20 Compt's die. 20	20 Figure of Justice with sword and scales on left; on right Goddess of Liberty with pole and cap; between them an eagle surmounting frame on which is a view of sunrise. Title of Bank running around them. 20	20 Ship. 20
50 Compt's die. 50	50 Female representing Commerce, resting her arm on a frame with an anchor on it; ship on the left. 50 GREENWICH BANK, New York City. Eagle.	50 Male portrait 50
100 Compt's die. 100	100 Female seated on the base of a column pointing to a ship in the distance; sheaf and rake. 100 GREENWICH BANK, New York City. Steamboat.	Male portrait 100 Male portrait
ONE Female seated with fig. 1	Compt's die. View of street, buildings, pedestrians, etc. GROCERS BANK, New York City.	1
TWO Female seated on bbl.	Compt's die. Female on either side of a fig. 2. GROCERS BANK, New York City. Bales and barrels.	2 Male portrait
3 Mechanic, sailor, farmer and fig. 3 THREE	Compt's die. Female reclining on merchandise; ships, cars, canal scene in distance. GROCERS BANK, New York City.	3
FIVE Three males; two females and letter V	Compt's die. Sailor seated with telescope; vessels in distance. GROCERS BANK, New York City.	5 Five females and fig. 5

Compt's die. Sailor erect; capstan, masts, etc.
10 Female on either side of ship; cars, vessels, etc., in distance. GROCERS BANK, New York City. Safe.
TEN 10

50 City Arms. 50
Compt's die. Female reclining on a view of sunrise; cars, steamer, &c., in distance. HANOVER BANK, New York City. Dragon and boy.
50 Female, horn of plenty, etc. FIFTY

Compt's die. 3 Indian reclining, and another approaching. Dolphin. THREE
IRVING BANK, New York City.
3 Male portrait 3

20 Mercury between 2 & 0.
Compt's die. Female between 2 and 0. GROCERS BANK, New York City. City Arms.
XX Ship and other vessels

100 Female with pole, cap and shield.
Compt's die. Female and cupid on either side of a view of sunrise. HANOVER BANK, New York City. Sailor reclining.
100 Ship and other vessels.

Compt's die.
Old man seated with gun. 5 Male portrait IRVING BANK, New York City.
5 Milkmaid seated.

50 Compt's die. 50
Ships and other vessels; city in distance. GROCERS BANK, New York City. Machinery, etc.
50 Male portrait FIFTY

ONE
Head of Washington. Ornamental figure 1. IMPORTERS' & TRADERS BANK. New York City. Compt's die.
ONE

10 Compt's die. 10
View of a cottage covered with vines. 10 IRVING BANK, New York City.
Ten Dollars Female with sword. Male portrait

Merchandise Compt's die. Cars.
100 Three females seated. GROCERS BANK, New York City. Bbls., bales, etc.
100 Male portrait

2 TWO
Title of Bank. Sailor and sailor boy. Compt's die. Secured, etc.
2 TWO

Cupid on a dolphin, holding aloft Compt's die. TWENTY
20 Two females on right of shield; eagle and vessel on left. IRVING BANK, New York City. Steamship.
20 Male portrait TWENTY

1 Compt's die.
Ship and other vessels 1 HANOVER BANK, New York City. Bbls. and bales.
ONE Female head. Horses with wings.

5 FIVE
Female seated; shield and eagle. Title of Bank. FIVE DOLLARS.
5 Compt's die. FIVE

Female. Compt's die.
50 Eagle and shield. IRVING BANK, New York City.
50

Compt's die. Indian princess erect.
2 Female seated with pole, cap, fig. 2, and eagle. HANOVER BANK, New York City. Sailor reclining.
2 Female portrait. TWO

X TEN
Two females, one erect, the other kneeling. NEW YORK TEN DOLLARS Title of Bank.
10 Compt's die.

Compt's die.
Eagle, shield, &c. IRVING BANK, New York City.
100 Male portrait 100

3 Compt's die. THREE
Winged female and cupid in act of raising drapery from shield on which is an eagle HANOVER BANK, New York City. City Arms
3 Female seated.

50 Female soaring in clouds with cornucopia of flowers.
Title of Bank. Large 50 in red dies. Compt's die
50 Female soaring in clouds

1 Compt's die. 1
Female on horse catching buffalo; hunting buffaloes in distance. ONE LEATHER MANUFACTURERS' BANK, New York City. Shield.
Cupid and grindstone. ONE

5 Compt's die.
Female with shield, pole and cap. Washington. HANOVER BANK, New York City. Safe.
5 Sailor erect, leaning on capstan.

100 New York.
Title of Bank. Large figures 100 in red die; on right sailor seated, and ship in distance; on left mower on the ground with scythe; trees, etc. Compt's die.
100

2 Compt's die. 2
2 TWO Title of Bank. Shield.
Same as vig. of ones. 2

Female seated; vessel & factory in distance. Compt's die
10 Female, shield and eagle soaring in clouds. HANOVER BANK, New York City. Boxes, bbls., &c.
10 Franklin. TEN

1 Steamship. Compt's die.
1 Head of Irving. 1 IRVING BANK, New York City
1 Steamboat. ONE

3 Compt's die. 3
3 Cupid and grindstone. 3 Title of Bank. 3
Gent's head. THREE Gent's head.

20 Mercury seated between 2 and 0.
Compt's die. Two females, bust and shield between them; ship in distance. HANOVER BANK, New York City. Bbls., bales, etc.
20 Jefferson.

Ship. Compt's die.
2 Head of Irving. 2 IRVING BANK, New York City.
Female with sheaf. TWO

5 Compt's die. 5
V Vig. Same as ones. 5 Title of Bank. 5
FIVE Female, vessel, cow, sheep, etc. V

Left end	Centre	Right end
10 Compt's die. 10	Cupid and grindstone. X Title of Bank. Steamboat.	Same as vig. of ones. 10
20 Compt's die. 20	20 Vig. Same as ones. TWENTY Title of Bank.	SAFETY Cupid and grindstone. FUND 20
50 Compt's die. 50	50 Title of Bank. 50 Cupid and grindstone.	FIFTY
100 Compt's die. 100	100 Vig. Same as ones. Title of Bank.	100
500 Compt's die. 500	Female with eagle; ships in distance. Title of Bank.	Statue of Washington 500
Die Compt's die. Die.	1000 Cupid and grindstone. 1000 Title of Bank.	1000 Full length Female with anchor.
1 Compt's die. 1	1 Male figure and Indian on either side of a shield, on which is a view of N. Y. harbor; female raising drapery from shield. MANHATTAN CO., New York City. Man reclining.	ONE Indian erect.
2 Compt's die. 2	Vig. Same as ones. 2 MANHATTAN CO., New York City. Man reclining.	TWO Indian with bow.
3 Compt's die. 3	Vig. Same as ones. 3 MANHATTAN CO., New York City. Man reclining.	THREE Indian with bow.
FIVE Compt's die. 5	V Title of Bank. Vig. Same as ones.	5 Head of Indian.

Left end	Centre	Right end
TEN Head of Indian.	Compt's die. MANHATTAN CO., New York City. Vig. Same as ones.	TEN X 10
TWENTY 20	Vig. Female reclining with jar of water; Indian in canoe, trees, etc. in distance. Compt's die. MANHATTAN CO., New York City. Man reclining.	Indian in act of drawing arrow.
FIFTY Compt's die. Head of Indian.	MANHATTAN CO., New York City. 50 Vig. Same as 20s. 50 Man reclining.	FIFTY
100 Compt's die. 100	MANHATTAN CO., New York City. C Vig. Same as twenties. Man reclining.	100 Head of Indian. 100
500 Compt's die. D	Vig. Same as twenties. MANHATTAN CO., New York City. Man reclining.	500 500
1000 Head of Indian.	Compt's die. Vig. Same as twenties. MANHATTAN CO., New York City.	1000 Letter M, and words "one thousand" around it.
Female, man with horses and gleaning machine. Compt's die.	MAN. & MERCH. BK N. Y. City, Female seated with mechanical implements; buildings, etc.	1 Anchor, bales, etc.
2 Compt's die. TWO	Title of Bank. Sailor on beach; steamer, ships, etc., in distance.	2 Female portrait TWO
FIVE Female with sewing machine. FIVE	Title of Bank. Sailor and Indian either side of shield, surmounted by eagle. Red tinted 5 either side.	5 Compt's die. 5
Sailor, quadrant, capstan vessels, etc. 10	Title Eagle. Female seated with bale, cloth, etc.; pedestrians, buildings, falls, etc. in distance. Red X either side.	X Compt's die.

Left end	Centre	Right end
L Female seated; buildings FIFTY	Title of Bank. Shipping and dock scene in general. Compt's die.	50 Two sailors and female seated.
C 100	Female seated with wheels, bales, etc.; buildings and steamer in distance. Title of Bank. Female portrait. Compt's die.	100 Female with spinning wheel; buildings.
ONE Male portrait	Compt's die. Steamship. MARINE BANK, New York City.	1 1
TWO Indian on cliff 2	MARINE BANK TWO DOLLARS Compt's die Large 2 New York Large ship under full sail	2
3	View of a shipwreck, mariners, etc. Compt's die. MARINE BANK, New York City.	3 Male portrait
FIVE Mechanic seated and sailor with flag and quadrant.	Compt's die. Male portrait. MARINE BANK, New York City.	5 V
Sailor seated with nautical implements, &c.; shipping in distance. X	X Compt's die. MARINE BANK, New York City.	TEN Male portrait
20 Male portrait	Female reclining on bales of goods. MARINE BANK, New York City. XX	XX Compt's die. 20
L	Ship under full sail. Compt's die. MARINE BANK, New York City.	50 Male portrait
100 Ship wreck scene.	MARINE BANK, New York City. Compt's die.	C Male portrait

Left end	Centre	Right end
1 Female with flowers.	Drovers and cattle; cars, bridge, buildings, &c., in distance. MARKET BANK, New York City. Dog, key and safe.	1 Compt's die.
TWO Male and female seated; anvil, &c. 2	Steamship and other vessels. MARKET BANK, New York City. Eagle.	2 Compt's die.
Three females; anchor, etc. THREE	3 Milkmaid and cattle; houses and trees in distance. 3 MARKET BANK, New York City. Steamboat.	3 Compt's die.
5 Female portrait.	Female reclining on bale of merchandise; ships in distance. MARKET BANK, New York City.	Female seated, holding out fig. 5; ship in distance. Compt's die.
10 Female bust.	Train of cars; in distance two other trains; water scene, houses; trees, etc. MARKET BANK, New York City.	10 Compt's die.
Henry Clay seated; dog by his side. 20	Spread eagle. MARKET BANK, New York City.	20 Compt's die.
50	Cattle and sheep. Female portrait. MARKET BANK, New York City.	50 Compt's die.
100 Sailor with flag, [illegible], bale and quadrant.	Three females in clouds; ships on right. MARKET BANK, New York City.	100 Compt's die.
Compt's die on a large fig. 1.	ONE Two mechanics, anvil, etc.; cars and ship in distance. ONE MECHANICS' BANKING ASSOCIATION, New York City. Steamship.	Washington on a large figure 1.
TWO Compt's die Carpenter at his bench.	Figure 2 with portrait of Washington and word two. Title of Bank.	Stone cutter seated. 2

Left end	Centre	Right end
Two females; figure 3 between them.	3 Indian princess, surrounded by flags, drums, cannon, etc. Title of Bank. Arm.	3
5 Female, eagle, safe, etc. FIVE	V Three females and a fig. 5; cars, shipping, etc., in distance. V Title of Bank. Arm.	5 Med. Head. FIVE
10 Same as fives TEN	Two females on either side of a shield; cars, buildings, canal, shipping, &c., in distance Title of Bank. Arm.	10 Two females, eagle etc. TEN
TWENTY Same as fives TWENTY	20 Female seated at table, scientific apparatus on her right; steamer in distance. 20 Title of Bank. Arm.	Die. XX Die
FIFTY Female seated; steamboat on right 50	Two Indians, and white man with gun. Medallion head and word fifty on either side of vig. Title of Bank. Arm.	FIFTY Female seated; house in distance. 50
HUNDRED Figure of Justice. 100	Two females on either side of a shield, surmounted by an eagle; shipping in distance. Med. head and figs. 100 on either side of vig. Title of Bank Arm.	ONE HUNDRED
500 Same as fives 500	500 Train of cars; steamboat and other vessels in distance. Title of Bank. Arm.	500
1000 Same as fives 1000	1000 Steamship, row boat, other vessels and view of city. Title of Bank. Arm.	ONE THOUSAND
Arm. ONE	1 Male and female; mechanical implements; ship, cars and bridge in distance. 1 MECHANICS' BANK, New York City. Horse.	Female. Compt's die. Female.
TWO Cooper at work. TWO	2 Vig. Same as ones. 2 MECHANICS' BANK, New York City. Locomotive.	Washington. Compt's die. Male portrait.

Left end	Centre	Right end
3 Compt's die. 3	3 Archimedes raising the world. MECHANICS' BANK, New York City. Arm.	3
5 Compt's die. 5	5 Vig. Same as three. MECHANICS' BANK, New York City. Arm.	V
Figure of Blacksmith TEN	MECHANICS BANK, 10 Eagle on rock. 10 TEN DOLLARS. City of New York.	10 Compt's die
10 Compt's die.	MECHANICS' BANK, New York City. Mechanic with hammer and anvil; buildings in distance. Red figs 10 on either side.	10
Figure of Justice, with sword and scales 20	20 Compt's die 20 MECHANICS BANK. TWENTY DOLLARS on XX City of New York.	Figure of blacksmith 20
Medallion head and word twenty. Compt's die.	20 Vig. Same as threes. MECHANICS' BANK, New York City. Arm.	20
50 50	MECHANICS' BANK, New York City. Arm and hammer.	Compt's die 50
100 Compt's die.	MECHANICS' BANK, New York City. Arm and hammer.	100 100
500	MECHANICS' BANK, New York City. 500 Female reclining. FIVE HUNDRED	Arm and hammer.
1000	1000 Vig. Same as threes. MECHANICS' BANK, New York City. ONE THOUSAND.	Arm and hammer.

Left	Centre	Right
1 Compt's die 1	Male with anvil ONE and hammer; ONE two females; ship on right, etc. MECH. & TRA. B'K. in the city of N. Y. ONE DOLLAR Arms	1 Clock 1
2 Compt's die 2	2 Vig. Same as ones. Title of Bank.	2 2
3 Compt's die 3	Vig. Same as ones. 3 Title of Bank.	3 Clock. 3
Vulcan with anvil and hammer and two females. V	5 Five Dollars Figure of Justice with scales; shipping in distance. MECHANICS' & TRADERS' BANK, New York City. Ship.	5 Compt's die. 5
5 Compt's die. 5	5 5 Title of Bank. Vig. Same as ones.	FIVE Female leaning on an urn 5
10 Compt's die. 10	Blacksmith with hammer and anvil. 10 Title of Bank.	Female with liberty cap, leaning on cornucopia. X
20 Compt's die 20	Male and female figure with frame between them enclosing three cupids. Title of Bank.	20 Mercury reclining on a bale. 20
50 Compt's die. 50	50 Two Cupids with globe and chart. 50 Title of Bank.	50 FIFTY 50
100 Compt's die. 100	100 Title of Bank.	Male and female; male with sickle.
ONE Female holding fig. 1, leaning on bale of merchandise.	Cupid. Compt's die. 1 MERCANTILE B'K., New York City.	ONE Female holding flag with emblematic figures around her.

Left	Centre	Right
TWO Indian female holding spear and bow	2 Compt's die. Cupid and fig. 2. MERCANTILE B'K., New York City.	TWO Female with fruit and flowers.
THREE Female with wheat in hand.	Cupid and fig. 3. Compt's die. Cupid and fig. 3. MERCANTILE B'K., New York City.	THREE Same as 3s.
FIVE	5 Female reclining with shield, anchor, and the word "Hope"; cars and building in distance. Compt's die. MERCANTILE B'K., New York City. Mechanic with hammer.	5 V 5
10 Mechanic with hammer. 10	X Emblematic group of females in clouds; one with keys. Compt's die. MERCANTILE B'K., New York City.	TEN
50	Female with eagle, shield, portrait of Washington, etc. Compt's die. MERCANTILE B'K., New York City.	50 Human figure with spear and shield.
100 Figure of Justice.	Compt's die. Female with pole, cap and eagle; letter C on shield. MERCANTILE B'K., New York City.	100
Male portrait Compt's die	(☞ Have Lyman's Protection.) ONE 1 MERCHANTS' BANK N. Y. City,	1 1 Title across large fig. 1.
Compt's die with word Two above and below and fig. 2 on right.	Male portrait 2 2 Title across large 2.	2
Compt's die. 3	Title of Bank. Child's head	3
5	V Child's portrait MERCHANT'S BANK,	5 Compt's die.

Left	Centre	Right
5 Compt's die. 5	5 Mercury seated with cornucopia and wand; safe, lion, etc.; cars, canal scene, vessels, etc., in distance. 5 MERCHANTS' BANK New York City. Bank building.	Male portrait Female erect building in distance.
10 Compt's die. 10	X Vig. Same as fives. X MERCHANTS' BANK New York City. Bank building.	Die. 10 Die
20 Compt's die. 20	20 Vig. Same as fives. 20 MERCHANTS' BANK New York City. Die.	Sea monsters Vessels. Sea monsters
50 Compt's die. 50	50 Vig. Same as fives. 50 MERCHANTS' BANK New York City. Die.	Sea monsters Same as fives Sea monsters
100 Compt's die. 100	C Vig. Same as fives. C MERCHANTS' BANK New York City. Bank building.	100 Boy's head. 100
Die Compt's die. Die.	Figs. 500, with Cupids on each figure. MERCHANTS' BANK New York City. Bank building.	Same as vig of fives. 500
1 Compt's die. ONE	MER. EX. BANK, New York City. Female seated with cornucopia and wand; bbls., quadrant, etc.; in distance vessels, buildings, cars, canal, &c.	1 Ship and other vessel.
TWO	MER. EX. BANK, New York City. Vig. Same as ones. Compt's die.	2 Female seated; buildings in distance.
Compt's die. THREE	MER. EX. BANK, New York City. Vig. Same as ones.	3 Mercury with wand, bag of coin and cornucopia.
FIVE	Vig. Same as ones. Compt's die. MER. EX. BANK, New York City.	5 Sailor leaning on capstan; masts in background.

Left	Centre	Right
10	Steamship and other vessels. Compt's die. MER. EX. BANK, New York City.	10 Female with flag, and 3 cupids.
Compt's die. Mercury seated between 2 and 0.	Spread eagle; steamship and other vessels in distance. MER. EX. BANK, New York City.	20 Female seated between a 2 and 0.
50 Female with spear and twig and a shield.	Compt's die. Female crowning eagle with wreath, right hand on portrait of Washington, in distance, vessels, cars, buildings, etc. MER. EX. BANK, New York City.	50 Ship and other vessels.
Compt's die. 100	Female, eagle, safe, balances, etc.; cars, buildings, and vessels. MER. EX. BANK, New York City.	100 Female seated; building in distance.
1 Compt's die.	METROPOLITAN BK New York City. Words "one dollar" over portrait of Washington in large die	1 Die.
2 Compt's die.	METROPOLITAN BK New York City. Words "two dollars" over a male portrait in large die.	2 Die
3 Compt's die.	METROPOLITAN BK New York City. Words "three dollars" over a male portrait in large die.	3 3
5 Compt's die.	METROPOLITAN BK New York City. Vig. Three females representing the Arts and Sciences; building in distance.	5 FIVE
Compt's die. 10	METROPOLITAN BK New York City. Vig. Three females in clouds.	10 X
Compt's die. Figure of buckles, coins, etc.	50 View of a building. 50 METROPOLITAN BK New York City.	FIFTY DOLLARS

Left	Centre	Right
100 Female seated with pole and cap; flowers, etc.	Compt's Die. Female reclining on a part of City Arms; vessels in distance. 100 METROPOLITAN BK New York City.	ONE HUNDRED C
500 Female erect and flowers.	500 Vig. Female reclining with pole, cap, eagle, drapery, &c.; vessels in distance. METROPOLITAN BK New York City. View of sunrise.	500 Compt's die
1000 Female with spear and shield; owl, globe, &c.	Compt's die. Female reclining with scroll, globe, etc.; ship and steamer in distance. METROPOLITAN BK New York City. View of sunrise.	1000
1 Franklin.	Faust, Guttenburg and Schoeffer, chests, wheels, books, etc. NASSAU BANK, New York City.	ONE Compt's die. 1
2 Compt's die. TWO	Steamer at sea. NASSAU BANK, New York City.	TWO Female portrait with grain. 2
3 Compt's die. 3	Five persons representing Agriculture, Manufacturers and Commerce. NASSAU BANK, New York City.	THREE Full length female figure with sickle and cornucopia; sheaf by her side.
5 Stone cutter at work.	Compt's die. View of the N. Y. Crystal Palace. NASSAU BANK, New York City.	FIVE V
TEN Compt's die	View of the Battery, Castle Garden and Governor's Island, New York city. NASSAU BANK, New York City.	X X
20 Compt's die	Vig. Same as tens. NASSAU BANK, New York City.	XX
L	Female reclining on a bale of merchandise; steamship and yacht in distance. NASSAU BANK, New York City.	50 Compt's die.

Left	Centre	Right
100 One hundred Compt's die.	Hunter with dog and gun warming himself by a fire, enclosed in a large ornamental letter C. NASSAU BANK, New York City.	C Dollars
1 Compt's die. 1	1 Male portrait. 1 NATIONAL BANK, New York City.	Statue of Washington.
2 Compt's die. 2	2 Male portrait. 2 NATIONAL BANK, New York City.	Statue of Washington.
3 Compt's die. 3	THREE Male portrait. THREE NATIONAL BANK, New York City.	3 Eagle. 3
Statue of Washington. FIVE	5 Compt's die. Male portrait NATIONAL BANK, New York City.	5 Female feeding an eagle.
10 Compt's die. 10	TEN TEN NATIONAL BANK, New York City. Vig. Female feeding an eagle.	Ten Dollars Statue of Washington.
20 Compt's die. 20	Female feeding an eagle. 20 NATIONAL BANK, New York City.	Statue of Washington.
50 Compt's die. 50	50 50 NATIONAL BANK, New York City.	Female feeding an eagle. Eagle.
100 Female feeding an eagle. Eagle.	100 Compt's die. 100 NATIONAL BANK, New York City.	Statue of Washington.
Female feeding an eagle. Compt's die.	1000 1000 NATIONAL BANK, New York City.	1000 Statue of Washington.

ONE ONE Compt's die.	Large vessel; ship and steamship on left. NEW-YORK COUNTY BANK, New-York City, N. Y. Female bathing.	1 Portrait of boy.

2 Compt's die. 2	Coat-of-Arms of the City of New-York. Title of Bank.	2 Portrait of a boy.

V Soldier with a musket.	State Arms. Title of Bank. Ducks.	5 Compt's die 5

10 Men shearing sheep.	Farmers at work loading hay. Title of Bank.	10 Compt's die.

20 XX	Indian in a canoe. Title of Bank. Compt's die.	20 Stay.

1 Female reclining; scroll globe, pole, cap, etc.	N. Y. EX. BANK, New York City. Vig. Female seated, with pole and cap; Compt's die on her left.	1 Female seated with balances.

TWO Male erect; female seated.	N. Y. EX. BANK, New York City. 2 2 Compt's die.	TWO Male erect; female seated.

3 Female beside bales, shield, etc.	N. Y. EXCH. BANK 3 New York 3 3 Compt's die 3	3 Female with sword beside shield.

3 Female reclining on a view of cars, mountains, &c	N. Y. EX. BANK, New York City. Compt's die.	3 Female seated in oval frame.

5 Compt's die. FIVE	N. Y. EX. BANK, New York City. Females and Cupids surrounding figure 5.	5 Male bust. FIVE

TEN Compt's die TEN	N. Y. EX. BANK, New York City. Steamship and other vessels.	10 Washington.

20 Compt's die. TWENTY	N. Y. EX. BANK, New York City. Train of cars; buildings, etc.	20 Female portrait.

50 Compt's die. FIFTY	N. Y. EX. BANK, New York City. Drover and cattle.	50 Female portrait.

100 Compt's die. 100	N. Y. EX. BANK, New York City. Female, harbor, city, etc.	100 Head of little girl.

ONE Compt's die. ONE	Hendrick Hudson landing in 1609; ship, etc. ONE ONE NORTH RIVER BK., New York City. Medallion Head.	Male portrait 1 Male portrait

TWO Compt's die TWO	2 Female, shield, indian, etc. 2 NORTH RIVER BK., New York City. Ship.	Washington. Male portrait

THREE Compt's die. THREE	3 Neptune, ship, etc. 3 NORTH RIVER BK., New York City.	Washington. Jefferson. Madison.

FIVE Compt's die. FIVE	5 Vig. Same as ones. 5 NORTH RIVER BK., New York City.	FIVE FIVE

TEN Compt's die. TEN	10 State Arms; cars and ship in distance. 10 NORTH RIVER BK., New York City.	X Ship. X

TWENTY Compt's die. TWENTY	20 Female seated, sheaf, cattle, etc. 20 NORTH RIVER BK., New York City	TWENTY

FIFTY Female 50	50 Two females; cars and vessels in distance. 50 NORTH RIVER BK., New York City. Steamboat.	50 Female portrait. 50

Washington. Sailor and blacksmith.	Compt's die. Two females, eagle, shield, etc. NORTH RIVER BK., New York City.	50 Male portrait

C	Steamship. Compt's die. NORTH RIVER BK. New York City.	100 Male portrait

Hundred Female Justice. 100	100 Two females, eagle and shield. 100 NORTH RIVER BK., New York City.	100 Med. Head. 100

1 ONE Compt's die	Neptune seated on sea-shell. pointing to vessels on the right 1 OCEAN BANK ONE DOLLAR New York Sea Dragon	Secured, etc. Large ship under sail ONE

II Man and female in row-boat.	OCEAN BANK, New York City. Vig. Same as ones.	II Compt's die Sailor seated

III 3 Female seated.	OCEAN BANK, New York City. Vig. Same as ones.	Die. 3 Die.

5 Sailor at wheel.	Ship loading; dray, boxes; sailor with glass; steamer and other vessels in distance. OCEAN BANK, New York City.	5 Compt's die 5

5 Compt's die. Word five and figure 5 across.	Vig. Neptune, steamship, &c. OCEAN BANK, New York City	FIVE Female erect on a rock; lighthouse, etc. FIVE

Sailor and letter X. Compt's die.	OCEAN BANK, New York City. Vig. Same as ones. Ship.	10 10

<table>
<tr><td>20
Compt's die.
TWENTY</td><td>OCEAN BANK,
New York City.
Vig. Same as ones.
Ship.</td><td>20
Dolphin.
TWENTY</td></tr>
<tr><td>50
Compt's die.
50</td><td>Vig. Same as ones.
OCEAN BANK,
New York City.</td><td>View of the bank building.
FIFTY</td></tr>
<tr><td>C
Compt's die.</td><td>Vig. Same as ones
OCEAN BANK,
New York City.</td><td>Indian.
100</td></tr>
<tr><td>1
Compt's die.</td><td>ORIENTAL BANK,
New York City.
Wood cutter seated, gold dollar on right; horse, wagon, trees, etc in distance.
Bird.</td><td>ONE
Oriental female reclining, playing with a bird; a fan in her right hand; fountain in background.</td></tr>
<tr><td>2
Same as on right of 1s.</td><td>ORIENTAL BANK,
New York City.
Compt's die. Farmer and milkmaid seated; two gold dollars, house cattle and trees in distance.
Bird.</td><td>2</td></tr>
<tr><td>3
Compt's die.
THREE</td><td>ORIENTAL BANK,
New York City.
Farmer, sailor and mechanic; three gold dollars on the ground.
Bird.</td><td>3
Same as ones</td></tr>
<tr><td>5
Two Elephants.
Compt's die.</td><td>Indian female, hunter with gun, five gold dollars and three cupids.
ORIENTAL BANK,
New York City.
Bird.</td><td>5
Same as ones</td></tr>
<tr><td>10
Machinists at work; ship and factory.
Compt's die.</td><td>ORIENTAL BANK,
New York City.
Machinist resting against piece of machinery with tools in his hand.
Bird.</td><td>TEN
Same as ones</td></tr>
<tr><td>XX
Female portrait.
Compt's die.</td><td>ORIENTAL BANK,
New York City.
View of ship yard, with two vessels on weighs.
Bird.</td><td>20
Same as ones</td></tr>
<tr><td>50
Compt's die.
FIFTY</td><td>Architect lying against fallen column with plans before him, compass in his hand; in the background, piece of architecture, two men, man with truck and horse.
ORIENTAL BANK,
New York City.
Bird.</td><td>50
Same as ones</td></tr>
</table>

<table>
<tr><td>100
Compt's die.
Female swimming with arm around neck of swan</td><td>Female reclining against box, bale and bbl.; shipping in distance.
ORIENTAL BANK,
New York City.
Bird.</td><td>100
Same as ones</td></tr>
<tr><td>1
Compt's die.
Dolphin.</td><td>Female reclining holding a fig. 1; cars and steamboat in distance.
PACIFIC BANK,
New York City.
City Arms.</td><td>1
Steamship.
ONE</td></tr>
<tr><td>Figure 2 supported by two mythological figures.
Steamship.</td><td>Compt's die. Train of cars.
PACIFIC BANK,
New York City.
City Arms.</td><td>2
Two dolphins</td></tr>
<tr><td>THREE
3
Compt's die.</td><td>Ship under full sail, vessels in distance
PACIFIC BANK,
New York City.
City Arms</td><td>Shell.
3
Steamship and dolphin.</td></tr>
<tr><td>5
FIVE
Compt's die</td><td>Sailor seated on ground beside barrels bales, etc. Ships in the distance.
PACIFIC BANK
FIVE DOLLARS
New York
City Arms</td><td>FIVE
Steamship.
5
Shipping.
FIVE</td></tr>
<tr><td>TEN
Compt's die
TEN</td><td>10 Two females, one crowning bust of Washington with wreath, bales, sheaf, etc.
PACIFIC BANK,
New York City.
City Arms.</td><td>TEN
Boy holding a shell, his foot on a dolphin.
TEN</td></tr>
<tr><td>XX
Compt's die.
20</td><td>Female reclining, right arm on a view of steamboat, &c.; cornucopia, safe, etc.; cars and steamship in distance.
PACIFIC BANK,
New York City.
City Arms.</td><td>20
Vessel.
TWENTY</td></tr>
<tr><td>50
Two dolphins
Compt's die.</td><td>Female with globe, quadrant, chart, book, pen and ink; shipping and factory in distance. 50
PACIFIC BANK,
New York City.
Steamship</td><td>Bale of goods.
City Arms.
Train of cars.</td></tr>
<tr><td>100
Compt's die.
Two ornamental male and female figures.</td><td>Female with eagle, shield, safe, &c; agricultural implements in background. 100
PACIFIC BANK,
New York City.
City Arms.</td><td>Ship.
Shell.
100</td></tr>
<tr><td>Sailor by side of shield, bbls. &c.
Compt's die.</td><td>PARK BANK,
New York City
Word one and figure 1. Word one and figure 1.
View of Park Fountain, and the City Hall.</td><td>Indian on cliff.
ONE</td></tr>
</table>

<table>
<tr><td>TWO
Compt's die.
Spread eagle and shield.</td><td>PARK BANK.
New York City.
View of Park, City Hall, Hall of Records, etc;</td><td>2
Portrait of girl.</td></tr>
<tr><td>Compt's die.
Mexican lassoing wild cattle.</td><td>PARK BANK,
New York City.
3 Three gold dollars. 3
Steamships and ships at sea.</td><td>3
Drove of cattle, sheep, hogs, &c.; house in distance.</td></tr>
<tr><td>5
Sailor and Indian seated by side of shield; eagle at top.</td><td>PARK BANK,
New York City.
Five cherubs and five silver dollars.
5</td><td>5
Compt's die
FIVE</td></tr>
<tr><td>10
Portrait of girl.</td><td>PARK BANK,
New York City.
Female seated with nine cherubs, shield, cornucopia and ten gold dollars; locomotive and steamboat in distance.</td><td>TEN
Sailor, bales, barrels.
Compt's die</td></tr>
<tr><td>TWENTY
Full length female with sword and scales.</td><td>PARK BANK,
New York City.
Three females representing agriculture, commerce and manufactures; ship in distance.
— Compt's die.</td><td>XX
Sailor and Indian seated by shield.</td></tr>
<tr><td>FIFTY
Full length female with spear and shield.</td><td>PARK BANK.
New York City.
Female and eagle in clouds, surrounded by American flag.
Compt's die.</td><td>50
Portrait of Washington</td></tr>
<tr><td>100
Male portrait</td><td>PARK BANK,
New York City.
View of the New York City Hall.
Compt's die.</td><td>100
Steamship.</td></tr>
<tr><td>500
Male portrait</td><td>PARK BANK,
New York City.
Sailor and Indian by side of shield; two females by side of State Arms; shipping in distance.
Compt's die.</td><td>500
D</td></tr>
<tr><td>1000
Sailor erect, flag, &c.</td><td>PARK BANK,
New York City.
Steamship at sea in storm.
Compt's die.</td><td>M</td></tr>
<tr><td>ONE
Compt's die.
Word one and fig. 1.</td><td>Train of cars passing under a bridge.
PEOPLE'S BANK.
New York City.</td><td>1
Portrait of Taylor.</td></tr>
</table>

TWO Compt's die. TWO	View of the bank building with sign on top. PEOPLES BANK, New York City.	2 Male portrait

3 Compt's die. THREE	Mechanic seated on machinery with hammer on his shoulder; cars and factory in distance. Title of Bank running around the vignette.	3 Male portrait

FI V VE Compt's die. FI V VE	One of the Peoples Line of steamers, with flag on it and words "Peoples Line." Dock on the right. PEOPLES BANK, New York City.	FIVE Portrait of Franklin

TEN Compt's die. 10	Female and Goddess of Liberty seated; ship on left; cars, sheaf, &c., on right. Title of Bank running around vignette.	X Head of Washington.

20 Compt's die.	Female representing Commerce, resting right arm on a bale of goods; shipping on the right. PEOPLES BANK, New York City. Eagle.	20 Male portrait

50 Compt's die.	Spread eagle, his feet on an olive branch and Am. shield. Title of Bank running over the shield. Horse.	50 Male portrait

100 Male portrait	Large steamship with shipping on right and left. Title of Bank running over the vignette.	100 Compt's die.

1 Compt's die. 1	1 Spread eagle. 1 PHENIX BANK, New York City.	1

2 Compt's die. 2	2 Spread eagle. 2 PHENIX BANK, New York City.	2

3 Compt's die. 3	3 Spread eagle. 3 PHENIX BANK, New York City.	3

5	Spread eagle. PHENIX BANK, New York City.	5 Compt's die. 5

10 Compt's die. 10	Spread eagle. PHENIX BANK, New York City.	10

20 Compt's die. 20	XX PHENIX BANK, New York City.	Spread eagle

50 Spread eagle.	Compt's die. 50 PHENIX BANK, New York City.	50

100	C Spread eagle. C PHENIX BANK, New York City.	100 Compt's die. 100

Compt's die.	500 Spread eagle. PHENIX BANK, New York City.	D

1000 Compt's die.	Spread eagle. PHENIX BANK, New York City.	M

Goddess of Liberty. Compt's die.	1 Female seated with frame on which is agricultural implements, &c.; shipping in distance. SEVENTH WARD BK New York City. Vessels.	1 Steamer. ONE

2 Compt's die. TWO	Female seated with mechanical implements; on right in distance cars and bridge; on left ship building. SEVENTH WARD BK New York City. Steamship.	2 Man-of-war. TWO

3 Compt's die. THREE	Male and female in sea car drawn by horses; man and female on left of car; steamship and steamboat in distance. SEVENTH WARD BK New York City. Steamship.	3 Ship building THREE

5 5	Title of Bank. 5 Female seated receiving horn of gold from Mercury; eagle on right of female. Eagle.	5 Compt's die. 5

10 Jefferson. 10	Launch of a vessel. Title of Bank. Launch of a vessel. Vig. Same as fives.	10 Compt's die 10

20 Female with book, torch, eagle and portrait. XX	XX Vig. Same as fives. XX SEVENTH WARD BK New York City.	20 Compt's die. 20

50 Compt's die. 50	50 Vig. Same as fives. 50 SEVENTH WARD BK New York City.	New York Safety Fund. Same as on left of 20s 50

100 Compt's die. 100	Washington. Title of Bank Male portrait. Vig. Same as fives.	100 Launch of a vessel. 100

FIVE HUNDRED	Compt's die. Vig. Same as fives. SEVENTH WARD BK New York City.	500 Launch of a vessel.

Compt's die. Launch of a vessel.	Vig. Same as fives. SEVENTH WARD BK New York City. 1000	1000 Launch of a vessel.

1 Female Portrait.	Men on horses catching wild cattle with lasso. SHOE & LEATH. BK. New York City. Spread Eagle.	1 Compt's die.

Compt's die. 2	SHOE & LEATH. BK. New York City. Vig. Same as ones. Steamboat.	2 Female Portrait.

Man carrying leather. Compt's die.	3 Vig. Same as ones. SHOE & LEATH. BK. New York City. Steamship.	3 Female portrait.

5 — FIVE — Two female children. | SHOE & LEATH. BK. New York City. Men on horses lassooing wild cattle. 5 5 | 5 — Compt's die.

X — 10 | Men on horses lassooing wild cattle. Female portrait. SHOE & LEATH. BK, New York City. Bee hive. | 10 — Compt's die.

Figure of Mercury holding bag of coin. — 20 | Same as ones. SHOE & LEATH. BK. New York City. 20 | 20 — Compt's die.

50 — Male head. | SHOE & LEATH. BK. New York City. Vig. Same as ones. | 50 — Compt's die.

Male head. — ONE — 100 | SHOE & LEATH. BK. New York City. HUNDRED. Vig. Same as ones. | 100 — Compt's die.

ONE — Male portrait. — Compt's die. | 1 View of the St. Nicholas Hotel. 1 ST. NICHOLAS B'K., New York City. Game Cock. | ONE — Santa Claus filling the stockings. — ONE

TWO — Male portrait. — Compt's die. | 2 Santa Claus riding over tops of houses. 2 ST. NICHOLAS B'K., New York City. Game Cock. | Merchandise. — City Arms. — Merchandise.

THREE — Male portrait. — Compt's die. | View of the St. Nicholas Hotel. 3 on left. ST. NICHOLAS B'K., New York City. Cock. | 3 — Santa Claus filling the stockings.

Compt's die. | Santa Claus in sleigh drawn by reindeers. ST. NICHOLAS B'K., New York City. Eagle. | 5 — Male portrait.

10 — Compt's die. | Santa Claus with sleigh and reindeer. ST. NICHOLAS B'K., New York City. Bee hive. | 10 — Bank building.

20 — Children asleep in bed; Santa Claus entering from chimney. | ST. NICHOLAS B'K., New York City. Compt's die. | 20 — Male portrait.

50 — Compt's die. | ST. NICHOLAS B'K., New York City. Children asleep in bed; Santa Claus entering from chimney. | 50 — Male portrait.

Compt's die. | U. S. Capitol; pedestrians, horses, carriages, etc. ST. NICHOLAS B'K., New York City. Gamecock. | 100 — Male portrait.

1 — Farmer with bundle under his arm, dog, horse, etc. | TRADESMEN'S B'K., New York City. Blacksmith shoeing horse; man seated on log; man in background. | 1 — Compt's die.

2 — Blacksmith's boy at forge. | Portrait of boy. 2 Portrait of girl. TRADESMEN'S B'K., New York City. | 2 — Compt's die.

3 — Two men at work on frame of cart. | Compt's die. Sailor seated on anchor smoking pipe, and apparently conversing with two others; ship in distance. TRADESMEN'S B'K., New York City. | 3 — Portrait of little girl.

5 — Compt's die. | Sailor reclining against bale of goods, supporting flag; vessels and light-house in distance. TRADESMEN'S B'K., New York City. | Figure 5, and large letter V, on this end.

X — Compt's die. | Stone cutter seated with mallet, chisel, etc. TRADESMEN'S B'K., New York City. | Figs. 10, and large letter X on this end.

TEN — Female with tablets; child at her feet. | X Sailor and two farmers; ship in distance. TRADESMENS' B'K. N. Y. City. | 10 — Compt's die.

TWENTY — Compt's die. | Eagle and figs. 20 on shield. Bull's head; horse, shipping, etc. TRADESMEN'S B'K., New York City. | TWENTY

Indian female, shield and eagle; steamer in distance. — XX | Compt's die. Title of Bank. | 20 — Cooper at work.

FIFTY — Female with sword and shield. — FIFTY | Compt's die. Man buying paper from boy; bales, barrels, etc. Title of Bank. | 50 — Female.

Compt's die. — 50 | 50 Vig. Same as twenties. TRADESMEN'S B'K., New York City. | FIFTY

C — 100 | Title of Bank. Compt's die. Sailor and Indian on either side of shield; eagle at top. | 100 — Female seated on bale with sword and cap; child at her feet.

ONE HUNDRED | 100 Vig. Same as 20s. 100 TRADESMEN'S B'K., New York City. | Med. head — Compt's die. — Med. head.

5 — Compt's die. — 5 | V Female reclining; vase of flowers, eagle, etc. V UNION BANK, New York City. Secured, etc. | FIVE — Figure 5 and a female. — FIVE

10 — Compt's die. — 10 | 10 Vig. Same as fives. UNION BANK, New York City. Secured, etc. | 10 — Female seated. — TEN

20 — Female seated. — TWENTY | Compt's die. 20 Vig. Same as ones. UNION BANK, New York City. Secured, etc. | 20 — Female seated. — TWENTY

50 — Compt's die. — 50 | 50 Vig. Same as fives. 50 UNION BANK, New York City. Secured, etc. | 50 — Female in oval frame. — 50

C — Compt's die. — C | 100 Vig. Same as fives. UNION BANK, New York City. Secured, etc. | 100

Die work. D Female seated feeding an eagle; clouds, etc. D 500
Compt's die.
UNION BANK,
New York City.
Die work Secured, &c.

Die work M Female seated with pole and cap; on her right shield with the words "Manufacturers and Commerce," over it; cornucopia at her feet; steamboat and cars in distance. M 1000
Compt's die.
Die work Title of Bank.
Secured, etc.

ONE on med. head. Spread eagle on shield in clouds. 1
ONE ADDISON BANK,
Addison, N. Y.
Compt's die. One Dollar One Dollar Female.

TWO TWO TWO 2 Rafting scene—man in boat with two birds; five males, female and child on raft; another raft in distance. 2 TWO TWO TWO
Compt's die.
TWO ADDISON BANK,
Addison, N. Y. TWO on med. head.
Two Dollars Two Dollars

F I V V E ADDISON BANK,
Addison, N. Y. 5
Three females with sickle, quadrant, cornucopia and compass. Compt's die.
Portrait of Martha Washington
Five Dollars Five Dollars FIVE

---

10 on med. head. ADDISON BANK,
Addison, N. Y. 10
Portrait of Washington; female, train of cars, scythe and grain on right; female, anchor, barrels, men and ship on left.
Male portrait Compt's die
Ten Dollars Ten Dollars

---

1 Compt's die 1 ALBANY
One male and two
CITY female BANK
figures
ONE DOLLAR
Building
O N E

Compt's die Indian, globe, city, female, eagle, &c. 1
ALBANY CITY BK.,
Albany, N. Y.
Head.

Compt's die. Vig. Indian and female with American eagle on the world over capitol. 2
Portrait of female. ALBANY CITY B'K.
Albany, N. Y.

---

2 2 Male, two females, anvil, sledge, etc. 2 TWO
Compt's die. ALBANY CITY BK.,
Albany, N. Y.
2 House.

Males, females, anvil, etc. Building. 3 3
ALBANY CITY BK., Compt's die.
Albany, N. Y.
3 3

---

3 Vig. Female pointing to shipping in distance. 3
Compt's die. ALBANY CITY B'K.
Albany, N. Y.

---

5 5 5 Capital.
Vig. Same as ones
Compt's die. 5
5 ALBANY CITY B'K
Albany, N. Y. Dwelling with trees.

---

10 X in wreath
ALBANY CITY B'K.
Compt's die. Albany, N. Y. Capital.
X X
10 Vig. Same as ones. 10

---

20 20 XX Male, two females, anvil and sledge.
Compt's die. ALBANY CITY BK.,
Albany, N. Y.
20 20

---

20 20
20 ALBANY CITY B'K. 20
Albany, N. Y.
Compt's die. Medallion head.
Vig. Female with wheat; cars in distance.
20 Capitol 20

---

50 House in die; words Fifty Dollars around it. 50 on right. Same as 20s.
Compt's die. ALBANY CITY BK.,
Albany, N. Y.
50 50

ONE HUNDRED Males, females, anvil, etc. 100 Build'ing. 100
Title of Bank C

---

1 Vig. Three artisans, shipping in distance. 1 ONE
ALBANY Compt's die.
EXCHANGE BANK,
Albany, N. Y.
Male portrait Female portrait Female portrait.

---

2 ALBANY EX. BANK 2
Female representing Liberty; child, etc. Compt's die
Male portrait TWO DOLLARS 2

---

5 V Vig. female seated in figure 5, females on either side. V 5
Compt's die ALBANY Medallion head.
EXCHANGE BANK,
FIVE Albany, N. Y. FIVE
Building.

---

10 Vig. Shield with female on either side, cars, shipping and buildings in distance. 10
Compt's die ALBANY State Arms
EXCHANGE BANK,
TEN Albany, N. Y. TEN
Building.

FIFTY Two Indians and boy; vessels on left in distance and on right a wood. On each side of vig. is a medallion head and word "Fifty" on it. FIFTY
Female with pole and cap. Female reclining with mechanical implements.
50 ALBANY EX. BANK
Albany, N. Y. 50
Building.

HUNDRED Two females reclining; eagle, &c.; vessels on left and bridge on right. Figs. 100 on med. head, on each side of vig. ONE HUNDRED
Justice. Title of Bank.
100 Building.

STATE OF N. YORK
1 Cannon, balls, bales, anchors, etc.; shipping in distance 1
ALONZO WOOD & CO.'S BK
ONE DOLLAR
Compt's die Eldridge Male portrait

STATE OF N. YORK
TWO Farming scene; mowing machine, horse rake, men, boy, wagon, etc. 2
Compt's die ALONZO WOOD & CO.S BK
TWO DOLLARS Two men, cloth, etc.
TWO Eldridge

---

1 1 Shipping. 1 Full length female on a large figure 1.
Compt's die. ATLANTIC BANK,
Brooklyn, N. Y.
1 Shield with anchor on it.

---

2 2 Shipping. 2 Liberty with cap, pole and cornucopia, standing in a large ornamental fig. 2
Compt's die. ATLANTIC BANK,
Brooklyn, N. Y.
2 Shield with anchor on it

---

3 3 Vig. Same as 1s 3 Female with flowers standing in a large ornamental fig. 3
Compt's die. ATLANTIC BANK,
Brooklyn, N. Y.
3 Shield with anchor on it.

---

5 5 Neptune riding in a sea shell on the sea drawn by two horses, female by his side. 5 FIVE
Compt's die. Ships.
5 ATLANTIC BANK,
Brooklyn, N. Y. FIVE
Sea shell.

10 X Vig. Same as fives. X TEN
Compt's die. ATLANTIC BANK, Brooklyn, N. Y. Shipping.
10 Sea shell. TEN

20 XX Vig. Same as 5s. XX 20
Compt's die. ATLANTIC BANK, Brooklyn, N. Y. Shipping.
20 Sea shell. XX

50 ATLANTIC BANK, Brooklyn, N. Y. 50
Compt's die. Vig. Same as 5s.
50 Letter L in med. die work 50

Compt's die. 100 Vig. Same as fives. 100
ATLANTIC BANK, Brooklyn, N. Y.
100 Sea shell. 100

Compt's die. 500 - Vig. Same as fives.
ATLANTIC BANK, Brooklyn, N. Y. 500
500

1000 Vig. Same as fives. 1000 Compt's die.
ATLANTIC BANK, Brooklyn, N. Y.
1000

ONE Compt's die. Rain bow and falls; female seated with one hand on figure 1; U. S. shield, &c. 1
AUBURN CITY BANK, Auburn, N. Y.
Full length female. Emblems of commerce and agriculture. Female portrait.

TWO Compt's die. Vig. Two females, figure 2 between them liberty pole, cap and balances. 2
Female holding liberty pole and cap; eagle feeding, horn of plenty. AUBURN CITY BANK, Auburn, N. Y. Female seated. Female portrait.

3 Fig. 3 on bale; female with distaff on left; two females on right. 3 THREE
Female portrait. AUBURN CITY BK., Auburn, N. Y. Female erect with shield, cap, etc.
Compt's die.

5 Vig. Ornamental 5 in centre; five females, sword, balances, &c.; horn of plenty, locomotive and building, in background; shipping in distance. 5
Compt's die.
FIVE AUBURN CITY BANK, Auburn, N. Y. Washington.

TEN Compt's die. Vig. Female reclining, eagle at her back, globe and liberty cap; shipping in distance. 10
Full length Indian, with bow, arrows and spear. Male portrait.
AUBURN CITY BANK, Auburn, N. Y. TEN

20 Female seated with rake between 2 and 0. 20
Compt's die. AUBURN CITY BK, Auburn, N. Y. Franklin
TWENTY Shield. TWENTY

Female with battle ax. AUBURN CITY B'K Auburn, N. Y. FIFTY
50
Compt's die Female and anchor.

ONE AUBURN EX. B'K. Auburn, N. Y. ONE on 1.
Red fig. one 1. Red silver dollar. Red fig. one 1. Two females, one at table; the other with horn in hand.
Male portrait.
Compt's die. Train of cars; load of hay drawn by two horses; men, cows, etc; city and bridge in distance.

TWO Spread eagle. 2
Compt's die. AUBURN EX. B'K. Auburn, N. Y.
Two females seated by side of shield Red silver dollar. Red silver dollar. Male portrait
TWO

Compt's die. 3 Cattle, sheep, two men, horses and dog; house in distance. 3
THREE
Male portrait AUBURN EX. B'K. Auburn, N. Y. Man feeding [illegible]

FIVE 5 Five cherubs and five silver dollars. 5
Compt's die.
Full length figure of Justice AUBURN EX. B'K. Auburn, N. Y.
Shield, bales and anvil. FIVE

X AUBURN EX. B'K. Auburn, N. Y. Indian looking over cliff.
10
Male portrait Train of cars; steamboat and hills in distance. Compt's die

20 AUBURN EX. B'K. Auburn, N. Y. XX
Indian and deer on ground; hills and water in distance. Eagle and shield; on either side is word twenty and figures 20. Female Indian reclining; deer in distance
TWENTY Compt's die.

Secured, &c. 1 Female with child ONE
BALLSTON SPA B'K. Ballston, N. Y.
ONE House. Female seated.

TWO 2 Female reaper seated. 2
Compt's die. BALLSTON SPA B'K. Ballston, N. Y. Artisan.
TWO Public building.

5 V Female seated in figure 5; female on both sides. V 5
Compt's die. BALLSTON SPA B'K. Ballston, N. Y. Medallion head.
FIVE Building. FIVE

10 Shield, with female on either side. 10
Compt's die. BALLSTON SPA B'K. Ballston, N. Y. State Arms.
TEN Building. TEN

TWENTY 20 Vig. Female seated with chemical apparatus, pointing to shipping in distance. 20
Compt's die. XX
BALLSTON SPA B'K. Ballston, N. Y.
TWENTY Building.

Secured by pledge, &c. 1 Vig. Female Die. with sword child, cornucopia, anchor, agricultural implements, &c; ship in distance. ONE
Female seated, cars and vessel in distance.
ONE BANK OF ALBION, Albion, N. Y. Dog's head.

TWO 2 Vig. Female seated; agricultural implements factory on left; canal boat and cars on right; steamboat in distance. 2
Compt's die. Mechanic seated, tools horn of plenty, &c. surrounded with corn.
TWO BANK OF ALBION, Albion, N. Y. Female reclining.

Secured by pledge, &c. 3 Vig. Female portrait in frame, surrounded by flags, drum, cannon, &c. 3
Male and female, figure 3 in centre. BANK OF ALBION, Albion, N. Y.
Compt's die. Female reclining.

5 Vig. Group of persons, centre female holding globe in one hand, key in the other, seated in chariot; lions at her feet; vessel and steamship in the distance 5
Compt's die. Female pointing towards cars in the distance; man cradling
FIVE BANK OF ALBION, Albion, N. Y. Female. FIVE

X Vig. Signing Declaration of Independence Compt's die X
Washington. BANK OF ALBION, Albion, N. Y. Martha Washington
10 Mechanics arm, hammer, anvil, &c. 10

1 BK OF AMSTERDAM Amsterdam, N. Y. 1
1 Female, smoking urn, flowers, etc. 1
Compt's die Male portrait

Left	Centre	Right
2 Compt's die.	BK OF AMSTERDAM Amsterdam, N. Y. Two on 2 Old man, child and bust of Washington Two on 2 TWO	2 Male portrait.
5 Male portrait	BK OF AMSTERDAM Amsterdam, N. Y. Corn grinding scene—three men, dog, etc.	5 Compt's die Five on 5
10 Female, co umn, steamer, etc	BK OF AMSTERDAM Amsterdam, N. Y. TEN Male portrait TEN	10 Compt's die
Secured, &c. ONE	1 Female with child. BANK OF ATTICA, Buffalo, N. Y.	ONE Female seated.
TWO Compt's die. TWO	2 Vig. Female reaper. 2 BANK OF ATTICA, Buffalo, N. Y. Drover and oxen,	Corn Artisan in circular die Corn
Secured, etc. Figure 3, female on either side. III	3 Vig. Portrait of female in oval die, with flags on either side. BANK OF ATTICA, Buffalo, N. Y. Oxen and trees.	3
5 Compt's die. FIVE	Vig. Vig. Group of females; plough, wheel, key, &c. &c. &c. BANK OF ATTICA, Buffalo, N. Y. Oxen and trees.	5 Female with shield reaper in distance. FIVE
TEN Public building, street, omnibus and people. Compt's die.	10 Farmer ploughing, with two horses. BANK OF ATTICA, Buffalo, N. Y.	10 Oxen and pigs.
TWENTY reaper sharpening scythe Compt's die.	20 Vig. Agricultural scene. BANK OF ATTICA, Buffalo, N. Y.	20 Female seated, holding 2 in right hand, 0 in left.
1 ONE Compt's die.	ONE ONE ONE ONE ONE Female, right arm resting on a fence; men and a mill in distance. BANK OF AUBURN, Auburn, N. Y. ONE ONE ONE ONE ONE	1 Female and fig. 1, with one on it. 1

Left	Centre	Right
1 ONE Compt's die.	Vig. Country scene; female figure, farm house and water mill in back ground. BANK OF AUBURN, Auburn, N. Y.	1 Female figure. 1
2 Compt's die. 2	Vig. Female seated with cap and liberty pole. BANK OF AUBURN, Auburn, N. Y.	2 Female figure. 2
Compt's die. Med head 3	THREE THREE Shield, eagle at top; on right two females with scales, cars in distance; on left, Liberty, ship in distance. BANK OF AUBURN, Auburn, N. Y. The word Three five times.	3 Female with flowers. 3
5 Compt's die. 5	Vig. Medallion head, supported on left by female figure of art and science, and on right by female figure of commerce. BANK OF AUBURN, Auburn, N. Y.	5 Medallion head. 5
Compt's die.	Vig. Eagle on rock, shipping, &c, on left. 10 BANK OF AUBURN, Auburn, N. Y.	TEN
ONE and 1 Male portrait	BANK OF BATH, Bath, N. Y. Vig. Blacksmith shop; smiths shoeing horse; one dollar.	1 Compt's die ONE
2 TWO Male portrait	Vig. Drover; cattle and sheep, cars in distance. 2 2 BANK OF BATH, Bath, N. Y. TWO TWO	TWO and 2 TWO Compt's die.
5 Male portrait	Vig. Harvest scene. 5 5 BANK OF BATH, Bath, N. Y. FIVE FIVE	5 F I V V E Compt's die.
TEN	Compt's Die. Drover on horse-back with boy in water and drove of cattle; trees, farmhouse, &c., in distance. BANK OF BATH, Bath, N. Y. Safe.	10 Male portrait
TWENTY	Female Portrait. Goddess of Liberty reclining with pole and cap in right hand; eagle on left. BANK OF BATH, Bath, N. Y. Compt's Die.	20 Male portrait

Left	Centre	Right
ONE Fillmore.	Compt's die. Vig. Female seated, holding figure one, cars in distance. BANK OF BING-HAMPTON. Binghampton, N. Y.	Female standing in large figure 1.
2 Female seated with scroll spear and globe.	BANK OF BING-HAMPTON, Binghampton, N. Y. Spread eagle on limb of tree; train of cars, canal, boats, &c. Figure 2 on either side of vignette. Compt's die.	2 Female seated with scales and sword; safe on left.
3 Female portrait.	Compt's die. Vig. Farmers at dinner. BANK OF BING-HAMPTON, Binghampton, N. Y.	3 Artisan in figure 3, art on either side. THREE
FIVE FIVE Compt's die.	5 Locomotive and cars. BANK OF BING-HAMPTON, Binghampton, N. Y. Safe.	FIVE Large figure 5 and five females.
Compt's die. Male portrait. TEN	10 Vig. 3 females. BANK OF BING-HAMPTON, Binghampton, N. Y. American Shield.	10 Goddess of liberty in wreath, with name of States and territories.
TWENTY Justice erect and Goddess of War seated.	20 Indian princess with shield. BANK OF BING-HAMPTON, N. Y. Shield, etc.	20 Female
FIFTY Indian female erect with bow and arrows.	Compt's die. Female portrait. 50 BANK OF BING-HAMPTON, Binghampton, N. Y. Horn of plenty and anvil.	Winged female erect; female seated at her feet, also an eagle.
ONE Compt's die. ONE	Vig. Indian and squaws in canoe. BANK OF CANAN-DAGUIA. Canandaguia. Fowls.	1 Male portrait.
TWO Compt's die.	Vig Wild horses. BANK OF CANAN-DAGUIA. Canandaguia. T W O Dog.	2 Male portrait.
V Railroad; train of cars.	BANK OF CANAN-DAGUIA. Canandaguia. Compt's die Vig. Female seated, arm resting on bale of goods; steamboat on left; vessel on right.	5 FIVE

Left	Centre	Right
TEN Female in field of grain.	Vig. Train of cars passing under bridge. Telegraph, &c. BANK OF CANANDAGUIA, Canandaguia. Dog.	X Compt's die.
1 Compt's die	BANK OF CANTON Men grooming horse 1 ONE DOLLAR 1 Canton, N. Y.	1 Male portrait
2 Compt's die TWO	BANK OF CANTON Girl and boy driving cattle through gate 2 TWO DOLLARS 2 Canton	2 Male portrait
Male portrait 5	BANK OF CANTON Female seated beside shield, ship, etc., ship and cars in distance 5 FIVE DOLLARS 5 Canton	5 Compt's die
10 Horse head	Male portrait X Spread eagle BANK OF CANTON TEN on TEN DOLLARS Canton	10 Compt's die
1 Portrait of Washington. ONE	Vig. Locomotive and cars. BANK OF CAYUGA LAKE, Painted Post, N. Y.	1 Compt's die
TWO Farmers loading grain TWO	Medallion head, with TWO on it. Compt's die. Medallion head with TWO on it. BANK OF CAYUGA LAKE, Painted Post, N. Y.	TWO Female seated in large figure 2
5 Male portrait	Medallion head. Vig. Signing the declaration of independence. BANK OF CAYUGA LAKE, Painted Post, N. Y.	FIVE Compt's die.
ONE	B'K OF CAZENOVIA. Cazenovia, N. Y. Large one in red die. Compt's die.	1 ONE 1
TWO DOLLARS Compt's die	B'K OF CAZENOVIA TWO DOLLARS TWO on large die Cazenovia, N. Y.	2 TWO 2

Left	Centre	Right
FIVE	BK. OF CAZENOVIA, Cazenovia, N. Y. Large five in red die.	5 Compt's die. FI V VE
TEN Washington	BK OF CAZENOVIA, Cazenovia, N. Y. TEN in large red die.	10 TEN Compt's die
Die. 20 Die.	BK OF CAZENOVIA, Cazenovia, N. Y. TWENTY in large red die.	20 Franklin.
1 Compt's die. ONE	Vig. Men loading hay. BANK OF CHEMUNG Elmira, N. Y. Wheelbarrow	1 Bridge and canal boat. ONE
TWO Compt's die. TWO	Vig. Female seated in figure 2. BANK OF CHEMUNG Elmira, N. Y. Load of hay.	2 Female with wheat. 2
5 Compt's die. FIVE	Vig. Oxen. BANK OF CHEMUNG Elmira, N. Y. Drov.	5 Fillmore.
Male portrait. Compt's die.	Vig. Female seated by bale; picture; sheep to the right. BANK OF CHEMUNG Elmira, N. Y.	10 Locomotive.
Female standing erect holding a shield. TWENTY	State arms. Vig. Capitol building. BANK OF CHEMUNG Elmira, N. Y.	20 Medallion head.
Full length male portrait. ONE	1 Vig. Canal boat and locks. Compt's die BK. OF CHENANGO, Norwich. Canal locks.	ONE Female, sheaf of wheat and cattle. 1
2 Canal boats and locks. 2	Vig. Cupid inscribing on rocks. BK. OF CHENANGO, Norwich. Canal locks	Full length figure with shield and spear. TWO

Left	Centre	Right
3 Female. THREE	Vig. Female with arm resting on wheel. BK. OF CHENANGO, Norwich. Canal locks.	Full length male figure. THREE
5 Compt's die. 5	5 Vig. Female seated. 5 BK. OF CHENANGO, Norwich.	Female seated, holding an eagle: three vessels on left in distance. V
10 Compt's die. 10	Vig. Atlas supporting globe; cars and village in distance. 20 each side. BK. OF CHENANGO, Norwich. Cupid riding deer.	Full length female. X
Full length female. 20	Vig. Two female figures soaring in the air. BK. OF CHENANGO, Norwich. Canal locks.	Full length male figure. 20
FIFTY	Vig. Cupid inscribing on rock. BK. OF CHENANGO, Norwich. Canal locks.	FIFTY
1 Compt's die.	Female reclining with bale, bbl., spinning wheel etc. BANK OF COHOES, Cohoes, N. Y.	1 Two on the erect; female seated; buildings.
Cupid and 2 Compt's die. TWO	Title of Bank. Two females at work on looms.	2 2
Compt's die. 3	Two females seated on bale; factory in distance. Title of Bank.	3 Girl's head.
Cupid and 5. Male portrait	Title of Bank. Eagle. Female seated by bale; factory and falls in distance.	5 Compt's die. 5
10 Two Indians on cliff; city in distance.	Two females seated by anvil; factory in distance. Title of Bank. 10 TEN TEN	10 Compt's die.

Left	Centre	Right
20 Female with sword and shield. TWENTY	Compt's die. Spread eagle. BANK OF COHOES. Cohoes, N. Y.	20 Female portrait.
1 Compt's die.	Vig. Female seated, with mirror, &c.; cars on right, steamer and ship on left. B'K OF COMMERCE, Carmel, N. Y.	ONE Female clasping figure 1
1 Compt's die	Wild horses. B'K OF COMMERCE, Carmel, N. Y. ONE on 1.	1 Female.
2 Compt's die. 2	B'K OF COMMERCE, Carmel, N. Y. 2 Horses, load of hay man and barn; load of hay in distance. 2	2 TWO
2 Compt's die.	Vig. Crystal Palace, N. Y. B'K OF COMMERCE, Carmel, N. Y. 2	Female seated in large figure 2. TWO
3 Compt's die.	Vig. Artisans; vessel cars and factory in distance. B'K OF COMMERCE, Carmel, N. Y. 3	111 Fig. 3 and Female seated on rocks.
FIVE Goddess of Liberty.	BK OF COMMERCE, Carmel, N. Y. Large V with FIVE running across it. Vig. Locomotive and cars, oxen and water in foreground.	5 Compt's die.
10 Male portrait	Cattle in pasture; one drinking. B'K OF COMMERCE, Carmel, N. Y. TEN and ten dollars across	10 TEN Compt's die.
20 Male portrait	Cattle and sheep; water in distance. B'K OF COMMERCE, Carmel, N. Y. Compt's die, X on TWENTY on left and X on DOLLARS on right.	20 XX
1 Portrait of Daniel Webster. Compt's die.	BANK OF COOPERSTOWN. Vig. Woodchopper, gold dollar; farm house and waggon in distance. Shield, etc.	1 Goddess of liberty supporting figure one.

Left	Centre	Right
2 Portrait of Franklin. Compt's die.	BANK OF COOPERSTOWN. Vig. Farmer, milk maid, two gold dollars, and cattle. Farm house in distance. Dog.	2 Indian with bow, spear, and arrows.
3 Portrait. Compt's die.	BANK OF COOPERSTOWN. 3 Vig. Farmer, mechanic and sailor, seated, holding implements; three gold dollars lapped. Goddess of liberty.	THREE Full length female.
FIVE Washington. Compt's die.	BANK OF COOPERSTOWN. Vig. Five figures and five gold dollars lapped. Safe.	5 Female holding balances; small figure 5; safe; and soldier in armor. FIVE
10 Compt's die. TEN	BANK OF COOPERSTOWN. Vig. Two females seated, hogshead and bale of goods; farmer plowing cars and steamship in the distance. Safe.	10 Female Indian holding ear of corn, and small X
1 Compt's die ONE	Vig. male ploughing. BANK OF COXSACKIE. Coxsackie, N. Y.	1 Indian seated with gun in hand.
Female, holding figure 2. Compt's die.	Vig. Horse running from locomotive in distance. BANK OF COXSACKIE. Coxsackie, N. Y.	2 Female milking cows
3 Portrait of Female. 3	BANK OF COXSACKIE. Coxsackie, N. Y. Vig. Female seated on safe, with dog and child.	3 Compt's die.
5 Compt's die.	B'K OF COXSACKIE, Coxsackie, N. Y. Female seated with anchor; city and shipping in background.	5 Portrait of Washington
State Arms. 10	Male portrait. BANK OF COXSACKIE. Coxsackie, N. Y.	10 Compt's die.
1 Compt's die. ONE	Vig. Man and two boys washing sheep, and dog. fig. 1 on left. BK. OF DANSVILLE. ONE DOLLAR. Banking house.	NEW YORK on fig. 1.

Left	Centre	Right
2 Die TWO	Vig. Agricultural scene, family group; horses and man in the distance. BK. OF DANSVILLE. TWO DOLLARS. Banking house.	2 Two female figures.
3 Die. THREE	Vig. Three figures, two male, one female, and a dog. BK. OF DANSVILLE. THREE DOLLARS. Banking house.	3 Three men one embracing or holding up figure 3.
5 Compt's die. FIVE	V Females and fig. 5. V BK OF DANSVILLE, Dansville, N. Y. Eagle.	5 Med head. FIVE
10 Compt's die TEN	Female either side of shield; vessels, etc., in distance. BK OF DANSVILLE, Dansville, N. Y. Grain, etc.	10 Arms. TEN
20 Compt's die.	Vig. Dairy scene, with maid in midst of cows, in sitting posture, with pail. BK. OF DANSVILLE. Machine	20 Banking house.
50 Compt's. die.	Vig. Indian sitting, bow in left hand, and viewing agricultural scene, chin resting on hand, elbow on words BK. OF DANSVILLE. Eagle	50 Portrait of Gov. Hunt.
Female seated, holding spear and branch; and large figure 1. Compt's die.	Female portrait; cupids on either side. BANK OF FAYETTEVILLE, Fayetteville, N. Y.	ONE Vig. Female soaring; sword in one hand, branch in the other eagle; steamship and vessels. 1
Female holding figure 2. Compt's die.	Male portrait; cupids on either side. BANK OF FAYETTEVILLE, Fayetteville, N. Y. Vig. Two females; mechanic reclining against safe; implements, cars, steamship, &c.	2 TWO
Female holding figure 3. Compt's die. THREE.	Franklin; cupids on either side. BANK OF FAYETTEVILLE, Fayetteville, N. Y. Vig. Boy plowing; Farm house, steamboat.	III 3
FIVE Girl. 5	Compt's die. Cupids on either side. BANK OF FAYETTEVILLE Fayetteville, N. Y. FIVE	FIVE Flower girl with basket of flowers. 5

Left	Centre	Right
X with inters TEN running across it. Female, liberty pole cap, &c.	BANK OF FAYETTE-VILLE, Fayetteville, N. Y. Vig. Farmer, sailor, and mechanic; implements, &c. Two vessels, cars, &c, in back ground.	10 Farm house and boat. Compt's die.
20 Indian woman, bow and spear.	BANK OF FAYETTE-VILLE, Fayetteville, N. Y. Compt's die. Vig. Train cars, village; female holding book and pen.	20
ONE Large figure 1 with portrait of Washington.	Vig. Train of cars; village in distance on left, steamboat on right. BANK OF FISHKILL Fishkill Village, N. Y. Secured, &c.	1 Compt's die.
2 Farmer ploughing. Female portrait.	BANK OF FISHKILL Fishkill Village, N.Y. Secured, &c.	2 Compt's die.
THREE Compt's die.	Vig. Horses drinking, pigs on right. 3 BANK OF FISHKILL, Fishkill Village, N. Y. Secured, &c.	3 Washington on horseback.
5 Compt's die. 5	Large ornamental figure 5, with word five on it. Vig. Artisans at work. BANK OF FISHKILL, Fishkill Village, N. Y. Secured, &c.	5 Portrait of Washington
Female with sheaf. Compt's Die.	X Milkmaid seated, one milking cow; sail vessels, cows, etc. BANK OF FISHKILL Fishkill Village, N.Y. Secured, etc.	10 Steamboat.
20 Female Indian.	BANK OF FISHKILL Fishkill Village, N.Y. X Vig. Eagle. X	20 Compt's die Secured, &c
1 Compt's die.	Vig. Locomotive and train of cars; canal boat and village in distance. BANK OF FORT EDWARD, Fort Edward, N. Y.	1 Male portrait.
2 Compt's die. TWO	Vig. Female with liberty pole and cap, shield, banners, cannon and drum. BANK OF FORT EDWARD, Fort Edward, N. Y.	2 Male portrait

Left	Centre	Right
3 Compt's die. 3	Vig. Drover, cattle and sheep; man horseback watering his horse. BANK OF FORT EDWARD, Fort Edward, N. Y.	3 Male portrait 3
FIVE Compt's die. FIVE	5 Vig. Two females, one reclining; liberty pole and cap, balances, sword, shield and eagle; ship in distance. BANK OF FORT EDWARD, Fort Edward, N. Y.	5 Franklin.
Compt's die. Female, liberty pole in one hand, the other resting on X.	Male portrait. 10 BANK OF FORT EDWARD, Fort Edward, N. Y.	TEN Two Indians, female kneeling between them, 10
Compt's die. Two indians and female. TWENTY	Male portrait. 20 BANK OF FORT EDWARD, Fort Edward. N. Y.	Vig. Canal boat, and cars crossing bridge; house
1 Compt's die. 1	Vig. Two females ONE with sword ONE balances, & spear; eagle mounted over a figure 1. BANK OF GENESEE, Batavia, N. Y.	1 Portrait of Washington ONE
2 Compt's die. 2	2 BANK OF GENESEE, Batavia, N. Y. Two dollars on die work.	Vig. Two females on either side figure 2; liberty cap, bee hive, and flowers. TWO
3 Compt's die. 3	3 Vig. Neptune in his car; female on left; ship in distance on right; canal on left. 3 BANK OF GENESEE Batavia, N. Y. Die	Full length Male portrait. THREE
5 Compt's die. 5	5 Vig. Three females; agricultural implements; sheaf of wheat, bee hive, &c. 5 BANK OF GENESEE, Batavia, N. Y. Die.	5 Male Portrait 5
10 Compt's die. 10	TEN TEN Vig. Agricultural implements, sheaf wheat, trees. BANK OF GENESEE, Batavia, N. Y.	10 Male portrait 10
Compt's die. Female head	1 Human Washington figure floating in air. BANK OF GENEVA. Geneva, N.Y.	1 Female figure holding fig. 1.

Left	Centre	Right
1 Compt's die.	Vig. Female seated ; sickle, grain, reapers at work. Portrait of Washington BANK OF GENEVA Geneva, N. Y.	1 Female, ship in distance. ONE
2 Compt's die.	Vig. Angel blowing trumpet. Male portrait. BANK OF GENEVA, Geneva, N. Y.	2 Two cupids seated on large figure 2
5 Compt's die. 5	Female seated on plow holding sheaf and sickle. 5 BANK OF GENEVA, Geneva, N. Y.	Female holding sheaf. 5
Portrait of male. Compt's die.	5 Vig. Man standing with flag and sword, others kneeling around BANK OF GENEVA, Geneva, N. Y.	5 Male portrait V
X Compt's die. 10	Vig. Harvest scene. BANK OF GENEVA, Geneva, N. Y. Locomotive.	10 Goddess of Liberty.
Mechanic at bench. Compt's die.	BANK OF HAVANA, Havana, N. Y. 1 Male portrait. 1	1 Female seated; houses in distance.
2 Compt's die. 2	Male portrait Vig. Female kneeling, with pail; cattle lying down, &c. BANK OF HAVANA, Havana, N. Y.	2 Male portrait
Compt's die. Male portrait	5 Portrait of Washington. 5 BANK OF HAVANA, Havana, N. Y. Canal boat.	FIVE Female standing, canal lock in distance.
1 ONE Compt's die.	Cattle and sheep. BANK OF KENT, Ludingtonville, N. Y.	1 Men gathering corn.
2 Compt's die. 2	Woodcutters at work. BANK OF KENT, Ludingtonville, N. Y	2 Men gathering corn.

Female seated by side of portrait of boy. V. — Men harvesting. BANK OF KENT. Ludingtonville, N. Y. — 5. Compt's die. 5.

Rip VanWinkle. Compt's die. — 1 Men washing sheep ONE on 1. BK of KINDERHOOK ONE DOLLAR ONE. — NEW YORK on large ornamental figure 1.

TWO. Compt's die. TWO. — 2 Female with wand, sickle, etc.; grain, buildings, etc. in background 2. BK of KINDERHOOK TWO Kinderhook. — Corn. Figure in oval frame. Corn.

5. Justice with scales and sword; eagle, safe, key, &c. FIVE. — Vig. Group of four figures, two lions, chariot, plough and rake, horn of plenty; ships in distance. BANK OF KINDERHOOK. Anchor between sigs. — 5. Minerva with head of Medusa on a shield; reapers in the distance. FIVE.

10. Justice with scales and sword; eagle, safe, key, &c. TEN. — Vig. Shield bearing coat of arms of the several States; female on either side; rake, plough, sickle, barrels; steamship, factory, train of cars, and city in the distance. BANK OF KINDERHOOK. Anchor between sigs. — 10. State Arms. TEN.

TWENTY. Compt's die. Man whetting scythe. — 20 Cattle, sheep, two men, horse and Dog. BANK OF KINDERHOOK. Kinderhook, N. Y. Bee hive. — Twenty across the Bill on either side of 20.

ONE. Webster. ONE. — 1 Two milkmaids, one erect, the other seated. 1. BANK OF LANSINGBURGH, Lansingburgh, N. Y. Horse's head. — Franklin. Compt's die. Male portrait.

TWO. Male portrait. TWO. — 2 Three reapers at work in field. 2. BANK OF LANSINGBURGH, Lansingburgh, N. Y. — Female head. Compt's die. Male portrait.

FIVE. V. A female sitting on the point of the 5. 5. — BANK OF LANSING BURGH. 5 Vig. Two men on horseback, driving cattle and sheep; dog; barn. In the distance, a small sloop. 5. — Head of Washington. State Arms. Chief Justice Marshall.

10 on med. head. Washington. — Compt's die. Eagle; light house, vessels, man plowing, etc., in distance. BANK OF LANSINGBURGH, Lansingburgh, N. Y. TEN. — 10 on med. head. Martha Washington.

20. State Arms. 20. — BANK OF LANSINGBURGH. 20 Vig. Two children; one astride a fish, surmounted with an eagle; one lying down; a steamboat in the distance. 20. — 20. Figure of Justice with scales; American eagle, head of Washington. 20.

50. State Arms. 50. — BANK OF LANSINGBURGH. 50 Vig. Three females sitting; sheaf of wheat, sickle, plough handle; haystack in rear. 50. — 50. Cattle and two men. 50.

Henry Clay. Compt's die. — 1 Boy on horse driving sheep; cows, colt, &c. BANK OF LIMA, Lima, N. Y. — 1. Cattle passing under and cars over arch.

TWO. Compt's die. TWO. — BANK OF LIMA, Lima, N. Y. Anvil; female on either side; cornucopia; factory in rear. — 2. Webster.

5. Male portrait. — Engine entering depot; cars leaving; two trains in distance. BANK OF LIMA, Lima, N. Y. — 5. Compt's die. FIVE.

10. Female and little girl seated; man drinking out of a jug. — Men reaping. Portrait of Washington. BANK OF LIMA, Lima, N. Y. — 10. Compt's die.

ONE. Female, sickle, etc. ONE. — Bird on branch of tree. BK OF LOWVILLE. Lowville, N. Y. — Female enclosed in large Ornament 1 fig. 1.

ONE. Female portrait. ONE. — 1 Eagle on branch of tree 1. B'K OF LOWVILLE ONE DOLLAR Lowville, N. Y. — Female figure in large figure 1.

TWO. Compt's die. TWO. — 2 Vig. Female reaper 2. B'K OF LOWVILLE, Lowville, N. Y. Dog's head. — Artisan pouring gold out of horn.

5. Compt's die. FIVE. — V Vig. Female in figure 5; female on either side. V. B'K OF LOWVILLE, Lowville, N. Y. Dog's head. — 5. Bust. FIVE.

10. Compt's die. TEN. — Vig. Wreath with female on either side; shipping, cars and buildings in distance. B'K OF LOWVILLE, Lowville, N. Y. Dog's head. — 10. State Arms. TEN.

Vig. Road, load of hay, canal boat, &c. 25. — B'K OF LOWVILLE, Lowville, N. Y. Male portrait. Cornucopia, bales, &c. — 25. Compt's die. 25.

ONE. Compt's die. ONE. — 1 Vig. Man on horseback watering his horse; drover and cattle. BANK OF MALONE, Malone, N. Y. — 1. Franklin.

2. Compt's die. TWO. — Saw mill, horses and waggon; yoke of oxen; men at work, &c. BANK OF MALONE, Malone, N. Y. — 2. Train of cars. TWO.

5. Compt's die. V. — Train of cars. BANK OF MALONE, Malone, N. Y. — Large ornamental 5; waterfall, cars, Indians &c.

10. Compt's die. 10. — Vig. Female seated; globe and cars behind her; wheel, &c, on right. BANK OF MALONE, Malone, N. Y. — 10. Franklin. 10.

20. Compt's die. TWENTY. — BANK OF MALONE, Malone, N. Y. Vig. Cattle and sheep; farm house in distance. — 20. Male Portrait. TWENTY.

1. ONE. Compt's die. — Blacksmith shoeing horse; old man by side of horse; man at anvil. B'K OF NEWARK, Newark, N. Y. — 1. Female portrait.

1. ONE. Compt's die. — View of harbor of New York, with steamship Pacific and ship. BANK OF NEWARK, ONE. Female bathing. — 1. Wayne co. Cattle, telegraph and railroad.

TWO. Two Indian chiefs with bows. — Railroad trains coming out of a tunnel; two laborers standing looking on. BANK OF NEWARK. TWO. — 2. Compt's die. TWO.

TWO TWO TWO 2 Compt's die. 2	Old man seated under tree with boy and dog; sheep in distance. Title of Bank.	2 Female with dove. TWO TWO TWO
5 Female feeding lamb.	Three females and bust of Washington. Title of Bank. Five Dollars Five Dollars	5 Compt's die FIVE
Compt's die. Five, V, 5.	Three female figures seated, with shield in centre and eagle perched on it. BANK OF NEWARK Locomotive.	5 Squaw and child seated.
TEN	Vig. Mechanic, sailor, and farmer making offerings to Goddess of Liberty, with eagle seated above the Goddess. BANK OF NEWARK.	10 Railroad with locomotive.
X Clay.	Female and two calves; canal scene, cars, cows, etc., in distance. Title of Bank.	10 Compt's die
TWENTY Eagle on shield, female with quadrant seated. TWENTY	BANK OF NEWARK. Vig. Ploughman and horses, with houses in distance.	20
Compt's die. 1	Vig. Train of cars, &c. BK OF NEWBURGH Newburgh, N. Y. Large figure 1 running lengthwise of the note.	ONE 1
2 Compt's die. 2	2 Vig. Female seated sickle in hand Wheat & cattle on either side. 2 BK OF NEWBURGH Newburgh, N. Y. Steamboat.	TWO Cupid engraving. TWO
Compt's die. 3	BK OF NEWBURGH, Newburgh, N. Y. Figure of Justice.	THREE 3
3 Compt's die. 3	3 Vig. Blacksmith at work, two females. 3 BK OF NEWBURGH Newburgh, N. Y. Steamboat	THREE Full length male figure. THREE

5 Compt's die. 5	5 Vig. Female leaning on a wheel, monument behind her. 5 BK OF NEWBURGH Newburgh, N. Y. Steamboat.	V Female seated one arm around a column the other extended. V
Compt's die. 10	BK OF NEWBURGH Newburgh, N. Y. X Vig. Two females seated, cask and bales in rear, canal boat in distance.	
Compt's die. XX	Vig. Mechanic seated leaning on anvil hammer on his shoulder, cars on right, &c. BK OF NEWBURGH Newburgh, N. Y.	20
FIFTY	50 BK OF NEWBURGH Newburgh, N. Y. Title of bank on each side of vignette. Vig. Female seated holding balances, anchor and small sail vessel. Compt's stamp on back of note.	
HUNDRED	100 BK OF NEWBURGH Newburgh, N. Y. Title of bank on each side of vignette. Vig. Female seated holding balances, sickle, wheat and small vessel. Compt's stamp on back of note.	100
1 Agricultural implements and products Compt's die.	Mowing and harvesting scene; load of hay in distance. BK OF NEWPORT. Newport, N. Y.	ONE Female portrait.
TWO Compt's die. TWO	Milkmaid seated; farmer reclining on ground; two gold dollars; cattle on left; farm houses on right. Title of Bank.	2 Cars.
Compt's die Cow. Three on 3	Farmer, sailor and mechanic; three gold dollars, &c. Title of Bank.	3 Cars passing over and cattle passing under arch
5 Clay.	Female seated either side of anvil. Title of Bank.	5 Compt's die 5
Full length statue on dark ground.	10 Cattle in stream; boy and child on bank. BK. OF NEWPORT, Newport, N. Y.	10 Compt's die

XX Youthful portrait with cap.	Compt's die. Boy on horse, colt, sheep, cattle, etc. Title of Bank.	20 Cooper at work on barrels.
Farmer with scythe. Compt's die	1 Indian and ornamental fig. 1. BANK OF NORWICH, Norwich, N. Y.	Word one and figure 1. Male portrait ONE
TWO Compt's die. TWO	Female on either side of fig. 2 TWO BANK OF NORWICH, Norwich, N. Y.	2 Male portrait
Compt's die. Male portrait	Three females and ornamental fig. 3; factory in distance. Fig. 3 on left. BANK OF NORWICH Norwich, N. Y.	Word three and fig. 3. Mechanic, sailor and farmer in fig. 3.
5 Male portrait FIVE	Five females, and fig. 5; shipping, and factories in distance. BANK OF NORWICH. Norwich, N. Y. Loading hay.	5 Compt's die FIVE
Male portrait TEN	Nine cherubs and ten gold dollars; female with cornucopia, shield, &c. BANK OF NORWICH Norwich, N. Y.	10 Agricultural implements. Compt's die.
TWENTY DOLLARS	BK. OF NORWICH, Norwich, N. Y. Female seated on either side of male portrait; sword, spear, bales, steamboat, cars, etc.	20
FIFTY	Boy on horse back; cows, sheep, etc. FIFTY. Compt's die. Title of Bank.	50 Male portrait
Female seated by side of fig. 1. Compt's die	Indian, squaw and child in canoe; wigwams, trees, etc. in distance. BANK OF OLD SARATOGA, Schuylerville, N. Y. Soldier and cannon.	1 Female seated and fig. 1
2 Compt's die 2	Indians on horse back viewing train of cars. Title of Bank. Sentinel and cannon.	2 Female and figure 2.

5 Male portrait	Female in clouds with shield, pole, cap and eagle. Title of Bank. Sentinel and cannon.	5 Compt's die. 5
TEN Spread eagle. 10	Surrender of Burgoyne. 10 BANK OF OLD SARATOGA, Schuylerville, N. Y. Soldier and cannon.	Justice. Compt's die
Two horses, man, dog, plow, etc. XX	Compt's die female each side. BANK OF OLD SARATOGA, Schuylerville, N. Y. Soldier and cannon.	20 Blacksmith with anvil.
1 Compt's die	BANK OF ONTARIO Men at work with cradling machines Die ONE DOLLAR Die Canandaigua, N. Y.	1 Male portrait
2 Compt's die	BANK OF ONTARIO Three children in oval die reading book Die Die	2 Male portrait
Medallion head. Compt's die. Medallion head.	1 Vig. Dairy maid with oxen. 1 B'K OF ORANGE CO. Goshen, N. Y. Dog's head.	ONE Female portrait. ONE
Female portrait. Compt's die. Female portrait.	2 Vig. Farmer with drove of cattle. B'K OF ORANGE CO. Goshen, N. Y. Eagle.	TWO Locomotive and cars. TWO
Female portrait. Compt's die. Female portrait.	5 Vig. Locomotive and cars. B'K OF ORANGE CO. Goshen, N. Y.	FIVE Male portrait FIVE
FIVE	5 Girl milking cow. V BK. OF ORANGE CO., Goshen, N. Y. Agricultural tools.	Compt's die.
FIVE Two girls with sheafs.	5 Boy, horses, colt, cows and sheep. BK. OF ORANGE CO., Goshen, N. Y.	5 Compt's die. FIVE

TEN Man sharpening scythe	X Milkmaid seated with hat on lap; dog, cars, etc. Title of Bank. Man plowing.	10 Compt's die.
TEN	10 Female churning. X B'K OF ORANGE CO. Goshen, N. Y. Agricultural implements	10 Compt's die
TWENTY	20 Female churning. 20 B'K OF ORANGE CO. Goshen, N. Y. Farming tools	Compt's die.
20 Cattle, telegraph, arch, cars, etc.	Milkmaid milking cow, etc. Title of Bank. Compt's die.	20 Men shearing sheep.
1 Compt's Die.	BK of ORANGETWN Orangeburg, N.Y. 1 Female with basket of flowers 1	1 Two children.
Two on 2 Compt's Die. TWO	BK of ORANGETWN Orangeburg, N.Y. 2 Female seated by wheel with flowers and smoking urn 2	2 Female seated with basket of fruit.
Female with lab'els on which is words "Five Dollars," child at her foot. FIVE	5 Two mermaids in water; vessels and ocean scene BK of ORANGETWN Orangeburg, N.Y.	5 Compt's Die. 5
1 surrounded by small 1's. Compt's die.	BANK OF OTEGO, Otego, N. Y. One Dollar on large 1. Portrait of Winfield Scott. One Dollar on large 1.	1 surrounded by words one. Female embracing child.
2 Compt's die. TWO	BANK OF OTEGO, Otego, N. Y. Two Dollars on Two Dollars on 2 Farmer seated on fence, holding scythe. 2	2 surrounded by small 2's and two. Female head.
5 in centre, with small 5's above and below it.	Dog's head. 5 Three children, with book open on table in an oval. BANK OF OTEGO, Otego, N. Y. FIVE DOLLARS.	5 Compt's die. 5

ONE Compt's die. Male portrait.	Vig. Portrait with females on either side; farmers at work; ship and steamboat in distance. BANK OF OWEGO. Wheelbarrow, &c.	ONE Female with sickle and grain. ONE
TWO Compt's die. Portrait of Taylor.	Vig. Three females surrounding frame on which is perched an eagle; ship and cars in distance. BANK OF OWEGO. Locomotive.	TWO Two Indians. TWO
5 Compt's die. 5	5 Vig. Female holding an eagle; horn of plenty at her feet; ships in distance. 5 BANK OF OWEGO. Raft.	V Female, eagle, &c. V
TEN	X Female holding an eagle; horn of plenty; ships in distance. X BANK OF OWEGO, Owego, N. Y. Spread Eagle.	10 Compt's die 10
TWENTY	20 Female holding an eagle; horn of plenty at her feet; ships in distance. 20 BANK OF OWEGO. Ark.	TWENTY Compt's die XX
FIFTY	L L BANK OF OWEGO, Vig. Female seated on rock, with eagle in left hand; horn of plenty at her feet. Canal boat.	50 Cattle. 50
ONE HUNDRED	100 100 BANK OF OWEGO. Female seated on rock, with eagle in left hand; horn of plenty at her feet. Ark.	ONE HUNDRED
1 Compt's die. ONE	1 Three cows and two females. 1 BK OF PAWLING, Pawling, N. Y.	1 Franklin. 1
2 Wm. Penn 2	Vig. Spread eagle. Compt's die. BK OF PAWLING	2 Spotted heifer. 2
3 Washington 3	THREE 3 DOLLARS Compt's die BANK OF PAWLING Pawling, N. Y.	3 Female with shield, etc. THREE

5 Washingt'n 5
Compt's die
B'K OF PAWLING
5 on FIVE DOLLS.
Farm scene; men and woman seated on ground; loading hay on r
Pawling
Secured, etc.
5 FIVE

X Compt's die. 10
Vig. Drove of cattle and sheep; driver on horse with arms and whip extended.
B'NK OF PAWLING.
10 Goddess with Liberty pole and cap and small eagle.

20
Compts die.
Vig. Drove of cattle and sheep; driver on horse with arms and whip extended.
B'NK OF PAWLING.
20 Female in an oval circle, dark ground.

FIFTY Female with sickle and sheaf of wheat on back. Compt's die.
Vig. Two females, one holding Liberty pole and cap; horse's head and neck between them.
B'NK OF PAWLING.
50 Female in circle, with Duchess cover.

100 Compts die. 100
BANK OF PAWLING
Goddess, American eagle and flag.
100 on head. Man with scythe.

ONE Male portrait.
Vig. Canal and boats hills on either side
BANK OF PORT JERVIS.
Port Jervis, N. Y.
1 Compt's die. 1

TWO Male portrait.
Vig. Men at work loading hay, horse and ox for the team.
BANK OF PORT JERVIS.
Port Jervis, N. Y.
2 Compt's die. TWO

Compt's die. Male portrait
Cattle and sheep.
BK of PORT JERVIS,
Port Jervis, N. Y.
3 Sailor

V Male portrait.
Vig. Train of cars, bridge and telegraph poles.
BANK OF PORT JERVIS,
Port Jervis, N. Y.
5 Compt's die.

X Compt's die
Vig. Female reclining on bale of goods, barrels and ships, in distance on right, steamship on left.
BANK OF PORT JERVIS,
Port Jervis, N. Y.
TEN Male portrait.

10 Compt's die.
Two females reclining; spinning wheel, sickle, etc.; cattle and factories in distance.
BK of PORT JERVIS,
Port Jervis, N. Y.
10 Penn.

20 Female kneeling with sheaf and sickle.
Compt's die.
Eagle on globe; shield, clouds and flags.
Title of Bank.
20; old issue has XX

Female with sickle and dog.
50 Interior of blacksmith, shop; four men and boy.
Title of Bank.
50 Compt's die 50
50 Female portrait

State of New York.
1 1 Compt's die.
BK. OF PORT BYRON
Farmer, horse, children, etc.
ONE DOLLAR
Port Byron.
ONE 1 1

2 Compt's die
New York
2 BK. OF PORT BYRON 2
TWO DOLLARS
Port Byron.
Sheep.
Ornamental dies Ornamental dies
Female portrait

Female portrait
STATE OF NEW YORK
Goddess of Liberty, eagle, etc.
BA V NK OF PORT BY V RON.
FIVE DOLLARS
Port Byron
on
FIVE
5 5 Compt's die 5

20 Male portrait
New York.
BANK OF PORT BYRON.
Compt's die. TWENTY DOLLARS
Port Byron.
Female portrait.
20

1 Female seated, eagle sword, balances, &c.
Vig. Milk maids cows, &c. Farm house in distance.
BANK OF POUGHKEEPSIE
Poughkeepsie, N. Y.
Building.
1 Compt's die.

2 Compt's die. 2
Small port. of Jefferson. Small port. of Washington
Vig. Female seated on plough holding sickle and grain; steamboat and cars in distance.
BANK OF POUGHKEEPSIE
Poughkeepsie, N. Y.
Building.
TWO Female Indian, liberty cap and pole. TWO

3 Female holding aloft a ... with flag on it, ship in background
3 Vig. Female leaning upon anchor, shipping and harbor in distance. 3
BANK OF POUGHKEEPSIE
Poughkeepsie, N. Y.
Building.
Female with wheat in her arms
Compt's die

Compt's die. 5
Vig. Spread eagle.
BANK OF POUGHKEEPSIE
Poughkeepsie, N. Y
Building.
5 Washington on horseback

10 Compt's die. 10
Vig. Large X in centre, Portrait on either side, the whole surrounded by scroll work, within which is seated cupids.
BANK OF POUGHKEEPSIE
Poughkeepsie, N. Y.
Building.
10 Washington

50 Steamboats shipping and harbor. 50
50 Compt's die.
Vig. Harvest field laborers at work man and woman in foreground, dog at their feet.
BANK OF POUGHKEEPSIE
Poughkeepsie N. Y.
Dog, key, and safe.
50 Indian in canoe.

Artist seated 100
BANK OF POUGHKEEPSIE
Poughkeepsie, N. Y.
Compt's die.
100 Vig. Cupid in clouds.
Dog, key, and safe.
Artist. 100

1 Lewis Cass. 1
Vig. Female looking at shipping in distance.
B'K OF RHINEBECK,
Rhinebeck, N. Y.
1 Compt's die.

Vig. Farmers at dinner; hay making in backgro'd
2
Portrait of Franklin.
B'K OF RHINEBECK,
Rhinebeck, N. Y.
2 Compt's die

3 Male portrait
Vig. Farmer with two horses; locomotive and cars in background.
B'K OF RHINEBECK,
Rhinebeck, N. Y.
3 Compt's die.

Portrait of Henry Clay. 5
B'K OF RHINEBECK,
Rhinebeck, N. Y.
5 Vig. Farmer with oxen and sheep. 5
5 Compt's die.

10 Female seated right hand on pail; cattle and trees on left.
X Farmer with child on right shoulder, female holding its hand. X
BK OF RHINEBECK,
Rhinebeck, N. Y.
10 Compt's die

ONE Man starting holding horn of plenty and wand, vessel in distance. Compt's die
Vig. Winged female, kneeling in front of large one, sword and balances.
BANK OF ROME,
Rome, N. Y.
Indian.
1

TWO 2 Vig. Farm house with maids, cows 2 Barn, &c. TWO
Compt's die. Two cupids, surrounded by large ornamental figure 2.
BANK OF ROME, Rome, N. Y.
TWO Indian's bust. TWO

THREE 3 Vig. Spread eagle on bow; canal boat, locks and train of cars. 3 3
Compt's die.
BANK OF ROME, Rome, N. Y.
Three females standing.
THREE Horse.

5 5 Vig. Five figures surrounding ornamental figure 5, vessel in distance. 5
Compt's die Female holding aloft figure 5.
BANK OF ROME, Rome, N. Y.
5 V 5

20 20 20
TWENTY
BANK OF ROME, Rome, N. Y.
Vig. Two females holding State Arms between; liberty pole and cap, sword and balance.
Round building with flag flying; view of cultivated fields, &c.
20

ONE State Arms. View of Rondout.
BANK OF RONDOUT.
Child's head. 1

10 Blacksmith and anvil. 2 State Arms. TWO
BANK OF RONDOUT.
TWO The letters TWO, with the words Two Dollars running across. Two female heads.

THREE on 3 Compt's die 3
Male standing and female seated beside milkpail.
BANK OF RONDOUT
THREE DOLLARS Washington
3 Secured, etc.

State Arms. 5
Two females supporting a figure 5 with three Cupids around them.
BANK OF RONDOUT.
The letters FIVE, with the word Five Dollars running across. Portrait.

Two females supporting a shield, on which is a small view of Rondout.
State Arms. 10
BANK OF RONDOUT.
TEN DOLLARS.
10 Portrait.

10 Female reclining on cornucopia; vessel in distance. Compt's die. 10
10 BANK OF RONDOUT, Rondout, N. Y. Male portrait

Two males with shield in an[illegible] grain; mechanics, sledge, anvil and safe.
BANK OF SALEM. 1
O N E
Farmer in cornfield, supporting ornamental figure 1.
Compt's. die. Vig. Train of cars; cattle drinking; steamship and vessel in distance.
Gold dollar.

2 Vig. Female reclining on bale of goods, with Liberty cap, &c.; cars, steamship and vessel in distance. 2
BANK OF SALEM.
Farmer in cornfield with basket of corn.
Compt's. die. T W O
Two gold dollars.

5 Vig. Drover on horseback; cattle and sheep. 5
Indians, locomotive and cars.
BANK OF SALEM.
Milkmaid seated; farmhouse in distance.
Compt's. die. Five gold dollars

Compt's die. Vig. Three figures, mechanic, farmer and sailor, implements, &c.; steamship and vessel in distance. 10
Female seated; horn of plenty and Liberty cap; village in distance.
BANK OF SALEM.
Female seated with balances and sword; locomotive in distance.

TWENTY TWENTY DOLLARS.
Female soaring in the air with garland of flowers in either hand; train of cars and houses in distance.
Compt's die.
Goddess of Liberty. BANK OF SALEM.
20

50 BANK OF SALEM. 50
FIFTY DOLLARS.
Female with sword in one hand, shield and branch in other.
Railroad depot. Compt's die.
Three figures, farmer, mechanic and sailor supporting die 50, with implements.

1 BANK OF SALINA. 1
1 Female standing. Indian sitting. Shield. 1
Compt's die. Eagle.
1 1 1

2 BANK OF SALINA. TWO
Compt's. die. Eagle on a rock. Female filling goblet from a pitcher.
Archimedes with lever and globe
2 Indian in a canoe between sigs TWO

3 BANK OF SALINA. THREE
Compt's. die. 3 Man lying and vase. Pump-house & saltworks. Portrait.
3 3 3

5 Female seated in FIVE chariot FIVE drawn by three lions 5
Compt's die
BANK OF SALINA
FIVE DOLLARS
Male portrait
5 Salina, N. Y. 5
Lion's head

NEW YORK
10 10 Female beside shield, male 10 figure in water-car, etc. TEN
Compt's die Female beside shield
BANK OF SALINA
TEN DOLLARS
10 Salina X

TWENTY BANK OF SALINA. 20
20 Vig. Woman with telescope on a pedestal; lion by her side, 20
Compt's. die.
20

50 BANK OF SALINA. 50
Man sitting. Face. Eagle. Face. Compt's. die.
50 50

Female. 1 Female with key and safe. Spread eagle 1
B'K OF SARATOGA SPRINGS.
Compt's die Saratoga, N. Y. Male portrait.
Secured by pledge of public stock.

Two men holding female in their arms 2 Vig. Mirror, with farmer on left, dairymaid on right. 2
B'K OF SARATOGA SPRINGS, Saratoga, N. Y.
Compt's die. Locomotive and cars.

Female seated in figure 5 Cupids Vig. Portraits of female. 5
B'K OF SARATOGA SPRINGS, Saratoga, N. Y.
Compt's die. Two females, one holding figure 5.

TEN 1 Female. 0 10
Building.
B'K OF SARATOGA SPRINGS. Saratoga, N. Y.
Compt's die. Female standing.

20 2 Female. 0 20
Building and street.
B'K OF SARATOGA SPRINGS, Saratoga, N. Y.
TWENTY Female holding 2 in right and 0 in left hand

FIFTY Compt's die Female on either side of shield and bust; ship in distance. 50
Indian princess. BANK OF SARATOGA SPRINGS. Saratoga Springs, N. Y. Female crest

Compt's die. Vig. Locomotive and cars crossing bridge, canal boats, &c. 1
Country road with cars, load of hay, &c.
BANK OF SENECA FALLS, N. Y.
Portrait of female.
Fire Engine.

5 — V Three females with fig. 5 in centre. V — 5
Compt's die. — BK of WATERVILLE, Waterville, N. Y. — Med head.
5 — Eagle. — FIVE

10 — Two females representing Agriculture and Commerce. — 10
Compt's die — BANK OF WATERVILLE, Waterville, N. Y. — State Arms.
TEN — Eagle and X. — TEN

20 — BK of WATERVILLE, Waterville, N. Y. — 20 on med. head.
Compt's die. — Cattle, cows, &c.
TWENTY — 20 Dog and safe. 20 — Fillmore.

50 — BK of WATERVILLE, Waterville, N. Y. — 50
Indian, squaw and papoose; shield; female instructing children.
50 — Compt's die. — 50

1 — Plank road, load of hay drawn by horses, group of cattle, men on horseback and standing, building, tree &c.
Vig. Lady reclining on bale of goods, with arms resting on large wheel; hammer and other implements lying about; in the distance, steam vessel to the right; railroad cars and building to the left.
BK. OF WEST TROY. — ONE — 1 — Compt's die

2 — Sailor standing, compass in left hand, and bale of goods, hogshead, &c., steamboat and vessel in the distance.
Vig. Two females weaving; weaving machine in the background to the right.
BK. OF WEST TROY. — TWO — Fire engine between sigs. — 2 — Compt's. die.

Portrait of D. Webster. — Vig. Two steamboats; three ships in the distance; dock and men. — 5
BK. OF WEST TROY. — FIVE — Fire engine between sigs. — 5 — Compt's. die.

10 — BK. OF WEST TROY. — 10
Portrait of Gen. Wool. — Vig. Man with flag and large cannon.
X — X — Compt's. die.

male sharpening scythe. — 1 Vig. Female reaper seated. — ONE
B'K OF WESTFIELD, Westfield, N. Y.
Compt's die. — Ship.

Compt's die. — 2 Vig. male ploughing. — 2
B'K OF WESTFIELD, Westfield, N. Y.
Pigs. — Female, churning.

Compt's die. — 5 Vig. Washing sheep. — 5
BK OF WESTFIELD, Westfield, N. Y.
Artisan. — Female standing by figure 5.

TEN — X Boy on horse; cattle, &c. — 10
BK OF WESTFIELD, Westfield, N. Y.
Blacksmith with sledge, beside anvil. — Compt's die.

1 — 1 Vig. Urn with eagle on top; mound, female with liberty cap and pole. 1 — 1
Compt's die. — Clock. Child on either side.
1 — B'K OF WHITEHALL, Whitehall, N. Y. — 1

1 — 1 Cattle, children and trees. 1 — 1
BK OF WHITEHALL, Whitehall, N. Y.
Compt's die. — ONE — Portrait of female.

TWO — Title of Bank. — 2
Compt's die. — Boy on horseback with another horse by trough, female, etc.
TWO — TWO — Female portrait.

2 — 2 Vig. Mechanic at work, tools, &c, lumber; two females, ship in distance. 2 — 2
Compt's die. — Ship on stocks.
2 — B'K OF WHITEHALL, Whitehall, N. Y. — Steamboat. — 2

Compt's die. — 3
Title and word THREE on large green die.
Female portrait. — Chickens.

3 — 3 Vig. Shield surmounted with eagle, female on either side; bales, ship, &c. 3 — 3
Compt's die. — Male portrait.
3 — B'K OF WHITEHALL, Whitehall, N. Y. — Locomotive. — 3

(Old Plate.)
FIVE — 5 Vig. Three females seated; agricultural implements, &c. — 5
B'K OF WHITEHALL, Whitehall, N. Y. — Cattle and sheep in river.
Steamboat. — 5

5 — Vig. Female seated; plow, sickle, wheat, &c. canal boat, cars, &c. — 5
Compt's die. — B'K OF WHITEHALL, Whitehall, N. Y. — Sailor leaning against capstan, glass in hand.
FIVE — Anchor, horn of plenty, &c.

(Old Plate.)
X Vig. Two females with liberty cap, pole, balances, &c., shield surmounted with eagle in centre. X — 10
Full length male portrait. — TEN 10 TEN
B'K OF WHITEHALL, Whitehall, N. Y. — Steamboat. — 10

10 — Vig. Female, key in one hand, liberty pole in other; balances on safe; spread eagle, ships, and cars in distance. — 10
Compt's die. — B'K OF WHITEHALL, Whitehall, N. Y. — Female churning.
TEN — Locomotive and cars.

20 — Compt's die. — Vig. Female holding liberty pole, seated between figures 2 and 0. — 20
Farmer sharpening scythe. — B'K OF WHITEHALL, Whitehall, N. Y. — Female raking hay.

50 — 50 Washington on horseback. 50
Head of McDonough. — BK OF WHITEHALL, Whitehall, N. Y. — FIFTY DOLLARS
50

1 — Vig. Farmers at lunch; loading hay in distance. — 1
Compt's die. — BANK OF WHITESTOWN, Whitestown, N. Y. — Goddess of liberty.

TWO — 2 Vig. Female seated with sickle, wheat, &c. 2
Compt's die. — BANK OF WHITESTOWN, Whitestown, N. Y. — Artisan with horn of plenty
TWO — Trees &c.

Washington and horse. — Vig. Oxen, sheep &c. — FIVE
BANK OF WHITESTOWN, Whitestown, N. Y. — Female with wheat.
Compt's die. — 5

10 — Vig. Mirror with female on either side; ships and cars in distance. — 10
Compt's die — BANK OF WHITESTOWN, Whitestown, N. Y. — State arms.
TEN — Trees, ox, &c. — TEN

TWENTY — 20 Female seated; scientific apparatus; steamship in distance. 20 — XX
Compt's die. — BANK OF WHITESTOWN, Whitestown, N. Y.
TWENTY — Cattle, trees, etc.

1 — Female portrait, Vig. Female and figure 1. — 1
BK OF YONKERS, Yonkers, N. Y.
Compt's die. — Secured, &c. — Bee hive.

2 | Vig. Three females and a child in water, the females are holding up the child. | 2
Female portrait. | BK OF YONKERS, Yonkers, N Y. Secured, &c. | Compt's die.

Compt's die. | BK OF YONKERS, Yonkers, N Y. | 5
Female portrait. | 5 Vig. A view of Yonkers; train of cars, sloops, etc. Secured, etc. | 5

10 | Vig. View of Yonkers, train of cars, sloops &c. | 10
Compt's die. | BK OF YONKERS Yonkers, N. Y. Secured, &c.
TEN | | Female Portrait.

Compt's die. | BK OF YONKERS Yonkers, N. Y. | 20
20 | Vig. Cattle, three of which are standing up and one laying down three sheep on left. Secured, &c. | Childs Portrait.

New York
1 | Cattle, female milking, and farmer with ladder | 1
Herkimer | BELLINGER BANK
Compt's die | ONE DOLLAR | Child's portrait

New York
TWO on 2 | 2 Man, child, horse, colt, etc. 2 | 2
Compt's die | BELLINGER BANK
TWO | TWO DOLLARS Herkimer | Two children

ONE | | 1
State Arms. | Vig. Milkmaid sitting with pail, cattle, &c. 1 | Boy and anvil.
ONE | BLACK RIVER B' Watertown, N. Y. | ONE

TWO | Two females; one with sickle; sheaf; ship in distance. 2 on med. head. | Female.
Compt's die. | BLACK RIVER BK., Watertown, N. Y. | Portrait.
TWO | | Female.

| BLACK RIVER BK. Watertown. | 3
Female with Liberty Cap. | Vig. Female with cornucopia; on right, female with shield, on which is inscribed the figure 3; to the left, an eagle soaring, with figure 3 under eagle.
State Arms.

FIVE | 5 Man plowing with two horses. | 5
Female with sickle and grain. | BLACK RIVER BK., Watertown, N. Y. | Compt's die.
FIVE

| 5 Female in clouds with cornucopia. | 5
Liberty street | BLACK RIVER B'K, Watertown, N. Y. | Compt's die.

TEN | X Two females; cars, vessels, etc. | 10
Compt's die. | BLACK RIVER BK., Watertown, N. Y. | Boy and anvil.
TEN | | X

20 | BLACK RIVER BK Watertown | 20
Forest, and cars crossing bridge. | Vig. Three females representing Hope, Industry, and Charity. Compt's die. | City, shipping, &c.

FIFTY | BLACK RIVER BK. Watertown. | 50
Female with Liberty Cap and shield. | State Arms. Angel and female on right receiving a bell, and one on left, extending hand to angel.

1 ONE | Drove of cattle; man on horseback, boy in water; trees, house, fence, etc. | 1
Compt's die. | BRIGG'S BANK OF Clyde, N. Y. Safe. | Portrait of female.

2 | Horse and oxen before load of hay; three men and a boy; trees, etc. Train of cars | 2
Compt's die. | BRIGG'S BANK OF Clyde, N. Y.
TWO | | Canal scene village in distance.

5 | Man plowing with two horses; trees and farmhouses in distance. | 5
Two men and dog; man and boy behind them; trees and house in distance. | BRIGG'S BANK OF Clyde, N. Y. | Compt's die
FI 5 VE

TEN | Two oxen before hay cart, men loading hay; three men at work in distance. On left of vig. letter X. | Word ten, figs. 10, and letter X.
Male, female, two boys, lamb, etc. | BRIGG'S BANK OF Clyde, N. Y. | Compt's die.

1 | 1 Three small male figures with compass, charts, globe, &c.; shipping on right. 1 | Female seated.
Compt's die | BROOKLYN BANK, Brooklyn, N. Y. Secured by pledge of public stock.
1 | | ONE

Two Doll's Two Doll's
2 | 2 Female on either side of a shield, on which is a fig. 2. 2 | Head laughing.
Compt's die | BROOKLYN BANK, Brooklyn, N. Y. Secured by pledge of public stock. | TWO
2 | | Head laughing.

3 | 3 Female seated with sickle, sheaf and plough; cattle lying on ground. 3 | Female with sickle.
Compt's die | BROOKLYN BANK, Brooklyn, N. Y.
3 | Secured by pledge of public stock. | THREE

5 | 5 Archimedes raising the world. 5 | FIVE
Compt's die | BROOKLYN BANK, Brooklyn, N. Y. | Winged female beside urn; with trumpet.
5 | Secured by pledge of public stock. | V

10 | Archimedes raising the world. 10
Compt's die | BROOKLYN BANK, Brooklyn, N. Y. | Horse.
10 | Secured by pledge of public stock. | TEN

20 | Horse with Title of Bank around him. Archimedes raising the world. | 20
Compt's die
20 | Secured by pledge of public stock. | XX

50 | BROOKLYN BANK, Brooklyn, N Y. | Horse.
Compt's die | FIFTY DOLLARS.
50 | 50 Secured by pledge of public stock. | FIFTY

100 | Archimedes 100 raising the world; Title of bank running around the vignette. 100 | Female with sword and scales; eagle with portrait of Washingt'n on breast.
Compt's die
100 | Secured by pledge of public stock.

ONE | Vig. Harvest scene; Lunch time. 1 | 1
Compt's die. | BROOME CO. B'K. Binghampton, N. Y. | Female
Female head. | | 1

2 | Vig. Spread eagle on branch, cars, &c. 2 | 2
Compt's die. | BROOME CO. B'K. Binghampton, N. Y. | Female, sickle, &c.
2 | | TWO

5 | Farming scene; farmer seated with scythe, load of hay in background. Fig. 5 on right and left. | 5
Comp's die. | | Female seated.
FIVE | BROOME CO. BANK, Binghampton, N. Y. | FIVE

5 | BROOME CO. BANK, Binghampton, N. Y. | Figure 5 with Cupid on left
Compt's die. | Vig. Farmer about to sharpen his scythe, canal and cars in distance.
FIVE | | Franklin.

10 Compt's die. 10	Vig. Harvest scene, female seated with infant. BROOME CO. BANK, Binghampton. N. Y.	10 Female, artist tools, &c.
1 Compt's die 1	Vig. Sailor with shipping in distance. BUFFALO CITY B'K. Buffalo, N. Y.	1 ONE Canal boat under bridge
2 Compt's die.	Vig. Indian female overlooking City in distance. BUFFALO CITY B'K. Buffalo, N. Y.	2 Sailor seated.
FIVE Vig. Three artisans, one holding wheel to goddess of liberty on throne, with eagle.	Compt's die. BUFFALO CITY B'K. Buffalo, N. Y.	5 5
X Bridge.	BUFFALO CITY B'K. Buffalo, N. Y. Vig. Three females seated. Compt's die	10 Shipping.
Head of Major Burnett. ONE Compt's die.	Vig. Dairy maid in sitting posture; one cow reposing in front of her, and one standing; farm-house, trees and flocks in background. BURNET BANK, Syracuse. Eagle.	1 Indian princess holding staff with Liberty Cap on it; hand resting on shield.
TWO Compt's die. Head of Major Burnett.	State Arms. BURNET BANK, Syracuse. [illegible] plough, rake, &c.	TWO Goddess of Justice; balance on left hand fore-finger; sword in right hand.
FIVE Male portrait 5	Cow and calf in stream; cattle and house in distance. Female portrait. BURNET BANK, Syracuse, N. Y.	5 Compt's die. 5
5 FIVE Compt's die.	BURNET BANK, Syracuse. 5 Vig. Goddess of Liberty; staff and Liberty Cap across her lap; starry drapery; shield on her left; United States Capitol on her left and rear. 5	5 Head of Major Burnett.
10 Soldiers seated; one with drum.	Male portrait. Male portrait BURNET BANK, Syracuse, N. Y.	10 TEN Compt's die.

ONE Man seated	CAMBRIDGE VALLEY BANK, North White Creek, New-York. Interior of a blacksmiths' shop; mechanic and tools.	1 State arms.
Word two and $ mark. Female drawing water from a well; steamboat on left.	Title of Bank. Horse on either side of a shield; eagle at top; cars crossing bridge and view of city on right; building on left.	2 State Arms.
5 Compt's die	Drover and cattle CAMBRIDGE VALLEY B'K No. White Creek, N. Y. FIVE DOLLARS	5 Two females, white and Indian
X State Arms.	Portrait of Washington; milk-maid with pail, and cattle on right; two females representing agriculture on left. Title of Bank.	10 Portrait of Jenny Lind.
XX Male portrait	State Arms. Liberty and eagle. Title of Bank.	20 Male portrait
1	CANAJOHARIE BK., Canajoharie, N. Y. Compt's die. The vig., extends the whole width and ends of the note. Vig. Hop scene, gathering hops; two horses attached to wagon; numerous male and female figures at work, trees, &c	1
2 Portrait of Calhoun.	CANAJOHARIE BK., Canajoharie, N. Y. Vig. Same as ones, only a different view with farm houses, &c.	2 Compt's. die.
3 Shearing sheep.	CANAJOHARIE BK., Canajoharie, N. Y. Compt's. die. 3	3 Two men gathering corn.
5 Compt's. die.	CANAJOHARIE BK., Canajoharie, N. Y. Five farmers at work, gathering hay; two oxen before hay wagon.	5 Clay.
X Two females, one churning; cars in distance on left.	CANAJOHARIE BK., Canajoharie, N. Y. X Portrait of a girl. X	10 Compt's. die.

ONE ONE Compt's die.	Indian behind rock watching deers; trees, etc. CANASTOTA BANK, Canastota, N. Y. Female bathing.	1 Girl.
2 Compt's die 2	Indian and female either side of shield; ship, etc. in distance CANASTOTA BANK TWO DOLLARS Canastota, N. Y. Dogs	TWO Two soldiers, one standing, the other seated
5 Two Indians on cliff viewing city.	Men at work harvesting; two oxen before cart. CANASTOTA BANK, Canastota, N. Y.	5 Compt's die. 5
TEN Two males on cliff.	X Load of hay drawn by two horses, female and child on top; blacksmith's shop and men at work; dog, girl and boy. CANASTOTA BANK, Canastota, N. Y.	10 TEN Compt's die
XX	Males and females gathering hops. CANASTOTA BANK, Canastota, N. Y. Compt's die. Twenty Dollars	20 Two horses before wagon; two men and dog; men in distance
1 Compt's die 1	ONE Vig. Female, shield and eagle; wheel and anvil on right; ships in distance on the left. ONE CATSKILL BANK, Catskill, N. Y. Steamboat.	Steamboat. 1 Steamboat.
2 Compt's die. 2	2 Vig. Ship and small boat, and hills in background. 2 CATSKILL BANK, Catskill, N. Y. Steamboat.	TWO DOLLARS
THREE Sheaf of grain. THREE	CATSKILL BANK, Catskill, N. Y. 3 Vig. Large ship, female seated in representation of commerce. 3 Ferry boat.	THREE Figure of Liberty erect supporting vase of flowers.
Two children with cattle, flowers, etc. FIVE	5 Child's head 5 CATSKILL BANK FIVE DOLLARS on FIVE and 5	5 Compt's die 5
5 Compt's die 5	V Vig. Female and eagle, female holds a goblet. V CATSKILL BANK, Catskill, N. Y. Eagle.	FIVE

Left	Center	Right
10 Female portrait	View of Catskill House on mountain CATSKILL BANK TEN DOLLARS Catskill	10 Compt's die
10 Compt's die. 10	Vig. Female with bucket, sheep on right, and cattle on left. X CATSKILL BANK, Catskill, N. Y.	Female reclining, and word TEN. 10
FIFTY	50 Vig. A Female seated working a spinning wheel. 50 CATSKILL BANK, Catskill, N. Y.	FIFTY DOLLARS
ONE HUNDRED	100 and medallion wreath. 100 Vig. A female seated large eagle and figures 100. CATSKILL BANK, Catskill, N. Y.	ONE HUNDRED
ONE Compt's die	1 Vig. Portrait of Washington. 1 CAYUGA Co. BANK. Auburn, N. Y. ONE DOLLAR. Child seated. ONE DOLLAR.	ONE Figure standing.
TWO Compt's die.	2 Vig. Male portrait; shipping and cars in background. Bee hive. CAYUGA Co. BANK. Auburn, N. Y. Man's head.	TWO Figure standing.
Compt's die. THREE	3 Vig. Portrait of Andrew Jackson, female on either side. CAYUGA Co. BANK. Auburn, N. Y. Eagle.	3 Indian in canoe. THREE
5 Compt's die. 5	Public building. Vig. Figure standing. Wheat &c. CAYUGA Co. BANK. Auburn, N. Y. FIVE	FIVE 5 FIVE
Compt's die. Man with scythe.	CAYUGA CO. BANK, Auburn, N. Y. Female with sheaf of wheat seated in large letter V.	5 Cattle and hogs.
Compt's die. Blacksmith.	CAYUGA CO. BANK, Auburn, N. Y. Large ornamental X enclosing figures of justice and liberty.	10 Figure of justice.

Left	Center	Right
10 Compt's die. 10	Locomotive and cars. Vig. Figure standing. Canal scene. CAYUGA Co. BANK, Auburn, N. Y. Indian in canoe.	TEN X TEN
XX Compt's die. 20	20 Female feeding Eagle. 20 CAYUGA CO. BANK. Auburn, N. Y. Eagle.	XX Justice. 20
50 Compt's die. 50	L Portrait of Washington. L CAYUGA Co. BANK, Auburn, N. Y. Sampson and lion.	Female with eagle. 50
1 Compt's die. ONE	CENTRAL BANK, Brooklyn, N. Y. Farmer and farm scene; boy with horse and sleigh.	1 Male portrait
2 2	Santa Claus drawn by reindeer. Compt's die. CENTRAL BANK, Brooklyn, N. Y.	TWO Male portrait
3 3	CENTRAL BANK, Brooklyn, N. Y. Female reclining on bale of goods; sail vessel on right, and steamboat on left.	3 Compt's die
5 Compt's die. V	CENTRAL BANK, Brooklyn, N. Y. View of the Brooklyn City Hall.	5 Male portrait
TEN Compt's die. X	CENTRAL BANK, Brooklyn, N. Y. X Ship under sail. X	TEN Male portrait
50 Compt's die. L	Goddess of Liberty and female representing Agriculture. CENTRAL BANK, Brooklyn, N. Y.	50 Male portrait
100	CENTRAL BANK, Brooklyn, N. Y. Compt's die. Male portrait.	C Three men at work.

Left	Center	Right
Medallion head. Compt's die. Medallion head.	One on medallion head. Vig. Farmer with oxen and sheep. One on medallion head. CENTRAL BANK, Cherry Valley, N. Y. Loading hay.	1 Female with rake. 1
Med. head Compt's die Med. head	2 on medallion head. Vig. Female seated in figure 2; two farmers in background. 2 on medallion head. CENTRAL BANK. Cherry Valley, N. Y. Dog's head.	TWO Female seated in figure 2 with balances and sword. TWO
Med. head. Compt's die. Med. head.	CENTRAL BANK. Cherry Valley, N. Y. THREE on Med. head. Two females with liberty pole and cap. THREE on Med. head. Wheat, &c.	Female cruel. 3
FIVE Compt's die. FIVE	5 Vig. Large figure 5, females on either side. 5 CENTRAL BANK, Cherry Valley, N. Y. Female with anchor.	FIVE Female. FIVE
X Compt's die. 10	Medallion head, with TEN on it. Female holding 1 in right, and 0 in left. CENTRAL BANK, Cherry Valley, N. Y.	X Portrait of female. 10
20 Compt's die 20	Female looking towards sea. 20 Female with sickle & sheep. CENTRAL BANK, Cherry Valley, N. Y.	20 Medallion head. 20
1 S. of N. York Female	Indian behind rock watching deer. Compt's die CENTRAL BK of TROY ONE DOLLAR Troy	1 ONE Male portrait
TWO Male portrait.	Title under vig. Vig. Locomotive, train of cars and depot; locomotive crossing bridge in the distance. Compt's die.	TWO 2
3 Compt's die.	Vig. Santa Claus riding in a car drawn by reindeers. CENTRAL BANK	3 Portrait of female
FIVE Male portrait. 5	Compt's die. Vig. Man on horseback; cattle and sheep. CENTRAL BANK.	V Head and shoulders of dog.

TEN Compt's die. X	CENTRAL BANK, Troy. Vig. Spread eagle.	TEN Male portrait.
20 XX 20	CENTRAL BANK, Troy. Vig. Miniature view of female reclining on bale of goods. Compt's die.	TWENTY Group of three females representing Agriculture, Commerce, &c.
ONE Stonecutter at work. ONE	Compt's die. Blacksmith shoeing horse; mule; locomotive in distance. CENTRAL CITY BK., Syracuse, N. Y.	1 Blacksmith anvil, hammer. ONE
Compt's die. Two cherubs Female portrait.	2 Farming scene—farmers at lunch; haying in background. CENTRAL CITY BK., Syracuse, N. Y. Agricultural implements.	2 Flower girl
Compt's die. Two sea nymphs. Steamship.	5 Three females representing Agriculture, Commerce and arts. CENTRAL CITY BK, Syracuse, N. Y.	5 Five figures around large V.
FIVE Spread Eagle and Shield. Compts die	Female crowning an Eagle with left hand, holding Portrait of Washington; with buildings on left; ships on right. CENTRAL CITY BK, Syracuse, N. Y. Agricultural implements	5 Five females around fig 5
10 Compt's die. TEN	Man looking at chart; two stonecutters, etc.; men, horses and cart in distance. Title of Bank.	10 Female head TEN
Female seated with scales. Compt's die.	20 View of N. Y. bay, vessels, etc. Title of Bank.	TWENTY Sailor hoisting flag.
1 Compt's die	CHAUTAUQUA CO. B'K Girl and boy with cattle in circular die ONE DOLLAR Jamestown, N. Y.	1 Basket of corn
1 Compt's die. 1	1 Vig. Man seated by die with 1 on it, an eagle on top with motto—"Internal Improvements." 1 CHAUTAUQUE Co. BANK, Jamestown, N.Y.	1 Oxen. 1

2 Compt's die TWO	Man and two horses in circular die. CHAUTAUQUA CO. B'K 2 TWO DOLLARS 2 Jamestown	2 Female with flowers
2 Compt's die. 2	2 Vig. Oxen in small die. 2 CHAUTAUQUE Co. BANK Jamestown, N. Y.	2 Vessel ready to launch. 2
Compt's die 3	Three children reading book in circular die CHAUTAUQUA CO. B'K 3 THREE DOLLARS 3 Jamestown	3 Dog's head
3 Compt's die 3	3 Vig. Oxen in small die. 3 CHAUTAUGUE Co. BANK Jamestown, N. Y.	3 Male portrait 3
5 Compt's die. 5	CHAUTAUQUE Co. BANK Jamestown, N. Y. Vig. Indian stringing bow.	FIVE Female Portrait. V
10 Compt's die. 10	Vig. Farmers mowing CHAUTAUQUE Co. BANK Jamestown, N. Y.	Oxen. Female Portrait. 10
Girl with dogs Compt's die	STATE OF N. Y. 1 Scene near blacksmith's shop, mending wheelbarrow. CHEMUNG CANAL B'K ONE DOLLAR Elmira	ONE on 1 Two girls with sickle, flowers, etc.
Compt's die. Steamer.	1 Vig. Locomotive and cars. CHEMUNG CANAL BANK, Elmira, N. Y. Farmer, plow, etc.	Figure 1 with "ONE" running across it. Female leaning on figure 1.
TWO Compt's die 2	CHEMUNG CANAL B'K Scene at flour mill by side of canal, cars, etc. in distance TWO DOLLARS Elmira	2 Female with torch beside column
Female Indian. Compt's die.	2 Vig. Dairy maid, cows, &c. CHEMUNG CANAL BANK, Elmira, N. Y. Dogs head.	2 Child with sheil, &c. TWO

3 Compt's die. 3	3 Cattle 3 CHEMUNG CANAL BANK, Elmira, N. Y. Indian in canoe.	3 Canal locks. 3
Compt's die. Portrait of female.	3 Vig. Farmer with oxen and sheep. CHEMUNG CANAL BANK, Elmira, N. Y. Wand and flowers.	3 Two females standing.
5 Compt's die. 5	5 5 Title of Bank. Two females, eagle, shield, cars, shipping, etc. Canal locks.	FIVE Male portrait 5
FIVE FIVE Compt's die	Two females, one of whom is crowning bust of Washington; ship in distance. 5 CHEMUNG CANAL BANK Elmira, N. Y. Cars.	FIVE Large ornamental fig. 5 FIVE
10 Eagle. Compt's die.	(New Plate.) Vig. Female seated, with shipping in the distance. CHEMUNG CANAL BANK, Elmira, N. Y. Wheat &c.	Bale of goods &c. 10 Train of cars.
10 Male portrait. 10	X Vig. Compt's die. X CHEMUNG CANAL BANK. Elmira, N. Y. Head of horse	Female holding the word "TEN." 10
20 Male seated, between figures 2 and 0	Compt's die. Female seated; bridge, train of cars, steamer, city, &c CHEMUNG CANAL BANK. Elmira, N. Y. Cog wheels, &c.	20 Female between a 2 and 0. TWENTY
Female erect with pole and cap. 50	50 Title of Bank 50 Compt's die. Boy astride a deer.	Female portrait. 50
100 Male figure destroying serpents. 100	100 Compt's die 100 Title of Bank. Canal locks.	100 Neptune in car; female soaring in air. 100
Two males with female on shoulders. Compt's die.	1 Vig. Female seated holding figure 1. CHESTER BANK, Chester, N. Y.	1 Female steering.

2 | Vig. Mirror with male on right, female on left. | 2
Compt's die. | CHESTER BANK, Chester, N. Y. | Locomotive and cars.
TWO

5 | Vig. Female with liberty pole, seated by American eagle with figure 5. | 5
Compt's die. | CHESTER BANK, Chester, N. Y. | Figure of Justice standing.
FIVE

Female seated between 1 and 0, with cornucopia and key. | Compt's die. | 10
CHESTER BANK, Chester, N. Y. | Men, cattle, and sheep.
10 | Secured &c.

Vig. Female holding 2 in right, and 0 in left hand. | Compt's die. | 20
CHESTER BANK. Chester, N. Y | Female portrait.
20

1 | Compt's die | Farmer chopping wood; farmhouse, etc. in distance. | ONE
CHITTENANGO B'K ONE DOLLAR Chittenango
Female figure erect | Female holding rake
Plough, wheat, etc.

1 | CHITTENANGO B'K, Chittenango, N. Y. | 1
ONE | Female seated by side of silver dollar; red figure 1 on either side. | Female seated with shield and sword.
Compt's die | Gold dollar.

2 | Female, cherub and two silver dollars | TWO
Compt's die. | CHITTENANGO B'K. Chittenango, N.Y. | Large figure 2 and female
2 | Rising Sun.

2 | Title under vig. Vig. Compt's die; cows lying and standing; milk maid sitting, pail on right arm; farmer with rake lying down, hat in left hand; two gold dollars before him. | 2
Portrait of female.
TWO | Dog, his name, "Wave," on collar. | Two females.

Compt's die. | Indian, squaw and pappoose in canoe; wigwams and hills in distance. | 3
CHITTENANGO B'K. Chittenango, N.Y. | Female with figure 3.
3 | Bales and cornucopia.

5 | Hunter, Indian, female, three cupids, five gold dollars, etc. | FIVE
FIVE | CHITTENANGO B'K FIVE DOLLARS Chittenango, N.Y. | Large ornamental figure 5
Compt's die | Man seated | FIVE

Female with balances; sheaf of wheat, etc. | 10 Harvest scene; farmers nooning; loading wagon, etc. | 10
CHITTENANGO BK., Chittenango, N. Y. | Squaw and pappoose.
Compt's die. | Female reclining.

XX | CHITTENANGO BK. Vig. Comptroller's die; Indian reclining on a shield, bow and arrow in right hand; eagle flying above him, water on his right and left; on his right deer and canoe in water; on his left three deers, one lying down and two standing. Safe. | 20
Portrait of D'l Webster.
Indian with lance and bow in right hand. | TWENTY

50 | CHITTENANGO BK. Vig. Commercial scene; vessels and houses in background; in foreground female sitting; cornucopia in right hand, sceptre in left, and sheaf of wheat on her right; cornucopia of coin on left; also, barrels, boxes, &c. Steamboat. | Angel or Cupid holding shield with 50 on it.
Portrait of Franklin Pierce. | Female standing.
Compt's die.

ONE | Portrait and flag. | Female in sitting posture, staff in left hand. | 1 | ONE
Female in standing position, left hand resting on ledge of rock, right arm elevated; monument in view.
State Arms. | A
ONE | CITIZENS' BANK, Fulton. | ONE

TWO | 2 Vig. Female resting, flag, &c.
Human figure seated, left foot slightly elevated, right arm extended. | CITIZENS' BANK, Fulton. | Large 2, word TWO twice, and portrait.
State Arms. | Sail vessel.

Fig. 5, cars, bridge, Indians, water, etc. | 5 Washington 5 | Female seated with sheaf.
CITIZENS' BANK, Fulton, N. Y. | 5
Compt's die. | Secured, etc.

Vig. Female in sitting position, left arm reclining upon shield; motto of U. S. inscribed; eagle, &c. | Figure 5 with representations of cupid. | FIVE
State Arms.
5 | B | CITIZENS' BANK, Fulton. | FIVE

State Arms. | 10 Vig. Two human figures—male and female; female holding sickle and sheaf of wheat; house and farm scene to the right in the distance; vessel under sail to the left. | 10
Monument. | X | Woman with spy-glass; boy in skiff. | Portrait.
CITIZENS' BANK, Fulton. | 10

Vig. Female reclining, holding in right hand a sledge hammer; in left, a pair of compasses; vessel under sail in the distance; four men working with horse on right in the distance. | State Arms with Cupid on either side. | TWENTY
Portrait of female.
20 | CITIZENS' BANK, Fulton. | 20

Word one and fig. 1. | View of Atlantic Basin, Brooklyn. | 1
Compt's die. | CITY BANK OF BROOKLYN, Brooklyn, N. Y. | Female resting on a large fig. 1; shield by her side.
ONE | Female with scales and money.

TWO | 2 Female with sickle and grain. | 2
Compt's die. | Title of Bank.
TWO | Female with scales. | Female raking hay.

Ship under sail. | 3 Train of cars. | 3
Title of Bank. | Ship on the stocks.
Compt's die. | Female with scales and money. | THREE

Merchandise and anchor. | FIVE Female and eagle on either side of a shield with fig. 5 on it. | 5
Compt's die. | Female with fig. 5 on a safe; warrior with shield and spear in background.
Train of cars. | Title of Bank.
Same as threes.

TEN | Compt's die. | Female seated between 1 and 0. | 10
View of the Ship houses at the Navy Yard; ships. | Title of Bank. | Two females; one with spear and shield, the other with sword and scales.
TEN | Same as threes.

20 | Compt's die. | Female seated between 2 and 0. | 20
View of the City Hall. | Title of Bank. | Female seated between, and holding a 2 and 0.
TWENTY | Same as threes.

Neptune with trident. | 50 Female on right of shield crowning bust of Washington with wreath; Goddess of Liberty and sheaf; on the left bbls., bales and ship on right. | 50
Compt's die. | Title of Bank. | Portrait of a child.
Same as threes.

100 | Female seated on either side of view of ship and water, surmounted by an eagle; bale of goods, cars, steamboat, &c. | 100
Compt's die.
100 | Title of Bank. | Female Portrait.
Same as threes.

ONE | Sailor and female seated; sheafs, quadrant, etc.; in distance, ship and house. | 1 | ONE
Compt's die. | Female seated; factory in distance.
ONE | CITY BANK, Oswego, N. Y. | ONE
Secured &c.

1 | Vig. Woodman kneeling, &c. Gold dollar. | 1
CITY BANK, Oswego, N. Y. | Public building.
Compt's die. | ONE
State Arms.

TWO | Male and female, two gold dollars, etc., cattle on left, farmhouse on right | 2
Eagle, shield, etc. | CITY BANK TWO DOLLARS Oswego, N. Y. | Banking house
Compt's die | Female | TWO

TWO 2 Vig. Ship in die. 2 Sailor.
Compt's die. CITY BANK, Oswego, N. Y.
TWO 2

FIVE Five human figures and five gold dollars. 5 FIVE
5 CITY BANK. Oswego, N. Y.
Compt's die Implements. Female feeding eagle

Large figure; cars crossing bridge; Indians. Vig. Female seated on bales; cars and shipping in distance. 5
CITY BANK, Oswego, N. Y. FIVE
Compt's die. 5

TEN 10 Amer. eagle. TEN
Sailor seated CITY BANK, Oswego, N. Y Female seated.
Compt's die. 10

20 Vig. Two females with mirror, eagle, &c. 20
CITY BANK, Oswego, N. Y.
Compt's die. Portrait of Washington

1 1 Cow, calf and sheep. 1 1
CITY BANK OF POUGHKEEPSIE, N. Y.
Compt's die. Dog and safe.

TWO Title of Bank. TWO on 2.
Compt's die. 2 Ox. 2 Female portrait.
TWO TWO

Compt's die CITY BANK of Poughkeepsie, N. Y. 3
Large red 3; on right boy and sheep; on left, female, gleaning scene, etc.
3 3

5 Title of Bank. 5
Female portrait. 5 Compt's die
Fowl. FIVE

10 Eagle—Ten Dollars above, red X each side. 10
Two females. CITY BANK of Poughkeepsie, N. Y. Compt's die

20 Compt's CITY BANK, die. Poughkeepsie, N. Y. 20
Full length figure of female.
20 Female portrait. 20
20

1 Female reclining, eagle behind; train of cars, bridge and city in distance. 1
CLINTON BANK, Buffalo, N. Y. Statue of DeWitt Clinton.
Compt's die. Horse.

2 Portrait of Clinton; city, steamboat, bridge and cars on right; farm scene on left. 2
Compt's die. CLINTON BANK, Buffalo, N. Y.
TWO 2 2 Two cherubs carrying with distaff and sheaf.

Compt's die. CLINTON BANK, Buffalo, N. Y. THREE
Three females reclining, representing Liberty, Agriculture and Manufacture. Justice erect and a female seated.
3 3 3

V CLINTON BANK, Buffalo, N. Y. 5
Fillmore. Truth reclining on safe looking at shield on which is ship on stocks and rising sun; sheep and sheafs on right. Compt's die.
FIVE 5 5 V across five

X Shield on which is word Hope and anchor; cars crossing bridge and factories on right; ship, steamboat and city on left. Webster. 10
Justice seated. CLINTON BANK, Buffalo, N. Y. TEN Compt's die

1 On die with words ONE and small 1s. COLUMBIA BANK, Chatham Four Corners, N. Y. 1 On die with words ONE and small 1s.
Portrait of Washington.
Compt's die ONE DOLLAR. Female representing agriculture

2 Compt's die. COLUMBIA BANK. Chatham Four Corners, N. Y. 2
Portraits of Andrew Jackson and Winfield Scott. Bust of Female holding flowers
2 TWO DOLLARS.

Compt's die Portrait of Webster, Franklin, and Clay. 3 On die with words THREE and small 3s.
3 On die with words THREE and small 3s. COLUMBIA BANK, Chatham Four Corners. N. Y. THREE DOLLARS

Figure of liberty erect, wreath in right hand shield beside her. Eagle clutching arrows, shield, and olive branch. 5
COLUMBIA BANK, Chatham Four Corners, N. Y. Compt's die
FIVE FIVE DOLLARS. 5

Female bust COLUMBIA BANK, Chatham Four Corners, N. Y. 10 On die with TEN.
10 On die with TEN. Three children with book on table, in oval.
TEN DOLLARS. X Compt's die

20 On die with small 20's. View of train of cars crossing bridge, canal boats, men, horses, &c. 20 On die with small 20's.
COLUMBIA BANK. Chatham Four Corners, N. Y.
TWENTY DOLLARS.
Compt's die.

Farmer ploughing with two horses, farm house in back ground. Compt's die 50 On die with small FIFTY'S
50 On die with small FIFTY'S. COLUMBIA BANK, Chatham Four Corners, N. Y.
FIFTY DOLLARS. Female bust.

Female holding child, grain, &c. Figure of Justice, with sword and scales, surrounded by clouds. Compt's die. 100 On die with small 100's.
100 On die with small 100's. COLUMBIA BANK, Chatham Four Corners, N. Y.
ONE HUNDRED DOLLARS.

1 1 Three females, sheaf of wheat, etc., ship on left ONE
Compt's die COMMERCIAL B'K DeWitt Clinton
ONE DOLLAR
1 Albany, N. Y. ONE
Secured, etc.

TWO on Med head. Vig. Female looking over a rock, cars, steamboat and canal on right. TWO
2 Compt's die. Franklin.
2 COMMERCIAL BANK Albany, N. Y. TWO
2 Secured, &c. 2

3 3 on Med. head. 3 on Med. head. THREE
Compt's die. Vig. Two females and shield, one on right holds a sickle. Portrait of Jackson.
3 COMMERCIAL BANK Albany, N. Y. THREE
3 Secured &c. 3

5 FIVE on Med. head Three females one pointing to ship in distance Compt's die 5
Washington COM. BK of ALBANY DeWitt Clinton
V FIVE DOLLARS Albany V
Secured, etc.

10 Med. head and word Ten. Compt's die. 10
Male portrait Vig. Three females seated sheaf of wheat, and quadrant on right trees in distance, on left ship in distance. Portrait of Washington.
10 COMMERCIAL BANK Albany, N. Y. 10

20 20 Vig. Two females reclining, ships in distance on right, and shield on left. Compt's die. 20
Male portrait. Portrait of Washington.
20 COMMERCIAL BK Albany, N. Y. 20
Secured, etc.

Left	Centre	Right
50 Portrait 50	Vig. Three females seated, representing agriculture and commerce. Medallion head and figure 50 on left of Vig. State Arms on right. COMMERCIAL BK. Albany, N. Y.	50 Male portrait 50
100 Portrait of Washington. 100	100 Vig. Three females seated, sheaf of wheat on right, and quadrant and ship on left in distance. Compt's die. COMMERCIAL BK. Albany, N. Y. Secured, etc.	100 Male portrait 100
ONE Compt's die. ONE	COMMERCIAL BK. Clyde, N. Y. 1 Vig. Female seated, ship in distance. 1	Cx. 1
II Compt's die. II	2 Vig. Female seated on bale, &c. 2 COMMERCIAL BK, Clyde, N. Y.	Female seated holding two. TWO
5 Compt's die. 5	5 Vig. Neptune seated with eagle, ship and cars in distance. 5 COMMERCIAL BK. Clyde, N. Y. Vessels.	Eagle. FIVE
Ten dollars. Mechanic, sailor and farmer making offering to Goddess of Liberty; implements, &c	Compt's die. COMMERCIAL B'K, OF CLYDE, N. Y.	10 Female
TWENTY Two males and two females with tablets and quadrant; city in distance	COMMERCIAL B'K, OF CLYDE, N. Y. 20 Compt's die.	20 Male, two females, dog and cattle.
Compt's die. Mechanic; safe and anvil; two females, steamship in distance.	1 Female in clouds over city, distributing flowers; view of rising sun. COMMERCIAL BANK Glenn Falls, N. Y. Secured, &c.	ONE Washington. ONE
Compt's die. Figure 2 with sailor and female.	Two female figures, Justice and Liberty; village on right, cars on left; eagle mounted between the two. COMMERCIAL BANK Glenn Falls, N. Y. Secured, &c.	TWO Figure 2 and female.
Compt's die. 3	Goddess of Liberty on globe; eagle and shield. COMMERCIAL BANK Glenn Falls, N. Y. Secured, &c.	THREE 3 Lighthouse and female seated.

Left	Centre	Right
Compt's die. Squaw; Indians in canoe; wigwams in distance.	V and letters FIVE. Spread eagle and shield. V and letters FIVE. COMMERCIAL BANK Glenn Falls, N. Y.	5 Female seated with book and pen.
Compt's die. Large X and ten scene.	COMMERCIAL BANK Glenn Falls, N. Y. Vig. Female blowing trumpet; steamboat and ship on right; village, load of hay and trees on left.	X and letters TEN Mechanic seated on a boiler. TEN
1 Washington. 1	1 Compt's die. Vig. Female leaning on rock, looking down on steamboat, &c. COMMERCIAL B'K. Rochester, N. Y. Plow, &c.	1 Female with liberty pole, U. S. shield, &c.
TWO Compt's die. TWO	2 Vig. Female with sword, sickle, &c. 2 cars on right, agricultural implements, &c, on left. COMMERCIAL B'K. Rochester, N. Y.	Mechanic seated; cornucopia; implements &c. surrounded with corn.
3 Male portrait 3	Vig. Female, bales, &c.; cars and ship in distance. 3 COMMERCIAL B'K. Rochester, N. Y. Eagle.	Compt's die 3 Female seated.
FIVE Female holding cap, eagle, ship, and U. S. flag Compt's die.	Vig. Shield with 5 in centre; Indians on left; female teaching children on right. COMMERCIAL B'K. Rochester, N. Y. Female.	5 Male portrait
TEN Female portrait. Compt's die	COMMERCIAL B'K. Rochester, N. Y. Vig. Three females, cornucopia, anchor, &c. Propeller	10 Male portrait TEN
20 Compt's die.	XX Vig. Three females, shield and eagle mounted in centre; cars on right, ship on left. COMMERCIAL BK, Rochester, N. Y.	Full length female standing on globe with word TWENTY on it.
50 Compt's die. 50	Vig. Two females, bales and bbls behind them; ship in the distance. 50 COMMERCIAL BK, Rochester, N. Y.	FIFTY Sailor leaning on a capstan, telescope in his hand, anchor behind him. FIFTY
Three females, anchor. 100	COMMERCIAL BK. Rochester, N. Y. Vig. Steamship and vessels.	100 Compt's die.

Left	Centre	Right
ONE Female and fig. 1. Compt's die.	COMMERCIAL B'K. Saratoga Springs, N. Y. ONE DOLLAR. ONE	1 Male reclining; sheep, dog, etc.; cars crossing bridge. 1
2 Compt's die. TWO	Female seated with distaff; ships and cars in distance. Title of Bank. [illegible]	TWO Man sharpening scythe; fig. 2 at his back.
5 Eagle. FIVE	Title of Bank. Female in clouds with eagle, pole, cap, shield and drapery. Rising sun.	Word five and letter V. Compt's die. 5
Letter X and word Ten. Sailor. TEN	Title of Bank. Two males and a female: train of cars, steamboat and city in distance. Eagle.	TEN Female and letter X. Compt's die.
20 Washington TWENTY	Title of Bank. Female portrait. Female seated blowing trumpet; ship, steamboat and city in distance. Compt's die. Tree.	XX Sailor; wharf scene. TWENTY
1 Female with wheat. 1	COMMERCIAL B'K, Troy, N. Y. 1 Female with pail on head, cows, &c. 1	1 Compt's die.
1 Compt's die	Spread eagle, clutching shield, arrows, and olive branch. COMMERCIAL B'K OF TROY, Troy, N. Y. ONE DOLLAR.	1 Female Portrait.
TWO Compt's die TWO	Man with two horses; house in the right. COMMERCIAL B'K, Troy, N. Y. TWO DOLLARS.	2 Girl's head.
2 Compt's die. TWO	Male portrait. Female seated on bales; steamer in distance. COMMERCIAL B'K, Troy, N. Y.	2 2
TWO Compt's die. TWO	2 Female seated with wheat, &c. 2 COMMERCIAL B'K, Troy, N. Y. Washington.	Artisan with gold.

Left	Centre	Right
Compt's die. 3	COMMERCIAL B'K, Troy, N.Y. Three children in circular die reading from book. THREE DOLLARS.	3 Horse's head.
3 Vig. 3 figures with printing press, &c., Faust, Gutenburg and Schoeffer.	COMMERCIAL B'K. Troy, N.Y. Compt's die.	3 Male portrait 3
5 Compt's die. FIVE	Five females with lions, keys, &c. COMMERCIAL B'K. Troy, N.Y. Coach.	5 Female with shield. FIVE
5 Farmer with corn.	COMMERCIAL B'K, Troy, N.Y. Laborers working; one smoking a pipe, another wheeling a barrow. 5 5	5 Compt's die. FIVE
10 Blacksmith at work.	Scene at depot: cars, steamboats, drays, etc. COMMERCIAL BK of Troy, N.Y.	X Compt's die.
10 Female, eagle, key, and safe. TEN	View of all the State Arms of the Union; two females on either side; steamship on left; on right men mowing, factories, etc. COMMERCIAL B'K Troy, N.Y. Portrait.	10 Two females, eagle, shield, cornucopia, &c. TEN
20 Male portrait	Three men shipyard, &c; ship on stocks on left, and steamboat, ship, and city on right. COMMERCIAL B'K. Troy, N.Y. Building small boat.	20 Compt's die
50 Ml portrait	Two wild horses alarmed at train of cars; trees, etc. COMMERCIAL B'K. Troy, N.Y. Female and anchor.	50 Compt's die.
100 Deer.	Indians spearing buffaloes. COMMERCIAL BK., Troy, N.Y. Compt's Die.	100 Dog and game.
ONE Compt's die.	Farmer ploughing. COMMERCIAL B'K, Whitehall, N.Y.	ONE Female.

Left	Centre	Right
2 Compt's die. TWO	Sailor. Portrait of Washington. Female reaper. COMMERCIAL B'K. Whitehall, N.Y.	2 Compt's die TWO
Compt's die. 3 State arms.	Steamboat leaving wharf. COMMERCIAL B'K. Whitehall, N.Y. Schooner.	3 Cupid. THREE
Female with sword. Compt's die.	5 Vig. Female seated with artisans tools, steamer in distance. COMMERCIAL B'K, Whitehall, N.Y.	5 Female with basket of corn.
Compt's die. Sailor with [illegible]. TEN	Cars; horse; house in distance. COMMERCIAL BK of Whitehall, N.Y.	10 Female seated. TEN
Compt's die. Sailor with quadrant; ship in distance.	Spread eagle on shield; cars and house in distance. 50 COMMERCIAL BK of Whitehall, N.Y.	Female seated on bag. 50
1 Compt's die.	CROTON RIVER B'K. Southeast N.Y. ONE DOLLAR	1 Female seated by side of silver dollar bales, anchor and house.
2 Compt's die 2	Cattle eating from hay rick 2 2 CROTON RIVER B'K TWO DOLLARS Southeast, N.Y.	2 Girl with fruit
2 Compt's die 2	Horse, cows and fence; bridge and train of cars in distance. CROTON RIVER B'K Southeast, N.Y. Dogs head.	TWO 2 Male portrait
Compt's die 3	Boy, girl, and cattle under tree. CROTON RIVER B'K THREE DOLLARS Southeast	3 Girl standing, with jug on fence
Cattle and sheep; boy on horse, trees, &c. V	FIVE Eagle. CROTON RIVER B'K. Southeast, N.Y. Locomotive and tender.	5 Compt's die 5

Left	Centre	Right
10 Boy with pigeon.	Cows, sheep, trees, house, &c. CROTON RIVER B'K. Southeast, N.Y. Dog's head.	10 Eagle and shield. Compt's die.
Male and female by side of wall; fences, etc; load of hay going in barn. 20	Compt's die. TWENTY DOLLARS. CROTON RIVER B'K. Southeast, N.Y. Cow's head.	20 Milkmaid with pail.
100	Man, woman, child, cows, chickens, fence, houses, etc. Compt's die. CROTON RIVER BK, South East, N.Y. Horse.	100 Letter C, female bust, sheaf, etc.
1 Compt's die.	CUBA BANK, Cuba, N.Y. Ornamental die work, on which is "One Dollar" in circular form, with portrait of girl at bottom; portrait of Washington on right; woodman felling a tree on left. Cottage.	1 Portrait of female.
2 Compt's die. 2	Train of cars approaching depot; passengers about to get aboard, train of cars crossing bridge in distance. CUBA BANK, Cuba, N.Y. 2	Ornamental die work, on which is "Two Dollars" in circular form, portrait at bottom. TWO
V Locomotive and cars coming down hill; cabin, trees and hills in distance.	Three men rolling log; two men on right, one of which is felling tree; and still another on left standing by side of oxen; trees, &c. CUBA BANK, Cuba, N.Y. Woodman felling tree.	5 Compt's die in square form. 5
Portrait of female. X	10 Two oxen before hay-cart; boy by side, with pitchfork on his shoulder; another boy lying on top of cart. CUBA BANK, Cuba, N.Y. Ducks and young ones.	TEN Indian head. Compt's die
Two females, one churning; the other turning out cheese; hen and chickens; cows in distance; shed, &c.	Compt's die. Female with pail; hand resting on fence-rail; two cows, one lying down; hens and rooster; shed, &c; two cows on right, with sheep in distance. CUBA BANK, Cuba, N.Y.	20 XX
1 Surrounded by ornamental die work.	1 Compt's die. 1 CUYLER'S BANK, Palmyra.	1 Female with scales and sword.
2 Surrounded by ornamental die work.	2 Compt's die. 2 CUYLER'S BANK, Palmyra.	2 Man with sheaf of wheat.

5 Surrounded by ornamental die work.	5 Compt's die. 5 CUYLER'S BANK, Palmyra.	5 Portrait of Lady Washington.
10 Ornamental die work.	X Compt's die. X CUYLER'S BANK, Palmyra.	10 Portrait of Washington
ONE Female portrait ONE	1 Eagle on branch of tree 1 DELAWARE BANK ONE DOLLAR Delhi, N. Y.	Large ornamental figure 1 enclosing full length female
TWO Compt's die. TWO	2 Female with sickle and wand 2 sheafs, mill, canal, railroad, etc. DELAWARE BANK, Delhi, N. Y. TWO Agricultural scene.	Ears of corn. Man surrounded by devices. Ears of corn.
Secured, etc. Two females and large figure 3 III	3 Indian girl in circular frame, female either side DELAWARE BANK THREE Delhi, N. Y. Cow and sheep	3
5 Compt's die FIVE	V Three females, large figure 5, etc. V DELAWARE BANK FIVE DOLLARS Delhi, N. Y. Cattle, trees, etc.	5 Medallion head FIVE
10 Compt's die TEN	DELAWARE BANK. Vig. Figures Agriculture and Commerce on each side of a shield; ships, railroad, canals, &c. in the distance. Agricultural scene.	10 Medallion work. TEN
TWENTY Compt's die. TWENTY	Title of Bank under vig. Vig. Female seated at a table, on which is a map, quadrant, compasses, &c.; scientific apparatus near her, and globe behind. Steamship in the distance. 20 each side Agricultural scene.	Die work. XX Die work.
ONE on 1 Wood cutting scene in forest.	DEPOSIT BANK ONE DOLLAR Deposit, N. Y. 1	1 Compt's die
ONE on fig. 1. Three woodmen, one seated; team of oxen and driver in distance.	DEPOSIT BANK. 1	1 Compt's die

2 Compt's die.	DEPOSIT BANK. Vig. Drove of cattle and sheep; drover on horseback; train of cars in distance. 2 on either side.	2 Male portrait
5 Compt's die	Vig. Train of cars; houses in background; small sail-boat on right. DEPOSIT BANK.	5 Drove of cattle, drovers, dog, telegraph wires, &c.
10 on seed head. Compt's die.	Male portrait; on right two females; on left three females in clouds; train of cars in distance on right. DEPOSIT BANK. Deposit, N. Y.	10 Two Indians erect.
XX Male Portrait	Compt's die. Three females. DEPOSIT BANK. Deposit, N. Y. Female bathing.	20
ONE Eagle, shield, &c. Compt's die.	DOVER PLAINS B'K, Dover Plains, N. Y. Farmer mowing with cradle; loading grain on left.	1 Deer in water.
2 Compt's die. 2	Engine and tender entering depot; train of cars leaving it. DOVER PLAINS B'K.	2 Two children playing with flowers.
5 Farmer with scythe.	V Drover on horse; drove of cattle, sheep, &c. V DOVER PLAINS B'K	5 Compt's die 5
X Cattle passing under, and cars passing over bridge.	Farmer ploughing with team of horses. DOVER PLAINS B'K.	10 Compt's die. TEN
20	DOVER PLAINS B'K. Drover on horse; drove of cattle, sheep, &c. Compt's die.	20 Milkmaid churning.
1 Compt's die.	Vig. Three horses prancing; farm houses in distance. ELMIRA BANK.	1 Female portrait.

2 Compt's die.	Vig. Three females bathing; cupid in centre. ELMIRA BANK.	2 Female portrait.
3 Compt's die.	ELMIRA BANK. Vig. Male and female with little child.	3 Female portrait.
5 Compt's die.	Vig. Raft, two men poling; female seated with child in arms. ELMIRA BANK.	5 Female portrait.
Compt's die.	Vig. Two trains of railroad cars; water and small vessel on the left; mountains in the distance. X ELMIRA BANK.	10 Portrait of Daniel Webster.
Male portrait 20	Vig. Train of cars, canal boat passing thro' lock; farmers at work. ELMIRA BANK.	20 Compt's die
1 Compt's die	E. S. RICH'S B'K OF EXCHANGE. View of Niagara Falls ONE DOLLAR Buffalo, N. Y.	ONE on 1 Male portrait
2 Compt's die TWO	Female with bird on her hand beside plants, etc. 2 E. S. RICH'S B'K OF EXCHANGE TWO DOLLARS Buffalo	2 Sloop
ONE Indian head. ONE	1 Vig. female seated with wheat. 1 ESSEX CO., BANK. Keeseville, N. Y. Eagle.	1 Compt's die. 1
2 2	TWO 2 Female 2 Indian ESSEX CO., BANK Keeseville, N. Y. Mechanics' arms.	2 Compt's die. 2
3 3 3	3 Vig. female seated by furnace with pestle and mortar. 3 ESSEX CO., BANK Keeseville, N. Y. steamer.	3 Compt's die. 3

5 Compt's die. 5	5 Female seated; Eagle. 5 ESSEX CO., BANK Keeseville, N. Y. cupid riding a deer.	FIVE
10 Compt's die. 10	10 Vig. 10 Eagle Goddess of liberty mechanics' arm and justice. ESSEX CO., BANK Keeseville. N. Y.	TEN
TWENTY	20 Vig. Archimedes raising the world with lever resting on mountain. 20 ESSEX CO., BANK Keeseville, N. Y. Artisan at work.	TWENTY
FIFTY	Male figure seated with left hand resting on wheel, anvil, hammer, etc., ship in distance, 50 either side. ESSEX CO. BANK, Keesville, N. Y.	FIFTY
1 Compt's die.	EXCHANGE BANK, Lockport, N. Y. Large die with male portrait and words one dollar in part circle across the top, red figure 1 on either side.	1 1
ONE Female bust with sickle. ONE	1 Vig. Eagle. 1 EXCHANGE BANK, Lockport. ONE in large ornamental letters.	Large ornamental figure one; full length female figure.
2 Compt's die 2	EXCHANGE BANK, Lockport, N. Y. Large die with male portrait and words two dollars across it in part circle; red figure 2 on either side.	2 TWO 2
TWO Compt's die. TWO	2 Vig. Female seated; farming implements; grain; factory on left, canal boat on left. 2 EXCHANGE BANK. Lockport. Eagle and safe.	Mechanic; die surrounded with corn.
Compt's die. 3	EXCHANGE BANK, Lockport. N. Y. Large die with portrait of Washington, and words three dollars in part circle at top; red figure 3 on either side.	Word dollars and figure 3. 3
Compt's die. 111	3 Vig. Female portrait surrounded by rays; two females on either side. 3 EXCHANGE BANK, Lockport. Eagle and safe.	3

5 Compt's die 5	V Vig. Two figures, one holding key; the other cornucopia; winged monster standing upon a safe. 5 EXCHANGE BANK, Lockport.	FIVE Full length female with balance and sword. FIVE
10 Compt's die. 10	Vig. Male figure soaring in clouds with cornucopia in arms. 10 EXCHANGE BANK, Lockport.	X Eagle perched upon a shield. TEN
1 Compt's die. 1	State arms. FALL KILL BANK, Poughkeepsie, N. Y.	1 View of falls.
Justice. Compt's die.	2 Drover watering his horse. FALL KILL BANK. Poughkeepsie, N. Y.	2 Falls.
Large figure 3, and female seated on rock, on top of which is lighthouse Compt's die	3 Mechanic seated on boiler FALLKILL BANK THREE DOLLARS Poughkeepsie, N. Y. Secured, etc	3 Engine crossing bridge, water fall, etc.
Falls. 5	Two female figures emblematic of manufacture. FALL KILL BANK, Poughkeepsie, N. Y.	5 Compt's die
TEN Female TEN	FALL KILL BANK. Poughkeepsie, N. Y. 10 Falls. 10	Liberty and large X. Compt's die
Falls. 20	FALL KILL BANK. Poughkeepsie, N. Y. 20 Washington. Compt's die.	TWENTY Liberty, ..., globe, &c
50 Falls.	Female portrait. Compt's die. FALL KILL BANK. Poughkeepsie, N. Y.	FIFTY Railroad. FIFTY
C 100	FALL KILL BANK. Poughkeepsie, N. Y. View of falls, American and Indian female on either side. Steamship.	Compt's die. 100

Secured by pledge, etc. ONE	1 Female and child, scroll, sword, cog-wheel, anchor, etc., ship on left Die FARMER'S BANK of Amsterdam ONE DOLLAR Man on horseback	ONE State of New York Female seated
TWO Figure of Justice with sword, scales, eagle &c. TWO	2 Female with sickle, wand, etc., grain factory and bridge in background. 2 FARMERS' BANK of Amsterdam, N. Y. TWO DOLLARS. Cattle, plow, tree, etc.	Corn. Male seat'd, cornucopia, anvil, etc. Corn
5 Female with scales; eagle, key, safe, &c. FIVE	Title under vig. V Vig. Three females in sitting posture; implements of agriculture, steamship, railroad cars, &c. V Two cattle, two trees, plough, sheaf of wheat	5 Med. head. FIVE
10 Female with scales; key, safe, &c. TEN	Title of Bank under vig. Vig. Two females; one on each side of a circle, one holding a sickle; implements of agriculture, steamship, casks, &c. Two cattle, two trees, plough, sheaf of wheat.	10 Two females, eagle, Liberty staff, cap, &c. TEN
FIFTY Female with distaff and shield; med head on shield and resting on pedestal.	FARMERS' BANK, Amsterdam, N. Y. Men mowing, gathering and loading wagons with wheat. Compt's Die.	50 on metal lion head. Female.
100 Man seated; scythe hanging on tree.	FARMER'S BANK, Amsterdam, N. Y. State Arms, with female and cows on right; two females and sheaf on left, horn of plenty at bottom.	100 Portrait of Washington.
1 ONE Compt's die.	Drove of cattle, four drovers on horseback; town in distance. FARMERS' BANK OF ATTICA, N. Y.	1 Female.
2 Compt's die. 2	Mechanic, sailor and farmer; man and horse in distance. FARMERS' BANK OF ATTICA, N. Y.	2 Female with bundle on her head
5 Farmer drinking.	FARMERS' BANK OF ATTICA, N. Y. 5 Male portrait 5	5 Compt's die. 5
Secured &c. ONE	1 Vig. Female with child, sheaf of wheat on right; ship in distance on left. Ornamental die. FARMERS BANK Hudson, N. Y. Man, dog and birds.	ONE Female seated.

Left	Centre	Right
TWO Compt's die. TWO	2 Vig. Female seated with sickle and grain 2 factory on left, and canal boat, locomotive and cars on right in distance. FARMERS BANK, Hudson. N. Y. Cattle.	Man seated with mechanical implements.
5 Compt's die. FIVE	Vig. Group of females, holding globe; dragon and lions. Steamship, and ship on right. FARMERS BANK Hudson, N. Y. cattle.	5 Female seated resting on shield, man mowing in distance FIVE
10 Compt's die. TEN	Vig. Two females seated resting on shield, steamship on right locomotive, factory, cars on left in distance. FARMERS BANK Hudson, N. Y. cattle.	10 State arms TEN
20 Male portrait.	Compt's die. Vig. Oxen, waggon and farmers loading grain. FARMERS BANK Hudson, N. Y.	TWENTY Full length female. TWENTY
ONE Compt's die.	FARMERS' BANK OF LANSINGBURGH, N. Y. Vig. Train of cars, bridge, canal boat; village in background, rural scenery, &c.	ONE Female and large figure 1.
TWO Compt's die 2	Indian girl seated beside shield, eagle, etc., wigwam in background. FARMER'S BANK of Lansingburgh, N. Y. TWO DOLLARS 2	2 Two children
TWO TWO	Vig. Drove of cattle, 2 men, one on horse back, and horse drinking from trough at a pump. Compt's die. FARMERS' BANK OF LANSINGBURGH, N. Y. 2	TWO Large figure 2, and a female with pail behind her.
Vig. Sailor, female, mechanic, ship and steamer on left; buildings viaduct &c., on right. Three females and a large ornamental V.	Compt's die. FARMERS' BANK OF LANSINGBURGH, N. Y. 5	FIVE Large figure 5, two Indians viaduct, train of cars, waterfall, and rural scenery.
Sailor, mechanic and farmer holding aloft a wreath on which is figures 10.	FARMERS' BANK OF LANSINGBURGH, N. Y. Vig. Two horses and a plow, man engaged in fastening the traces to plough, horse on right; steamboat on left.	Large X with ten across; milkmaid with pail, cow, viaduct train of cars &c. Compt's die.
1 Compt's die. 1	1 Vig. Male and female erect, female has a wreath in left hand, on left a sheaf of wheat, on right an anvil. 1 FARMERS' BANK, Troy, N. Y. Female reclining with sheaf of wheat.	Female erect with staff, shield and eagle on left. ONE

Left	Centre	Right
2 Compt's die. 2	2 Vig. Two females, shield and figure 2, one on left holds scales, one on right a sickle, on right a sheaf of wheat, on left a ship in distance. 2 FARMERS' BANK, Troy, N. Y. 2	Female erect with staff, shield and eagle on left 2
3 Compt's die. 3	3 Man erect with mantel around him, a plough on right, shield, cap and spear on left. 3 FARMERS' BANK, Troy, N. Y. Female reclining.	Female erect with staff, shield and eagle on left. 3
5 Compt's die. 5	FIVE Vig. Man FIVE erect and oxen; on left in distance. FARMERS' BANK, Troy, N. Y. Secural &c.	5 Large vase Horse.
X Farmers at work. 10	TEN Vig. Dog TEN laying down; large safe and house in distance. FARMERS' BANK, Troy, N. Y.	10 Compt's die. X
20 Compt's die. 20	Vig. Man on horseback; cattle, &c. Female portrait. FARMERS' BANK, Troy, N. Y. Farmers at work.	20 Cars and men with wheelbarrow 20
L Compt's die. 50	Vig. Man on horseback; cattle, sheep, &c. FARMERS' BANK, Troy N. Y. Dog, safe and key.	FIFTY Female standing holding scales.
Compt's die.	Female seated, flowers, &c.; factories and man plowing in distance. FARMERS' BANK OF WASHINGTON CO. Fort Edward, N. Y.	1 Female shading her eyes with her hand.
2 Compt's die 2	Farmer at lunch; boy, girl, dog, horses, &c. FARMER'S B'K OF WASHINGTON CO. TWO DOLLARS. Fort Edward, N. Y. Monument.	2 TWO
2 Compt's die. 2	Farmer seated, girl and horses on right; boy and dog on left. Title of Bank. Tomb of Jane McCrea.	2 TWO
Compt's die 3	Female reclining on grain; farm scene on right. 3 FARMER'S B'K OF WASHINGTON CO. THREE DOLLARS.	3 Dog and safe.

Left	Centre	Right
5 Portrait of a boy	Female seated on grain; houses, cattle, loading hay, etc., in distance. Title of Bank.	5 Compt's die. FIVE
X Female seated with sword; word TEN on shield.	Two horses before load of hay; man on one of the horses, woman and child on top of hay; boy with rake and girl with flowers; dog; blacksmith with sledge and interior of shop with men at work. Title of Bank.	10 Building, pedestrians etc Compt's die
20 XX 20	Female with pole and cap on right of shield; female with sickle on left. Compt's die below. FARMERS' BANK of Washington Co., N. Y.	20 Man with musket.
50 Female seated under tree.	Title of Bank. Compt's die.	50 Farmer carrying corn stalks.
Compt's die. Road scene; drovers and cattle, load of hay, etc	1 Female with ears of corn; vessels and city in distance. FARMERS' & CITIZENS' BK OF LONG ISLAND, Williamsburg, N. Y. Agricultural implements.	1 Train of cars, houses, etc., in distance.
2 Compt's die TWO	Shipwright at work; vessels, men, etc. Title of Bank. Steamship.	2 Female seated with tablets.
3	Horses drinking from trough, man seated; female feeding hogs, buildings, etc. Compt's die. Title of Bank. Eagle.	3 Female with shield, etc.
Three females, one above the other. FIVE	Title of Bank. Female with trident seated in a shell; vessels in distance.	5 Compt's die
10 Female portrait.	Steamship and other vessels. Title of Bank. Eagle.	10 Compt's die.
Female seated with sword, etc. TWENTY	Title of Bank. Milkmaid seated, cows; house in distance. Steamboat.	20 Compt's die

Sailor erect, flag; female reclining. FIFTY	Title of Bank. Female with pole, cap and shield; buildings in distance.	50 Compt's die.
Mercury with wand and bag of coin. 100	Title of Bank. Indian, shield, eagle, female and letter C.	100 Compt's die.
ONE Female portrait. ONE	1 Vig. Eagle on branch of tree. 1 FARMER'S & DROVER'S BANK, Somers, N. Y. View of Croton dam between signatures.	Female in standing position, figure 1 full width of note.
TWO Compt's die TWO	2 Vig. Female seated; agricultural implemenns, factory on left; canal boat and cars on right; steamboat in distance. 2 FARMER'S & DROVER'S BANK, Somers, N. Y. Men and cattle.	Mechanic seated, tools, horn of plenty, &c., surrounded with corn.
3 Compt's die III	3 Vig. Female portrait in frame, surrounded by flags, drum, cannon, &c. FARMER'S & DROVER'S BANK, Somers, N. Y. Men and cattle.	3
5 Female seated, balances, eagle, key, safe, &c. FIVE	V Vig. Three females seated; surrounded by ornamental figure 5. V FARMER'S & DROVER'S BANK, Somers, N. Y. Men and cattle.	5 Medallion head. FIVE
10 Female adjusting scales, eagle, key, safe, &c. TEN	Vig. Two females representing agriculture, &c., spread eagle in min. case, farming implements, locomotive and cars, houses &c. on left; steamship, barrels, &c. on right. FARMER'S & DROVER'S BANK, Somers, N. Y. Men and cattle.	10 Two females liberty cap mounted eagle, vase flowers, &c. TEN
TWENTY Same as two. TWENTY	20 Vig. Female in sitting posture, globe by her side, steamship in the distance. 20 FARMER'S & DROVER'S BANK, Somers, N. Y. Men and cattle.	XX
1 Compt's die. 1	1 Eagle. 1 FARMERS AND MANUFACTURES BK Poughkeepsie, N. Y. Head of horse.	ONE Portrait 1
2 Compt's die. 2	Title under vig. Male Portrait. Portrait of Washington. Arm	2 Farmer with cradle. TWO

3 Compt's die 3	3 Ship and other smaller vessels. FARMER'S AND MAN. BANK, Poughkeepsie. Barrels, &c.	THREE Portrait. 3
5 Compt's die. 5	Title under vig. 5 Vig. Two human figures, male erect; female reclining. 5	FIVE 5 FIVE
Male and female, male erect, female reclining. 10	10 Compt's die. FARMERS' AND MANUFACT'RS BK. Poughkeepsie.	TEN 10 TEN
TWENTY	XX Compt's die. XX FARMERS' AND MANUFACT'RS' BK. Poughkeepsie.	Male and female; the one reclining, the other erect. XX
Male and female; male standing, female reclining. 50	FIFTY FARMERS' AND MANUFACT'RS BK. Poughkeepsie. Eagle between signatures.	Compt's die. 50
Male and female; the one reclining, the other erect. 100	ONE HUNDRED FARMERS' AND MANUFACT'RS' BK. Poughkeepsie. Eagle between signatures.	Compt's die 100
Secured by pledge of &c. ONE	1 Vig. Female with sword, child, cornucopia, anchor, agricultural implements, &c; ship in distance. FARMERS & MECHANICS' BANK OF GENESEE, Buffalo, N. Y.	ONE Female seated, cows, and vessel in distance.
TWO Compt's die. TWO	2 Vig. Female seated, agricultural implements factory, canal boat and cars; steamboat in distance. 2 FARMERS' AND MECHANICS' BANK OF GENESEE, Buffalo, N. Y.	Mechanic seated, tools, horn of plenty, &c. surrounded with corn.
5 Compt's die. FIVE	V 11 5 VZ V Vig. Three females, centre one seated in large figure 5; factories, cars, and agricultural implements on the left, vessels and articles of commerce on the right, wheat, &c. FARMERS' & MECHANICS' BANK OF GENESEE, Buffalo, N. Y.	5 Medallion head. FIVE
10 Two Indians.	Portrait of Franklin surrounded by five females. FAR. & MECH. B'K. OF GENESEE, Buffalo, N. Y.	10 Compt's die

Yatch race, various male and female figures, XX	Compt's die. Title of Bank.	20 Female seated; cars and factories in distance. TWENTY
ONE Compt's die. ONE	1 Vig. Female and child, ship in distance. Oval die. FARMERS AND MECHANICS' BANK, Rochester, N. Y. Anvil, etc	ONE Female seated, cars in distance.
TWO Compt's die. TWO	2 Vig. Female reaper seated. 2 FARMERS' AND MECHANICS' BANK, Rochester, N. Y. Farmer gathering corn.	Artisan with horn of plenty.
Female on either side of figure 3. III	3 Vig. Portrait of female in wreath, with flags, drum, &c. FARMERS' & MECHANICS' BANK, Rochester, N. Y. Farmer gathering corn.	3
5 Compt's die. FIVE	Vig. Female with Hand, key, &c. Title of Bank. Farmer gathering corn.	5 Portrait of female. FIVE
10 Compt's die. TEN	Vig. Wreath with female on either side, cars, shipping, &c., in the distance. Title of Bank. Arm	10 State Arms. TEN
TEN Female feeding fowls.	X Men, horse, dog, cattle and sheep. FAR. & MECH. BK., Rochester, N. Y.	10 Male portrait
TWENTY Compt's die. TWENTY	Vig. Female with chemical apparatus, pointing to steamer in distance. 20 20 Title of Bank. Arm	XX
1 Compt's die.	FLOUR CITY B'K. Rochester, N. Y. Farming scene.	1 Man and barrels
TWO Compt's die. TWO	Two cherubs; two silver dollars; train of cars and cattle in background. FLOUR CITY BANK. Rochester, N. Y.	2 Male portrait

Left	Centre	Right
5 Male portrait	FLOUR CITY BANK. Rochester, N. Y. Two flowry barrels, sheafs of wheat; men in distance.	5 Compt's die. FIVE
X Two figures carrying sheafs.	Male portrait in frame; winged female on left; cherub on right. FLOUR CITY BANK. Rochester, N. Y.	TEN Compt's die
20 20	Compt's die. Milkmaid seated; cows on left; dog and pail on right. FLOUR CITY BANK. Rochester, N. Y.	TWENTY Mechanic; barrels, bale; ship in distance, TWENTY
1 Female with spear, figure one at her feet.	Compt's die. Vig. Milkmaid seated, and cattle. FORT PLAIN BANK, Fort Plain, N. Y. Dog.	ONE on fig. 1 Female portrait. ONE
TWO Compt's die. TWO	2 Vig. Female; sheaf of wheat, plow, canal, railroad cars &c. 2 FORT PLAIN BANK, Fort Plain, N. Y. Round building, &c.	Mechanical tools, and horn of plenty surrounded with corn.
Compt's die.	3 Vig. Three females; one in frame. FORT PLAIN BANK, Fort Plain, N. Y. Round building.	3
5 Compt's die. FIVE	Vig. Group of females; centre one in car; lions at her feet; key in one hand; globe in other. FORT PLAIN BANK, Fort Plain, N. Y. Round building.	5 Female seated; one at feet; man standing. FIVE
10 Compt's die. TEN	Vig. Two females, cars and horses on left; steamship, barrels and bales on right. FORT PLAIN BANK, Fort Plain, N. Y. Round building.	10 Two females in round frame. TEN
Man seated, holding 0 and bag of coin. Compt's die. TWENTY	FORT PLAIN BANK, Fort Plain, N. Y. Vig. Steamboats; cars; female seated, holding balances, &c; safe, steamship coin, &c.	20 Female portrait.
50 Compt's die. FIFTY	FORT PLAIN BANK, Fort Plain, N. Y. Farmers at lunch, loading hay, &c.	50 Full length female Indian.
100 Spread eagle Compt's die.	FORT PLAIN BANK, Fort Plain, N. Y. Cattle and sheep; drover on horse back.	100 Full length female; liberty pole and cap.
Compt's die. Water scene, bridge, boat, etc.	1 Indian seated; agricultural scene. FORT STANWIX BK Rome, N. Y.	ONE Female with grain and sickle. ONE
Med head and TWO. Compt's die.	Man plowing with two horses. FORT STANWIX BK Rome, N. Y. Locomotive.	2 Female head. TWO
Portrait of Wm. Penn. Compt's die.	FIVE on med. head. Signing the Declaration of Independence. FORT STANWIX BK Rome, N. Y.	5 FIVE on Med. head. 5
TEN on med. head. Compt's die.	Goddess of Justice, Liberty and Truth. FORT STANWIX BK Rome, N. Y.	X TEN on med. head. 10
TWENTY on med. head. Indian family contemplating the progress of civilization.	FORT STANWIX BK, Rome, N. Y. Two females.	20 on med. head. Compt's die.
L on med. head. Compt's die.	FORT STANWIX BK, Rome, N. Y. Scene in the battle of New Orleans.	50 on med. head. Male portrait
1 Compt's die. ONE	Vig. Cupid rolling gold piece; locomotive in distance. FRANKFORT BANK Frankfort, N. Y. Dog.	1 Female seated with shield and figure 1.
2 Compt's die. TWO	Vig. Two children fencing, with gold pieces for shields, one standing; locomotive in distance. FRANKFORT BANK, Frankfort, N. Y.	2 Female seated with figure 2
3 Compt's die. THREE	Vig. Three children with three gold pieces. FRANKFORT BANK, Frankfort, N. Y. Loading hay.	3 Large figure 3 with three men, one in centre, and one on either side.
5 Compt's die. FIVE	Vig. Five children with 5 gold pieces. FRANKFORT BANK, Frankfort, N. Y. Corn.	5 Female seated with scales and figure 5.
10 Compt's die. TEN	Vig. Sailor, Indian, and two females with eagle, liberty pole and cap, bust, &c, FRANKFORT BANK, Frankfort, N. Y. Bee hive.	10 Female portrait.
20 Compt's die. TWENTY	Vig. Oxen, sheep, farmers, &c. FRANKFORT BANK, Frankfort, N. Y. Two horses.	20 Female portrait,
1 ONE Compt's die.	Female and fig. 1; cars and steamboat in distance. ONE FREDONIA BANK, Fredonia, N. Y.	Indian on cliff. ONE
TWO Compt's die. TWO	Farmer and milkmaid; two gold dollars; cows, houses, etc. 2 FREDONIA BANK, Fredonia, N. Y.	TWO Two females erect. TWO
Compt's die. THREE Mechanic, sailor, farmer and figure 3	3 Three females representing Agriculture, Commerce and Manufactures; ship in distance. FREDONIA BANK, Fredonia, N. Y.	3 Female.
5 Female.	Five females, fig. 5 in centre; shipping, factory, locomotive and tender in distance. 5 FREDONIA BANK, Fredonia, N. Y.	5 Compt's die. 5
TEN Blacksmith, anvil, hammer, forge, etc. TEN	FREDONIA BANK, Fredonia, N. Y. 10 Nine cherubs making offering to female seated with cornucopia and ten gold dollars.	10 TEN Compt's die
XX Portrait of girl with curls.	Female representing Agriculture; ship in distance. 20 FREDONIA BANK, Fredonia, N. Y Compt's die.	TWENTY Female erect with spear and shield. TWENTY
1 Compt's die.	Female milking cow; cornfield, men, boy, trees, house, etc. FRONTIER BANK. Potsdam, N. Y. Locomotive.	1 Female with sewing machine.

Left	Centre	Right
Female with hammer and anvil. Compt's die.	1 Portrait of Washington. FRONTIER BANK Potsdam, N. Y.	1 Female seated with sheaf of wheat.
Child standing. Compt's die.	2 Male portrait. FRONTIER BANK Potsdam, N. Y.	2 Female portrait.
2 New Compt's die TWO	York Two children, cattle, etc., under tree Eagle Potsdam FRONTIER BANK TWO DOLLARS	2 Two children
Compt's die 3	Men building log cabin, door on horse's back, etc FRONTIER BANK THREE DOLLARS Potsdam	3 Two children
Large figure 5 with Indian at the bottom. Compt's die.	5 Male portrait. 5 FRONTIER BANK Potsdam, N. Y.	Sailor standing. 5
5 Female in 5.	View of a street. Title of Bank. FIVE V on FIVE. FIVE	5 Compt's die. 5
Large X, figure 10, sailor looking through a telescope and a sailor in a boat. Compt's die.	10 Male portrait 10 FRONTIER BANK Potsdam, N. Y.	TEN Ship at sea. TEN
10 Hatter at work.	Old man on horse; boy on rail fence; colt, sheep, etc.; house in distance. Male portrait. Title of Bank. 10	10 X Compt's die
Mechanic at work. Compt's die.	FULTON CO. BANK Gloversville, N. Y. 1 Vig. Male portrait. 1	1 Deer. ONE
2 Deer TWO	Mechanics at work Compt's die FULTON CO. BANK TWO DOLLARS Gloversville, N. Y. Bales of goods	2 Female bearing pail

Left	Centre	Right
5 Female seated.	FULTON CO. BANK Gloversville, N. Y. Compt's die. Vig. Mechanics at work Bales of goods.	5 Portrait of George Washington.
TEN Geo. Washington. Compt's die.	Vig. Large eagle resting on liberty cap. X FULTON CO. BANK, Gloversville, N. Y. Bales of goods.	10 Mechanic at work. TEN
ONE Compt's die. ONE	1 Vig. Goddess of Industry, child, bale of goods, anchor, plow; &c. Ship in distance. GENESEE CO. BK. Leroy.	ONE Female seated; railroad cars, &c
TWO Compt's die. TWO	2 Vig. Female seated, sickle in hand, plow and grain house; cars and canal boat in distance. 2 GENESSE CO. BK. Leroy. Trees and cattle.	Mechanic seated; hammer and cornucopia in his hands; die surrounded by corn.
3 Franklin 3	Compt's die. Vig. Farmer plowing. GENESEE CO. BK. Leroy.	3 Female with sickle and grain in each hand. 3
5 Compt's die. FIVE	V Vig. Three female figures; middle one surrounded by ornamental figure 5; steamer in distance, on right; cars on left. V GENESEE CO. BK. Leroy. Trees and cattle.	5 Medallion head. FIVE
X Male portrait. TEN	Compt's die. Goddess of Liberty. Vig. Signing declaration of independence. GENESEE CO. BK. Leroy.	X Male portrait. TEN
Female holding figure 1. Compt's die.	Vig. Female seated, with basket of corn; river and vessels in distance. GENESEE RIVER BANK, Mount Morris, N. Y. Sheaf of wheat and agricultural implements	1 Female Indian with bird and pole.
2 Portrait of female.	Vig. Locomotive and cars going over bridge; canal boats and hay makers. GENESEE RIVER BANK, Mount Morris, N. Y.	Compt's die 2
Compt's die. 5	Vig. Cattle and sheep, some standing and some lying down. GENESEE RIVER BANK, Mount Morris, N. Y.	5 Indian reclining.

Left	Centre	Right
10 Compt's die.	GENESEE RIVER BANK, Mount Morris, N. Y.	10 Man felling a tree; oxen; children seated on ground.
20 Compt's die.	Vig. Indian seated, gun in right hand; city in distance, and steamship. GENESEE RIVER BANK, Mount Morris, N. Y.	20 Female with tablet, resting on column.
Female with rake. Compt's die.	1 Vig. Female seated with oxen. GENESEE VALLEY BANK. Genesee, N. Y. Safe.	1 Cows, and pigs.
2 Compt's die. TWO	Vig. Farmer seated with jug, basket, dog, &c. GENESEE VALLEY BANK Genesee' N. Y. Wheat	2 Two Females standing.
5 Spread eagle Compt's die.	Vig. Oxen and sheep. GENESEE VALLEY BANK, Genesee, N. Y. Ox.	5 Female leaning on figure 5.
Indian. Compt's die.	10 Vig. Farmers at dinner; loading hay, &c. GENESEE VALLEY BANK, Genesee, N. Y. State Arms.	10 Male portrait
20 Compt's die. XX	Two females, shield, buildings, etc. GENESSEE VALLEY BANK, Genesee, N. Y. Sheaf.	20 Male portrait TWENTY
1 Compt's die. ONE	Female portrait in centre; angel on left, cupid on right. GEORGE WASHINGTON BANK, Corning, N. Y. Wheat, plow, anvil &c.	1 Washington.
2 Compt's die. TWO	Vig. Washington. GEORGE WASHINGTON BANK, Corning, N. Y. TWO Shield.	2 Lady Washington.
5 Male portrait	V Vig. Indian seated beside slain deer. GEORGE WASHINGTON BANK. Corning, N. Y. Female portrait.	5 Compt's die

TEN — X Martha George Wash'n Wash'n — 10
GEO. WASHINGTON BANK, Corning, N. Y.
Washingt'n. — Compt's die. — Dog's head.

TEN — X Vig. Sailor, Indian, Justice and Liberty. — 10
GEORGE WASHINGTON BANK, Corning, N. Y.
Full length Washington. — Compt's die. — Dogs head.

1 — Vig. Milk maids—one milking cow; farm house on right, vessel on left. — 1
GLENN'S FALLS BK. Glenn's Falls, N. Y.
Female with sheaf of wheat on her shoulder. — Compt's die. — Sow-hive.

2 — Vig. Female seated; eagle at her feet; bags of coin and pick-axe on her right; vessels in distance on left; cars on right end. — 2
GLENN'S FALLS BK. Glenn's Falls, N. Y.
Hunter, dog and gun. — Compt's die. — Agricultural implements.

3 — Vig. 3 females,—one holding sword and balances; ship on right. — 3
GLENN'S FALLS BK. Glenn's Falls, N. Y.
Man, woman, and child. — Compt's die — Eagle.

Female with Liberty cap; large building in back ground. — 5
GLENN'S FALLS BK. Glenn's Falls, N. Y. Male Portrait.
5 5 — Indian.
5 — Compt's die.

10 — Vig. Spread eagle. — 10
GLENN'S FALLS BK. Glenn's Falls, N. Y.
Indian, gun and waterfall — Compt's die

1 — Compt's die. 1 Female seated on sheaf of wheat cars on right and steam boat on left. — 1
GOSHEN BANK, Goshen, N. Y.
Female seated. 1 — Female erect.

2 — Vig. Farming scene; on right man loading hay. — 2
GOSHEN BANK, Goshen, N. Y.
Compt's die. TWO — Sheaf of wheat plough &c. — Female seated, bucket on each side.

FIVE — Vig. Drove of cattle and man on horse. — 5
GOSHEN BANK, Goshen, N. Y. Female.
Compt's die. FIVE — 5, and group of females.

TEN — 10 Vig. Train of cars, house and steam boat on left. — 10
GOSHEN BANK, Goshen, N. Y.
Compt's die. X — Ox. — Female erect shield on left.

20 — XX Vig. Female seated, safe, sheaf of wheat, farming implements and cars on right, steamship on left. — 20
GOSHEN BANK, Goshen, N. Y.
Eagle, shield &c. Compt's die. — Man shearing a sheep. — 2 Female seated. 0

ONE — Compt's die. Vig. Wood chopper seated on fallen log; horse and waggon in back ground; gold dollar on left. — 1
Two large buildings; shade trees, cattle, &c. — HAMILTON BANK, Hamilton, N. Y. — Female erect holding figure one.
ONE — Dog.

2 — Compt's die. Vig. Man and woman; rake and pail; two gold dollars; cattle and farm house. — 2
Two large buildings; shade trees, cattle &c. — HAMILTON BANK. Hamilton, N. Y. — Female raking.
TWO — Mechanic.

FIVE — Vig. Five human figures; five gold dollars lapel. — 5
Female portrait. Compt's die. — HAMILTON BANK, Hamilton, N. Y. — Ornamental 5 surrounded by five human figures.
Farming tools.

10 — Vig. Female reclining upon a chest; locomotive on left, female and cattle on right. — 10
Compt's die. TEN — HAMILTON BANK. Hamilton, N. Y. — Female portrait. TEN
Anvil and horn of plenty.

1 — HAMPDEN BANK, Northcastle, N. Y. — 1
ONE Male portrait ONE — Female erect with flag and shield; Indian female at her feet.
Compt's die — One Dollar.

1 — HAMPDEN BANK. Farming implements, etc. — 1
Compt's die — North Castle, N. Y. — Daniel Webster

2 — Zouaves charging. — 2
HAMPDEN BANK, North Castle, N. Y.
Compt's die TWO — Henry Clay

TWO — Man, two horses, pig, ducks, etc., at pump; cattle and barn in distance. — 2
HAMPDEN BANK, Northcastle, N. Y.
Compt's die. Two on 2 — Beehive.

5 FIVE 5 — HAMPDEN BANK. Soldier with gun & flag. 5 surrounded by: oval dies on which are name of bank and five. — 5 Compt's die 5
North Castle, N. Y. FIVE DOLLARS.

5 — Train of cars; steamboat; men, horses, canal boat, etc. — 5
Head of Liberty surrounded by stars. — HAMPDEN BANK, Northcastle, N. Y. — Compt's die 5

1 — STATE OF NEW YORK. Two children driving cattle through gate — 1
Compt's die — H. D. BARTO & CO'S BK. ONE DOLLAR Trumansburgh — Male portrait

TWO — Scene at door of house; men, woman, children, horse, etc. — 2
Compt's die TWO — H. D. BARTO & CO'S BK. TWO DOLLARS Trumansburgh — Male portrait

5 — Child on horse, man, boy, etc. — 5
Male portrait — H. D. BARTO & CO'S BK. FIVE DOLLARS Trumansburgh — Compt's die 5

1 — HERKIMER Co. B'K. Little Falls, N. Y. — Female seated with wheat.
Compt's die. 1 — 1 Portrait of child with wheat and sickle. 1 — 1

2 — HERKIMER Co. B'K. Little Falls, N. Y. — Female standing in large figure 2.
Compt's die. 2 — 2 Vig. Female seated with sheaf of wheat. 2

3 — 3 Title of Bank Vig. Eagle on branch of tree; train of cars. 3 — THREE
Compt's die. 3 — TH 3 REE — Portrait of child. THREE

5 — HERKIMER Co. B'K. Little Falls, N. Y. — FIVE Female seated in large figure 5.
Compt's die. 5 — 5 Vig. Oxen, sheep, &c 5 — 5 — FIVE

10 — TEN TEN HERKIMER Co. B'K, Little Falls, N. Y. — TEN
Compt's die. 10 — Vig. Female seated with eagle, &c. — State arms X

Left	Centre	Right
100 Goddess of liberty with eagle; Union is strength; E Pluribus Unum. 100	HERKIMER Co. B'K, Little Falls, N. Y. Male portrait. Male portrait. Vig. Man killing snakes with club.	100 Female churning.
Male portrait. Compt's die	1 H. G. HOTCHKISS & Co.'s BANK, Lyons, N. Y. Boy on horse, colt, female, etc., at trough.	1 Child's head.
Compt's die Male portrait.	Title of Bank. 3 Man, two horses, pig, etc at pump; cattle, barn, etc. in background.	3 THREE
1 Compt's die 1	HIGHLAND BANK 1 View of Hudson River, steamer, ship at dock, etc. 1 1	1 Male portrait ONE
2 Compt's die. 2	HIGHLAND BANK, Newburgh. Portrait of Washington. Head of Clinton. Vig. Same as above. TWO DOLLARS. 2	2 A man gathering corn.
3 Compt's die. 3	HIGHLAND BANK, Newburgh. 3 Head of Clinton. Vig. Same as above. THREE DOLLARS.	3 3
5 Compt's die. 5	5 5 Vig. Same as above. HIGHLAND BANK, Newburgh. FIVE. Head of Washington.	Head of Lafayette. Washington on horseback.
10 Compt's die. 10	10 10 Vig. Washington's head-quarters at Newburgh. HIGHLAND BANK, Newburgh. TEN DOLLARS. X	TEN Same as the vig. of 1s, 2s, 3s, and 5s, except the schooner, which is not seen. TEN
20 Compt's die. 20	20 Vig. Washington's head quarters at Newburgh. HIGHLAND BANK, Newburgh. TWENTY DOLLARS. Head of Washington.	XX Head of Jas. Clinton 20
50 Compt's die. 50	Vig. Washington's head quarters. HIGHLAND BANK, Newburgh. FIFTY DOLLARS.	50 Head of De Witt Clinton. 50

Left	Centre	Right
100 Compt's die. 100	Vig. Washington's head-quarters. HIGHLAND BANK, Newburgh. ONE HUNDRED DOLLARS	100 Head of De Witt Clinton. C
FIVE. FIVE. Female portrait 5	STATE OF NEW YORK. Farmer, children, horses, etc. H. J. 5 Horse's head V MESSENGER'S BK. 5	FIVE. FIVE. 5 Compt's die 5
20 Horse fair.	M. J. MESSINGER'S BANK. TWENTY DOLLARS on 20 New York. Compt's die	20 Male portrait
1 Compt's die.	Steam mill, carts, boat, etc. H. J. MINER & Co's BANK, Dunkirk, N. Y.	1 Female [illegible] flowers.
2 Compt's die. 2	Locomotive and depot. Title of Bank.	2 Girl
V Woman with wheat.	Steamboats and vessels. Title of Bank.	5 Compt's die. Secured, etc.
TEN Mechanic with sledge.	River and wharf scene—barge and steamboat with tow. Title of Bank.	10 Secured, etc. Compt's die.
1 Compt's die.	H. J. MESSINGER'S BANK, Marathon, N. Y. Milkmaid, cows, etc.; house and trees in distance.	1 Male portrait
2 Compt's die. TWO	Title of Bank. Horses alarmed at lightning; cows in distance.	2 Male portrait
5 5	Drove of cattle and sheep; men bargaining. Title of Bank. Horse	5 Compt's die

Left	Centre	Right
10 Man plowing with two horses; boy leading horses.	Title of Bank. 10	10 Compt's die
Anchor against rock ONE Compt's die	STATE OF NEW YORK HOPE B'K of Albany ONE DOLLAR 1 1 Albany ONE Orna die	1 mental work
2 Compt's die 2	HOPE B'K of Albany Scene in saw mill TWO DOLLARS Albany TWO Orna die	2 mental work
5 Female, grain, sickle, etc.	HOPE B'K of Albany Canal, boat, road, cars, men, etc. FIVE DOLLARS Albany	5 Compt's die V
1 Compt's die. 1	1 Vig. Farmers at work in field; bee hive, plough, rake &c. 1 HUDSON RIVER B'K, Hudson, N. Y. Steamboat.	ONE
2 Compt's die. 2	2 Vig. Two children seated, in centre sheaf of wheat, on right ships in distance, on left steamboat. 2 HUDSON RIVER B'K, Hudson, N. Y. Steamboat.	TWO
3 Compt's die. 3	Two children seated, sheaf of wheat in centre, on right a ship, on left a steamboat. 3 HUDSON RIVER B'K, Hudson, N. Y. Steamboat.	THREE
5 Compt's die. 5	5 Male and female reclining, monument &c. 5 HUDSON RIVER B'K, Hudson, N. Y. Portrait of Washington.	FIVE
10 Compt's die. 10	10 Vig. Large ship under sail, small boat and whale on left in distance, vessels in distance on right. 10 HUDSON RIVER B'K, Hudson, N. Y. Male portrait.	TEN
20 TWENTY 20	Vig. Male portrait with female on the right and male on left. HUDSON RIVER B'K Hudson, N. Y.	20 20

Left	Centre	Right
L Female standing erect. L	50 Vig. Three females, liberty pole and cap, beehive on left. 50 HUDSON RIVER B'K Hudson, N. Y.	50 Portrait of Washington. 50
Female and eagle. Compt's die.	1 Vig. White men trading with Indians. HUGUENOT BANK New Paltz, N Y Shield.	1 Book staff and torch. ONE
TWO Book staff and torch. Compt's die.	2 Vig. White men trading with Indians. HUGUENOT BANK New Paltz, N. Y. Dog.	2 Two females standing erect.
Compt's die Book, liberty cap, torch, etc. FIVE	5 Indian hunter, three cupids, five gold dollars, etc. HUGUENOT BANK FIVE DOLLARS New Paltz, N. Y.	5 Five females entwined in large figure 5
10 Compt's die. X	Vig. Females and males; on right, horses and load of hay. HUGUENOT BANK New Paltz, N. Y. Sheaf of wheat plough &c.	10 Book torch and staff. TEN
XX Portrait of Washington. Compt's die,	Vig. Female seated, goods and boats on right, cars and vessels on left. HUGUENOT BANK New Paltz, N. Y. Female seated.	20 Book torch and staff. TWENTY
ONE Compts die.	figure 1 on shield. Female milking cows. HUNGERFORD'S. BK Adams, N. Y.	1 Female with rake. 1
Figure 2 on shield. Male portrait.	Compts die. Loading hay. HUNGERFORD'S B'K Adams, N. Y. Female portrait.	2
3 Compts die.	HUNGERFORD'S BK Adams, N. Y. 3 Vig female with shield; steamer in distance. 3	3 on medallion head. female portrait.
5 Compt's die.	Vig. horses, colt, trees, &c. HUNGERFORD'S B'K Adams, N. Y.	5 Canal boat and bridge. 5

Left	Centre	Right
TEN male portrait.	Compts die. Vig. drove of sheep man on horse; mill in background. HUNGERFORD'S BK Adams, N. Y. Wheat, plough, &c.	X on shield
20 Male portrait	Compt's die. Men loading hay; oxen, etc. HUNGERFORDS' BK, Adams, N. Y.	TWENTY Full length figure in Roman costume TWENTY
1 Compt's die	Vig. Dairy maid, cows, &c. 1 ILLION BANK, Illion, N. Y. Dog.	ONE Artisan.
Indian standing. Compt's die.	2 Mirror, female with pail on right; man with rake on left. ILLION BANK, Ilion, N. Y. Dog.	2 Two females.
3 Medallion head.	Compt's die. Vig. Three females seated. ILLION BANK, Ilion, N. Y. Dog.	3 Figure 3 and three men. THREE
Compt's die. Large V and females, sailor and two men.	5 Female with mirror, liberty pole and cap, motto Agriculture and Commerce. ILLION BANK, Ilion, N. Y.	FIVE Figure 5 and five females
10 Eagle. Compt's die.	Female seated with scales, and sword; ship, house, train, sun and cupid. X ILLION BANK, Ilion, N. Y. Dog's head.	Deer. 10 Buffalo.
20 Compt's die. TWENTY	Drover on horseback; drove of cattle and sheep. ILION BANK; Ilion, N. Y.	20 Female with rake; female in distance.
Goddess of Liberty. Compt's die.	1 Vig. Male portrait; female with trumpet and wreath of flowers on left; Cupid on right. 1 INTERNATIONAL BANK, Buffalo. Shield.	1 Female, Falls, rainbow and figure 1.
2 Male portrait.	Compt's die. Vig. 4 figures, sailor, Indian, Goddess of Liberty and Justice head in centre. INTERNATIONAL BANK Buffalo. Mechanic reclining on anvil.	2 Male portrait.

Left	Centre	Right
3 Male Portrait THREE	Compt's die. Vig. Two men and horse, dog, cattle and sheep. INTERNATIONAL BANK. Buffalo. Two horses.	3 Male portrait THREE
FIVE Male portrait. Compt's die.	5 Vig R R depot, locomotive, drayman loading goods harbor and ships INTERNATIONAL BANK Buffalo. Canal locks.	Five human figures surrounding ornamental figure 5. FIVE
10 Portrait of male.	Compt's die. 10 Vig Female seated bale of goods, shipping &c; lighthouse and canal boat. INTERNATIONAL BANK Buffalo. Farmers loading hay.	Two female figures one erect, the other seated, liberty cap and eagle.
20 Suspension bridge, two steamboats and falls. TWENTY	Compt's die. Vig. Female figure seated, three cupids riding sea animal. INTERNATIONAL BANK Buffalo. Goddess of liberty.	20 Portrait of Male
Compt's die. Male portrait	50 INTERNATIONAL BANK Buffalo. Vig. Steamship on left, ship on right, ship and steamer in distance.	50 Male portrait
1 Compt's die.	Vig. Santa Claus in sleigh drawn by reindeers. IRON BANK, Plattsburgh, N. Y.	ONE Smith with hammer on his shoulder.
TWO Compt's die.	IRON BANK, Plattsburgh, N. Y. Large red 2. Vig. Female seated on bale; steamboat in distance.	2 2
3 Mechanic and sailor.	3 Compt's die. IRON BANK, Plattsburgh, N. Y. Large red 3 length wise of note.	3 Dog's head.
5 V	Vig. Indian hunting deer. Compt's die IRON BANK, Plattsburgh, N. Y.	5 Female seated in harvest field.
TEN Compt's die.	IRON BANK, Plattsburgh, N Y. Vig. Steamboat and vessel; train of cars, light house &c. in distance.	X

N. Y. STATE.	N. Y. STATE.	N. Y. STATE.
1 Men at work with cradling machines 1 J. A. CLARK & CO.'S BANK Compt's die ONE DOLLAR Pulaski, N. Y. Girl's head	Female with cornucopia. JEFFERSON CO. BK, Watertown, N. Y. 10 Figs. 10, words Ten Dollars on three red dies. X Horse. Compt's die.	1 1 Three children in circular die reading book 1 1 JOSHUA PRATT & CO.'S BANK ONE DOLLAR Sherburne, N. Y. Compt's die Female portrait
2 J. A. CLARK & CO.'S BANK 2 Compt's die 2 Male portrait 2 2 TWO DOLLARS Cow and calf	XX JEFFERSON CO. BK, Watertown, N. Y. 20 Figs. 20 and words Twenty Dollars on three red dies. Female gathering wheat. Compt's die. Female with flowers.	2 Agricultural implements, etc 2 JOSHUA PRATT & CO.'S BANK Compt's die TWO DOLLARS Sherburne TWO Female beside barrel, grain, etc.
Female with sheaf of wheat and sickle in her hand. JAMESTOWN BANK, Jamestown, N. Y. 1 Compt's die Vig. Farmer, sailor, and mechanic; city, locomotive and ship in distance. ONE ONE	ONE Chasing buffaloes. ONE J. N. HUNGERFORD'S BANK, Compt's die Corning, N. Y. Daniel Webster.	New York Compt's die Girl and boy with cattle 3 JOSHUA PRATT & CO.'s BANK THREE DOLLARS Sherburne 3 Girl's head
2 JAMESTOWN BANK, Jamestown, N. Y. TWO Vig. Two females seated; steamboat, factory, cars, canal, &c., in the distance. Compt's die. Female seated on large figure 2.	ONE Hunters killing buffaloes. ONE State of N.Y. J. N. HUNGERFORD'S BANK, Corning, N. Y. Compt's die. Webster	JOSHUA PRATT & CO.'S BANK Men at work with cradling machine 5 FIVE DOLLARS 5 Compt's die 5 Sherburne 5
FIVE Compt's die. Vig. Farmer and Indian seated on either side of frame; Indian huts on left; cars and canal on right. Franklin Pierce. FIVE JAMESTOWN BANK, Jamestown, N. Y. V	2 Man and boy plowing with two horses. 2 Compt's die. Title of Bank. TWO Child's head.	X Cars crossing bridge; canal, lock, boats, men, horses, etc. 10 JOSHUA PRATT & COMPANY'S B'K Compt's die Sheep etc. TEN DOLLARS Sherburne
ONE JEFFERSON CO. BK Watertown, N. Y. 1 Male portrait Vig. Compt's die. Locomotive and cars.	Compt's die. Dogs pursuing deer. 3 Title of Bank. 3 Girl's head.	X X JOSHUA PRATT & COMPANY'S B'K Figure of Justice Sherburne 20 X X TWENTY DOLLARS Compt's die Two children Washington
3 3 Female with an Eagle and shield 3 Compt's die. JEFFERSON CO. BK Watertown, N. Y. Female portrait. 3 American eagle.	Five inverted Rafting scene on river; steamboat, etc. 5 Compt's die. Sailor seated with female, ships, etc. above him. Title of Bank. Cow, horse, bale, etc.	Male portrait 1 Milkmaid, cattle, sheep, &c. 1 1 J. T. RAPLEE'S BK Penn Yan, N. Y. Compt's die ONE Female portrait.
Compt's die. Farmer seated with sickle loading hay in distance 3 JEFFERSON CO. BK Large figure 3 and three cupids. Watertown, N. Y. Female portrait. Secured, etc.	STATE OF N. YORK 1 Man on horse, 1 boy on fence, colt, sheep, etc. 1 ONE on 1 J. N. WESTFALL & CO.S BK ONE DOLLAR Compt's die Jordan Male portrait	2 J. T. RAPLEE'S BK, Penn Yan, N. Y. 2 Compt's die. 2 2 Two young girls holding flowers. 2 Male portrait
5 Shipping, steamer &c. 5 Compt's die. JEFFERSON CO. BK Watertown, N. Y. Female with wheat.	2 STATE OF N. Y. Girl with sheep, grain, etc. 2 Child's head Compt's die J. N. WESTFALL & CO.S BK TWO DOLLARS TWO Jordan 2 Male portrait	Two Indians overlooking water fall; deer. Indian camp. V Webster V 5 J. T. RAPLEE'S BK, Penn Yan, N. Y. Compt's die. Fig. 5, with dies on each side. Farmer seated on plow 5
10 X Two females with safe key horn of plenty &c X TEN Compt's die. JEFFERSON CO., BK. Watertown, N. Y. Farmer ploughing 10 Locomotive and cars. 10	J. N. WESTFALL & CO BK 5 Compt's die FIVE DOLLARS STATE OF New N. YORK 5 on mill be- on 5 side canal 5 Male portrait	10 X Males, two horses, canal boat, cars, steamboat, mountains, etc., in distance. X 10 Male portrait TEN J. T. RAPLEE'S BK., Penn Yan, N. Y. Compt's die.

20 — Title of Bank. 20 Female erect column, steamer, etc. 20 — 20
Two girls, vase on left. — XX Compt's die. XX — Male portrait

1 — Vig. Am. eagle, E Pluribus Unum; shipping &c. — 1
Compt's die. ONE — JUDSON BANK, Ogdensburgh, N. Y. — Female portrait.

2 — JUDSON BANK, Ogdensburgh, N. Y. — Compt's die.
Locomotive. — Vig. Indians feeding horse. — 2

Locomotive and train of cars — 5
JUDSON BANK FIVE DOLLARS Ogdensburgh, N. Y. — Compt's die
FIVE — FIVE

ONE — 1 Vig. female seated on safe, Dog and child; ship in distance on right, plough on left. — 1
Female reclining. — KINGSTON BANK Kingston, N. Y. Park. — Compt's die.

Compt's die. — Female on either side of a shield on which is a ship, plow, etc.; vessels and city in distance. — 2
Farmer seated with scythe. — KINGSTON BANK, Kingston, N. Y. Building, &c. — Carpenter at the work bench.

THREE — Vig. Three females seated on a shield, ships on right, wheel of wheat and cars, on left — Compt's die — 3
3 — KINGSTON BANK Kingston, N. Y. 3 A park. 3 — Steamboat.

FIVE DOLLARS — 5 Vig. State arms ship on right, cars on left. 5 — V
KINGSTON BANK Kingston, N. Y. — Compt's die.
Hands joined together. — V

TEN — X Vig. Female; sheaf of wheat and plough, and cattle on left. X — 10
Cupid, grindstone &c. — KINGSTON BANK Kingston, N. Y. Steamboat. — Female and wheel.
10 — 10

NEW YORK
1 — Deer beside wood — 1
LAKE BANK ONE DOLLAR Skaneateles
Compt's die — Male portrait

NEW YORK
2 — Scene at door of house, men, woman, children, horse, etc. — 2
Compt's die — LAKE BANK
2 — TWO DOLLARS — Fowl

NEW YORK
Compt's die — Herd of deer beside brook — 3
LAKE BANK THREE DOLLARS Skaneateles Fruit
3 — Female portrait

FIVE — Scene at dock; vessels, men at work etc. — 5
Compt's die
Man on rock; sheep etc. — LAKE BANK FIVE DOLLARS Skaneateles — 5

FIVE — Man plowing with two horses — Women and child — 5
Compt's die
THE LAKE BANK FIVE DOLLARS Skaneateles
5 — 5

10 — Horse-fair. — 10
NEW YORK — LAKE BANK
Skaneateles — TEN DOLLARS — Compt's die

1 — LAKE ONTARIO BK, Oswego, N. Y. — ONE
Female representing Agriculture, sailor and blacksmith with implements; ship city and cars in distance.
Compt's die. — Anchor on shield. — Male portrait

2 — Vessels at sea. — TWO
Compt's die. — LAKE ONTARIO BK, Oswego, N. Y.
2 — Anchor on shield. — Male portrait

Scene on wharf; various vessels in port at distance; men at work on dock; horse cart, etc. — Male portrait — 5 on Five.
LAKE ONTARIO BK, Oswego, N. Y. Anchor on shield. — Compt's die.
V — 5

1 — Drovers, cattle, and sheep. — 1
View of Street men and cattle end of bay, town in distance. — LAKE SHORE B'K, Dunkirk, N. Y. — State Arms.

2 — LAKE SHORE B'K, Dunkirk, N. Y. — 2
Sailor leaning on capstan. — Catching wild horse. — State Arms.

Compt's die. — 3 Male portrait. 3 — 3
Indians hunting buffaloes. — LAKE SHORE BANK, Dunkirk, N. Y. — Man cutting tree; two children, oxen, etc.

5 — Landing of the pilgrims. — 5
Female artist and implements. — LAKE SHORE B'K, Dunkirk, N. Y. — State Arms

10 — Title of Bank. Sailor on ship with quadrant. — 10
Anchor, bales, bbls., etc. — Compt's die.

ONE — Drove of sheep, dog, &c.; man on horseback; mill and trees in distance. — 1
LEONARDSVILLE BANK, Leonardsville, N. Y. — Cattle, telegraph and railroad.
Compt's die. — Agricultural Implements.

2 — Horses, cattle and sheep; boy, trees, fence and house in distance. — TWO
Compt's die. — Title of Bank.
TWO — Dog, key and safe. — Male, female, boy, girl, dog, hen and chickens.

Compt's die. — Two females and a male at work making cheese. — 3
Title of Bank.
3 — THREE Fish. — Pig pen, pigs and chickens

FIVE — Title of Bank. Man tending large machinery. — 5
Blacksmith, hammer and anvil; factories in distance. — 5 Arm. 5 — Compt's die. V across five

X Title of Bank — 10
Liberty erect with pole, cap, shield and eagle. — Indian on shield; eagle at top, horse each side; steamboat in distance on right; cars, factory and canal boat on left. TEN TEN — Compt's die.

XX — Title of Bank. — 20
Spread eagle on ball of the globe.
Farmer, tree and scythe. — 20 Compt's die. 20 — Sailor seated with telescope.

1 — LINCOLN BANK. Portrait ONE of DOLLAR Abraham Lincoln. — 1
Compt's die — Clinton, N. Y.

2 | LINCOLN BANK. Portrait of Abraham Lincoln. Compt's die. Clinton, N. Y. TWO | 2 DOLLARS

Compt's die. 3 | Portrait of Abraham Lincoln. LINCOLN BANK. THREE DOLLARS. Clinton, N. Y. | 3

1 | Vig. Female seated on rock, canal boats, steamboat, &c., village in distance. Compt's die. LOCKPORT CITY B'K. Lockport, N. Y. | 1 Canal boat and bridge.

TWO Compt's die TWO | Vig. Anchor and Hope above in scroll, city, factories, etc., on right; canal boat and harbor on left. LOCKPORT CITY B'K Lockport, N. Y. | 2 Drove of cattle, cars &c

3 Train cars 3 | Vig. Ship and schooner under full sail; steamboats and cars in distance. LOCKPORT CITY B'K Lockport, N. Y. | 3 Compt's die THREE

5 Female portrait | LOCKPORT CITY B'K FIVE DOLLARS Lockport, New York Five cupids and large ornamental 5 5 5 | FIVE Compt's die

FIVE Indian with bow and tomahawk. | LOCKPORT CITY B'K Lockport, N. Y. Compt's die. Vig. vessels, steamboat and harbor. Large 5 across note. | V with letters Five running across it.

X Squaw. | LOCKPORT CITY B'K Lockport, N. Y. View of the Suspension Bridge. | 10 Compt's die

20 XX | LOCKPORT CITY B'K Lockport, N. Y. Cattle; stream of water, trees, etc. | 20 XX

Lockport. 50 Niagara Co. | LOCKPORT CITY BK View of Crystal Palace, etc. Fifty Compt's die. Dollars. | 50 NEW YORK.

L | LOCKPORT CITY B'K Lockport, N. Y. View of the Crystal Palace; pedestrians, horses, carriages, etc. Compt's die. | 50

Compt's die. | Soldier on a galloping horse. ONE LONG ISLAND B'K, Brooklyn, N. Y. Deer. | Washington. Female resting on a rock.

2 Compt's die. 2 | Same vig. as ones. TWO 2 Title running around the vig. Fish. | TWO

3 Compt's die 3 | 3 Vig. Same as ones. LONG ISLAND B'K, Brooklyn, N. Y. Chicken. | THREE

5 Compt's die. 5 | Male figure seated on rock in clouds; buildings in background. 5 LONG ISLAND B'K, Brooklyn, N. Y. Deer. | FIVE

X Compt's die. X | 10 Title of Bank. Vig. Same as fives. Fish. | TEN

50 Compt's die. | Indian standing beside block of stone, in his right hand a sword; in background an ox with plow. 50 LONG ISLAND B'K, Brooklyn, N. Y. Deer. | Die Work. Franklin. Die Work.

100 Compt's die. | 100 Vig. Same as fifties, with the Title running around it. 100 | Med. head. Washington. Med. head.

ONE Female with sickle and grain. ONE | 1 Eagle on limb of tree. 1 LYONS BANK, Lyons, N. Y. | Female erect in large fig. 1.

TWO Female seated with safe, scales, eagle, etc. TWO | 2 Female seated with sickle and wand; factory and canal in distance. 2 Title of Bank. Farmer cradling. | Vulcan seated with implements; ears of corn above and below him.

5 Justice, safe, eagle, scales, etc. FIVE | V Three females and fig. 5, cars, ships, farm scene, etc., in distance. V Title of Bank. Farmer cradling. | 5 Med. head. FIVE

10 Man seated on ground with cradle and basket. Compt's die | LYONS BANK. TEN X DOLLARS | 10 Female seated on bales and boxes.

1 Female with pen and tablets. | Sailor steering ship. MANUFACTURERS' BANK of Brooklyn, N. Y. | 1 Compt's die.

Indian on cliff. 2 | Title of Bank. Mechanic with hammer, anvil, cog-wheel, etc. | 2 Compt's die.

THREE View of wharves, vessels, etc. THREE | Milkmaid and cows; houses in distance. Title of Bank. | 3 Compt's die.

5 Female portrait | Title of Bank. Mechanic erect in a letter V; anvil, hammer, cog wheel, etc.; buildings, &c., in distance. | 5 Compt's die.

10 | Spread eagle; buildings, street, etc. Female portrait. Title of Bank. | 10 Compt's die.

20 Arm and hammer. 20 | Title of Bank. Figures 20, winged female on either side; two cupids between 2 and 0. | 20 TWENTY Compt's die

50 50 | Three females and winged cupid floating in water. Compt's die. Title of Bank. | 50 Female with compass, &c.

100 Female reclining with sheaf and sickle. | Cattle and stream of water. Title of Bank. | 100 Compt's die

N. Y. STATE.

Left	Centre	Right
Female and figure 1. Compt's die.	Mechanics at work in an iron mill; large wheel in distance. 1 MANUFACTURERS' BANK, Troy, N. Y. Secured, &c.	ONE Female seated. ONE
TWO Compt's die. 2	Vig. Train of cars; steamboat on right, trees and rocks on left. MANUFACTURERS' BANK, Troy, N. Y. Secured, &c.	TWO Boiler makers seated on boiler. TWO
Compt's die Cupid and dolphin. THREE	Vig. Sailor seated holding a quadrant; female with sheaf of wheat and sickle, on right sheaf of wheat and men at work in distance, on left steamship in distance. MANUFACTURERS' BANK. Troy, N. Y. Secured, &c.	THREE Female portrait. 3
FIVE Male portrait. Compt's die.	Vig. Large iron mill and houses, large house in distance on a hill, on left waggon, on right houses in distance. MANUFACTURERS' BANK, Troy, N. Y. Secured, &c.	Blacksmith at work. FIVE
TEN Liberty by X Compt's die.	MANUFACTURERS' BANK, Troy, N. Y. Large steamboat leaving wharf. Secured &c.	Man with scythe. 10
20 Compt's die.	Two females seated; factory in distance. MANUFACTURERS' BANK, Troy, N. Y. Secured, etc.	20 Female seated on bale
1 ONE	MAN. & TRADERS' BANK, Buffalo, N. Y. Compt's die. Blacksmith anvil and hammer; city in distance.	1
2 TWO	Title of Bank. Compt's die. Ship yard; men at work and ship on stocks.	TWO Figure 2, in top curve is figure 2.
3 THREE	Compt's die. Bull's head on shield; on left female binding sheaf; on right man dressing leather. Title of Bank.	THREE Large figure 3 in top curve is fig. 3.
5 FIVE	Title of Bank. Three cherubs with lever, &c., breaking stone. 5	5 Compt's die. FIVE

N. Y. STATE.

Left	Centre	Right
X TEN	Title of Bank. Five cherubs with globe, anvil hammer, &c. X	Word ten, letter X and figure 10. Compt's die.
ONE Ship in full sail.	Compt's die. 1 Vig. Houses and shipping, sailor in foreground. MARINE BANK, (Buffalo, N. Y.)	ONE Ship in full sail.
2 Compt's die.	TWO TWO Shipping and marine view. MARINE BANK, Buffalo, N. Y.	2 Sailor holding flag.
5 Compt's die.	FIVE FIVE Marine view. MARINE BANK, Buffalo, N. Y.	5 Canal boat passing under a bridge
X Compt's die.	X Whaling scene. X MARINE BANK, Buffalo, N. Y.	10 Ship in full sail
1 ONE	Farmer seated with scythe. Sailor seated. On demand, and one dollar in red die. MARINE BANK, Oswego, N. Y. Compt's die.	1
TWO TWO Compt's die.	2 2 MARINE BANK, Oswego, N. Y. Female with wheat. 2 Female with flowers.	TWO DOLLARS
Compt's die. THREE 3	Ships and other vessels; city in distance. 3 MARINE BANK, Oswego, N. Y.	THREE
5 Compt's die. FIVE	View of N. Y. Harbor, with a steamer and ship. MARINE BANK, Oswego, N. Y.	5 FIVE
10 Sailor by capstan.	Three horses drinking from trough; sheep, &c.; farm scene in general. MARINE BANK, Oswego, N. Y.	X Ship on stocks. Compt's die

N. Y. STATE.

Left	Centre	Right
XX Two sailors and female in a boat.	TWE Compt's die. NTY MARINE BANK, Oswego, N. Y.	20
1 Compt's die. ONE	Vig. Farmers at work; cars in distance. MARKET BANK, Troy, N. Y.	1 Female, sheaf of wheat and sickle.
Compt's die. 2	Vig. Two farmers and man on horse, sheaf of wheat on right, and trees on left. MARKET BANK, Troy, N. Y.	2 Female portrait.
Compt's die. 5	Vig. Man on horse, cattle and sheep, houses and waggons on right. MARKET BANK, Troy, N. Y.	5 Group of children with shield and spear.
X Bull's head. X	MARKET BANK, Troy, N. Y. Three females, two seated and one in centre erect, one on right is drawing, on left playing a harp; house in background.	10 Compt's die. X
50 Drove of cattle.	MARKET BANK, Troy, N. Y. Two females on either side of Washington; on right, steamboat and ship; on left, sheaf and men mowing.	50 Compt's Die.
1 Compt's die.	Blacksmiths shoeing horse. MECHANICS' BANK, Brooklyn, N. Y.	1 Squaw and papoose.
2 Compt's die.	Stone cutters at work. Title of Bank. Female portrait	2 Franklin.
3 Compt's die.	Carpenter at work; tools lying on the bench. Head of Washington. MECHANICS' BANK, Brooklyn, N. Y.	3 Mechanics' arms, with hammer, anvil, and cog wheel.
5 Compt's die.	MECHANICS' BANK, Brooklyn, N. Y. Three Cupids with press and levers trying to raise a large stone.	5 Locomotive and tender.

Left	Center	Right
10 Compt's die.	Masons working on scaffold, building a house, man coming up a ladder with hod. MECHANICS' BANK, Brooklyn, N. Y.	10 Jenny Lind.
50 Compt's die	Two females reclining inside a kind of shell, with bee hive between them; female on left has sword and scales. MECHANICS' BANK, Brooklyn, N. Y.	50 Blacksmith resting on hammer and anvil; female in background.
100 Compt's die. 100	View of the Brooklyn City Hall. 100 MECHANICS' BANK, Brooklyn, N. Y.	C Female seated with Am. shield beside her.
Compt's die ONE	1 Man seated on a boiler, with sledge in right hand. 1 MECHANICS' BANK, Syracuse, N. Y.	Man bearing a hide. ONE
II Compt's die.	Female seated; boiler, anvil, etc.; ship in distance. MECHANICS' BANK, Syracuse, N. Y.	II Blacksmith with forge and anvil.
3 Compt's die. 111	MECHANICS' BK. Syracuse. Vig. Two females sitting; factory, canal, cars, steamboat, &c., in the distance.	3 Indian viewing a ship.
5 Compt's die. 5	MECHANICS' BANK, Syracuse, N. Y. Two Indians one with gun and the other lying down. Secured, etc.	FIVE 5 Cars. Waterfall. FIVE
X Sailor, light house, etc Compt's die.	Locomotive and cars. MECHANICS' BANK, Syracuse, N. Y.	10 Female and anvil. 10
Female with sword in right hand. Compt's die. TWENTY	MECHANICS' BK. Syracuse. Vig. Female sitting; two sheafs of wheat, scroll, and globe; cat in distance.	20 Canal view.
Three males supporting 50.	Girl's head. MECHANICS' BANK, Syracuse, N. Y. Cupids and 50.	L Compt's die.

Left	Center	Right
100 Liberty seated.	Girl's head. MECHANICS' BANK, Syracuse, N. Y. Compt's die.	100 Stone cutter.
1 Compt's die. 1	1 Vig. Female, male, grain, farmers' and mechanics' tools, &c. 1 MECHANICS' AND FARMERS' BANK, Albany.	ONE Head of Washington ONE
2 Compt's die. 2	2 Title of Bank. II Vig. Same as ones.	2 Washington 2
3 Compt's die. 3	3 Title of Bank. 3 Vig. Same as ones.	3 Washington 3
5 Compt's die	MECH. & FAR. BK., Albany, N. Y. Blacksmith seated by anvil, forge, factories, vessels, etc. FIVE	5 Agriculture.
5 Compt's die.	Male, female, grain, etc. 5 MECH. & FAR. B'K of ALBANY, FIVE DOLLARS Albany, N. Y.	FIVE Female erect, with left hand pointed upwards, and right holding shield, on which is figure 5
X Compt's die.	MECHANICS' AND FARMERS' BANK, Albany. Vig. Female, male, grain, farmers' and mechanics' tools, &c.	X TEN
50 Male and female seated.	MECH. & FARMERS B'K. Albany, N. Y. FIFTY DOLLARS Compt's die.	50 Male portrait.
50 FIFTY 50	MECHANICS' AND FARMERS' BANK, Albany. Vig. Mechanic seated. FIFTY DOLLARS 50	
C Male portrait. 100	MECH & FARMERS BK. Albany, N. Y. One Hundred Dollars. Compt's die.	100 Male and female seated

Left	Center	Right
ONE HUNDRED	MECHANICS' AND FARMERS' BANK, Albany. Vig. Mechanic seated, ONE HUNDRED 100	
Male Portrait ONE Compt's die.	MERCANTILEBANK Plattsburgh, N. Y. Vig. Two Indians in the forest—one reclining on the ground, the other in the back ground.	1 Male figure clasping ornamental figure 1.
Compt's die. Male Portrait	MERCANTILEBANK Plattsburgh, N. Y. Vig. Steamer coming into the dock. Small vessel on left.	TWO Large 2. Man sharpening a scythe.
Male Portrait. Compt's die.	MERCANTILEBANK Plattsburgh, N. Y. Vig. Mechanics at work, machinery, &c.	THREE Large 3. Female seated. Man in small boat.
5 Male Portrait	MERCANTILEBANK Plattsburgh, N. Y. Vig. Train of cars. Cattle drinking	Large 5. Indians, and train of cars. Compt's die.
1 DeWitt Clinton	Cars crossing bridge, scene on canal, haying, etc. MERCHANT'S BANK ONE DOLLAR Albany, N. Y.	1 Compt's die
2 Head of Washington.	Vig. Female figure representing Agriculture in the foreground; Hudson River in the distance. MERCHANTS' BK. Albany.	2 State Arms.
Head of female. 3	Vig. Three female figures supporting the figure of Cupid. MERCHANTS' BK. Albany.	3 State Arms
5 Head of John Hancock.	Vig. Railroad scene on the Susquehanna River; train of cars in the foreground; bridge over the river in the distance. MERCHANTS' BK. Albany.	5 State Arms
X 10	Vig. Very fine view of one of the Collins' line of steamers at sea, under both sails and steam. Head of John Jay MERCHANTS' BK. Albany.	10 State Arms.

20 | MERCHANTS' BK. Albany. | 20
Female figure. | Vig. Goddess of Liberty; eagle to the left of the figure. |
TWENTY | | State Arms.

Female with sword and shield. | X Two children, cows, sheep, etc. | 10
TEN | MERCHANTS' B'K in Poughkeepsie, N. Y. | Compt's die.

Female. | Vig. Locomotive and train of cars. | II
| MERCHANTS' BANK OF WESTFIELD, N.Y. | 2
Compt's die. | | TWO

ONE | MERCHANTS' BK. Lancaster. Title under vig. | 1
State Arms. | Vig. Spread eagle, cask, bale, shield, &c.; village, dam, cars, &c. in background | Female reading book, guard chain on her neck, chin resting on hand, in circle.
ONE | | ONE

20 | Compt's die. 20 Male figure sitting; hammer in hand, &c. |
Female erect. | MERCHANT'S BK in Poughkeepsie, N. Y. |
| | 20

5 | Vig. Cattle and sheep. | 5
Compt's die | MERCHANTS' BANK OF WESTFIELD, N.Y. |
FIVE | | Portrait of Washington.

TWO | 2 Female with eagle, child, flowers, etc. | 2
Compt's die | MERCHANTS BANK TWO DOLLARS Lancaster | Female
TWO | Secured, etc. | TWO

50 | Infant figure holding shield with figs. 50; cask and cornucopia on the left; money chest and dollars on the right. | 50
Compt's die | MERCHANTS B'K in Poughkeepsie, N. Y. |
50 | |

Compt's die. | 1 Vig. Female, one hand extended over child's head, agricultural implements, anchor &c.; sail vessel in distance. Die. | ONE
ONE | MERCHANTS' AND FARMERS' BANK, Ithica, N. Y. Building. | Female seated, liberty pole and cap.

5 | MERCHANTS' BK. Lancaster. | 5
State Arms. | Vig. An old gentleman, two young men, and one lad, washing sheep; trees, dog, and water factories in the background. | Female standing with wreath in right hand and leaning other arm on large figure 5, with Liberty Cap.
FIVE | |

100 | Goddess of Liberty, eagle and shield, with letter C in centre of it. | 100
Compt's die | MERCHANT'S B'K in Poughkeepsie, N. Y. |
100 | |

TWO | 2 Vig. Female seated, wand in left hand extended, sickle, wheat &c.; houses and railroad in distance. 2 | Mechanic seated, horn of plenty &c.
Compt's die. | MERCHANTS. AND FARMERS' BANK, Ithica, N. Y. Steamboat. |
TWO | |

10 | MERCHANTS' BK. Lancaster. | 10
State Arms. | Vig. An old man sitting nearly naked, sledge in right hand, chin on the left; shield with letter X on it; anvil, anchor, &c. Water, steamship, vessel, cars, &c. in the background | Female standing, right hand on capstan and left hand hold of her dress.
TEN | |

1 | Man plowing with two horses. | 1
Compt's die. | MERCHANTS' BANK Syracuse, N.Y. |
1 | | Haymakers.

5 | V Vig. Female seated within large 5, female on either side; implements of agriculture, cars, bales, steamboat &c. V | 5
Compt's die. | MERCHANTS' AND FARMERS' BANK, Ithica, N. Y. Die. | Medallion head.
FIVE | | FIVE

ONE | 1 Female; shield in left hand; cornucopia beneath; ship in distance | 1
Compt's die | MERCHANTS B'K in Poughkeepsie, N. Y. |
ONE | | ONE

2 | Three females; setting sun; ship in distance. | 2
| MERCHANTS' BANK Syracuse, N. Y. | Female portrait.
Compt's die. | | TWO

10 | Vig. Two females, shield between them, sickle, balances, implements of agriculture, barrels, bales, shipping, manufactories &c. | 10
Compt's die. | MERCHANTS' AND FARMERS' BANK, Ithica, N. Y. Steamboat. | Two females, horn of plenty, liberty pole, cap &c.
TEN | | TEN

TWO | 2 Female seated with globe, wheel, pen, scroll, etc. | 2
| MERCHANT'S BANK in Poughkeepsie, N. Y. | Female portrait
Compt's die | TWO DOLLARS Secured, etc. |

5 | MERCHANT'S BANK Female reclining; ship and plough on shield; safe, sheep, cornucopia, etc. | 5
Compt's die | FIVE DOLLARS Syracuse, N. Y. | Female portrait

ONE | MER. & MECHANICS' BANK, Troy, N. Y. | 1
Compt's die. | Male portrait; sailor on right; farmer on left. | Man carrying lumber.

3 | 3 Female seated with pole, twig and shield; steamboat and sheep in distance. | 3
Compt's die | MERCHANTS' BANK Poughkeepsie, N. Y. | Female head
THREE | | THREE

Ship. | 10 Female reclining on cornucopia. | X
| MERCHANTS' BANK Syracuse, N. Y. | Female portrait.
Compt's die. | Still born. |

One on 1 | Female seated; sheaf, vessels, etc. 1 on med. head on each side. | ONE
Med. head. | MERCHANTS' AND MECHANICS' BANK Troy, N. Y. | Compt's die.
1 | | ONE

V | Title of Bank under vig. | 5 Compt's die. 5
| Vig. Female holding stalk of corn in right hand and sickle in left; grain and ripe fruits at her feet, left of the centre. Canal and railroad in the distance. No margin at the left. | Wm. Penn.
5 | | FIVE

20 | MERCHANTS' BK. Syracuse. | 20
| Vig. Three females, cornucopia, anchor, cars crossing bridge, trees, water, &c.; State arms, ship, city in distance. | Ocean ship.

2 | Title of Bank. | 2
| Three men erect; shipping, &c. in distance. |
Compt's die. | TWO DOLLARS |

10 | Compt's die. 10 Eagle, &c. | X
Female head. | MERCHANTS B'K in Poughkeepsie, N. Y. | 10
TEN | |

ONE | MERCHANTS' BANK OF WESTFIELD N.Y. | 1
Female. | Vig. Female seated, leaning on a shield; ship and steamboat in the distance on the left. | Portrait of Daniel Webster.
Compt's die. | |

TWO | Blacksmiths at work; one at anvil and one at bellows. 2 on med head on either side. | TWO
Justice. | Title of Bank. | Compt's die
TWO | | TWO

Left end	Centre	Right end
Compt's die. 3	Title of Bank Indian princess with shield etc; steamer in background.	3 Male portrait
3 Washington. 3	Title of Bank under vig. 3 Vig. Female sitting on bale of goods; in background, on left, vessels, &c.; in background, on right, cars, &c. 3	THREE State Arms.
5 State Arms.	Title of Bank under vig. 5 Medallion head. Medallion head. 5 Vig. Signing Declaration of Independence. Steamboat	5 Bo 5 ad. 5
TEN Compt's die TEN	Water scene, vessels, steamboats, etc. Ten on med head either side. Title of Bank. Eagle	X TEN and med. head. 10
L Franklin FIFTY	50 Female seated by shield; male figure in a car drawn by sea monsters. 50 MER. & MECH B'K. Troy, N. Y. Die.	Full length male figure
100 Washington. 100	MER. & MECH. B'K. Troy, N Y. 100 100 Vig. Same as Fifties.	100 Three cherubs. 100
1 Compt's die.	MIDDLETOWN B'K, Middletown, N Y Male and female hatters at work.	1 Boy's head.
Secured by image, &c. ONE	1 Vig. Female with sword child, cornucopia, anchor, agricultural implements, &c; ship in distance. Die MIDDLETOWN B'K, OF ORANGE CO. Middletown, N. Y. Girl milking.	ONE Female seated, cars and vessel in distance.
TWO Compt's die. TWO	2 Vig. Female seated; agricultural implements; factory on left; canal boat and cars on right; steamboat in distance. 2 Title of Bank. Female milking	Mechanic seated, tools, horn of plenty, surrounded by ears of corn
2 Compt's die. TWO	Title of Bank. Boy and horses; cars in distance.	2 Girl's head.

Left end	Centre	Right end
5 Two children	Cows, milkmaid, man, ladder, tree, dog, etc. Title of Bank. 5 FIVE 5	5 Compt's die. Female portrait.
5 Compt's die. FIVE	Vig. Group of persons, centre female holding a globe in one hand, key in the other seated in chariot lions at her feet; vessel and steamship in the distance. Title of Bank. Female milking.	Female pointing towards cars in the distance; man cradling FIVE
10 Compt's die. TEN	Vig. Two females seated, shield, balances and sickle between them; mill, agricultural implements, cars, steamboat, barrels, &c. MIDDLETOWN BK. OF ORANGE CO. Middletown, N. Y. Female milking.	10 State die. TEN
Male portrait 10	MIDDLETOWN BANK, Middletown, N. Y. Farmer, sailor and mechanic.	10 Compt's die.
Two females and two rapids with fig. 20. 20	Compt's die. Title of Bank. TWENTY	20 Male portrait
and TWENTY Compt's die. TWENTY	20 Vig. Female seated, left hand extended towards steamboat, chemical apparatus, table and writing implements' globe, &c. 20 Title of Bank Female milking	XX
FIFTY Female with sheaf and sickle	Compt's die. Man reclining; sheep, etc. Title of Bank.	50 Two children
100 Apotheosis to Art.	Title of Bank. Compt's die. Fig 100 and words ONE HUNDRED.	100 Two children
1 Compt's die. 1	1 Vig. Indian seated in canoe going through rapids. 1 MOHAWK BANK. Schenectady, N. Y. Locomotive and cars.	1 Female seated. 1
2 Compt's die. 2	MOHAWK BANK. Schenectady, N. Y. 2 Vig. Indian seated in canoe going through rapids. 2	TWO TWO

Left end	Centre	Right end
3 Compt's die.	MOHAWK BANK, Schenectady, N. Y. 3 Vig. Indian seated in canoe going through rapids. 3 Secured, &c.	THREE Female, sheaf of wheat, sickle &c. 3
5 Compt's die. 5	5 Indian seated in canoe going over rapids. 5 MOHAWK BANK, Schenectady, N. Y.	FIVE Male portrait 5
5 Female portrait.	MOHAWK BANK Schenectady, N. Y. Indian in canoe going over rapids. Canal lock	5 Compt's die. FIVE
5 Female portrait.	MOHAWK BANK, Schenectady, N. Y. 5 Indian seated in canoe going through rapids. 5 Canal lock.	FIVE Compt's die 5
10 Compt's die. 10	Title of Bank Vig. Indian seated in canoe going through rapids. X	10 Male portrait. 10
TEN Male portrait	MOHAWK BANK, Schenectady, N. Y. Indian in canoe going over rapids. Loading hay.	10 Female portrait. Compt's die
Farmer ploughing with two horses. 50 Compt's die.	L Indian seated in canoe going through rapids. MOWHAWK BANK, Schenectady, N. Y. Cars.	FIFTY Old soldier loading 50
1 Secured, &c. Compt's die	Three Indians; train of cars, hill, &c. in distance. 1 MOHAWK RIVER BANK, Fonda, N. Y.	ONE and 1 Male portrait
2 Compt's die. 2	Title of Bank. Three Indians; suspension bridge, etc. TWO Train of cars.	2 Male portrait
Compt's die. Building. 3	Three Indians; THREE cars, hills, etc., in distance. Title of Bank.	3 Male portrait

5 Male portrait. | Title of Bank. Three Indians; cars, hills, etc. Secured &c. | 5 Compt's die. FIVE

10 Three Indians erect, etc. | Title of Bank. Large X across the title. TEN Male portrait. DOLLARS TEN | 10 Building. Compt's die.

ONE Female seated, holding figure. ONE | 1 Compt's die. Cupid. MOHAWK VALLEY BANK, Mohawk, N. Y. | ONE Indian with bow and spear.

Indian drawing bow. Compt's die. | 2 Vig. Farmers harvesting; two seated at lunch; female holding rake, and pouring drink. 2 MOHAWK VALLEY BANK, Mohawk, N. Y. | Female portrait surrounded by corn.

Indian drawing bow. Compt's die. | 3 Vig. Female portrait in frame, surmounted with eagle; antelopes, on either side. Vessel in distance. MOHAWK VALLEY BANK, Mohawk, N. Y. | 3

Indian drawing bow. Compt's die. | 5 Vig. Deer and Indians in canoe hunting them. MOHAWK VALLEY BANK, Mohawk, N. Y. | FIVE Full length male figure.

Indian drawing bow. Compt's die. | 10 10 Two females seated; shield between them; sickle and hammer; barrels and steamship on right; train of cars and houses on left. MOHAWK VALLEY BANK, Mohawk, N. Y. | Eagle and deer. Secured, etc. Deer.

50 Compt's die. 50 | 50 Vig. Farmer plowing. MOHAWK VALLEY BANK, Mohawk, N. Y. | 50 Female portrait.

100 Compt's die. 100 | Vig. Indian seated, canoe on right, deer on left, letter C. 100 MOHAWK VALLEY BANK, Mohawk, N. Y. | Reaper with sheaf of wheat and sickle. 100

1 Compt's die. | Men moulding in iron mill. MONROE CO. BANK, Rochester, N. Y. ONE | 1 Factory.

TWO Compt's die. 2 | Male portrait. Anchor on shield; shipping, city and cars in distance. MONROE CO. BANK, Rochester, N. Y. TWO | 2 View o. cattle, telegraph, railroad, etc.

Compt's die. 3 | Female seated by chest, shield with ship on stocks; sheep, sheaf, &c. MONROE CO. BANK, Rochester, N. Y. THREE | 3 View of canal.

5 Male portrait. | Milkmaid seated with pail by side of shield on which is cars; sheaf, on right; cabin on left. MONROE CO. BANK, Rochester, N. Y. FIVE | 5 Compt's die. FIVE

X Men dressing leather. | Male portrait with female, cars, sheaf, etc, on right; female, horses, bbls., men and steamer on left. MONROE CO. BANK. Rochester, N. Y. | 10 Compt's die.

XX Bricklayers at work. | Male portrait; Justice, bridge and cars on right; manufactories on left. MONROE CO. BANK, Rochester, N. Y. Compt's die. | 20 Female sewing shoes.

1 Compt's die. | Man and woman watering horses at trough. MONTGOMERY CO. BANK, Johnstown, N. Y. | 1 Milkmaid, cow, calf and ducks.

1 Compt's die. 1 | Vig. Female seated with bucket and dog at her feet, cattle on either side. 1 MONTGOMERY CO. BANK Johnstown, N. Y. Farming implements. | Large house. 1 Church.

2 Compt's die. 2 | Man and boy plowing with two horses. Title of Bank. | 2 Fowls.

3 Compt's die. | Vig. Farmers washing sheep. 3 MONTGOMERY CO BANK Johnstown, N. Y. 3 sheafs of wheat and rake. 3 | Large house.

5 Compt's die. | Vig. Farmers ploughing, large V with five running across. MONTGOMERY CO. BANK Johnstown, N. Y. 5 Large house. 5 | 5 Church.

V Clay. | Cattle, sheep, etc. Title of Bank. | 5 Compt's die. V

X Washington. | Man and three horses at well; goats, kids, sheep, houses, etc. Title of Bank. | 10 Compt's die.

10 Compt's die. | Vig. Farmers at work. 10 MONTGOMERY CO BANK Johnstown, N. Y. X | House. X Church.

50 Female seated with eagle. 50 | MONTGOMERY CO. BANK. Johnstown, N. Y. L Vi. Female erect and large eagle. L | 50 Female, shield and anchor. 50

100 Male sculptor on his knees. 100 | C Vig. Female and two males; canal, locks, cars and houses in distance. C MONTGOMERY CO BANK. Johnstown, N. Y. | Female erect and large eagle. 100

ONE Compt's die. | MUTUAL BANK, Troy, N. Y. Vig. Artisans at work. | 1 Male portrait.

2 Female portrait. | Compt's die. Vig. Artisans at work. MUTUAL BANK, Troy, N. Y. | 2 TWO

Vig. Artisans at work. 3 | 3 Compt's die. MUTUAL BANK, Troy, N. Y. | 3 Male portrait.

V Male portrait. | MUTUAL BANK, Troy, N. Y. Compt's die. 5 | 5 Vig. Old man seated talking to children.

TEN Male portrait. | 10 Vig. Old man seated talking to children. 10 MUTUAL BANK, Troy, N. Y. TEN | X Compt's die.

XX | Old man seated talking to children. XX | 20
Compt's die. | MUTUAL BANK, Troy, N. Y. XX | Male portrait.

ONE | View of Fulton Ferry, City Railroad Station, etc.; New York in distance. | ONE
Compt's die | NASSAU BANK, of Brooklyn, N. Y. | Boy and rabbits.

2 | Two Cupids and two silver dollars; cattle, locomotive, etc.; in distance | 2
Compt's die. TWO | Title of Bank. | Female portrait

Compt's die. 3 | Launching the Adriatic. Title of Bank. | 3 Franklin

V | Sailor reclining on beach; steamer and vessels in distance. | 5
Female | Title of Bank. | Compt's die

10 | Spread eagle. Title of Bank. | 10
Girl's portrait. | | Compt's die.

20 | Title of Bank. Three females seated with compass, sickle, etc. | 20
Steamboat; Governor's Island in distance. | Compt's die. | Ship

50 | Title of Bank. Female reclining with shield, flag, etc.; ship in distance. | 50
Washington. | Compt's die. | Female seated and figs. 50.

100 | Spread eagle; Compt's steamer, building, die, etc.; in distance. Title of Bank. | 100
| | Sailor and captain.

1 | Vig. Large steamboat. | 1
Compt's die. 1 | NEW YORK & ERIE BANK, Buffalo, N. Y. | Portrait of Franklin.

2 | Vig. Female with sheaf of wheat and sickle; farm house, viaduct with train of cars passing over it in the distance. | 2
Compt's die. TWO | NEW YORK & ERIE BANK, Buffalo, N. Y. | Locomotive

5 | Vig. Locomotive and train of cars passing under a bridge. | V
Compt's die. FIVE | NEW YORK & ERIE BANK, Buffalo, N. Y. | Portrait of Washington.

Vig. Cattle and sheep, some lying down. TEN | Compt's die. NEW YORK & ERIE BANK, Buffalo, N. Y. | X Portrait of Webster.

20 | Vig. Spread eagle, holding the American flag in its talons. | 20
Portrait of Gen. Taylor. | NEW YORK & ERIE BANK, Buffalo, N. Y. | Compt's die.

1 | NEW YORK STATE BANK Albany, N. Y. | ONE
Compt's die. 1 | 1 Vig. State arms. 1 Male portrait.

2 | 2 NEW YORK STATE BANK. Albany, N. Y. Vig. Two females, eagle &c. female on left holding scales, on right ship in distance. Male portrait. | 2
Compt's die 2 | | 2

3 | 3 Vig. State arms 3 | THREE
Compt's die. 3 | NEW YORK STATE BANK Albany, N. Y. Male portrait

Die Work | 5 Vig. State arms. 5 | Die Work
Compt's die | NEW YORK STATE BANK Albany, N. Y. | 5
Die work | Secured &c. | Die Work

Med. work | 10 Vig. State arms. 10 | Medallion work.
Compt's die. | NEW YORK STATE BANK Albany, N. Y.
Med. work | Secured, &c.

20 | Female on either side of shield on which is eagle, etc. 20 on right and left. | XX
Compt's die. 20 | N. Y. STATE BANK, Albany, N. Y. Secured &c. | Canal scene, buildings, etc. 20

50 | 50 Vig. Two Females with scales &c, on right a ship in distance. 50 | FIFTY
State Arms 50 | N. Y. STATE BANK Albany, N. Y. Secured, etc

100 | 100 N. Y. STATE BANK, Albany N. Y.
Compt's die | State arms.
100 | Male head | 100

1 | Henry Clay. | ONE
ONE | NIAGARA CO. B'K. Lockport, N. Y. Compt's die.

TWO 2 | NIAGARA CO. B'K. Lockport, N. Y. 2 | 2 TWO
Compt's die. Male Portrait.

THREE | Compt's die. NIAGARA CO. B'K Lockport, N. Y. Stone cutters at work. | 3

FIVE | Male portrait. 5 NIAGARA CO. B'K. Lockport, N. Y. Female, sheaf, plow, &c; in distance, cars, bridge, canal lock, boat, &c. | 5 Compt's die FIVE

X TEN | NIAGARA CO. B'K Lockport, N. Y. Mechanic with anvil and [illegible]; city in [illegible]. X | 10 Compt's die.

TWENTY | NIAGARA CO. BK. Lockport, N. Y. Two cherubs in clouds. Red die with figure 20 and words twenty dollars. Compt's die | 20 Sheep.

ONE | 1 Group of females, pans, cattle, etc 1 | ONE
Compt's die | ONEIDA BANK ONE DOLLAR Utica, N. Y. | Canal, ship, etc
ONE | | ONE

TWO | 2 Train of cars, steamboat, etc. | II
Compt's die. | ONEIDA BANK, Utica, N. Y.
TWO | | Canal boat and sloop.

3 Compt's die. 3	3 Three females and an iron chest guarded by a dragon. ONEIDA BANK, Utica, N. Y.	III Train of cars
5 Compt's die.	5 Title of Bank. 5 Female, Cupids and a figure 5.	FIVE Female portrait. 5
10 Compt's die. 10	X Train of cars; building with cupola. X ONEIDA BANK, Utica, N. Y. Canal Locks	10 Female. 10
20 Portrait of a female. 20	ONEIDA BANK, Utica. XX XX Vig. Reapers with sickles and sheaf of wheat.	20 20
100 Factory, ship, cars, etc. 100	ONEIDA BANK, Utica, N. Y. Male figure seated in clouds with staff, lightning, eagle and shield. C each side	100 Cherub with basket of flowers. 100
1, with letters one running across. Vig. Cattle, man plowing	ONEIDA CENTRAL BANK, Rome, N. Y. Compt's die.	1 Henry Clay
2 Compt's die 2	ONEIDA CENTRAL BANK, Rome, N. Y. Vig. Blacksmith shop; smith shoeing horse.	2 2
FIVE Man and woman; two boys and sheep.	Vig. Two females with sword and balances; beehive, &c. ONEIDA CENTRAL BANK, Rome, N. Y.	5 Compt's die. 5
TEN Compt's die. 10	X Vig. Group of ten figures; ten gold dollars; steamboat in distance. ONEIDA CENTRAL BANK, Rome, N. Y.	10 X
20 Female portrait. Compt's die.	Vig. Female sitting; three cupids sporting on water. ONEIDA CENTRAL BANK, Rome, N. Y.	XX 20

1 With two small images on either side. Compt's die. ONE	ONEIDA CO. BANK. Vig. Three small figures with scythe, anvil, and capstan; ship and railroad cars in the dis- distance. Gold dollar between sigs.	1 Man clasping ornamental figure 1.
2 Compt's die. TWO	ONEIDA CO. BANK. Vig. Two females with man reclining on anvil and safe; steamship and railroad cars in the distance.	Large figure 2, with man whetting scythe. TWO
V With word Five running across. Compt's die. 5	ONEIDA CO. BANK. Vig. Shield, Indian and farmer on either side; canoe, Indian tents, and railroad cars in the distance. Dog between signatures	FIVE Portrait of a female.
10 Compt's die.	ONEIDA CO. BANK. Vig. Drover with cattle and sheep.	10 Female reclining with pen and book.
Female holding frame, on which is mechanic, anvil and hammer; locomotive, steamship and vessel in the distance. 20	Comptroller's die. ONEIDA CO. BANK	Shepherd reclining, with dog and flock around him, cars in distance. 20 TWENTY
ONE Indian Squaw Compt's die	1 Female, eagle, safe, key, etc. ONEIDA VALLEY BK ONE DOLLAR Oneida, N. Y. Grain, etc	1 Female with corn in right hand and figure 1 in left.
Indian with bow and arrows, &c. Compt's die.	ONEIDA VALLEY BK 2 Vig. Female, eagle, Cap of Liberty. Title to the right. State Arms.	2 Two females with spear, sword and scales. TWO
Indian with bow and arrows in right hand and a compass belt in left,	ONEIDA VALLEY BK 3 Vig. Female, shield; staff with Cap of Liberty. Steamboat and railroad in the distance. Dog and safe.	3 Female, sword and scales.
5 Med. head. FIVE	Compt's die. Shield surmounted by an eagle; man on right; female with sword and scales on left. ONEIDA VALLEY BK Oneida, N. Y. Compt's die.	5 Female with flowers and anchor.
Compt's die Female bust.	Vig. Goddess lifting drapery from an eagle. X ONEIDA VALLEY BK Safe.	Harvest scene. TEN

Compt's die Mermaid and Neptune blowing sea horn. Ship.	20 Baronial coat of arms. ONEIDA VALLEY BK Female in sitting posture.	20
Male head.	ONONDAGA BANK Syracuse, N. Y. Vig. Cattle standing in water.	1 Compt's die
Compt's die. Plank road, cattle, &c	Vig. Indian on rock and city in distance. ONONDAGA BANK Syracuse, N. Y. Beehive.	2 Male head.
3	Vig. Blacksmith shoeing horses, &c. ONONDAGA BANK Syracuse, N. Y.	3 Sea nymph in shell
Compt's die. Indian looking over a rock.	ONONDAGA BANK Syracuse, N. Y. Vig Drover selling oxen to Farmer.	5
10 Compt's die.	ONONDAGA BANK Syracuse, N. Y. Three sea nymphs supporting Cupid in water.	10 Female head
Boys head. Compt's die.	Vig. Horses running, prominent feature, three horses. ONONDAGA BANK Syracuse, N. Y.	50 Female head
Female head.	Vig. Capitol at Washington. ONONDAGA BANK Syracuse, N. Y.	100 Male head.
1 Compt's die	STATE OF NEW YORK Two children driving cattle through gate O. PADDOCK & CO'S BK. ONE DOLLAR Watertown	1 Female portrait
2 Compt's die 2	Man plowing with two horses O. PADDOCK & CO'S BK. TWO DOLLARS Watertown	2 Two men, cloth, etc.

Left	Centre	Right
Compt's die 3^{1}	Scene at door of house; men, woman, children, house, etc. O. PADDOCK & CO'S BK. THREE DOLLARS Watertown	3 Female with pen and scroll
Girl's portrait 5	Cattle in water; cars passing over bridge, etc. O. PADDOCK & CO'S BK. FIVE DOLLARS Watertown	5 Compt's die 5
1 Compt's die.	Man and boy plowing with two horses. ORLEANS CO. B'K, Albion, N. Y.	1 Female feeding fowls.
2 Compt's die. TWO	Milkmaid milking cow; one reclining; man, ladder, dog, houses, etc. Title of Bank.	2 Girl's head.
Compt's die. 3	Man drinking, two horses, plow, boy, etc. Title of Bank	3 Male portrait
Male portrait 5	Black and white horse alarmed at lightning; cattle in distance. Title of Bank	5 Compt's die. 5
10 Girl's head.	Farmer grinding scythe; negro turning; men mowing, house and barn in distance. Title of Bank.	10 Compt's die. TEN
ONE Compt's die. 1	Vig. Female resting on a sofa, on right females, cattle &c, on left locomotive. OSWEGATCHIE B'K Ogdensburgh, N. Y. Blacksmith.	1 Female Portrait.
2	Vig. Water scene, female and children. Compt's die. OSWEGATCHIE B'K Ogdensburgh, N. Y.	2 Female Portrait.
FIVE Compt's die. V	Vig. Female seated on right, bales of goods, steamship and ship, and on left vessels &c. in distance. OSWEGATCHIE B'K Ogdensburgh, N. Y.	5 Male Portrait.

Left	Centre	Right
TEN Compt's die. 10	10 Vig. Train of cars leaving depot; people &c. OSWEGATCHIE B'K Ogdensburgh, N. Y.	10 Male portrait. TEN
XX Compt's die. 20	Vig. Large eagle on which a female is reclining with an American flag around her. OSWEGATCHIE B'K Ogdensburgh, N. Y. Men loading hay.	20 Male portrait.
Female in clouds, small figure 1 to left. Compt's die.	OSWEGO RIVER BK. Fulton, N. Y. Indian seated by fig. 1; trees, water fall, hills, &c in distance	1 Male portrait
TWO Compt's die. TWO	OSWEGO RIVER BK. Fulton, N. Y. Figure 2, with female on either side. Canal Lock.	2 Male portrait
5 Male portrait	OSWEGO RIVER B'K. Fulton, N. Y. Female reclining; 5 in front of her; ships in distance. 5	5 Compt's die 5
X Two girls with sheafs of grain.	Men harvesting; man seated on sheafs; farm scene. OSWEGO RIVER BK. Fulton, N. Y. Beehive.	10 Male portrait Compt's die.
XX Male portrait TWENTY	Indian reclining, deer on ground at his back; stream of water, hills, &c. in distance. OSWEGO RIVER BK. Fulton, N. Y. Compt's die.	TWENTY Female erect with shield and spear. TWENTY
1 Compt's die. 1	Vig. Three females seated, agricultural implements, beehive, sheaf of wheat, &c. 1 OTSEGO COUNTY B'K Cooperstown, N. Y. Eagle.	ONE DOLLAR
2 Compt's die. 2	Female with scroll in each hand, on which is two dollars. 2 OTSEGO COUNTY B'K Cooperstown, N. Y.	Deer in frame surmounted with eagle; female on either side, with sword, spear and balances. 2
3 Compt's die. 3	3 Vig. Man seated within large figure 3; spears, gun, battle axe, &c. 3 OTSEGO COUNTY B'K Cooperstown, N. Y.	3 Female with sword and balances; portrait of Washington. 3

Left	Centre	Right
FIVE FIVE FIVE	5 Vig. Pillar on which is the word Otsego and V, male and female on either side; implements of war, science and arts. Compt's die. OTSEGO COUNTY B'K Cooperstown, N. Y. Fish.	FIVE FIVE FIVE
X Male portrait. 10	10 Vig. circular die on which is X surmounted with scroll on which is Otsego; male and female on either side implements of war, science and arts. Compt's die. OTSEGO COUNTY B'K Cooperstown, N. Y. Fish.	X TEN 10 TEN X
1 Compt's die	Sailor and Indian on either side of shield; ship on left. PALISADE BANK. ONE DOLLAR. Yonkers, N. Y.	1 Female and child.
2 Compt's die 2	PALISADE BANK. Canal, boat, road, cars crossing bridge. etc. TWO DOLLARS. Yonkers, N. Y.	2 Artisan leaning against machinery.
Compt's die 3	PALISADE BANK. Three children in circular frame, reading from book. THREE DOLLARS. Yonkers, N. Y.	3 Bee hives.
1 Compt's die.	PERRIN BANK, Rochester, N. Y. Indians hunting buffaloes. ONE ONE	1 1
2 Compt's die. 2	Title of Bank. The word two running down and repeated six times; on left, conflict between dog and bear, man with uplifted axe, on right, mower at work, house in distance. TWO TWO	2 2
5 Male portrait	Train of cars; two men at work; hills and large body of water in distance. PERRIN BANK, Rochester, N. Y. FIVE FIVE	5 Compt's die 5
1 Compt's die.	Indian seated with fig. 1 1 1 P. R. WESTFALL'S BANK, Lyons, N. Y.	ONE
2 Compt's die. 2	Liberty and Justice seated with fig. 2. Male portrait. Title of Bank.	2 2

Left	Centre	Right
5 Justice seated in fig. 5.	5 Boy, cattle and trees. Title of Bank.	5 Compt's die. 5
10 Female portrait.	Nine cherubs, female, shield and ten gold dollars Title of Bank.	10 Compt's die.
with letters one running across it. Female portrait.	PULASKI BANK, Pulaski, N. Y. 1 1 One dollar in part circle Male portrait.	1 Compt's die Large figure 1 and one dollar.
2 Compt's die. 2	Vig. Two women over wash tub; mechanic at work, machinery, &c. PULASKI BANK, Pulaski, N. Y. 2 2	2 2, with letters TWO running across. 2
3 Compt's die. THREE	PULASKI BANK, Pulaski, N. Y. Vig. Three men, one holding pole. 3 3	3 THREE 3
5 Compt's die.	PULASKI BANK, Pulaski, N. Y. Vig. Two horses; eagle mounted; figure 5 in centre; steam boat on right, cars, &c, on left. 5 5	5 5, with letters FIVE running across it. 5
X Compt's die. TEN	Vig. Woman reclining on chest male portrait, horn of plenty, sheep, &c. PULASKI BANK, Pulaski. N. Y. X X	10 X 10
1 Train of cars, boys, telegraph wires, Washington's head quarters, &c.	QUASSIACK BANK, Newburgh, N. Y. Bust in oval. Compt's die.	1 Scene on a plank road, carriage, man on horse back, sheep, omnibus, load of hay, &c.
2 Same as on ones.	QUASSIACK BANK, Newburgh, N. Y. Bust in oval, Compt's die.	TWO Same as on ones.
5 Train of cars; boys, telegraph wires, Washington's head-quarters, &c.	QUASSAICK BANK, Newburgh, N. Y. Bust in oval. Compt's die.	5 Man and merchandise on wharf; steamboat, barges, vessels, &c

Left	Centre	Right
V Same as on 1s and 2s.	QUASSIACK BANK, Newburgh, N. Y. Bust in oval, Compt's die.	V Man and merchandise on wharf; steamboat, barges, vessels, &c.
X Vig. Indian with gun, behind a ledge of rocks, watching deer.	QUASSIACK BANK, Newburgh, N. Y. Compt's die.	TEN Bust in oval.
XX Vig. Same as tens.	QUASSIACK BANK, Newburgh, N. Y. Compt's die.	20 Bust in oval.
FIFTY DOLLARS. Two Continental soldiers, one sitting with pipe in hand—the other standing, and reclining on his gun.	Compt's die. Vig. Indians in a canoe, rocks, trees, and mountains. QUASSIACK BANK, Newburgh, N. Y.	50 Little girl sitting at a table, with left hand over left eye to protect it from the light.
100 Man and boy with guns.	Compt's die. Vig. Buildings, viaduct, locomotive and train of cars on right: Indians and wigwams on left. QUASSIACK BANK, Newburgh. N. Y.	100 C
ONE on 1 Q. Compt's die	NEW YORK W. WELLINGTON & CO'S BANK Man with child on knee, pointing to bust of Washington ONE DOLLAR Corning	1 Eagle on rock
TWO on 2 Q. Compt's die TWO	W. WELLINGTON & CO'S BANK TWO on 2 Male portrait 2 2 surrounded by smaller figures 2	2 Dog on safe
1 Male portrait.	Compt's die. Vig Milk maid seated, cattle, &c. RANDALL BANK, Cortland, N. Y.	ONE Female, sword and balances.
2 Male portrait	Vig. Three females, sword, balances, horn of plenty, &c.; vessels on right. Compt's die. RANDALL BANK, Cortland, N. Y.	2 Full length female.
5 Male portrait FIVE	Vig. Train of cars; group of persons; some seated; most prominent one holding gun; hat in hand extended. Compt's die. RANDALL BANK, Cortland, N. Y.	5 Female portrait.

Left	Centre	Right
Female seated, holding frame, on which is man chopping; locomotive, steamship and vessel in distance. 1	Vig. Male portrait in frame, cupids on either side. RENSSALAER COUNTY BANK, Lansingburgh, N. Y. Gold dollar.	1 Compt's die. ONE
2 Compt's die. TWO	RENSSALAER COUNTY BANK, Lansingburgh, N. Y Vig. Two females holding liberty cap sword and balances, two gold dollar and eagle mounted between them; cars on left; village on right.	2 Portrait of Washington.
3 Indian maiden reclining with bow and arrow	RENSSELAER CO. B'K III Compt's die III 3 3 THREE DOLLARS Male portrait 3 gold dols. 3 gold dols	3 Female seated
FIVE Compt's die. 5	Male portrait in frame, Cupid on either side. RENSSELAER COUNTY BANK, Lansingburg, N. Y. Five gold dollars lapped.	Vig. Boy seated, basket and dog beside him; flock of sheep, cars in distance. 5 FIVE
Compt's die. Light house, large X small 10 on it, two sailors, one in boat, the other standing with glass in hand.	RENSSELAER COUNTY BANK, Lansingburgh, N. Y. Vig. Drover on horseback; drove cattle and sheep.	TEN Male portrait. 10
20 Compt's die.	RENSSELEAR COUNTY BANK, Lansingburgh, N. Y. Vig. Two females reclining, with liberty cap, sword and balances; sun rise, eagle and vessel in distance.	20 Male portrait.
Male figure pouring coin from horn of plenty. FIFTY	RENSSELAER COUNTY BANK, Lansingburgh, N. Y. 50 Male portrait 50 Compt's die.	Female soaring in the clouds, right arm extended over title of Bank; sickle in one hand, sheaf of wheat in the other. FIFTY
Male portrait 100	RENSSELEAR COUNTY BANK, Lansingburgh, N. Y. Vig. Mechanic reclining on anvil and safe, rule in one hand, hammer in the other, square, tongs, &c., beside him; two females: steamship on right, cars on left.	100 Compt's die.
1 Compt's die	R. L. INGERSOLL & CO.S BK ONE on 1 Girl, boy, cattle, etc. ONE on 1 ONE DOLLAR Pulaski, N. Y.	1 Female and child
2 TWO Compt's die	R. L. INGERSOLL & CO.S B'K 2 on Three children in circular die reading book 2 on DOLLARS TWO DOLLARS Pulaski	2 Stephen A. Douglas

5 Statue of R. America 5 | Man with two horses | L. INGERSOLL & CO.S. B'K | FIVE DOLLARS | Pulaski | 5 Compt's die 5

Figure 1 with one running across it. Washington. | Vig. Female seated, farmers loading hay in background. | ROCHESTER BANK, Rochester, N. Y. | 1 Compt's die.

2 Goddess of liberty. | Vig. Dog and safe. Compt's die. | ROCHESTER BANK, Rochester, N. Y. | 2 Female seated.

3 Compt's die. | Vig. Female seated on safe, with dog and child. Portrait of female. | ROCHESTER BANK, Rochester, N. Y. | THREE Female reaper.

5 Compt's die. 5 | Washington Jefferson Vig: Female with sheaf of wheat. | ROCHESTER BANK, Rochester, N. Y. | 5 Locomotive 5

X Compt's die. | Vig. Male portrait, with female on each side. | ROCHESTER BANK, Rochester, N. Y. | Eagle. | TEN Male portrait TEN

20 Compt's die. | Vig. Male portrait, with female on left, with liberty pole; two females on right. | ROCHESTER BANK, Rochester, N. Y. | Locomotive. | 20 Portrait of Fillmore.

1 Compt's die. ONE | Vig. Female seated, clasping large figure one. 1 | ROCHESTER CITY BANK, Rochester, N. Y. | ONE Full length squaw, holding bow and spear.

2 Compt's die. TWO | Vig. Mechanic seated, with tools around him, cars and steam factory in distance. | ROCHESTER CITY BANK, Rochester, N. Y. | 2 Two females with spear, balances, &c.

3 Compt's die THREE | Vig. Farmer; team of horses and plow; steam boat in distance. | ROCHESTER CITY BANK, Rochester, N. Y. | 3 Female seated.

5 Compt's die. FIVE | Vig. Female reclining on bale of goods; shipping in distance on right; canal locks and boat on left; cars, &c. | ROCHESTER CITY BANK, Rochester, N. Y. | 5 Male portrait.

10 Compt's die. TEN | Vig. Female seated, holding horn of plenty, &c; steam ship and shipping on right; canal boat, town on left. | ROCHESTER CITY BANK, Rochester, N. Y. | 10 Male portrait.

Compt's die. Man seated, holding 0, and bag of coin. 20 | 20 Washington. | ROCHESTER CITY BANK, Rochester, N. Y. | Columns. | XX Female portrait.

50 Compt's die. 50 | Vig. Eagle on limb of tree, railroad cars, canal boats, &c. | ROCHESTER CITY BANK, Rochester, N. Y. | Columns. | 50 Male portrait FIFTY

Compt's die. Female seated. | ROCHESTER CITY BANK, Rochester, N. Y. | 100 Vig. Female holding liberty cap and pole; spread eagles, C between them. | Columns. | 100 Benjamin Franklin.

Female, wheel, and urn. State Register's seal. | 1 Child's head. 1 | ROCHESTER EXCHANGE B'K. Rochester, N. Y. | 1 on ONE. Justice resting on pillar.

TWO on 2 Compt's die TWO | ROCHESTER EX. B'K | TWO Man seated with boy, pointing to bust of Washington TWO on 2 on 2 | TWO DOLLARS | 2 Canal boat and locks

ROCHESTER | Two females. FIVE | V Merchant, bales, boxes, barrels, &c. Boy with news papers. | EXCHANGE BANK. Rochester, N. Y. | 5 State Register's seal. FIVE

Cars, canal boats, horses, men, &c. 10 | ROCHESTER 10 | EXCHANGE BANK, Rochester, N. Y. | 10 State Register's seal.

20 Dog on safe. | ROCHESTER | XX State Register's seal. XX | EXCHANGE BANK. Rochester, N. Y. | 20 Female resting on pillar, torch in hand, &c.

Female writing on scroll, child at her feet | FIFTY 50 | ROCHESTER | L Compt's die L | EXCHANGE BANK | FIFTY DOLLARS | Rochester | 50 Girl's head FIFTY

Two children in large circular die 100 | ROCHESTER EXCH. BANK | Compt's die | One Hundred Dollars | 100 Indian girl

Large spread eagle across top of bill | ROCHESTER EXCHANGE B'K | FIVE HUNDRED | 500 D Compt's die D 500 | State of New York

Statue of Liberty with sword and American shield ONE 1000 | ROCHESTER EX. BK | 1000 Compt's die 1000 | THOUSAND DOLLARS | 1000 Eagle on shield

1 Compt's die. | ROCKLAND CO. B'K, Nyack, N. Y. | Green die with ONE on it. | 1 | 1 Eagle.

Two on 2 Compt's die Two on 2 | Steamboat "Armenia." | ROCKLAND CO. B'K Nyack, N. Y. | 2 TWO 2 | Two on 2 Female head

Compt's die 3 | ROCKLAND CO. B'K Nyack, N. Y. | Steamboat "Armenia." | 3 THREE 3 | 3 Female head

FIVE Washington. | 5 Female, cows, sheep, etc. | Title of Bank. | FI 5 VE | 5 Compt's die. 5

10 Machinist at work. | Title of Bank. | X Female pouring water in trough, sheep drinking. X | 10 Train of cars. Compt's die.

1 1 | ROME EXCHANGE BANK. | Vig. Locomotive with train of cars. | 1 | ONE Female with sheaf, and mechanic. Compt's die.

2

Three horses drinking at large trough; man seated; woman on left feeding pigs, farmhouse, etc., in distance. Large 2 across bill.

2

ROME EXCH. BANK
TWO DOLLARS
Rome, N. Y.

Compt's die. Secured, etc. Female with grain.

---

5 Milking scene 5 FIVE

5

Compt's die. ROME EXCHANGE BANK. Female with scales and sword.

---

10 Vig. Falls of Niagara in the distance; female figure in foreground. X 10

Compt's die. ROME EXCHANGE BANK. Head of Washington.

---

20 ROME EXCHANGE BANK. XX 20

Compt's die. Reaping scene. Femalehead.

A female seated, resting her elbow on the head of a barrel. State Arms. Vig. Load of salt barrels drawn by two horses; man on top of load. ONE

Portrait.

1 SALT SPRINGS BK. Syracuse. 1

---

2 State Arms. Vig. Indians boiling salt, and white man sitting on a log learning the trade. Scene near the shore of a lake, canoe close by. 2

Cupid sitting on a large ball.

TWO SALT SPRINGS BK. Syracuse. Portrait.

A large figure 5 in the background, an arched bridge over a river, and in front two Indians and guns. State Arms. Vig. Large coat of arms of this State, which is a little inclined to right of the centre of the bill. FI 5 VE

Portrait.

SALT SPRINGS BK. Syracuse. FIVE

TEN State Arms. Man boiling salt, &c.

Portrait. 10 10

TEN SALT SPRINGS BK. Syracuse. 10

TWENTY State Arms. TWENTY

Portrait. 20 20 Salt-house.

20 SALT SPRINGS BK. Syracuse. 20

ONE DOLLAR SARATOGA CO. BK. 1

Vig. Oxen, plough, man, &c. 1 Compt's. die.

ONE

1 Female sitting, [illegible] 1

---

2 2 Harvest scene; reapers; farming utensils and beehive. 2 TWO DOLLARS

Compt's die.

2 SARATOGA CO. BK., Waterford, N. Y. TWO

---

3 THREE

Compt's. die. Vig. Sheaf, two youths, steamboat, vessels, &c.

3 SARATOGA CO. BK. Portrait.

---

5 SARATOGA CO. BK. 5

Compt's. die. Portrait. Vig. Eagle drinking; female with pitcher; urns.

FIVE Fire engine. Figure of Justice

---

10 10 Cattle, sheep, &c. 10 X

Compt's die. SARATOGA COUNTY BANK, Waterford, N. Y. Med head.

10 Cornucopia, &c. X

---

10 SARATOGA CO. BK.

Portrait. Vig. Head of Washington, female with Liberty cap and wreath in hand; eagle and shield.

Compt's. die. Fire engine. 10

---

50 SARATOGA CO. BK. 50

Vig. Two females.

Compt's. die. 50 Likeness.

50 Small die. 50

---

1 SAUGERTIES BANK, Saugerties. N. Y. 1

Scene in a stone quarry.

Compt's die. Female portrait.

---

2 Two cows; female milking one; cornfield, house, man and dog in distance. 2

Compt's die. Title of Bank.

2 Female portrait.

Two men plowing with two horses. Milkmaid; cows in distance. 5

Title of Bank. Compt's die.

FIVE FIVE

Large X, female each side. 10 Scene in Iron mill. 10

XX Title of Bank. Train of cars.

Compt's die.

Female Eagle. Female, column, steamer, etc. 20

Compt's die.

20

---

1 1 Vig. Indian drawing his bow. 1 ONE

Compt's die. Houses &c.

1 SCHENECTADY B'K Schenectady, N. Y. ONE

Compt's die. 2 Vig. train of cars. 2 Indian drawing his bow

SCHENECTADY B'K Schenectady, N. Y.

2 Canal locks. 2

---

5 Vig. Indian drawing his bow. 5 FIVE

Compt's die. SCHENECTADY B'K Schenectady, N. Y.

5 Indian drawing his bow

X Vig. Indian drawing his bow. X Houses &c.

Compt's die. SCHENECTADY B'K Schenectady, N. Y. 10

10 Canal locks. Train of cars.

---

20 SCHENECTADY B'K Schenectady, N. Y. 20

Female with torch, eagle and medallion head of Washington. XX XX Vig. Indian with bow and arrow. Female with torch, eagle and medallion head of Washington

20 20

---

50 Vig. Female with torch, and medallion head of Washington. Indian with bow and arrow.

Buildings L L

50 SCHENECTADY B'K Schenectady, N. Y. Eagle. 50

Vig. Indian with bow and arrow. 100 N. Y. Safety Fund.

Female with torch, eagle and medallion head of Washington.

100 SCHENECTADY B'K Schenectady, N. Y.

Eagle. 100

Female seated, wheat and balances. 1 Vig Farmers sitting at lunch; female children and dog; team of horses. ONE

SCHOHARIE CO. BK. Schoharie, N.Y.

Compt's die. 1 Female holding rake.

Indian with bow and arrows. 2 Vig. Gathering corn; church and cars in back ground. 2

SCHOHARIE CO. BK. Schoharie, N.Y. Female portrait.

Compt's die. Building. TWO

Left	Centre	Right
FIVE FIVE Compt's die.	Vig. Cattle, &c. SCHOHARIE CO. BK. Schoharie, N.Y. Building.	5 5, five figure around, and balances, &c.
Vig. Spread Eagle,—flags on either side. TEN	Male Portrait SCHOHARIE CO. BK. Schoharie, N.Y. Dog.	X Compt's die.
1 Compt's die. ONE	Mechanic seated with sledge and anvil, cars and factories in distance. SENECA CO. BANK, Waterloo, N. Y. Female bathing.	1 Justice.
1 Compt's die. 1	One Dollar One twice. 1 Spread eagle. 1 SENECA CO BANK, Waterloo, N Y. Steamboat. One Dollar four times	bust Franklin. ONE
1 Two females sitting, with eagle and balances between. 1	SENECA CO. BANK. Vig. Locomotive and train of cars Machine	Shield with large figure 1 on it. Medallion head. ONE
2 Compt's die TWO	Man plowing with two horses 2 SENECA CO BANK TWO DOLLARS Waterloo, N. Y. Eagle	Statue of Liberty, with shield, etc
2 Compt's die. 2	Two Dollars Two Dollars. 2 Female either side of fig 2 on shield; motto "speed the plow" at bottom; vessel in distance. 2 Title of Bank. Canal scene Two Dollars Two Dollars.	Male figure erect. TWO
3 Two females sitting, eagle and balances between. 3	SENECA CO. BANK. 3 Females reclining on monument; bunch of grain in hand, vessel in distance 3 Canoe	3 3
3 Compt's die 3	Title of Bank 3 Female erect beside monument, sloop, hills, etc., in background. 3 Indian in canoe	3 Lafayette 3
5 Two females sitting, eagle and balances between	Sheaf of wheat, sickle, basket and child. Child in sail vessel, an eagel above. SENECA CO. BANK	5 Medallion head.

Left	Centre	Right
5 Compt's die. 5	5 Female, sheaf, cattle and plow. 5 SENECA CO. BANK, Waterloo, N. Y. Female.	Upright figure. FIVE
10 Two females sitting, &c. 10	10 Vig. Man reclining; left arm on vessel containing fluid, which is running out. SENECA CO. BANK. Eagle.	10
20 Two females sitting, &c. 20	SENECA CO. BANK. XX Indian full length. XX	Gentleman, with hat and cane in hand.
FIFTY	SENECA CO. BANK. 50 Indian full length. Two females sitting, eagle and balances.	FIFTY
Indian.	100 C Two females sitting; eagle, balances, &c SENECA CO. BANK.	C 100
One on 1 Compt's die	SETAUKET BANK, Setauket, N. Y. Female pouring water into trough, from which sheep are drinking	1 Sailor, mechanic, stranger, &c.
Two on 2 Compt's die Two on 2	Title of Bank. Sailor, farmer, boy, dog, capstan, anchor, boats, etc.	2 Female at work with sewing machine
5 Ship carpenter.	Title of Bank. Boy and girl; boy cutting stick; girl reclining; cattle.	5 Compt's die 5
Farmer erect in field leaning on rye; the small village in distance. Compt's Die.	Farmers loading cart with grain; two horses in front. SMITH'S BANK OF PERRY, N. Y. Secured, &c.	1 ONE
2 Compt's die. 2	Barnyard scene—female seated on sled another erect; fowls, cows, haystacks, &c. SMITH'S BANK OF PERRY, N. Y. Secured, &c.	2 Boy and rabbits.

Left	Centre	Right
5 Little girl and fowls.	SMITH'S BANK OF PERRY, N. Y. 5 Male portrait. 5 Secured, &c.	Large 5 and word five on either side. Compt's die. FIVE
10 Male portrait	X Female portrait. X SMITH'S BANK OF PERRY, N. Y. Secured &c.	10 Compt's die.
ONE Compt's die.	SPRAKER BANK, Montgomery Co., N.Y. 1 Vig. Man and boy at work; horse and sled 1	1 Portrait of Gen. Cass.
2 Indian, small vessel in distance. TWO	SPRAKER BANK, Montgomery Co., N.Y. 2 2 Compt's die.	2 Waterfall hunter on his knees drinking.
3 Compt's die	Vig. Two females; cars on right, vessels on left. SPRAKER BANK, Montgomery Co., N.Y. Large red 3 lengthwise	THREE Portrait of Webster.
Hunter warming himself at fire; dog and gun.	V Compt's die SPRAKER BANK, Montgomery Co., N.Y. Large figure 5 lengthwise of note	5 Male portrait
TEN Male Portrait	Vig. Spread eagle with U. S. flag in talons. SPRAKER BANK. Montgomery Co., N. Y.	X Compt's die. TEN
1 Female leaning on pedestal with tablet in hand.	Vig. Milk maid and cows; farm house in distance. STATE BANK, Troy. Grain and farming implements.	1 Compt's die.
Portrait of female. TWO 2	Vig. Iron works with forges and workmen. STATE BANK Troy. Steamboat.	2 Compt's die
3 Sheaves of wheat	Vig. Cattle standing in water. Sheep grazing. STATE BANK Troy. Eagle	3 Compt's die

5
Female sitting on anvil; mechanical tools, &c.
Vig. Shield, females on either side with liberty cap and balances; ship and steamboat in distance.
STATE BANK
Troy.
Farming implements.
5
Compt's die.

Female with sickle.
10
10 Vig. Female 10 reclining on bale of goods barrels, &c.; house and ship in distance.
STATE BANK
Troy.
Eagle.
Female sitting on bale of goods.
Compt's die.

50
FIFTY
50
STATE BANK,
OF TROY, N. Y.
Female portrait; on right female, column, steamer; on left, female, cow, calf, etc.
Compt's die.
50
DOLLARS
50

ONE
Compt's die
ONE
Vig. Farmer and Indian on either side of a shield.
STATE OF NEW YORK BANK,
Kingston, N. Y.
Gold dollar,
1
Man dressing leather.

Compt's die
2
State Arms.
STATE OF NEW YORK BANK,
Kingston, N. Y.
Schooner.
2
Stone cutter at work.

3
Portrait of Dewitt Clinton.
STATE OF NEW YORK BANK,
Kingston, N. Y.
Vig. Sailor, woman, mechanic; ship and steamboat in the distance.
3
Compt's die.

V
Compt's die.
Vig. Kingston Academy, with wagon loaded with flag stone, horses, and driver.
STATE OF NEW-YORK BANK,
Kingston, N. Y.
Clasped hands.
FIVE
5
Male portrait.

Figure 10 with cupids on either side
View of Washington Irving's residence.
STATE OF NEW YORK BANK,
Kingston, N. Y.
Letter X with Ten running across it.
Compt's die

50
Washington
STATE OF NEW YORK BANK,
Kingston, N. Y.
Indian reclining with dead deer.
Compt's die.
50
Cars.

ONE
Girl leaning on bundle of grain.
Compt's die
Farm scene. 1 ONE on 1
STEUBEN COUNTY BANK.
ONE ONE 1 ONE DOLLAR
Bath, N. Y.
ONE
Full length figure of General Steuben.
ONE

ONE
Compt's die.
ONE
1 Vig. Female, soaring eagle, shield, liberty cap and pole, cornucopia &c. 1
STEUBEN CO. BANK,
Bath, N. Y.
Cornucopia, anchor &c.
Full length portrait of an officer.
ONE

TWO on 2
Compt's die
TWO on 2
2 Female reclining; quadrant, globe, map, books, &c.
STEUBEN COUNTY BANK.
Two Dollars.
Bath, N. Y.
TWO
Full length figure of General Steuben.
New York.

TWO
Compt's die.
TWO
2 Vig. Female seated on bale, train of cars, sickle, grain &c.; factory in distance. 2
STEUBEN CO. BANK,
Bath, N. Y.
Agricultural implements
Same as one's,
TWO

3
Compt's die.
3
3 Vig. Farmers at lunch. 3
STEUBEN CO. BANK,
Bath, N. Y.
Agricultural implements
Same as one's.
THREE

V
Full length figure of General Steuben.
STEUBEN COUNTY BANK.
FIVE on 5 Male portrait. DOLLARS on 5
Five Dollars.
5
Compt's die
5

V
Compt's die.
V
5 Vig. Large ornamental 5, female on either side, cupids &c. 5
STEUBEN CO. BANK,
Bath, N. Y.
Dog and safe.
Same as one's.
FIVE

10
Male portrait.
STEUBEN COUNTY BANK.
TEN DOLLARS. Full length figure of General Steuben. TEN DOLLARS.
10
Compt's die

10
Compt's die.
10
Vig. Female portrait in frame, surrounded by banners, drum, cannon &c. 10
STEUBEN CO. BANK,
Bath, N. Y.
Agricultural implements and wheat.
Same as one's.
TEN

Full length figure of General Steuben.
XX
20 Compt's die. 20
STEUBEN COUNTY BANK.
Twenty Dollars.
TWENTY.
XX
Male portrait.

20
Compt's die,
20
20 Vig. Spread eagle on bale and shield, cask, anchor; falls and train of cars in distance. 20
STEUBEN CO. BANK,
Bath, N. Y.
Agricultural implements and wheat.
Same as one's.
TWENTY

50
Female seated, key and wand.
50
STEUBEN CO. BANK.
Bath, N. Y.
Vig. Horse. 50
Full length portrait of a military officer.

Red 1.
Compt's die.
Man and boy plowing with two horses.
Female portrait.
STISSING BANK.
Pine Plains, N. Y.
Red 1.
Indian with gun.

2
Compt's die.
TWO
Title of Bank.
Portrait of boy.
Males, horse, colt, cart, etc., in corn field.
Red 2.
Indian erect

Red 5.
Female seated in fig. 5.
Girl's portrait.
Man with bag, horse, colt, mill etc.; boys on bridge.
Title of Bank.
Red 5.
Compt's die
FIVE

Red X.
Two females either side of X with cupid either side.
Cow and calf in stream; sheep, house, etc., in distance.
Title of Bank.
TEN
10
Compt's die.

20, XX and twenty.
Two winged females, figures 20 and two cupids.
Girls' portrait.
Title of Bank.
TWENTY Compt's die. DOLLARS
Red 20.
Fowls.

50
Boy's head.
STISSING BANK,
Pine Plains. N. Y.
Red die with 50 on it.
Compt's die.
50
Two children

Goddess of Liberty.
Compts die.
1 Whaling scene; two ships, whale and whale boat.
SUFFOLK CO. BANK
Sag Harbor, N. Y.
ONE
Bust of female.
ONE

TWO
Compt's die.
TWO
Vig. Two females, box, barrel, sheaf of wheat; on left female with sickle in hand, and ship in distance.
2
SUFFOLK CO. BANK
Sag Harbor, N. Y.
2
Medallion head of female.
2

3
Compt's die
Eagle 3
Two females in clouds, one holding cornucopia, the other holding die on which is large figure 3
SUFFOLK CO. BANK
THREE
Sag Harbor
State of New York
THREE

FIVE Compt's die. | Ship under sail. 5 Vig. Three females sitting; box; compass and sheaf of wheat (the female on left is pointing to ship. SUFFOLK Co. BANK Sag Harbor, N. Y. | FIVE Medallion head. FIVE

10 Compt's die. | Vig. Steamboat; ship under full sail leaving port, ship in distance 10 SUFFOLK Co. BANK Sag Harbor, N. Y. | Full length female.

TWENTY Compts die | 20 Female, sitting; ship in distance at left of female. Eagle and shield SUFFOLK Co. BANK Sag Harbor, N. Y. | 20

Figure 1 with word one running across. Train of cars. | Vig. Indian seated with bow; hut, plow, sheaf of wheat, &c. on left. SUSQUEHANNA VALLEY BANK, Binghampton, N. Y. | Same as on left. Compt's die.

Female with flowers; birds flying on left. 2 | Compt's die. Vig. Shield with word Excelsior, on right of which is a female, three children, globe, &c.; on left Indian, squaw and child. Title of Bank. | 2

5 Indian head | Title of Bank. Compt's die. Vig. Two females seated on right of a shield, on which is agricultural implements; on right public building, on left train of cars. | Figure 5, a V and word Five. Female with arm resting on pail.

Head of Webster. 10 | Vig. Female seated with sickle sheaf of wheat, plow &c., train of cars and canal lock in distance. Bridge, canal boat, horse, village and spire in the distance. Title of Bank. | Figure 10, a letter X and word Ten. Compt's die

BROOME COUNTY. Goddess of liberty, eagle, shield, liberty pole and cap. | TWENTY DOLLARS. Compt's die. Three females, one with wings, represented as soaring, the others in the act of receiving gift from her. Title of Bank. | 20 STATE OF N. Y.

Compt's die Load of hay &c. ONE | Vig. Female resting on sheaf of wheat, and on left a farming scene. fig. 1 on left. SYRACUSE CITY B'K Syracuse, N. Y. Dogs head. | ONE Female standing erect. and fig. 1.

Compt's die. Indian standing erect. | 2 Vig. Indians and white man holding a council. SYRACUSE CITY B'K Syracuse, N. Y. Deer. | 2 Indian female and pappoose. TWO

Female seated on rock. Compt's die. | 5 Vig. Water scene water gods &c. SYRACUSE CITY B'K Syracuse, N. Y. Train of cars. | 5 Female standing erect.

Compt's die. Indian with bow and spear in right hand. | TEN Vig. Deer and water scene. SYRACUSE CITY B'K Syracuse, N. Y. A Buffalo. | 10 Female standing holding an ear of corn X

1 Compt's die. 1 | 1 Vig. Male and female, most prominent figures group in rear, also train of cars. TANNERS BANK Catskill, N. Y. Cars. | 1 Cattle. 1

2 Compt's die. 2 | Vig. same as ones. 2 TANNERS BANK Catskill, N. Y. | TWO

FIVE | 5 Vig. same as ones and twos 5 TANNERS BANK Catskill, N. Y. | 5 Compt's die. 5

10 Female, liberty pole and cap. 10 | Vig. frame with vessel surmounted with eagle, female on either side, cars on right, shipping on left. 10 TANNERS BANK Catskill, N. Y. | 10 Compt's die 10

1 T. O. Compt's die | Indian girl beside eagle, shield, wigwam, etc GRANNIS & CO.'S ONE DOLLAR Utica, N. Y. | 1 B'K Child's head

Compt's die T. O. 3 | Female seated, grain, sheep, etc. farm house in distance GRANNIS & CO.'S THREE DOLLARS Utica | 3 B'K Two children

5 T. O. Female portrait | Female reclining beside chart globe, book, etc. GRANNIS & CO.'S FIVE DOLLARS Utica | 5 BK Compt's die 5

1 Compt's die. Female portrait. | Female with spear; bales on left; quadrant, urn, pallet, etc., on right. TOMPKINS CO. BK Ithaca, N. Y. | ONE Female 1 ONE

2 Compt's die 2 | Vig. Female reclining liberty cap and safe. TOMPKINS CO., B'K Ithica, N. Y. | TWO Large figure 2 and female standing. TWO

Female sitting on shield 5 | Vig. Large figure 5, with five at top, female at each side. TOMPKINS CO., B'K Ithica, N. Y. | 5 Compt's die

10 Female in air with vase in left hand ships in distance. TEN | Female portrait X Female portrait TOMPKINS, CO., B'K Ithica, N. Y. Bee Hive. | 10 Compt's die.

20 Medallion head. 20 | 20 on med. head. Vig. Female, shield and sheaf of wheat; ship in distance. 20 on med. head. TOMPKINS CO. BK. Ithica, N. Y. B | 20 Medallion head. 20

100 Medallion head and figures, 100. C | Medallion head and fig. 100 Vig. Eagle standing on a log on the left a steamboat. Medallion head and fig. 100. TOMPKINS CO. B'K Ithica, N. Y Letter A. | 100 Medallion head and figure, 100. C

1 Compt's die. | Female pouring water in to trough from which sheep are drinking. TRADERS' BANK, Rochester, N. Y. | 1 Two children

2 Compt's die. TWO | Indian female, eagle, shield, etc; steamer in distance. Title of Bank. | 2 Six figure 2's on small die.

FIVE Female with pen and tablets; child at her feet. | Man buying paper of newsboy; hogsheads, cars, steamer, etc. Title of Bank. | 5 Compt's die. 5

10 Man and dog; barn and men on right | Female seated pointing to factory; pedestrians, falls, etc. Title of Bank. | 10 Compt's die.

1 Compt's die. 1 | 1 Vig. Two females one seated and other erect holding a sheaf of wheat figure 1, in centre, on right plough rake &c. 1 TROY CITY BANK Troy, N. Y. Steamboat. | 1 Male portrait. ONE

2 Compt's die. 2 | TROY CITY BANK Troy, N. Y. 2 Vig. Female standing erect and Indian seated holding a gun in left hand. Vessel. | TWO 2

3 Compt's die. 3 | 3 Vig. Large steamboat under way. 3 TROY CITY BANK Troy, N. Y. Female reclining. | THREE Female standing erect with scales in right hand. 3

5 Compt's die. 5 | V Vig. Female seated holding scales in left hand, on right ships barrels and male at work. V TROY CITY BANK Troy, N. Y. Steamboat. | 5 Female erect with grain in left hand. V

5 Portrait of Washington. | Large letter V with female seated within. 5 TROY CITY B'K Troy, N. Y. | Compt's die. Female.

5 Male portrait. | Vig. Large eagle resting on tree; falls in background. TROY CITY BANK Troy, N. Y. Horse | Compt's die 5

X Male portrait. 10 | X Vig. Female seated with key in left hand X TROY CITY BANK Troy, N. Y. Steamboat. | TEN Two females one on right holding a sheaf of wheat on left a rake. 10

10 Male portrait. | Vig. Large eagle and shield on right a vessel under sail, on left a vessel. TROY CITY BANK. Troy, N. Y. Farm implements. | Compt's die TEN X

TWENTY Female with trumpet and staff. 20 | Vig. Two females and two children supporting the figures 20. TROY CITY BANK. Troy, N. Y. Eagle. | 20 Female. Compt's die

50 Female with wand, reclining. 50 | TROY CITY BANK, Troy, N. Y. L Spread eagle on rock. L FIFTY DOLLARS. Steamboat. | 50 Female holding scales, seat'd 50

100 Female seated, with eagle and olive br'nch 100 | Female seated, pouring liquid into urn, eagle on left. 100 100 TROY CITY BANK. Troy, N. Y. ONE HUNDRED DOLLARS. Steamboat. | 100 Female seated, with grain and sickle. 100

1 Compt's die. 1 | 1 Vig. Two females hands clasped, harvest field on left, cars on right in distance. 1 ULSTER COUNTY BK Kingston, N. Y. | 1 Horse. 1

2 Compt's die 2 | ULSTER CO. New York BANK 2 Three children around grindstones, screw, lever, etc. TWO DOLLARS Kingston Secured, etc. | TWO Male portrait TWO

3 Compt's die. 3 | Vig. Female in skiff. 3 ULSTER COUNTY BK Kingston, N. Y. | Man seated within large ornamental figure 3. 3

5 Compt's die. 5 | 5 Vig. Female in square frame with balances &c. ship in full sail on right. ULSTER COUNTY BK Kingston, N. Y. | FIVE

10 Compt's die. 10 | ULSTER COUNTY BK Kingston, N. Y. 10 Vig. Female in square frame with spear, implements of agriculture, grain, beehive, horn of plenty on each side. Male portrait. | 10

20 Compt's die. 20 | 20 Female on either side of shield on which is 20; ship in distance. ULSTER CO. BANK, Kingston, N. Y. Die. | TWENTY

50 Compt's die. 50 | 50 Vig. Knight on horseback. 50 ULSTER COUNTY BK Kingston, N. Y. | New York Safety Fund

1 ONE Compt's Die. | Vig. Wild Horses. UNADILLA BANK, Unadilla, N. Y. | 1 Child and rabbits.

ONE Compt's die. ONE | 1 Vig. Female in the air and figure 1. 1 UNADILLA BANK. Unadilla, N. Y. Secured, &c. | 1 Female seated, resting on shield 1

2 | Drover and Cattle. Compt's Die UNADILLA BANK. Unadilla, N. Y. | 2 Female Portrait.

TWO Compt's die. TWO | 2 Vig. Two females seated, on right plough and sheaf of wheat, on left ships in distance. 2 UNADILLA BANK. Unadilla, N. Y. Secured, &c. | 2 Man with an axe in right hand; cows &c. in distance.

5 | Two men, one a stone cutter; masons at work in background. UNADILLA BANK, Unadilla, N. Y. | 5 FIVE Compt's. Die.

5 Compt's die. 5 | 5 Vig. Female seated, in right hand a sickle, sheafs of wheat and horse on right, on left cars. 5 UNADILLA BANK. Unadilla. N. Y. | 5 Female portrait, in left hand a sickle. V

Female gathering wheat. 10 | UNADILLA BANK, Unadilla, N. Y. Words ten dollars and figure 10. | TEN Female with cornucopia. Compt's die

20 Two females with sheaf &c. | UNADILLA BANK, Unadilla, N. Y. TWENTY DOLLARS. Compt's die. | XX Milkmaid with tub.

ONE 1 Compt's die. | Vig. Building, load of hay, &c. UNION BANK, Albany, N. Y. Canal boat | ONE 1 Male portrait.

TWO 2 Compt's die. | Vig. Buildings, street, &c. UNION BANK, Albany, N. Y. Beaver. | 2 Male portrait.

FIVE 5 Compt's die | Vig. Male portrait, with locomotive on left factory on right UNION BANK, Albany, N. Y. Secured, etc | FIVE 5 Portrait of Washington.

TEN Male portrait. 10 | UNION BANK, Albany, N. Y. X Vig. Cupids with wheat. X | Large X with the word "TEN" running across it and 10. Compt's die 10

TWENTY Male portrait. 20 | 20 Vig. Female with shield, American eagle, &c. UNION BANK, Albany, N. Y. Secured, etc. | XX Compt's die XX

Left	Centre	Right
Compt's die. Figure 1 and the words one dollar.	One Vig. Female sitting with pail on her lap, cows, &c., UNION BANK Kinderhook, N. Y.	1 Bust of female with sheaf of grain; in an oval frame
2 2	Vig. Female reclining, factories in an oval frame, sheep, grain, &c Compt's die. UNION BANK Kinderhook, N. Y.	2 Two females one standing and the other kneeling.
3 Compt's die	UNION BANK Kinderhook. N. Y. 3 3 Vig. Eagle on branch of a tree, cars, &c., in the distance.	The word "Three" with the figure 3 running across Female walking with pail.
5 Compt's die.	UNION BANK. Kinderhook. N. Y V Vig. Three females sitting, the middle one a little above the others one with a quadrant, another with a pair of compasses and the middle one with sickle. V	5 Man driving cattle; trees, bridge, telegraph poles &c.
Female standing, and resting on her left elbow. TEN	UNION BANK Kinderhook, N. Y. Compt's die Three females seated, one of whom is reclining, and a pair of compasses in her hand.	10
XX Man talking to a boy who is sitting on the ground.	UNION BANK Kinderhook. N. Y. Compt's die.	20 Mechanic sitting with hammer in right hand factories &c
1 Compt's die	Canal boat nearing lock, cars passing over bridge, etc. UNION BANK, Medina. N. Y.	1 Female portrait.
2 Compt's die 2	Man with two horses; canal, farmhouse, &c in distance. UNION BANK. Medina, N. Y.	2 Male portrait.
5 FIVE 5	Statue of the Goddess of Liberty wreath, shield, etc. UNION BK, Five Dollars & extending nearly across bill.	5 Compt's die 5
ONE Compt's die. 1	Vig. Boy ploughing, steamboat on left; Farm house on right. UNION BANK Monticello, N. Y.	1 Man dressing leather.

Left	Centre	Right
2 Compt's die. TWO	Vig. Cattle and sheep, farm house in distance. UNION BANK Monticello N. Y.	2 Blacksmith at work.
3 Compt's die.	Vig. Saw mill and men at work. UNION BANK OF MONTICELLO, N. Y. Secured, &c.	3 Female with sheaf of wheat,
Large ornamental 5 car, &c. Compt's die.	Vig. Sailor and female seated. UNION BANK Monticello, N. Y.	5 Man carrying basket of corn.
X Compt's die. X	Vig. Two females, sword balances &c. eagle on left. UNION BANK Monticello, N. Y.	10 Cars. 10
20 Compt's die. 20	20 Vig. Public buildings &c. man on horseback and one on foot. UNION BANK Monticello, N. Y.	Female with sword and balances Locomotive TWENTY
Female standing resting on shield Compt's die.	1 Vig. Female seated shield &c. figure 1, and falls on left. UNION BANK OF ROCHESTER, N. Y.	1 Eagle and shield. ONE
2 Male and female figures and steamship	Compt's die. Vig. figure 2 on each side a female and the one on right, holding scales, and one on left a spear. UNION BANK OF ROCHESTER.	2 Two females standing erect.
5 Group of males and females, and large V,	Compt's die. Vig. figure 5, five females one in centre holding scales, on right large house and locomotive, steamship and vessels UNION BANK OF ROCHESTER, N. Y.	5 Portrait of Washington FIVE
10 Compt's die. 10	Vig. Two females liberty cap and eagle in centre on right cars and steamship in distance, on left a man ploughing, ship and mill in distance. UNION BANK OF ROCHESTER N. Y. Wheels and bale of goods	10 Male portrait. TEN
20 Compt's die. XX	Vig. Female with scales in centre, fort vessels and steamboat, in distance, on right cupid. UNION BANK OF ROCHESTER, N. Y. Sheaf of wheat rake plough and shovel.	20 Female eagle and money.

Left	Centre	Right
FIFTY Female standing erect with looking glass in right hand.	Vig. Female reclining large eagle and globe, on left steamships and ship in distance. UNION BANK OF ROCHESTER, N. Y. Shield.	50 Compt's die.
100 Female resting on anchor.	UNION BANK OF ROCHESTER, N. Y. Vig. Two females seated, eagle and shield in centre; cars and steamboat in distance. Shield.	100 Compt's die
Merchandise Compt's die Train of cars	1 Female with horn of plenty; bundle of sheafs at her feet. UNION BANK, Troy, N. Y. Wheels, bale, etc.	One on 1 Female with fig. 1.
ONE Compt's die.	UNION BANK OF TROY, N. Y. View of large building, street, etc.	1 ONE 1
2 Compt's die. 2	Title of Bank. Vig. Same as above ones.	2 Male portrait
Female standing. Compt's die.	Vig. Farmer with basket of corn. 2 on left. UNION BANK, Troy. Barrels and boxes between signatures.	2 Drove of cattle TWO
THREE Female surrounded by circle with names of the different states inscribed thereon. Compt's die	Vig. Locomotive and cars; depot in distance. fig. 3 on left UNION BANK, Troy. Steamboat between signatures,	THREE Figure three with blacksmith, sailor and farmer THREE
5 FIVE Compt's die.	Vig. Figures of females, one holding wreath over head of Washington. UNION BANK, Troy. Wheels, bale, etc	FIVE 5 surrounded by females.
10 Two male and female figures, lower extremities like a fish. Steamer	Compt's die. Vig. Eagle on branch; canal locks on right, and railroad cars on left. UNION BANK, Troy. Sailor	TEN 10 Sea horses
XX Male portrait. Compt's die.	Vig. Two females on either side of shield; eagle perched on top in centre; hogshead and bale on left; cars and steamship on right. UNION BANK. Troy. Bale.	20 Vessel in circular die. TWENTY

1 — Vig. Indian and sailor seated on either side of frame, surmounted by an eagle. Compt's die. — UNION BANK, Watertown, N. Y. — 1 — Female reaper. — 1

2 — Vig. Three mechanics; on right, bridge, factory, &c, in the distance. Compt's die. — UNION BANK, Watertown, N. Y. — 2 — Locomotive and tender. — 2

5 — Vig. Three females, two seated, and the other reclining. Compt's die. — UNION BANK, Watertown, N. Y. — 5 — Two females, one with arm resting on shield. — 5

Compt's die. — 10 — UNION BANK, Watertown, N. Y. — Vig. Man, woman, girl, boy and dog, rural scenery, &c. — TEN — Sailor in the act of hoisting a flag.

20 — Compt's die — UNION BANK, Watertown, N. Y. — Vig. Spread eagle, seated on the globe. — 20 — 20

1 — Compt's die — UTICA CITY BANK — Female with sword, child with scales, etc. 1 1 — ONE DOLLAR — ONE on 1 — Boy with fruit

1 — Compt's die. — UTICA CITY BANK. — Vig. Head of Martha Washington. — 1 — Head of a girl.

TWO on 2 — Compt's die — TWO on 2 — UTICA CITY BANK — Three men, grain, etc., ship in distance 2 2 — TWO DOLLARS — 2 — Two children

Compt's die. — Mower sharpening scythe. — Vig. Liberty and Ceres; shield with crest of the head of a horse; iron chest, vessels, &c.; horn of plenty, sheaf of wheat, &c. — UTICA CITY BANK. — TWO — Blacksmith at a forge.

Compt's die. — Head of Franklin on dark ground. — Vig. Indian and woodman; shield. — UTICA CITY BANK. — Secured, etc. — 5 — Girl with a hay rake.

Compt's die. — Head of Washington on dark ground. — UTICA CITY BANK. — Vig. Two half length female figures. — 10 — Female with ear of corn in right hand and figure X in left.

Compt's die. — 20 — UTICA CITY BANK, Utica, N. Y. — Female with the wand of Mercury; factory, viaduct, cars, steam vessels, etc. — XX XX — Secured, etc. — 20 — State of New York. — Female seated between 2 and 0.

1 — Compt's die. — WALLKILL BANK, Middletown, N. Y. — Cars and view of Mathews Hunt & Co.'s Warehouse. — 1 — Female Portrait.

2 — Compt's die. — TWO — Cattle in water, trees etc. — Title of Bank. — TWO — TWO — Female feeding fowls.

5 — Lady Washington. — FIVE — View of cars and saw manufactory. — Title of Bank. — FIVE — FIVE — Compt's die. — FIVE

10 — Building. — Bull's head on shield; man dressing leather on right; female sewing shoes on left. — Title of Bank. — TEN — 10 — Compt's die

XX — Female with dove. — Compt's die with female and children on right; squaw and papoose on left. — Title of Bank. — TWENTY — 20 — Male portrait

Secured by pledge &c. — ONE — 1 Vig. Female and child; on left an anchor and vessel in distance. Die. — WASHINGTON CO. BANK Greenwich, N. Y. — Portrait of Washington. — ONE — Female seated.

TWO — Female seated with scales. — TWO — 2 Vig. Female seated holding sickle, on right bridge &c. left sheaf of wheat and mill in distance. 2 — WASHINGTON CO BANK Greenwich, N. Y. — Man at work. — Female seated.

Secured &c. — THREE — Two females, one on left holding scales. — Compt's die. — 3 Vig. Two Females and in centre a female portrait, on left cars in distance. — WASHINGTON CO. BANK, Greenwich, N. Y. — Man at work. — 3

5 — Female holding scales, eagle, safe and key — FIVE — V Three females and in centre figure 5, on right barrels, and steamship in distance, on left a plough, &c. and cars in distance. V — WASHINGTON CO. BANK. Greenwich, N. Y. — Man at work. — 5 — Medallion head. — FIVE

10 — Female with scales, eagle, safe and key. — TEN — Vig. Two females, in centre a shield with scales at top, on right barrels and steamship in distance, on left houses and cars in distance. — WASHINGTON CO. BANK, Greenwich, N. Y. — Man at work. — 10 — State arms. — TEN

TWENTY — Female with scales eagle safe &c. — TWENTY — 20 Vig. Female seated steamship on right and globe on left. 20 — WASHINGTON CO. BANK Greenwich, N. Y. — Man at work. — XX

Medallion head and ONE — Compt's die. — Vig. Three blacksmiths at work. — WATERTOWN B'K AND LOAN CO. Watertown, N. Y. — Female in water. — 1 — Medallion head. — ONE

TWO — Compt's die. — Vessels and cars. — Three females reclining, two on left and one on right, eagle and shield in centre; ships on left in distance, bridge and cars on right. — WATERTOWN B'K AND LOAN CO., Watertown, N. Y. — Female in water. — 2 — Train of cars. — TWO

FIVE — Compt's die. — Male portrait. — Vig. Train of cars; in the background large rocks and a man on right, houses and hills in distance. — WATERTOWN B'K AND LOAN CO., Watertown, N. Y. — Female in water. — 5 — Female portrait. — 5

TEN — Compt's die. — Portrait of Washington. — Vig. Signing of the Declaration of Independence. — WATERTOWN B'K AND LOAN CO., Watertown, N. Y. — Eagle. — 10 — Male portrait. — TEN

Compt's die. — 25 — Vig. Mechanic seated hammer in hand, anvil; factories and cars in distance. — WATERTOWN B'K AND LOAN CO., Watertown, N. Y. — Deer — 25 — Two females, one blind folded holding balances, the other seated playing on harp.

50 — Compt's die. — Three females representing Liberty, Commerce and Agriculture. — WATERTOWN BK AND LOAN CO., Watertown, N. Y. — Safe. — FIFTY — Female giving eagle drink. — L

1 — Compt's die. — WAVERLY BANK, Waverly, N. Y. — Large Die. — 1 — ONE

2 WAVERLY BANK, Waverly, N. Y. 2
Compt's die. Die. Die.
2 2 DOLLARS. American shield.

Die. Die. Die. Die. Die.
V WAVERLY BANK, Waverly, N. Y. Compt's die
FIVE Female. 5

TEN X WAVERLY BANK, Waverly, N. Y. 10
Male portrait Compt's die

TWENTY XX WAVERLY BANK, Waverly, N. Y. TWENTY 20
Male portrait

Male portrait. WEEDSPORT BANK, Weedsport, N. Y. ONE
Vig. Five boys sporting in wheat. 1 1
Large build'g
Compt's die. One with figure 1 across.

TWO WEEDSPORT BANK, Weedsport, N. Y. 2
Female erect with right hand resting on compt's die.
Male portrait with female on either side; buildings on right in distance.
Portrait of Washington.
Canal Locks

5 Female portrait. Portrait of Washington. Female portrait. 5
WEEDSPORT BANK. Compt's die
FIVE DOLLARS
Weedsport 5

FIVE 5 Vig. Frame surmounted by an eagle, on either side is a female. 5
WEEDSPORT BANK, Weedsport, N. Y.
Compt's die. Canal boat. Male portrait

Farmer, woman, child, dog, etc. NEW YORK. BANK 10
WEEDSPORT Henry Clay.
TEN DOLLARS
10 Weedsport. Compt's die

Male portrait WEEDSPORT BANK, Weedsport, N. Y. 10
Female, eagle and shield.
X Compt's die.

1 Female beside shield, on which is eagle and Am. Arms Compt's die ONE
WESTCHE STER CO. BK Capture of Major Andre; Andre offering his purse
ONE DOLLAR
ONE Peekskill, N. Y.
Sloop ONE

Capture of Andre. 2 Compt's die. TWO
WESTCHESTER CO. BANK, Peekskill, N. Y. Female and sheafs.
2 Steamboat. TWO

WESTCHE STER Capture of Major Andre; Andre offering his purse COUNTY B'K
3 3 3
Compt's die
THREE DOLLARS 3
Peekskill, N. Y.
3 THREE THREE

5 WESTCHESTER CO. BANK. FIVE
State Arms. Capture of Andre. Sheaves of wheat.
5 Woman. FIVE

10 X TEN TEN
WESTCHESTER CO. BANK.
State Arms. Gold Dollars
Capture of Andre.
10 Barrels, ships, &c. TEN

20 XX XX Capture of Andre.
State Arms. WESTCHESTER CO. BANK.
20 Barrels, ships, &c. 20

Capture of Andre. WESTCHESTER CO. BANK. 50
50 State Arms
50 50

100 WESTCHESTER CO. BANK. Portrait of Lieut. Gov. Van Cortlandt.
State Arms. Capture of Andre.
100 100

1 Vig. Cows, three sheep reclining. 1
WEST WIN FIELD, West Win field, N. Y.
Load of hay, drove of cattle &c. Compt's die.

Drove of cattle and sheep. Compt's die. 2
WEST WIN FIELD, West Win field, N. Y.
2 Female.
Locomotive.

5 WEST WINFIELD BANK. West Winfield, N. Y. 5
Locomotive and train of cars crossing bridge; mountains in distance. Compt's die

Compt's die. Steamship. 10
WEST WIN FIELD BANK West Win field, N. Y.
Sailor, bbl. bale of cotton &c. Blacksmith, large anvil, anchor, &c

Compt's die. Vig. Capitol at Washington. 20
WEST WIN FIELD BANK, West Win field, N. Y.
Portrait of Jackson. Portrait of Webster.

ONE 1 Vig. Indians hunting buffaloe. 1 1
Compt's die. WHITE'S BANK OF BUFFALO, N. Y. Female
ONE Secured, &c. 1

TWO 2 Vig. Female reclining, shield &c. in centre, on right train of cars, on left steamboat. 2
Compt's die. WHITE'S BANK OF BUFFALO, N. Y. 2
TWO Secured, &c.

5 5 Vig. Steamboat and vessels. 5 FIVE
Compt's die. WHITE'S BANK OF BUFFALO, N. Y. 5
5 Secured, &c. female, etc
FIVE

TEN Vig. Female holding a vase, steamship on right, sheaf, canal, cars and mills on left. 10
Male and female figures. Sailor and Indian, in centre a shield.
Compt's die. WHITE'S BANK OF BUFFALO, N. Y. X
Safe.

2 Sailor with flag; anchor, bbl., quadrant and bale. Ship building; view of city in distance. 1
WILLIAMSBURG CITY BANK, Williamsburg, N. Y.
ONE Sloop. Compt's die

Female portrait. Female seated, eagle, etc.; in distance cars, city, vessels, &c. 2
TWO Title of Bank.
2 Eagle. Compt's die.

Indian on cliff. Female seated with shield; Falls in the distance. 3
Title of Bank.
3 Bee hive. Compt's die

N. Y. STATE.

Female seated holding a figure 5. FIVE | Vessels and view of city. Title of Bank. Head of Indian. | Female seated holding a 5; masts in background. Compt's die.

10 Female with flowers in her apron. | Female reclining on bales; vessels in distance. Title of Bank. Locomotive and tender. | 10 Compt's die.

50 Drovers and cattle, load of hay, etc.; road scene in general. | Farmers at rest and mowing; loading hay in distance. Title of Bank. Yacht Una. | 50 Compt's die.

Spread eagle. 100 | Compt's die. Title of Bank. Dog, key and safe. | 100

ONE Female portrait. ONE | 1 Vig. Eagle on a branch. 1 WOOSTER SHERMAN'S BANK, Watertown, N. Y. Male portrait. | Female standing in large figure one.

TWO Compt's die. TWO | 2 Female seated with wheat &c. 2 WOOSTER SHERMAN'S BANK, Watertown, N. Y. | Artisan with horn of plenty.

Figure 3 with female on either side. III | 3 Female portrait, female on either side. WOOSTER SHERMAN'S BANK, Watertown, N. Y. | 3

5 Compt's die. FIVE | V Female seated in large figure V, female on either side. WOOSTER SHERMAN'S BANK, Watertown, N. Y. Male portrait. | 5 Medallion head. FIVE

ONE | Male portrait. Farming scene. WORTHINGTON BK. Cooperstown, N. Y. | 1 State arms.

TWO DOLLARS | State arms. Man plowing with oxen; little girl on right with pail and jug. WORTHINGTON BK. Cooperstown, N. Y. | 2 Male portrait.

N. JERSEY.

3 THREE | Compt's die. Five females and a male gathering vines. WORTHINGTON BK, Cooperstown, N. Y. Male portrait | 3

FIVE | State arms. Farming scene; men at work. WORTHINGTON BK. Cooperstown, N. Y. | 5 Male portrait.

X TEN | Male portrait. Hunter shooting a deer; dog, trees and stream. WORTHINGTON BK, Cooperstown, N. Y. | 10 Compt's die.

1 ONE Compt's die | Two horses, boy on one; man attaching plow, etc. WYOMING CO. B'K ONE DOLLAR Warsaw, N. Y. | ONE Benjamin Franklin

2 State Arms. | Vig. Train of railroad cars passing under bridge; also, telegraph posts; stage coach crossing a bridge. WYOMING CO. BK. | TWO Head of Washington TWO

3 State Arms. | Vig. Blacksmith shop; smith shoeing horse, and another at the bellows. WYOMING CO. BK. | 3 Head of Webster.

V 5 V State Arms. | Vig. Liberty with a sheaf of wheat in right hand, sickle in left; men cradling grain; farm-house in distance; train of cars crossing a viaduct. WYOMING CO. B'K. | FIVE Head of Seward.

TEN State Arms. | Vig. Portage Bridge, and train of cars passing over. WYOMING CO. B'K. | 10 X Indian bow and arrows slung at his side.

ONE | 1 Blacksmith shoeing horse, man looking on, another by anvil. BK OF JERSEY CITY Jersey City, N. J. | 1 Compt's die.

2 TWO | Female portrait. Ship under sail. Compt's die. Two on 2. Title of Bank. | 2 TWO

N. JERSEY.

3 THREE | THREE Eagle on shield; female seated with anchor and quadrant. 3 Title of bank on right of vignette. | 3 Compt's die.

5 FIVE | V BK OF JERSEY CITY Jersey City, N. J. Locomotive and cars. 5 | 5 Compt's die. FIVE

X TEN | BK OF JERSEY CITY Jersey City, N. J. Female with cornucopia. American shield; female instructing children on right; Indian, squaw and papoose, on left. TEN TEN | 10 Compt's die.

XX Female with wheat. | BK OF JERSEY CITY Jersey City, N. J. XX Compt's die. XX | 20 Female with flowers in her apron.

50 Ship. | BK OF JERSEY CITY Jersey City, N. J. Red letter L on a shield; sailor, ship in distance on right; farmer with scythe on left. | 50 Compt's die.

100 | Steamboat, hills and raft. BK OF JERSEY CITY Jersey City, N. J. | 100 C Compt's die.

ONE on 1 State Arms. | BK OF NEW JERSEY New Brunswick, N. J. Portrait of Columbus and words one dollar. | ONE on 1. Shipping, bridge and cars.

Female portrait in ornamental die with TWO, 2, TWO, over top N. | TWO DOLLARS BANK OF NEW JERSEY Brunswick N. J State Arms | Female portrait in ornamental die with TWO, 2, TWO, on top ersey

Female with pen and tablets; child at her feet. THREE | 3 Female reclining with chart, dividers, quadrant, globe, &c. BANK OF NEW JERSEY, New Brunswick, N. J | 3 Boy.

Heavy ornamental engraving with figure 3 the middle and word THREE round the top. | BK. of NEW JERSEY, New Brunswick, N. J. State Arms enclosed in a heavy ornamental border with words THREE DOLLARS round the top. | Heavy ornamental engraving with figure 3 the middle and word THREE round the top.

5 | A large ornamental V with the word FIVE across it. | Word FIVE letter V and figure 5.
Female bust with sickle and wheat. | BK. of NEW JERSEY, New Brunswick, N. J. Anvil, &c. | State Arms.

Same as on right. | A large ornamental X with word TEN across it | Word TEN letter X and figure 10.
Female Portrait. | BK. of NEW JERSEY New Brunswick, N. J. Figure of Commerce, shipping, &c. | State Arms.

XX | A large ornamental 20 with word TWENTY across it. | 20
Female bust with sickle and wheat. | BK. of NEW JERSEY New Brunswick, N. J. | State Arms.

50 | BK. of NEW JERSEY. A large ornamental letter L with female figure engraved and word FIFTY across it. | 50
State Arms. | New Brunswick, N. J.

100 | A kneeling Female figure with sickle and sheaf of wheat, farm houses and mowers on right; railroad cars on left; the whole surrounded by a large ornamental letter C. | 100
State Arms. | BK. of NEW JERSEY New Brunswick, N. J. | C

ONE on 1 | STATE OF N. JERSEY Deer pursued by dogs | ONE on 1
Dog on safe | BANK of OCEAN CO. ONE DOLLAR Tom's River | Female at sewing machine

2 | STATE OF N. JERSEY BANK OF OCEAN CO. Two men and two women pick ing grapes | Child's head wreathed TWO DOLLARS Tom's River | 2
2 | | Vessels, lighthouse, etc.

3 | BK OF OCEAN CO. 3 Vessels at sea 3 | 3
Dog watching dead deer | THREE DOLLARS Tom's River | Girl beside bank

5 | STATE OF N. JERSEY. Landing of Columbus. | 5
Sailor with glass; girl, boy, etc. | BANK OF OCEAN CO. 5 DOLLARS. 5 | Girl and three dogs.

X | STATE OF N. JERSEY Train of cars at depot, etc. | X
Two children | BANK OF OCEAN CO. TEN DOLLARS Tom's River. | Sailor at helm.

20 | Tom's River. STATE OF N. JERSEY Bust of Washington, female on left, sailor on right. | 20
Machinist, arm upon column, on which is bust. | BANK OF OCEAN CO. TWENTY DOLLARS | Horse's head.

1 | Female seated on a log with a pail, train of cars, sheaf of wheat &c. 1 | ONE
State Arms. ONE | BELVIDERE BANK, Belvidere, N. J | Female erect ONE

Two children with grain | Belvidere Cow and calf in stream; sheep in distance | 1.25 New Jersey
1.25 | BELVIDERE BANK One dollar & twenty-five cts | Boys head

Boy watering horse in trough; with pail, etc. | female portrait | Female portrait | 1.50
1.50 | BELVIDERE BANK One Dollar & fifty cents | Female beside cattle

TWO | BELVIDERE BANK. Belvidere, N. J. | 2
Female with cakes sweet and figure 2. TWO | Farmer at work leading wheat, one holds horse. | State Arms.

THREE | Drove of sheep; Man on horse; dog; mill on left in distance. Boo right. | Female erect
Female erect with liberty pole and cap. 3 | BELVIDERE BANK, Belvidere, N. J. | THREE

Male portrait | 5 Two houses, farmers wagon, cattle, horses, trees, &c., hills in background. 5 | Portrait of Franklin.
Portrait of Washington. Male portrait | BELVIDERE BANK. Belvidere, N. J. State Arms. | Male portrait Male portrait

Horse head. | 10 Female seated on rock with spear; arm around eagles neck; cows in bank in distance. 10 | Flowers. Female, Bust of Washington on pedestal with eagle and shield at bottom.
Male Figure standing in front of fig. X | BELVIDERE BANK. Belvidere N. J. | 10

Female head. | 20 Three females, two seated, one erect. 20 | TWENTY
Male erect. | BELVIDERE BANK. Belvidere, N. J.

Female erect with cornucopia. | 50 Three females seated on bales &c, one nude looking toward vessels; on right sheafs of grain; farm house, rake, &c., on left. 50 | Female erect with sheaf of grain and sickle.
50 | Title of Bank. State Arms. | 50

1 | Locomotive and train of cars turning a curve. | 1
ONE State Arms. | BORDENTOWN BANKING CO., Bordentown, N. J. | Male portrait

TWO 2 | Two horses, one man riding and one leading other horse crossing railroad track; locomotive and two cars in the distance. 2 | TWO
State Arms. TWO | Title of Bank. | Male portrait 2

5 | A female sitting on a log with a bucket in her lap; two sheafs; locomotive and cars, | 5
State Arms. FIVE | Title of Bank | Head of Washington

10 | Title of Bank. | TEN
Male portrait | Two Indian figures and child. State Arms. Female, three children, and globe. Locomotive. | Milkmaid. TEN

50 | Title of Bank. | 50
Male portrait | Female sitting on money chest. State Arms. Sheaf and two sheep. Locomotive | 50

100 | Title of Bank. | C
Male portrait | Female fig. and horn of plenty. State Arms. Female handing $100 bill to other fig. | Locomotive and cars.

Male portrait | BURLINGTON BK., Burlington, N. J. | 1
1 | 1 Milkmaid with stool in left hand, leaning on cow; cows, sheep, &c. 1 | Child and rabbits.

Male portrait | BURLINGTON BK., Burlington, N. J. | 1
1 | Steamboat John Stevens, and view of town. | Child and rabbits.

2 | BURLINGTON BK., Burlington, N. J. | 2
Farmer with scythe; church spires in the distance. | Farming scene; farmers at work. | Head of William Penn.

3 | BURLINGTON BK., Burlington, N. J. | 3
Farmer drinking. | Three females, liberty, commerce and manufacture. | Portrait of Henry Clay.

Left	Centre	Right
5 Male portrait	BURLINGTON BK., Burlington, N. J. Steamboat John Stevens, and view of town in distance. Locomotive and cars.	5 Male portrait
Male portrait X	BURLINGTON BK., Burlington, N. J. Canal scene, and cars crossing bridge; houses on left.	Male portrait 10
20 Male portrait 20	Spread eagle on shield; ship on left. 20 BURLINGTON BK., Burlington, N. J.	Female with cornucopia TWENTY
FIFTY Male portrait L	BURLINGTON BK., Burlington, N. J. Factories and train of cars.	50 Male portrait
Girl with grain on head; farming scene in the distance. 100	BURLINGTON BK., Burlington, N. J. C State Arms of N. J.; factories on left.	100 Portrait of Washington.
ONE Indian. 1	Harvest scene. 1 BURLINGTON COUNTY BANK, Medford, N. J.	ONE Two females, one with sickle and grain.
TWO Cattle. TWO	2 Liberty in large figure 2. 2 BURLINGTON COUNTY BANK, Medford, N. J.	2 Milkmaid.
THREE Man seated on rock. State arms.	3 Vig. Female representing agriculture; cars crossing bridge on right. 3 BURLINGTON COUNTY BANK, Medford, N. J.	THREE Female drawing water from a well; steamboat in distance.
5 Letter V on medal. head. FIVE	5 Vig. Cattle and teaming; view of town; bridge and coach in background. 5 BURLINGTON COUNTY BANK, Medford, N. J.	5 Letter V on medal head. FIVE
5 Male portrait	BURLINGTON CO. BK Medford, N. J. Drover and farmer bargaining for bull; negro, boy, dog, horse, sheep, barn, etc.	5 Male portrait

Left	Centre	Right
10 Male portrait	Title of Bank. Female, calves, canal scene, cars, etc.	10 Male portrait
10 Franklin. 10	10 Three female figures representing Agriculture, Science and Art. 10 BURLINGTON CO. BANK, Medford, N. J.	X Franklin. X
20 Male portrait XX	20 Interior of a manufactory, men at work, houses in foreground. 20 BURLINGTON CO. BANK, Medford, N. J.	20 Male portrait XX
50 Male portrait 50	50 William Penn, treating with the Indians. 50 BURLINGTON CO. BANK, Medford, N. J.	50 Male portrait 50
100 Washington. 100	100 Signing the Declaration of Independence 100 BURLINGTON CO. BANK, Medford, N. J.	100 Male portrait 100
1 State arms. ONE	CENTRAL BANK, Hightstown, N. J. Train of cars passing under bridge.	ONE Male portrait.
2 Man, peach basket trees, &c.	State arms. Train of cars passing under bridge. CENTRAL BANK, Hightstown, N. J.	TWO TWO
3 Portrait.	State arms. Men, oxen, load of hay, &c. CENTRAL BANK, Hightstown, N. J.	3 3
FIVE State arms. FIVE	Train of cars passing under bridge CENTRAL BANK, Hightstown, N. J.	V Man, peach basket trees, &c.
TEN State arms.	CENTRAL BANK, Hightstown, N. J. Railroad scenery.	X Male portrait.

Left	Centre	Right
20 State arms.	Male portrait, on either side of which is a female, ship, sheaf of wheat, &c., on left; on right train of — CENTRAL BANK, Hightstown, N. J.	20 XX
50	CENTRAL BANK, Hightstown, N. J. Market house, shipping, &c. State arms.	L Male portrait.
C 100	Male portrait on either side of which is a female; ship, sheaf of wheat, &c., on left; on right, train of cars. CENTRAL BANK, Hightstown, N. J.	C State Arms.
1 Two Indians on a cliff viewing city.	Various vessels. CITY BANK of Perth Amboy, N. J. Female bathing.	1 State Arms. ONE
TWO	Female reclining on bales; Girl. steamboat in distance. Title of Bank. Dog.	2 Train of cars. 2
3 Female with bird.	Group of men, horses, etc. CITY BANK of Perth Amboy THREE DOLLARS Stage Coach.	3 3
5 Factory.	State Arms. Title of Bank Ducks.	V Male portrait
ONE Female feeding fowls.	State Arms. CLINTON BANK of NEW JERSEY, Clinton, N. J.	1 Male portrait
2 Head of Franklin.	Farmer watering horses at a well; buildings, sheep, goats, &c. Title of Bank.	2 Washington
3	Three men, farmer, mechanic and tradesman. Title of Bank.	3 Female head

5 — Female with sickle, grain, &c. — FIVE
Title of Bank.
Blacksmith standing; anvil and tools.
5 — Girl's head

X — Female with flowers — TEN
Title of Bank.
Head of Clinton.
10 — Boy's head

TWENTY — Female seated; eagle, &c.
Title of Bank.
House, flag, etc.
20 — Female with horn of plenty, grapes, &c.

1 — Female and column
1 Washington on horseback, officers, cannon, etc. 1
THE CITY BANK of Trenton
ONE DOLLAR
Trenton, N. J.
1 — State die

2 — Head and bust of girl
Locomotive, cars, etc.
THE CITY BANK of Trenton
TWO DOLLARS
2 — State die

L — Compt's die
CITY BANK
Eagle on rock — Two females with book, wand, etc: city and bridge in distance
FIFTY DOLLARS
Trenton
50

100 — Compt's die
CITY BANK of Trenton
Figure of Justice with sword and scales
One Hundred Dollars
100 — Two children

Liberty, female, shield, starry drapery, and liberty pole.
Spread eagle.
1 Indian seated viewing the improvements of the white man.
CUMBERLAND B'K, Bridgeton, N. J.
Female bathing.
ONE — Milkmaid. — ONE

ONE
1 on med. head. — Eagle on a shield. — 1 on med. head.
CUMBERLAND BK, Bridgton, N. J.
1 — ONE on med. head. — 1

THREE — Justice. — 3
Female seated, eagle, rock, shield, etc.; ships in distance. 3 on med. head on either side of vig.
CUMBERLAND BK., Bridgton, N. J.
THREE — Ship. — THREE

Liberty. — THREE
Spread eagle
Harvest scene; men at work in distance. — Figure 3, and word three on either side.
CUMBERLAND B'K, Bridgeton, N. J.
Two females, one with sickle and grain.

5 — Med. head. — FIVE
V Spread eagle on a rock. V
CUMBERLAND B'K, Bridgeton, N. J.
Med. head. — FIVE 5

5 — Male bust.
Man feeding cows with cornstalks; sheep, heifer, etc. Red V either side.
CUMBERLAND B'K, Bridgeton, N. J.
5 — Female with flowers.

Cupid with sheaf. — TEN
Title of Bank.
10 Boy's head. 10
Cupid with cornucopia. — TEN

10 — Cupid and farming implements. — 10
Med. head. — State arms of N. J. — Med. head.
CUMBERLAND B'K, Bridgeton, N. J.
X — Cupid. — X

20 — Female soaring in air.
Female seated; safe, flags; eagle at top of shield; ship on right.
CUMBERLAND B'K, Bridgeton, N. J.
Horse.
20 — Man sowing

Liberty and shield.
50 Eagle on limbs of tree.
CUMBERLAND B'K, Bridgeton, N. J.
Farming implements.
Female representation of Fame, Globe, and figures 50.

100 — Indian on horse.
CUMBERLAND BK, Bridgeton, N. J.
Washington.
100 — Sailor boy.

1 — Boy's head
Carpenter at work. — ESSEX CO BANK
1
ONE DOLLAR
Newark, N. J.
ONE
1 — Girl's head

1 — Boy's head.
Carpenter at bench. — ESSEX CO. BANK,
Newark, N. J.
1 — Girls' portrait

2 — Girls portrait
2 Farmers at rest, one seated, one leaning against fence. 2
Title of Bank
2 — Fowls.

THREE 3 — Anchor, bales, &c.
Title of Bank.
Mechanic, tradesman and sailor.
THREE 3 — Girls' head

V on 5 — Two children
Title of Bank.
Man in boiler shop.
5 — Man dressing leather.

10 — Head of sailor. — TEN
Title of Bank.
Four females—one reading.
10 — Blacksmith.

L — Clay.
Three female figures—liberty, protection, etc.
Title of Bank.
50 — Milkmaid and cows

C — Sailor.
Title of Bank.
Four female figures representing the Union.
100 — Webster.

ONE DOLLAR — ONE on 1 — Compt's die
EXCHANGE BANK
1 Cows and calf in water 1
of New Jersey
Tom's River
ONE DOLLAR
ONE on 1 — Dog's head — ONE DOLLAR

TWO
Scene near blacksmith's shop; girl with sheaf, etc.
2 Female portrait 2
EXCHANGE BK of N. J.
TWO DOLLARS
Tom's River
2 — 2 — Compt's die — TWO

Female portrait — Compt's die
THREE
3 Man with horses at trough, etc. 3
EXCHANGE BK of N. J.
THREE DOLLARS
3
Sloop

5
EXCHANGE B'K
V Dog on safe V
Female reclining beside chart, globe, compass, etc.
of New Jersey
FIVE DOLLARS
Tom's River
Compt's die
5 — Eagle on rock

Farmer giving hay to horse. TEN. TEN DOLLARS. EXCHANGE BANK of New Jersey. TEN. Female, grain, sheep, etc. TEN. 10. Compt's die.

1. ONE. Portrait of Franklin. Men on horse, dog and drove of sheep, mill in distance. FARMERS BANK OF N. JERSEY, Mt. Holly. 1. Portrait of Washington. ONE.

3. Portrait of Washington. THREE. Two horses (one white and the other black), and a train of cars. FARMERS BANK OF N. JERSEY, Mt. Holly. 3. Portrait of Franklin.

FIVE DOLLARS. 5 Cow and Calf. 5. FARMERS BANK OF N. JERSEY, Mt. Holly, Eagle. FIVE DOLLARS.

Female reclining on sheaf. 5. FARMERS BANK OF NEW JERSEY Mount Holly. V. 5 Hens. 5. 5. Male portrait.

10. X. Title of Bank. Farmer watering horses; pigs, cattle, &c. TEN. Sheep. X. 10. Male portrait.

TEN. 10 Drove of cattle and sheep; man on horseback. 10. FARMERS BANK OF N. JERSEY, Mt. Holly. Deer. TEN.

FIFTY. Female with a sheaf of wheat in her hands. FARMERS BANK OF N. JERSEY, Mt. Holly. 17 miles from Phila.

ONE HUNDRED. A Group of three females. FARMERS BANK OF N. JERSEY, Mt. Holly. 17 miles from Phila.

I. FARMERS BK of WANTAGE. ONE. Man and boy ploughing with two horses. 1. ONE DOLLAR. Deckertown NEW JERSEY. Milkmaid with pail on head. ONE.

2. 2. Shield, three plows and horse's head, female seated on each side. 2. Title of Bank. TWO. Female erect with staff and cap of Liberty.

3. 3. Man with hammer leaning on anvil; locomotive, foundry, etc. THREE. Title of Bank. Female erect with sickle, sheaf of grain, etc.

5. FIVE. 5 Floating female with horn of plenty; ships, etc. V. Title of Bank. Indian with bow and arrow.

TEN. Small Indian with bow and arrow. X Shield, three plows, and horse head, female sitting either side. Title of Bank. 10. 10.

20. Male portrait. Floating female with horn of plenty; ships, etc. Title of Bank. XX.

1. Men at work in mine. Two females seated; cows in distance. FAR. & MECHANICS' BANK, Camden, N. J. Bee-hive. 1. Three blacksmiths.

2. Justice. Farmer, blacksmith, girl with rake; boy, etc. Title of Bank. Female bathing. 2. Wm. Penn.

3. Factory. Scene in an iron foundry. Title of Bank. Ducks. 3. Female with grain, etc.

V. Girl. FARMERS' AND MECHANICS' BANK, Camden, N. J. Load of hay; woman and boy on top; two horses, man on one; dog, boy and girl; blacksmith shop and men at work. Dog. 5. FIVE. 5.

X. TEN. X. Title of Bank. Blacksmith shop, four men at work; boy, &c.; man plowing, house and trees in distance. Dog. 10. Female portrait.

XX. Two male figures, sailor and blacksmith on board ship. Title of Bank. Figure of liberty, right arm resting on shield, on which is portrait of Washington; drapery with stars on it, over the portrait. Dog. 20. Boy carrying bundle of corn stalks; boy and horse behind him.

50. Female with sheaf and sickle. Title of Bank. State Arms with female on either side; ship and cars in distance. Dog. 50. Shipwright seated; woman with bundle of chips; ship on stocks.

Portrait of Washington. ONE C HUNDRED. Title of Bank. Boy reclining on load of hay, drawn by two oxen; boy with fork side of oxen. Dog. C. 100. C.

Die. 500. Die. Title of Bank. Female seated with sheaf and sickle; houses, trees and man mowing on right; train of cars cross ing bridge on left. Dog. 500. Blacksmith shop; man at forge, anvil, &c.

ONE. Milkmaid. ONE. [Old Plate.] 1 Long ornamental figure 1 enclosing a full length Female figure. FARMERS and MECHANICS BANK, Rahway, N. J. View of Town. 1. ONE.

ONE. Figure of Liberty leaning on an ornamental figure 1, with word ONE in center. [New Plate.] 1 Long ornamental figure 1 enclosing a full length female figure. FARMERS and MECHANICS BANK, Rahway, N. J. Banking House. 1.

Milkmaid and cows. 2. [Old Plate.] Ornamental figure enclosing a full length female figure. FARMERS and MECHANICS BANK, Rahway, N. J. 2. Female Head.

TWO. Female Portrait. TWO. [New Plate.] 2 Ornamental figure 2 enclosing a full length female figure. FARMERS and MECHANICS BANK, Rahway, N. J. Banking House. 2.

THREE. Female Portrait. THREE. 3 Ornamental figure 3 enclosing a full length figure, the word THREE at top and small figure 3 at bottom. FARMERS and MECHANICS BANK, Rahway, N. J. Banking House. 3.

Banking House. 5. Ornamental figure 5 enclosing a full length figure of Washington. FARMERS and MECHANICS BANK, Rahway, N. J. FIVE 5. Male and female supporting a small ornamental 5.

TEN on 10 Blacksmith, anvil, etc.	FARMERS' & MECH. B'K of Rahway. State of N. Jersey. X Female, sheaf grain, etc. X TEN DOLLARS. Rahway.	TEN on X Man carrying corn.
Oval Die. Female. Oval Die.	10 Two females supporting a shield. FARMERS and MECHANICS BANK, Rahway, N. J. Railroad cars.	TEN Female resting on pillar and shield. TEN
20 N. Jersey Female reclining; reaping machine at work in the distance. XX	20 Girl's head. 20 Rahway. FARM. & MECH. BK. of Rahway.	20 Cooper at work.
20 Female Portrait. 20	20 Male figure resting on book with torch in hand; eagle &c. FARMERS and MECHANICS BANK, Rahway, N. J. A	20 Female Portrait. 20
50 Farmer with axe and sickle. 50	50 Country scene, beeves, plough sheaf of wheat &c. 50 FARMERS and MECHANICS BANK. Rahway, N. J.	50 Female figure; plow, sheaf of wheat. 50
C Indian Female C	100 Male figure, leaning on an ox; plow, cattle, &c. 100 FARMERS and MECHANICS BANK, Rahway, N. J. Ship.	Figure of Justice 100
500 Female Portrait. 500	500 Two females supporting shield; shipping on left and building on right. FARMERS and MECHANICS BANK, Rahway, N. J. Head of Female.	500 Woman churning; country scene in distance.
ONE Female erect with sword and scales. ONE	1 Agricultural scene, plowing, oxen, &c. 1 FAR. & MER. BANK. Middletown P't. N. J. 1	1 Washington. ONE
1 Farmer carrying sheafs of grain. ONE	Title of Bank Horse running away; boys endeavoring to stop him.	1 Female portrait.
Red end with white 2 2 Anchor, bales, &c	FAR. and MER. BK, Middletown Pt, N. J. Two Dollars on large ornamental die. Eagle and Shield.	2 Female with flowers. Red end with white 2

Unicorn. Eagle on shield. 2	2 Mercury. 2 Title of Bank.	TWO Washington 2
2 Female portrait.	Drover buying cattle. FAR. & MER. BANK, Middletown P't, N. J.	2 Male and female seated TWO
3 Drove of cattle, wagon &c.; scene upon road.	FAR. & MER. BANK, Middletown P't, N. J. Country scene—man on horse which is drinking from trough; female, sheep, &c.	3 Portrait of a little girl.
3 Plough, rake, &c. 3	3 Female seated upon bale; ships in background; water, &c. 3 FAR. & MER. BANK. Middletown P't. N. J.	3 Flowers. 3
FIVE Female with sword and scales. 5	5 State arms of N. J.; female on either side. 5 FAR. & MER. BANK, Middletown P't. N. J. V	FIVE Female leaning on ornamental figure 5.
Spread eagle on rock overlooking sea. TEN	10 10 FAR. & MER. BANK. Middletown P't. N. J. Plough, rake, &c. X	Goddess of Liberty seated. TEN
TWENTY	20 20 FAR. & MER. BANK. Middletown P't. N. J. Female seated on bale, water before her; anchor, &c.	XX Unicorn. XX
Female erect between ornamental 5 and 0. FIFTY	50 Female reclining on state arms. 50 FAR. & MER. BANK. Middletown P't, N. J.	Female erect with cornucopia. FIFTY
100 Female erect feeding eagle from cup.	Female reclining on shield. FAR. & MER. BANK, Middletown P't, N. J.	Same as 50's
ONE Head of girl.	State Arms. Female seated resting on shield, on which is fig. 1 FREEHOLD BANKING CO. Freehold, N. J.	1 Male portrait

Female seated by portrait of boy. 2	2 Two oxen before hay cart, boy asleep on top, another boy walking by side. Title of Bank.	2 Girl.
3	Two horses before hay cart; on top, woman and child; man on one of the horses; boy, girl, blacksmith shop, &c. Title of Bank.	Male portrait Word three and figure 3. Webster.
5	Title of Bank. The vig. extends across the whole lower part of the note, and is men shearing sheep on left and men gathering corn right.	5
10 Train of cars	Title of Bank. Female in clouds with eagle and sword.	10 Male portrait
XX Female with sickle and sheaf.	Title of Bank. Shield with female on either side; train of cars and ship in distance.	20 Male portrait
50 Male portrait	Title of Bank. State Arms.	50 FIFTY 50
Shield, bust of female, soldier and war implements and female. C	Male portrait. Title of Bank. Letter C with words one above and hundred below.	Die. Die.
1 Blacksmiths boy at forge. ONE	GLOUCESTER CO. BK Woodbury, N. J. Vig. female on either side of a shield surmounted by horse's head; steamer and cars in distance.	1 ONE Female milking cow; little girl and another cow.
3 Horse running away, boys trying to stop him; horse, colt and house in distance.	GLOUCESTER CO. BK, Woodbury, N. J. Female on either side of a shield, surmounted by head of horse.	3 Head of a little girl.
5 Farmer seated with scythe in hand; village cars, factory, building, &c. in distance.	GLOUCESTER CO. BK Woodbury, N. J.	5 Male portrait

10	Cows standing in water; one reclining on bank; sheep on left. Small head of a girl. GLOUCESTER CO. BK Woodbury, N. J.	10 Female portrait.
20 Farmer, horse, dog, and pigeons.	GLOUCESTER CO. BK Woodbury, N. J. Blacksmith shoeing a horse; man seated on log looking on; man in distance.	20 Female portrait.
Full length male figure with scroll. FIFTY	Drovers and drove of cattle; in distance village, train of cars, building, &c. GLOUCESTER CO. BK, Woodbury, N. J. Bee-hive.	50 Carrier at work.
100 Male portrait 100	GLOUCESTER CO. BK, Woodbury, N. J. Signing the Declaration of Independence.	100 Portrait of Washington. 100
Farm scene; female at table blowing horn; three men in distance.	1 State Arms. HACKETTSTOWN BK, Hackettstown, N. dog.	1 ONE
TWO Head of girl.	Title of Bank. An ox and a sheep standing, three cows and two sheep lying down.	2 Female head.
3 Ox.	Two oxen before hay cart, boy asleep on top and another walking by the side of oxen. Title of Bank.	3 State Arms. 3
FIVE Locomotive and train of cars: trees, house, &c.	Female and Indian on either side of Portrait of Jackson; tents and trees on right, ships and city on left. Title of Bank.	5 Girl.
TEN X	Farm scene; men at work mowing, raking and loading wagon; two oxen before wagon. Title of Bank.	10 Boy.
XX Child.	Two cows one standing the other lying down; milkmaid, chickens, cows and sheep; on right in distance trees, shed, &c. Title of Bank.	20 Female head.

50 Portrait of Washington.	Two boys one on horse driving sheep the other holding gate open. Title of Bank.	50 Henry Clay.
1 Compt's die	HIGHLAND BANK ONE DOLLAR on 1 · Portrait of General Scott · ONE DOLLAR on 1 Hudson City, N. J.	1 Horse's head
Compt's die 2	Group of men, cattle, sheep, etc. HIGHLAND BANK TWO DOLLARS Hudson City	2 Daniel Webster
5 Compt's die Hudson City 5	HIGHLAND BANK Man seated on fence FIVE DOLLARS	5 5 5
Compt's die New Jersey 10	HIGHLAND BANK. Two horses, man, houses in distance, etc. TEN DOLLARS Hudson City.	10 Bull's head
TWENTY Sheep TWENTY	STATE OF N. JERSEY Cattle grazing: men, horse, factory in distance, etc. HIGHLAND BANK TWENTY DOLLARS Hudson City.	20 Compt's die
Male portrait ONE	HOBOKEN CITY BK, Hoboken, N. J. Treas die · Fig. 1; farmers at lunch; boy playing with dog, &.	1
TWO Boy.	Treas. die and 2. Team of oxen; load of hay, two boys and fig. 2. HOBOKEN CITY BK, Hoboken, N J. Dog.	2
Male portrait Treas die.	Indian, squaw and papoose in canoe. HOBOKEN CITY BK, Hoboken, N. J.	Three across 3. THREE Three dogs.
FIVE Train of cars. Coal heaver standing with pick; large white V across.	Men heaving coal. View of a yacht sailing. HOBOKEN CITY BK, Hoboken, N. J. Portrait of Buchanan. 5	5 Treas die.

TEN Train of cars with large white X across.	Treas. die. Shipbuilding; two carpenters in the foreground. 10 in white across. HOBOKEN CITY BK, Hoboken, N. J.	10 Girl with horn.
50 Male portrait	Female nursing child; boy and dog; reapers in background. Letter L across vignette. Treas. die. HOBOKEN CITY BK, Hoboken, N. J.	50 Female portrait.
1 Compt's die. 1	Jersey City ferry landing; ferry boat "Arcesseh" coming in the slip. HUDSON CO. BANK. Jersey City, N. J. Steamship.	1 Blacksmith with anvil and hammer.
2 Compt's die	Farmer with two horses and a plough. HUDSON CO. BANK, Jersey City, N. J. Implements of war.	2 Man with basket of corn.
3 Compt's die. 3	Locomotive and cars; factory on left. HUDSON CO. BANK, Jersey City, N. J. Schooner.	THREE Steamer. 3
3 Treas. die 3	Sailor, farmer, and blacksmith HUDSON CO. BANK THREE DOLLARS Jersey City, N. J. Schooner	THREE Steamer 3
State Arms FIVE	5 White and Indian females seated, city, canoe, etc. in distance. HUDSON CO. BANK Jersey City, N J. Beehive	5 Washingt'n FIVE
State Arms. FIVE	5 Two females, shield, cornucopia, &c. Title of Bank Beehive	5 Washington FIVE
State Arms. FIVE	5 Same as ones. HUDSON CO. BANK, Jersey City, N. J. Sea monster.	5 Locomotive. 5
X, 10; two sailors, boat, telescope and light-house, &c Compt's die.	10 View of a large building, &c. HUDSON CO. BANK, Jersey City, N. J. Shells.	10 Mechanic seated on a boiler; cars in distance.

Left	Centre	Right
X, 10, two sailors, telescope, lighthouse, etc. Compt's die.	10 View of a large building, etc. Title of Bank.	10 Female with cornucopia.
Compt's die. Female instructing children.	Steamship and sail-vessel; city in distance. HUDSON CO. BANK, Jersey City, N. J. Bales of goods.	20 Locomotive.
FIFTY Two males and two females with tablets and quadrant; city in distance.	HUDSON CO. BANK, Jersey City, N. J. Compt's die.	FIFTY Male, two females, dog and cattle.
Indian family on cliff contemplating the progress of civilization.	HUDSON CO. BANK, Jersey City, N. J. Compt's die.	100 Mechanic seated with hammer; factory in distance.
Large figure 1, which covers the whole end of the bill. ONE	Female bathing. ONE. State Arms. HUNTERDON CO. BANK, Flemington, N. J. Locomotive	1 ONE Female
2 Train of cars 2	HUNTERDON CO. BANK, Flemington, N. J. Cheese press, two females and man at work. 2 2	2 Bridge and drove of cattle. 2
THREE Loading hay; two men and a horse; scene, &c.	HUNTERDON CO BANK, Flemington, N. J. Three Dollars Head of dog.	3 Milkmaid
5	Large V, word "Five;" man with sickle in hand, sheaf of wheat in and around it. HUNTERDON CO. BANK. Flemington, N. J. Quails.	Letter "V" and word "Five." Female bust FIVE
Figure 10, word TEN, and letter X Bull's head.	View of State House. HUNTERDON CO BANK. TEN DOLLARS. Flemington, N. J.	Figure 10, word TEN, and letter X Female.
Horses and cattle. XX	Canal and vessels. HUNTERDON CO. BANK, TWENTY DOLLARS. Fish.	20 Female.
L inverted State portrait	Red 50 on die; on right, old man, boy, dog, etc; on left milkmaid seated; Steamboat in background. HUNTERDON CO BK, Flemington, N. J.	L inverted Female portrait with bonnet on.
100 Female portrait	Four females; one erect, reading. C C HUNTERDON CO. BANK. One Hundred Dollars.	ONE HUNDRED.
Word one and figure 1 across. State Arms.	View of large building; horses and carriage in street. IRON BANK. Morristown N. J.	1 Train of cars going under bridge; load of hay passing over bridge.
2 Child in shell resting on water	Scene in an iron foundry IRON BANK TWO DOLLARS Morristown, N. J.	2 Two farmers with dog, etc; men in background
2 State Arms.	Men at work in iron mill. IRON BANK,	2 Two men and dog in foreground, man, boy in background.
3 Milkmaid, cows, etc.	IRON BANK THREE DOLLARS Morristown N. J. View of the Crystal Palace.	3 on THREE View of cattle, telegraph, railroad, etc.
3 State Arms	IRON BANK, N. J. View of New York Crystal Palace. Three dols Three dols	Word three and figure 3 View of cattle, telegraph and railroad
FIVE	IRON BANK, 5 View of part of the globe with eagle on top.	5 State Arms
FIVE	5 IRON BANK, Morristown, N. J. V Eagle on half of the globe.	5 State Arms
TEN Bank building	Working in an iron foundry; IRON BANK, ... N. J.	10 Compt's die TEN
20 Foundries.	IRON BANK, Morristown, N. J. View in rolling mill; men and machinery.	20 State Arms.
Sailor, mechanic, two females, lighthouse and city in distance.	THE IRON BANK. FIFTY DOLLARS Morristown, State of N. Jersey. 50	50 Sailor reclining beside anchor, capstan, compass, etc ships in distance.
50 Foundries.	Title of Bank. Same vig. as 20s.	50 State Arms
One Hundred Dollars. Goddess of Liberty with eagle, shield, pole, etc.	Three females in clouds. THE IRON BANK, Morristown, New Jersey.	100
500	THE IRON BANK Five Hundred Dollars Morristown, N. Jersey. Steamer, ship, city in distance. D	Goddess of Liberty with eagle, shield, pole, etc.
1 ONE	LAMBERTVILLE BK Lambertville, N. J. Sheep shearing scene. Female head Treas. die.	1 ONE
2 TWO	Title of Bank. Treas. die. Railroad scene—train of cars, mountains, river, etc.	2 Female head. TWO DOLLARS
THREE 3 Girl with a dove.	Title of Bank. Treas. Die. Pigs, geese, chickens, etc.	3 THREE
5 Treas. die. 5	Title of Bank. Interior of iron mill—men at work. FIVE	5 Indian boy paddling canoe.
10 Treas. die. 10	Title of Bank. Mining scene—two men digging coal in mine. TEN	X Female seated; two males behind bar.

Left end	Centre	Right end
20 / 20	Rafting scene—men, woman and child on raft; skiff; raft in distance. Treas. dle. Title of Bank. 20	20 / Male portrait
ONE / Mechanic seated. / ONE	1 Ferry wharf; view of river and vessels. MECHANICS' BANK, Burlington, N. J.	1 / Male portrait / ONE
TWO / Mechanic and anvil. / TWO	2 Female in frame, farming implements on either side. 2 MECHANICS' BANK, Burlington, N. J.	TWO / Portrait of Franklin. / TWO
THREE / Female in fig. 3. / THREE	3 Harvest scene; girl, boy and dog, farmers at work in distance. 3 MECHANICS' BANK, Burlington, N. J.	THREE / Male portrait. / THREE
Spread eagle.	5 Vig. Five Cupids and fig. 5. 5 MECHANICS' BANK, Burlington, N. J.	Portrait of Washington.
10 / View of river, steamboats &c. / 10	10 Female between two males, cars on right. MECHANICS' BANK, Burlington, N. J. TEN	TEN / Male portrait / TEN
20 / Ship. / 20	20 Cupid holding wand, dog, safe and key. 20 MECHANIC'S BANK, Burlington, N. J.	20 / Male portrait / 20
50 / Male portrait / 50	View of river, steamboat and tow boat, also village. MECHANIC'S BANK, Burlington, N. J.	50 / Train Cars. / 50
Indian with bow and arrow. / 100	100 Locomotive and train of cars. 100 MECHANICS' BANK, Burlington, N. J.	Washington and his horse. / 100
1 / Female with sheaf.	Mechanic seated; anvil, &c.; train of cars, buildings, hills, &c., in distance. MECHANICS' BANK, Newark, N. J. Arm.	1 / ONE

Left end	Centre	Right end
ONE / Male seated supporting the world with a lever. / 1	1 on med. head. Female seated with book in hand; anvil, sledge, &c.; in distance on left ship. 1 on med. head. MECHANICS' BANK, Newark, N. J.	ONE / Male figure seated with tablets. / 1
TWO / Male supporting the world. / 2	MECHANICS' BANK, Newark, N. J. 2 on med. head. Female seated with child in her arms; basket, sheaf of wheat; farmers mowing in background. 2 on med. head. Arm.	TWO / Female seated with book / 2
2 / Two farmers with rakes; two in distance and house.	Three males apparently in conversation; view of city in distance on right. MECHANICS' BANK, Newark, N. J. Arm.	TWO / 2
THREE / Male supporting the world, &c. / 3	3 Three females seated; trees on right; ship in distance on left. 3 MECHANICS' BANK, Newark, N. J. Arm.	Full length female with sickle. / 3
3 / Portrait of Jenny Lind.	Frame surmounted by an eagle; two females on right and female on left; ship, train of cars crossing bridge, in distance. MECHANICS' BANK, Newark, N. J. Arm.	THREE / 3
5 / Blacksmith at work. / V	Med. head and fig. 5. Train of cars, man leaning on fence. Med. head and fig. 5. MECHANICS' BANK, Newark, N. J. Arm.	V / Sailor with hat in hand; masts in distance. / 5
X / Canal scene; buildings in distance. / X	Med. head and letter X. Man seated on log with left hand on dog's head, trees, &c. Med. head and letter X. MECHANICS' BANK, Newark, N. J. Arm.	10 / Brig. / 10
20 / Sheaf. / 20	20 Female seated with sword, in left hand scales; lion on right; steamboat on left. 20 MECHANICS' BANK, Newark, N. J. Arm.	20 / Ship. / 20
50 / Beehive. / 50	50 Female seated, arm resting on shield, on which is anchor; ship on left. 50 MECHANICS' BANK, Newark, N. J. Arm.	50 / Eagle. / 50
100 / Plough, &c. / 100	100 Shield on which 100 in figures 100, on either side of which female; reaping scene and steamboat in distance. MECHANICS' BANK, Newark, N. J. Arm.	ONE HUNDRED

Left end	Centre	Right end
500 / Female erect, supporting shield on which is med. head.	Med. head and fig. 500. Female reclining looking up; steamboat on right; building on left. Med. head and figs. 500. MECHANICS' BANK, Newark, N. J. Arm.	500 / Female erect with sword. / 500
1000 / Two med. heads and figures 1000. / M	1000 Female seated on bale of goods, right arm resting on shield. 1000 MECHANICS' BANK, Newark, N. J. Arm.	Same as on left end.
ONE on 1 / Children with horse.	MECH. & MAN. B'K Trenton. ONE on 1 Mechanic with anvil and hammer ONE on 1. New Jersey	1 / Washingt'n
ONE / Male portrait. / 1	1 Horse and two horsemen in the distance. 1 MECH. & MAN. B'K, Trenton, N. J. Train of cars.	ONE / Drovers and cattle. / 1
Mechanic at work / 2	MECH. & MAN. B'K Trenton, N. J. 2 Blacksmiths at work 2 TWO DOLLARS	Henry Clay / 2
2 / Washington. / 2	2 Horse terrified by a train of cars; buildings in the distance. 2 MECH. & MAN. BK. Trenton, N. J.	2 on Medallion. / Liberty reclining on a figure 2; cars in distance.
3 / Male portrait / 3	3 MECHANIC'S & MANUF. B'K 3 Farmers mowing. Trenton THREE DOLLARS New Jersey Canal lock	3 / Female beside wheel / 3
Carpenters at work / THREE	MECHANIC'S AND MANUFACTURER'S B'K 3 Male portrait 3 THREE DOLLARS Trenton	Two males standing, and female seated with cap and pole
FIVE / Shield with Liberty on right, and eagle on left, and motto "E Pluribus Unum." / 5	(Old Plate.) 5 Eagle and shield, Justice on left, Liberty on right; train of cars and bridge in distance. Title of Bank. Oaks, shipping, &c.	FIVE / Female feeding an eagle.
FIVE / Male Portrait / 5	Same as above. 5 Title of Bank. Oaks, &c.	Precisely the same as above.

Left	Centre	Right
Indian springing a bow ; landscape in distance. 10	10 Mechanic with anvil, &c.; two females, offering the one fruit; the other, money ; shipping in distance. Title of Bank. Head of a horse.	X Franklin. 10
Female feeding an eagle ; stars of America around. 20	XX State Arms. XX Title of Bank. Eagle feeding its young.	20 Three figures typifying home and plenty; lave, wheel, water mill, &c., in distance. 20
FIFTY 50 Mechanic, anvil, &c.	L Beehive, flowers &c. L Title of Bank.	Same as on left of twenty. 50
Same as tens. 100	100 Benjamin Franklin seated. 100 Title of Bank.	Full length statue of Washington. 100
ONE Compt's die. ONE	Masons at work building a house. MECHANICS' AND TRADERS' BANK, Jersey City, N. J. ONE	1 Blacksmith with sledge.
Blacksmith shoeing a horse. 2	Compt's die. Title of Bank. TWO	2 Sailor with telescope.
THREE	MECH. & TRA. B'K Jersey City THREE DOLLARS 3 on Carpenter at work on 3 STATE OF N. JERSEY THREE	3 Compt's die
FIVE Mechanic, sailor and farmer making offering to winged female.	Compt's die. Title of Bank.	5 5
10 MECH Compt's die	STATE OF N. JERSEY ANICS' & TRADERS' TEN DOLLARS Jersey City. Train of cars. TEN.	10 BANK Female portrait.
X Compt's die.	Title of Bank. Locomotive and cars TEN.	10 TEN

Left	Centre	Right
L Compt's die. Die Work.	Title of Bank. Portrait of Washington. Figures 50, letter L and words FIFTY each side. L L	L 50 Die Work.
100 Compt's die.	ONE HUNDRED surrounded by ornamental die work. Title of Bank.	100 C 100
1 Female portrait.	ONE ONE View of church, woods, park, fountain, etc. MERCANTILE B'K ONE DOLLAR Orange, N. J.	1 Female beside barrel, plow, &c.
Female portrait 2	Park entrance ; porter's lodge; etc. MERCANTILE B'K TWO DOLLARS Orange	2 Female portrait
3 Wharf scene, men, boxes, etc.	Park entrance: porter's lodge, woods, flagstaff, fountain etc. MERCANTILE BANK THREE DOLLARS Orange	3
Large 5 with smaller 5's above and below.	MERCANTILE B'K Park entrance ; porter's lodge, woods, etc. Female with Union shield, wreath, etc. 5 FIVE DOLLARS Orange	Large 5 with smaller 5's above and below
Goddess of Liberty with arms resting upon column. X	STATE OF N. JERSEY MERCANTILE BANK Genius of America, eagle, scenery, etc. TEN DOLLARS.	10 ORANGE. X
Tomb of Washingt'n at Mount Vernon 50	MERCANTILE B'K Orange Three females crowning bust of Washington, Union shield, etc. FIFTY DOLLARS	50
1 Female with sheaf and sickle	MILLVILLE BANK, Millville, N. J. Scene in a glass blowing establishment. Dog.	1 Factory, &c.
2	Scene in a factory ; girls working at looms. Female portrait. Title of Bank. Ducks.	2 Mechanic.

Left	Centre	Right
3 Portrait of Boy.	Title of Bank. Female seated with infant child offering birds nest.	3 State Arms. 3
5 Female portrait.	Same as ones. Title of Bank.	5 Three Blacksmiths at work.
10 Reaper girl holding sickle and bonnet.	Title of Bank. Two men conversing ; one reclining on anvil ; the other has his right arm around boy beside him.	10 Female portrait
XX Farmer bearing bundle of grain.	Scene in a ship yard. Title of Bank. XX	20 Justice
1 Female seated with cornucopia.	Pigs and fowls Chickens in pen. MT. HOLLY BANK, Mt. Holly, N.J. One on red die.	1 Treas. Die.
1 Female seated with cornucopia	New Jersey Cupid rolling a silver dollar ; train of cars on right, city in the distance MOUNT HOLLY B'K Mount Holly	1 Head of Charles Bispham
1^{25} Head of Charles O Bispham	MT. HOLLY BANK Wharf scene; horses, drays, train of cars, and steamboats ; ships and warehouses in background One doll. & twenty five cts Mt. Holly	1^{25} Head of two girls
1^{50} Male portrait	MT. HOLLY BANK Express wagons, etc. One dollar & fifty cents Mt. Holly, N. J.	1^{50} Male portrait
TWO DOLLARS 2 Three Cupids	State seal; horse's head on shield ; three plows, two females seated, cars and factory in distance MOUNT HOLLY B'K Mount Holly State of New Jersey	2 Head of Charles Bispham
TWO DOLLARS 2 Three cherubs	State Arms ; cars and factory in distance. MT. HOLLY BANK, Mt. Holly, N. J. Two on red die.	2 Treas. die.

5 | MOUNT HOLLY B'K. View of State Capitol at Trenton. Mount Holly. State of New Jersey. | 5
Head of Gen. G. B. McClellan. | Head of Charles Bispham.

5 | MT. HOLLY BANK, Mt. Holly, N. J. View of large building and street. 5 5 | 5
Henry Clay. | Treas. die.

10 | Man watering three horses from a trough by side of well; goat, kid, sheep, trees and house. MOUNT HOLLY B'K. Mount Holly. State of New Jersey. | X
Female seated. | Head of Charles Bispham.

10 | Man watering three horses from trough by side of well; goat, kid, sheep, trees and house. MT. HOLLY BANK, Mt. Holly, N. J. | X
Treas. die. | Male portrait.

20 | Three men reaping grain with machine; barn and trees in distance. MOUNT HOLLY B'K. Mount Holly. State of New Jersey. | 20
Head of Charles Bispham. | Female seated.

20 | Three men at work with two horses and patent mowing machine; house in distance. MT. HOLLY BANK, Mt. Holly, N. J. | 20
Treas. die. | Female seated.

50 | MOUNT HOLLY B'K. Drover on horse, boy with a drove of cattle drinking; farmhouse, etc. in distance. Mount Holly. State of New Jersey. | 50
Female with flowers in apron. | Head of Charles Bispham.

50 | MOUNT HOLLY BK, Mount Holly N. J. Drover on horse; boy and drove of cattle; farm house etc., in distance. | 50
Female with flowers. | State Arms.

1 | NEW JERSEY. Ships at sea. NATIONAL BANK. ONE DOLLAR. Paterson. | 1
Compt's die. | Girl with pen, etc.

2 | NEW JERSEY. Ships, steamer, tugs, etc. NATIONAL BANK. TWO DOLLARS. Paterson. | 2
Compt's die. | Woman and child.

3 | NEW JERSEY NATIONAL BANK. Cannon, ammunition, ships, etc. THREE DOLLARS. Paterson. | 3
Compt's die. | Girl with flowers.

V | STATE OF NEW JERSEY. Female Sailor Female portrait with portrait bundle. NATIONAL BANK. FIVE DOLLARS. Paterson. | 5
Washingt'n. | Compt's die.

20 Statue of America with wreath, shield, etc. | Spread eagle on shield. NATIONAL BANK. TWENTY DOLLARS. | 20
Compt's die.

Children. ONE | NEWARK BANKING COMPANY, Newark, N. J. Milkmaid under tree, boy pointing. | 1
Male portrait.

ONE DOLLAR | 1 Squaw contemplating progress of civilization; railroad and canal boat in distance; city in extreme distance. NEWARK BANKING COMPANY. Newark, N. J. Eagle. | 1
Portrait of Franklin.

2 Portrait of Washington. 2 | 2 Two females, sheaf of wheat and ships in distance. Title of Bank. | 2
Female entwined in figure 2.

TWO | 2 Ornamental figure 2, with two females entwined. Title of Bank. Implements of war. | Ornamental die. Portrait of Washington. Ornamental die.

2 | Scene at canal locks; train of cars crossing bridge and harvesting scene in distance. NEWARK BANKING COMPANY. Newark, N. J. | 2
Girl's head. | Male portrait.

3 | 3 Two females by loom. Title of Bank. | 3
Male portrait. | Blacksmith.

3 Female with pole and cap; eagle and shield; ship in distance. | Title of Bank. Miniature; train of cars. | Three females on ornamental figure 3; one representing Liberty, Justice, &c. THREE

3 Ornamental figure 3, with three females. | Title of Bank. | Arms of the State of New Jersey; ship in distance.

5 Med. head, with V on it. 5 | Title of Bank. Female seated on bale of goods, with arm resting on shield. | 5 Med. head, with V on it. 5

5 Female with scales, seated on a barrel; cars in distance. | Goddess of Liberty resting on American shield. Ornamental figure, with two females and cherub. Title of Bank. | FIVE DOLLARS

5 Male portrait. | Title of Bank. V Cattle and children. V | 5 Female with spinning wheel.

5 Female with balance, anchor and shield. | Arms of the State of New Jersey; ship in distance. Ornamental figure 5, with two females and cherub. Title of Bank. | Ornamental die. Portrait of Washington. Ornamental die.

10 Male portrait. | Horse. Eagle. Female seated on grain; sheep, etc. Title of Bank. TEN | 10 Male portrait.

10 Med. head with X on it. 10 | Med. head. View of blacksmith shop; one at bellows and one at anvil; cars in distance. Med. head. Title of Bank. | Med. head. TEN Med. head.

20 Med. head, with Twenty on it. 20 | Med. head, with two cherubs on left, and one on right. Title of Bank. | 20 Med. head, with Twenty on it. 20

50 Canal boat. 50 | State Arms; cars in distance. 50 NEWARK BANKING COMPANY. Newark, N. J. | Justice full length. FIFTY

100 State Arms. 100 | Spread eagle; cars on left; factory on right. 100 Title of Bank. | Full length female. 100

1 Portrait of female. NEWARK CITY BK., Newark, N. J. Vig. Machinist and heavy turning lathe. 1 Female reaper.	2 on TWO Head of male Title of Bank. Word TWO in red, TWO 2 TWO 2 Female reclining on bales; steamboat and schooner in distance.	Head. 100 Head. 100 Female in a chariot drawn by two horses and enveloped in clouds. 100 ORANGE BANK, Orange, N. J. Head. 100 Head.
2 Portrait of female. NEWARK CITY BK., Newark, N. J. Vig. Stone-cutters at work. TWO Female with small globe.	THREE Male portrait ORANGE BANK 3 Female seated beside implements; cars and factories in the distance 3 THREE DOLLARS 3 State Arms 3	1 Compt's die. Blacksmith shop, three men at work, and two more at work in background. PASSAIC CO. BANK, Paterson, N. J. 1 Male portrait
3 Leather dresser. NEWARK CITY BK., Newark, N. J. Three females reclining, representing liberty, agriculture and art. 3 Arm hammer, and anvil.	THREE on 3. Male portrait Title of Bank. 3 Female seated with mechanical implements; cars, bridge and factory in distance. Red 3 on vig. 3 THREE 3 3	2 Compt's die. PASSAIC CO. BANK, Paterson, N. J. Large machinery, machinist standing, &c. 2 Male portrait
V Fireman. Two females, one seated; horn of plenty. NEWARK CITY BK., Newark, N. J. 5 Locomotive and tender.	Half length female figure. 3 Train of cars; water and hills in the distance. 3 ORANGE BANK, Orange, N. J.	5 on red head. Trees, die. Train of cars; large chimney, trees, houses, sloop, &c., in background. PASSAIC CO. BANK, Paterson, N. J. Peg, key and safe. Five, V, 5. Portrait of a female
10 Farmer resting. NEWARK CITY BK., Newark, N. J. Three females representing music, poetry, and painting. 10	FIVE Farming scene, boy playing with dog; girl, horses, etc. 5 Train of cars ORANGE BANK FIVE DOLLARS and FIVE V 5 Male portrait	ONE Train of cars coming through arch; two laborers. PHILLIPSB'RGH BK Phillipsburgh, N. J. 1 Puddling in an iron-mill
50 State Arms. NEWARK CITY BK., Newark, N. J. L FIFTY Male figure, and two females seated; agricultural scene.	Farming scene and 5 across, V Large white V across note. Train cars. ORANGE BANK, Orange, N. J. 5 Male portrait	2 TWO Female feeding fowls. 2 Six men at work in an iron mill. PHILLIPSB'RGH BK Philipsburgh, N. J. 2 TWO
100 Two Indians. State Arms Title of Bank. One hundred. Two females, one seated, the other erect. 100	TEN Male portrait ORANGE BANK, Orange, N. J. 10 Boy with birdnest; woman, child, dog, &c.; farmers in the rear. 10 10 Male portrait	3 PHILLIPSB'RGH BK Philipsburgh, N. J. Bull's head on a shield; men dressing leather on right and female sewing shoes on left. 3 Milkmaid with pail.
State Arms. Same as right end. NEWARK CITY B'K, Newark, N. J. Female with tablets; child at her feet. Small D either side and words Five Hundred below. 500 D and words Five Hundred Dollars on red die.	TEN TEN Head. TEN 10 Female resting on a globe, with shield and eagle. 10 ORANGE BANK, Orange, N. J. TEN DOLLARS	Female with flowers. 5 PHILLIPSB'RGH BK Phillipsburgh, N. J. Bridge, two men on a raft; trees, houses and a raft in distance. 5 5 V Locomotive.
1 Girl Two horses before hay cart; various male and female figures; blacksmith's shop. ORANGE BANK Orange, N. J. ONE ONE 1 Head of male	TWENTY Head. TWENTY 20 Figure of Justice, with a picture of Washington in her left hand; an eagle at her feet. 20 ORANGE BANK, Orange, N. J. TWENTY	Female with cornucopia. 10 PHILLIPSB'RGH BK Phillipsburgh, N. J. Men at work in a glass manufactory; horses in distance. 10 Blacksmith; anvil hammer and horses.

Left	Centre	Right
Indian family contemplating the progress of civilization. 20	Figure 20 with word Twenty, six times, around it on red die. PHILLIPSB'RGH BK Phillipsburgh, N. J.	20 Mechanic and implements.
50 Female with cornucopia.	Fig. 50 and words Fifty dollars on three red dies. PHILLIPSB'RGH BK Phillipsburgh, N. J. Spread eagle.	50 Female with quadrant.
ONE HUNDRED Female erect.	PHILLIPSB'RGH BK Phillipsburgh, N. J. Fig. 100 and words One hundred dollars on three red dies.	Helmeted female. ONE HUNDRED
1 Soldiers raising a breastwork.	PRINCETON BANK, Princeton, N. J. State arms; in distance, on right, steamship; on left, train of cars.	1 Head of a boy.
2 2	Drover buying cattle. Picture of Buck. 2 PRINCETON BANK, Princeton, N. J. Eagle	Head of a girl.
3 Female with veil.	Farm scene; milk-maid and two cows, one lying down. PRINCETON BANK. Princeto n, N. J.	3 Portrait of Washington.
V Woman with scales; eagle, &c. V	PRINCETON BANK, Princetown, N. J. 5 Death of Gen. Mercer. 5 Eagle.	5 Portrait of Madison. 5
10 Washington. 10	Portrait of female. Two females, one standing and the other seated; small ship in distance. 10 PRINCETON BANK. Princeton, N. J. Pump, pony, and boy.	X Madison. X
20 Madison. 20	Female portrait. State Arms. 20 PRINCETON BANK, Princeton, N. J. Man and cow.	XX Male portrait. XX
50 Male portrait. 50	Female portrait. Female in car. 50 PRINCETON BANK, Princeton, N. J. Pony and boy at a pump.	50 Male portrait. 50

Left	Centre	Right
100 Male portrait. 100	Female portrait. Female holding cup to an eagle. 100 PRINCETON BANK, Princeton, N. J. Eagle.	100 Male portrait. 100
1 One in med. head. 1	Word one and figure 1. Female with child in arms, &c. Word one and figure 1. SALEM BANKING CO., Salem, N. J.	1 One on med. head. 1
3 Med. head. 3	3 Shipping. 3 SALEM BANKING CO., Salem, N. J.	3 Washington 3
5 Female holding goblet to an eagle.	V Female reclining against iron chest; ship in distance, &c. V SALEM BANKING CO., Salem, N. J.	5 Two female figures.
Portrait of Franklin.	10 Two female figures; 10 tree, sheep, &c. SALEM BANKING CO., Salem, N. J. Eagle.	Portrait of Washington.
TWENTY	20 Female erect, resting on anchor. 20 Female figure. SALEM BANKING CO., Salem, N. J. Eagle.	Portrait of Franklin.
Portrait of Washington.	50 Female; ocean scene. SALEM BANKING CO., Salem, N. J. Eagle.	50 Two females.
100 State arms. 100	Three females; eagle, cars, ship, &c. SALEM BANKING CO., Salem, N. J. Steamboat.	C Portrait of Washington.
ONE Male portrait ONE	1 Female on either side of Unicorn with horn of plenty, liberty pole and cap, cars and factories on the left. SOMERSET CO. B'K, Somerville, N. J.	Female with wreath of flowers. ONE
2 Man Woman and dog.	Head of Franklin. Farmer with pipe seated on plow, yoke of cattle on right, farm house on left. SOMERSET CO. B'K. Somerville, N. J. Farm implements.	2

Left	Centre	Right
Indian with bow and arrow. THREE	3 Harvest scene farmers at lunch. SOMERSET CO. B'K. Somerville, N. J.	THREE Female THREE
5 Female.	SOMERSET CO. B'K. Somerville, N. J. Vig. Same as Ones. FIVE in circular Die. Farming Implements.	5 Franklin. 5
10 Washington. 10	Vig. Drove of cattle and sheep; man on horseback; public house on left. SOMERSET CO. B'K, Somerville, N. J. Farming implements.	10 Female with spear and balances; eagle and small portrait of Washington
XX Female. XX	SOMERSET CO. B'K, Somerville, N. J. 20 Vig. Man plowing with two horses, also man with spade on his shoulder. Female.	20 Two farmers with cradle and grain.
50 Two females with wand and spyglass seated on merchandise	SOMERSET CO. B'K. Somerville, N. J. Vig. Two females seated, with cornucopia and wand; steamboat on right; anchor and vessel on left. 50	50 Male portrait.
Female erect with sword, cornucopia at her feet. HUNDRED	SOMERSET CO B'K. Somerville, N. J. 100 Vig. Two females with flag overlooking the sea, on which is seen a ship in distance; eagle on right. 100	
1 Med. head. 1	Camden N. Jersey 1 State Arms of New Jersey. 1 STATE BANK AT CAMDEN	ONE
3 Dog's head. 3	Female, boy, anvil, rake, plow, etc. STATE BANK, Camden, N. J	3 Dog's head 3
5 Male portrait V	Medal. Head. Harvest scene. Reaper reclining. Medal. Head. STATE BANK, Camden, N. J.	V Male portrait 5
10 Male portrait X	Medal. Head. Liberty and shield, view of river, town, &c. Medal. Head. STATE BANK. Camden, N. J.	X Male portrait 10

20 — Harvest Scene. — XX | Two Medal. Heads. Female reclining with wand. Two Medal. Heads. STATE BANK, Camden, N J. | XX — Harvest Scene. — 20

FIFTY | Man plowing. STATE BANK, Camden, N. J. Spread eagle. | 50 — State Arms. — 50

100 — Portrait of Franklin. — 100 | Vig. State Arms. STATE BANK, Camden, N. J. Spread eagle. | C — 100 — Hundred.

FIVE HUNDRED | 500 Two females, Liberty and shield. Title of Bank. 500 D | 500 — 500

ONE — Portrait of Male. — ONE | Medallion head. Shield with female figure on either side, the one holding liberty cap and pole, the other a cornucopia. Medallion head. STATE BANK, Elizabethtown, N. J. | ONE — Portrait of Male. — ONE

2 — Medallion Head. — 2 | Male Portrait. Shield with Female figure on either side, the one on right holding a sickle. Male Portrait. STATE BANK, Elizabethtown, N. J. | TWO

3 — Medallion Head. — 3 | Male Portrait. Shipping, steamer, buildings in distance. Male Portrait. STATE BANK, Elizabethtown, N. J. | 3 — Medallion Head. — 3

Circular Die. — Female Portrait. — Circular Die. | [Old Plate.] 5 Two females supporting an ornamental figure 5, and three boys representing Cupid, Mercury and Love. 5 STATE BANK, Elizabethtown, N. J. | Circular Die — Female Portrait. — Circular Die.

5 — Female Portrait. | [New Plate.] Neptune driving sea-horses in a shell car with Female seated therein; mermaid &c. in the water; steamer in distance. STATE BANK, Elizabethtown, N. J, 5 and Cupid. | 5 — Portrait of Girl.

5 — Portrait of girl. | Female, safe, shield, sheep, sheaf, etc. STATE BANK AT ELIZABETH, N. J. FIVE | 5 on head. — Male portrait

10 — Franklin — 10 | Three females and bust of Washington. Title of Bank. TEN | TEN — Portrait of girl. — TEN

Circular Die. — Female Portrait. — Circular Die. | 10 Two females supporting shield; steamer on right and church on left. 10 STATE BANK, Elizabethtown, N. J. 10 | Oval Die. — Female Portrait. — Oval Die.

20 — Shield and eagle with outstretched wings. — 20 | Female figure reclining; scene representing agriculture on right; railroad cars and shipping on left. STATE BANK, Elizabethtown, N. J. Mechanic and anvil. | 20 — Female Portrait.

50 — Female Portrait. | Female reclining with liberty cap and pole; eagle on right; globe on left; shipping in distance. STATE BANK, Elizabethtown, N. J. Sheaf of wheat and plow. | FIFTY — Full length female figure leaning on anchor; ships in distance.

100 — Portrait of Male. — 100 | Female reclining on bales and other articles of commerce; ship on left and steamer on right in distance. 100 STATE BANK, Elizabethtown, N. J. Dog. | Full length figure of Liberty. — 100

500 — Male Portrait | Shield supported by two females, the one on right holding liberty cap and pole, one on left ears of corn; steamship and railroad cars on right and factory on left. STATE BANK, Elizabethtown, N. J. Female. | 500

1 — ONE | Female reclining on horn of plenty; pole and cap, eagle and shield. STATE BANK, Newark, N. J. State Arms. | 1 — ONE

2 — Goddess of liberty and justice. | Two females seated; ship on left; train of cars and factory on right. STATE BANK, Newark N. J. Eagle. | 2

3 — Female and ornamental figure 3. | Three females seated; cars on left and ship on right. STATE BANK, Newark N. J. State Arms. | 3

5 — Ship, water in commotion. | View of banking house and church. STATE BANK, Newark, N. J. Eagle. | 5 — 5

10 — Female with cornucopia. | Vig. Same as 5's. STATE BANK, Newark, N. J. Head of Horse. | 10 — X

FIFTY — Cooper at work. — L | 50 Female seated, agricultural scene on left; blacksmith shop on right. 50 STATE BANK, Newark, N. J. State Arms. | FIFTY — Female seated. — 50

Figure of Justice. — 100 | C Female reclining on anchor; ship in distance. STATE BANK, Newark, N. J. State Arms. | ONE HUNDRED.

500 — Female seated; ship, &c., in distance. | State Arms; train of cars on left; Steamboat on right. STATE BANK, Newark N. J. Agricultural Implements. | D

STATE OF N. JERSEY
1 — Female portrait | Dog's head. STATE BK of N. BRUNSWICK. ONE DOLLAR. State Arms | ONE on 1 — 1

1 STATE B'K OF N. BRUNSWICK 1
Cars, canal boats, etc | ONE DOLLAR. Female portrait in ornamental die. ONE ONE | Grain, etc.

1 — Female standing. | State Arms with female on either side; buildings in distance. 1 STATE BANK. New Brunswick, N. J. | ONE — Female bust. — ONE

TWO — N. JERSEY — Female portrait | State Arms. New Brunswick on 2. STATE BK of N. BRUNSWICK. TWO DOLLARS | 2 — Dog's head

TWO 2 — Female portrait — TWO | New Jersey State Arms, horse's head on shield; female either side. STATE BANK AT NEW BRUNSWICK. TWO DOLLARS. New Brunswick | 2

STATE OF N. JERSEY
3 — State Arms | Female portrait. N. Brunswick. STATE BK of N. BRUNSWICK. THREE Dog's head | 3 — DOLLARS

Left end	Centre	Right end
3 Female bust	Same as Ones. STATE BANK, New Brunswick, N. J.	3 Female Indian. THREE
FIVE Cattle and farmers in a circle. 5	Portrait of Washington. State Arms supported by two females, the one on left seated. Portrait of Franklin. STATE BANK, New Brunswick, N. J. Railroad cars.	FIVE Cattle and farmers in a circle. 5
TEN Venus in a sea shell, and ship in distance. 10	10 Same as Fives. 10 STATE BANK, New Brunswick, N. J. Schooner.	TEN Venus in a sea shell, and ship in distance. 10
20 State arms supported by two females, the one on left seated. 20	20 Male figure seated, with torch in left and scroll in right hand; eagle on left, with miniature of Washington round his neck. 20 STATE BANK, New Brunswick, N. J. Figure of Agriculture.	XX A shield supported by figure of agriculture on right, commerce on left; shipping &c., in distance. 20
50 Female Portrait. FIFTY.	State arms supported by two females seated; train of railroad cars, shipping, &c., in distance. STATE BANK, New Brunswick, N. J.	50 A ship and shipping.
100 Stone cutter.	Same as Fifties. STATE BANK, New Brunswick, N. J. Figure of Agriculture.	100 Blacksmith.
On this end the words five hundred dollars and portrait of Washington.	Same as Fifties. STATE BANK, New Brunswick, N. J.	500 Female Portrait.
ONE State Arms 1	Female seated with pail on her lap; cows on left and right of her. 1 SUSSEX BANK, Newton, N. J.	Large fig. 1, whole length of note.
ONE	SUSSEX BANK, Newton, N. J. Men Loading Hay.	1 ONE
TWO	Man seated; Girl and boy playing with dog; houses. SUSSEX BANK, Newton, N. J.	2 Girl seated with horn in hand.

Left end	Centre	Right end
2 Washington. 2	Two females with eagle in centre; anchor and ship on right; cornucopia on left. SUSSEX BANK, Newton, N. J.	2 Female with pole and cap; figure 2.
THREE Female erect with cap of liberty. THREE	Portrait of Franklin, with female on either side; on right a sheaf of wheat, &c., on left steamboat, and ship. SUSSEX BANK, Newton, N. J.	3 State Arms. 3
5 Female. 5	5 Two females one reclining on a sheaf with sickle in her left hand; the other on a shield containing a plow in its centre, her left hand on a cornucopia 5 Title of Bank. Portrait of Washington.	FIVE
F I V E FIVE V	Female seated with flowers around her; man plowing on left; buildings on right. SUSSEX BANK, Newton, N. J. Female bathing.	5 V
TEN	10 Two sloops of war in an engagement. 10 SUSSEX BANK, Newton, N. J. Male Portrait with hat on	NEW JERSEY
TWENTY	20 Female seated on sheaf of wheat, sickle in right hand; farming utensils on her left. XX Title of Bank.	NEW JERSEY
50 Horse's head. 50	50 Female seated with sickle in right hand; left hand resting on sheaf of wheat; and two cows at her right. 50 Title of Bank. Portrait of Jefferson.	FIFTY
100 Boy's Head.	SUSSEX BANK, Newton, N. J. State Arms, female on either side.	100 Female portrait
1 Female portrait.	TRENTON BANKING COMPANY Trenton, N. J. Milkmaid erect; boy pointing.	1 Female portrait.
ONE Medallion Head. ONE	Female figure seated supporting figure 1. Water; mill in distance. Female figure seated supporting figure 1. TRENTON BANKING COMPANY, Trenton, N. J. Engine and coal cars	ONE Medallion Head. ONE

Left end	Centre	Right end
2 Female portrait.	Title of Bank. Female seated with agricultural implements and products.	2 Scott.
TWO A seated female with cornucopia, &c. TWO	Medallion head and 2. Dairy maid and cows; farm house in distance. TRENTON BANKING COMPANY. Trenton, N. J.	TWO Male portrait TWO
3 Three cherubs with bunches of grapes. 3	3 View of Old Trenton Bridge. 3 TRENTON BANKING COMPANY, Trenton, N. J. Row Boat.	3 Three cherubs with bunches of grapes. 3
3 Beehive	Title of Bank. Female seated with sheaf and sickle.	3 Child's head
5 Boy and girl.	Horse, colt, man with bag on back, mill, wheel, boys on bridge, etc. Title of Bank.	5 Male head.
5 Milk maid and pail.	TRENTON BANKING COMPANY, Trenton, N. J. View of Trenton State House.	5 5 in ornamental engraving.
X Female portrait.	Title of Bank. Female seated with right arm on rock; factories and man plowing in distance.	10 Children and butterfly
Ornamental Die. Male portrait Ornamental Die.	10 Figures of Agriculture, Labor and science, with heads of cattle in distance. 10 TRENTON BANKING COMPANY. Trenton, N. J.	Ornamental Die. Male portrait Ornamental Die.
20 Male portrait 20	State Arms of N. J., water mill on left agriculture on right in distance. TRENTON BANKING COMPANY, Trenton, N. J.	20 Male portrait 20
XX Female portrait.	Title of Bank. Female erect reading, two others seated listening.	20 Female portrait.

50 Male portrait 50	50 Shield with the words "liberty and prosperity" on base; figure of agriculture on left, and Minerva on right, holding a shield with the word FIFTY thereon. 50 TRENTON BANKING COMPANY, Trenton, N. J.	50 Male portrait 50
50 Squaw.	Girl's portrait. Title of Bank.	50 Female with pen and tablets.
100 Cattle, telegraph, railroad, etc.	Female seated pointing with right hand to ship. Title of Bank.	100 Portrait of girl.
10 0 Male portrait 100	State Medallion Head. Arms of N. J. Medallion Head. TRENTON BANKING COMPANY, Trenton, N. J.	100 Male portrait 100
1 1	Blacksmith at work. UNION BANK AT DOVER ONE DOLLAR Dover, N. J.	ONE Factories, steamer, river, etc.
1 Female portrait. ONE	UNION BANK, Dover, N. J. 1 Figure of America reclining on shield; goods on left; steamboat on right. 1	Full length female. ONE
2 2	UNION BANK OF DOVER, N. J State arms of N. Jersey TWO DOLLARS.	2 Train of cars.
Ornamental work. Med. head with word two thereon. Ornamental work.	Small md. head and word 2. Coat of arms of N. J., Small md. head and word 2. supported by two female figures; bridges and cars on left in distance. UNION BANK, Dover, N. J.	TWO Figure of America. TWO
THREE Male portrait. THREE	Female figure apparently flying, typifying plenty; ships in distance. UNION BANK, Dover, N. J.	3 3
FIVE Male portrait FIVE	UNION BANK, Dover, N. J. V State Arms supported by two females, cars in distance on left; steamship on right.	5 FIVE

TEN Female portrait. X	X Mechanic with hammer, anvil, &c. buildings and cars on right. UNION BANK, Dover, N. J.	X 10
20 Farmer and Plough. XX	XX Large vig. of cars, track, and telegraph wires. UNION BANK Dover, N. J.	20
Full length figure of Justice. 50	50 Female figure of science seated, balances, &c.; factory and water-mill in distance. 50 UNION BANK, Dover, N. J. State arms supported by two females.	Full length figure of Justice. 50
Hunter loading rifle; deer. ONE	Two oxen before cart; men loading it with hay; men, trees, and haystack in distance. UNION BANK, Frenchtown, N. J.	1 Registers die
2 Washington.	Female reclining; shield on which is deer in water; on right sheep and wheat; on left chest and bags of coin. UNION BANK, Frenchtown, N. J.	2 Registers die
Word Three and figure 3. Female feeding chickens.	Train of cars; trees, houses, sloop, etc, in distance. UNION BANK, Frenchtown, N. J.	3 Registers die
5 Registers die	UNION BANK, Frenchtown, N. J. Portrait of Washington; eagle at top; two females on right, one on left; cars and ship in distance.	5 Three dogs, two birds in trees.
Registers die X	UNION BANK, Frenchtown, N. J. Shield on which is cars; sheafs and fruit on right; milkmaid seated on left, in distance farmhouse, cows and trees.	TEN Female reclining; Indian female erect
XX Drove of cattle.	UNION BANK, Frenchtown, N. J. Portrait of Washington; female on either side; on right ship and steamboat in distance; on left sheaf and men mowing.	Figures 20, word twenty and two XX. Reg. die.
1 Female erect beside column; steamer, building, etc., in distance. ONE	UNION COUNTY BK, Plainfield, N. J Female reclining on ground beside scroll, shield, etc; view of falls in background.	1 Female feeding fowls.

2 Beehive.	Boy and horses at trough; female, ducks, etc.; horses in distance. 2 Title of Bank.	2 Female beside column; steamer, building, &c.
UNION THREE	COUNTY BANK Farmer, horse; wheelwright and men loading cart, etc. Female beside column; steamer, building, etc.	3 Female seated
5 Female beside column; steamer, building, etc. FIVE	FIVE DOLLARS. Man on horse at trough, man, boy, sheep; loading hay, etc. Title of Bank.	5 Girls head.
10 Female beside column; steamer, etc.	Title of Bank. Hunter, farmers, etc, viewing train of cars.	10 Female portrait.
20 Female beside column; steamer, building, etc.	Cattle, sheep, etc. Title of Bank.	20 Female with trident seated on shell.
Three females with anchor. FIVE	V Steamship and sail vessels. B'K. OF COMMERCE, Philadelphia, Pa.	5 Female seated with spy glass; ship in distance.
Die. 5 Die.	V Men loading truck with bales. V B'K OF COMMERCE, Philadelphia, Pa. 5 Indian head. 5	Die. 5 Die.
Old man, child and bust of Washington. 10	Title of Bank. 10 X Wheels.	10 Sailor.
TEN Sailor with flag and female at his feet; cornucopia, anchor bales, barrels, &c.	10 Shipping; storehouse on right; city on left. B'K. OF COMMERCE, Philadelphia, Pa.	10 Liberty with pole, cap and shield. TEN
Statue of Liberty with pole and cap.	20 Shipping. 20 B'K. OF COMMERCE, Philadelphia, Pa.	20 Artist seated with brush and canvass. 20

Left	Centre	Right
FIFTY	Med. head Female with 50 on it, seated with eagle perched on shield on right; ship on left. Med. head male with 50 on it. B'K. OF COMMERCE, Philadelphia, Pa.	50 Cupid seated with pencil and paper. 50
100 C 100	100 Female seated and giving eagle drink. 100 B'K. OF COMMERCE, Philadelphia, Pa.	100 C 100
500 Neptune with trident, seated in sea shell.	Female seated on bale of goods with wand in her right hand; shipping on left. B'K. OF COMMERCE, Philadelphia, Pa. Medallion head.	500 Ship under full sail.
POST Ship in a storm. NOTE	Neptune with trident seated in a shell on the sea. B'K. OF COMMERCE, Philadelphia, Pa.	POST Med. head. NOTE
1 Indian princess	Child's head BANK OF GERMANTOWN Phila., Pa. 1 on ONE Sailors in boat attacked by a white bear	ONE on 1 1 on ONE
2 Two children.	BANK OF GERMANTOWN, Philadelphia, Pa. 2 Cows browsing on haystack. 2 TWO DOLLARS.	2 Gen. Scott.
5 Head of Wm. Penn. 5	Vig. Boy and man on horseback; drove of sheep and cattle; boy reclining at foot of tree; farmer, &c in the distance. BANK OF GERMANTOWN, Philadelphia, Pa.	5 Head of Franklin. 5
Cupid and 5. Male portrait V	BANK OF GERMANTOWN, PA. Farmer gathering corn; horse, colt and wagon.	5 and Cupid. V Male portrait
10 Farmers at lunch.	Male portrait. Boy watering horses; girl standing beside, &c. BANK OF GERMANTOWN, PA.	10 Male portrait
Female representing Agriculture, with sickle in hand. TEN	10 Vig. Harvest scene, farmers reclining; female seated with child in arms, basket and pitcher by her side. BANK OF GERMANTOWN, Philadelphia, Pa.	10 Head of J. Q. Adams. TEN

Left	Centre	Right
10 Head of Washington. 10	Vig. Harvest scene; three men seated, taking lunch, hat and basket, house in the distance. BANK OF GERMANTOWN, Philadelphia, Pa. Agricultural implements.	10 Head of Penn. 10
20 Medallion head of female. 20	Vig. Man representing the mechanic arts; wheel, sledge hammer, compass and square; two men and house in the distance. BANK OF GERMANTOWN, Philadelphia, Pa.	20 Female seated, holding sheaf and sickle on right shoulder, left hand extended up wards. 20
50 Head of Marshall. 50	Vig. Female in sitting posture, holding a stock of grain in her right hand, reclining on a bale of cotton; tobacco stalk and hogshead, farm scene in the distance. BANK OF GERMANTOWN, Philadelphia, Pa.	50 Washington on horseback.
100 Head of Lafayette. 100	Vig. Dairy scene, female in sitting posture, and woman milking, little girl in sitting posture; mill and farm house in distance. BANK OF GERMANTOWN, Philadelphia, Pa.	100 Head of Gen. Taylor 100
500	BANK OF GERMANTOWN, Philadelphia, Pa. Vig. Eagle on globe, with female holding stalk of grain in her right hand on right; and Indian with rifle on left. Five Hundred 500 Dols.	500
1 Phila. Male portrait.	BANK OF NORTH AMERICA. Camp scene. 1 Officers, one on horseback, cannon, tents, &c. 1 ONE	1 Public building
5 Word Five and fig. 5. 5	BK OF NORTH AM., Philadelphia, Pa. Portrait of Franklin. Indian the centre of a V; eagle, shield, pole and cap. Female portrait.	5 Locomotive. 5
10 Portrait of Wm. Penn. TEN	Female and Indian on either side of a frame enclosing ship, plough and sheafs; cattle and factory in background. BK OF NORTH AM., Philadelphia, Pa. Dog, key and safe.	10 Franklin. TEN
20 Male portrait 20	Female seated on bale; shield, barrel, sheaf, &c. BK OF NORTH AM., Philadelphia, Pa.	20 Female with arms extended resting on anchor; shipping in background.
50 Lafayette. 50	Female reclining; on left eagle, shield, flags, etc.; on right, shipping. BK OF NORTH AM., Philadelphia, Pa. Sheaf, plow, &c.	50 Justice. 50

Left	Centre	Right
100 Washington 100	Eagle on a rock; shipping on either side. BK OF NORTH AM., Philadelphia. Dog, key and safe.	100 Liberty with pole and cap. 100
Ornamental work. Dog and safe. Ornamental work.	500 Ship with sails set. 500 BK OF NORTH AM., Philadelphia, Pa. Spread eagle.	Ornamental work. Sailor with telescope. Ornamental work.
Ornamental work. Dog and safe. Ornamental work.	1000 Ship with sails set. 1000 BK OF NORTH AM., Philadelphia, Pa. Spread eagle.	Ornamental work. Sailor with telescope. Ornamental work.
Med. head of Franklin. 1000	BANK OF NORTH AMERICA. Philadelphia, Pa. Vig. Female seated with eagle and globe. Letter M either side. ONE THOUSAND in red.	Med. head of Washington. 1000
5 Med. Head and word five. V	Eagle mounted on escutcheon; group of persons representing various pursuits—Agriculture, Commerce, Manufactures, Justice, Liberty, and so on; ship on right. B'K. OF NORTHERN LIBERTIES, Philadelphia, Pa.	V Med. head and word five 5
10 Washington X	Vig. Same as fives. B'K. OF NORTHERN LIBERTIES, Philadelphia, Pa.	X Med. head and word ten. 10
20 Med. head. 20	Vig. Same as fives. B'K. OF NORTHERN LIBERTIES, Philadelphia, Pa.	20 Washington 20
FIFTY Group of persons, Liberty, Justice, spear horse, eagle, &c. FIFTY	Med. head and 50 on it. State Arms. Med. head and 50 on it. B'K. OF NORTHERN LIBERTIES, Philadelphia, Pa.	50 Washington 50
100 Washington 100	Female with babe in arms, shipping and sheafs; life boat; steamboat in distance. Med. head and 100 on it, on either side of the vignette. Title of Bank.	100 Same as on left of 50s. 100
500 Med. head. 500	Liberty and Justice on either side of escutcheon, surmounted by eagle; ship and plow in centre; heads of two horses. 500 Title of Bank. State Arms	Escutcheon, mounted on globe and group of persons.

Left	Centre	Right
	1000 [illegible] mounted eagle, Goddess of Liberty, Justice, female with horn of plenty, and other persons; ship on right and two horses on left. Vig. on left end of note. Title of Bank.	POST Child's head. NOTE
Tomb of Washing't'n 1 surrounded by words ONE.	Group of three children with book on table, in an "oval." BANK OF PENN TOWNSHIP, Philadelphia Pa. ONE DOLLAR.	1 surrounded by words ONE. Portrait of Washingt'n
Bust of Female. 2 surrounded by words TWO.	Ocean view, ships, &c. BANK OF PENN TOWNSHIP, Philadelphia, Pa. TWO DOLLARS.	2 surrounded by words TWO Portrait of Winfield Scott.
5 Bust of Penn FIVE	Agricultural scene; group of five persons. BANK OF PENN TOWNSHIP, Philadelphia, Pa.	5 Washington on horseback
Goddess of Liberty. Wm. Penn. Goddess of Liberty.	10 Female seated, sickle, cornucopia, farming implements, house, etc. 10 Title of Bank.	Spread eagle. Washington Spread eagle
20 Franklin. 20	Title of Bank. Portrait of Penn. Two females embracing each other; safe in foreground; ship in background; steamboat on left.	Washington 20
50 Locomotive and cars; Train of cars ascending hill. 50	Portrait of Penn. Female seated on bale of goods; houses and spires in distance. Portrait of Washington. Title of Bank.	50 Franklin. 50
100 Washington 100	Title of Bank. Portrait of Penn.	Milkmaid erect; cottage in distance. 100
Dis. FIVE HUNDRED Dis.	Three females seated; cornucopias, etc. Figs. 500 on either side of vig. Title of Bank. Eagle	Dis. Head of Penn Dis.
Dis. 1000 NOTE Dis.	1000 Washington and others on horseback; soldiers and cannon. 1000 Title of Bank. Spread eagle	Dis. Wm. Penn. Dis.

Left	Centre	Right
1 1 1	Philadelphia Indian girl beside shield, on which is figure 1 1 City Arms of Phila. CITY BANK ONE DOLLAR	1 1
2 2	Two females either side of shield in which is ship. Phila. Pa CITY BANK 2 across TWO 2 TWO DOLLARS	2 Female with flag and shield; Indian girl seated.
5 Portrait of a boy 5	CITY BANK, Philadelphia, Pa. Signing of the "Declaration of Independence."	5 Portrait of a girl. 5
Female erect with vase of flowers. 10	Two females seated on either side of a shield; in centre of shield, a ship; the female on the left holds a scroll. CITY BANK, Philadelphia, Pa.	X Sailor at the helm.
20 XX	CITY BANK. Philadelphia, Pa. Head of Washington on shield; right Indians and female with pole and cap; on left a Continental soldier. Portrait of Penn on right of vignette, and Franklin on left.	20 XX
50 Large anchor, box, barrel and bale of goods	CITY BANK, Philadelphia, Pa. Portrait of Washington. State arms.	50 Beehive and flower bush on.
100	CITY BANK Philadelphia, Pa. Female reclining, and eagle; on left, train of cars crossing a bridge; view of a harbor and city in distance. 100.	100
Female seated with sickle and portrait of Washington. 500	Male portrait CITY BANK, Philadelphia, Pa.	Shield and letter D. bust of female at top; male on right, female at left. 500
M Shearing sheep.	1000 Female reclining on shield, on which is a scroll and tree; drapery with stars over the shield. CITY BANK, Philadelphia, Pa.	1000 M
1 Man paper barrels, ship, 1	COMMERCIAL BK. buying of hay, bales, &c. Large green 1 on ONE. Sailors reefing sail. Philadelphia, Pa.	1 Female head ONE

Left	Centre	Right
2 TWO across 2	COMMERCIAL BK, Philadelphia, Pa Ship towed by tug. Female. TWO across 2	2 TWO across 2
FIVE Sailor with flag.	Shipping; schooner on the right with figure 5 on the sail; on left small steamboat. COMMERCIAL BANK OF PENNSYLVANIA, Philadelphia, Pa.	5 Locomotive. Landscape, etc.
10 Anchor and bale of goods	Sailor on deck of ship with quadrant; shipping in background. Title of Bank running over the vignette.	10 Female Portrait.
Die Work. Washington Die Work.	20 Two females representing Agriculture and Manufactures; between them shield with 20 on it; ships on left, and sheep on right. 20 Title of Bank. Spread eagle.	Die Work LaFayette Die Work.
Die Work. Franklin. Die Work.	50 Female seated on anchor, right arm resting on shield with 50 on it; sheaf, ship, &c. 50 Title of Bank.	Die Work. Male portrait Die Work.
Die Work. Male portrait. Die Work.	100 Female seated, eagle beside; shipping in distance. 100 Title of Bank. Sword.	Die Work. Male portrait Die Work.
Figures 500 written with a pen. Med. head. Figures 500 written with a pen.	Med. head. Female reclining with sprig and wand; shipping in distance. Med. head. Title of Bank.	Same as on left.
Figs. 1000 written with a pen. Med. Head. Figs. 1000 written with a pen.	Med. head. Vig. Same as 500s. Med. head. Title of Bank.	Same as on left.
1 Horses, men &c., in circular die.	Ships, steamers, &c; Philadelphia COMMONWEALTH BANK ONE DOLLAR.	1 Cars, canal boat, &c in circular die
Goddess of Liberty resting her arm upon pillar, on which is the word TWO.	2 Portrait of Gen. Scott Two Dollars. COMMONWEALTH BANK Philadelphia	2

Left	Centre	Right
Die. 5 Die.	COMMONWEALTH BANK, Philadelphia, Pa. Male portrait. Figure 5 on word FIVE either side.	Die. 5 Die.
5 Farmer, dog, horses' head, implements, bird flying, &c.	Girls' head. Man, horse, colt, bridge, two boys; hills in background. COMMONWEALTH BANK, Philadelphia, Pa. FIVE FIVE FIVE	5 Two sailors pulling rope, etc.
10 Mechanic and bench.	Title of Bank. Two females seated representing Agriculture and Commerce; factories and buildings on right; cows, sheep and village in distance on left.	10 Sailor; ships, houses, etc., in background.
20 Female seated, dog beside her.	Three male figures erect beneath motto with "Faust, Guttenberg, and Schoeffer, upon it; printers frames on left; press, &c., on right. Title of Bank.	20 Wm. Penn.
50 Female shading her eyes with hand.	Title of Bank. Circular die containing outline map of Penn, N. Y., O., Va., Md., N. J., surmounted by bust of Washington; soldier on right; goddess of liberty, cannon, &c., on left.	50 Sailor seated.
100 Franklin.	Title of Bank. State Arms.	100 Scene in an iron mill.
ONE across 1 1	CONSOLIDATION BANK. View of ship yard and ship launch. Philadelphia, Pa.	ONE across 1 1
2 TWO on 2 TWO	CONSOLIDATION BK. Large public building. Philadelphia, Pa	2 TWO on 2 TWO
5 Portrait of Wm. Penn.	CONSOLIDATION BANK, Phila., Penn. Steamer Quaker City under way, and view of Phila. Harbor. Portrait of Female Child.	5 Portrait of Governor Pollock.
10 Female on a platform working a mechanical instrument.	A Drove of Cattle and drovers driving them in the water; house and trees in background and church in the extreme distance. CONSOLIDATION BANK, Phila., Penn. Portrait of a Female Child	10 Sailor seated with spy glass.

Left	Centre	Right
20 Interior view of a blacksmith shop.	CONSOLIDATION BANK, Phila., Penn. Raft floating down a river, man in boat holding up two birds on the right, another raft in background, trees, hills, &c.	20 Workman dressing leather.
50 Cattle, telegraph poles and wires; cars and bridge in background.	CONSOLIDATION BANK, Phila., Penn. The Globe or the world, and an eagle surmounting it. Portrait of a boy.	50 Woodman erect, hand resting on axe.
100 Female with liberty pole and cap, left hand resting on a shield, eagle sitting on the ground.	Title of Bank. C 100 Female erect holding sickle in right hand, and grain in left.	100 Sailor, blacksmith and anchor.
Female with flowers in her apron. D	CONSOLIDATION BK. Philadelphia, Pa. Ornamental portrait of Gen. Scott. D D Five Hundred Dollars.	500 Female feeding fowls.
1000 Man seated; scythe hanging on tree.	CONSOLIDATION BK. Philadelphia, Pa. Horses drinking from trough by a well; man, goat and kid, sheep, etc. house in background. One Thousand Dollars.	M Female portrait.
1 Female with sickle and sheaf of wheat.	CORN EXCHANGE BANK, Philadelphia, Pa. ONE across 1 Portrait of Gen. Scott. ONE across 1	1 Female resting on bank basket of fruit at feet.
2 Male portrait.	CORN EXCHANGE BANK, Philadelphia, Pa. TWO across 2 Female stepping into pool of water. TWO across 2	TWO across 2 Dog on safe.
5 Portrait.	CORN EX. BANK, Philadelphia, Pa. Miller and farmer beside wagon: two horses, one drinking out of trough: mill in back ground. Farmer seated on plow.	5 Female head.
10 Female glaner.	X Sailor, farmer and blacksmith. Title of Bank.	10 Male portrait.
TWENTY Male portrait.	CORN EX. BANK, 20 Philadelphia, Pa.	Corn husking scene. 20

Left	Centre	Right
50 50	Western steamers, etc. 50 Title of Bank.	FIFTY Milkmaid, erect with stool; cows etc.
C 100	Marine view—ships sailing C Title of Bank. 100	100 Two farmers gathering corn.
500	CORN EX. BANK, Philadelphia, Pa. Train of cars, men, horses, steamboat, &c. 500	500
5 Sailor seated.	FAR. & MECH. B'K., Philadelphia, Pa. Blacksmith, farmer and horses; spire in distance.	5 Female seated; house in background.
X Female portrait. 10	Female seated between 1 and 0; agricultural scenery, house, &c. 10 on right. FAR. & MECH. B'K., Philadelphia, Pa. Arm, anvil and hammer.	X Female portrait. 10
10 Female with sheaf.	Blacksmith shop, farmer, two horses, plow, rake, etc. FAR. & MECH. BK., Philadelphia, Pa.	10 Mechanic and lathe.
20 20	Title of Bank. Female with bundle of grain. Cogwheels, etc.	20 Farmer, two horses, plow, blacksmith, anvil, etc. TWENTY
20 Farmer leaning against a tree; female seated. 20	Two cupids, flag, vessel; &c., word Twenty and Medallion head each side. FAR. & MECH. B'K., Philadelphia, Pa.	XX Blacksmith at forge. XX
50 Female seated; house in distance. FIFTY	Blacksmith, farmer, horses, farming utensils, &c., spire in distance. FAR. & MECH. B'K., Philadelphia, Pa. Bee-hive.	50 Sailor seated, vessel, &c. FIFTY
C Vig. same as right of 20.	Mechanic and lathe. Title of Bank. 100	100 C 100

Left end	Centre	Right end
Female seated with shield and spear. 100	FAR. & MECH. B'K., Philadelphia, Pa. 100 Female, harvest scene, vessel, horses, &c. 100	100 Word hundred on Med head. 100
FIVE HUNDRED	Female seated; anvil, screw, hammer, &c. Steamboat in distance. FAR. & MECH. BANK. Phila. Pa.	Female sheaf wheat, plow and ship. 500
ONE THOUSAND	FAR. & MECH. B'K., Philadelphia, Pa. 1000 Vulcan.	ONE THOUSAND
ONE	GIRARD BANK, 1 Philadelphia. Pa. Female seated on bales, water mill on right. canal lock on left. ONE	ONE Female with sickle and grain. ONE
5 Female portrait.	GIRARD BANK, Philadelphia, Pa. Goddess of Liberty and eagle.	5 Female portrait.
10 Male portrait X	10 Market scene; wagons, horses, pedestrians, &c. 10 GIRARD BANK, Philadelphia, Pa.	X Male portrait 10
10 Washington	GIRARD BANK, Philadelphia, Pa. Portrait of Girard; plow and ship. Word Ten on either side.	10 Male portrait
20 Head of Girard. XX	20 Female reclining; anvil and hammer; cars in distance. 20 GIRARD BANK, Philadelphia, Pa.	XX Head of Girard 20
L Head of Girard. 50	Two females seated on bale of goods, shipping, &c. Word Fifty on either side of vig. GIRARD BANK, Philadelphia, Pa.	50 Head of Girard L
100 HUNDRED 100	Female seated in chariot drawn by sea horses. Head of Girard on either side of vignette. GIRARD BANK, Philadelphia, Pa.	100 HUNDRED 100

Left end	Centre	Right end
500 Head of Girard. 500	View of the Bank building. Figures 500 on either side of vig. GIRARD BANK, Philadelphia, Pa.	500 Head of Girard. 500
1000 Head of Girard. 1000	Female seated representing Commerce, Manufactures and Arts; ship and engine in distance. Word Thousand on either side of vignette. GIRARD BANK, Philadelphia, Pa.	1000 Head of Girard. 1000
ONE Mechanic resting arm upon colu'n on which is the word ONE; with bust on top.	KENSINGTON BK. Philadelphia, Pa. 1 across ONE. Female with fan in hand. 1 across ONE.	ONE across 1 Mechanic at work in ship yard.
2 Female figure leaning against column.	2 across TWO Wm. Penn surrounded by Indians, etc. KENSINGTON BK. Philadelphia, Pa	2 Female portrait
5 Female bust. V	Vessels, ship building and houses in distance Double med. head on either side of vig. KENSINGTON B'K., Philadelphia, Pa.	V Female portrait. 5
10 Female erect and vessel in distance. X	Med. head. Rafts, boats, and other water craft; mountain scenery, houses, etc. Med. head KENSINGTON B'K., Philadelphia, Pa.	X Female and spinning wheel. 10
Die. Columbus. Die.	20 The Old Elm Tree; harbor or city in distance. 20 KENSINGTON B'K., Philadelphia, Pa. Sword.	Die. Wm. Penn. Die.
20 Indians contemplating the progress of civilization.	KENSINGTON B'K., Philadelphia, Pa. Vig. Same as 20s above. Large red 20 in centre of bill. XX XX	20 Portrait of Wm. Penn.
Die Work. Male portrait. Die Work.	50 Two females seated; escutcheon between; eagle and ship; ship in distance. 50 KENSINGTON B'K., Philadelphia, Pa. Eagle.	Die Work. Washington Die Work.
50 Franklin.	KENSINGTON B'K., Philadelphia, Pa. Female seated in a letter L with machinery, etc.; cars on left; factory on right. Female in water.	50 Washington

Left end	Centre	Right end
Justice and head of Washington	100 Female seated and cupids; cattle, harvest scene, houses, agricultural implements, &c. Title of Bank on either side of vig. 100 Male figure.	Die Work. Lafayette. Die Work.
C 100 C	KENSINGTON B'K., Philadelphia, Pa. View of ship yard, three vessels on stocks. Large red C. 100 PENNSYLVANIA 100	100 Female with sheaf and sickle.
500 Interior of a rolling mill.	KENSINGTON B'K. Philadelphia, Pa. Steamship at sea; large red letter D. PENNSYLVANIA.	500 Factory and creek.
ONE on 1 Girl's head.	State Arms of Penn. MAN. & MECH'NICS' BANK Philadelphia, Pa.	1 Figure of Justice.
2 Two females with sickle and grain.	State Arms of Penn. MAN. & MECH'NICS' BANK Philadelpaia, Pa.	2 Girl's head
5 Portrait of little girl.	MAN. & MECH. B'K Philadelphia, Pa. Vig. Two horses; houses, shrubbery &c. in background. 5	5
10 Female and cows; farm scene.	MAN. & MECH. B'K Philadelphia, Pa. Large 10 and words ten dollars. X	10 Log-rolling, forest, yoke of oxen, &c.
20	MAN. & MECH. B'K Philadelphia, Pa. Canal scene, men unloading wood and coal from canal boats; men, horse and cart, &c., city in distance. The vig. extends across the whole lower part of note.	20
50	MAN. & MECH. B'K Philadelphia, Pa. City Arms, with female on either side; train of cars and sheaf on right; steamboat and barrel on left. The vig. extends across the whole lower part of note.	50
100 C	MAN. & MECH. B'K Philadelphia, Pa. Trains of cars, bridge, factory, &c.; cars, hills and houses in distance.	100 C

Left end	Centre	Right end
500 Male portrait	MAN. & MECH. BK., Philadelphia, Pa. Five Hundred Dollars in ornamental die work. Red letter D. The State House as it looked in 1776.	500
1000 M	MAN. & MECH. BK., Philadelphia, Pa. Frame enclosing view of shipping. M M	1000 M
1 Henry Clay	MECHANICS BANK Green 1 across ONE — Mechanic's arm and hammer. — Green 1 across ONE Phila. Penn.	1 Child's head
2 Andrew Jackson	MECHANICS BANK Green 2 across TWO — Man pouring oil on machinery. — Green 2 across TWO Phila. Penn.	2 TWO
Bank building. 5	5 Portrait of a female; globe, &c. 5 MECHANICS' BANK, Philadelphia, Pa. Blacksmith's arm.	Washington and horse. 5
5 Sailor leaning on capstan.	MECHANICS' BANK, Philadelphia, Pa. Mechanic, letter V and mechanical implements, factories in distance; FIVE across V on left; on right DOLLARS across V.	5 Female head.
TEN Female with cornucopia. TEN	10 Blacksmith reclining on anvil; house in distance. 10 MECHANICS' BANK, Philadelphia, Pa.	Liberty. TEN
20 XX	MECHANICS' BANK, Philadelphia, Pa. Penn. Goddess of Liberty holding bust of Washington; soldier and two Indians looking at it. Franklin.	20 XX
TWENTY Miniature view of female reclining on hogshead, etc.; locomotive in distance.	MECHANICS' BANK, Philadelphia, Pa. 20 Spread eagle on trunk of fallen tree; cars on left; depot on right. Mechanics' Arm.	20
50	MECHANICS' BANK, Philadelphia, Pa. Train of cars crossing bridge; vessel at the farther end; trees, wagon, horses, etc. Goddess of Liberty.	50 Vessels and harbor.

Left end	Centre	Right end
50 Male portrait Dis.	Two females representing Agriculture and Commerce. MECHANICS' BANK, Philadelphia, Pa. Mechanics' Arm.	50 Washington Dis.
100 Mechanics' arm. 100	MECHANICS' BANK, Philadelphia, Pa. Agricultural implements.	ONE HUNDRED
500	MECHANICS' BANK, Philadelphia, Pa. 500 View of the building formerly occupied by the Bank. 500	FIVE HUNDRED
1000	MECHANICS' BANK, Philadelphia, Pa. 1000 Vig. Same as 500s. 1000	ONE THOUSAND
Two females and Goddess of Liberty. 5	PHILADELPHIA BK, Philadelphia, Pa. 5	FIVE Female seated with bird, globe and spear.
5 Male portrait	Female either side of shield on which is ship; building, factories, cars, etc., in background. Red V below. PHILADELPHIA BK, Philadelphia, Pa.	5 Male portrait
10 Male portrait	Vig. Same as 5s. Title of Bank. Red X.	10 Clay.
TEN Female portrait. TEN	Female seated on bale of goods; shipping and lighthouse. Figs. 10 on either side of vignette. PHILADELPHIA BK, Philadelphia, Pa. Dog's head.	TEN Female portrait. TEN
20 Wm. Penn. 20	Female on either side of escutcheon; vessels and houses in distance. Portrait on either side of vignette. PHILADELPHIA BK, Philadelphia, Pa. Spread eagle.	20 Franklin. 20
20	PHILADELPHIA BANK, Philadelphia, Pa. TWENTY. TWENTY Male Portrait. DOLLARS.	20

Left end	Centre	Right end
50 Franklin. 50	PHILADELPHIA BK, Philadelphia, Pa. Vig. Same as 20s. Washington	50 Wm. Penn. 50
Male Portrait.	50 PHILADELPHIA BANK, Phil'adelphia, Pa. FIFTY Franklin.	50 DOLLARS
100 Male portrait 100	PHILADELPHIA BK, Philadelphia, Pa. Vig. Same as 20s. Bee-hive.	100 Male portrait 100
100 Male head.	Female either side of ship, on shield, buildings and vessels in distance. PHILADELPHIA BANK, Philadelphia, Pa. Bee hive.	100 Male head.
Med. head. Female erect	View of impending cliff; locomotive, omnibuses, forest trees, &c. Figures 500 on either side of vig. PHILADELPHIA BK, Philadelphia, Pa. Ship.	Med. head. Three females.
Female statue 1000	PHILADELPHIA BK Philadelphia, Pa. Female seated and raising lid of chest; cars in distance. Figures 1000 on either side of vignette. Male reclining.	Female erect with horn of plenty. 1000
Justice eagle and head of Washington	SOUTHWARK BANK Philadelphia, Pa. 5 Large fig. 5, two females, cupid and eagle. 5 Eagle.	Dis. Wm. Penn. Dis.
5 Portrait	Spread eagle on a rock; ship and steamboat in distance. Large V and two figure 5s in red ink. SOUTHWARK BANK Philadelphia, Pa.	5 Wm. Penn.
10 Indian on rock with bow and arrow.	Two females reclining; city, vessels and lighthouse in distance. SOUTHWARK BANK Philadelphia, Pa.	10 Female with eagle and portrait of Washington TEN
X on a med. head. Justice and head of Washington on breast of eagle.	SOUTHWARK BANK Philadelphia, Pa Female representing the Arts, angel; sea horses and car and man therein; Vessel on left.	TEN Indian with bow and arrow. TEN.

Left end	Centre	Right end
20 Indian with bow and arrow.	SOUTHWARK BANK Philadelphia, Pa. Two females representing Agriculture and Commerce. 20	Justice and head of Washington on breast of eagle. Washington
Indian with bow and arrow. 50	SOUTHWARK BANK Philadelphia, Pa. Two females reclining; cars and vessels in distance. 50	Same as 20s. Female portrait.
Same as 50s. 100	SOUTHWARK BANK Philadelphia, Pa. Goddess of Liberty and eagle; vessels, etc. Figs 100 on either side of vig. Steamboat	Same as 20s C
Indian with bow and arrow.	SOUTHWARK BANK Philadelphia, Pa. 500 Steamboat.	
FIVE Blacksmith and female seated. 5	5 Female seated, supporting arm; vessels on right. 5 TRADESMEN'S B'K., Philadelphia, Pa. Steamship.	FIVE Blacksmith erect. FIVE
Female encircled by heavy folds of dress, left arm extended.	10 Goddess of Liberty and spread eagle. TRADESMEN'S B'K., Philadelphia, Pa. X	10 Franklin. TEN
TWENTY Bust of Penn TWENTY	20 Two females; one reclining on cornucopia, the other apparently elevated in the air. XX TRADESMEN'S B'K., Philadelphia, Pa.	
50 Canal scene; bridge, houses and spire. FIFTY	Female with right arm leaning on hogshead; cars and vessel on left; house on right. Portrait of female on either side of the vignette. TRADESMEN'S B'K., Philadelphia, Pa.	50 Ship. FIFTY
100 Indian squaw and papoose. 100	C Group of three mechanics; vessel on right; man and horse on left. TRADESMEN'S B'K., Philadelphia, Pa.	100 Med. head. 100
500 Washington 500	Spread eagle; houses on right; cars on left. TRADESMEN'S B'K., Philadelphia, Pa. Female bathing.	Two females; one standing the other kneeling. 500

Left end	Centre	Right end
Die work. 1	UNION BANK. Philadelphia. ONE ONE 1 across ONE. Officer on horse receiving returns. 1 across ONE.	1 Die work.
TWO Soldier leaning on musket.	UNION 2 BANK, Philadelphia. 2 2 2 across TWO. Female globe, shield, &c. 2 across TWO.	TWO Sailor seated on gun.
5 FIVE	UNION Eagle. BANK. Female, column, steamer, buildings, etc. Red V. Female head. Philadelphia, Pa.	5 FIVE
Cupid with sheaf. X	Title of Bank. Female in clouds with shield, pole, cap, eagle, etc. Sailors hoisting TEN.	10 Girl's portrait.
20 Sailor and farmer each side of shield on which is deer and tree	UNION Washington BK., TWENTY.	20 S. C. arms, Cupid, female, soldier, etc.
50 Female with sledge hammer; factories, etc.	Calhoun. Title. Webster. Female and Mercury; ships on right, canal and railroad scene on left.	50 Sailor boy; two sailors and man of war in distance.
100 UNION One Hundred	Med. head of Franklin. HUNDRED. Med. head of Washington. Penn's treaty with the Indians.	100 BANK. One Hundred
500	Title. 500. Mechanic and boy repairing cart; farmer, horse, etc. Child's head. Red 500. Red D.	Goddess of Liberty.
1000 1000	Female head. Title of Bank, Female seated with shield, starry drapery, pole and cap across her lap; building in distance. Red M.	1000 Female holding glass; ship, water, etc.
5 FIVE	WESTERN BANK, Philadelphia, Pa. Indian, squaw and papoose; buildings, etc. FIVE	5 Female kneeling, buildings and spars.

Left end	Centre	Right end
5 Boy gathering corn. Med. head.	5 Farmers reposing beneath a tree and enjoying their dinner; basket, horses, etc. WESTERN BANK, Philadelphia, Pa. Agricultural Implements.	5 Female representing Agriculture; figure 5. 5
5 Farmer sharpening scythe.	WEST[illegible] Philad[illegible] Large V.	5 Mason at work on wall
FIVE 5 FIVE	Female erect with shield, etc. Eagle and shield WESTERN BANK, Philadelphia, Pa.	5 Female with flowers.
10	Deer grazing, trees, waterfall, etc. WESTERN BANK, Philadelphia, Pa.	10 Female portrait.
Two Indians, one erect the other kneeling; wigwam, &c.	WESTERN BANK, Philadelphia, Pa. 10 Female representing agriculture; cars crossing bridge in distance. Mechanics arm.	Letter X and word Ten. Female reclining.
10 Indian warrior on horseback.	Title of Bank. Large X.	TEN Female erect with shield on which is med. head.
X Med. Head. X	10 Female with trumpet, globe and eagle. 10 WESTERN BANK, Philadelphia, Pa. Steamship.	X Med. head X
Female seated on bale. 20	WESTERN BANK, Philadelphia, Pa. Two females seated; ship, steamboat and small sail vessel on left; cars on right. Med. head [illegible] word Twenty on [illegible] of vignette. Steamboat and sail vessel	20 Med. head. 20
Human figure reclining. 50	WESTERN BANK, Philadelphia, Pa. Portrait of Washington. Instructor and pupil; house on right. Med. head figs. 50 on it. Dog's head.	50 Med. head. 50
100 Med. head. 100	WESTERN BANK, Philadelphia, Pa. C Eagle; ship and other small sail vessel. C Steamboat and life-boat.	Female erect with horn of plenty. 100

Left	Center	Right
500 Female representing Agriculture. 500	Indian seated; grain, agricultural implements, etc.; house seen amid the wood. WESTERN BANK, Philadelphia, Pa. Female bathing.	500 Liberty reclining.
1000 Med. head. 1000	Goddess of Liberty and two other females; eagle surmounted; ship and cars in distance. WESTERN BANK, Philadelphia, Pa. Spread eagle.	1000 Milkmaid erect
1 Female with rake.	Western river scene—steamboats, raft, men, etc. ALLEGHANY BANK Pittsburgh, Pa.	1 One Dollar.
Farmer with scythe seated on fence. TWO	Man, boy and girl in factory; machinery, etc ALLEGHANY BANK Pittsburgh, Pa.	2 Two Dollars
Five on 5. Locomotive and tender.	Steamboat; city and steamboat in distance. ALLEGHANY BANK, Alleghany, Pa. FIVE	5 Female portrait.
X Female with dove.	Three cherubs with lever, sledge, wedge and stone. ALLEGHANY BANK, Alleghany, Pa.	10 Head of bull
20 Girls portrait	Two females and shield on which is farming implements; cars and factory in distance. ALLEGHANY BANK, Alleghany, Pa.	20 Negro holding bull; sheep, fence etc.
50 Female portrait.	View of the wharf at Pittsburg with steamboats receiving and discharging freight. ALLEGHANY BANK, Alleghany, Pa.	50 Indian portrait.
100 Female with sickle and grain.	Mexican lassoing wild cattle. ALLEGHANY BANK Alleghany, Pa	C Portrait of boy.
1	Man, horse, cow, pig, fowl, &c., at trough; cattle, barn, &c. Female portrait ALLENTOWN B'K, Allentown, Pa.	One on 1. Spread eagle

Left	Center	Right
2 Clay.	2 Horse either side of shield surmounted by an eagle. 2 ALLENTOWN B'K, Allentown, Pa.	2 Female with sewing machine.
5 Boy and rabbits.	Drovers and drove of cattle; city on right, in distance. ALLENTOWN BK., Allentown, Pa. Sheaf of wheat, rake &c.	5 Female portrait.
Female erect with sheaf of wheat on her head. 10	ALLENTOWN BK., Allentown, Pa. Farmer, sailor and blacksmith; farmer seated, and holds sickle and sheaf of wheat; anvil, horse and man on right; sheaf of wheat on left. X on left.	10 Male portrait
TWENTY Farmer reclining; female seated.	ALLENTOWN BANK Allentown, Pa. 20 XX	Female with fowl. 20
Female with cornucopia. FIFTY	50 Farmers loading wagon with hay; two horses &c. Title of Bank. L L	50 Female portrait
100 inverted Blacksmith, anvil, and sledge.	Title of Bank. C Washington C 100 100	100 inverted Locomotive
Sailor with flag, female at his feet.	1 ANTHRACITE B'K, Tamaqua, Pa. Miners at work in mine.	1 Washingt'n on horseback
Two on 2. Washingt'n	2 ANTHRACITE BANK, 2 Tamaqua, Pa. Milkmaid milking cow; one cow reclining; man, dog, &c. TWO 2 TWO	2 Drummer boy and soldiers.
5 Three sheep; two laying down; one standing. 5	Train of cars, &c.; mining view, iron furnace, &c.; train of cars on left, in distance. ANTHRACITE BK., Tamoqua, Pa.	5 Portrait of Henry Clay.
X Portrait of Gov. Pollock. TEN	10 Farmers at work, loading hay. ANTHRACITE BK., Tamoqua, Pa. Female bathing.	10 TEN 10

Left	Center	Right
20 XX 20	ANTHRACITE BK., Tamoqua, Pa. Portrait of boy. Female reclining with sheaf of wheat and sickle; farmers at work on right; train of cars and bridge on left.	20
Miners at work and a coal shaft; train of cars in background. FIFTY	50 Portrait of Gov. Pollock. ANTHRACITE BK., Tamoqua, Pa.	50 L
100 ONE 0 HUNDRED. 100	Portrait of a girl. Woodmen at work; yoke of oxen on left, in background. ANTHRACITE BK., Tamoqua, Pa.	C Portrait of Webster.
V	Farmer seated; girl and team of horses on left; boy and dog, boy on his back on right. V BK OF BEAVER CO, New Brighton, Pa. Dog.	5 Franklin.
Full length flying female country scene, river, steamboat, locomotive, &c; in background.	Title of Bank Two females seated representing Agriculture and Manufactures; factories on right; cows, &c., on left.	10
1 Eagle.	BK OF CATASAQUA. Catasaqua, Pa. ONE DOLLAR. Female portrait. ONE DOLLAR.	1 Man working at vice.
2 Soldier in battle TWO	B'K of CATASAUQUA Catasauqua, Pa. 2 Farmers resting; female, child, etc. Eagle	2
V Male plowing	BK OF CATASAUQUA, Catasauqua, Penn. Depot, factory, etc. FIVE	5 Squaw and papoose.
10 Female feeding fowls.	Scene in barnyard—farmer and drover bargaining for ox. Title of Bank. 10	10 Female with sheaf and sickle.
20 Train of cars.	Title of Bank. Female head.	20 Men at work in coal mine

50 — Hunter loading rifle. | Man at work in iron mill. Title of Bank. FIFTY | 50 — Scene on a canal.

100 — Farmer and family. | Title of Bank. Letter C on large red die. | 100 — Squaw.

1 — Benjamin Franklin seated in library. | B'K OF CHAMBERSBURG, Chambersburg, Pa. ONE on 1 1 1 | 1 — Old man seated with child, pointing to bust of Washington.

2 — Two fem'les with sickle and grain. | Agricultural implements. BANK OF CHAMBERSBURG, Chambersburg, Pa. TWO DOLLARS on TWO | 2 — Fem'l. with wreath on her head.

Portrait of Washington. 5 — Male portrait. | 5 Vig. Two female reclining, farming implements, &c. 5 BANK OF CHAMBERSBURG, Pa. | Male portrait. 5 — Male portrait.

X — Medallion head and word "TEN" — 10 | Med. head TEN on it. Vig. Instructor and pupil; house in distance on right. Med head TEN on it. BANK OF CHAMBERSBURG, Pa. | Female representing Agriculture — X

10 — Med. head of Washington. | Man with bag, horse, colt, mill, etc.; boys on bridge. BK OF CHAMBERSBURG, Chambersburg, Pa. | 10 — Printer at his stand

20 — Bust of Penn — XX | Med. head. Vig. Spread eagle. Med. head. BANK OF CHAMBERSBURG, Pa. | XX — Bust of Washington — 20

50 — Med. head. — 50 | Vig. Female reclining on safe; commerce and agriculture; two sheep on right. BANK OF CHAMBERSBURG, Pa. | 50 — Male portrait — FIFTY

100 — Mal. portrait — 100 | Vig. Wild horses. BANK OF CHAMBERSBURG, Pa. | Med. head and figures "100" on it — 100

Medallion portrait of late Cashier of the bank. — 5 | Vig. Female seated on ground, with right hand on a milking pail. Cows near; cottage and cattle in the distance. BANK OF CHESTER COUNTY, Westchester, Penn. | 5 — Male portrait.

10 — Half length figure of a city lady, with basket of flowers in her hand. — TEN | Vig. Farmer with scythe in hand seated on ground, dinner basket beside him; haymakers, acqueduct, and warehouses in background. BANK OF CHESTER COUNTY, Westchester, Penn. | 10 — Country girl with sheaf of wheat on her shoulder. — TEN

20 — Drove of cattle, waggon load of hay, and travelers on a plank road. | Vig. Female seated on ground; basket of corn, melons, grapes, &c., at her side; bay, vessels, town and mountains in the distance. BANK OF CHESTER COUNTY, Westchester, Penn. | 20 — Locomotive. — 20

50 — Daniel Boone and dog. | Vig. Female seated on the ground, left arm resting on shield; both hands holding a bundle of fasces; Niagara falls in distance. BANK OF CHESTER COUNTY, Westchester, Penn. | 50 — Indian seated gun in hand.

100 — Portrait of lady. | Female figure seated in chair; eagle on shield at her feet, &c; city, bay, and mountains in the distance. B'K OF CHESTER CO., Westchester, Pa. | 100 — Milkmaid, cattle, &c. — 100

500 — Medallion head of Washington. — 500 | Vig. Two men standing and one seated on a stone in the foreground; railroad, viaduct, and city in the background; mountains in the distance. 500 on Medallion head. BANK OF CHESTER COUNTY, Westchester, Penn. | Full length figure in Roman toga. — 500

Female head. 1000 — Female head | Vig. Locomotive and train of passenger cars, coming round a rocky bank; city and mountains in distance. BANK OF CHESTER COUNTY, Westchester, Penn. | 1000 — Medallion head of Washington. — 1000

5 — Male portrait | Bridge at Coatesville; iron works; mule team; hills in the background. BANK OF CHESTER VALLEY, Coatesville, Pa. FIVE | 5 — Male portrait

10 — Female with sickle and rake; dog; houses in distance. | Title of Bank. Interior of a rolling mill. TEN | 10 — Wm. Penn

XX — Three smiths at work at anvil. | Title of Bank. Female seated on sheaf with sickle; farm building and men loading hay in distance. XX Goose and goslings. | 20 — Female shading her eyes with her hands.

50 — FIFTY — 50 | Title of Bank. Oxen before load of hay; driver with fork; man reclining on top of hay. FIFTY | 50 — Male portrait

100 — Buchanan. | Vig. Same as fives. Title of Bank. 100 | 100 — Clay.

ONE on 1 — Three Deer | BK OF CRAWFORD CO. 1 Loading hay; two men, oxen, dog, etc. 1 ONE DOLLAR Meadville. | ONE on 1 — Pennsylv'a — Male portrait

1 surrounded by words ONE. — Girl and child with sickle and grain. | Scene at a mill, man, horse, dog, child, poultry, etc. Woman crossing bridge in distance. B'K OF CRAWFORD CO. ONE DOLLAR, Meadville, Pa. | 1 surrounded by words ONE. — Basket of corn.

2 — Female portrait | BK OF CRAWFORD CO. Pennsylvania. TWO DOLLARS Meadville. TWO on 2 Female, sheep, grain, etc. TWO on 2 | 2 — Male portrait

2 — Man seated on fence with scythe. | B'K OF CRAWFORD CO. Meadville, Pa. Herd of deer in forest Water fall in distance. TWO DOLLARS. | 2 — Female, child, poultry, dog, etc.

5 | STATE OF PENN. Horse drinking at trough, men, shop, etc. 5 Boy watering horses two B K of CRAWFORD CO. Meadville FIVE DOLLARS on FI VE | 5 — 5

5 — Buchanan. | Man and boy plowing with horses; trees, dog and fence, in distance. Girls Head on each side of vig. BK OF CRAWFORD COUNTY, Meadville, Pa. FIVE FIVE | Fig. 5 invertal. — Female feeding fowls.

X — 10 | Farmer eating lunch; horses, hay, plow, etc in background. Eagle Childs head Title of Bank. TEN TEN | X — Male portrait

20 — Farming implements and products. | Coal mining scene; men resting, men hewing timber; cars, etc. Title of Bank. TWENTY | 20 — Male portrait

50 — Surveying scene. Head of Penn. 50. Title of Bank. Two sailors with boat; sailor boy in front; man of war in distance. 50. FIFTY.

100 — Title of Bank. 100. Two Beavers knawing limbs of trees. Farmer feeding pigs; head of horse over fence. Washington. 100.

1 — B'K OF DANVILLE, Danville, Pa. 1. Female seated, with flowers; smoking urn, &c. Words "One Dollar" across ONE. Farmer with scythe, &c. 1. ONE. 1.

Old man, child, bust on table. 2 Female reclining with scroll quadrant, globe, &c. 2. Two on 2. B'K OF DANVILLE, Danville, Pa. 2. Dog and safe.

5 — BANK OF DANVILLE, Pa. FIVE. FIVE. Vig. Large letter "FIVE" and mechanic in standing position, anvil, cog wheel, &c., houses in background. Bust of female on either side of vig. Iron furnace. 5. FIVE.

10 — Female. Vig. Puddling Furnace. Female portrait. Male portrait. X. Female representing Justice. BANK OF DANVILLE, Pa. TEN. Dog's head. 10.

20 — BANK OF DANVILLE, Pa. 20. Female portrait. Vig. Spread eagle, Am. shield, olive leaves, &c. Male portrait. Goddess of Liberty, Am. flag in one hand and Roman shield in the other. Washington on horseback. Implements of manufacture.

50 — BANK OF DANVILLE, Pa. 50. Female portrait. Train of cars. Vig. Landscape, cows talking; vessel in distance. 50. 50. Wagon Team.

100 — Vig. View of Danville, furnaces, canal, river, &c. Female portrait. 100. Goddess of Liberty in Indian costume, with shield, pole and Liberty cap. Female portrait. BANK OF DANVILLE, Pa. 100. Agriculture Implements. 100.

1 — 1 Milkmaid beside cows; farmhouse in distance. 1. 1. Med. head. B'K OF DELAWARE COUNTY. Med. head. 1. ONE DOLLAR. Chester, Pa. 1.

2 — 2 Ships, steamer, city, etc. 2. 2. Med. head. B'K OF DELAWARE COUNTY. Med. head. 2. TWO DOLLARS. Chester, Pa. 2.

5 — Pat Lyon at forge. Five on med. head each side. 5. Medallion head. BANK OF DELAWARE CO., Chester, Pa. Medallion head. V. Locomotive and cars. V.

10 — View of sea with ships, &c. X. Double Medallion head and TEN. BANK OF DELAWARE CO., Chester, Pa. Double Medallion head and TEN. X. 10.

Man and boy plowing with two horses. 10. BK. OF DELAWARE COUNTY, Chester, Pa. 10. Vessel and lighthouse. Girl's head.

20 — (Old Plate.) 20. Medallion head. Title of B'k. 20. Vig. Harvest field, farmer under tree, boats in distance. Medallion head. 20. 20.

20 — (New Plate.) 20. Vig. View of Upland, a manufacturing village. Head of Wm. Penn. BANK OF DELAWARE CO., Chester, Pa. Head of female.

Female with rake. Vig. Female reclining under sheaf of wheat. Female with rake. FIFTY. BANK OF DELAWARE CO., Chester, Pa. FIFTY. Female with rake. Female with rake.

100 — Vig. Female figures of Justice and Liberty with shield between them, also eagle and ships. 100. Medallion head. BANK OF DELAWARE CO., Chester, Pa. Medallion head. 100. 100.

500 — Vig. Eagle to the right, factory to the left; locomotive and train of cars. 500. Head of Wm. Penn. BANK OF DELAWARE CO., Chester, Pa. Steamship. Female head. D.

1 — BANK OF FAYETTE COUNTY, Uniontown, Pa. 1. In centre of circular die with words one and small 1's in red all over it. Cattle passing through a gate. Female, child, poultry, &c. In centre of circular die with words one, and small 1's in red all over it. ONE DOLLAR.

2 — In die with words TWO. BANK OF FAYETTE COUNTY, Uniontown, Pa. Poultry. Circular Ducks, die with words TWO, and 2. 2 In circular die with words TWO. Two Dollars 2 on ornamental die. Lane and ornamental 2. Two and 2 on ornamental die. TWO DOLLARS.

V — BK OF FAYETTE CO., Uniontown, Pa. 5. Female seated with culvert; canal and railroad scene on left. Clay. Penn.

10 — Title of Bank. X. Drovers and cattle in stream; country scene in distance. Jackson. Female's head.

20 — Title of Bank. 20. General reaping scene with "patent reaper;" city in distance. Washington. Lafayette.

Female with sickle and grain. TWO Females reclining beside chart, globe, books, etc. 2. 2. PENNSYLVANIA. BK OF GETTYSBURG. 2. TWO on 2. TWO DOLLARS. Gettysburg. Dog on safe.

5 — Vig. American shield in centre containing figures of ship, plough, and sheafs of wheat. On left two Indians male and female with child, mountains in distance. On right female with three children, sheaf of wheat, trees and farm houses in distance. 5. Female head. BK OF GETTYSBURG, Gettysburg, Pa. Female head. FIVE. Loading hay. FIVE.

TEN — Vig. Two females supporting shield, containing the arms of the different states, with a representation of an eagle. TEN. head. head. X. BK OF GETTYSBURG, Gettysburg, Pa. 10. Female bathing.

20 — Vig. Washington mounted by an eagle, on the left female seated having in right hand pole with liberty cap, on the right, two females, one reclining and the other kneeling behind her; ship on the left, and railroad bridge on right in distance. XX. Female holding cup, eagle in the act of drinking. Female head. -XX. Title of bank. 20. Agricultural implements.

L — Vig. Three farmers harvesting in foreground; town and water on right in distance, trees and hay stacks on left. Medallion head of female with 50 on it. 50. BK OF GETTYSBURG, Gettysburg, Pa. L. 50. Eagle.

One on 1. Man feeding pigs, horses, &c. Fig. 1 either side. One on 1. Female with sickle and dog. B'K OF LAWRENCE COUNTY, Newcastle, Pa. Dog & safe.

2 | 2 State arms. 2 | 2
TWO
B'K OF LAWRENCE COUNTY, Newcastle, Pa.
Female and sewing machine.

Cupid and ornamental work | 5 Man and boy plowing with two horses. | 5
BK of LAWRENCE COUNTY, Newcastle, Pa.
Merchants with sledge. | Girl's portrait.

X | 10 Surveyors at work. | 10
Female | Title of Bank.
TEN | Female feeding fowls.

1 | Rafting scene. | 1
BANK OF MIDDLETOWN, Middletown, Pa.
Portrait of Gen. Scott. | Head of girl
ONE DOLLAR.

TWO DOLLARS.
2 on red 2. | Female head. Female with sheaf and sickle. Female head. | 2 on red 2.
2 | BANK OF MIDDLETOWN, Middletown, Pa. | 2

5 | V Female on either side of shield; eagle at top. V | 5
Female Portrait. | BANK OF MIDDLETOWN, Middletown, Pa | Female with grain, &c.
5 | 5

5 | Female seated with child; reapers and house in distance. 5 on die; head on either side of vig. | FIVE
Male portrait | BANK OF MIDDLETOWN, Middletown, Pa.
V

5 | 5 Spread eagle. 5 | FIVE
Sleeper seated. | BANK OF MIDDLETOWN, Middletown, Pa. | Female erect with shield and helmet.
FIVE | FIVE

5 | V Two females, eagle, &c. V | 5
Female head | BANK OF MIDDLETOWN, Pa. | Female head with grain, &c.
5 | 5

Shield on which is letter X—female bust at top; soldier and war implements on right; female on left, and head of female on right of vig. | 10
TEN | BK OF MIDDLETW'N Middletown, Pa. | 10

10 | 10 on medallion. Vig. Two horses, medallion shield in centre, surmounted with eagle, scroll with virtue, liberty and independence. 10 on medallion. | TEN
Ten on Medallion
10 | BANK OF MIDDLETOWN, Pa.

Die. | 20 Milkmaid and two cows; other cows in distance. | 20
Title of Bank.
Male portrait | Dog. | Female head.

20 | 20 Vig. Female seated with sickle, grain, &c.; house, &c. in distance. 20 | XX
Medallion head, twenty across it. | BANK OF MIDDLETOWN, Pa. | Twenty on Medallion head.
20 | XX

50 | Female in clouds with sword and eagle. Female with grain. | 50
Title of Bank.
Male portrait | Male portrait

50 | 50 Vig. Cupids at work at press, lever and sledge. 50 | 50
Artist seated at work. | BANK OF MIDDLETOWN, Pa. | 50 across medallion head.
50 | 50

5 | Vig. View of Norristown and bridge. | 5
Male portrait. | BANK OF MONTGOMERY CO., Pa. | Male portrait.
FIVE | Vessel, trees, houses, &c. | FIVE

10 | Portrait of Washington. Goddess of Liberty reclining. Portrait of Rittenhouse. | 10
Canal boat and scenery. | BANK OF MONTGOMERY CO., Pa. | Male and female.
X | Train of cars. | X

TEN | Male portrait. View of building, trees and part of street. Male portrait. | 10
BANK OF MONT. CO. Norristown, Pa.
Male portrait | Dog. | Male portrait

XX | Men at work in iron mill. Bank building. | 20
Title of Bank.
Male portrait | Dog's head. | Male portrait

20 | Portrait of La Fayette. Vig. Signing the Declaration of Independence. Portrait of Washington. | 20
Male portrait. | BANK OF MONTGOMERY CO., Pa. | Portrait of Rittenhouse.
20 on medallion head. | 20 on medallion head.

100 | Vig. Cattle, sheep, &c.; steamboat in distance on right. | 100
Goddess of Liberty. | BANK OF MONTGOMERY Co., Pa. | Portrait of Washington.

ONE | 1 Spread eagle on shield; female, etc. 1 | 1
Female erect with pen, etc. | B'K of NORTHUMBERLAND Northumberland, Pa. | Male portrait
1 | State Arms | 1

TWO | 2 Female either side of portrait of Wm. Penn. 2 | TWO
Female and Cupid | BANK OF NORTHUMBERL'ND Northumberland, Pa.
TWO | State arms.

5 | BANK OF NORTHUMBERLAND, Pa. | 5
Vig. Farmers loading hay, canal and boat, train of cars.
Female head. | Girls head.

Three female figures, anchor, &c. | BANK OF NORTHUMBERLAND, Pa. | 10
Male head.
TEN | Vig. Female seated, scythe, sickle and pitcher; train of cars in distance, grain and implements. | TEN

20 | Vig. Spread eagle on rock, ship on either side. | Female with grain.
Dog. | BANK OF NORTHUMBERLAND, Pa.
20 | 20

1 | Views of factory, railroad, canal, boats. | 1
In die with small 1s. | BANK OF PHOENIXVILLE. Phoenixville, Pa. | In die with small 1s.
Child in chair holding kitten, poultry, &c. | ONE DOLLAR on ONE | Bust of Female.
Phoenix.

Portrait of Andrew Jackson. | Herd of cattle, two drovers, one on horse; factory in distance. | 2 On die with two.
BANK OF PHOENIXVILLE, Phoenixville, Pa.
2 In die with two's. | TWO DOLLARS on TWO | Head of Newfoundland Dog
Phoenix.

5 | BANK OF PHOENIXVILLE, Phoenixville, Pa. | 5
Cars. Washington at Valley Forge. Eagle
Male portrait | Phoenix. | Female feeding fowls.

X | Man holding horse, sack on back; wheelwrights repairing cart. | 10
Clay. | Title of Bank
[illegible] | Phoenix. | Cars.

Cupid and 20. Penn.
BANK OF PHŒNIXVILLE, Phœnixville, Pa.
Train of cars; others in distance.
20 Phœnix. 20
20 and engine. Female portrait.

50 Farmer at lunch; horses, plow, etc. L
Title of Bank. Buchanan.
FIFTY Phœnix FIFTY
50 Man on gate; one on horse; colt, sheep, dog, etc. L

100 Washington.
Title of Bank. State Arms—horse either side; steamer in distance.
Phœnix.
100 Franklin.

5 Female and sheaf of wheat, sickle in left hand, grain in right. FIVE
Vig. Three artisans with implements, ship yard factory and bridge in distance.
BANK OF PITTSBURG, Pa.
5 Train of cars. FIVE

X Locomotive and tender. TEN
Vig. Blacksmith in sitting posture hammer in right hand; anvil train of cars crossing a bridge in distance, workshops; river and hills in distance.
BANK OF PITTSBURG, Pa
10 Head of Washington X

20 Head of Dewitt Clinton. 20
20 Vig. Blacksmith sitting with forge and anvil to right; cars crossing bridge in distance. 20
BANK OF PITTSBURG, Pa.
20 Head of Jefferson, 20

50 Medallion head 50
50 Vig. Female reclining with stalks of grain in left hand, shipping and farm house in distance. 50
BANK OF PITTSBURGH, Pa.
Die Figure of Justice. Die

Female with harp.
100 Vig. Female sitting on a bale; Mercury descending; shipping in distance. 100
BANK OF PITTSBURG, Pa.
Figure of Justice.

Artisan and sailor standing; two females sitting; spinning wheel and capstan to right, view of city in distance.
D Vig. Shield on which is a view of a city; Indian, squaw, and child on left; female teaching group of children on right.
BANK OF PITTSBURG, Pa.
500

1000 Two blacksmiths at work.
Vig. Group of three, farmer and two artisans, half length figures
BANK OF PITTSBURG, Pa.
1000 Female standing among grain, sickle in right hand. 1000

1 On die with one's on it. Male Portrait.
B'K OF POTTSTOWN, Pottstown, Pa.
State arms of Pa. Two horses rearing on shield with ships, plough, and grain on it. Motto "virtue, liberty, and independence."
ONE DOLLAR on die
1 On die with words ONE. Male Portrait.

2 On die with words TWO. Portrait of Abe Lincoln.
Agricultural group, men, female, children, horse, dog swine, chickens, poultry, &c. One man lifting child.
B'K OF POTTSTOWN, Pottstown, Pa
TWO DOLLARS on large ornamental die.
2 On die with words TWO. Portrait of General Scott.

Bust of Female with basket of flowers. 3 On die with words THREE
Train of cars crossing stone bridge, cattle in stream below, boy with fishing rod, shrubbery, &c
B'K OF POTTSTOWN, Pottstown, Pa.
THREE DOLLARS on die.
3 On die with words "THREE." Portrait of Wm. H. Seward.

5 5
BK OF POTTSTOWN, Pottstown, Pa.
Buchanan on left of title and female portrait on right.
V Farmer and boy plowing with two horses. V
5 5

Cupid, sheaf, etc. Female portrait.
10 Title of Bank. 10
X Scene at grist mill; carrying out grain; horses; boys on bridge. X
10 10
Cupid, cornucopia, etc. Male portrait

1 STATE OF NEW YORK Compt's die
BK of TRUMANSBURG
Deer beside tree
ONE DOLLAR Trumansburg
1 Male portrait

2 Compt's die 2
STATE OF N. YORK
Cattle in stream; cars passing over bridge, etc.
BK of TRUMANSBURG
TWO DOLLARS
2 Male portrait

5 5 5
STATE OF NEW YORK
BK of TRUMANSBURG
View of waterfall 5
FIVE DOLLARS
5 Compt's die 5

View of waterfall TEN
STATE OF N. YORK.
Trumansburg X Male portrait
BK of TRUMANSBURG
TEN DOLLARS
10 Compt's die

Male portrait
STATE OF N. YORK
BK of TRUMANSBURG
Oxen, cart, men, corn, etc.
Compt's die
TWENTY DOLLARS
20 Female, barrel, plow, etc.

1 ONE 1
CITIZENS' BANK, Pittsburgh, Pa.
Two females seated; anvil, hammer, &c.
1 1 ONE

Man oiling machinery. TWO
CITIZENS' BANK, Pittsburgh, Pa.
Steamboat. 2 Cars.
2 2
TWO TWO
2 Girl.

Hhds., bales, pig lead, ship, steamboat, &c. THREE
CITIZEN'S BANK, Pittsburgh, Pa.
Word "Three" across white 3 on red die.
Female; steamer in distance.
3 Word "Dollars" across white 3 on red die.

5 Female head.
CITIZENS' BANK, Pittsburgh, Pa. Male portrait.
Scene in a grist mill; man leading horse with grain; boys fishing in brook.
5 Blacksmith with hammer in hand, standing beside anvil.

X Female.
Interior of an iron foundry. Female with flowers.
CITIZENS' BANK.
10 Female standing beside pillar.

Girl seated. TWENTY
CITIZENS' BANK.
Robert Morris. Coal heaver leaning against cart.
20

50 Battle scene, soldier charging bayonet.
Female head. Blacksmith mending cart; farmer standing beside him with horse
CITIZENS' BANK.
50 Thomas Jefferson

C Boy's head.
CITIZENS' BANK.
Farmer riding horse; boy on fence.
100 William Penn.

1 Auditor's die 1
PENNSYLVANIA
Woodcutter resting against rock 1 Dog and game
CLEARFIELD CO. BK
ONE DOLLAR
O N E
Clearfield
1 Girl and fruit

State Arms Raft scene on Western river
5 CLEARFIELD CO. BK
Clearfield, Pa.
Bear.
5

State Arms. 10
Woodcutting scene in forest. X each side. CLEARFIELD CO. BK. Clearfield, Pa. Die.
10 Female portrait.

ONE Wm. Penn. ONE
1 Male and female gleaning; harvest scene in general. 1 COLUMBIA BANK, Columbia, Pa. Locomotive.
ONE Female clasping 1. ONE

2 Washingt'n. 2
2 Spread eagle, cars, bridge, &c. 2 COLUMBIA BANK, Columbia, Pa. Indian head.
TWO Female, cupid, &c. TWO

V Female seated in letter V. 5
5 Five cupids encircling figure 5. 5 COLUMBIA BANK. Columbia, Pa. Dog's head.
V Female seated in 5. 5

5 Washington. V
COLUMBIA BANK, Columbia, Pa. Vig. Female and cupid with wand seated, vessel in distance. 5 on medallion head.
5 Train of cars. V

10 Male portrait 10
COLUMBIA BANK, Columbia, Pa. Vig. Wood chopper seated, dog and axe beside him.
X Medallion head with ten across it.

20 Franklin 20
COLUMBIA BANK Columbia, Pa. Medallion head. Vig. Horse and train of cars. Medallion head.
Goddess of liberty. 20

50 Wagon, horses, bales unloading on ships. 50
50 on medallion head. Vig. Pat. Lyon in his shop. 50 on medallion head. COLUMBIA BANK, Columbia Pa.
50 Cattle; landscape in distance. 50

Medallion head. 100 Medallion head.
COLUMBIA BANK. Columbia. Pa. Female figure seated on bale of merchandise, right arm resting on a shield, with plough in centre and ship above it. 100 on medallion head. ONE HUNDRED.
HUNDRED Female standing, her right hand over shield resting on a pedestal, head of man on shield. HUNDRED

5
DOWNINGTON B'K. Downington, Pa. Cattle on bank and in stream. State arms 5
5 Female head.

10
Scene at mill; two men, two horses, wagon, &c State arms. DOWNINGTON B'K. Downington, Pa.
10 Male head.

ONE Drummer boy and soldiers.
DOYLESTOWN B'K. Doylestown, Pa 1 Scene in grist mill, men at work. 1
1 Female head

2 2 2
DOYLESTOWN B'K. Doylestown, Pa. Man, two horses, plough, boy, trees, &c. Scott.
2 2 2

5 FIVE on figure 5. 5
William Penn. A large V and a female between the heavy part of the letter and the light part. Franklin. DOYLESTOWN B'K. Doylestown, Penn.
5 Man sharpening scythe 5

10 Female and sailor.
Vig. Haymakers, agricultural scene. DOYLESTOWN B'K. Doylestown, Penn. State Arms.
10 Female Indian sitt'g.

20 Blacksmith. 20
Vig. Female sitting, haymakers, railroad in the distance. DOYLESTOWN B'K. Doylestown, Penn. Eagle.
20 Portrait of Chief Justice Marshall.

50 Head of female. 50
50 Vig. Female, plough, oxen, two children, anvil, &c. 50 DOYLESTOWN B'K. Doylestown, Penn.
50 Head of female. 50

100 Drove of cattle. 100
100 Vig. View of Fairmount water works, female, two trains. 100 DOYLESTOWN B'K. Doylestown, Penn.
100 Drove of cattle. 100

Man plowing with two horses. 1
EASTON BANK, Pennsylvania ONE DOLLAR Chartered 1814
1 Female with flowers

2 5 dies with name of b'k and word two. 2
Figure of Angel. EASTON BK, Pennsylvania. Figure with wreath shield, &c. Chartered 1814.
2 Horse's head.

5 Male portrait.
Scene at mill—horse, man, wheel; boys on bridge. EASTON BANK, Easton, Pa. Red 5
5 Male portrait.

5 Hunter with rifle. 5
Medallion head, 5 on it. Vig. Wood chopper, seated, dog and axe beside him, cabin in distance. Medallion head, 5 on it. EASTON BANK Easton, Pa.
5 Male Portrait. 5

10 Girl's head.
EASTON BANK, Easton, Pa. Female with two calves; canal and railroad scene on left. 10
10 Female head.

10 Male portrait. 10
Medallion head ten across it. Vig. Indian seated bow and arrow, canoe in distance. Medallion head ten across it. EASTON BANK Easton, Pa.
10 Medallion head. 10

20 Washington. 20
Child seated reading, plow and wheat. Vig. child in canoe, house in distance. Child seated, tools in hand, &c. EASTON BANK Easton, Pa. Locomotive and cars.
20 Male Portrait. 20

50 Male portrait. FIFTY
Vig. Female seated, agricultural implements wheat, &c., cars locks, &c., in distance. Female portrait EASTON BANK Easton, Pa.
50 Male portrait. FIFTY.

100 Head of male 100
Vig. Female seated, shield, sickle, &c., two Indians on right. Female portrait on right. EASTON BANK Easton, Pa.
100 Head of male 100

ONE Two Females.
1 Cows and fowl 1 EXCHANGE BANK, Pittsburgh, Pa.
One on 1.

2 Man and girl at well, man drinking.
2 Horse drinking at brook, boy on his back, dog, trees, &c. 2 EXCHANGE BANK OF PITTSBURGH, Pittsburgh, Pa.
2 Female Portrait.

5 Male portrait 5
Vig. View of the city of Pittsburgh; spread eagle on the other side of the river. EXCHANGE BANK, Pittsburgh, Penn. State Arms.
5 Portrait of Millard Fillmore. 5

PENN.	PENN.	PENN.
5 — EXCHANGE BANK of Pittsburg, Pa. — 5 Girl's head. — View of Pittsburg, river bridge, boats, etc. — Female feeding fowls	5 — Farmer reclining against tree, woman seated holding child; harvest scene and house in distance. FIVE on med head either side. — V Wm. Penn. — Washington. V — FARMERS' BANK of BUCKS CO., Pa. — 5	X — [New Plate.] Vig. Farmers at work loading hay, horse and ox for the team on right hay stack & trees on left large tree. — X Female blowing dinner horn, table &c., farmers and load of hay. — TEN FARMERS BANK OF LANCASTER, Pa. — X
10 — Steamboat—"Mail packet Pittsburgh," on wheel house. — 10 Title of Bank. Female portrait. — Indian warrior on horse.	10 — FARMERS' BANK OF BUCKS CO., Pa. — X Portrait of Washington. — 10 Vig. Same as above. — Head of Penn. 10 — Medallion head. — X	Female with portrait and sickle. — FARMERS' BANK OF LANCASTER, Pa. — 20 Man at lunch, girl, horses, dog; boy on his back, etc. XX — State Arms. — Farmer [illegible] resting [illegible]
10 — Female portrait. Vig. View of the interior of a rolling mill; men at work. — 10 Figure of Wm. Penn standing. — Male portrait. EXCHANGE BANK, Pittsburgh, Penn. Steamer. — TEN	20 — FARMERS' BANK OF BUCKS CO., Pa. — 20 Portrait of Penn. — Vig. View of bridge over canal; houses, teamster, cattle, &c., cupid on right of vig. — Portrait of Washington. 20 — 20	20 — Med. head with twenty across it. Med. head with twenty across it. Vig. Woodman seated, dog, and axe beside him. Female with rake; load of hay, &c. — Same as left. 20 — FARMERS BANK OF LANCASTER, Pa.
20 — Title of Bank. Vig. Train of cars. — 20 Portrait of Gen. Scott. — Female with sheaf. TWENTY — TWENTY	FIFTY — FARMERS' BANK OF BUCKS CO., Pa. — 50 Farmers loading a wagon with grain. — Large die with 50, and words FIFTY DOLLARS thereon. — Portrait of Washington.	50 — Med. head with fifty across it. Med. head with fifty across it. Vig. Medallion head, cupids on either side, spinning wheels, &c. — 50 Man and dog. — Man and dog. 50 — FARMERS BANK OF LANCASTER, Pa. — 50
50 — State arms — Goddess with horn of plenty in the clouds over landscape. Male portrait. — EXCHANGE BANK, Pittsburgh, Penn. — 50	100 — FARMERS' BANK OF BUCKS CO., Pa. — C Male reclining with sickle in hand. — Vig. Female reclining on safe or chest; Escutcheon bearing the Arms of State. — Portrait of Washington. 100 — Farming implements. — 100	[New Plate.] — 50 Farmer sowing seed. — L Large building, people, trees, &c. FARMERS' BANK OF LANCASTER, PA. — Portrait of boy
100 — Vig. Eagle standing on a shield. — 100 Male portrait. — Male portrait 100 — EXCHANGE BANK, Pittsburgh, Penn. — 100	ONE — 1 Dog on safe. 1 Cattle, sheep, &c. Farm house in distance. Female stepping in pool of water. — FARMERS BANK OF LANCASTER, Pa. ONE DOLLAR. — 1	100 — FARMERS BANK OF LANCASTER, Pa. — 100 Vig. Harvest field farmers at work. Washington. — Female, [illegible] shield, [illegible] and [illegible] pole and cap
500 — Medallion head. Vig. A female sitting with a plant in her hand; steamboat in the distance. Medallion head. — A figure in the act of pouring a liquid from a vessel. Female holding a medallion head on a pedestal, in left a staff with two serpents coiled around it. — EXCHANGE BANK, Pittsburgh, Penn. — 500	2 — Horse either side of shield surmounted by eagle. Child's head. — TWO TWO across — FARMERS BANK OF LANCASTER, Pa.	1 — Female holding lamb; two sheaves of wheat, wai-Penn. State Arms, sickle, etc. — 1 1 — FARMER'S BANK Mt. Joy, Pa. — Two children
Small medallion head. — Infant figure. Vig. Eagle standing on a log; steamer in the distance. Infant figure. — Small medallion head. 1000 — 1000 Small medallion head. — EXCHANGE BANK, Pittsburgh, Penn. — Small medallion head.	Figure of Justice — Cattle in the water; one lying down; sheep in the distance. — FIVE Two females, one standing; sickle wheel, &c. 5 — FARMERS B'K OF LANCASTER, Pa. Dog and safe. — FIVE	State Arms — Two shields; sheaf of wheat in one, plow and ship in the other; angel blowing trumpet, soldier, female, etc. — 5 5 — FARMER'S BANK Mt. Joy, Pa. — Female portrait
1 — Female with pail, cows, &c.; ONE on med. head either side. — 1 ONE on Med. head. — ONE on Med. head 1 — FARMERS BANK OF BUCKS CO., Bristol, Pa. — 1	FIVE — Vig. Farmers at lunch. Female with basket seated, load of hay, and farm house in distance. 5 — Pennsylvania. Man on horseback talking with a farmer. — Two females standing, sickle, wheat, &c. FIVE — FARMERS BANK OF LANCASTER, Pa. Dog, boy, and Safe. — FIVE	20 FARMERS' BANK OF MT. JOY. XX Twenty Auditor's die. Dollars — Girl and dogs. Female, grain, machinery, etc. — TWENTY DOLLARS Mt. Joy, Pennsylvania.
Urn of Pa. 2 — 2 Eagle on branch of tree. 2 — TWO Med. head. — FARMERS BANK OF BUCKS CO. TWO DOLLARS — Female seated in large figure 2 2 — TWO	10 — Medallion head with ten across. Medallion head with ten across. — 10 Drove of cattle in circle. — Vig. Female seated, canal locks in front of her, wheat in rear. — Boy with spade and basket of flowers, man spading, women sprinkling. 10 — FARMERS BANK OF LANCASTER, Pa. — 10	ONE on 1 — 1 Cattle, boy and girl, trees, &c. 1 — 1 Girl, boy, and pitcher. — FARMERS' BANK. Reading, Pa. — Dog and safe.

Left	Centre	Right
2 2	FARMERS' BANK, Reading, Pa. Female with sword and shield. Gen. Scott.	2
FIVE Portrait of female, with sickle and sheaf. V	Vig. Milkmaid and cows. 5 FARMER'S BANK, Reading, Penn. Wagon load of hay.	5 Child in imitation of blacksmith. 5
TEN Two females representing agriculture and commerce. TEN	X Vig. City Hall and scenery. FARMER'S BANK, Roading, Penn. X Farming implements. X	X Portrait of female. 10
Female reclining, shield, &c. 20	20 Vig. Farmer ploughing. FARMER'S BANK. Reading, Penn. Dog and safe.	20 medallion head. 20
50 Double medallion head 50	Male Portrait. Male Portrait. Vig. Large house, with cupola, spire, and smaller house in back ground. FARMER'S BANK, Reading, Penn.	50 Double medallion head. 50
L 50	(New Plate.) Cattle, and drovers driving them in the water; houses and trees in background; a church in extreme distance. FARMERS' BANK OF READING, PA. Locomotive.	50 Female erect with vase of flowers.
C Two female figures; one reclining	(New Plate.) FARMERS' BANK OF READING, PA.	100 Male and female; two boys, dog and a hen.
100 Medallion Head and figure 100 inscribed. 100	Head of Washington. Vig. Three houses. Head of Lafayette. FARMER'S BANK, Baading, Penn.	100 Medallion Head, and figure 100 inscribed. 100
ONE Male portrait. ONE	Men on horses, and dogs pursuing fox. FARMERS' B'K OF SCHUYLKILL CO., Pottsville, Pa.	1 Male head.
5 Male portrait FIVE	5 5 Vig. Two females, shield, mansion, cars, &c. in distance. FARMERS BANK OF SCHUYLKILL CO. Pottsville. Pa.	V and Five Male portrait FIVE

Left	Centre	Right
TEN Female. TEN	X Vig. Female in a sitting posture with a sickle and sheaf. X FARMERS BANK OF SCHUYLKILL CO. Pottsville, Pa. Locomotive.	10 Bridge, boat, horse, house, &c. in distance. TEN
20 Portrait of Wm. Penn.	Vig. Female sitting on a log with hands resting on a pail; cottage, steamboat, &c. FARMERS BANK OF SCHUYLKILL CO. Pottsville, Pa. Safe; dog with key in left paw.	20 Portrait of Ben. Franklin.
100 Male portrait	Man watering three horses at trough; sheep, &c.; house and trees in distance. FARMER'S BK. OF SCHUYLKILL CO. Pottsville, Pa. 100	100 Male portrait
500 Portrait of Washington. 500	Vig. Female sitting on a plough, left hand with sickle resting on sheaf of wheat, right hand uplifted with stems of wheat. 500 FARMERS' BANK OF SCHUYLKILL CO. Pottsville, Pa.	500 Portrait of Marshall. 500
ONE	Female reclining on sheaf of grain, hat resting on arm. mowing machine in background. FARMERS' & DROVERS' BANK, Waynesburgh, Pa ONE DOLLAR on ONE and 1.	1 Girl reclining, with basket of flowers.
2 Two children, with bundles of grain.	2 2 Farmer, two horses drinking at trough, woman with pails, ducks, &c. FARMERS' & DROVERS' BANK, Waynesburgh, Pa TWO DOLLARS.	2 Female feeding poultry.
5 Cattle. 5	(Old Plate.) Medallion head. Vig. Farmer leaning against a tree, female sitting along side of him; farmers reaping on right, also farm house. Medallion head. FARMERS & DROVERS BANK Waynesburg, Pa.	FIVE Cattle. FIVE
5 Portrait of Washington. FIVE	(2d. Plate.) Vig Cattle; farmers reaping on right, and farmer ploughing with oxen and horse on left. FARMERS & DROVERS BANK. Waynesburg, Pa.	5 Female. FIVE
FIVE Female with sheaf of wheat and sickle.	(3d. Plate) Vig. Farmer and boy loading hay cart and horse before cart. FARMERS & DROVERS BANK, Waynesburg, Pa.	5 Female portrait
10 Farmer and dog. 10	(Old Plate.) X on med. head. Vig. Male and female male with pitchfork in right hand, farmers loading hay, &c. X on med. head. FARMERS & DROVERS BANK, Waynesburg, Pa.	X Farmer and dog. X

Left	Centre	Right
X Bull's head TEN	(New Plate.) Vig. Man on horseback, another holding pitchfork in hand and another tying up bundle of grain. X FARMERS & DROVERS BANK, Waynesburg. Pa.	Two females, one with sickle and sheaf of wheat. TEN
10 Sheep.	FAR. & DROVERS' BANK. Waynesburg, Pa. Harvesting scene; man bearing sheaf on shoulder; boy on his knees apparently unhitching team of horses.	10 Female with dove.
20 Female with pitchfork. 20	(New Plate.) Vig. Country wagon and four horses and head drove of cattle crossing a stream of water; bridge, houses mail coach, wharf, &c in background. FARMERS & DROVERS BANK. Waynesburg, Pa.	20 Female with pitchfork 20
XX Milkmaid. TWENTY	New Plate. Vig. Drover on horseback, dog and flock of sheep; mill in background on left. FARMERS & DROVERS BANK, Waynesburg, Pa.	20 Female seated.
20 Female portrait.	Title of Bank. Shield containing a portion of N. Y., Pa., and Va.; farmer seated on right, locomotive, etc.; female with rake seated on left.	20 Female portrait
1 One Dollar.	FAR. & MECH. B'K., Easton, Pa. 1 in red. Portrait of Gen. Scott. 1 in red	1 One Dollar
2 Basket of corn.	Railroad, canal, road and farming scene in general. FAR. & MECH. B'K. Easton, Pa.	2 Clay.
5 surrounded by ornamental dies. FIVE DOLLARS Ornamental die.	FARMERS & MECHANICS BANK, Easton, Penn. Agricultural Implements. This bill has 5 repeated 87 times around border.	5 surrounded by ornamental dies FIVE DOLLARS Ornamental die
5 Small head. FIVE	Vig. Harvest scene four human figures, cradler sharpening his scythe. 5 FARMERS & MECHANICS BANK OF EASTON, Pa.	FIVE Mechanic, anvil, tools &c. FIVE
TEN Farmer with scythe	10 ornamental dies. [illegible] & MECH. B'K. 10 in ornamental dies. Easton, Pa. TEN DOLLARS. This bill has X repeated 40 times around border.	TEN Blacksmith at work.

Full length female with shield, wand, &c. TEN	10 on medallion head. Vig. Public buildings. FARMERS AND MECHANICS BANK OF EASTON, Pa.	10 Male portrait
TWENTY Female figure, one arm resting on a pedestal, the other on shield.	20 on medallion head. Vig. Female seated, leaning against safe; sheep on right, church in centre, cornucopia, &c. FARMERS AND MECHANICS BANK OF EASTON, Pa.	XX 20
Goddess of Liberty; fifty on shield and eagle.	50 on medallion head. FARMERS AND MECHANICS BANK OF EASTON, Pa. Vig. Milkmaid seated on a log, farm house on left, steamboat on right.	50 50
100 on medallion head. Farmers going to work house in the distance.	FARMERS AND MECHANICS BANK OF EASTON, Pa. Vig. Mechanic seated, sledge in hand, viewing factories and train of cars, &c. 100	Two females, one seated with sickle and bunch of grain. C
5 Head of Ben Franklin. FIVE	FRANKLIN BANK, Washington, Pa. Vig. Men loading hay on waggon; oxen. Head of female.	5 Washington. FIVE
10 Franklin. TEN	Man on horse, sheep, dog and mill. Washington. FRANKLIN BANK, Washington, Pa. Eagle.	TEN Milkmaid TEN
20 Franklin XX	Harvest scene; man with fork, female with rake; men loading wagon with hay. 20 on med. head on either side. FRANKLIN BANK, Washington, Pa.	XX Washington 20
50 Fifty on medallion head. 50	Wash-ington. Vig. Harvest scene, reapers man standing by a tree with arms folded, sickle in his hand, female sitting, child on her lap, baskets, &c. Frank-lin. FRANKLIN BANK, Washington, Pa.	50 FIFTY on med head 50
1 Female writing on tablet, child at feet.	HARRISBURG B'K, Harrisburg, Pa. Large portrait of Gen. Scott.	1 Two females, flowers, &c.
2 Female, bee hive, and flowers.	HARRISBURG B'K. Harrisburg, Pa 2 Sailor seated on gun-carriage. Soldier resting on flags, fort in the distance. 2 2 2	2 Female leaning on pillar, with torch in hand, foot resting on [illegible].

5 Boys head. V	HARRISBURG B'K Harrisburg, Pa. Female figure erect. FIVE FIVE	5 5 Girl's head. V
FIVE Two male figures; [illegible] females [illegible] house and city in distance.	HARRISBURG BK. Harrisburg, Pa 5 State House.	5 Male figure; two females sitting; yoke of oxen and dog.
10 Two females seated; vessel in distance. 10	Female seated with liberty cap and book in lap; houses on left. TEN on either side of vig. HARRISBURG B'K., Harrisburg, Pa.	X Same as left X
Indian. 20	20 Vig. State House. HARRISBURG BK. Harrisburg, Pa. Eagle.	20 Washington. 20
50 Figure of Justice. 50	Female in stooping posture; man in boat, and State House on right, in distance 50 50 HARRISBURG B'K, Harrisburg, Pa.	L Figure of Justice. L
100 Cupid reading; plow, sheaf of wheat, &c. 100	Female seated, holding liberty cap; State House in distance on right. 10 10 HARRISBURG B'K, Harrisburg, Pa.	100 Cupid reading; plow, sheaf of wheat, &c.
Boy whittling under tree, child reclining, cows and sheep. 1	1 Male Portrait HONESDALE B'K, Honesdale, Pa. ONE DOLLAR.	ONE on 1. Dog watching safe.
2 Male portrait	HONESDALE BANK, Honesdale, Pa. 2 Interior of mine, men at work. 2 TWO 2 DOLLARS. 8	2 Girl seated, with fruit, &c.
V Female sitting; arm resting on shield. V	5 Vig. Three human figures; winged monster standing upon safe; cars in distance on right; vessel on left. 5 HONESDALE BANK, Honesdale, Pa. Dog.	V Female seated; book, portrait, eagle, &c. V
TEN	X Vig. Male and female seated; Jupiter in rear, anvil, hammer, &c. X HONESDALE BANK, Honesdale, Pa.	X

Female seated; ship on left; State Arms on right. XX	20 Vig. Cupid soaring in clouds. XX HONESDALE BANK Honesdale, Pa. Eagle.	TWENTY
TWENTY	XX State Arms. HONESDALE BANK, Honesdale, Pa.	20 Male portrait
FIFTY inverted. FIFTY	Mining scene. Title of Bank.	50 Male portrait
FIFTY	50 L on circular die. HONESDALE BANK, Honesdale, Pa. Head of dog.	Vig. Female seated, arm resting on bale of goods, Jupiter and eagle with scroll in mouth. 50
100 Mining scene	C Indian seated with left arm resting on shield. Title of Bank.	100 Male portrait
Female Portrait. ONE on 1	IRON CITY BANK, Pittsburgh, Pa 1 Military men, horse, cannon, balls, drum, &c. 1	ONE on 1 Blacksmith, anvil, &c.
2 Female erect, beside column, steamer in distance.	2 Female reclining, with chart, compass, globe, &c. 2 IRON CITY BANK, Pittsburgh, Pa.	2 Male Portrait
5 Agricultural implements and products	Male portrait Scene in a rolling mill; two men at work, etc. IRON CITY BANK, Pittsburgh, Pa.	5 5
10 Female portrait.	View of Banking House. 10 Title of Bank.	Pennsylvania Smith at forge. TEN
Male portrait 20	Title of Bank. Wharf scene, railroad depot, steamboats, vessels, cars, men, horses, carts, etc.	20 Portrait of girl.

50 — Launch of the Adriatic. Female portrait. Title of Bank. 50 — Fowls. 50

100 — Half length figures of the inventors of printing; press, &c. Male portrait. Title of Bank. One Hundred in red. 100 — Male portrait.

IRON CITY BANK, Pittsburgh, Pa. 500 — Raft scene, steamboat in distance. Eagle. Female portrait.

IRON CITY BANK, Pittsburgh, Pa. 1000 — Boiler makers at work in shop. Female portrait. Cupid and cornucopia.

1 Female portrait. 1 — JERSEY SHORE B'K, Jersey Shore, Pa. Male portrait.

Five. JERSEY SHORE BK, Jersey Shore, Pa. 5 — Scene on a raft, etc. Men at work in mine.

5 — JERSEY SHORE B'K, Jersey Shore, Pa. 5 — V Old man and child, bust of Washington on table. V — Female portrait. Male portrait.

JERSEY SHORE BK, Jersey Shore, Pa. 10 — Female seated on a log ... with cars on ... sheaves of grain ... farm house in distance on left. Male portrait.

JERSEY SHORE BK, Jersey Shore, Pa. 20 — Bull's head on shield; ... Female portrait.

1 — KITTANNING B'K. 1 — Man plowing with two horses. ONE DOLLAR. Kittanning, Pa. Female portrait. Two children.

Five on 5. KITTANNING BK., Kittanning, Pa. 5 — Three females representing the Arts and Sciences, head of Washington. FIVE. Female head. Male portrait.

10 — Title of Bank. 10 — Four females on globe; shield, flag and sword. Girl with dove. Male portrait.

LANCASTER CO. BANK, Lancaster, Pa. 1 — Female reaper seated with grain and sickle, straw hat beside her. 1 — Continental soldiers, one on horse, one with pennant, cannon, tents, &c. 1 surrounded by small 1's. One Dollar.

2 surrounded by small 2's down, and two. — Milkmaid with pail and stool, cows lying down, farmhouse in distance. 2 surrounded by small 2's, and two. LANCASTER CO. B'K, Lancaster, Pa. Eagle on rock. 2. 2 — Female with flowers.

FIVE — 5 Vig. Farm scene, harvesters at lunch. 5 — Reaping scene. LANCASTER CO. BANK, Pa. V — Dog's head. FIVE. 5

Female and churn. Vig. Female representing a flax spinner. X — Agricultural scene. LANCASTER CO. BANK, Pa. 10 — Dog's head. TEN

XX — Med head. 20 Med head. Head on ... Farmer gathering corn. LANCASTER CO. BK, Lancaster, Pa. XX — 20 — Eagle.

50 — Vig. Farmers cradling grain; houses in back ground. L — 50 surrounded by the words fifty dollars. Medallion head. LANCASTER CO. BK, Lancaster, Pa. Farmer sowing grain, another harrowing. 50 — Dog's head.

100 — Vig. Landscape, load of hay drawn by oxen, man on horseback, mill, viaduct, train of cars &c in distance. 100 — Allegorical figure representing manufactures, water in distance. LANCASTER CO., BANK, Pa. Farmer ploughing. 100 — Dog's head.

ONE — 1 Female seated on rock with eagle, shield, &c.; vessels, &c. 1 — 1 — Med. head. LEBANON BANK, Lebanon, Pa. 1

2 — 2 Two females, one pointing to vessels on ocean. 2 — Med. head. LEBANON BANK, Lebanon, Pa. Med. head. 2. 2

FIVE — LEBANON BANK Lebanon, Pa. FIVE — Female trampling on cornucopia. 5 Vig. Female seated on barrel of merchandise, anchor, vessel, houses &c. V — Justice erect and head of Washington. FIVE — Child's head.

X 10 TEN — LEBANON BANK Lebanon, Pa. TEN — 10 Vig. Female seated; eagle at her feet; shipping in background. X — Child's head. Same as five.

TWENTY — LEBANON BANK, Lebanon, Pa. 20 — 20 Vig. Female seated representing agriculture and commerce. XX — Same as five.

50 — 50 Vig. Male and female agricultural scene. 50 — 50 — Female with sword in right hand. LEBANON BANK, Lebanon, Pa. Female standing with sword in left hand. FIFTY — Babe. FIFTY

100 — 100 Vig. Two females; one of whom Goddess of liberty is seated on a stone on which the figures "1776," are inscribed. 100 — 100 — Female seated on bale of goods; ship in distance. LEBANON BANK, Lebanon, Pa. Female seated on bale of goods, ship in distance. 100 — Deer. 100

Figure 1 surrounded by small 1s. LEBANON VALLEY BANK, Lebanon, Pa. Same as left end. Cows and calf passing through gate; female and boy. ONE DOLLAR.

2 — LEBANON VALLEY BANK, Lebanon, Pa. 2 — TWO DOLLARS. Chickens 2 Ducks. TWO DOLLARS

5 — LEBANON VALLEY BANK, Lebanon, Pa. 5 — Female erect; cow, sheep, etc. Clay. Female seated with pole and cap. Beehive.

TEN — Title of Bank. 10 — Three military men; one on horseback; flag in distance. Justice. Eagle.

Twenty inverted. Man with sheaf. 20	Title of Bank. Spread eagle; town, etc., in distance.	20 Female head
50 Med. head. 50	Goddess of Liberty reclining against U. S. Arms; Indian on right; two females on left. Title of Bank.	50 Men with corn, basket, etc.
100 Blacksmith and anvil.	Title of Bank. C Horses at through railroad and canal scene; steamboat, etc.	100
1 Male portrait.	LEWISBURG BANK. Lewisburg, Pa. Two soldiers and drummer.	1 Male portrait
5 Male portrait	Two females seated; factories, &c., on right; cows sheep, &c, on left. LEWISBURGH BK, Lewisburgh, Pa. Ducks.	5 Male portrait
10 Male portrait	Title of Bank. Blacksmith with hammer; farmer with scythe; girl with rake; child with fruit. Female bathing.	10 Male portrait
LEWIS 20	BURG BANK. Lewisburg, Pa. Boys attempting to catch running horse; dog, horses, etc. Male head	20 Man carrying corn stalks.
1 Soldier with flag beside cannon	STATE OF PENN. LOCKHAVEN BANK 1 ONE DOLLAR Lockhaven	ONE on 1 General Scott
2 Portrait of Henry Clay.	LOCKHAVEN B'K. Lockhaven, Pa. 2 Revolutionary scene, man firing on enemy, woman loading gun. 2	2 Portrait of Jackson.
5 Woodmen falling trees; oxen in background.	LOCKHAVEN BANK. Lockhaven, Pa. Female with sheaf of wheat.	Male portrait 5

Male portrait TEN TEN	LOCKHAVEN BANK. Lockhaven, Pa. DOLLARS Men at work with patent mowing and raking machine drawn by two horses.	10
XX 20	LOCKHAVEN BANK, Lockhaven, Pa. Field with train of cars and rising sun; on right, sheafs and sheep; on left female seated with tub; house in distance.	20 Portrait of Washington
Male portrait 50	LOCKHAVEN BANK, Lockhaven, Pa. State Arms with horse on either side; cars, boats, factories, etc.	50
100 C	LOCKHAVEN BANK, Lockhaven, Pa. Female with small tub.	100 Eagle on branch of tree; cars, canal, factories, etc.
1 Male portrait. ONE	ONE DOLLAR. MAUCH CHUNK BK. Mauch Chunk, Pa. Two females	1 Female head. ONE
2 Girl & boy at well.	MAUCH CHUNK BK, Mauch Chunk, Pa. 2 Female reclining with torch, &c. 2 2 TWO DOLLARS.	2 Male portrait.
5 Male portrait FIVE	Vig. Mining scene; loaded coal car two miners leaning against it; two seated on wheelbarrow upturned; two men at work, and stationary engine in distance on left. MAUCH CHUNK BK. Mauch Chunk, Bk. Bear.	5 Head of young girl with curls. FIVE
10 Harvest scene; male and female seated; man in act of drinking from pitcher.	Head of young girl. Title of Bank. Vig. Lumbering scene; man falling tree; another seated; horses dragging a log; saw mill in distance. TEN DOLLARS.	
Man, horse, dog, &c, in field of grain; man with sheaves under right arm.	20 Train of cars passing a group 20 of people; some seated, consisting of hunters, hay makers, women, &c. Title of Bank. Childs Head.	Young girl erect with glass in her hand.
50 Scene upon road, drovers among herd of cattle; Hay wagon &c, in distance.	Vig. Scene on canal; boat looking through; harvest scene and cars on viaduct in background. Title of Bank.	50 Locomotive and train of cars coming round curve; steamboat in distance.

C Woman with basket on left arm, feeding chickens. 100	100 Vig. Cupid surrounded by three mermaids floating on water. MAUCH CHUNK BK. Mauch Chunk, Pa. Spread eagle.	C Head of female.
1 Beehive.	MECHANICS' BANK of Pittsburgh, Pa. Mechanic at work at vice, etc.	1 Female with flowers
Mechanic and machinery. 2	Males, female, child, horse, dog, hogs, fowls, etc. MECHANICS' BANK of Pittsburgh, Pa	2 Female and child
5 Two men at work on a locomotive boiler.	MECH. BANK OF PITTSBURGH, PA.	5 Female portrait.
X Carpenter sawing a board; bench at his back.	MECH. BANK OF PITTSBURGH, PA. Portrait of Washington.	10 Man in shirt sleeves erect; houses in background.
Word "twenty" in part circle running up. Blacksmith erect; anvil and sledge; building in distance.	MECH. BANK OF PITTSBURGH, PA. 20	Three figures reclining; one on left is Mercury; the middle one holds pole and cap. 20
FIFTY Female erect with sword.	50 Sailor, farmer and mechanic; farmer holds a sickle and sheaf of wheat; man and horse and anvil on right; sheaf on left. MECH. BANK OF PITTSBURGH, PA.	50 Boy and rabbits
Two men erect; in distance, two masons at work. 100	C Mechanic, farmer, wheel, tree, horse, &c.; in background, bridge and buildings. MECH. BANK OF PITTSBURGH, PA.	100
Farmers loading wheat; yoke of oxen, horse, &c.	MECH. BANK OF PITTSBURGH, PA. 500	500 Female Indian erect.
Farmer standing with scythe, &c. 1000	M Interior view of an iron mill, and men at work. MECH. BANK OF PITTSBURGH, PA.	1000 Female portrait.

1000 Farmer erect with scythe. | Train of cars crossing bridge; in background another train and city. MECHANICS' BK OF Pittsburg, Pa. | M Female portrait.

5 State Arms 5 | MECHANICSBURG BANK, Mechanicsburg, Pa. Old man, child, and bust on table. | 5 5

10 State arms. 10 | MECHANICSBURG BANK, Mechanicsburg, Pa. TEN DOLLARS on X Man at pump, two horses, pig, cattle, &c. | 10

1 Female with tablets child at her feet. | MER. & MAN BANK of Pittsburgh, Pa. ONE One on 1 ONE ONE | 1 Male portrait.

Two females at looms. TWO | TWO DOLLARS across 2 MER. & MAN. B'K, Pittsburgh, Pa. Dog's head. | Male portrait. 2

THE MER CHANTS' & PITTSBURGH, General wharf scene. Indian head. MANU FACTURERS BK of Pittsburgh, Pa. 5 | 5 Sailors on ship hoisting.

5 Canal boat passing under a bridge. FIVE | Vig. Group of three. Farmer and two artisans; half length figures. MERCHANTS AND MANUFACTURERS BANK. Pittsburgh, Pa. Blacksmith's arm, hammer and anvil. | FIVE Medallion head. FIVE

X | View of city, bridge canal, steamboat and river scenes. Child's head. MER. & MAN. B'K, Pittsburgh, Pa. TEN DOLLARS across 10 | 10 X

10 Blacksmith with hammer in right hand resting on anvil. 10 | MERCHANTS AND MANUFACTURERS BANK. Pittsburg, Pa. Vig. Female figure, left hand resting on a vase Pitcher in right hand pouring water into a vase out of which an eagle is drinking. | 10 Blacksmith with right hand resting on an anvil. 10

20 Farmer cleaning scythe. Railroad bridge, locomotive and cars in background. | MERCHANTS AND MANUFACTURERS BANK. Pittsburg, Pa. Vig. Three female figures. Right end figure of Justice with sword and scales. Centre figure with wand of Mercury in left hand; left end figure with basket of fruit. Machinery | 20 XX 20

50 Female with hands on spinning wheel. 50 | Med. head of Franklin. Vig. Female sitting on a rock sketching, anvil and hammer at her feet. Railroad bridge locomotive and cars in the background. Med. head of Franklin. Title of bank. | 50 Female with hands on spinning wheel. 50

50 | Scene in a rolling mill; men at work. MERCHANTS' AND MANUFACTURERS' BANK of Pittsburg, Pa. Anvil. | 50 Portrait of girl.

100 Scene in an iron foundry, men carrying metal, etc. | Title of Bank. Letter C. | 100 Men engaged in moulding.

100 Steamboat. 100 | Medallion head. Vig. Mercury with wand pointing to a steamboat, female with right arm resting on bale of goods. In the background Neptune drawn by horses. Medallion head. Title of Bank. | 100 Canal boat. 100

500 Franklin. D | Vig. Locomotive and train of cars. MERCHANTS AND MANUFACTURERS BANK. Pittsburg, Pa. Safe. | 500 Figure resting on shield sextant and compass at her feet, in right hand a bow.

1000 Washington. 1000 | Vig. Blacksmith seated, left arm resting on an anvil; Factories, shipping in the background. Med head on right. MERCHANTS AND MANUFACTURERS BANK. Pittsburg, Pa. | 1000 Female head and bust. M

Cupid. Words "Secured," &c., on red die. FIVE | MIFFLIN CO. BANK Lewistown, Pa. V FIVE V Female and calves: canal and railroad scene on left. | 5 Male Portrait

X 10 | MIFFLIN CO. BANK, Lewistown, Pa. Scene at mill, two men, two horses, wagon, &c. Words "Secured," &c., on red die. Cars. | 10 Male portrait

ONE on 1 Auditor's Die. ONE on 1 | 1 Barnyard scene; men, horses, etc. 1 MILTON BANK ONE DOLLAR Milton Pennsylvania | ONE on 1 Soldier loading gun

TWO Auditor's die. | Scene in Mill. TWO on 2 MILTON BANK TWO DOLLARS | 2 Two females, Indian and white with shield, flag, etc.

ONE Washingt'n ONE | 1 Blacksmith at work. 1 MINERS' BANK, Pottsville, Pa. Locomotive. | ONE Milkmaid seated. ONE

TWO Female, Cupid, &c. 2 | 2 Blacksmith shoeing horse; boy, dogs, cars, &c. MINERS' BANK, Pottsville, Pa. Agricultural implements and products. | TWO Male portrait. 2

5 Washington. 5 | Vig. Train of cars, village in the distance. MINERS BANK OF POTTSVILLE, Pa. Eagle. | 5 Female. 5

10 Webster. TEN | Head of Randolph. Vi. Eagle on branch of tree; train of cars and canal and boats in the distance. MINERS BANK OF POTTSVILLE. PA. | 10 Fillmore. TEN

20 Female. 20 | Columbus. Vig. Winged female blowing a trumpet, globe, eagle, flags &c. Washington. MINERS BANK OF POTTSVILLE, PA. Dogs Head. | 20 Female 20

50 Female 50 | Franklin Vig. A female seated between 5 and 0, barrel, bales, &c. ship on left. Fulton. MINERS BANK OF POTTSVILLE, PA. Eagle. | 50 Female. 50

C Portrait of Washington. | Vig. Eagle on branch of tree; view of Niagara Falls, in the background. MINERS BANK OF POTTSVILLE. PA. Horse | 100 Franklin.

Medallion head of Washington. | MONONGAHELA B'K Brownsville, Pa. 5 Vig. Large V, with female and sheaf of wheat in centre of V. 5 | Fame blowing a trumpet, and holding pole with liberty cap. 5

X Medallion head. X | 10 Vig. Harvest scene, and farmers taking lunch. MONONGAHELA BK Brownsville, Pa. | Large X with persons supporting it on either side; sledge and anvil at bottom.

Female portrait. | 20 Vig. Goddess of Liberty, with pole and cap, reclining against U. S. Coat of Arms. MONONGAHELA BK Brownsville, Pa. | 20 Portrait of Washington.

Left	Centre	Right
1 Officer with drum and sword.	MOUNT JOY BANK, Mount Joy, Pa. Female head. Men and two horses at pump; pig, cattle, &c	1
2 Girl's head.	Boy and girl under a tree; cattle, sheep, &c. MOUNT JOY BANK. Mount Joy, Pa.	2 Female with basket of fruit.
Female reclining on sheaf; reaping scene. 5	Female portrait. MOUNT JOY BANK, Mount Joy, Pa. Turkey.	5 Man carrying corn stalks.
X Mt. Joy Bk Mt. Joy, Pa. Female head. X	Milkmaid, cows, man, dog, &c TEN DOLLARS	10 10
Cupid and 20 Boy's head.	MOUNT JOY BANK, Mount Joy, Pa. Corn gathering scene; man, horse, colt, dog, &c	20 and Cupid. Cars, telegraph, cattle, &c.
State Arms of Penn. ONE on 1	NATIONAL BANK of Pennsylvania. Girl's head. 1 Girl's head. Pottsville. ONE DOLLAR on ornamental work.	1 Auditor's die
2 Workman beside machinery.	Auditor's die Scene in Iron foundry 2 NATIONAL BANK of Pennsylvania. TWO DOLLARS. Pottsville.	2 $2
5 Soldier with flag beside cannon.	NATIONAL BANK of Pennsylvania. V Auditor's die V 5 on FIVE DOLLARS.	5 Mechanic with hammer, etc.
100 Female beside machinery.	Camp scene, group of officers, etc. NATIONAL BANK of Pennsylvania. One Hundred Dollars.	100 Auditor's die C
ONE on 1 Male portrait	NORTHUMB'RLAND CO. BANK Female seated on ground beside flags, eagle, safe, shield, etc. ONE DOLLAR Pennsylvania	1

Left	Centre	Right
2 Male portrait.	NORTHUMB'RLAND CO. BANK, Shamokin. TWO across 2 Blacksmith at work; tools, &c. Pennsylvania.	2 Female portrait
5 Henry Clay	NORTHUMB'RLAND CO. BANK, Shamokin, Pa. Girl seated on sheaf of wheat; engine and cars on right. Pennsylv'ia State arms on left.	5 Gen. Scott.
1 Female seated with pail, cows, &c.	OCTORARA BANK, Oxford, Pa. Cows, mill, stream, &c.	One on 1. Female seated with basket of fruit.
Indians on skiff watching deer. 2	2 Boy's portrait. OCTORARO BANK. Oxford, Pa.	2 Boy's head.
5 Plowman and horses.	OCTORARO BANK, Female with two calves, tree; canal boat, cars, etc., in distance. Oxford, Pa. V V V V	V Female with dove.
10 Washington	Four females—one erect. Title of Bank. TEN TEN	X Two girls, &c.
20 Bulls head.	Title of Bank. Reaper man at work in field of wheat; town in distance. TWENTY	20 Rams head.
ONE Female at well. ONE	PITTSTON BANK, Pittston, Penn. Man hunting Buffaloes.	ONE across figure 1. Female.
Eag'e, shield, etc. TWO across figure 2.	2 Female PITTSTON BANK, Pittston, Penn.	2
Female soaring above buildings, river, cars, steamboat, etc.; on upper right country scene.	Coal train and mine. PITTSTON BANK, Pittston, Pa.	5 Indian.

Left	Centre	Right
10 Female seated and dog's head.	Title of Bank. Female seated among implements; cars on bridge and factories in distance.	10 Female with sheaf. 10
Men with pick; coal-pit and men shoving coal car.	Title of Bank. Men at work with wheelbarrows on dock, horse, cart, coal, etc.	10
Mechanic with sledge. 20	Moonlight scene on canal, men, horses, boat, bills, and distant city. Title of Bank.	20 Female portrait
1 Die work.	STROUDSBURG B'K. Stroudsburg, Pa. ONE Man DOLLAR and dog fighting with bear in woods ONE ONE	1 Die work
2 TWO 2	STROUDSBURG B'K. Stroudsburg, Pa. Train of cars. TWO TWO	2 DOLLARS 2
5 Franklin.	STROUDSBURG BK Stroudsburg, Pa. Men dressing leather. FIVE	5 Wm. Penn.
X Washington	Man watering three horses from trough by side of well; goat, kid, sheep, trees and house. Title of Bank.	10 Lady Washington.
20 View of cattle, telegraph and railroad.	Washington—female, scythe, sheaf, cars, etc., on right; female, anchor, men, boxes, barrels and steamer on left. Title of Bank.	XX Two cherubs with sheaf and distaff. XX
50 Locomotive.	Title of Bank. Rafting scene; man on raft. FIFTY	50 Male portrait
100 Farmer seated at lunch.	Horse on either side of shield; eagle at top; cars, factory and steamboat in distance. Title of Bank.	C ONE HUNDRED

Left end	Centre	Right end
1 Portrait of Washingt'n	Farmer seated, with boy, girl, and dog; two horses, &c. TIOGA COUNTY B'K, Tioga, Pa. ONE DOLLAR.	1 Indian seated, with axe.
2 Two on 2 2	TIOGA COUNTY B'K, Tioga, Pa. Train of cars in an oval.	2 Portrait of Jefferson.
5 Female with hand head	TIOGA COUNTY BK, Tioga, Pa. Men and children with load of hay; mechanic standing near anvil and column. V Ducks V	5 Penn
10 Male portrait	Title of Bank. Jolly raftsmen on Western river; steamboat on left. X X	10 Sailor
20 Franklin.	Title of Bank. Mining scene	20 Washington.
50 Buchanan.	Farmer at lunch; girl, boy, dog, horses, etc. Title of Bank.	50 Indian seated.
C 100 C	Locomotive. Title of Bank.	100 Male portrait.
FIVE Female seated with grain and sickle.	5 Washington on horseback with his staff around him. UNION BANK OF Reading, Pa.	5 Male portrait
10	Miller and farmer beside wagon; two horses, one drinking from trough; mill in background. UNION BANK OF Reading, Pa.	Male portrait X Female portrait
Farmer with pitcher, etc. 20	UNION BANK, Reading, Pa. Man cutting a stick; horse, cow, sheep and trees.	20 Female with flowers.

Left end	Centre	Right end
50	Two men and horse; factories in distance. 50 Title of Bank.	FIFTY Milkmaid; boy pointing.
100 Female with sword and scales.	C Two females and machinery. C Title of Bank.	Farmer seated with sickle; men reaping in distance.
Blacksmith mending wheelbarrow; female with grain, etc. 1	VENANGO BANK across 1 1 1 Franklin, Pa.	State die
2 Large half length figure of female seated in chair	VENANGO BANK 2 Female seated with sheaf and sickle 2 Franklin, Pa.	2 State die
5 Girl beside brook 5	FIVE DOLLARS 5 State die 5 VENANGO BANK FIVE	5 FIVE
Female with flag, shield, etc.	WEST BRANCH BK. Williamsport, Pa. Canal, railroad and farming scene.	One on 1. Man loading gun.
2 Female with sword and scales.	WEST BRANCH BK. Williamsport, Pa. 2 Men mowing in field; female seated. 2	2 2 Female feeding fowls.
5 Justice reclining.	Vig. View of a public building, miniature view of female on right of vig. WEST BRANCH BK. Williamsport, Pa. Dog and safe.	5 Sailor and shipping in background
5 Washington 5	Farmers at lunch. Franklin. WEST BRANCH BK. Williamsport, Pa. Agricultural Implements.	5 Canal and boats. 5
10 Medallion head. 10	Vig. Spread eagle poised on trunk of tree; locomotive and cars in background 10 WEST BRANCH BK. Williamsport, Pa. Arms of Pa.	Portrait of Washington TEN Portrait of Harrison.

Left end	Centre	Right end
XX Miniature view of farm girl drawing pail of water from well.	Vig. Iron furnace, locomotive and cars; forest scenery in background; locomotive and cars on left of vig in foreground. WEST BRANCH BK. Williamsport, Pa. Indian paddling canoe.	20 Portrait of Lafayette. 20.
1 Medallion head	ONE Female ONE on either side of on 1 bee-hive 1 WYOMING BANK Wilkesbarre, Pa.	1 Medallion head
2 Med. head. 2	2 Milkmaid beside cows, farm-house in distance. WYOMING BANK at Wilkesbarre, Pa. TWO DOLLARS	TWO Figure of Justice with sword and scales, seated in large fig 2 TWO
5 5 on Med. head 5	5 Two females, shield and eagle. 5 WYOMING BANK Wilkesbarre, Pa.	5 5 on Med. head. 5
5 Franklin. V	(Old Plate.) Vig. Female with sheaf of wheat, pole boat with two men in distance. 5 5 WYOMING BANK, Wilkes Barre, Pa. State Arms.	5 Jackson; V
5 head of son. Franklin. FIVE	(New Plate.) WYOMING BANK, Wilkes Barre, Pa. Agricultural Implements.	Large V a figure 5 and FIVE. Male portrait.
FIVE 5 5	FIVE DOLLARS Female portrait. 5 Statue of Liberty WYOMING BANK, Wilkesbarrie, Pa.	Same as left
Fig. 10 inverted. X	Railroad, bridge, canal, haying and country scenes. Title of Bank.	10 Female with flowers
X Mars. X	(Old Plate.) Vig. Female with rake sitting on plough, and small figures working at forge. 10 10 Title of Bank. State Arms.	Canal locks, boats passing through.
10 Two Indians in front of tent, one standing, the other on right knee.	(New Plate.) WYOMING BANK, Wilkes Barre, Pa. Girl bathing	10 Male portrait. TEN

PENN.

Canal, lock, and boats passing through.	20 Female on either side of a shield, surmounted by an eagle. 20 WYOMING BANK, Wilkesbarre, Pa. State Arms.	20 Washington. 20
50 Canal scene 50	50 on medallion head. State Arms. 50 on medallion head. WYOMING BANK, Wilkes Barre, Pa.	Female with sickle and wheat. 50
100 Portrait of Washington. 100	100 on medallion head. Signing of Declaration of Independence. 100 on medallion head. WYOMING BANK, Wilkes Barre, Ea.	100 Portrait of Dewitt Clinton. 100
1 Medallion head. 1	Milkmaid, cows, &c.; ONE on medallion head either side. YORK BANK, York, Pa.	1 Medallion head. 1
TWO Female seated in fig. 2. TWO	2 Old man and youth with plow; mill in distance. 2 YORK BANK, York, Pa.	2 Medallion head. 2
5 Male portrait. FIVE	Vig. Public buildings, stage coach, teamsters, shrubberry, &c. YORK BANK. York, Pa.	5 Male portrait. FIVE
10 Male portrait. TEN	Vig. Daguerreotype view of York. YORK BANK. York, Pa.	10 TEN Male portrait.
Pennsylvania 1 YORK COUNTY BANK 1 Continental Congress, 1776 1	General Scott 1 ONE DOLLAR Eagle	1 Indian girl
2 Farmer seated	YORK COUNTY B'K Female with rake in hand; loading hay in background 2 2 TWO DOLLARS	2 Female portrait
5 Half length figure of girl.	Corn husking scene. YORK COUNTY BK. York, Pa.	5 Blacksmith at forge

DELAWARE.

5 Farmer sitting, woman with rake and pitcher, dog behind her.	FIVE Vig. Boy plowing with two horses; boy by his side with shovel on his shoulder YORK COUNTY B'K. York, Penn. Female with sickle.	5 Wm. Penn. 5
Farmer seated holding glass and scythe; woman with victuals.	Jefferson. Males and females and train of cars. Title of Bank.	X
Female with grain and sickle. 10	Vig. Two boys on horse back, driving cattle and sheep; boy sitting beside a tree, dog behind him. YORK COUNTY B'K. York, Penn. Farming utensils.	10 Portrait. 10
XX Portrait. XX	Vig. Blacksmith shop; one smith at work on anvil, another shoeing horse; man standing in door. YORK COUNTY B'K. York, Penn. Farming utensils.	20 Washington.
1 Female figure.	State arms; locomotive and ship in background. B'K OF DELAWARE, Wilmington, Del.	1 Ship.
Female erect ONE	Scene at sea; lighthouse and vessels. 1 on med. head on either side. BK. OF DELAWARE Wilmington, Del.	ONE DOLLAR
TWO Washington TWO	Shipping scene, houses, etc.; 2 on med head on each side. BK OF DELAWARE Wilmington, Del.	TWO DOLLARS
2 Half of the State Arms.	Spread eagle on a tree, ship and steamboat in background. B'K OF DELAWARE. Wilmington, Del.	2 Other half State Arms.
5 Dog, key, and safe. V	State arms. B'K OF DELAWARE, Wilmington, Del. Chartered 1795.	5 FIVE V
X Two harvest men, with dog.	Female with sheaf of wheat, sickle, &c. B'K OF DELAWARE, Wilmington, Del.	10 Female 10

DELAWARE.

TWENTY	B'K OF DELAWARE, Wilmington, Del. 2 Female figure. 0	20 Gen. Taylor. XX
FIFTY	Figure 50 and female head. Two ships and whale boat out. Figure 50 and female head. B'K OF DELAWARE, Wilmington, Del. Engine and cars.	FIFTY
100 Brig.	Female; in background, engine and cars; shot tower. B'K OF DELAWARE, Wilmington, Del. Railroad train.	100 Female holding anchor.
1 Male portrait	Man on horse; man harvesting in distance. BANK OF NEWARK, Newark, Del. Sheep.	1 Head of girl.
Male figure erect. TWO	2 Blacksmith shoeing horse, driver seated on log; blacksmith in background. BANK OF NEWARK, Newark, Del. Cock.	2 Male portrait
5 Washington.	Milkmaid seated with pail, cows, &c.; farm house in distance. BANK OF NEWARK, Newark, Del.	5 Chalkens
10 X	Drove of cattle, pigs, &c; two men on horseback; train of cars, bridge and village in distance BANK OF NEWARK, Newark, Del. Beehive.	10 X
Man gathering corn. TWENTY	20 Head of girl. 20 BANK OF NEWARK, Newark, Del.	Mower sharpening scythe TWENTY
1 One and head of female. 1	Man reaping, child, dog, and agricultural implements in the foreground. 1 1 BANK OF SMYRNA. Smyrna, Del. Female.	1 One and head of female. 1
1 ONE 1	Man watering horses from trough; sheep, goats, trees and house. B'K OF SMYRNA, Smyrna, Del.	1 Washington.

Left	Centre	Right
TWO DOLLARS	2 Drover bargaining for ox; negro, boy, horse, cattle, dog, etc. BANK OF SMYRNA, Smyrna, Del.	2 Female feeding fcwls.
TWO Female seated in large figure 2. TWO	Female seated with child in her arms; shipping in the distance. ? on med. head each side BANK OF SMYRNA, Smyrna, Del. State arms.	TWO Same as left. TWO
3 Drove of cattle. 3	Med. Three. Shipping—three men in small boat; town in distance. Med. Three. BANK OF SMYRNA, Smyrna, Del.	3 Head of Washington. 3
5 Head of female, 5	Med. Five. Country scene—male and female; four reapers in distance. Med. Five, BANK OF SMYRNA, Smyrna, Del.	5 Head of female, 5
5 Female, male, boy, girl, dog and chickens.	Female driving cows home; train of cars and city in distance. B'K OF SMYRNA, Smyrna, Del.	V 5
10 Female portrait.	Drover and drove of cattle; boy in water; trees, and house in distance. BANK OF SMYRNA, Smyrna, Del.	10 X
10 Female with rake in hand. 10	Med. X. Woodman seated on a log with his left hand on his dog's head. Med. X. BANK OF SMYRNA, Smyrna, Del.	10 Drove of cattle. 10
Head of Franklin.	20 Female seated on a rock; left hand resting on a stalk of corn, right resting on a cornucopia, 20 BANK OF SMYRNA, Smyrna, Del Double med. head.	Head of Washington.
Lathe work with statue in niche.	Med. 50. State arms, with female on either side, representing Agriculture and Commerce. Med. 50. BANK OF SMYRNA, Smyrna, Del. Male portrait,	Same as left.
100 State arms with female on either side. 100	Female portrait. Country scene; two men loading hay; pair of oxen to wagon. BANK OF SMYRNA, Smyrna, Del. Steamboat.	100 Ship under sail. 100

Left	Centre	Right
1 Female portrait. ONE	Sailor reclining, coil of rope, anchor, windlass, horn, &c. Ships on left in distance. WILMINGTON AND BRANDYWINE B'K, Delaware. Wheelbarrow, &c.	1 Mechanic. ONE
2 TWO Female seated on barrel, scales, &c.	Sailor and Indian, eagle, shield, &c; Ship on right in distance, tents on left. WILMINGTON AND BRANDYWINE B'K, Delaware. Arm, anvil, &c.	2
FIVE Farmer reclining with sickle. FIVE	Three men erect, one holds a pole; village and water on right. WILMINGTON AND BRANDYWINE B'K, Delaware. Locomotive.	5 Female, sheaf of wheat, &c.
X TEN on Med. Head. 10	Man and boy seated; man is drawing; mill on right; Med. Head and word TEN on either side. WILMINGTON AND BRANDYWINE B'K. Delaware.	10 Man seated drawing. X
20 Portrait of Washington. 20	Two females seated, shield, eagle, &c.; Med. Head and word TWENTY on either side. WILMINGTON AND BRANDYWINE B'K, Delaware.	20 Male portrait 20
50 Ship under weigh. 50	Female seated, plow, barrel, bale of goods, &c.; portrait of Washington on left; portrait of Lafayette, vessels, &c., on right. WILMINGTON AND BRANDYWINE B'K. Delaware. Cupid.	50 Steamboat and small boat. 50
100 Female seated, shield &c. 100	Cars and People, Steamboat on left in distance. WILMINGTON AND BRANDYWINE B'K, Delaware. Ship.	100 Female seated, letter C, eagle, shield, &c. 100
1 Machinist.	CITIZENS' BANK. Middletown, Del. 1 Man sharpening scythe on grindstone; negro turning; men at work in distance. 1	1 Girl's head.
2 2 Cupid.	2 2 Title of Bank. Girl's head. 2 2 2 Female portrait. TWO TWO	2 2 Cupid.
5 Female portrait.	Hunter and farmer with implements on either side of shield; vessels in distance. Title of Bank 5 Man and plow. 5	5 Male portrait

Left	Centre	Right
10 Female portrait.	Girl with rake; child, farmer and blacksmith. CITIZENS BANK. X Middletown, Del. X 10	10 Male portrait.
20 Washington.	Group of male and female figures looking at train of cars. Title of Bank. 20 Wheels. 20	20 Girl's head.
1 Head of Wm. Penn. ONE	Female figure and bale; man loading hay wagon on right. DELAWARE CITY BANK, Del.	1 Locomotive, train of cars, and bridge. ONE
2 Head of J. Quincy Adams. TWO	Female figure with sickle and sheaf of wheat in left hand, and bunch of grain in right, plow in background DELAWARE CITY BANK, Del.	2 Steamboat. TWO
3 Head of Wm. Penn. 3	Three females in a sitting posture, the one on the left with sickle and sheaf of wheat. DELAWARE CITY BANK, Del.	Goddess of Liberty. THREE
5 Medal. Head Washington. 5	[Old Plate.] State Arms, ship in background. DELAWARE CITY BANK. Del. Dee Hive.	5 Canal Boat Train of cars in the distance. 5
5 Head of Female.	[New Plate.] DELAWARE CITY BANK. Del. State Arms; mill, &c., in background. Chicken.	5 Medal. Head J. M. Clayton
TEN Man and woman in a sitting posture; man with hammer in right hand, woman with sheaf of wheat. 10	Two female figures one has her left hand on a cogwheel; shipbuilding in background. DELAWARE CITY BANK, Del. Dee Hive.	10 Medal, Head Washington, 10
20 Medal. Head Washington. 20	Man Plowing. DELAWARE CITY BANK, Del. Dee Hive.	TWENTY Washington on horseback TWENTY
Male portrait.	ONE Female seated and figure 1. 1 FARMERS BANK OF DELAWARE. Three cupids reclining.	Female standing with sickle. ONE

Left	Centre	Right
1 Man dressing leather.	FARMERS' BANK OF THE STATE OF DELAWARE, Dover, Del. Three males and female, harvest scene; cars and house in distance.	1 Washing sheep; horses in distance.
2 Wood cutter,	Title of Bank. Deer and tree on shield; on right, sailor, ship in distance; farmer with scythe on left. Locomotive.	2 Female erect and another kneeling.
Male portrait	TWO Female with sickle, figure 2 and cupid. 2 FARMERS BANK OF DEL. Female seated and sheep.	Female standing with sickle. TWO
Male portrait	3 Three females, eagle, figure 3, &c. 3 FARMERS BANK OF DEL. Male reclining.	Female erect with scales. THREE
Male portrait	5 Drove of cattle, man on horse, &c. 5 FARMERS BANK OF DEL. Female erect.	Male portrait
Portrait of Franklin.	10 Two females, sheep, shield, &c. 10 FARMERS BANK OF DEL, Double med, head.	Portrait of Wm. Penn.
Portrait of Washington.	20 Two females reclining; ship on right. Two cupids, beehive, and figs. 20. FARMERS BANK OF DEL.	Male portrait
50 Sailor erect with American flag. 50	FARMERS BANK OF DEL. Four cupids with baskets, sheaf of wheat, sickle, &c.; house in background.	50 Med. head and figs. 50. 50.
100 Med. head and word Hundred. 100	FARMERS BANK OF DEL. View of the landing of Columbus; boats on right; Indians on left in background.	Female erect with shield and pole. 100
Interior of blacksmith's shop, with men at work; cottage in distance. 1	MECHANICS' BANK, Wilmington, Del. Portrait of Washington. Fire Engine.	1 1

Left	Centre	Right
2 Two dollars. 2	MECHANICS' BANK, Wilmington, Del. Three blacksmith's at work with their tools; anchor and boiler; on the left of vig. portrait of female; on right portrait of male.	2 TWO 2
5 Female portrait.	MECHANICS' BANK, Wilmington, Del. Ship yard with vessels on the stocks, and men at work; city and sloop in distance. V Eagle V	5 Female feeding chickens.
10 Blacksmith at forge.	Portrait of female. Sailor seated on anchor smoking pipe, and conversing with two other men. MECHANICS' BANK, Wilmington, Del. Cock.	10 10
20 Sailor leaning on capstan; bale, etc.; ship in distance.	Five men at work at a puddling furnace. MECHANICS' BANK, Wilmington, Del.	20 Figure of Justice.
50 Farmers at dinner in field.	Train of cars; city in distance. MECHANICS' BANK, Wilmington, Del. Steamboat.	50 Female portrait.
100 C	MECHANICS' BANK, Wilmington, Del. Female seated; factories in the distance; on right of vig. male portrait; on left female portrait.	100 C
1 Milkmaid and churn.	NEW CASTLE CO. BANK, Cantwell's Bridge, Del. Blacksmith's shop—two smiths shoeing horse, farmer with hand on horse's back; two men at anvil in background.	Female bathing. ONE
2 Bridge and train of cars; yacht in foreground.	Farmer ploughing with two horses; farm-house in distance. Title of Bank.	2 2
5	Title of Bank. Scene reaping—two men, negro and two horses; barn in distance. V	V 5
X TEN	10 Female between 1 and 0, with basket and plow at her feet; on right man plowing with two horses, farm house in distance; on left man plowing with two oxen. Title of Bank.	Female loosely dressed standing; shield. TEN

Left	Centre	Right
XX 20	Title of Bank. Female seated on log; train of cars; wheat; cattle and house in distance.	20 Sailor leaning on rail of ship.
Farmer feeding hogs; horses, etc. 1	REAL ESTATE BANK OF DELAWARE. ONE	1 Penn.
2 Female with sheaf and sickle. TWO Two on 2.	Title of Bank. Scene in iron foundry.	Female with flowers. 2 Dollars on 2 TWO
5	Man watering horses at trough; pigs, cattle, &c. Female portrait. Title of Bank. FIVE V FIVE	5 Jefferson.
10 TEN TEN	Title of Bank. Farmers nooning—four males, female and child. X each side.	10 TEN TEN
Steamboat. Female and and fig. 1. Cars.	1 Female Portrait. sheaf of wheat, &c. UNION BANK OF DELAWARE. Arm.	1
2 Farmer seated; dog, sheaf of wheat, &c.	UNION BANK OF DELAWARE.	Two females reclining; safe, &c.; steamboat on left. 2
5 Train of cars, house, &c.	UNION BANK OF DELAWARE.	Figure 5, and five cupids. 5
10 Train of cars. X	X Farmers at work in corn-field, X UNION BANK OF DELAWARE. Steamboat.	10 Sheaf of wheat, &c. X
Ship. 20	20 View of harbor and village. 20 UNION BANK OF DELAWARE. Pump.	Farmer erect, dog and pitchfork. 20

Left	Centre	Right
50 Male portrait 50	State Arms; steamship on right; cars and bridge on left. UNION BANK OF DELAWARE.	50 Male portrait 50
100 Female with pitcher and rake. 100	100 Spread eagle, shield &c. 100 UNION BANK OF DELAWARE. Female Portrait.	100 Portrait of Washington. 100
5 Med. head. V	Med. head with 5 on it. Sailor and farmer on either side of shield eagle at the top. Med. head with 5 on it. BK OF BALTIMORE, Baltimore, Md.	5 Med. head. V
10 Med. head. 10	Med. head with Ten on it. Same as fives. Med. head with Ten on it. BK OF BALTIMORE, Baltimore, Md.	10 Med head. 10
20 Portrait of Z. Taylor. 20	BANK OF BALTIMORE, Baltimore, Md, Head of Indian female.	Fame as vig. of fives. 20
50 Portrait of Webster. 50	Same as fives. BK OF BALTIMORE, Baltimore, Md.	50 Female with flag and shield
100 Male portrait 100	Same as fives. 100 BK OF BALTIMORE, Baltimore, Md.	ONE HUNDRED
FIVE HUNDRED	500 Med. head. Same as fives 500 Med. head. BK OF BALTIMORE, Baltimore, Md.	Female representing Agriculture. 500
Female erect with wand shield, pillar sustained head 1000	1000 Three females seated with grain, sickle, quadrant, &c.; ship in distance. BK OF BALTIMORE, Baltimore, Md. ONE THOUSAND	ONE THOUSAND
1 Girl's head ONE	Scene on dock; men rolling barrels, etc. B'K OF COMMERCE ONE DOLLAR Baltimore, Md.	1 Girl's head. ONE

Left	Centre	Right
5 Ship at sea.	Sailor seated and two standing; cannon, boxes, barrels, &c., on left; and a ship on right. B'K OF COMMERCE, Baltimore, Md.	5 Squaw seated with cap, pole and shield.
FIVE Three females over figure 5.	B'K OF COMMERCE, Baltimore, Md.	5 Female head
10 Female head X	Harvest scene; four men, etc. B'K OF COMMERCE, Baltimore, Md.	X Bailor.
10 Male portrait	Large vessel; steamship and another vessel in the distance. Title of bank running around vignette.	10 Portrait of a girl.
20 Mechanic reclining on a boiler; cogwheel; foundry in distance.	Large steamship; vessels in distance. B'K OF COMMERCE, Baltimore, Md. Female head.	20 Sailor seated; box, bales and barrels
Ship. 50	B'K OF COMMERCE, Baltimore, Md. 50 Portrait of Henry Clay. 50	FIFTY Female erect with sword and shield; fruit and flowers at her feet.
Blacksmith erect with hammer and anvil. 100	B'K OF COMMERCE, Baltimore, Md. C Portrait of Washington. C	100 Locomotive.
D Portrait of a girl.	B'K OF COMMERCE, Baltimore, Md. Three females representing Agriculture, Commerce and Manufactores.	500 Sailor with quadrant; steamship in distance.
View of a depot, buildings, factories, &c., cars dock, drays, steamboat, vessels, boxes, bales, men, &c. M	Male portrait B'K OF COMMERCE, Baltimore, Md.	1000 Vessel, houses, &c.
Indian with bow and arrow. FIVE	Fox chase. BANK OF WESTMINSTER, Md. Wagon.	5 Indian squaw.

Left	Centre	Right
10 10	Vig. Blacksmith shoeing a horse. 10 BANK OF WESTMINSTER, Md.	Female with wreath of flowers.
20 20	20 Vig. Female sitting on a rock, bag of coin, mile stone, 28 miles to B. 20 BANK OF WESTMINSTER, Md	Female head
50 50	50 Vig. Female with sickle in hand inclined on mile stone, marked 28 miles to B. 50 BANK OF WESTMINSTER, Md.	50
Female with sword. FIVE	5 Female with shield. 5 CECIL BANK. Port Deposit. Md. Raft and timber.	FIVE Female with horn of plenty. FIVE
TEN Justice. 10	10 Reapers. CECIL BANK, Port Deposit. Md. Raft and timber.	10 Female reclining.
Full length figure of an Indian drawing bow. 20	Vig. Two females, steamboat on the right and vessel on left of them. CECIL BANK. Port Deposit, Md. Raft and timber.	20 Head of Washington. TWENTY
Farmer erect in act of drinking from mug. 50	CECIL BANK, Port Deposit, Md Milkmaid erect holding stool in left hand; shading her eyes with right; hay beside; cows, etc.	50 Female head
Farmer drinking 50	Female erect with stool, etc. CECIL BANK, Port Deposit, Md.	50 Portrait of female
100 Farmer with scythe; village, etc.	Milkmaid with stool, cows, sheep, etc. Title of Bank. Steamer.	100 Female with flowers.
1 1	CENTRAL B'K OF FREDR'K, Frederick, Md. Female with pen and tablet, child at her feet with wreath. Old man with child, bust of Washington. ONE DOLLAR	1 ONE

5 — head of female.
CENTRAL BK OF FREDERIC, Md.
Vig. Female seated with pail, two cows, farm house and trees in the background.
5 — head of Webster.

10 — 10
CENTRAL BK OF FREDERIC, Md.
Vig. Female with sheaf of wheat in left hand, sickle in right; a cow and grain field in background. Medallions of Clay and Chief Justice Marshall on either side of vig.
10 — 10

20 — Medallion portrait.
Vig. Three nymphs swimming, supporting a winged cupid.
CENTRAL BANK OF FREDERIC, Md.
20 — Milkmaid, child, two cows.

50 — Medallion portrait of Pierce.
CENTRAL BANK OF FREDERICK, Md.
Vig. Cattle, stream of water; three sheep in background.
50 — Medallion portrait of Fillmore.

Am shield surmounted by eagle. — C
Vig. Medallion portrait of Washington.
CENTRAL BANK OF FREDERICK, Md.
100

1 — Figure of Justice with sword and scales.
Male and female in shell drawn by three sea-horses; two other figures in water.
CHESAPEAKE B'K
ONE DOLLAR
Baltimore, Md.
Steamship
1 — Sailor with spyglass, etc.

5 — Train of cars; bridge with cars passing over. — 5
V View of a harbor with shipping. V
CHESAPEAKE B'K
Baltimore, Md.
5 — Washington — 5

TEN — Jackson. — 10
CHESAPEAKE B'K, Baltimore, Md.
10 Female seated; Mercury approaching with cornucopia; spread eagle with scroll. 10
Eagle.
TEN — Van Buren — 10

20 — Jackson. — 20
20 Indian and Sailor on either side of a shield surmounted by an eagle; schooner on right. 20
CHESAPEAKE B'K., Baltimore, Md.
Ship.
20 — Van Buren. — 20

Female feeding an eagle. — 50
Male portrait 50 Male portrait
CHESAPEAKE B'K., Baltimore, Md.
[illegible]
Indian with bow and arrow. — 50

FIFTY — Blacksmith.
50 Vessel; others in distance.
CHESAPEAKE B'K, Baltimore, Md.
50 — Female portrait.

Male portrait — 100 — Male portrait
Female with torch seated on a globe; on her left eagle with Washington on its breast. Figures 100 on each side of the vig.
CHESAPEAKE B'K, Baltimore, Md.
Schooner.
Female with sea horses at her feet; cupid in the air. — 100

100 — Girl's head.
Title of Bank.
C Sailor reclining; anchor, boat, etc.; steamer in distance.
100

1 — Female reclining with sickle, grain etc. — 1
CITIZENS BANK of Baltimore, Md.
ONE DOLLAR
Train of cars.
1 — Indian seated. — 1

2
CITIZEN'S BANK of Baltimore
2 Sailor with bundle on shoulder 2
TWO DOLLARS
2

3 — Baltimore
CITIZEN'S BANK
3 Three children reading book in circular die 3
THREE DOLLARS
3

V — Female seated with rake in right hand, shield, etc. — V
5 Wharf scene—bales, barrels, boxes, &c., steamboat, shipping, &c. 5
CITIZENS' BANK, Baltimore, Md.
Clasped hands.
Female representing Agriculture; Vulcan with hammer and anvil; Mercury with a bag. — V

V — FIVE — 5
CITIZENS' BANK OF Baltimore, Md.
FIVE Female DOLLARS on V. portrait. on V.
V — FIVE — 5

Same as on upper right [illegible] of the [illegible] — [illegible]0
10 Same as fives. 10
CITIZENS' BANK, Baltimore, Md.
Clasped hands.
10 — Franklin seated with pen and book; book at his feet with motto on it. — 10

Same as on right of 5s. — 20
20 Ship at sea. 20
CITIZENS' BANK, Baltimore, Md.
Clasped hands.
20 — Female with scales; on right eagle on shield; [illegible]bble, bales, &c. — 20

Same as on right of 5s. — 50
50 Female seated; her left arm resting on a shield on which is a building.
CITIZENS' BANK, Baltimore, Md.
L — Female with torch; eagle with portrait of Washington on its breast.

C — Same as on right of 10s.
Vig. Same as 50s. 100
CITIZENS' BANK, Baltimore, Md.
Same as on right of 5s. — 100

Same as on right of 5s. — 500
D 500
CITIZENS' BANK, Baltimore, Md.
Clasped hands.
500

1000
1000 M
CITIZENS' BANK, Baltimore, Md.
Clasped hands.
Same as on right of 5s. — 1000

Farmer seated on fence, scythe in hand — ONE
Ships at sea
COM. & FAR. BANK of Baltimore, Md.
ONE DOLLAR
Baltimore
1 — Female portrait

5 — Schooner. — 5
Cars. Two females; wagon and four horses on right; building on left. Cars.
COMMERCIAL AND FARMERS' BANK, Baltimore, Md.
5 — Female with rake and pitcher. — 5

10 — Ship. — 10
X Sailor and farmer with hands clasped; landscape in distance. X
Title of Bank.
10 — Eagle on a shield. — 10

10
Horse, colt and cattle running away from cars.
COMMERCIAL AND FARMERS' BANK. Baltimore, Md.
Female seated with horn of plenty; anchor, etc.
10 — Male portrait

20 — Schooner. — 20
Med. head. Two females with shield between them with XX on it, and surmounted by an eagle. Med. head
Title of Bank.
20 — Agricultural implements. — 20

50 — Ship. — FIFTY
Med. head. Female seated with sickle; vessels on right; plow, bales, boxes, trees, etc., on left. Med. head
Title of Bank.
50 — Statue of female with sheaf and sickle.

Left	Centre	Right
100 Female seated with cornucopia, cap, money, wand and book. 100	Med. head. Shipping; sheafs on right; plow on left. Med. head. Title of Bank.	100 Female seated with chart. 100
500 Med. head. 500	Female seated on a bale surrounded by boxes, bales, &c., anchor and shipping. Title of Bank. Five Hundred Dollars	500 Justice.
1000 Female seated, bales, shipping, &c. 1000	Title of Bank. Three females representing Agriculture, Manufactures, and Commerce. ONE THOUSAND.	1000 Female seated with sickle. 1000
ONE Train of Cars. ONE	CUMBERLAND B'K. OF ALLEGHANY, Cumberland, Md. Head of female. 1 on ONE Head of child. ONE DOLLAR on ONE	1 ONE on 1
5 Female with horn of plenty. 5	A CUMBERLAND B'K. OF ALLEGHANY, Md. Vig. View of Cumberland with drover and cattle; road waggon in front; medallion head on each side	FIVE Female with horn of plenty. FIVE
5 Indian seated. 5	B Vig. Same as above CUMBERLAND B'K. OF ALLEGHANY, Md	5 Indian seated. 5
5 Drove of cattle 5	C Vig. Same as above CUMBERLAND B'K OF ALLEGHANY, Md.	FIVE Reaper lying down. FIVE
10 Drove of Cattle 10	Medallion of Franklin. Medallion of Franklin. CUMBERLAND B'K. OF ALLEGHANY, Md Vig. Blacksmith sitting on his anvil.	10 Waggon unloading near a market woman. 10
20 Female with horn of plenty.	Vig. Female seated with a sheaf of wheat, bridge in background and medallions on either side CUMBERLAND B'K OF ALLEGHANY, Md	20 Same as on other end.
50 Female seated, sheaf of wheat in her lap. L	Vig. Reaper, male and female, seated on a rock in the woods. Medallion on either side. CUMBERLAND B'K. OF ALLEGHANY, Md	L Female seated, sheaf of wheat in her lap. 50

Left	Centre	Right
1 Farmer leaning on fence caressing dog.	EASTON BANK OF Maryland, Easton, Md. 1 Boy and child under tree, cows, etc. 1 ONE DOLLAR on ONE	1 ONE on 1
5 Indian girl kneeling, sickle in right hand, female standing behind with bow and arrow.	EASTON BANK OF MARYLAND. FIVE on lathe strip, large medallion V on face of note. Anvil.	5 FIVVE 5
Large X on medallion shield. Hebe sitting on wheat, suckling eagle; ship in distance.	EASTON BANK OF MARYLAND. TEN on lathe strip; Large medallion X on face of note. Justice standing; barrels and ships behind.	10 X 10
20 Medallion head of Ariadne. XX	Vig. Representing Commerce, Agriculture, &c., with portrait of Franklin between. EASTON BANK OF MARYLAND.	TWENTY
50 Large ship, full sail; another ship in distance	Shield draped with American flag, females with girl and globe on right, Indian Squaw and child on left. EASTON BANK OF MARYLAND.	L 50 L
100 Farmers loading wagon with bundles of wheat, boy holding horse.	EASTON BANK OF MARYLAND. Spade, rake, sheaf of wheat, bee-hive and plow.	100 Portrait of Jenny Lind.
FIVE Two females with sickle, &c. FIVE	Drove of cattle and sheep; man sitting down on left. FARMERS' BANK OF MARYLAND.	FIVE 5 FIVE
Female erect, shield, sword, &c. TEN	10 Farmers at work in wheat-field. 10 FARMERS' BANK OF MARYLAND.	TEN Female with sickle and sheaf of wheat. TEN
1 ONE on 1	FAR. & MER. BANK 1 Group of sheep 1 ONE DOLLAR Elkton, Md.	1 ONE on
2 Two children	FAR. & MER. BANK Female pouring 2 water into trough; 2 sheep drinking, etc. TWO DOLLARS Elkton, Md.	2 Eagle on rock

Left	Centre	Right
20 Two children with grain	FAR. & MER. BANK Man, two horses, cattle, etc., in barn-yard Elkton, Md. TWENTY DOLLARS	20 Female with basket of fruit
Female with scales, portrait of Washington and anchor, ship masts are in distance.	5 Vig. Two females—one with helmet on her head, and the other a winged female with wand, ship on right. V FARMERS & MECHANICS BANK OF FREDERICK CO., Md.	FIVE
TEN Portrait of Washington. TEN	10 Vig. Female with sickle cornucopia, &c., clouds back of female. 10 FARMERS AND MECHANICS BANK OF FREDERICK CO., Md.	Male portrait.
Male portrait.	20 Vig. Drover and cattle, drover on horseback. 20 FARMERS AND MECHANICS BANK OF FREDERICK CO., Md	Male portrait.
Portrait of Lafayette.	50 Vig. Female, child, and another child stirring fire, yoke of oxen, plough, anvil, rake, &c. 50 FARMERS & MECHANICS BANK OF FREDERICK CO., Md.	Portrait of Washington.
Portrait of Washington.	100 Vig. Female seated on bales, barrels, sheaf of grain, cornucopia, rake, &c. two houses and a man in the distance on left. 100 FARMERS & MECHANICS BANK OF FREDERICK CO., Md.	Portrait of Jefferson.
5 Franklin. 5	Vig. Milkmaid seated. 5 FARMERS AND MECHANICS' BANK, of Carroll County, Westminister, Md. Horses and Waggon.	FIVE Female portrait. FIVE
FIVE	5 Female seated with boy leaning on her lap; man entering gate, and little girl running towards him; dog, fence, trees, etc. FARMERS' & MECHANIC'S BANK, Westminister, Md	5 Male portrait.
TEN Women drawing water from a well.	Vig. Man on horse; farmer harvesting. FARMERS' AND MECHANICS' BANK, of Carroll County, Westminister, Md.	X Washington. TEN
20 Washington. TWENTY	FARMERS AND MECHANICS' BANK, of Carroll County, Westminister, Md. Vig. Cattle, farmer plowing in distance.	Medallion head with figure 20 on it. Male portrait.

50 Two male portraits. FIFTY
Vig. Farmer plowing.
FARMERS' AND MECHANICS' BANK of Carroll County, Westminster, Md.
Spread eagle.
50 Ship.

ONE HUNDRED 100 Milkmaid with a pail
FARMERS' AND MECHANICS' BANK OF CARROLL CO. Westminster, Md.
100 Female ONE HUNDRED

---

5 Washington
Man watering three horses at trough; house in background. Female portrait
FAR. & MECH. BK. OF KENT CO., Chestertown, Md.
Beehive.
5 Cooper at work.

---

10 Female seated; X on a shield.
Man on horse; reaping scene etc., on right.
FAR. & MECH BANK OF KENT CO. Chestertown, Md.
Machinery.
10 Female portrait

---

20 Male portrait
Female seated leaning on a bale; vessels in distance.
FAR. & MECH. BANK of Kent Co, Md.
20 Franklin.

Goddess of Liberty. FIFTY
Title of Bank.
Female reclining in corn field; negro gathering corn.
50 FIFTY

---

100 Female with sickle and sheaf.
Female seated holding ear of corn; men, boats and village in distance.
Title of Bank.
100 Female portrait

---

5 Portrait of Girl. 5
FARMERS' & MERCHANTS' BANK, Baltimore, Md.
Vig.—Farming scene—farmer with sickle over his shoulder, female with grain under her arm; sailor with hands in his pocket; ship in distance on left.
Five and 5. Five and 5.
5 5 5

Steamboat. 5
5 Female representing Agriculture. 5
FARMERS' & MERCHANTS' BANK, Baltimore, Md.
Steamboat. 5

TEN Shearing sheep. TEN
10 Female seated; stages, etc. 10
Title of Bank.
TEN Ship. TEN

10
Title of Bank.
Vig. Same as fives. Letter X and words Ten Dollars.
TEN
10 Milkmaid; cow, calf, ducks, &c.

---

20 Female; steamship and buildings in distance.
Title of Bank.
TWENTY
20 Vig. same as fives.
20

---

20 Sheep. 20
20 Female spinning; houses bar; bar, etc. 20
Title of Bank.
20 Sail vessel. 20

FIFTY
Female representing Agriculture. Figs 50 on left, and 50 and L on the right of vig.
Title of Bank.
Die. FIFTY DOLLARS Die

Cherub. Female portrait.
50 Surveying scene.
Title of Bank.
FIFTY DOLLARS
50 Anchor, bales, bbls., &c.

100
Female reclining on bales; ship, cornucopia, etc Figs. 100 on either side.
Title of Bank.
ONE HUNDRED

---

100 Man with corn stalks.
Sailor boy. Sailors; one looking through telescope; one seated on broken mast; one resting his face on hand; ships in distance on right; man seen in distance on left.
Title of Bank.
ONE HUNDRED
100 Female feeding fowls.

500
Farmer loading hay on ox team. Girls portrait
Title of Bank.
500
500 Sailor boy; ship on right; sailors on left.

1000 Sailor leaning on capstan; ship in distance.
Farmer plowing; boy at horses head with branch; dog, basket, etc.
Title of Bank.
1000
1000 Maryland Girl's portrait.

---

1 Female portrait. ONE
Female seated, supporting shield, resting on cornucopia; steamboat, ship, etc., on left.
FAR. & PLANTERS' BANK
Baltimore, Md.
ONE DOLLAR
Head.
Large figure 1 enclosing full length female with sickle and grain.

FIVE
5 Female representing Agriculture with sheaf and sickle; cattle on left. 5
FARMERS' AND PLANTERS' BANK, Baltimore, Md.
Schooner.
Statue of Washington. FIVE

TEN
X Two men cradling; house in distance. X
Title of Bank.
Vessel.
Female with sheaf and sickle; reapers in distance. Drovers and cattle.

TWENTY
XX Female erect with bundle of grain, another seated with rake; shield with plow on it XX
Title of Bank.
Schooner.
Mowers mowing; house in distance. Man ploughing with two horses.

FIFTY
50 Same as tens. 50
Title of Bank.
Schooner.
Man ploughing with two horses. Men farming with two horses; distant houses.

ONE HUNDRED
100 Same as fives. 100
Title of Bank.
Schooner.
Man gathering corn. 100

500
500 Same as 50s. 500
Title of Bank.
Schooner
Milkmaid churning in dairy.

1000
Two females soaring with wand, bag, grain and sickle; figures 1000 each side.
Title of Bank.
Schooner.
Female erect with scroll. 1000

---

1 ONE or 1
Launching a vessel, city steamboats, &c.
FELLS POINT BANK, Baltimore, Md.
Printed in green tint.
1 Dog and safe.

---

5 Clay.
FELLS POINT SAVINGS INSTITUTION of Baltimore, Md.
Two sailors, one seated on merchandise, the other smoking a pipe; coil of rope, anchor, trumpet, bbls., bales, sails, etc.; steamship, schooner and brig in distance.
5 Washington

Female with flowers. TEN
10 Large steamship at sea; ship in the distance.
Title of Bank.
TEN

20
Thomas Jefferson
Indian and two females beside American shield
FELL'S POINT B'K
TWENTY DOLLARS
Baltimore, Md.
20
Female portrait

20
Ship under full sail.
Three men with plans on a table; ship yard scene, man and two horses; on right steamship.
Title of Bank.
20
Female seated representing Commerce.

Ship and other vessels at sea
50
FELL'S POINT B'K
FIFTY DOLLARS
Baltimore, Md.
Female portrait
50
Eagle on shield

50
Webster.
Three vessels; lighthouse on right in distance.
Title of Bank.
FIFTY
Sailor with telescope, leaning on capstan.
FIFTY

100
Child with hen and and chickens in her arms.
View of the Capitol at Washington.
Title of Bank.
100
Sailor with telescope seated on a bale; capstan vessel, etc.

5
Franklin.
FIVE
Shield with figure of Justice on it; on left Indian, squaw and papoose; on right female instructing children with globe.
FRANKLIN BANK,
Baltimore, Md.
Head of female.
5
Milkmaid.

TEN
Franklin.
TEN
X Milkmaid seated; cattle, etc.
FRANKLIN BANK,
Baltimore, Md.
TEN

20 20
Ship.
20 20
Female with quadrant, chart, globe, compass, &c., fruit at her feet; man in the water. Franklin on either side of vig.
FRANKLIN BANK,
Baltimore, Md.
Steamboat
20
Ship.
20

XX
20
FRANKLIN BANK,
Baltimore, Md.
Portrait of Franklin; on right sailor; farmer on left.
20
20

50
50
Ship. Franklin. Ship.
FRANKLIN BANK,
Baltimore, Md.
Man reclining.
50
50

50
Franklin.
FRANKLIN BANK,
Baltimore, Md.
Figure 50 and words Fifty Dollars on three large red dies.
50
Female feeding fowls.

100
Franklin.
100
Female representing Agriculture; farmers mowing in distance. Eagle on either side of vig.
FRANKLIN BANK,
Baltimore, Md.
Dog, key and safe.
100
Franklin.
100

100
Female with flowers in apron.
FRANKLIN BANK,
Baltimore, Md.
Portrait of Franklin.
ONE HUNDRED
100
Female seated; two men, cog wheel, buildings, etc.

Female seated representing Manufactures.
500
500 Franklin. 500
FRANKLIN BANK,
Baltimore, Md.
Justice.
Female seated with scroll; bridge and wagon in distance.
500

Three females grouped, one in centre has helmet; grain on the ground.
1000
1000 Franklin 1000
FRANKLIN BANK,
Baltimore, Md.
Justice.
Same as on left.
1000

5
Portrait of Washington.
5
Head of Clay. Vig. Female resting on anchor; harbor and shipping. Head of Cass.
FREDERICK CO. BK.
Frederick, Md.
Bee-hive.
5
3 Females supporting globe.
FIVE

10
Dog.
10
Train of cars. X Large heads of ten of the Presidents. Farmers with loading hay.
FREDERICK CO. BK.
Frederick, Md.
10
TEN
10

XX
20
Vig. Female with sword and balances; farmer ploughing, &c.
FREDERICK CO. BK.
Frederick, Md.
MARYLAND

Franklin.
50 50
Vig. Female on either side of 50; sheep; spinning wheel; ship in distance, &c.
FREDERICK CO. BK.
Frederick, Md.
Female and sheep.
Washington

Male head.
Full length figure with spear and shield.
100 100
Vig. Female sitting on plough; child; agricultural implements; oxen, &c.
FREDERICK CO. BK.
Frederick, Md.
Spread Eagle.
Washington.

ONE on 1
1 on ONE
ONE DOLLAR
Two females with sickle, and basket of flowers
Large 1 on ONE
Female with basket of flowers
FREDERICKTOWN SAVINGS INSTITUTION
Maryland
ONE on 1
1 on ONE

Portrait of Franklin.
TEN'S
FREDERICK TOWN SAVING INSTITUTION, Md.
Vig. harvest scene, harvesting wheat, &c.
Justice with scales.

20
Boy and rabbits.
Female, cows and sheep.
FREDERICKTOWN SAV. INSTITUTION,
Frederick, Md.
Man seated on plow.
20
Female.

ONE on 1
On
1 Cattle, milkmaid, etc.
FROSTBURG BANK
ONE DOLLAR
Frostburg, Md.
1
Eagle on rock

Figure of Justice.
FIVE
Train of cars, and two men; steamboat and hills in distance; figure 5 on left of vig.
FROSTBURG BANK.
Frostburg, Md.
Mechanical Implements.
5
Die.
5

10
Two girls with sheafs of grain.
X Spread eagle. X
Title of Bank.
Two horses.
10
Indian on cliff.

Female.
XX
Men harvesting; farm scene. Figs. 20 on either side of vig
Title of Bank.
Female.
20

1
Two females.
1
1 Banking House. 1
HAGERSTOWN B'K
ONE DOLLAR
Hagerstown, Md.
Eagle
Four Cupids raising column upon pedestal, on which is the word
ONE

5
5 on Die.
5
5 Vig. Two female 5 soaring in the clouds, one with rake, sickle, spade and pitchfork.
HAGERSTOWN B'K.
Hagerstown, Md.
5
5 on Die.
5

X
Ten on medallion head.
10
10 on die. Boys bearing flowers on pole, another with sickle. 10 on die.
HAGERSTOWN B'K.
Hagerstown, Md.
Female with sickle and sheaf of wheat.
X

Left	Centre	Right
20 Female with babe in her arms. 20	Medallion head. Vig. Two females, ships in distance on right. Medallion head. HAGERSTOWN B'K, Hagerstown, Md.	20 Man and cattle. 20
50 Portrait of Washington. 50	Medallion head. Vig. Boy in boat, with cupid soaring over him; another boy in the act of digging. Medallion head. HAGERSTOWN B'K, Hagerstown, Md.	50 Female with rake and sheaf of wheat. 50
100 Female with sickle and sheaf of wheat. 100	100 on medallion head. Vig. Female with liberty pole and cap, eagle, and shield; vessels in distance on either side. 100 on medallion head. HAGERSTOWN BK, Hagerstown, Md.	100 Male with tablet. 100
ONE on 1. Two children.	HAGERSTOWN SAVINGS BANK, Hagerstown, Md. 1 Boy whittling under a tree child reclining, cows, sheep, &c. 1 ONE DOLLAR on ONE	1 Girl seated, with flowers and fruit at her foot.
2 Man, two horses drinking at trough. Female with pails. Poultry, farmhouse, &c. 2	Female head. HAGERSTOWN SAVINGS BANK. Hagerstown, Md TWO DOLLARS on TWO	TWO Man with armful of corn.
5 Two females on either side of bee' ive in dark relievo.	HAGERSTOWN SAVINGS BANK, Hagerstown, Md. Large V, on which is Five Dollars on lathe strip.	5, V & FIVE. Bust of Blacksmith.
X Washington	American shield; on right is female instructing children; on left is Indian, squaw and papoose. Title of Bank.	10 Female reaper.
20 XX	Title of Bank. Cows; men mowing and house on right; man plowing on left. XX	20 Woodcutter.
5 Male portrait FIVE	Male portrait; female on left with pole and cap; on right two females reclining. HOWARD BANK, Baltimore, Md. Spread eagle.	F I V E Milkmaid and pail; house on the right.
10 Clay. 10	Female on either side of portrait of Washington; ships, farmers, etc. HOWARD BANK, Baltimore, Md. Locomotive.	X Med head and word Ten.

Left	Centre	Right
20 J. Q. Adams. TWENTY	Steamship, vessel, fort, etc.; city in distance. HOWARD BANK, Baltimore, Md. Anvil.	20 Portrait of a Sailor.
50 Franklin.	Female seated: safe, money bags, etc.; on her right shield with view of Monument; sheep, grain, fruit, etc. HOWARD BANK, Baltimore, Md. Ship.	50 Interior of blacksmith's shop; smith resting.
100 Female leaning on a railing.	[illegible] harbor; on right schooner with letter C on the sail; city in distance. HOWARD BANK, Baltimore, Md. Shells.	100 Jackson.
1 Medallion head. 1	ONE on Med. head. Three women; ships in distance, &c. ONE on Med. head MARINE BANK, Baltimore, Md.	ONE Man reclining; basket, rake, sheaf of wheat, &c. ONE
2 Medallion head. 2	Baltimore, Maryland. Female; eagle on shield, &c. MARINE BANK OF BALTIMORE. TWO DOLLARS.	2 Girl with sheaf of wheat. 2
2 Female head. 2	TWO on Med. head. Female seated on rock; eagle on right; ships in distance. TWO on Med. head. MARINE BANK. Baltimore, Md.	2 Female with rake. 2
5 Girl's portrait.	MARINE BANK, Baltimore, Md. Ships, &c.	5 Sailor raising sail.
Die Work. Male portrait Die Work.	5 Ornamental figure 5 and two females with trident and figure 5; cupid, scales and eagle. 5 MARINE BANK, Baltimore, Md. Sword and scales.	Justice; part of column, shield, anchor, &c. FIVE
10 Sailor reclining on capstan.	MARINE BANK, Baltimore, Md. X Large Ship eagle. Ship X	10 Female; bale, &c.; ship in distance.
10 Sailor with flag; bales, shipping, &c. 10	X on med. head. Neptune in a shell with trident; ship on right. X on med. head. MARINE BANK, Baltimore, Md.	X Ship under full sail. X

Left	Centre	Right
Female portrait. TWENTY	MARINE BANK, Baltimore, Md. 2 XX 0 Arctic explorers' boat, dogs, &c.	20
20 Med head. 20	Med. head. Sailor with flag; warehouses, bales, boxes, shipping, dock, &c. Med. head. MARINE BANK, Baltimore, Md.	XX Med. head. XX
50 Figure of vessels	MARINE BANK, Baltimore, Md. Hope; in distance. Female portrait. 50	50 Anchor with bales of goods.
50 Med. head 50 Med. head	50 Female seated with anchor; 50 shipping in distance. MARINE BANK, Baltimore, Md. Dog, and safe.	50 Med. Head with 50 on it FIFTY
C C	Ship building. MARINE B'K, Baltimore. Sailor with Am. flag. C seated on bale; &c. ONE HUNDRED.	100 Maryland. Eagle. 10[illegible]
Med. head with 100 on it. Male portrait. Med. head with 100 on it.	Med. head with 100 on it. Female with wand representing Commerce seated on bales, shipping on left. Med head with 100 on it. MARINE BANK, Baltimore, Md. Two cherubs in a boat.	Full length portrait of Lafayette.
FIVE Blacksmith with implements. 5	5 Washington penning his Farewell Address. 5 MECHANICS' BANK, Baltimore, Md. Justice.	FIVE Ship at sea. 5
Letter X between two females.	10 Ship carpenter at work; ship on way in background. MECHANICS' BANK, Baltimore, Md.	TEN Ship under full sail. TEN
Ornamental scroll work. Stone cutter seated with tools. Ornamental scroll work	20 Archimedes raising the world with lever; cars on right; steamb[illegible] MECHANICS' BANK, Baltimore, [illegible]	20 Female with sword and scales. [illegible]
FIFTY	50 Steamboat on the water; men in a small boat in foreground; sloop on the right in background. 50 MECHANICS' BANK, Baltimore, Md. FIFTY	50 Head of Indian 50

50 — FIFTY — Steamer, city, etc. — MECHANICS' BANK OF BALTIMORE, Md. — 50 Indian head. 50 — 50 — FIFTY

Indian head — 100 — Title of Bank. — Cars, factory, cow and dog. — C Wheels. C — 100 — 100

100 — Landscape, arched bridge in background. — 100 — Old fashioned train of cars; rocks, trees, &c. — MECHANICS' BANK, Baltimore, Md. — 100 — Train of cars crossing an arched bridge. — 100

500 — Cut through a rock with rail track. — 500 — Male figure seated with pole, machinery; ship in distance on left. Figs. 500 on either side. — MECHANICS' BANK, Baltimore, Md. — Head of Indian. — View of a monument.

1000 — Statue of Washington — Female seated her left arm resting on a large cog-wheel; on her left base and part of a column — MECHANICS' BANK, Baltimore, Md. — Spread eagle. — 1000 — Car track, rocks, trees, &c. — 1000

1 — Female portrait — ONE — Ships steam-boats, etc. 1 — MERCHANTS BANK Baltimore, Md. — ONE DOLLAR — Female erect with wheat and sickle. — ONE

V — Shipping, harbor, city in distance. — V — 5 Female seated with key in her hand; Phoenix upon a safe; Mercury approaching with cornucopia of money; coin at side of female. 5 — MERCHANTS' BANK Baltimore, Md. — FIVE — Schooner. — FIVE

FIVE across and fig. 5 on it. — V Female reclining, anchor, bales, cornucopia, etc. 5 — MERCHANTS' BANK of Baltimore, Md. — FIVE DOLLARS across and V on it.

Sailor barrel, shield, etc. — 10 and X Same as 5s. — Title of Bank — 10&X — Weighing cotton bales.

10 — Female seated with wand anchor on shield beside her. — 10 — X Vig. Same as fives. X — MERCHANTS' BANK Baltimore, Md. — 10 — Female seated with a torch; eagle with portrait of Washington on his breast. — 10

TWENTY DOLLARS — 20 — Justice seated. — Same as 5s. — Title of Bank. — 20

20 — Female with scales; eagle on shield; bbls., bales, &c. — 20 — XX Vig. Same as fives. XX — MERCHANTS' BANK Baltimore, Md. — 20 — Schooner. — 20

FIFTY DOLLARS — 50 — 50 — Title of Bank. — Same as 5s. — 50

50 — Cupid on one knee looking at scroll with the words, "Capital $2,000,000." — 50 — L Vig. Same as fives. L — MERCHANTS' BANK Baltimore, Md. — 50

100 — Sailor on bale and female with cornucopia. — Title of Bank. — Same as 5s. — C — 100

100 — C Vig. Same as fives. C — MERCHANTS' BANK Baltimore, Md. — ONE HUNDRED — 100

500 — 500 Vig. Same as fives. 500 — MERCHANTS' BANK Baltimore, Md. — FIVE HUNDRED — 500

$500 — Same as 5s. — Title of Bank. — D — 500

ONE THOUSAND — 1000 — $1,000 — Title of Bank. — M Same as 5s. — STATE OF MARYLAND

1000 — 1000 Vig. Same as fives. 1000 — MERCHANTS' BANK Baltimore, Md. — ONE THOUSAND — 1000

5 — Male portrait — Five on 5 — PEOPLES' BANK, Baltimore, Md. — Train of cars; canal scene, city, and general view of country in background. — 5 — Cupid with cornucopia. — FIVE on 5.

10 — Vessels at sea. Female portrait. — Title of Bank. — Eagle. — 10 — TEN on large X; milk-maid, cow, etc.

20 — Female seated with spear and shield. — Cattle; horse looking over fence. — Title of Bank. — Man and sheaf — 20 — Blacksmith beside anvil.

50 — Mechanic holding a lifter. — Sailor, female and blacksmith seated; city, bridge, vessels, etc., in distance. — Title of Bank. — Schooner — 50 — Washington.

100 — Franklin. — 100 on Dollars — Male and female at well; barn, load of hay, etc. — Title of Bank. — Eagle in clouds. — 100 — 100 on Dollar

ONE on 1 — Beehive — ONE — Maryland — Female seated on ground beside sheep, etc. — SOMERSET & WORCESTER SAVINGS BANK — 1 ONE DOLLAR 1 — Salisbury — ONE DOLLAR — ONE on 1 — Boy with bird's nest

2 — Man with dog beside fence — Maryland — SOMERSET & WORCESTER SAVINGS BANK — Woman milking; farmhouse and farmer with ladder in distance — TWO DOLLARS — 2 — 2 — Girls with dog

Female head — Maryland — 3 — THREE 3 — Scene near blacksmith's shop: girl with grain, etc. — SOMERSET & WORCESTER SAVINGS BANK — THREE DOLLARS — 3 — Female with roses

5 — Two females with grain and sickle — SOMERSET & WORCESTER SAVINGS BANK — V Cow and calf in stream; ship in distance V — FIVE DOLLARS — Maryland — 5 — Cooper at work

ONE — Female seated with wand and quadrant; anvil, etc. — ONE — 1 Child playing with dog; safe, etc. in the background. — UNION B'K — ONE DOLLAR — Baltimore, Md. — Female head — 1

MARYLAND.

5 | 5 Male seated at a table, with pens and chart on it; column in back. 5 | 5
Milkmaid with pail on her head, and stool in hand. | Reaper with sickle.
UNION BANK OF MARYLAND, Baltimore, Md.
5 | Cars. | 5

10 | Title of Bank. Female on either side of a Male portrait in a frame.
Washington
Title of Bank.
10 | Vessel. | 10

Portrait of Washington with female seated on either side. Title of Bank. | 20
Male portrait
20 | Steamship. | 20

50 | Female seated with pen and chart; Mercury flying toward her with wand and bag of coin; Neptune with sea horses on right, ship on right. | 50
Female erect with sword and scales. | Male portrait
Title of Bank.
50 | 50

Die Work. | 100 Title of Bank. | ONE HUNDRED
Male portrait | Female holding scales, with shield beside her. Words one hundred on the left, and on right word dollars.
Die Work.

500 | Spread eagle holding in his beak a shield, with 500 on it. | 500
Med. head. | Med. head.
Title of Bank.
500 | 500

1000 1000 | Three figures representing Agriculture, Manufactures and Commerce. | 1000 1000
Med. head. | Med. head.
Title of Bank.

5 | Train Vig. Female Canal boat: cars, plough, with and sickle, &c., coupling scene on her right hand; mill scene on her left. | 5
Spread eagle on shield. | Bust of Washington.
WASHINGTON CO. BANK, Williamsport, Md.
5 | 5

TEN | 10 Bust of Washington surmounted by an eagle, female on either side. 10 | TEN
Justice with sword and scales, scroll with inscription under figure. | Female and dog.
WASHINGTON CO. BANK, Williamsport, Md.
TEN

Two females with American flag furled between. | 20 Vig. Washington on horse with staff; artillery, river, &c. in distance. 20 | Blacksmith and forge
WASHINGTON CO. BANK, Williamsport, Md.
Locomotive and cars.

DIST. COL.

FIFTY | 50 Vig. Female sitting at table, reading the "Farewell Address;" large mill, water, &c. in the distance. 50 | Full length portrait of Washington in citizens dress.
WASHINGTON CO. BANK. Williamsport.

5 | 5 Mercury seated with globe, wand, cornucopia, &c.; safe, scales, lion, etc. 5 | Washington in a large fig. 5.
Med head.
WESTERN BANK, Baltimore, Md.
5 | Dog's head.

Male and female reapers, dog, etc. | X Vig. Same as fives. X
Med. head.
WESTERN BANK, Baltimore, Md.
TEN | Dog's head. | 10

Winged head surrounded by flags, anchor, etc.; eagle at top. | 20 Farmers mowing; female with raking sheafs, etc.
XX
Head of Vulcan with hammer.
WESTERN BANK, Baltimore, Md.
Dog's head. | 20

50 | WESTERN BANK, Baltimore, Md. | 50
Canal scene. | L Village with men, teams, cattle, &c. L | Female representing Commerce.
FIFTY | Sheafs. | FIFTY

100 | WESTERN BANK, Baltimore, Md. | 100
Sloop; city in distance. | C Female seated; eagle on right, with medal in his beak; bbls., bales, boxes, etc. C | Female seated representing Art, carrying a male bust.
100 | 100 | 100

500 | Cupid. 500 Cupid. | 500
WESTERN BANK, Baltimore, Md.
Ship.

1 | Large spread eagle on shield. | 1
B'K OF COMMERCE, Georgetown, D. C.
Abraham Lincoln. | ONE DOLLAR. | Female portrait.

Figure of Liberty leaning on column, on which is the word "TWO." | 2 in ornamental die. Portrait of General Scott. | 2 in ornamental die.
B'K OF COMMERCE, Georgetown, D. C.
TWO DOLLARS.

FIVE | B'K OF COMMERCE, Georgetown, D. C. | 5
Female | Portrait of Washington, surmounted by spread eagle; female on either side; sickle, cornucopia and anchor. | Liberty resting on coat of arms of U. S.; spread eagle.
FIVE | Female

DIST. COL.

X | B'K OF COMMERCE, Georgetown, D. C. | 10
Cars crossing viaduct in the distance and a sloop in foreground.
Same as 5's.
TEN | Female

20 | B'K OF COMMERCE, Georgetown, D. C. | 20
Canal boat passing under a bridge.
Same as 5's.
TWENTY | Female.

50 | B'K OF COMMERCE, Georgetown, D. C. | 50
Same as 5's
Female Figure. | Female and anchor. | Shipping, city in the distance.
FIFTY

100 | B'K OF COMMERCE, Georgetown, D. C. | 100
Female with sheaf of wheat.
Same as 5's.
100 | Female and anchor. | Large ship sails spread

V | 5 U. S. Capitol. 5 | U
Female—Goddess of Liberty. | BANK OF THE METROPOLIS, Washington, D. C. | Eagle.
V | S

X | 10 U. S. Capitol. 10 | U
Female—Goddess of Liberty. | BANK OF THE METROPOLIS, Washington, D. C. | Eagle.
X | S

The 20s are the same as 10s all through, with the exception of the denomination.

L | 50 U. S. Capitol. 50 | U
Goddess of Liberty. | BANK OF THE METROPOLIS, Washington, D. C. | Eagle.
L | S

Letter C. | 100 U. S. Capitol. 100 | U
Goddess of Liberty. | BANK OF THE METROPOLIS, Washington, D. C. | Eagle.
Letter C. | S

FIVE | B'K OF W'SHINGTON, Washington, D. C. | Ship under sail.
Med. head of Washington. | Two female figures, one standing and one sitting, both leaning on figure 5.
FIVE | 5

Female standing, in her right a sword and her left hand resting on a shield.
10 Head of Washington 10 surrounded by flags and trophies; quadrant, &c.
BK OF W'SHINGTON
Washington, D. C.
X TEN 10

XX Head of Washington. XX
20 Two females one seated, and one kneeling; ship and steamboat in background.
BK OF W'SHINGTON
Washington, D. C.
20 Female leaning on gate with pails.

FIFTY Head of Washington. FIFTY
50 Farmer seated on plough, lighting a pipe, cattle in the background.
BK OF W'SHINGTON
Washington, D. C.
50 Female seated with pole and cap.

100 Female seated with cornucopia and wheat. HUNDRED
Head of Washington supported on right by sailor with anchor, and on left by figures representing agriculture and mechanics.
BK OF W'SHINGTON
Washington. D. C.
HUNDRED A representation of Washington monument.

5 Portrait of Washington 5
Farmer seated sharpening his scythe, another farmer erect on right, basket on left.
FARMERS' & MECH. BANK,
Georgetown, D. C.
Eagle.
5 Female seated. V

10 Portrait of Washington
Canal and boat. Female seated, holding bucket, two others in background and one is milking; house in distance on right; two ships on left.
Title of Bank.
10 Blacksmith at work.

20 Female erect with basket. 20
Portrait of Washington. Female shield, eagle horn of plenty, liberty pole and cap.
Title of Bank.
Plow, sheaf of grain, &c.
20 Two blacksmiths in shop. 20

50 Portrait of Washington. 50
Female in the air with a horn; globe and eagle, American colors on left. Ship on the stocks.
Title of Bank.
Wheel, &c.
50 Farmer standing, another in background plowing.

100 Milkmaid. 100
Washington Male figure supporting the globe on lever.
FAR. & MECH. BK.
of Georgetown, D. C.
100

[illegible] boy, with a flag; [illegible] usher, &c., in background.
[F]IVE
5 Female seated, resting her right elbow on the Coat-of-Arms of the U. S.
PATRIOTIC BANK,
Washington, D. C.
5 Female sitting.

10 Washington standing by his horse
Vig. Same as Five's.
PATRIOTIC BANK.
Washington, D. C.
10 Female; scales in her left hand, &c

Female with a sickle in her right hand. TWENTY
20 Vig. same as 5's.
PATRIOTIC BANK.
Washington, D. C.
20 Female figure, with U. S., flag in her right hand; staff resting on the ground; shield, &c., in her left.

50 Female holding scales; eagle under the scales. 50
Vig. Same as the 5's. 50
PATRIOTIC BANK.
Washington, D. C.
Female figure. 50

100 Female figure sitting, holding scales in her left hand; a sword in her left.
Female figure sitting, resting her right elbow on the Coat of Arms of the U. S.
PATRIOTIC BANK.
Washington. D. C.
100 Figure of a man with scythe, &c., buildings in background.

State arms—Justice trampling upon the neck of a tyrant. 5
B'K OF WHEELING.
Wheeling, Va.
Vig. Large letter V and the word FIVE.
5 Medallion Head.

10 State arms—Justice trampling upon the neck of a tyrant.
B'K OF WHEELING.
Wheeling, Va.
Large letter X and words TEN DOLLARS.
Female—Justice and Commerce.
10 Locomotive and cars. 10

ONE on 1. 1 1
FAIRMONT B'K,
Fairmont, Va
Woman feeding horse, poultry, &c.
ONE DOLLAR
on ONE
Train of cars.
1 Hunters making fire Horse, dogs and game. 1

2
Female reclining on grain straw hat beside her, mowing machine in distance.
FAIRMONT B'K, Fairmont, Va.
Sheep. Two females with grain. Fowls.
TWO on 2
2 TWO DOLLARS.
TWO
2

V Dog's head. V
Man on horseback, driving cow and sheep; boy holding gate open; cattle, trees, &c. in distance; at right of vig. Trea's sig.
FAIRMONT BANK,
Fairmont, Va.
5 Men loading wagon with hay.

X Train of cars coming down grade, house in background, two males in foreground.
Indian crouching behind rock with gun, watching two deers. Trea's sig.
FAIRMONT BANK,
Fairmont. Va.
TEN Dog's head.

5 Male portrait. FIVE
MANUFACTURERS' AND FARMERS' BK.
Wheeling, Va.
Vig. Interior of a glass work establishment; hands at work.
5 Female treading the neck of a tyrant. 5

X TEN
MANUFACTURERS' AND FARMERS' BK.
Wheeling, Va.
Vig. Group of seven persons; three males and four females; commerce, agriculture, &c.; harbor and lighthouse in distance
10 State arms.

5 5
MER & MEC. BANK
of Wheeling, Va.
Man and three horses at wall; goats, kids, etc.
5 Female head.

Cars on bridge; cattle, stream, etc.
Merchants' and Mechanics' B'k
Wheeling, Va.
5

V Male portrait. 5
FIVE Vig. Large FIVE wagon and horses, steamboat, houses, &c.
MERCHANTS' AND MECHANICS' BANK.
Wheeling, Va.
5 Male portrait. V

5 Bull's head.
Female seated with two calves; canal and railroad scene on left.
Title of Bank.
5 Female with flowers.

5
Red tinted V and 5 blended with sailor seated with glass, bales, bbls, etc.; ship in distance on left, and female with cog-wheel, bals, etc. on right, and Mer. and Mech. Bank above and below either vignette.
Dog's head.
5 Girl's portrait.

5 Bust of Washington. V
Medallion head and figure 5. Medallion head and figure 5.
Vig. Harvest scene; bundles of grain; urchin sleeping.
Title of Bank.
5 Male portrait. V

5 Male portrait. 5
Female portrait. Vig. Dog and safe. Female portrait.
Title of Bank.
5 Male portrait. 5

Red TEN inverted. Red TEN inverted.
Title of Bank.
Cattle and sheep on bank; cow in stream.
Male portrait X
Eagle.
TEN to right of fig. 10. Jefferson.

Female, cows, sheep, ducks, etc. 10 TEN
Title of Bank.
X Red TEN Red TEN Hunter lead leg gun; deer at his feet.

Red 10. MERCHANTS' AND MECHANICS' BK., Wheeling, Va. Red 10.
Sailor with quadrant; vessels. TEN on red X. Wash-ington. TEN on red X. Wheelwr'gt at work.

X TEN Vig. Mechanic reclining on an anvil; house in background. TEN 10
Portrait of Washington. Male portrait.
10 Title of Bank. X

Washingt'n Female portrait. 10
MERCH & MECHS BK Wheeling, Va.
X Basket of corn. Cattle, tree, etc.

Female head. Eagle and shield 20
MERCH & MECHS BK Wheeling, Va.
20 Head of horse.

50 Med. head. Vig. male figure in standing position. Med. head 50
Medallion head. Medallion head.
50 Title of Bank. 50

100 Med. head. Vig. Harvest scene, houses and shrubbery in background. Med. head. 100
Cattle shrubbery, &c. Cattle.
100 Title of Bank. 100

FIVE on med. head. NORTH-WESTERN BANK, Wheeling, Va. 5
View of Suspension bridge; steamboats and houses.
Male portrait. Male portrait.

Med. head and word five. Indian and female reclining on either side escutcheon or arms of the State of Virginia. 5
Locomotive and tender.
Title of Bank.
FIVE Female bathing. Med. head.

5 NORTH-WESTERN BANK of Virginia. 5
Female, bale, bbls.; factories, vessels, etc., in distance. Youthful portrait with cap. Mechanic seated, wheel, hammer, etc.; two farmers, houses, etc. in distance.

5 Washington V Three females seated; ship in distance. 5 on reel. head on either side of vig. NORTH-WESTERN BANK, Wheeling, Va. FIVE

Male portrait FIVE NORTH-WESTERN BANK, Wheeling, Va. 5
Suspension bridge.
Male portrait. Locomotive. Med. head.

TEN Title of Bank. 10
Male and female and two children, one holding a sheep, &c. Large die containing the word ten, figures 10, and letter X. Female with sickle. 10

X Title of Bank. 10
Scene in blacksmith's shop.
Female portrait. Female with dove
10 10

X NORTH-WESTERN BANK OF VIRGINIA 10
Female portrait. Female portrait.
10 Three blacksmiths at work by anvil. 10

TEN Title of Bank. 10
Male and female and two children, one holding a sheep. Large die containing word ten, figures 10, and letter X. Female with sickle in hand.
10

X Med. head and word Ten. Female reclining, and representing Agriculture. Med. head and word Ten.
Med. head and word ten thereon. Word Ten in ornamental italics.
10 Title of Bank.

TEN Med. head and word ten. Indian seated and gazing on vacancy. Med. head and word ten. TEN
Female erect holding sword and sickle.
10 Title of Bank.

20 Med. head. Instructor and pupil. Med. head. 20
Portrait of Washington. Med. head.
20 Title of Bank. 20

Med. head. 50 Group of three females representing Agriculture, Commerce, &c. 50 Med. head.
50 50
Med. head. Title of Bank. Steamboat. Med. head.

5 Spread eagle. 5
Compt's die. BK OF AMERICA, New Orleans, La.
FIVE Half of Globe. Men shearing sheep.

10 Spread eagle. 10
Title of Bank.
TEN
Compt's die Half of Globe. Cars passing over and cattle under arch.

TWENTY Spread eagle. TWENTY
20 Title of Bank. 20
Compt's die.
TWENTY Half of Globe. Two females.

Cattle. Title of Bank. Train of cars
50 Spread eagle. 50
Compt's die. Half of Globe. Female on stocks.

100 Title of Bank. 100
Spread eagle.
Compt's die.
Boy and girl with grapes. Half of Globe. 100

FIVE 5 Large figure 5, two females, cupid, eagle, etc. 5 FIVE
BK. OF LOUISIANA New Orleans, La.

TEN Female erect leaning on shield; ship in distance; 10 either side. TEN
BK. OF LOUISIANA, New Orleans, La.

Steamboat. 10 Two females with pole, cap and shield; portrait of Washington, bales, bbls., and ship on right; sheaf of grain, &c., on left. 10
10 BK OF LOUISIANA, New Orleans, La.
Steamship Bank building. Indian female with ear of corn and letter X

TWENTY Man on horseback, going at full speed; 20 on either side. TWENTY
BK. OF LOUISIANA, New Orleans, La.

FIFTY Female reclining by a grove; 50 on either side. FIFTY
BK. OF LOUISIANA, New Orleans, La.

Left end	Centre	Right end
50 Bank building. FIFTY	Female seated, representing Commerce; bales, bbls., &c.; shipping in distance. B'K OF LOUISIANA, New Orleans, La. Shield.	50 Two females representing Justice and Wisdom.
ONE HUNDRED	Two females; 100 on either side. BK. OF LOUISIANA, New Orleans, La.	ONE HUNDRED
100 Indian female with bow, arrows, and spear.	Train of cars; factories on left; steamboat on right. B'K OF LOUISIANA. New Orleans, La. Bbls., bales, &c.	100 Female seated with hand on capstan.
Die. Portrait of Washington Die.	Female Eagle Female reclining, and and a shield, and sheep. figures 500. BK. OF LOUISIANA, New Orleans, La.	FIVE HUNDRED
500 Female seated with shield, horn of plenty, pole and cap. L500	View of New Orleans from opposite side of river; ships in distance. B'K OF LOUISIANA. New Orleans. La. Safe.	500 Portrait of female. $500
ONE THOUSAND	1000 Sailor seated against bales; ships in distance. B'K OF LOUISIANA. New Orleans, La. Bank building.	1000 1000
Auditors die. Figure 5 and [illegible] by five females	Indian female, western hunter, cupids, and five gold dollars. BANK OF NEW ORLEANS, La. Safe.	5 Female portrait. FIVE
TEN [illegible] erect [illegible] pole, [illegible] 10	[illegible] with sheaf of wheat, cornucopia of flowers and corn, compass, quadrant, etc., laying around, in distance factories, bridge, train of cars, ships, steamboats, &c. BANK OF NEW ORLEANS. La. Two sheep.	10 Blacksmith, etc. TEN
Auditors die. Mercury seated on bale of cotton, right [illegible] and left hand supporting 0 on [illegible] TWENTY	Train of cars; steamboat and depot in background. BANK OF NEW ORLEANS. La. Agricultural implements.	20 Figure of Hope erect, left hand on anchor. TWENTY
50 Marine God and Goddess with dolphin [illegible] Auditors die.	State arms of N. Jersey with female on either side, motto "Prosperity and Liberty." In background factories, steamship, train of cars etc. BANK OF NEW ORLEANS, La. [illegible]	50 Head of Franklin. FIFTY
100 Neptune in a shell on the sea; steamboat in distance. One Hundred	Auditors die. Steamboat under way with the name Crescent City, on the wheel house. BANK OF NEW ORLEANS, La.	100 Female seated on plow, with sickle, sheaf of wheat, fruits &c. One Hundred
500 Justice seated. Five hundred	Auditors die. Female seated on bale of goods with eagle; ship and steamer in the background. BANK OF NEW ORLEANS, La.	500 Head of female. 500
5 Portrait of Washington. 5	CANAL BANK, New Orleans, La. Large figure 5 surrounded by five females; figure 5 on either side.	5 Portrait of Lafayette. 5
Large V, with two females and three males. 5	5 Local view in New-Orleans; vessels, houses, wharfs, &c. CANAL BANK. New-Orleans, La. Bales and wheels.	5 Large V, with five females entwined. FIVE
10 Spread eagle with shield, &c. TEN	View of large public building; houses, &c. 10 CANAL BANK. New-Orleans. La. Steamship.	TEN Figure of female, with pole cap and shield, inside of a wreath around which is names of all the States. 10
10 Columbus 10	Large letter X, medallion heads of Washington and Franklin; four cupids. CANAL BANK, New Orleans. La.	10 Male portrait 10
10 [illegible]	Spread eagle. CANAL BANK, New Orleans, La.	10
20 Male portrait 20	Figures 20, two angels and cupid; figures 20 on either side. CANAL BANK, New Orleans, La.	20 Female portrait. 20
Ornamental figure 20, supported by 2 marine figures. Steamship.	Three females representing agriculture, commerce and manufactures. 20 CANAL BANK, New-Orleans, La. Bales, barrels, &c.	Eagle. Goddess of Liberty. TWENTY
50 Jackson. 50	Female, figures 50, bales, shipping, etc.; female portrait on either side of vig. CANAL BANK, New Orleans, La.	50 Lafayette. 50
50 Female seated on a barrel; ship and steamship in background. FIFTY	Female figure representing manufactures, seated on bale, with arm resting on barrel; bale of goods, anchor, ships, &c. CANAL BANK, New-Orleans, La. Pelican feeding her young.	Female with arms and balances. 50
100 Franklin 100	Sailor seated on bale of merchandise; shipping, etc.; figures 100 on left. CANAL BANK, New Orleans, La.	100 Washington 100
100 Portrait of Washington,	C [illegible] on a levee, loading steamboat [illegible] with bales unloading wagon, &c.; locomotive, horses and wagons; numerous male figures; trees, &c. CANAL BANK, New-Orleans, La. Steamboat.	100 Female seated on chest with cap and pole; also, cornucopia.
500	Two females conversing; shipping on left; cars on right. CANAL BANK. New Orleans, La. Steamship.	500
500 Portrait of female, supported by two marine figures.	Sea view, with steamship in front; another steamship on left, and a ship on right. CANAL BANK, New-Orleans, La. Steamboat.	500 Cherub on sea monster. 500
1000	CANAL BANK, New Orleans, La. Spread eagle. Head of Washington.	1000
1000 Female seated, with helmet and breast plate on arm, resting on shield, spear in one hand; scroll in the other	Arms of the U. S., with female on either side, representing liberty and plenty; boxes, &c.; ships and steamship on right; man plowing, and factories on left. CANAL BANK, New-Orleans. La.	1000 Steamship. 1000
1 Sailor at wheel	CITIZENS' BANK of Louisiana. ONE on 1 Sloop ONE on 1 ONE DOLLAR	1 Male portrait
2 Male portrait	CITIZENS' B'K of LA. Female seated between TWO side bales; TWO ships in distance 2 TWO DOLLARS 2	2 Two men with glass looking at ship in distance
3 Female with globe and book	CITIZEN'S B'K of LA. Hunters lighting fire, deer on horse, etc. THREE DOLLARS New Orleans	3 Ship-carpenter at work

Left end	Centre	Right end
FIVE	5 Female with pole and cap, left arm resting on shield. 5 CITIZENS' BANK, New Orleans, La. Pelican	CINQ
Five on 5. Male portrait	Title of Bank. Two females seated; factories on left. Green 5 either side. 5	Five on 5. Female portrait.
5 Girl's head FIVE	CITIZENS BANK, of La. V Sailor, farmer, boy, dog, ocean scene, etc. V	5 Male portrait CINQ
TEN	DIX Vig. Same as 5s. CITIZENS' BANK, New Orleans, La. Phœnix.	TEN X TEN
10 Washington.	CITIZENS' BANK of Louisiana. Sailor reclining on beach; steamer and vessels in distance.	10 DIX Female portrait. TEN
X Male portrait	Storm at sea—steamers, vessels, etc. CITIZENS' BANK of Louisiana. X	10
10 Male portrait	CITIZENS' BANK, of Louisiana. Old man child and bust. Letter X either side. 10	10 Female seated with pole and 10 on shield.
20 Sailor with flag; barrel bale, anchor, etc.	CITIZENS' BANK OF Louisiana. XX Male portrait. 20	20 Female with sword and shield.
20	Female with pole and cap; left arm on shield. CITIZENS' BANK, New Orleans, La VINGT	20 Phœnix. XX
FIFTY Female, anchor, steamer and light house in distance.	Title of Bank. L Female pouring water in trough; sheep drinking. L	50 Male portrait

Left end	Centre	Right end
50 Sailor and captain.	Title of Bank. L Three females and squaw on globe. L	50 Female with dove. FIFTY
50 L	CITIZENS' BANK, New Orleans, La. Pelican.	Goddess of Liberty. 50
100	C Female with liberty cap and pole; cornucopia, &c. C CITIZENS' BANK, New Orleans, La. Phœnix.	Cent Piastres. 100 Cent Piastres
100 Female portrait.	Title of Bank. Three females and bust. Green C each side.	100 Male portrait
500 Pelican 500	CITIZENS BANK, New Orleans, La.	Goddess of Liberty. 500
1000	1000 Goddess of Liberty. 1000 CITIZENS BANK, New Orleans, La Pelican.	1000
5 Three males, two females and large V.	Compt's die. Indian family seated contemplating city, &c. CRESCENT CITY BK, New Orleans, La. A crescent.	V Five females entwined in fig. 5.
10 Blacksmith and forge; carson right.	Compt's die. Nine cherubs making offering to female; ten gold dollars, &c. Title of Bank. A crescent.	10 Female portrait. TEN
TWENTY Female feeding fowls.	Compt's die. 20 Negroes picking and carrying cotton. Title of Bank. A crescent.	20 Martha Washington TWENTY
Compt's die Girl. FIFTY	50 Female seated on either side of anvil; buildings on right. Title of Bank. A crescent.	50 Weighing cotton. FIFTY

Left end	Centre	Right end
100 Compt's die. Two cherubs 100	Drove of wild horses. Title of Bank. A crescent.	100 Female, portrait 100
5 Female holding sickle in right hand. FIVE	LOUISIANA STATE BANK. New Orleans, La. Female seated, right arm resting on a bird.	5 Eagle in the act of flying away from base on which is a shield.
Female figure seated.	5 Steamship and other vessels. Title of Bank. Pelican.	5 Sailor erect ship in distance.
V	Harbor scene—steamer, steamboats, sail vessels, etc. Female portrait below between name of Bank. LA. STATE BANK. New Orleans, La.	5
10	Steamboat loaded with cotton; raft on right. LA. STATE BANK, New Orleans, La Cotton Bales.	10
10 Male bust. 10	X Female seated, left arm resting on an escutcheon. Title of Bank.	Roman senator in robes with casque. TEN
10 Female seated with spear and branch	Triton in his car conducting a female. Title of Bank. Farmer leaning on plough.	10 Ship.
20 View of the Cathedral and adjoining buildings N. O. TWENTY	20 2 Female. 0 Title of Bank	20 Female seated between 2 and 0.
20 Female bust, 20	Title of Bank. Female seated, bale, cask, &c.; view of city in distance.	XX Female seated, pail at her feet.
FIFTY A bust. 50	L Child seated holding an escutcheon; sons around him. Title of Bank.	FIFTY Roman bust 50

LOUISIANA.

50 — Female seated resting left arm on an escutcheon; on right the head of a bird appearing; cornucopia by her side. Title of Bank. Steamboat. — 50
Left: Female bust. Right: Female erect and three children playing around her.

50 — LOUISIANA STATE BANK, New Orleans, La. Female seated on bale with sword and liberty cap; shield with scales at her feet; ship and steamship in distance. — 50
Left: Beehive. Right: Female reclining with chart, compass, globe, &c. FIFTY

100 — Five men, boy, dog, anchor, boat, barrel, etc., ship in distance. Title of Bank. — 100
Left: Female with scroll; child at her feet. Right: Female.

100 — 100 — Three ships under way, with all sail set. Title of Bank. — 100
Right: Female with pails and can. 100

100 — Head of Washington surmounted by an eagle, with female on either side, ship, steamboat, &c., in distance. Title of Bank. Pelican. — 100
Left: Public building. 100. Right: View of town and steamboats. 100

Left: Two men bearing a female on their shoulders. 500 — 500 Portrait of Mrs. Washington 500. Title of Bank. Pelican. — Right: Female seated holding basket of flowers; at her feet the letter D. 500

Left: Figures 1000 supported by two nymphs. Portrait of Washington. — Sea view—steamship and three ships. Title of Bank. Pelican. — 1000

5 — FIVE Mechanic seated and resting arm on anvil, holding in left hand a sledge, factories and a stream of water in the background. MECH. & TRADERS' BANK, New Orleans, La. Steamship. — 5
Left: Auditor's die; pelican feeding her young. 5. Right: Female with a sheaf. 5

10 — Auditor's die. Female seated, globe at her right; in distance sea, ship, and steamship. MECH. & TRADERS' BANK, New Orleans, La. Mechanical implements, &c. — 10
Left: Train of cars. TEN. Right: Female seated.

20 — Auditor's die. Female seated on a rock; cupids sporting with a dolphin. MECH. & TRADERS' BANK, New Orleans, La. Plow, sheaf, &c. — 20
Left: Sailor boy holding the end of an oar. XX. Right: Portrait of Franklin. XX

LOUISIANA.

50 — Auditor's die. Mechanic seated with hammer and chisel in hands, in background men at work on boiler; foundry; vessel on right. Title of Bank. Mechanic's arms and hammer. — 50
Left: Sailor with spyglass. FIFTY. Right: Female seated, left arm on a screw wheel. 50

Auditor's die. 100 — Female seated on an eagle in full flight. Title of Bank. Interior of a blacksmith's shop; anvil, screw wheel, and the hand of a mechanic with hammer. — 100
Left: Female seated. 100. Right: Four men with sledge. 100

V — Female seated with wand pointing at ship on left; cornucopia on right. MERCHANTS' BK. New Orleans, La. — 5
Left: Comptr's die. FIVE. Right: Female portrait.

TEN — Title of Bank. Female seated beside grain; ship on left; lighthouse and promontory on right. — 10
Left: Comptr's die. X. Right: Female portrait.

State Arms. TWENTY. XX — Two females seated; eagle, anchor, globe, etc.; temple of Fame and steamship in distance. MERCHANTS' BK., New Orleans, La. — 20
Right: Female portrait.

Comptr's die. Female portrait. FIFTY — 50 Female figure representing miner pointing at steamer on left; mirror, safe, grain cornucopia, &c. on left. Title of Bank. — FIFTY
Right: Statue of Justice with sword and scales.

FIVE — 5 Figure 5 surrounded by five females, house, cars, and ships in distance. SOUTHERN BANK, New Orleans, La. Plough and sheaf. — FIVE
Left: State arms. 5. Right: 5

10 — State arms. White trading with Indians; wigwams in distance. SOUTHERN BANK, New Orleans, La. Man seated with sledge; steamer in background. — 10
Left: Male with quadrant; globe, hhd., and ship. Right: Portrait of female with flowers in hand. TEN

20 XX — State arms. Spread eagle; pole, liberty cap, building on right, steamship on left. SOUTHERN BANK, New Orleans, La. — 20
Left: Female seated with pole and cap. Right: Female in a reclining posture, pair of scales in her hand. TWENTY

FIFTY — 50 Female with pole and cap, and dog partly around her; eagle over her right shoulder, and globe over her left; ship and steamship in distance. Title of Bank. Cornucopia, bale, &c. — 50
Left: State arms. Two sea monsters. Right: Head and bust of Washington. 50

LOUISIANA.

State arms. Male head and bust. 100 — Female reclining on a box; plough before her; on right two females and two cows; on her left steamer and other evidences of civilization, foundry, ship, &c., a cluster of fruits partly over the woman. Title of Bank. American shield. — 100
Right: Indian woman seated with child. 100

500 — State arms. Female and eagle soaring in the air, horn of plenty, the contents of which she is scattering; shield in claws of eagle. SOUTHERN BANK, New Orleans, La. — 500
Left: Head and bust of a female. Right: Steamship; ship in background.

5 — Eagle on shield. 5. UNION BANK of LA. New Orleans, La. 5
Left: FIVE. State arms. Right: Figure 5 and full length portrait of Washington.

10 — View of a Western steamboat loaded with cotton. UNION BANK of LA. New Orleans, La. — TEN
Left: State arms. Ten Dollars. Right: Female feeding an eagle. 10

Female with spear. TWENTY — State arms. Signing Declaration of Independence. UNION BANK of LA. New Orleans, La. Eagle. — XX
Right: Bust of a female. 20

50 — State arms. Marine diving with the British officer. UNION BANK of LA. New Orleans, La. Female seated. — 50
Left: Female figure. Right: Farmer seated with sheaf of wheat by his side. FIFTY

100 — View of the Capitol at Washington as enlarged. UNION BANK of LA. New Orleans, La. Figure of Justice seated. — 100
Left: State arms. Right: Spread eagle and shield. 100

Left: Figure of Justice and a female seated at her side. $500 — State arms. Female with pole and cap crowning an eagle with wreath, shield, anchor, and a portrait of Washington. UNION BANK of LA. New Orleans, La. Sailor seated. — 500
Right: Female with sickle and sheaf. 500

OHIO.

Woman and three little children on left. ONE — BK. OF COMMERCE, Cleveland, Ohio. Male portrait. — Girl, lamb, &c., man shearing sheep. One dollar in parti circle.

3 — Male Portrait. BK. OF COMMERCE, Cleveland, Ohio. — 3
Left: Man, Woman and two children. Grape Scene, making wine. Right: 3

Left	Centre	Right
Figure 5, and man drinking from brook.	B'K OF COMMERCE Cleveland, Ohio. Male portrait.	V Library scene; Calhoun and Webster talking. FIVE
Group of ten fig. male and female.	Male Portrait. B'K OF COMMERCE, Cleveland, Ohio.	TEN X
1 Figure of Justice.	Map of Ohio, Indian seated on left, female on right; wigwams, building, cars, etc., in distance. B'K OF DELAWARE, Delaware, Ohio.	1 Male portrait
3 Male portrait	Frame holding map of State of Ohio, with cupids on right. Title of Bank.	3 Two children and butterfly
5 Female portrait.	Map of Ohio, with three females and eagle on right; Indian squaw and white man on left. Title of Bank.	5 Agricultural implements and products FIVE
10 Two girls with grain.	Battle scene; white men, Indians, etc. Title of Bank.	10 Map of Ohio. TEN
20 Arms. 20	Male portrait. Female seated between 2 and 0. Title of Bank. Man on plow.	20 Male portrait 20
1 State Arms. ONE	Male portrait. Female with sickle and sheaf, plow & canal boat in ground. BANK OF GEAUGA Painesville, Ohio	1 Female portrait Male portrait. 1
3 State Arms. THREE	Female portrait. Male portrait. Female portrait. BANK OF GEAUGA, Painesville, Ohio.	3 Male portrait THREE
5 State Arms. FIVE	Portrait of Clay. 5 Female. BANK OF GEAUGA. Painesville, Ohio. Female.	5 Male portrait FIVE

Left	Centre	Right
10 State Arms. TEN	Male portrait. 1 Female with sheaf. 0 BANK OF GEAUGA, Painesville, Ohio. Sheaf, plow, &c.	10 Male Portrait. TEN
Mother and three children and grape vine. ONE	Male portrait: Girl with pet lamb and man shearing sheep on right. B'K OF MARION, Marion, Ohio.	1 One Dollar, in part circle
3 Wine harvest	Male portrait B'K OF MARION, Marion, Ohio.	3 3
FIVE Hunter drinking from brook; gun by his side.	BANK OF MARION, Marion, Ohio. Male portrait FIVE	5 Library scene with J. C. Calhoun seated and D. Webster erect. FIVE
Four Male and six Female figures representing the Arts and Sciences.	Male Portrait. B'K OF MARION, Marion, Ohio. TEN	X 10
1 Bust of child.	1 Child seated on rock, steamboat in distance. 1 B'K OF OHIO VALLEY, Cincinnati, O. ONE DOLLAR on ONE	ONE DOLLAR with small 1s.
3 Head of girl with cap.	3 Child seated on rock. B'K OF OHIO VALLEY, Cincinnati, O. THREE DOLLARS on THREE	THREE
5 Child seated on rock, steamer in distance.	B'K OF OHIO VALLEY, Cincinnati, O. FIVE Female erect, with torch, pointing with right hand, books at her feet. DOLLARS.	5 Male portrait.
10 surrounded by small 10s. Male portrait	B'K OF OHIO VALLEY, Cincinnati, O. TEN Child seated on rock, steamer in distance. DOLLARS	10 surrounded by small 10s. TEN
1 Girl's head.	Indian and female either side of map of Ohio. CHAMPAIGN CO. BK Urbana, Ohio.	1 Washington.

Left	Centre	Right
3 Washington.	Female and four cupids with map of Ohio. Title of Bank.	3 Girl's head.
V Hunter drinking out of his hand.	CHAMPAIGN CO. BK. Urbana, Ohio. Male portrait.	FIVE Library scene: Webster and Calhoun. FIVE
Six females and four males.	Male portrait. CHAMPAIGN CO. BK. Urbana, Ohio.	X 10
1 State Arms. ONE	Female with sheaf, sickle and plow; female head on right, male head on left; town in distance CITY BANK, Cleveland, Ohio.	1 Male portrait
3 State arms. THREE	Male head in centre; female head on each side. CITY BANK.	3 Male head. THREE
5 State arms. FIVE	Title of Bank under vig. Head of Henry Clay on the left; female head on the right. Female seated.	5 Portrait of male. FIVE
10 State Arms. TEN	CITY BANK, Cleveland, Ohio. Male portrait. Female seated, sheaf of wheat between figures 1 and 0. Farming Implements.	TEN Portrait of Harrison. TEN
10 State arms. TEN	CITY BANK, Cleveland, O. Male portrait. Vig. Female seated with sheaf of wheat, wreath, &c. Agricultural implements.	10 Portrait of Harrison. TEN
	CITY BANK, Columbus, Ohio. For a description of the notes of this, see those of any of the Ohio Independent Banks, they all being nearly alike.	
	COMMERCIAL BK., Cincinnati, Ohio. For a description of the notes of this, see those of any of the Ohio Independent Banks, they all being nearly alike.	

Left end	Centre	Right end
Female and three children. 1	Male portrait. FOREST CITY BANK, Cleveland, Ohio.	Female and dog; farmer shearing sheep, cars in distance. ONE DOLL'R
3 Man, woman and two children, grape scene, making wine.	Male portrait. FOREST CITY BANK, Cleveland, O.	3 3
V Man drinking from brook.	Male portrait. FOREST CITY BANK, Cleveland, O.	5 Webster and Calhoun conversing. FIVE
Group of ten figures, male and female.	Male portrait. FOREST CITY BANK, Cleveland, O.	10 10
1	Vig. Male portrait; on right, female and three children; on left, lady and lamb, man shearing sheep, and train of cars in distance. FRANKLIN BANK, of Portage Co., Ohio	1 One dollar in semi circle.
3 Wine harvest—men, women and children.	Male portrait. FRANKLIN BANK, of Portage Co., Ohio	3 3
FI V VE Hunter on his knees, drinking out of his hand.	FRANKLIN BANK, of Portage Co., Ohio. Male portrait.	V Library scene; Webster and Calhoun talking. FIVE
Males, females, spinning wheel, and agricultural and other implements.	Male portrait. FRANKLIN BANK, of Portage Co., Ohio	TEN 10
V Man drinking from a brook.	IRON BANK, Ironton, Ohio. Male portrait.	5 Calhoun and Webster conversing. FIVE
Group of 10 figures, male and female.	Male portrait. IRON BANK, Ironton, Ohio.	10 X
1 State Arms. ONE	Male head. Female with sheaf and sickle, plough, &c.; train of cars on a viaduct. MAHONING CO., BK., Youngstown, Ohio.	1 Male head.
3 State Arms. THREE	Female head. Male head. Female head. MAHONING CO., BK., Youngstown, Ohio.	3 Male head. THREE
5 State Arms. FIVE	Head of Clay. Female head. MAHONING CO., BK., Youngstown, Ohio.	5 Head of Corwin. FIVE
10 State Arms. TEN	Male head. Female with sickle and sheaf of wheat; shield; steamboat in distance. MAHONING CO., BK., Youngstown, Ohio.	10 Male portrait. TEN
1 Wharf scene; men, horses, barrels, etc.	MARINE BANK, Toledo, Ohio. 1 Vessel at sea.	1 Building.
5 Building.	Harbor scene; steamship, steamboats, sail vessels, etc. MARINE BANK, Toledo, Ohio	5 Clay.
10	Vessels at sea. Building. MARINE BANK, Toledo, Ohio.	10 Male portrait
	MERCHANTS BANK, Massillon, Ohio. For a description of the first plate of the Merchants' Bank see Springfield Bank, Ohio	
Woman, and three children on left. 1	Male portrait. Female and dog; man shearing sheep; also cars. MERCHANTS BANK, Massillon, Ohio.	One dollar in part circle.
3	Man, woman, and children; grape scene—making wine. Male portrait. MERCHANTS BANK Massillon, Ohio.	3 Three and figure 3.
V5V Man drinking from brook.	MERCHANTS BANK, Massillon, Ohio. Male portrait.	Five and letter V. Calhoun and Webster conversing together. FIVE
	Group of ten figures, male and female. Male portrait. MERCHANTS BANK, Massillon, Ohio.	X 10
ONE on 1	Cows in brook; boy, girl, &c. MOUNT VERNON BANK. ONE DOLLAR. Mount Vernon, Ohio. 1	ONE on 1 Female Portrait.
3 Two children.	Two children at foot of tree; cows, sheep, &c. MOUNT VERNON BANK. THREE DOLLARS Mount Vernon, Ohio	3 Dog and safe.
FIVE on 5 Female seated in letter V	MOUNT VERNON BANK. Farmer gathering FIVE corn. DOLLARS. Mt. Vernon, Ohio.	FIVE on 5 Girl's head
10 Farmer and dog.	MOUNT VERNON BANK. TEN Girl's head. DOLLARS. Mt. Vernon, Ohio.	10 Cooper at work.
1	Male Portrait; on left Female with three children, on right Female with lamb, Men shearing sheep, Railroad cars in distance. PICKAWAY CO. B'K., Circleville, Ohio.	1 ONE DOLLAR in semi-circle.
3 Scene, Wine Harvest.	Male Portrait. PICKAWAY CO. B'K., Circleville, Ohio.	3 3
5 Hunter kneeling by brook drinking from his hand.	PICKAWAY CO. B'K., Circleville, Ohio. Male Portrait.	V Library scene Calhoun seated, Webster standing by his side. FIVE
Harvest scene, group of ten figures.	Male Portrait. PICKAWAY CO. B'K., Circleville, Ohio.	X TEN

1 State arms. ONE	Male portrait. Female, sheaf of wheat, &c. Female portrait. SANDUSKY CITY BANK, Sandusky, Ohio.	1 Male Head.
3 State arms. THREE	Female portrait Male portrait and large figure 3. Female portrait SANDUSKY CITY BANK, Sandusky, Ohio.	3 Male portrait THREE
5 State arms. FIVE	Portrait of H. Clay. Five and large figure 5. Female portrait SANDUSKY CITY BANK, Sandusky, Ohio.	5 Male portrait FIVE
10 State arms, TEN	Male portrait. Female seated; sickle and sheaf of wheat. SANDUSKY CITY BANK, Sandusky, Ohio.	X Male portrait TEN
1 ONE on 1	Female milking cows. SPRINGFIELD B'K, Springfield, O.	1 Female portrait.
2 TWO on 2	Eagle on shield 2 SPRINGFIELD B'K, Springfield, O.	2 Female, spinning wheel, factory, &c.
3 Portrait of Henry Clay	SPRINGFIELD B'K Springfield, O Old man and child, bust of Washington on table.	3 Female leaning on pillar, torch in hand, &c.
5 FIVE Cattle and sheep.	[First Plate.] Female on either side of shield, on which is a view of rising sun, &c., surmounted by an eagle; steamer, train of cars, factories man ploughing, &c., in distance. Title of Bank. Same as ones.	5 FIVE Train of cars
5 Hunter kneeling by stream to drink; woodland scenery.	SPRINGFIELD B'K, Springfield, O. Male portrait	V Vig. Webster and Calhoun conversing in a library; books, globe, papers, & scattered around. FIVE
10 Spread eagle TEN	[First Plate.] Female on left of shield, on which is a view of rising sun, steamboat, &c. steamboats, steamer, ships, train of cars, &c. Title of Bank. Same as ones.	10 Spread eagle TEN

Group of males and females, ten in number.	[Second Plate.] Male portrait. SPRINGFIELD B'K, Sprigfield, O.	10 X
5 Man drinking from a brook	STARK CO. BANK, Canton, Ohio. Male portrait. Webster and Calhoun conversing together.	V FIVE
	Ten figures, male and female. Male portrait STARK CO. BANK, Canton, Ohio.	X TEN
Four males and one female. 1	STATE BANK OF OHIO. Male portrait.	1 ONE
1 Male portrait ONE	State Arms; sailor on right; two men on left one is seated. STATE BANK OF OHIO,	ONE Full length female.
1 Portrait of Washington 1	State Arms; farmer reclining with sickle; sheaf on right. STATE BANK OF OHIO, Dog's head.	ONE Full lenght female. ONE
Webster. 2	STATE BANK OF OHIO.	2 Two horses, two men, canal scene, railroad, etc.
2 Male portrait 2	Shield; Indian and female on either side STATE BANK OF OHIO. Dog's head.	TWO Female TWO
2 Male portrait	STATE B'K OF OHIO. TWO on 2 Females gathering grapes from vine. TWO on 2	2 Male portrait.
THREE Male portrait THREE	3 Group of four females; spinning wheel &c. STATE BANK OF OHIO.	3 Male head.

3 Male portrait 3	Shield; Indians on right; female on left. 3 STATE BANK OF OHIO. Mutual Liability.	THREE Female erect THREE
3 surrounded by small 3s. 3 on THREE	STATE B'K OF OHIO Two females, one pointing to wheel, two others in background. Male portrait. Male portrait.	3 surrounded by small 3s. 3 on THREE
Same as on right. Male Portrait.	STATE BANK OF OHIO. Group of five male figures.	Figure 5 and words FIVE DOLLARS on wreath. Male head.
5 Franklin. 5	Shield; on right two Indians, on left three females city in distance 5 STATE BANK OF OHIO.	FIVE Full length figure. FIVE
FIVE Female seated within large V. 5	Franklin. Large ornamental fig. 5, surrounded with cupids. STATE BANK OF OHIO. Wheat, &c.	5 5
10 Male portrait 10	Letter X on shield; female on right; farmers, train of cars on left. STATE BANK OF OHIO.	TEN Female with sword and balance. TEN
10 Male Portrait. TEN	Two females, shield, plow and steamboat; female on right is seated and holds grain; on left anchor and ship in extreme distance STATE BANK OF OHIO.	X Male portrait. TEN
10 X on TEN. 10	STATE BANK of Ohio. Three men—smith, student, farmer; tools, etc. TEN	10 Male portrait
10 Harrison. 10	State Arms; Indians on right on horseback; on left woodchopper and hunter; men plowing, cars, &c., in distance. STATE BANK OF OHIO. Dogs head.	TEN Full length female. TEN
20 Clay.	STATE BANK OF OHIO.	Female with spinning wheel; steamboat in the distance 20

Left	Centre	Right
20 Male portrait. 20	State Arms, with female on right and houses in distance; on left man on horseback. STATE BANK OF OHIO. Dog's head.	20 Female Indian representing liberty. XX
50 Male head 50	State Arms; female on left and steamboat in distance; on right Indian in canoe and figs. 50. STATE BANK OF OHIO. Dog's head.	50 Female artist seated. 50
1 State arms ONE	Male portrait. Female seated, with sheaf and sickle; train of cars, &c., in distance. Female portrait. WESTERN RESERVE BANK, Warren, Ohio	1 Male portrait
3 State arms. THREE	Female portrait. Male portrait in top of large figure 3. Female portrait. WESTERN RESERVE BANK, Warren, Ohio	3 Male portrait THREE
5 State arms FIVE	Portrait of Clay. 5 Female portrait WESTERN RESERVE BANK, Warren, Ohio	5 Male portrait FIVE
10 State arms TEN	Male portrait. Female seated, with medal between arms, mental figure 1 and 0, steamboat, shield, &c WESTERN RESERVE BANK, Warren, Ohio	10 Male portrait TEN
ONE 1 ONE	Men and women picking grapes BANK OF CORYDON ONE DOLLAR Corydon, Ind.	1 Female portrait
Word Five and 5 V	Female, eagle and shield; steamer in distance. BANK OF CORYDON, Corydon, C. H. Ind.	Word Five and 5. V
1 ONE	BANK of ELKHART. Elkhart, Ind. Portrait of Washington and words "one dollar" at top.	1 ONE
5 FIVE	BANK of ELKHART, Elkhart, Ind. Female bust. Duck.	5 FIVE

Left	Centre	Right
ONE Auditor's die	BANK OF GOSHEN, Goshen, Ind. Vig. One dollar in circular die. Spread eagle.	ONE ONE
3 3	BANK OF GOSHEN, Goshen, Ind. Circular die. Auditor's die. Circular die.	3 3
5 V	BANK OF GOSHEN, Goshen, Ind. Auditor's die and five circular dies in semicircle below it.	5 V
X TEN	Ten dies in semi circle. Auditor's die. Title of Bank.	X TEN
1 ONE	Cupid and gold dollar: train of cars, steamboat and village in the back ground. BANK OF MOUNT VERNON, Mount Vernon, Ind., Man mowing.	A large figure 1 and goddess of Liberty.
THREE Portrait of Henry Clay.	Three females and figure 3. BANK OF MOUNT VERNON, Mount Vernon, Ind., Man plowing.	A large figure three with female small 3 and word Three.
State Arms Letter V surrounded by five human figures.	Large 5 surmounted by five human figures; ships and factory in distance. BANK OF MOUNT VERNON. Mount Vernon, Ind., 5	Large 5, Washington and word Five thereon.
State Arms Portrait of Martha Washington. TEN	BANK OF MOUNT VERNON, Mount Vernon, Ind. TEN X DOLLARS	10 Portrait of Washington. TEN
1	Cupid rolling silver dollar; cars in the distance. BANK OF PAOLI, Paoli, Ind.	1 Female portrait. ONE
5	Five cherubs and five silver dollars. BANK OF PAOLI, Paoli, Ind.	Female holding sheaf of wheat seated in large V.

Left	Centre	Right
2	Two cupids and two silver dollars; cars in distance. 2 BANK OF SALEM. New Albany, Ind.	TWO Female leaning on bale of goods.
Female holding grain seated in large V. 5	Five cupids and five silver dollars. Title of Bank. Hog.	5
1 Male portrait	BANK OF THE STATE OF INDIANA One Dollar across circular die. 1 ONE 1	ONE 1 Male portrait
3 Male portrait	Title of Bank. 3 Three across large die. 3 Three.	3 Male portrait
5 Male portrait	Female seated; sheep, house, sheep, etc. BK. OF THE STATE OF INDIANA.	5 Male portrait
10 Male portrait	Four male figures seated, city in distance. BK. OF THE STATE OF INDIANA.	10 Male portrait
20 Male portrait	BK. OF THE STATE OF INDIANA. Sailor, male and dog; sloop in distance.	20 Male portrait
50 Male portrait	BK. OF THE STATE of Indiana. Male portrait. Three more; one seated.	50
100 Male portrait	Title of Bank. Two males and two females.	100 Male portrait
5 Male Portrait.	Vig. Female soaring in clouds, eagle, shield, &c. CAMBRIDGE CITY BANK, Cambridge City, Ind. Eagle.	5 Male Portrait.

Left	Center	Right
5 Male Portrait. 5	5 Farmer feeding hogs in pen; two horses looking over bars. CAMBRIDGE CITY BANK. Cambridge City, Ind.	5 Male Portrait. 5

Left	Center	Right
FIVE Male Portrait. FIVE	5 Vig. Female seated on barrel, holding a pitcher; mechanical implements laying around; ships on right in distance. 5 CAMBRIDGE CITY BANK, Cambridge City, Ind.	FIVE Male Portrait. FIVE

Left	Center	Right
10 Male Portrait. 10	10 Vig. A large X, with portraits of ten of the Presidents of the United States thereon. 10 CAMBRIDGE CITY BANK. Cambridge City, Ind. Eagle.	10 Male Portrait. 10

Left	Center	Right
1 Fars and basket of corn.	Boy on horse, girl, dog, two men, mill, chickens and female crossing bridge EXCHANGE BANK, of Attica, Ind.	1 Sheep, house etc.

Left	Center	Right
FIVE Female and child feeding fowls.	Cars crossing bridge; drover and cattle coming down hill. Title of Bank.	5 Female with flowers.

Left	Center	Right
Word one and fig. 1. Milkmaid with tub.	EXCHANGE BANK, Greencastle, Ind. Circular die with portrait of Henry Clay, and words one dollar in half circle over his head; large figure 1 with the word one twice on each figure.	Word one and fig. 1. Auditors die.

Left	Center	Right
FIVE Two males erect, one leaning on capstan; two females seated drawing; city in distance.	EXCHANGE BANK, Greencastle, Ind. V Auditor's die.	5 Male figure erect, and two females seated on the ground: dog, cattle, sheaf, &c.

Left	Center	Right
Female head. State arms.	INDIANA BANK. Madison, Ind. Harvest maid, with sickle, in reclining posture; railroad train crossing a bridge in distance.	1 Flower girl.

Left	Center	Right
Female head. State arms.	INDIANA BANK. Madison, Ind. Milkmaid and cows.	3 Figure 3 and three cupids.

Left	Center	Right
Head of Fillmore. State arms.	INDIANA BANK. Madison, Ind. Locomotive and railroad train; town or city in distance.	5 Figure 5 supported by a female figure

Left	Center	Right
Head of Gov. Wright. State arms.	INDIANA BANK, Madison, Ind. Railroad trains crossing the Susquehanna River on Pennsylvania Railroad Bridge.	10

Left	Center	Right
5 Med. head. FIVE	Cars, horses, trees, large chimney and sloop. INDIANA FARMERS BANK. Franklin, Ind Quails.	5 Washingt'n

Left	Center	Right
10 Female with sheaf of wheat. TEN	INDIANA FARMERS BANK, Franklin, Ind Milkmaid seated with pail; cows, etc. Eagle.	10 on medallion head. Franklin.

Left	Center	Right
1 ONE	ONE ONE KENTUCKY STOCK BANK, Columbus, Ind. ONE DOLLAR.	1 State arms.

Left	Center	Right
5 5	KENTUCKY STOCK BANK, Columbus, Ind. Coat of arms.	5 5

Left	Center	Right
10 Three dies. TEN	KENTUCKY STOCK BANK, Columbus, Ind. Ten dollars Ten dollars Train of cars; two dies on either side.	10 Three dies. TEN

Left	Center	Right
20 Three dies. TWENTY	Female portrait; three dies on each side. Title of Bank. Twenty Twenty Still; four dies each side.	20 Three dies. TWENTY

Left	Center	Right
Indian lying behind rock watching two deers. ONE	ONE Woodman cutting a tree, buffalo. LA GRANGE BANK. Lima, Ind.	ONE Portrait of Female.

Left	Center	Right
TWO Two females holding aloft sheaf of grain and sickle.	Vig. Man with sheaf of grain on shoulder, boy loading a sled to which a horse is attached; on right stacks of grain, and on left house. LA GRANGE BANK, Lima, Ind.	2 Woodman felling a tree; buffalo.

Left	Center	Right
V FIVE	LA GRANGE BANK, Lima, Ind. Vig. Cattle and sheep on right steamboat in distance, on left in distance cattle and house.	5 Same as on Twos.

Left	Center	Right
2 Female portrait. TWO	Farming country, ox in foreground PARKE CO. BANK, Rockville, Ind. Canal lock.	2 Male portrait TWO

Left	Center	Right
3 Portrait of Gen. Scott.	Cattle and sheep. PARKE CO. BANK, Rockville, Ind. Hog.	3 Portrait of a female.

Left	Center	Right
5 Female portrait. FIVE	Cattle scene and milkmaid. PARKE CO. BANK, Rockville, Ind. Anvil and cornucopia.	5 Male portrait FIVE

Left	Center	Right
10 Female portrait. TEN	Stone quarry. PARKE CO. BANK, Rockville, Ind. Loading hay.	10 Portrait of Gen. Scott TEN

Left	Center	Right
1 Male Portrait.	Vig. Train of Cars; on left in distance village; on right steamboat and sloop. PRAIRIE CITY B'K, Terre Haute, Ind.	1 Woodman in the act of cutting; buffalo.

Left	Center	Right
Female with sheaf of grain on right shoulder.	Vig. Man seated on trough; three horses, one drinking; girl feeding swine; house in background. PRAIRIE CITY B'K, Terre Haute, Ind.	2 Same as Ones.

Left	Center	Right
3 Female with flowers.	Vig. Three females in clouds; flowers, &c.; on right train of cars, canal lock, boat, &c. PRAIRIE CITY B'K, Terre Haute, Ind.	3 Same as Ones.

Left	Center	Right
Male Portrait. 5	Vig. Steamship, and four ships under sail PRAIRIE CITY B'K, Terre Haute, Ind.	5 Same as Ones

Left	Center	Right
Three females, one above the other; anchor, sheaf of grain, &c. TEN	Vig. Four cows and three sheep; stream of water, trees, &c. PRAIRIE CITY B'K, Terre Haute, Ind.	10 Same as Ones.

Left	Center	Right
1 State Arms.	SALEM BANK, Ind. Female portrait in circle, with words "one dollar" at top.	1 Female with sheaf of wheat; ships in distance.

Left	Center	Right
Portrait of a girl; words two dollars on the upper margin of the circle. 2	SALEM BANK, Ind. Female with sheaf of wheat on her shoulder.	Same as on left.
5 V 5 V	Female and two cows; in the distance, fence and country scene. SALEM BANK, Ind. Female bathing.	5 State Arms.
V 5	Indian; two Squaws and papoose in canoe. SALEM BANK, Ind.	5 State Arms.
1 head of Washington. ONE	Indian reclining on left arm; another Indian coming out of a copse SOUTHERN BANK. Terre Haute, Ind. Secured, &c.	1 State Arms. ONE
2 head of Clay. TWO	Train of cars; depot, steamboat, &c., in distance. SOUTHERN BANK. Terre Haute, Ind. Secured, &c.	2 State Arms TWO
Large figure 5; in background, train of cars, water fall, Indian, &c FIVE	Portrait of Webster; Cupid on either side; flowers and scroll. SOUTHERN BANK, Terre Haute, Ind. Secured, &c	FI 5 VE State Arms FIVE
State Arms. Female X TEN	SOUTHERN BANK, Terre Haute, Ind. Word ten, and figures 10, across. Traveler on horse, watering him at trough; birdsman, sheep, cows &c Secured, &c.	10 Indian hunting on a tree, ship in distance.
1 Auditor's die ONE	Capitol at Washington; eagle, steamer, &c. 1 ALTON BANK. Alton, Ill. Steamboat.	ONE Female standing with shield, &c.
TWO Sailor, windlass &c.	Auditor's die. Female and eagle; railroad and steamboat in the distance. ALTON BANK. Alton, Ill. Horn of plenty and anvil.	2 Female portrait.
THREE Large fig. 3, with mechanic, sailor and farmer. Auditor's die	Eagle on top of a shield, with a female figure sitting on each side; man plowing, railroad and steamboat, and factories in the distance. ALTON BANK. Alton, Ill. Bull.	3 Female portrait. THREE

Left	Center	Right
5 Female portrait. FIVE	Auditor's die. Female and eagle. ALTON BANK. Alton, Ill. Dog	FIVE Large figure 5 with five females.
10 Female seated on safe with scales and sword.	ALTON BANK. Alton, Ill. State Arms on large X.	10 Train of cars
Scene in a mill; carrying out grain ONE	B'K OF BLOOMINGTON, Illinois. Compt's die.	1 Male portrait
2 Compt's die.	B'K OF BLOOMINGTON. Girl's head.	Cupid supporting figure 2. Farmer and boy ploughing with horse.
3 Surveyors measuring ground.	B'K OF BLOOMINGTON. Girl's head; Farmers loading hay. Girl's head.	3 Compt's die.
5	B'K OF BLOOMINGTON. Scene in the arctic regions; men pushing boat off of ice. Compt's die.	5 James Buchanan.
1 Portrait of Franklin.	BANK OF GALENA. Galena, Ill. Two drovers with cattle and hogs.	1 State arms.
State arms. TWO 2	BANK OF GALENA, Galena, Ill. Locomotive and cars.	2 Female portrait.
3 Cattle, drovers, load of hay, &c.	Female. 3 Man with sickle and bundle of grain. BANK OF GALENA. Galena, Ill.	3 State arms.
5 Female portrait.	Female with arm resting on bale; right of vignette, load of hay. State arms. BANK OF GALENA. Galena, Ill.	5 Portrait of Webster.

Left	Center	Right
1 Auditor's die	CITY BANK, Ottawa, Ills. Milkmaid with stool in left hand, leaning on cow; cows, sheep, &c.	1 Female portrait.
Fig. 5, with word Five on each side	Indian hunters overlooking deer; squaw and wigwam in background. Aud. Die CITY BANK, Ottawa, Ills.	5 Child and rabbits.
1¼ Auditor's die	State of Ills. Eagle EXCHANGE BANK Albion One Dollar & twenty-five cts.	1¼ Female portrait
2½ Girl's head	State of Train of cars Illinois EXCHANGE BANK Two dollars & fifty cents Albion	2½ Auditor's die
1 State Arms	GRUNDY COUNTY BANK. Scene in yard; men, horses, &c. ONE DOLLAR. Morris, Ill.	ONE on 1 1
GRUNDY Cows feeding from hay stack. 5	COUNTY BANK. FIVE Morris Ill. FIVE DOLLARS.	5 State Arms
1 Three children with horse	HOME BANK Children and cattle under tree ONE DOLLAR on ONE 1 ONE Elgin, Ill.	1 Auditor's die
2 Fowls	HOME BANK TWO on 2 Female stepping into water DOLLARS on 2 2	2 Auditor's die
Auditor's die ONE Cattle; cars passing over arch.	Female seated by safe, shield, etc.; on left men, locomotive, shipping, etc, on right females and cows. KANE COUNTY BK. Geneva, Ill.	1 Male portrait
2 Girls with sheafs.	Auditors' die. Milkmaid, cows, dog, pail, etc. Title of Bank	2 Men washing sheep.

ILLINOIS.

Left	Centre	Right
Auditors' die Justice.	Agricultural scene—man seated—others standing and loading wagon; farm-house, steamboat and vessel in distance. Title of Bank.	3 Female, churn; cow and barn in distance.
Auditors' die FIVE Washington.	Drover, cattle and sheep. Title of Bank.	5 Liberty with flg. &c.
ONE Man standing with American flag; barrel, bale, &c.	[Old Plate.] Vig. Ships at dock, warehouse, &c. MARINE BANK, Chicago, Ill. Steamboat.	1 State arms.
American eagle, two mermaids. Steamship.	[New Plate.] 1 Vig. Train of cars building, &c. MARINE BANK, Chicago, Ill. Barrel, bale, &c.	Figure 1, with one running across it.
Male with American flag; female, bale, anchor, &c.	MARINE BANK, Chicago, Ill. Vig. Ships at sea.	2 State arms.
3 Female standing inside of circle; shield, &c.	American eagle. Vig Neptune riding in car, sea nymphs, &c. MARINE BANK, Chicago, Ill. Safe.	3 Female portrait. THREE
Three female figures, &c. FIVE	[Old Plate.] Vig. Steamship, ships, &c. at sea. MARINE BANK, Chicago, Ill.	5 State arms.
FIVE Indian standing with spear, &c.	[New Plate.] American eagle. Vig. Two females standing, male in centre barrel, bale, &c.; ship on right; sheaf of wheat, &c. on left. MARINE BANK, Chicago, Ill. Dog.	FIVE Five female figures encircled with large figure 5
American eagle. Two mermaids. Steamship.	10 Vig. Steamship, ships, &c. at sea. MARINE BANK, Chicago, Ill. Female sitting.	10 Sailor standing, barrels, &c.
ONE Drovers, oxen, and sheep. ONE	Harvest scene; laborers (with woman and children) reaping; dog in front; load of grain and horses in distance. 1 McLEAN CO. BANK, Bloomington, Ill. Hog.	ONE Ox. Auditor's die.

ILLINOIS.

Left	Centre	Right
2 Spread eagle and shield. Auditor's die	Drove of cattle and sheep; man on horseback. McLEAN CO. BANK, Bloomington, Ill. Pig.	TWO Female figure, with small mirror
1 Boy, girl, child, horse &c.	MECHANICS' BANK, Hardin, Ill. Female with basket of flowers.	1 Aud. die.
2 Boy.	MECHANICS' BANK, Hardin, Ill. Man and negro at grindstone; men, barn, etc.; red 2 each side	2 Aud. die.
3 Aud. die.	MECHANICS' BANK, Hardin, Ill. Boy, child, cattle, sheep, trees, etc.	3 Girl, deer and 2 dogs.
Five on V Aud. die.	MECHANICS' BANK, Hardin, Ill. V Old man, child; & bust of Washington.	5 Dollars.
ONE Female and 1. ONE	REAPERS' BANK, Fairfield, Ill. Farmer in field whetting cradle and scythe.	1 Auditors' die
TWO Men gathering corn. TWO	Title of Bank. Large TWO in front of two females; building, ocean scene, etc., in distance.	TWO 2 Auditors' die
Boy and girl. 3	Man on horse conversing with farmer, another on ground. Title of Bank. Three gold dollars.	3 Auditors' die
5 FIVE Female with 5 on shield.	Patent reaping machine at work in field; city, etc. in distance Title of Bank.	5 Auditors' die
ONE on 1 State Arms. ONE	Children at foot of tree; cows, sheep, &c. Child's head. SYCAMORE BANK, Sycamore, Ill.	1 Fowls.

KENTUCKY.

Left	Centre	Right
V Female figure seated. FIVE	5 Female with sickle and grain. 5 SYCAMORE BANK, Sycamore, Ill.	V State Arms. FIVE
1 Figure of Justice with sword and shield. ONE on 1. 1	ONE on 1 State Arms. ONE on 1 TRADERS BANK. 1 on ONE. Chicago, Ill.	1 1 Girl's head. 1
FI5VE Cow under tree	TRADERS BANK STATE OF ILLINOIS Sailor, with trumpet in hand V V FIVE DOLLARS Chicago	FI5VE Compt's die
2 Man loading barrels 2 Public building	Griggsville TREASURY BANK Locomotive, male, female, wagon and horses in distance 2 Dog's head	2 ILLINOIS Auditor's die
Female reclining on sheaf of grain; mowing scene in distance. 1	Auditors' die UNION BANK, Benton, Ills.	Men and sheep. 1
2 Auditors' die	Title of Bank Female beside column; steamer, etc. in distance	2 Sheep.
ONE across 1 Farmer gathering corn.	Female figure surrounded by agricultural products, &c. BANK OF ASHLAND, KENTUCKY, Ashland.	ONE across 1 Mechanic at work.
5 Continental soldier charging bayonet.	Girl's head. Five men at work in Iron Foundry Girl's head. BANK OF ASHLAND Ashland, Ky. Machinery.	5 Female portrait.
TEN	BANK OF ASHLAND Ashland, Ky. Male and female on either side of a shield on which is a head; two Indians on left.	10 Female head.
Train of cars another train crossing bridge in distance 20	BANK OF ASHLAND Ashland, Ky.	20 Clay.

ONE
Two men standing, two women sitting.
Woman swimming. Portrait of H. Clay. Woman swimming.
ONE ONE
B'K OF KENTUCKY.
ONE
Man standing, two women sitting.

5
Clay
FIVE
Portrait Female sitting on a bale, holding sheaf of wheat; oxen with wagon load of hay; in the distance locomotive and cars. Portrait of Jefferson.
B'K OF KENTUCKY.
Dog's head.
5
Washington.
FIVE

Henry Clay.
Male figure sitting with scroll in left hand.
B'K OF KENTUCKY.
5 Hunting scene—hunter, game, &c. 5
Portrait of Shelby.
Female figure.

10
Washington.
10
Portrait of Boone. Globe with eagle on top, Indian on one side, female on the other. Portrait of Shelby.
10
B'K OF KENTUCKY
Dog's head.
10
Clay.
10

10
Daniel Boone hunting
B'K OF KENTUCKY.
Woman in a chariot drawn by three horses.
Indian in a canoe.
10

20
Webster.
B'K OF KENTUCKY.
Marion offering the British officer sweet potatoes; camp in distance.
Dog's head.
20
Male portrait

Portrait of Shelby.
Female figure
Boone.
20 Female in the clouds holding flowers in the left hand; ship in the distance. 20
B'K OF KENTUCKY.
Agricultural implements and grain.
Med. head.
Female figure.

Female portrait.
50
Marion offering the British officer sweet potatoes; &c.
B'K OF KENTUCKY.
Dog's head.
50
Male portrait

100
Male portrait
100
Male portrait. Two females sitting; bbl., anchor, &c.; steamboat in the distance
B'K OF KENTUCKY.
Horse's head.
100
Portrait of Boone.
Washington
100

FIVE HUNDRED
500 Indian queen with bow in right hand surrounded by a circle composed of the arms of the different States, flags, drums, &c. 500
B'K OF KENTUCKY.
500
FIVE HUNDRED

Fig. 1 inverted.
Female portrait
ONE
BK OF LOUISVILLE, KY.
Female seated—in front large ornamental ONE; barrels, ships, &c., in background.
1
Female with figure 1.

ONE
1 1
B'K OF LOUISVILLE, Kentucky.
Female sitting on a bale.
ONE
Full length portrait of Clay in a speaking attitude
ONE

2
2 2
B'K OF LOUISVILLE, Kentucky.
Female leaning on a pedestal sitting.
TWO
Female with shield.
TWO

FIVE
Female sitting in letter V.
5
5 Eagle with wings extended. 5
B'K OF LOUISVILLE, Kentucky.
Locomotive under headway.
FIVE
Female sitting in figure 5.
5

5
V
BK OF LOUISVILLE, Kentucky.
5 Woman, boy and girl. 5
5
V

5
Justice.
V
Med. head on frame; female seated on either side.
BANK OF LOUISVILLE, Ky.
V
Justice.
5

5
Female with shield, etc.
BANK OF LOUISVILLE, Ky.
Male portrait
5
5
Female representing Manufactures.

Washington.
Female portrait, with reaper and grain.
Boone.
10 Female sitting on a bale, pointing to a ship in the distance; lighthouse in the background. 10
B'K OF LOUISVILLE, Kentucky.
Eagle with extended wings.
10
Female portrait.
10

10
Female figure spinning
X
Med. head. Female sitting, with pole and Liberty cap in right hand; river and steamboat in distance. Med. head.
B'K OF LOUISVILLE, Kentucky.
X
Female spinning.
10

10
Woman, boy, child.
BANK OF Louisville, Ky.
X
10
Boy with hat on.

10
10
BANK OF LOUISVILLE, Ky.
Female, eagle, shield, etc. Webster on right; Clay on left.
10
10

20
Indians hunting buffalo.
BANK OF LOUISVILLE, Ky.
Female portrait.
20
Man felling a tree; oxen, children, houses, etc.

20
Washington.
Two female figures with ships and cars in the distance.
B'K OF LOUISVILLE, Kentucky.
Agricultural implements and grain.
20
Med. head with helmet

50
Female with horn of plenty.
50
Female figure. Female kneeling with sickle in hand; flowers around her. Female figure.
B'K OF LOUISVILLE, Kentucky.
50
Female with horn of plenty.
50

HUNDRED
Med. head and helmet.
HUNDRED
Female with wings, blowing a trumpet; globe and eagle. 100 100
B'K OF LOUISVILLE, Kentucky.
Indian with quiver of arrows.
HUNDRED
Med. head and helmet.
HUNDRED

100
Female with rake, etc.
C
Med. head. Female reclining on bale with spear; steamboat in distance. Med. head.
BK OF LOUISVILLE KENTUCKY.
C
Female with rake, &c.

ONE on 1.
ONE
ONE on 1.
Map of Kentucky with State arms on upper corner; on right, hunters in canoe; on left, squaw.
COMMERCIAL BK. OF KENTUCKY.
Bell.
1
Female with dove.

Female and figure 1.
1
Rafting scene; male, female and child.
COMMERCIAL BK. OF KENTUCKY.
Words "State of Ky.," on shield.
Female with figure 1.
1

ONE
Steamboat on stocks.
ONE
Wood chopper with axe; house, trees, and dollar gold piece.
COMMERCIAL BANK OF KENTUCKY.
State Arms.
1
Male portrait
ONE

2
Female portrait.
Vig. Same as above ones.
Title of Bank.
Dog.
TWO
TWO
TWO

3
Boy and rabbits.
Vig. Same as above ones.
Title of Bank.
Canal lock.
3
Youthful figure with cap.

THREE
Male portrait.
THREE
Three men sitting; Farmer, Sailor, and Mechanic; 3 one dollar gold pieces.
COMMERCIAL BANK OF KENTUCKY.
State Arms.
3
Steamboat on stocks.
THREE

5
Male portrait.
FIVE
Indian woman, three cupids and hunter, and 5 gold dollar pieces.
Title of Bank.
State Arms.
FIVE
View of Harrodsburg Springs.
FIVE

FIVE
V. two females and three males.
5 Five females, fig. 5; factory, locomotive and tender on right; steamer, etc., on left.
COMMERCIAL BK. OF KENTUCKY.
State Arms.
FIVE
Pierce.
5

10
Male portrait.
TEN
Steamboat running; small one in the distance.
X on right.
Title of Bank.
State Arms.
TEN
Harrodsburg Springs.
TEN

20
Harrodsburg Springs.
TWENTY
Woman reclining; locomotive and vessels, woman and cows in distance.
Title of Bank.
State Arms.
XX
Clay.
TWENTY

XX
Male portrait.
TWENTY
Woodcutter seated; oxen, horse, etc., on right, men fishing on left.
COMMERCIAL BK. of Kentucky.
XX
Steamboat on stocks.
TWENTY

50
Clay.
FIFTY
50 Female reclining holding liberty pole and cap in left hand; eagle and globe; ships in the distance.
Title of Bank.
State Arms.
50
Crittenden.
FIFTY

100
Male portrait.
100
100 Traders and Indians.
Title of Bank.
State Arms.
100
Male portrait.
100

1
1
FARMER'S BANK, of Kentucky.
Corn gathering scene.
Male and female portrait.
Beehive.
1
1
1

1
Male portrait.
ONE
Pasture two horses running, negro boy and dogs, mules standing and reclining.
FARMER'S BANK OF KENTUCKY.
Bee Hive.
1
Female Portrait.
ONE

2
Female Portrait.
TWO
FARMER'S BANK OF KENTUCKY.
Indian on horseback; Prairie Buffaloes in distance.
2 Bee Hive. 2
2
Male Portrait.
TWO

Man and boy plowing with two horses.
V
Title of Bank.
Male and female portrait.
Beehive.
5
5

5
Male Portrait.
5
Drove of cattle and hogs, 2 Drovers and dog, river, covered bridge, rail road bridge, cars in distance.
FARMER'S BANK, OF KENTUCKY.
Bee Hive.
5
Female Portrait.
5

10
Male portrait.
Female with sickle by barrel; negroes at work and steamboat in distance.
Title of Bank.
Beehive.
10
Man gathering corn-stalks.

10
Male Portrait.
10
Female reclining against hogshead tobacco plant, 2 negroes cutting tobacco, wagon on left and steam boat on right in distance.
Female Portrait.
FARMER'S BANK, OF KENTUCKY.
Bee Hive.
X
TEN
10

Female Portrait.
Male Portrait.
20 White man standing by two horses geared, cart; negro breaking hemp; hemp shock in background; cabin, locomotive and cars in distance.
FARMER'S BANK OF KENTUCKY.
Bee Hive.
20

Female portrait.
Male portrait.
20 Two men, two horses, cart, oars, hut, etc.
FARMERS' BANK of Kentucky.
Beehive.
20

Three female figures on rock with anchor in the centre.
50 Portrait in frame, on the ground on each side agricultural implements.
FARMER'S BANK OF KENTUCKY.
Bee Hive.
50
Male Portrait.
50

100
Male Portrait.
100
Three female figures (steamboat and town in distance.
Female Portrait.
FARMER'S BANK OF KENTUCKY.
Bee Hive.
ONE HUNDRED

Head of Clay.
1
Female figure sitting; city in distance, cows, &c.
Female head.
NORTHERN BANK OF KENTUCKY, Lexington, Ky.
1
Head of Washington

1
Boy's head.
NORTHERN BANK of Kentucky.
Drovers, cattle, sheep, etc.
1
Girl's head.

5
Head of Clay.
5
Title of Bank.
5 Same as ones. 5
Dog and safe.
5
Head of Washington
5

X
10
X
Head of Washington
Same as ones.
Head of Clay.
Title of Bank.
Dog and safe.
X
10
X

50
Head of Washington.
50
50 Same as ones.
Title of Bank.
Dog and safe.
50
Head of Clay
50

100
Head of Washington.
100
Same as ones 100
Title of Bank.
Dog and safe.
100
Head of Clay
100

1
Farmer seated under tree; scythe hanging on limb.
Tobacco plantation; two men, one holding leafs of tobacco; hogshead, etc.
PEOPLES BANK, Bowling Green, Ky.
1
1

2
Female portrait.
TWO TWO
Female seated in fig. 2; farming scene on right and left.
PEOPLES BK OF KY.
2
Boy and girl

THREE
Female portrait.
THREE
THREE THREE
Female seated on plow with sheaf, sickle; cars and canal scene in distance.
Title of Bank.
3
Female portrait.

5
V
Farmer and drover bargaining for ox.
PEOPLES BANK, Bowling Green, Ky.
5
Female.

X — TEN — TEN — Female seated between 1 and 0; farming scene on right and left. Title of Bank. — 10 — Female portrait. — Man plowing.

20 — 20 Same as ones. 20 — Title of Bank. — Dog and safe. — 20 — Head of Washington — 20 — Head of Clay — 20

20 — TWENTY — TWENTY — Female with eagle, pole, cap and motto "Excelsior" above. Title of Bank. 20 on red die. — 20 — Female with lora. — Clay.

ONE — Female on ground, globe, books, chart, &c. BK OF THE STATE OF MISSOURI. St. Louis. — 1

2 — Steamboat. BK OF THE STATE OF MISSOURI. St. Louis. — 2 — State Arms. — Dog & safe.

Female, wheel, &c. — THREE — Negro beating hemp. B'K OF THE STATE OF MISSOURI. St. Louis — 3

5 — B'K OF THE STATE OF MISSOURI, St. Louis. Scene in the arctic regions; men pushing boat off ice. — 5 — Male portrait — Male portrait

X — 10 Steamboat Pike running, sloops &c.; Indian kneeling, and white men in the foreground. 10 — BK OF THE STATE OF MISSOURI. — X — Male portrait — X — Male portrait — X

Male portrait — Eagle — Male portrait — 20 Two females sitting, iron chest; steamboat in distance. 20 — BK OF THE STATE OF MISSOURI. — Male portrait — Eagle — Male portrait

50 — B'K OF THE STATE OF MISSOURI. Female sitting; bridge, rail cars, houses, ships, hills, &c. in distance. — Female holding portrait of Washington — 50 — Hunter with dog and gun.

100 — 100 Indian on horseback shooting a buffalo, hunters and buffalo in distance. 100 — B,K OF THE STATE OF MISSOURI. — Male portrait — 100 — Male portrait — Indian portrait. — 100

1 — Indians hunting buffalo. BANK OF ST. LOUIS, St. Louis, Mo. ONE DOLLAR on ONE — 1 — Female head. — Dog and safe.

2 — White and black horse alarmed by lightning; cattle in stream. BANK OF ST. LOUIS, St. Louis. Mo TWO DOLLARS on TWO — 2 — 2 — Head of child.

5 — BANK OF St. Louis, Man with bag horse, mill, mill, two boys on bridge, etc. — 5 in red. — Female head — 5 Missouri. — Eagle on shield — FIVE

X — Steamboat; city, etc., on left; flat boat on right. Title of Bank. — 10 — Female head. — Male portrait

X — View at steamboat landing. BANK OF ST. LOUIS, St. Louis, Mo. TEN — 10 — Men dressing leather. — Male portrait

XX — Portrait of Washington with female, scythe, care sheaf, etc., on right; female, men, boxes, bbls and steamer on left. BANK OF ST. LOUIS, St. Louis, Mo. 20 — 20 — Male portrait — Female portrait

20 — Title of Bank. Men and boy plowing with two horses. Figs. 2 and 0 blended either side. — 20 — Children and butterfly. — Girls' portrait.

FIFTY — Title of Bank. 50 — FIFTY — Female with battle axe and shield. — Compt's die. — Female and anchor.

5 — EXCHANGE BANK of St. Louis, Mo. Local scene; view of iron mountain; mule team, locomotive, cars, men, trees, etc., in foreground. — 5 — Male portrait — Female portrait.

10 — Title of Bank. 10 Male portrait. 10 TEN — 10 — Reaper girl seated; dog beside her. — Bank building.

20 — Men at work in iron furnace. Girl seated at table. Title of Bank. — 20 — Male portrait — Male portrait

50 — Female seated on either side of shield, enclosing ornamental L with spread eagle at top; river and steamboat on right; cars on left. Title of Bank. — 50 — Male portrait — State Arms.

Full length floating female; city and country, locomotive, river, etc., in background. — Male portrait: letter C either side. Title of Bank. 100 — 100 — Bank building.

Corn husking scene, negroes wheelbarrow, &c. — 1 — Eagle on rock. — FARMERS' B'K OF MISSOURI, Lexington, Mo. ONE DOLLAR on ONE 1 ONE — ONE on 1 — Female bust.

Two cows, one lying down, mill, stream, &c. — 2 — Dog and safe. — FARMERS' B'K OF MISSOURI, Lexington, Mo. TWO 2 TWO — TWO — Fem'le with wreath on head.

5 — Two females seated; factories on right; cows, sheep, etc., on left. FARMERS' BANK OF MISSOURI, Lexington, Mo. Dog. — 5 — Portrait of Boy. — Washington

10 — Six mules before load of cotton; negro reclining on one of them. Title of Bank. Ducks. — 10 — Male portrait — Indian seated

20 — Title of Bank. Frame containing bust of Washington; male seated on right, locomotive &c; female seated on left, steamboat, &c. XX XX — 20 — Male portrait — Female portrait.

Female seated with sickle in right hand, left resting on portrait of girl. — FIFTY — Two men conversing; one reclining on anvil; the other has his right hand round little boy at his side. Title of Bank. L L — 50 — Female portrait

Left end	Center	Right end
100 Male portrait	River scene—steamboat; three men in small boat. Title of Bank. C C	100 Justice.
1 1 1	Figure of liberty, leaning on column with cap, pole, and cornucopia, with fruit at her feet. Eagle clutching arrows, shield and olive branch ONE DOLLAR MECHANICS' B'K, St. Louis, Mo.	1 surrounded by "ONE." Portrait of Henry Clay.
Statue of Liberty, with wreath and shield, on which is figure 2	St. Louis Three children in circular die reading book MECHANICS' BANK TWO DOLLARS	2 Girl's head
3 Blacksmith	Girl and boy with cattle St. Louis MECHANICS' BANK THREE DOLLARS	3 Female and child
FIVE	MECHANICS BANK St. Louis, Mo. Scene in a blacksmith shop. Girl's head. FIVE	5 Farmer carrying corn.
Girl seated TEN	MECHANICS BANK. 10 TEN	Cupid. Mechanic's arm and hammer.
20 Boy and girl	MECHANICS BANK, Public buildings, fountains, pedestrians, horses, carriages, etc. St. Louis, Mo.	20 Male portrait
50 Clay	Three females and bust of Washington. Title of Bank	50 Steamboat discharging.
500 in center of black die with red border. Missouri.	MECHANICS' BANK. FIVE Male portrait St. Louis,	HUNDRED
5 5 in red.	Negroes rolling hogshead, pigs of lead, bales, etc.; sea, man and dray on left; steamboat on right. V MERCHANTS BANK, of St. Louis, Mo. FIVE FIVE	5 Portrait of a Boy.

Left end	Center	Right end
10 Portrait of girl.	Title of Bank. X in red. Vig. Same as fives.	10 in red.
20 inverted. TWENTY 20	Portrait of girl. Title of Bank. Vig. Same as 5s. Twenty in red.	20 in red. DOLLARS 20
Title of	Bank. 50 FIFTY in red. Vig. Same as fives. 50 in red.	50 in red. Male portrait
Male portrait C in red.	Title of Bank. Figs. 100 in red and words One Hundred across in black. Vig. Same as fives.	100 C in red.
Female resting on pillar, holding torch in hand, &c. ONE	ONE on 1 SOUTHERN B'K OF ST. LOUIS, St. Louis, Mo.	ONE on 1 Female portrait.
TWO Female, wheel, anvil, screw, &c.	SOUTHERN B'K OF ST. LOUIS, St. Louis, Mo. 2	2 Female seated, resting on wheel.
FIVE Male portrait	SOUTHERN BANK, St. Louis, Mo. Steamship.	5 Female erect pointing to pillar on which is inscribed "Union"
10 Girls head.	SOUTHERN BANK, St. Louis, Mo. X Man tanning leather.	Men working at bench.
Female seated. TWENTY	20 Engineers surveying land. SOUTHERN BANK, St. Louis, Mo. Eagle.	20 20 TWENTY
100 C	Title of Bank. State Arms; sailor on right and Indian on left. Girls head.	100

Left end	Center	Right end
ONE Negro boy beating hemp. ONE	UNION BANK OF MISSOURI, St. Louis, Mo. ONE DOLLAR and ONE on oval ornamental die.	1 Female head.
2 2 Fem'le with pen and scroll, child at her feet 2 2	UNION BANK OF MISSOURI, St. Louis, Mo. TWO DOLLARS and TWO on ornamental die.	2 Indians gazing on waterfall.
5 Male portrait	UNION BANK of Missouri. Indians attacked by wild animals.	5 Man, woman and child.
Full length statue on a dark ground.	Cupid and 10. Title of Bank. Male portrait; steamboat, mast, etc.	10 and Cupid TEN on red X.
20 Female head XX	Cass. Webster. Title of Bank. Hunters, horse, game, dogs, &c, trees, etc.	20 Child's head XX
50 Clay.	Title of Bank. Two females erect crowning female seated; buildings in distance.	50 Indian head
C	Title Apotheosis of Washington; female, soldier, and two Indians. Female, eagle, shield, etc. Game cock.	100 Fillmore.
1 1 Fem'le seated on rock, with grain in hand.	1 WESTERN BANK OF MISSOURI, St. Joseph, Mo. Man beating hemp. 1	1 1
2 2 Female portrait. TWO	WESTERN BANK OF MISSOURI, St. Joseph, Mo. Two females.	2 Female portrait.
5 Bear either side of frame and motto at bottom. 5	WESTERN BANK OF MISSOURI. Cattle, sheep, stream, &c	5 Child's head.

10	Train of cars; steamboat, horses, canal boat and men.	10
	Title of Bank.	
Portrait of female.	X	Female feeding fowls.

20	Title of Bank.	20
	Hunters killing buffaloes.	
Beavers.	20	Male portrait

ONE on 1	STATE OF MICHIGAN. Three cows under tree; children playing, etc.	ONE on 1
	BK OF MICHIGAN.	
Female portrait	ONE DOLLAR Marshall.	Dog's head

THREE	MICHIGAN. THREE DOLLARS	THREE
	3 Flock of Sheep, etc 3 Marshall	
Old man with child pointing to bust of Washington	BK OF MICHIGAN THREE DOLLARS	Female with sheaf of grain.

5	MICHIGAN 5 Scene at blacksmith's shop, mending wheelbarrow, girl with grain, etc.	5
Deer	B'K OF MICHIGAN	
5	FIVE DOLLARS Marshall	Female with roses

Continental Congress, 1776	MARSHALL, MICH X Spread eagle on rock	TEN on X
	B'K OF MICHIGAN	
10	TEN DOLLARS	Female with basket of fruit

Girl's portrait	Pontiac Three children reading from book Mich	1
	BANK OF PONTIAC	
1	ONE DOLLAR	Ducks

TWO	Cattle in water, cars crossing bridge, etc.	2
	BANK OF PONTIAC	
Woman, child, fowl, etc.	TWO DOLLARS Pontiac	Female portrait

FIVE	Canal, boat, cars, road, men, horses, etc	5
	BANK OF PONTIAC	
Boy on rock tending sheep	FIVE DOLLARS [illegible]	Female with sheaf [illegible]

Deer	1 Vig. Female reclining	1
State arms.	FARMERS' AND MECHANICS' BANK.	
Deer.	Detroit, Mich. Steamboat	Eagle and shield.

Deer.	2 Vig. State arms.	2
State arms.	FARMERS' AND MECHANICS' BANK, Detroit, Mich.	Female with sword and balances.
Deer.	Steamboat.	

Deer.	3 Vig. Woodland scene; water, deers, canoe in water, &c. 3	THREE
State arms.	FARMERS' AND MECHANICS' BANK.	Female figure with bow and arrow, quiver at her back.
Deer.	Detroit, Mich. Steamboat.	THREE

FIVE	(Old Plate.) 5 Vig. Large figure 5 with female either side; three cupids. 5	Deer.
	FARMERS' AND MECHANICS' BANK,	State arms.
	Detroit, Mich. Steamboat.	Deer.

Deer.	(New Plate.) 5 Vig. Large figure 5 with female either side; three cupids 5	Deer
State arms.	FARMERS' AND MECHANICS' BANK,	State arms.
Deer.	Detroit, Mich. Steamboat.	Deer.

Deer.	10 Vig. Female, eagle, and shield.	10
State arms.	FARMERS' AND MECHANICS' BANK,	Female sitting under canopy.
Deer.	Detroit, Mich. Steamboat.	TEN

FIFTY	50 Cupid sharpening knife on grindstone.	FIFTY
	FARMERS' AND MECHANICS' BANK,	Steamboat, vessels, bales of goods, &c.
	Detroit, Mich. Arm and hammer.	50

ONE HUNDRED	100 Vulcan, sledge, and anvil; nude female seated on his left; another figure in back ground.	100 ONE
	Title of Bank.	Male portrait HUNDRED
	Beaver.	100

ONE	(Old Plate.)	Female standing.
Female.	Vig. Female sitting on a log; steamboat on right; house in distance on left. 1	
ONE	MICHIGAN INS. CO., Detroit, Mich	1

1	(New Plate.) MICHIGAN INS. CO., Detroit, Mich	1
Words one dollar, and figure 1 under.	Vig. ONE, with ornamented die work.	Words one dollar, and figure 1 under

TWO	(Old Plate.) TWO on Medallion head. Vig. Two females sitting, bale of goods, &c.; ship on right.	2
Male resting arm on shield, &c.		Female resting her arm on figure 2; cars &c.
TWO	MICHIGAN INS. CO., Detroit, Mich	

2	(New Plate.) MICHIGAN INS. CO., Detroit, Mich.	2
TWO		2
2	Vig. TWO DOLLARS, with ornamental die work.	TWO

Female.	3 on Medallion head. Vig. Men, women, children, &c.	3
	MICHIGAN INS. CO., Detroit, Mich	
3	Female.	Portrait of Washington.

Indian in full costume.	(Old Plate.) 5 Vig. Farmer plowing; dairymaid and house in distance.	
FIVE	MICHIGAN INS. CO., Detroit, Mich. Sail vessel.	5

5	(New Plate.) Secured by individual liability. Vig. FIVE, with ornamented die work.	5, V, Five
V with word five running across it.	MICHIGAN INS. CO., Detroit, Mich.	FIVE

Female standing with pole, liberty cap, &c.	10 Vig. Female reclining, &c.	TEN
	MICHIGAN INS. CO., Detroit, Mich. Eagle.	Full length female.

Female.	20 Vig. Portrait of Washington, with female on either side, &c.	
Portrait of Franklin.	MICHIGAN INS. CO., Detroit, Mich.	
Female.	Fish.	20

Female standing with pole, liberty cap, shield, &c.	50 Vig. Three females reclining, &c.	50
	MICHIGAN INS. CO., Detroit, Mich.	

1	Two females reclining with eagle and shield; cars on right; steamboat on left.	1
	PENINSULAR BANK, Detroit, Mich	
Male great, barrels, &c.	Plow, sheaf of wheat, &c.	Vessel under full sail

2	Female reclining, sheaf of wheat, country scene, &c.	2
	PENINSULAR BANK Detroit, Mich.	Female sitting.
Two female portraits		TWO

THREE.	Female sitting, barrels, &c.; ship on right; cars and factory on left.	3
	PENINSULAR BANK Detroit, Mich.	Floating figure.
Female, pole, liberty cap, &c.	Safe.	THREE

IOWA.

FIVE 5 FIVE	Female reclining on bale of goods, barrel, &c.; vessels on right; cars on left. PENINSULAR BANK Detroit, Mich. Safe.	5 Female sitting; male with shield; figure 5, sails, &c.
TEN Indian standing with bow and arrow.	10 Female sitting, pole, liberty cap, spread eagle, &c. PENINSULAR BANK Detroit, Mich. Plow, sheaf of wheat, &c.	TEN Squaw and papoose. TEN

THE STATE BANK OF MICHIGAN.

These notes are printed on what is known as "Lyman's Protection" which consists in grading the portion of the bill covered by the note proper according to the denomination of the bill, thus:—
1s, one third the length of the paper.
2s, one-half the " " "
3s, two-thirds the " " "
5s, three-fourths " " "
and are also done in colors.

1 Two children and butterfly	Title of Bank. Eagle on shield; deer either side; steamboat on right; cars on left.	1 Detroit 1 on ONE State Bank of Michigan. One Dollar.
Red 2.	Title of Bank. Indians spearing buffaloes.	2
Female portrait. White word Three.	Title of Bank. Large white 3.	3 Man carrying corn stalks.
5 on red die. 5	Steamboat 5 Title of Bank.	5 Anchor, bales, barrels, etc.
ONE	Farm scene—man leaning on gate, woman milking; farm house in distance. Male portrait STATE BANK of IOWA.	1 Man carrying corn.
2 Military scene—officer, men with implements.	Drovers, cattle, sheep, and hogs. Title of Bank.	2 Boy's head.
3 Female THREE	Husking scene. Title of Bank.	3 Deer crossing stream.

WISCONSIN.

5	Title of Bank. Emigrant train.	5 Portrait of Antoine Le Claire.
10 Cars crossing bridge.	Map of Iowa with steamer "Iowa," farming implements, etc., on left, and female, factory, etc., on right. Title of Bank. Building.	10 Male portrait
1	STATE BK OF IOWA Iowa City. Figure of Justice with sword and scales. ONE DOLLAR.	1
Female leaning on column on which is word Two.	II STATE BK OF IOWA Iowa City. Henry Clay.	2
3	Man plowing with two horses; house in distance; STATE BK OF IOWA Iowa City.	3 Male portrait
V	STATE BK OF IOWA Iowa City. Washington.	5 FIVE
X Webster.	STATE BK OF IOWA Iowa City. Three females; one crowning bust of Washington; shield, etc.	10 Ten Dollars
	The plates of the branches of the State Bank, of Iowa, are the same as those of the Principal Bank.	
1 Female seated with arms uplifted on bale; bbl. &c, ships in distance. ONE	Boy reclining watching flock of six sheep; in distance. Compt's. die on fig. 1. BANK OF BELOIT, Beloit, Wis.	1 Female erect with flag and shield.
2 2	Four males seated and reclining; female with child, basket, &c; in distance men loading wagon with hay, two oxen before wagon; horse &c. Compt's. die on fig. 1. Title of Bank.	2 Washington on horseback

WISCONSIN.

Three females one above the others; anchor on which topmost female has right hand. THREE	3 St. George fighting the Dragon. BANK OF BELOIT, Beloit, Wis.	3 Compt's. Die
5 Compt's Die.	Female seated with sheaf of grain within a large ornamental V. BANK OF BELOIT, Beloit, Wis.	5 Female within a figure 5.
Female portrait.	10 Spread eagle; cars, city and shipping in distance. 10 BANK OF BELOIT, Beloit, Wis. Horse.	Compt's die.
1 Washington.	Landing of Columbus. B'K OF COLUMBUS, Columbus, Wis.	1 Compt's die.
2 Male portrait	B'K OF COLUMBUS, Columbus, Wis. Men at work surveying.	2 Compt's die.
5 Indian on a horse.	Two males, two females and child, dog and Indians. B'K OF COLUMBUS, Columbus, Wis.	5 FIVE Compt's die.
ONE inverted 1	Shield—on which is Am. shield, shovel, plow, arm, pick and motto "E Pluribus Unum," surmounted at top by weasel; mechanic on right; sailor on left. Bank of Compt's die. Fox Lake, Fox Lake, Wis. Figure 1.	Indian, female and fig. 1. Male portrait
2 Farmer sharpening scythe.	Female on either side of an eagle and words "Two Dollars" between. BANK OF FOX LAKE Fox Lake, Wis. Cornucopia, bales, etc.	2 Compt's die.
V	Cattle, sheep, etc. Female portrait. BANK OF FOX LAKE Fox Lake, Wis. Anchor, bales, bbls, etc.	5 Compt's die.
ONE	Male, female, boy, girl, dog, etc. 1 E. B. HINCKLEY & CO.'S BANK OF GRANT CO., Platteville, Wis.	1 Compt's die.

Left	Center	Right
2 TWO	Title of Bank. 2 Drove of cattle and sheep; boy in water; man on horseback; house in distance.	2 Compt's die.
5 Compt's die.	Men at work in mine. Title of Bank.	5 5
X Compt's die.	Title of Bank. Man plowing with two oxen.	10 Agricultural implements. TEN
Female portrait. Compt's die.	Cars. BK. OF GREEN BAY, Green Bay, Wis. Man seated at lunch, two horses, plow, etc.	1 Female portrait
2 Compt's die.	Corn gathering scene. Title of Bank. Female beside shield, on which is anchor and word "Forward;" vessels in distance.	2
1 Girl with basket.	Man, two horses and pig at pump, cattle and barn in distance. BK of the INTERIOR Warsaw, Wis.	One on 1 Compt's die
Two on 2 Compt's die.	BK of the INTERIOR Warsaw, Wis. Milk-maid and cows.	2 Dog & safe.
Female seated in chair. FIVE	BANK OF THE INTERIOR, Wausau, Wis. Compt's die. Female with eagle, and "America" on globe.	5 Female, cow, calf, fowls, etc.
10 Compt's die. Wisconsin.	Title of Bank. Girl's head. Farmer eat lunch under a tree; female, horses, etc.	10 Portrait of Girl
1 Female seated; cow, sheaf, sickle, etc.	Compt's die. Indians surprised at appearance of white men. BK OF JEFFERSON, Jefferson, Wis.	1 Farmer cleaning scythe; mill, canal and railroad scene in distance.

Left	Center	Right
2 Compt's die.	Indians welcoming white man in boat. Jefferson Title of Bank.	2 Farmer carrying corn stalks.
1 soldier loading gun, drum, at his feet.	B'K OF LA CROSSE, La Crosse, Wis. Female with grain and sickle. ONE DOLLAR.	ONE on 1. Compt's die
3 surrounded by small 3's. Compt's die	B'K OF LA CROSSE, La Crosse, Wis. 3 Old man seated, holding child, pointing to bust of Washington on table. 3 THREE DOLLARS.	3 Female erect holding torch.
1 Boy and dog.	BANK OF MADISON, Madison, Wis. 1 Female with sword and scales. 1	1 Compt's die.
2 Compt's die.	Title of Bank. 2 Cow calf and sheep. 2	2 Male portrait.
1 Deer.	BK OF MANITOWOC, Manitowoc, Wis. Scene at depot and on wharf. Bust of Washington on right and Franklin left. ONE ONE	1 Compt's die
2 TWO Compt's die.	BK OF MANITOWOC, Manitowoc, Wis. Horse and colt, two boys, man with bag of grain, bridge, falls, etc. TWO	TWO Female seated representing Commerce.
5	BK OF MANITOWOC, Manitowoc, Wis. Female portrait and V. Male and female on either side of shield, on which is 5; horse, man, boy and steamboat in distance.	5 Compt's die. Wisconsin.
1 Man leaning against a tree with a drum; man sitting on a log; others in background.	Vig. Three females in water; Cupid, &c. BK. OF MILWAUKEE, Milwaukee, Wis.	1 State arms.
2 Man with gun; trees, dog, &c.	Three females—one with balances; two ships on right, &c. BK. OF MILWAUKEE, [illegible], Wis.	2 State arms.

Left	Center	Right
5 State arms.	Vig. Children in bed asleep; Santa Claus with toys on his back. Large figure 5 encircled with title of the Bank.	5 Female portrait.
Figure of America leaning on column, on which is letter X	TEN DOLLARS BK OF MILWAUKIE Milwaukie Wis.	10 Compt's die
Girl and boy driving cattle through gate 20	Wisconsin Compt's die BK OF MILWAUKIE TWENTY DOLLARS Milwaukie	20 Female portrait
V Compt's die	BANK OF MONEKA, Viroqua Wis. Indians viewing train of cars on prairie.	5 on Five. Indian female.
X Compt's die.	Female seated on cliff, city, cars, locks, etc., below. Title of Bank.	10 Squaw and papoose.
Hunter loading rifle; deer at his feet. ONE	Drover and farmer bargaining for ox; farm yard scene. BANK OF MONROE, Monroe, Wis.	1 Compt's die ONE
Male, female, boy, girl, dog and chickens. TWO	Portrait of Washington; milkmaid and cows on right; two females on left. BANK OF MONROE, Monroe. Wis.	2 Compt's die.
Female feeding chickens. THREE	Drover and drove of cattle; boy in water; trees and house in distance. BANK OF MONROE, Monroe, Wis.	3 Compt's die. THREE
Female gathering wheat. 5	Man watering three horses from trough; sheep, goats, trees and house. BANK OF MONROE, Monroe, Wis.	5 Compt's die.
1 Deer.	B'K OF THE NORTH-WEST, Fondulac, Wis Man, woman, and child.	1 State die. ONE

Left end	Centre	Right end
2 State die. TWO	B'K OF THE NORTH-WEST, Fondulac, Wis. Raft scene.	2 Female with grain on her shoulder.
3 Female with spyglass seated on merchandise vessel on left.	Train of cars, group of male and female figures. B'K OF THE NORTH-WEST. Fondulac, Wis.	3 State die. THREE
5 State die. FIVE	Cattle and sheep; buildings in background. B'K OF THE NORTH-WEST. Fondulac, Wis.	5 Farmer sharpening his scythe.
3 Female THREE	BK OF OSHKOSH, Oshkosh, Wis. 3 Loaded wagon, two boys and two oxen.	3 Compt's die.
FIVE V Female and fig. 5.	Compt's die. BK OF OSHKOSH, Oshkosh, Wis. 5	5 Two men plowing with two horses; dog, etc.
ONE Compt's die.	Steamboat Prairie du Chein and St. Paul. 1 BANK OF PRAIRIE DU CHEIN, Prairie du Chein, Wis. Cars.	Indian. ONE
2 Two children	Wild horses. Title of Bank. Dog.	2 Compt's die.
3 Compt's die.	Rafting scene. Title of Bank. Dog's head.	3 Farmer.
5 Farmer.	Title of Bank. Compt's die. Load of hay, cars, city and bridges.	5 Two females.
1 Country road, with oxen load of hay &c.	BANK OF RACINE, Racine, Wis. Vig. Man watering horse; female feeding pigs; house &c., in distance.	1 State arms.

Left end	Centre	Right end
2 Female Portrait. 2	Vig. Locomotive and train of cars; steamboat on right; city in distance on left. BANK OF RACINE, Racine, Wis.	2 State arms.
3 Three cupids encircled with large figure 3	BANK OF RACINE, Racine, Wis. Vig. Man watering horse; dogs, pigs, child, &c.	3 State arms.
5 Washington. FIVE	Vig. Harvest scene; wagon, loading grain; female with child; men, basket, pitchers. &c., State Arms. BANK OF RACINE, Racine, Wis.	5 Male portrait. FIVE
1	Four cows and three sheep. Girl's head. BANK OF RIPON, Ripon, Wis. Farming utensils.	1 Compt's die.
2 Compt's die.	Train of cars; city and town. BANK OF RIPON, Ripon, Wis.	2 Female feeding fowls.
5 Farming utensils.	Female portrait. Men at work surveying. BANK OF RIPON, Ripon, Wis.	5 Compt's die.
1 Compt's die	BK OF SHEBOYGAN Sheboygan, Wis. 1 Blacksmith, hammer, anvil; city in distance. 1	1 Woodcutter.
TWO TWO TWO 2 Locomotive.	Yacht scene—various male and female figures on the beach. BK OF SHEBOYGAN Sheboygan, Wis.	2 Compt's die. TWO TWO TWO
3 THREE 3	3 Ship yard scene; men at work. BK OF SHEBOYGAN Sheboygan, Wis.	3 Compt's die
5	American shield; on right female instructing children, house in distance; on left Indian, squaw and child. 5 BK OF SHEBOYGAN Sheboygan, Wis.	5 on FIVE Compt's die.

Left end	Centre	Right end
1 Compt's die. Wisconsin.	Indians on horseback fighting wild animals. Child's head. 1 BANK OF SPARTA, Sparta, Wis.	1 Female feeding fowls.
Cupid and fig. 2. Man, horse, dog, pigeons, etc.	Boy on horse; pony, female, ducks, trough; houses, etc., in distance. Title of Bank.	2 Compt's die. WISCONSIN
Soldiers of the Revolution. THREE	3 Man and boy plowing with two horses. Title of Bank.	3 Compt's die. WISCONSIN
FIVE	Title of Bank. Surveyors at work, &c. Portrait of boy.	5 Compt's die WISCONSIN
5 Stevens Point Compt's die	Wisconsin B K OF STEVENS POINT 5 Henry Clay 5 FIVE DOLLARS	5 Grain, etc.
10 Stevens Point 10	Wisconsin BANK OF STEVENS POINT Goddess of Liberty with pole, cap, etc. TEN DOLLARS X	10 Compt's die
Female bust. 1	BANK OF WATER-TOWN, Watertown, Wis. Vig. Female reclining in a sea shell; water scene.	1 Compt's die
TWO Female figure erect.	BANK OF WATER-TOWN, Watertown, Wis. Vig. Indian and female reclining on globe, spread eagle between them. 2	2 Compt's die.
3 Compt's die.	Vig. Man on horseback; boys, sheep, and load of hay in distance. BANK OF WATER-TOWN, Watertown, Wis.	3 Three Cherubs.
5 5	Vig. Two farmers inspecting drove of cattle. Female bust. BANK OF WATER-TOWN, Watertown, Wis.	5 Compt's die

1 Female portrait. 1
BANK OF WEYAUWEGA, Weyauwega, Wis.
Hunters, fire, horse, game, dogs, etc.
1 Compt's die.

2 Two Dollars Compt's die.
Man whittling stick; horse, cow, sheep; boy on gate; man in distance.
Title of Bank.
2 2
2 Two Dollars Dog and game.

1 Compt's die.
BANK OF WHITEWATER. Whitewater, Wis.
Farmers at work, mowing and loading wagon—one in foreground resting.
ONE
1 Boy and girl.

Three on 3. Compt's die.
Title of Bank.
Female seated with dog and pail, cows, etc.
THREE
3 Cars.

1 Male portrait
BK OF WISCONSIN, Madison, Wis.
ONE Battle scene—old man and female; soldiers in distance. ONE
ONE ONE
1 Compt's die

2 Male, female and child.
BK OF WISCONSIN, Madison, Wis.
Compt's die. Horse and colt, man and child; barn, etc.
2 TWO

5
BK OF WISCONSIN, Madison, Wis.
Arctic regions—men fixing boat; dogs, ship, etc. 5
5 Compt's die.

ONE on 1. Boy and girl at well.
BATAVIAN BANK, La Crosse, Wis
Gir's head. 1 Girl's head.
ONE DOLLAR.
ONE on 1 Compt's die

Female with pen and tablet, child at her feet. FIVE
V Female reclining with chart, compass, and quadrant. V
BATAVIAN BANK, La Crosse, Wis.
FIVE DOLLARS.
5 surrounded by small 5's. Compt's die

1 Compt's die. 1
Female surrounded by fruit and corn; in distance trees, river, shipping, village, &c.
CENTRAL BANK OF WISCONSIN, Janesville, Wis.
Locomotive.
1 Portrait of female. 1

2 Compt's die. TWO
Farm scene; man watering three horses at a trough; female feeding pigs; buildings in distance.
Title of Bank.
Steamboat.
2 Female with folded hands. 2

3 Compt's die. 3
Title of Bank.
Train of cars.
Agricultural implements.
3 Portrait of Washington. 3

1 CITY B'K OF GREEN BAY 1
Farmer plowing with two horses
TWO DOLLARS
Compt's die Green Bay, Wis.
Girl's head

Girl and boy driving cattle through gate
of Green Bay
Female and child
CITY B'K
FIVE DOLLARS
5 Green Bay
Wisconsin
5 Compt's die

1 Compt's die. ONE
Vig. Indian and horse on right buffaloes, train of cars, &c.
CITY BANK, Kenosha, Wis.
Safe.
1 Indian female seated and child.

2 Compt's die. TWO
Vig. Large public building; men and women, horses and carriages, &c., in front
CITY BANK, Kenosha, Wis.
2 Locomotive and tender.

THREE Female seated with quadrant, spread eagle, standing on frame.
3 Vig. Indian and boy feeding horse; Indians seated on left.
CITY BANK, Kenosha, Wis.
3 Compt's die. THREE

Blacksmith at forge. ONE
1 Justice seated; eagle, shield, etc.; cars, bridge, village and shipping in the distance.
CITY BANK OF PRESCOTT, Wis.
ONE
1 Compt's die. ONE

2 Three men—one on horseback watering horse from trough; shop, hay wagon, etc.
Title of Bank.
Compt's die.
2
Eagle.
2 Two horses, boy, girl and duck by trough.

3 3
Cars. Justice.
Title of Bank.
3 Compt's die.

V 5
Title of Bank.
Cattle and sheep, water, trees, houses, etc. Girl's head.
FIVE
5 Compt's die. FIVE

1 ONE State arms.
COLUMBIA CO. BK. Portage City, Wis.
Railroad train.
ONE Portrait of Penn.

2 State arms.
Rural scene—cattle, sheep, land, water,
COLUMBIA CO. BK. Portage City, Wis.
2 Female.

5 State arms. FIVE
Chariot of the Sun.
COLUMBIA CO. BK. Portage City, Wis.
5 Train of cars

ONE Compt's die. Milkmaid and cows.
COMMERCIAL BANK Racine, Wis.
Farmer, horse and dog. Blacksmith, anvil and forge.
1 Sailor with implements.

1
COMMERCIAL BANK Racine, Wis.
Wharf scene—cars, drays, males, females, shipping, etc. Girl.
1 Compt's die.

2 Female.
COMMERCIAL BANK Racine, Wis.
Train of cars, men, trees, etc.; cars, bridge and hills in distance.
2 Compt's die.

3 Female portrait.
COMMERCIAL BANK Racine, Wis.
Female portrait.
Compt's die.
3 Female portrait.

Female portrait. 1
1 Female representing Commerce with implements.
CORN EX. BANK, Waupun, Wis.
1 Compt's die

Male portrait 2
Spread eagle and shield. 2
CORN EX. BANK, Waupun, Wis.
2 Compt's die.

Left	Center	Right
Compt's die. 3	Three females and fig. 3; factories in distance. 3 CORN EX. BANK, Waupun, Wis.	3 Male portrait
5 Female portrait	CORN EX BANK, Waupun, Wis. Farmers, etc., in cornfield.	5 Compt's die. FIVE
Female blowing dinner horn, table, etc.	CORN PLANTER'S BANK, Waupacca, Wis. Large red tinted 5. Compt's die.	5 Female with pail on fence; open gate, etc.
Two men in corn field. X	Title of Bank. Two men, wagon, mill, horses drinking at trough; chickens, etc.	10 Compt's die.
ONE Compt's die.	DANE CO. BANK, Madison, Wis. Female reclining upon a rock viewing lake with city on opposite side; cars passing around lake shore. 1	1 ONE
TWO Compt's die.	DANE CO. BANK, Madison, Wis. Two females; cars on the right and steamboat on left in the background. Safe.	TWO 2
3 Compt's die.	DANE CO. BANK, Madison, Wis. Three females joining hands. 3	3
FI5VE Compt's die.	Indian, squaw and child; female and child; between them a shield with word five thereon. DANE CO. BANK, Madison, Wis. Eagle.	5 Med. head.
X Compt's die.	View of church, buildings and trees. DANE CO. BANK, Madison, Wis.	10 Med. head.
TWENTY Female with shield. Wisconsin.	DANE CO. BANK, Madison, Wis. 2 Female portrait. 0	TWENTY Compt's die.

Left	Center	Right
1 Compt's die. ONE	ELKHORN BANK, Elkhorn, Wis. Elk's head. ONE Cupid. ONE Cupid	1 Female and figure 1.
TWO Female portrait. Compt's die.	ELKHORN BANK, Elkhorn, Wis. Lovers at a well; barn in distance. Man.	2 Elk's head.
THREE Female portrait. Compt's die.	ELKHORN BANK, Elkhorn, Wis. Train of cars; hills and village in distance. Beaver.	3 Elk's head. THREE
1 Farmer seated; scythe hanging on limb of tree.	Shipping, ships, steamboat, pilot boat and city. EXCHANGE BANK OF DARLING & CO., Fond du Lac, Wis. Capital $50,000.	1 Compt's die. ONE
2 Compt's die.	Western steamboat; hills, &c. Title of Bank. Capital $50,000.	2 Squaw.
Hunter loading gun; deer at his feet. THREE	Indian portrait; female instructing children on right; house in distance; on left squaw and papoose. Title of Bank. Capital $50,000.	3 Compt's die.
1 Compt's die. 1 1	Farm scene, horses drinking from trough, man, cows, poultry, hogs, &c.; barn in background. FARMERS' BANK. Beaver Dam, Wis. ONE DOLLAR.	1 1 Female seated, flowers at her feet. 1
Compt's die. 5	5 Cattle eating from hay mow; pitchfork, birds, &c. 5 FARMERS' BANK. Beaver Dam, Wis. FIVE DOLLARS.	5 Dog and safe.
Man with bag on back; horse, colt, mill; two boys on bridge. 1	FOND du LAC, The Farmers and Mechanics' Bank, ONE DOLLAR ONE ONE	1 Compt's die Wisconsin.
FARMERS TWO	and MECHANICS' BK Man erect with horse; wheelwrights at work. Portrait of Boy. FOND du LAC, TWO	2 Compt's die. Wisconsin.

Left	Center	Right
1 ONE Head of Henry Clay.	Female sitting down; cars and load of hay in background. FARMERS' & MILLERS' BANK, Milwaukee, Wis. Eagle.	1 State Arms.
Portrait of female. 2	Two men reposing under a tree; hay-field in the background. FARMERS' & MILLERS' BANK, Milwaukee, Wis.	2 State Arms.
5 Locomotive. 5	FARMERS' & MILLERS' BANK, Milwaukee, Wis. Female sitting down by a shield; State House in background.	5 State Arms.
TEN on X Two females	FAR. & MILLERS BK Scene at grist mill Milwaukie TEN DOLLARS	TEN Compt's die TEN
1 Compt's die.	FOREST CITY BANK Waukesha, Wis. Load of hay, men, horses, barn, etc. Dog's head.	ONE 1
2 Compt's die.	FOREST CITY BANK Waukesha Wis. Liberty, eagle and shield, on half globe. Shield.	TWO Female and fig. 2.
Compt's die. 3	FOREST CITY BANK Waukesha, Wis. Ship and other vessels at sea. Hands.	3 Sailor at wheel.
Female seated holding shield on which is V and 5. Compt's die	Two men, child, anvil, wheel, etc. FRONTIER BANK, Stevens' Point Wis.	5 Sailor seated with pipe.
Female soaring above houses, cars, steamboat, etc; on right upper is cattle, houses, etc.	Comp's die. Title of Bank.	10 Mechanic at bench.
ONE Mower with scythe seated.	Female seated; dog and pail on right, cows on left. GERMAN BANK, Sheboygan, Wis.	1 Compt's die.

TWO Compt's die.	Women at work on cotton machines. GERMAN BANK, Sheboygan, Wis.	2 Train of cars.
Compt's die. Word three and fig. 3.	GERMAN BANK, Sheboygan, Wis. Three females; ship in distance.	3
5 Steamboat.	GERMAN BANK. Sheboygan, Wis. 5 Compt's die.	FIVE
ONE Soldier with gun.	Indians hunting buffaloes. GREEN BAY BANK, Oconto Wis.	1 ONE Compt's die.
TWO 2 Compt's die.	Backwood's scene—men at work clearing. GREEN BAY BANK. Oconto Wis.	2 Female; cow and calf.
TWENTY DOLLARS 20 Compt's die	GREEN BAY BANK TWENTY Figure DOLLARS on of on Die America Die Wisconsin	20 Female beside barrels, grain, etc. TWENTY DOLLARS
Compt's. Die. Harvestman, sharpening cradle.	1 Indian and white man, with upright shield between. JEFFERSON COUNTY BANK, Watertown, Wis. Bull	1 Blacksmith.
THREE Indian warrior.	Compt's. Die. American officers; Indian Chiefs in council. JEFFERSON COUNTY BANK, Watertown, Wis. Female.	3 Indian mother and child sitting.
5 Large V., with group of male and female figures.	Compt's. Die. Locomotive and train of cars. JEFFERSON COUNTY BANK, Wa ertown, Wis. Cornucopia.	5 Washington. FIVE
1 Indians on horses hunting buffaloes.	JUNEAN BANK, Milwaukie, Wis. Large Male portrait.	1 Compt's die. Wisconsin.

5 Two men at work: wheel, sledge, etc.	JUNEAN BANK, Milwaukie, Wis. Male portrait. Compt's die and 5.	5 Female feeding fowls.
X White men in boat; Indians on shore. TEN	JUNEAN BANK, Milwaukie. Wis. Large male portrait. TEN DOLLARS.	10 Compt's die.
1 Steamboat.	Vig. Female seated State holding a dagger Arms and supporting a silver dollar. KENOSHA CO. BANK Kenosha, Wis. Capital Stock, &c.	1 Female holding large figure 1.
Vig. River scene, Indian, squaw and child in a canoe. 2	State Arms. KENOSHA CO. BANK Kenosha. Wis Capital Stock, &c.	Female holding large figure 2. TWO
5 Large 5, two Indians, water fall, cars and bridge.	Lumber, loading wagon, &c.; shed, men and water falls in distance. LUMBERMANS' BK., Viroqua Wis. Shield.	5 Compt's die. FIVE
10 Hunter seated; dog at feet.	Indian reclining; another in distance. LUMBERMANS' BK., Wis. Woodcutter.	10 Compt's die TEN
Three children in circular die reading book 5	FIVE on 5 Female portrait MERCHANT'S BANK FIVE DOLLARS Milwaukie, Wis.	5 Compt's die
Female reclining on grain; men at work in distance V	V Child's head V FIVE DOLLARS MILWAUKIE CO. BK FIVE DOLLARS Wisconsin	5 Auditor's die
TEN Washingt'n TEN	View of Niagara Falls MILWAUKIE CO. BK TEN DOLLARS on 10	10 Auditor's die
Fig 5 inverted Compt's die.	Man with white and black horse; cars, water scene, building, etc. MONROE CO. BANK, Sparta, Wis. Indian.	Fig. 5 inverted. Female seated with pail, cows, church, etc., in distance.

1 Compt's die. ONE	Vig. Factory, train of cars, horses, canal, boat, houses, trees, &c.; in the distance a train of cars crossing aqueduct. NORTHERN BANK Howard, Wis. Capital $50,000, &c.	1 Indian princess seated, figure 1, rainbow, shield &c.
2 Compt's die. TWO	Vig. Drove of cattle and sheep, drovers, horse, and dog. NORTHERN BANK Howard, Wis. Capital $50,000, &c.	2 Two Females erect.
3 Compt's die. THREE	Vig. Harvest scene, farmers at lunch, female and children, boy climbing, dog, &c., in distance man, 4 horses, and load of hay. NORTHERN BANK Howard, Wis. Capital $50,000, &c.	3 Figure 3 and three male figures, sailor, farmer, & mechanic.
FIVE Blacksmith with sledge, anvil, etc.; locomotive and factory.	NORTHERN BANK Green Bay, Wis. Compt's die.	5 Train of cars; cars, etc, in distance.
10	Large Spread eagle. NORTHERN BANK Green Bay, Wis. Compt's die.	10
1 Compt's die. ONE	Man watering three horses from trough by side of well; goat, kid and sheep; cattle and house in distance. OSHKOSH COMMERCIAL BANK, Oshkosh, Wis.	ONE Female seated with shield.
2 Farmer's family scene.	Title of Bank. Indians on horseback hunting buffaloes.	2 on TWO. Compt's die. TWO
3 THREE	Indian family contemplating the progress of civilization. Title of Bank around Compt's die.	Fig. 3 on DOLLARS Female with flowers in her apron.
5 FIVE Compt's die.	Title of Bank. Prairie scene—Indians and horse; train of cars, buffaloes and rising sun in distance.	5 on FIVE Squaw and papoose.
2 Two children	PRAIRIE CITY B'K. Ripon, Wis. Boy and dog; house in distance.	2 Compt's die TWO

ONE Goddess of liberty with spear in left hand.	State arms. RACINE CO. BANK. Racine, Wis. Portrait of Washington cupid on either side.	1 Female child with basket.
TWO Little girl. 2	State arms. RACINE CO. BANK, Racine, Wis. Two females and male reclining, the female on right has sickle in right hand and sheaf of wheat in left; anvil, sledge, &c.; train of cars on left, vessel on right. Clasped hands.	2 TWO
3 Sailor with left hand on rudder block.	State arms. RACINE CO. BANK. Racine, Wis. F[illegible]ted, with blacksmith on right and sailor on left, [illegible] in distance on left [illegible]; city on right.	3
FIVE State arms. 5	RACINE CO. BANK, Racine, Wis. FI 5 VE Three cows standing in water, train of cars, farm house, &c.	FI 5 VE Blacksmith, sailor and farmer.
1 Man erect with drum, two others seated, one with pipe.	Blacksmith shoeing horse; man seated and one erect. ROCK COUNTY B'K, Janesville, Wis.	1 Compt's die
Portrait of boy. Compt's die.	Men gathering ears of corn; horse, colt, cart and dog. ROCK COUNTY B'K, Janesville, Wis. Dog, key and safe.	2 Portrait of female.
Head of girl. Compt's die	Group of persons viewing and applauding train of cars; in distance, forest house, cart, &c. ROCK COUNTY B'K, Janesville, Wis. Dog's head.	3 Female seated with sheaf and sickle.
5 Compt's die.	Cattle, hogs, &c.; town on right. ROCK COUNTY B'K. Janesville, Wis.	5 Henry Clay. 5
1 Country road oxen, horses, load of hay, men, &c.; houses, &c. in distance.	Vig. Man and female on either side of a shield on which is inscribed figure 1, and word one; on left steamboat, and on right, drover, drove of hogs and a negro. ROCK RIVER BANK, Beloit, Wis.	1 Compt's die.

Female seated holding figure 3, sheaf of wheat on left. Compt's die.	ROCK RIVER BANK, Beloit, Wis. Portrait of female.	Female seated holding figure 3; masts and bbls., bales, &c. on right. 3
5 Female portrait. 5	ROCK RIVER BANK, Beloit, Wis. Vig. Female seated, shield, &c., in background hills, &c.	5 Compt's die
Cupid with sheaf. 2	ROCKWELL & Co's BANK, Hunter with gun and dog. Fig. 2 to right and cupid with cornucopia above. Compt's die. Two Dollars. Elkhorn, Wis.	2
Portrait of female.	3 Title of Bank. Female, column, steamer, etc. Sheep.	3 Compt's die.
1 Compt's die. Wisconsin.	SAUK CITY BANK, Sauk City, Wis. ONE DOLLAR	1 Female reclining with shield, pole, cap, eagle &c
2 Portrait of girl. Wisconsin.	Title of Bank. Compt's die. Man on load of hay in front of building, man in window; horse, colt, shop, etc. Dog's head.	2 TWO
ONE Compt's die. ONE	SAUK COUNTY B'K, Baraboo, Wis. Blacksmith shop; shoeing horse; man at forge; farmer, etc.	1 Indian female.
TWO	SAUK CO. BANK, Baraboo Wis. Shield; farmer seated town, etc., on right; Indian, hills, etc., on left. 2	2 Compt's die. TWO
3 Female with love	SAUK CO. BANK, Baraboo, Wis. Cattle, trees, stream of water, etc.	3 Compt's die. THREE

Compt's die One on 1	1 Three men, dog, machinery, etc., in grist mill. SHAWANAW BANK Chilton, Wis.	1 Female with flower
Compt's die 2	Corn husking scene—males, female, negro, dog, etc. SHAWANAW BANK Chilton, Wis. TWO	2 Child's head.
V Five cherubs with anvil, globe and sledge.	SHAWANAW BANK Shawanaw, Wis. Compt's die.	5 Five cherubs with tablet and rake.
X Train of cars	SHAWANAW BANK Shawanaw, Wis. Compt's die.	10 Indian seated; plow, cabin, wheat, etc.
Compt's Die. 1	Indian with spear and horse; train of cars. STATE BANK, Madison, Wis.	1 Mechanic seated; buildings in distance.
Compt's Die. 2	STATE BANK, Madison, Wis. Three females, one with lyre; another seated painting, and middle one with tablet.	2 Train of cars.
FIVVE Compt's Die. FIVVE	STATE BANK, Madison, Wis. View of the Capitol building of Wisconsin.	5 Indian reclining; huts in background.
1 Portrait of Webster.	STATE BANK OF WISCONSIN, Milwaukee, Wis. Vig. Farming scene at noon.	1 State Arms.
2 Female Portrait.	STATE BANK OF WISCONSIN, Milwaukee, Wis. Vig. Female reclining on bale of goods, barrels, &c., ship on right; factory, &c., on left.	2 State Arms.

WISCONSIN.

Left	Centre	Right
5 5	Vig. Three females in water, cupid, &c. Male Portrait. STATE BANK OF WISCONSIN, Milwaukee, Wis.	5 State Arms.
10 Male portrait	Vig. Land and water scene, train of cars running to the left, one crossing bridge in distance. STATE BANK OF WISCONSIN, Milwaukee, Wis.	10 State Arms.
FIVE Eagle on cliff Compt's die.	Men propelling raft on river ST. CROIX VALLEY BANK, St. Croix Falls, Wis. Sunset.	Five on 5 5, Indians, cars, water falls, etc.
10 X, female, cows, cars, etc.	Steamboat Indian. Title of Bank. Compt's die.	10 Indian, water etc.
2 2	SUMMIT BANK, Milkmaid, man, ladder, house, etc. Female portrait. Oconomowoc. Wis.	2 Compt's die. TWO
3 Compt's die. THREE	Title of Bank. Man drinking; boy, horses and plow.	3 Boy and two horses at trough.
Man plowing with two horses 5	Wisconsin Female portrait UNION BANK FIVE DOLLARS Columbus	5 Compt's die
TEN DOLLARS Female portrait UNION	Figure of Justice Female portrait BANK Columbus TEN DOLLARS	10 Compt's die
1 Female feeding chickens	WALWORTH CO. BK Delavan, Wis. State die.	1 Man, horse and dog.
TWO Smith's shop	WALWORTH CO. BK Delavan, Wis. 2 Female; bale of goods; houses in distance. 2	2 State die.

WISCONSIN.

Left	Centre	Right
5 Head of female.	Horse Market. WALWORTH CO. BK Delavan, Wis.	5 State die.
1 Female seated on stone, with pail.	WAUKESHA CO. BK. Waukesha, Wis. 1 Female seated on bale beside silver dollar, anchor, trees, &c. 1 Girl's head.	1 Compt's die.
TWO Compt's die. TWO	WAUKESHA COUNTY BANK, Waukesha, Wis. Corn husking scene—two males, two females, dog, fowls, etc.	TWO Female head
Agricultural implements, grain, etc. 5	Wisconsin Female and child WHEAT GROWERS' BK Sun Prairie FIVE DOLLARS	5 Compt's die
10 Female portrait 10	TEN DOLLARS WHEAT GROWERS' BK Sun Prairie Compt's die Scene at door of mill, boy on horse: child, dog, etc.	10
ONE	Vig. same as the above 2. WISCONSIN BANK, Madison, Wis. Badger	1 Compt's die. ONE
TWO	Male portrait with Indian, wigwams and canoe on right; farmer, sheaves, cars, bridge, canal boat, etc., on left. WISCONSIN BANK, Madison, Wis.	2 Compt's die. TWO
5 Compt's die.	Two females representing Liberty and Justice on either side of male portrait; cars, bridge, factory, steamer, &c., in distance. WISCONSIN BANK, Madison, Wis. Bull	5 5
10 Male portrait	WISCONSIN BANK, Madison, Wis. Compt's die on X. Indian.	10 Reaper seated; loading wagon in the distance TEN
State Arms Male standing with American flag, female sitting at his feet, anchor, bale, barrels, &c.	WISCONSIN MARINE AND FIRE INSURANCE CO. Milwaukee, Wis. Vig. Female sitting, resting right arm on anchor; ships on right and left.	2 Female Portrait.

MINNESOTA.

Left	Centre	Right
3 State Arms. Three female figures reclining each above the other; anchor, &c. THREE	Title of Bank. Vig. St. George on horse, and the dragon.	3 Female Portrait.
State Arms. Indian with gun, &c.	Title of Bank. Vig. Man, woman, and child.	5 Female with bundle of straw on her back.
ONE on 1 Boy with dog.	STATE OF MINNESOTA. BANK OF HASTINGS 1 Steamboat on Western River. 1 ONE DOLLAR. Hastings.	ONE on 1 Female with bundle of grain
MINNESOTA. Female with sheaf of grain and sickle. TWO	Two Dollars. 2 Dog's head. 2 BANK OF HASTINGS TWO DOLLARS Hastings.	2 Locomotive and train of cars. TWO on 2
Scene at blacksmith's shop; mending wheelbarrow, etc.; girl with grain THREE	3 Dollars 3 STATE OF MINNESOTA. Girl's head. BANK OF HASTINGS. THREE DOLLARS.	3 Fowls.
V Reaper with grain sickle etc	BK OF HASTINGS. 5 FIVE DOLLARS. 5 Hastings, Minn's. Minn's. 5 Cow under tree. 5	V Farmer seated, scythe in hand.
ONE on 1 Female with basket of flowers	ONE DOLLAR 1 Agricultural implements 1 B'K OF MINNESOTA ONE DOLLAR Saint Paul 1	1 Female with pitcher, etc.
2 Eagle TWO	B'K OF MINNESOTA 2 View of waterfall 2 TWO DOLLARS	2 Eagle TWO
5 Man with dog FIVE	B'K OF MINNESOTA V on FIVE Two children V on FIVE FIVE DOLLARS Saint Paul	5 Female with bundle of grain 5
Engineers surveying land 10	at work X Girl's head X B'K OF MINNESOTA TEN DOLLARS Saint Paul	10 Female on bank, with basket of [illegible]

MINNESOTA.

Indians on cliff | BK OF RED WING | ONE DOLLAR | Red Wing. | State of Minns's | Two horses, man with bag of grain, etc. | 1 | 1 | Steamboat loading

2 | TWO | BK OF RED WING | TWO DOLLARS | Minnesota. | Female feeding calves, cows, boat, train of cars in distance. | Red Wing. | 2

3 | Reaper, horses' head dog, pigeon etc. | Shield, Indian on left, reaper on right. | BK OF RED WING | THREE DOLLARS | Red Wing, Minnesota. | 3 | Three Cupids on large ornamental fig. | 3

5 | Indian with bow and hatchet. | STATE OF MINNESOTA. | Steamboat on Western River. | BK OF RED WING | FIVE DOLLARS | Red Wing. | 5 | Man with bundle of corn.

ONE on BK 1 | Female portrait | ONE DOLLAR. | OF SO. MINNESOTA | One Dollar. | Winona. | Train ONE of cars, ONE etc. | ONE on 1 | Portrait of farmer.

TWO | Three deer | BK OF SOUTHERN MINNESOTA. | Winona. Female, sheep, grain, etc. | State of Minn's. | 2 DOLLARS. 2 | TWO | Female portrait

FIVE | BK OF | Boy feeding horse, two children, etc. | State of Minns's | Group of cattle. | SOUTHERN MINNESOTA. | FIVE DOLLARS | FIVE | FIVE | Female reclining; basket of flowers, etc.

ONE on 1 | Girl playing with dogs | MINNESOTA | Cupid rolling silver dollar; train of cars in distance | THORNE'S BANK | ONE DOLLAR | Hastings | ONE on 1 | Male portrait

2 | Hastings | Male portrait | MINNESOTA | Two cupids and two silver dollars; cars in distance on right | THORNE'S BANK | 2 DOLLARS 2 | 2 | Horse's head

V | MINNESOTA. | Dog on safe | THORNE'S BANK | FIVE | Five cupids and five silver dollars | FIVE | FIVE DOLLARS | Hastings | 5 | Male portrait | FIVE

CANADA.

Dis. | Queen Victoria. | Dis. | Five Shillings. | BANK OF B. N. AMERICA, | Hamilton, Canada. | Arms of the Bank; or sailor, husbandman, &c. | Dis. | Prince Albert. | Dis.

TEN SHILLINGS | Victoria | TWO DOLLARS | Arms of the Bank; $2 or sailor husbandman, &c. $2 | Title of Bank. | Albert | TEN SHILLINGS

ONE | Female reclining. | POUND | Title of Bank. | Three females seated; $4 agriculture, commerce, &c. 1£ | Arms of Great Britain. | FOUR | Indian Chief seated. | DOLLARS

Twenty-five | Arms of the Bank, &c. | SHILLINGS | Title of Bank. | Two females seated; $5 shipping, merchandise, &c. £1. 5. 0 | Arms of Great Britain | FIVE | Victoria the Royal Chair. | DOLLARS

Ten | Miniature of three females. | DOLLARS | Title of Bank. | £2. 10. 0. Large beehive, surrounded by shrubbery, etc. $10 | Arms of Great Britain. | FIFTY | Miniature of plow, sheep, vessel, tree, water, &c. | SHILLINGS

Portrait of Queen Victoria. | FIVE SHILLINGS | BANK OF BRITISH NORTH AMERICA, | Kingston, Ca. | 1 Arms of the Bank; or sailor, husbandman, dove, beehive, &c. 1 | Portrait of Prince Albert

TEN Shillings. | Portrait of Queen Victoria. | TWO DOLLARS | $2 Arms of the Bank; or sailor, husbandman, &c. $2 | BANK OF BRITISH NORTH AMERICA, | Kingston, Ca. | Portrait of Prince Albert | TEN Shillings

QUATRE | Indian chief seated. | PIASTRES | Title of Bank. | 4 Female reclining representing Commerce; bale of merchandise, anchor, shipping, &c. 4 | British arms. | FOUR | Female surrounded by shrubbery, &c.; farming implements at her feet. | DOLLARS

CINQ | Victoria seated in the royal chair. | PIASTRES | BANK OF BRITISH NORTH AMERICA, | Kingston, Ca. | 5 Two females; lion and unicorn. 5 | British arms. | FIVE | Indian chief seated. | DOLLARS

DIX | Miniature view of town or city. | PIASTRES | BANK OF BRITISH NORTH AMERICA, | Kingston, Ca. | 10 Two females reclining, shipping, &c. X | British arms. | TEN | Arms of the Bank. | DOLLARS

CANADA.

VINGT | Female standing erect with spear in left hand; right hand resting on a shield. | PIASTRES | BANK OF BRITISH NORTH AMERICA, | Kingston, Ca. | 20 Female reclining on bale of under. 20 | British arms. | TWENTY | Miniature view of town or city. | DOLLARS

50 | Miniature view of group of three females. | PIASTRES | Title of Bank. | CINQUANTE Female FIFTY reclining, representing Commerce, Justice, and Agriculture. | British arms. | 50 | Miniature view of Indian, canoe, tent, trees, &c. | DOLLARS

One Dollar | Portrait of Queen Victoria. | Five Shillings | BANK OF BRITISH NORTH AMERICA, | Montreal, Ca. | Arms of the Bank, or sailor, husbandman, beehive, dove, cornucopia, &c. | Montreal. | Portrait of Prince Albert | UnePiastre

Two Dollars. | Arms of Great Britain or lion and unicorn fighting for the crown. | DeuxPiastres | BANK OF BRITISH NORTH AMERICA, | Montreal, Ca. | $2 | Montreal. | Arms of the Bank. | Ten Shillings

Four Dollars. | Indian seated | Quatre Piastres. | BANK OF BRITISH NORTH AMERICA, | Montreal, Ca. | 4 Large sail vessel; small one in background. 4 | British arms. | Quatre Piastres. | Miniature view of female reclining, representing Commerce. | Four Dollars

FIVE | Monument. | DOLLARS | BANK OF BRITISH NORTH AMERICA, | Montreal, Ca. | 5 Large sail vessel; smaller one in distance. 5 | British arms. | CINQ | Her Majesty seated in the royal chair | PIASTRES

$10 | Tent, canoe, persons, trees, &c. | Ten Dollars | BANK OF BRITISH NORTH AMERICA, | Montreal, Ca. | Female reclining on bale of mdse., representing Commerce, shipping, &c., in background. | British arms. | DIX | View of entrance to harbor; houses, vessels, &c. | PIASTRES

20 | View of public buildings in Montreal. | PIASTRES | BANK OF BRITISH NORTH AMERICA, | Montreal, Ca. | VINGT Group TWENTY of three females, Agriculture, Commerce, &c. | British arms. | 20 | Monument, houses, &c. | DOLLARS

Cinquante | Arms of the Bank. | PIASTRES | BANK OF BRITISH NORTH AMERICA, | Montreal, Ca. | 50 Steamship. 50 | British arms. | FIFTY | View of monument public buildings. | DOLLARS

Dis. | Queen Victoria. | Dis. | FIVE SHILLINGS. | BANK OF BRITISH N. AMERICA. | Toronto, Ca. | Arms of the Bank, or sailor, husbandman, &c. | Dis. | Prince Albert | Dis.

Left	Centre	Right
TEN SHILLINGS. Queen Victoria. TWO DOLLARS.	$2 Arms of the Bank $2 or sailor, husbandman, &c. Title of Bank.	Prince Albert. TEN SHILLINGS.
QUATRE Female seated on bale of merchandise shipping, &c. PIASTRES	Title of Bank. £1 £1 British arms.	ONE Arms of the Bank. POUND
QUATRE Female seated; shipping, &c. PIASTRES	Title of Bank. 4 4 British arms.	FOUR Arms of the Bank. DOLLARS
CINQ Miniature view of house, rural economy, &c. PIASTRES.	Title of Bank. 5 5 British arms.	FIVE Female seated. DOLLARS.
CINQ Same as 5s. PIASTRES	Title of Bank. 25s. 25s. British arms.	Twenty-five Same as 5s. SHILLINGS
DIX Miniature of Cataract of Niagara. PIASTRES	Title of Bank. 10 X British arms.	TEN Queen Victoria seated in the royal chair. DOLLARS
ONE Court House.	Cattle, &c. BANK of the COUNTY OF ELGIN, St. Thomas. Can.	1 Fowls.
2 Male head.	Cars, &c. BANK of the COUNTY OF ELGIN, Canada.	2 Court House.
5 Male portrait.	Man, three horses, sheep, house, &c. BANK of the COUNTY OF ELGIN, Canada.	5 Buildings, &c.
10 Male head.	Cars, men, &c. BANK of the COUNTY OF ELGIN, Canada.	10 Court House.

Left	Centre	Right
	B'K. OF MONTREAL AND BRANCHES, Canada. These notes all have the place from which they are issued printed in the same manner as we have shown in the second description of the ONE.	
Female in a large figure 1.	[Old Plate.] B'K. OF MONTREAL AND BRANCHES, Canada. Steamer towing. FIVE SHILLINGS. City Arms.	Female in a large figure 1.
MONTREAL City arms supported by two Indians, the female seated.	[New Plate.] B'K. OF MONTREAL AND BRANCHES. Canada. FIVE SHILLINGS. ONE DOLLAR.	Steamship and shipping, and large figure 1. MONTREAL
ONE Female portrait.	B'K OF MONTREAL, Canada. 1 Two Indians either side of shield; beaver at top. 1 ONE	1 Female with sheaf.
Indian either side of shield. 1	BK OF MONTREAL, Canada. ONE DOLLAR	1 Queen Victoria.
TWO St. George and dragon.	Title of Bank. 2 Queen Victoria. Prince Albert. 2 2	2 Same as vig. of 1s.
Female figure in large figure 2. 2	[Old Plate.] B'K. OF MONTREAL AND BRANCHES. Canada. Female seated. 2 Female standing. TWO SHILLINGS. City Arms	Female figure in large figure 2. 2
Same as on Ones.	[New Plate.] Title of Bank. TEN SHILLINGS. TWO DOLLARS.	Female shipping and figure 2, and horn of plenty.
4 DOLLARS Female.	Royal Arms with motto. B'K. OF MONTREAL AND BRANCHES, Canada City Arms.	4 DOLLARS Female
City Arms supported by two Indians, the female seated.	B'K. OF MONTREAL AND BRANCHES. Canada. TWENTY SHILLINGS. FOUR DOLLARS.	Female holding sheaf and sickle, lamb at her feet; large 4 resting on back of another lamb

Left	Centre	Right
FOUR Same as vig. of 1s.	Title of Bank. 4 Male portrait. 4 FOUR	4 Female seated by bale.
FIVE DOLLARS FIVE Same as vig. of 1s.	5 Building. 5 Title of Bank. FIVE	5 Blacksmith seated.
5 Female bust. FIVE	B'K. OF MONTREAL AND BRANCHES, Canada. Large V, with female; figure 5 on either side. City Arms	Bust of female. FIVE
City Arms supported by two Indians, the female seated. 5	B'K. OF MONTREAL AND BRANCHES. Canada. TWENTY-FIVE SHILLINGS. FIVE DOLLARS.	Indian erect, one seated and two on horseback in distance, and 5
TEN Female seated with wand in hand, vessels in distance	B'K OF MONTREAL TEN DOLLARS on X Male portrait on X Ornamental die	10 Indian either side of shield
TEN Female seat by bale; steamer in distance.	Title of Bank. X Male portrait. X TEN	10 Same as vig. of 1s.
10 Female. TEN	B'K. OF MONTREAL AND BRANCHES, Canada. TWO POUNDS TEN X SHILLINGS currency	10 Female. TEN
City Arms supported by two Indians, female seated. 10	B'K. OF MONTREAL AND BRANCHES. Canada. FIFTY SHILLINGS. TEN DOLLARS	Steamboat prospective with large 10
50 Bust of Her Majesty. 50	B'K. OF MONTREAL AND BRANCHES, Canada. A large ship in full sail and gulliott. TWELVE POUNDS TEN SHILLINGS. City Arms.	50 Bust of Prince Albert. 50
100 Female figure representing Justice. 100	B'K OF MONTREAL AND BRANCHES, Canada. Queen Victoria seated. TWENTY-FIVE POUNDS. City Arms.	100 Female representing Commerce. 100

1 / Cooper at work. / UNE / 1 Farmer with sheaf and scythe; buildings in distance. 1 / LA BANQUE DU PEUPLE, Montreal, Canada. / 1 / Four cherubs and fig 1.	TEN / Beaver. / BANK OF TORONTO, Toronto, Canada. / City Arms. / 10 / Train of cars.	5 / Queen Victoria. / V / 5 Lion with his paw upon a shield. 5 / Title of Bank. / Same as on ones. / 5 / Prince Albert / V
2 / Farmer sharpening scythe. / DEUX / Blacksmith and ship carpenter with implements; cars and ships in distance. / LA BANQUE DU PEUPLE, Montreal, Canada / 2 / Dog, key and safe. / TWO	1 / Female seated on chest with sword and scales. / BANK OF UPPER CANADA, Toronto, Canada. / ONE St. George and the dragon. ONE / 1 / Female with trident and shield.	5 / Wild horse. / FIVE / Title of Bank. / Queen Victoria; lion and unicorn on either side. / Same as on ones. / 5 / Dog and safe / FIVE
Ship carpenter seated with tools. / 4 Milkmaid seated; female milking cow; vessels in distance. / Title of Bank. / Dog's head. / 4 / Blacksmith at work. / 4	1 / Miniature view of female head. / 1 / BANK OF UPPER CANADA. / 1 Female seated half reclining, hand resting on figure 1. 1 / St. George and dragon. / 1 / Miniature view of female seated, dog, figure 1, &c. / 1	X / Female portrait. / Title of Bank. / X Same as 4s. X / 10 / Female with trident and shield.
Two females with large X / TEN / Four cherubs, X, Prince Albert, Queen Victoria. / Title of Bank. / Agricultural implements. / Two females with large X. / DIX	1 / Indian with bow and arrow, &c. / Train of cars and village in distance. / Title of Bank. / St. George and dragon. / 1 / Female seated.	X / Portrait of Girl. / BANK OF UPPER CANADA / Two females seated, with owl, bust, anchor, etc.; ocean scene on left; building, etc., on right. / Toronto, Canada, / 10 / Cattle, telegraph, cars, bridge, etc.
20 / Sailor. / 20 / Title of Bank. / Man plowing with two horses. / Steamship. / 20	2 / Female portrait. / Sailor reclining; anchor, boat, etc.; steamship in distance. / Title of Bank. / 2 / Female with trident and shield.	TEN / Miniature view of flower girl. / TEN / 10 Female representing the Arts and Sciences. 10 / Title of Bank. / Same as on ones. / TEN / Statue of Minerva. / TEN
50 / Canal scene. / 50 / Title of Bank. / Sailor with flag reclining on bale; ship in distance. / Female head. / Steamboat.	TWO / Female representing agriculture / 2 / Title of Bank. / 2 Two flying griffins, figure 2 between. 2 / Same as on ones. / TWO / Portrait of Female. / 2	10 / Sailor with hand on Jack staff. / Steamship; other vessels in distance. 10 / Title of Bank. / Bale, bbls. and anchor. / British arms.
100 / Female portrait. / C / General view of city, wharf and shipping. / Title of Bank. / Arms. / 100 / Portrait of female. / C	2 / Train of cars / TWO / Hogs, cattle, drovers, &c.; train of cars and village in distance. / Title of Bank. / Same as on ones. / 2 / Milkmaid and two cows / TWO	20 / Miniature view of flying griffin. / TWENTY / Two female figures; locomotive, vessel, &c., in background. / Title of Bank. / Same as on ones. / 20 / Miniature of Minerva, spear, shield, &c. / TWENTY
ONE / Justice. / 1 Farmer seated on grain; reapers on left; loading hay on right. / BANK OF TORONTO, Toronto, Canada. / 1 / Indian seated supporting fig. 1.	figure 4. / Queen Victoria. / figure 4. / Female seated holding spear, shield, &c.; lion, implements of war, &c. Fig. 4 on either side. / Title of Bank. / Same as on ones. / 4 / Female representing agriculture. / 4	TWENTY / 20 Two females on either side of shield, crown at top; house and vessels in distance. / Title of Bank. / 20 / Stonecutter at work.
4 / Farmers and scythe. / Three females seated representing Agriculture, Commerce, and Arts. / BANK OF TORONTO, Toronto, Canada. / City Arms. / FOUR / Portrait of an Indian Chief.	4 / Female with cornucopia. / Title of Bank. / Two females, Royal arms, lion and unicorn. / 4 / Mechanic reclining.	50 / Miniature of cupid. / 50 / L Locomotive and car; shipping, merchandise, &c. L / Title of Bank. / Flying griffin. / Miniature view of monument, trees, shrubbery, &c. / 50
5 / Female portrait. / BANK OF TORONTO, Toronto, Canada. / British Arms. / City Arms. / 5 / Female seated, large fig. 5; bales, ships, &c.	5 / Sailor, barrel, capstan, etc. / V Same as 4s. V / Title of Bank. / 5 / Prince Albert	50 / Female figure seated; agriculture. / FIFTY / Female seated between lion and unicorn. / Title of Bank. / Same as on ones. / 50 / Female seated, armory, &c.; vessel in the background. / FIFTY.

Left	Centre	Right
50 Agricultural implements.	Title of Bank. Same as 20s	50 Female with sickle.
100 100	Same as 20s. Title of Bank.	100 Female, whale shipping, &c.
Die. 100 Die.	100 Arms of Great Britain, or lion and unicorn. 100 Title of Bank. Flying griffin.	Miniature of monument, trees, shrubbery, &c. 100
100 Miniature view of female seated.	Queen Victoria seated between lion and unicorn. Title of Bank. Same as on ones.	100 Male head.
—	Bank building. 1 CITY BANK, Montreal, Canada. Crown, sceptre, &c.	ONE Female. ONE
ONE	ONE and figure 1. Female Figure spinning; wheel and buildings in rear. ONE and figure 1. CITY BANK, Toronto, Canada. 1	Victoria.
1 Bust of William 4th UNE	1 1 LA BANQUE DE LA CITE. Montreal, Canada. Indian with bow. UNE PIASTRE.	1 The City Bank will pay the bearer on demand one dollar. ONE
TWO	2 Female figure, Agriculture and Commerce in rear. 2 CITY BANK. Toronto, Canada 2	Victoria.
2	Bank building. 2 CITY BANK. Montreal, Canada.	TWO Male and female.
2 The City Bank will pay the bearer on demand two dollars. DEUX	LA BANQUE DE LA CITE, Montreal, Canada 2 Indian in canoe. 2 DEUX PIASTRES.	2 Bust of William 4th. TWO

Left	Centre	Right
4 Victoria with crown. 4	4 Bank building. 4 CITY BANK, Montreal, Canada.	ONE POUND.
Lion and Unicorn.	5 Figure sustaining the globe with a lever. CITY BANK Toronto, Canada.	V Bust of William 4th. V
5 Bust of a female. FIVE	City arms supported by two Indians. 5 Bank building. CITY BANK, Montreal, Canada	5
5 Male portrait FIVE	Group of persons viewing train of cars. CITY BANK, Montreal, Canada.	5 Male portrait FIVE
CINQ Lion and Unicorn. PIASTRES	5 Figure sustaining the globe with a lever. 5 CITY BANK, Montreal, Canada.	V Bust of William 4th V
10 Male portrait.	CITY BANK, Montreal, Canada St George and the dragon	10 Male portrait.
TEN 10 TEN	Bank building. CITY BANK, Montreal, Canada.	10
10 Bust of William 4th 10	CITY BANK, Montreal, Canada DIX Lion and Unicorn. 10	X La Banque de la Cite payera au porteur sur demande Dix Piastres. X
10 Bust of William 4th. 10	10 CITY BK. 10 Toronto, Canada. Lion and Unicorn.	X Female Figure. X
20 La Banque de la Cite payera au porteur sur demande Vingt Piastres. XX	VINGT Bust of William 4th; Lion on right, Unicorn on left. CITY BANK, Montreal, Canada	TWENTY

Left	Centre	Right
20 Female Figure. XX	20 Bust of William 4th, Lion and Unicorn 20 CITY BANK, Toronto, Canada.	TWENTY
Female. XX	20 Bank building CITY BANK, Montreal, Canada.	20
50	Bank building. CITY BANK. Montreal, Canada.	50
100 Prince Albert.	Bank building. CITY BANK. Montreal Canada.	100 Queen Victoria.
1 Indian on rock. ONE	COMMERCIAL BK OF CANADA, Kingston, Ca. Farming scene; cars and city in distance.	1 Female Indian. ONE
1 Farm boy standing erect, holding sickle and bundle of grain.	COM. BANK, M. D Kingston, Ca. Female reclining; figure 1, cornucopia, &c. 1	1 Sailor standing erect.
1 Portrait of Prince Albert 1	1 Female erect holding a robe; canoe, &c. 1 COMMERCIAL BANK M. D., Montreal, Canada. National arms.	1 Portrait of Queen Victoria in ornamental frame. 1
2 Fowls TWO	Cattle in water, etc. Title of Bank	2 Female feeding fowls.
2 Justice and Liberty erect	COM. BANK, M. D., Kingston, Ca. Two females seated, cornucopia at their feet. 2	2 Two females standing erect, in representation of Agriculture and Commerce.
2 Portrait of Prince Albert 2	2 Two females seated, cornucopia; ship on left; sheaf of wheat and plough on right. 2 COMMERCIAL BANK M. D., Montreal, Canada National arms.	2 Same as ones 2

4 Female portrait. QUATRE	Locomotive and train of cars; city in the background; trees, houses, load of hay, &c. COM. BANK, M. D., Kingston, Ca.	4 Female portrait. FOUR
5 Portrait of Prince Albert. V	Two females, cupids, and three ornamental 5s. COMMERCIAL BANK M. D., Montreal, Canada. National arms.	5 Same as ones V
FIVE Portrait of Queen Victoria.	5 Large figure 5 enclosing female, the whole surrounded by four cupids. 5 COM. BANK, M. D., Kingston, Ca. British arms.	FIVE Portrait of Prince Albert
5 Engineers surveying land. FIVE	Farming scene; cars and city in distance. Title of Bank.	5 Man with pickaxe, shovel; &c.
V	5 Mercury seated, representing Commerce, Justice, &c., lion at his feet. COM. BANK, M. D., Kingston, Ca.	5 Portrait of female.
10 Portrait of Queen Victoria.	X Female seated in position to divide the figures 10, supporting cornucopia and key. X COM. BANK, M. D., Kingston, Ca.	10 Portrait of Prince Albert
X	10 Floating female. COM. BANK, M. D., Kingston, Ca.	10 Miniature view of shipping.
10 Portrait of Queen Victoria.	COMMERCIAL BANK M. D., Montreal, Canada. National arms.	10 TEN
10 Queen Victoria.	Title of Bank. Three sailors, anchor, bales, &c; ship on right.	10 Female portrait.
20 Portrait of Queen Victoria.	Female seated dividing the figures 20, rake in her right hand. COM. BANK, M. D., Kingston, Ca.	20 Portrait of Prince Albert

Portrait of Queen Victoria surrounded by the lion and unicorn.	COM. BANK, M. D., Kingston, Ca. 50	50
100	Miniature of female, representing the Arts and Sciences. C COM. BANK, M. D., Kingston, Ca.	100 British arms. 100
ONE HUNDRED	COMMERCIAL BANK of Canada. C View of large building, pedestrians, etc.	100 Female portrait. $100
1000	Title of Bank. M Male portrait M	ONE THOUSAND
1000	COMMERCIAL BANK M. D., Montreal, Canada. Portrait of the Empress of France.	ONE THOUSAND
ONE Queen Victoria.	EASTERN TOWNSHIP BANK, Sherbrook, Canada. Falls, mills, bridge, buildings, etc.	Indian on cliff. ONE
2 Queen Victoria.	EASTERN TOWNSHIP BANK, Sherbrooke, Canada. Cattle, pigs, and men on horseback; cars and bridge in distance.	2 Prince Albert.
4 Male portrait.	Fall, bridge, mills, etc. EASTERN TOWNSHIP BANK, Sherbrooke, Canada.	4 Male portrait.
5 Female with book.	Man with sack on back; mill, horse, colt, wheel; boys on bridge. Title of Bank.	5 Man cleaning scythe.
TEN Hunter by fire, dog, etc.	Boy watching sheep. Title of Bank.	10 Cars; buildings in distance.

XX Female, wheel, building, etc.	Man plowing with two horses; man harrowing, city, etc., in distance. Title of Bank.	20 Female with spear and XX on shield.
Ornamental work 1 Ornamental work	1 Large building, and arms of Great Britain. 1 ONE ONE GORE BANK, Hamilton, Canada.	Ornamental work 1 Ornamental work
2 Ornamental die, enclosing the words 'Honi Soit Qui Mal Y Pense.' 2	TWO Two females seated between the lion and Unicorn. TWO Title of Bank.	2
ONE POUND 4 FOUR DOLLARS	4 IV Arms of Great Britain, or lion, unicorn, &c. Title of Bank.	4 FOUR DOLLARS 4
TEN Miniature view of shipping; bales of merchandise, &c. TEN	X Miniature view of a man mounted on horseback, spearing a dragon. 10 Title of Bank.	TEN
1 Male figure erect.	Female seated with branch and shield; fort in distance. Fig. 1 on ONE either side. LA BANQUE NATIONALE. Quebec, Canada.	1 Male figure.
2 Two females.	Same as ones with fig. 2 on word DEUX either side. Title of Bank.	2 Male portrait. 2
5 Agricultural implements.	V Two men plowing with two horses. V Title of Bank.	5 Female with flowers.
10 Boy with sheep.	Locomotive and train of cars, men, etc.; steamboat in distance. Title of Bank. X TEN X	10 Female seated with spear and shield.
Female seated, holding figure 1, sheaf of wheat. 1	MOLSON'S BANK. Montreal, Canada. Vig. Steamship and other vessels.	Female seated, holding figure 1; bbls., bales and ships masts. 1

ONE Female portrait ONE	MOLSONS BANK, Montreal. Canada. 1 Female reclining with fig. 1 1	1 Sailor.
TWO Portrait of female.	Title of Bank. Two females seated by fig. 2. 2	TWO Female and two fig. 2s.
Large figure 2, portrait of Prince Albert, and two figure ones.	MOLSON'S BANK, Montreal, Canada. Vig. Female seated; on right men loading hay, train of cars, houses, &c,	2 Portrait of Queen Victoria.
Three females, with anchor, sheaf of wheat, &c. CINQ.	5 MOLSON'S BANK, Montreal, Canada. Vig. Female seated, with tub, two cows, one lying down; in distance cows trees, house, &c. Agricultural implements,	5 FIVE 5
10 Bee hive. DIX	MOLSON'S BANK, Montreal. Canada. Large X and three Cupids. Steamboat.	10 Female portrait. TEN
20 Indian in frame TWENTY	Vig. Steamship and five vessels, all under way. MOLSON'S BANK. Montreal, Canada. Man on horseback.	20 Man erect, with whip; horse and steamboat in distance.
50 Country road, drove of cattle, load of hay, horses, men, &c.	MOLSON'S BANK, Montreal. Canada. Portrait of Queen Victoria. 50	50 Train of cars, village in distance.
1	View of Niagara Falls. 1 NIAGARA DISTRICT BANK, St Catherines, Ca	Five Shil's 1
1 Milkmaid.	Register's die. Lion and unicorn on either side of the crown. NIAGARA DISTRICT BANK, St. Catharines, Ca.	1 ONE
Head of Queen Victoria. 2	NIAGARA DISTRICT BANK, St. Catherines, Ca. Ship on stocks; female reclining on safe on left; on right sheaf of wheat and sheep.	2 Locomotive and tender.

2 Prince Albert.	NIAGARA DISTRICT BANK, St. Catharines, Ca. Register's die. 2	2
FOUR Male portrait.	NIAGARA DISTRICT BANK, St. Catherines, Ca. View of N. Y. harbor with steamship and ship.	4 Ship in canal trees, houses, &c.
5 Male portrait.	NIAGARA DISTRICT BANK, St Catherines, Ca. Three men looking at chart on a stone; ship on stocks, shipping and city.	5 and word Five. Royal Arms.
5 Ship building	NIAGARA DISTRICT BANK, St Catharines, Ca. Portrait of the Queen of England.	Register's die. 5
Canada 10 Sailor with glass, girl, boy, etc	NIAGARA DISTRICT BANK TEN Figure of Justice with sword and scales TEN	West 10 Female with basket of fruit
ONE Agricultural implements and products ONE	1 Ox, sheep, horse, etc. 1 ONTARIO BANK, Bowmanville, Canada ONE	1 ONE Men shearing sheep.
TWO Mechanic with sledge, anvil; locomotive, etc.	Two and 2. Female seated, hat on lap, dog, cows, etc Title of Bank TWO	2 TWO 2
FIVE Male portrait Five and green V	ONTARIO BANK, Bowmanville, Canada Five and Cg 5. Man sharpening scythe. 5 and Dollars	5 and green V FIVE Bull's head.
10 and green X. Canal and railroad scene.	Indian with shield on which is usual scene, sun, steamer, man plowing, etc; bison on right; deer on left. Title of Bank	10 and green X. Cattle, cars, telegraph, bridge, etc.
20 Female reclining on sheaf. 20	20 on green die. ONTARIO BANK, Bowmanville, Canada	20 Boy and sheep. Prince Albert. XX

Female with sickle. 50	ONTARIO BANK, Bowmanville, Canada 50 Male portrait. 50	50 Female with flowers
100 Male portrait	Female either side of anvil; factories in distance. ONTARIO BANK, Bowmanville, Canada	100 C
1 Sailor 1	QUEBEC BANK 1 Arms of the Bank 1 ONE DOLLAR on ONE 1 ONE	1 Men at work in water
1 Anchor, bales, bbls, &c	Men chopping trees; cattle, horse, &c., in background. QUEBEC BANK, Quebec, Canada. St. George and the Dragon.	1 Bee hive surrounded by flowers.
1 Medallion head with one on it. 1	1 Vig. Indians hunting buffaloes. 1 QUEBEC BANK, Quebec, Canada. 1	Large figure 1 and female on it.
1 ONE 1	1 Vig. Two females on either side of a shield, surmounted by a crown and lion, train of cars in distance. 1 QUEBEC BANK, Quebec, Canada.	1 ONE 1
2 Female erect with spear, globe, &c	Vig. Male and female seated, male with scroll in right hand and rod in left. QUEBEC BANK. Quebec, Canada 2	2 Female with pail.
TWO on 2 Ships on ways	QUEBEC BANK 2 Arms of the Bank 2 TWO DOLLARS	TWO on 2 Ships at sea
TWO	2 British coat of arms. 2 QUEBEC BANK, Quebec, Canada	2 Female portrait with helmet. 2
4 Girl, boy, and sailor with glass	4 Arms of the bank 4 QUEBEC BANK FOUR DOLLARS	4 Female figure with shield, on which is FOUR across 4

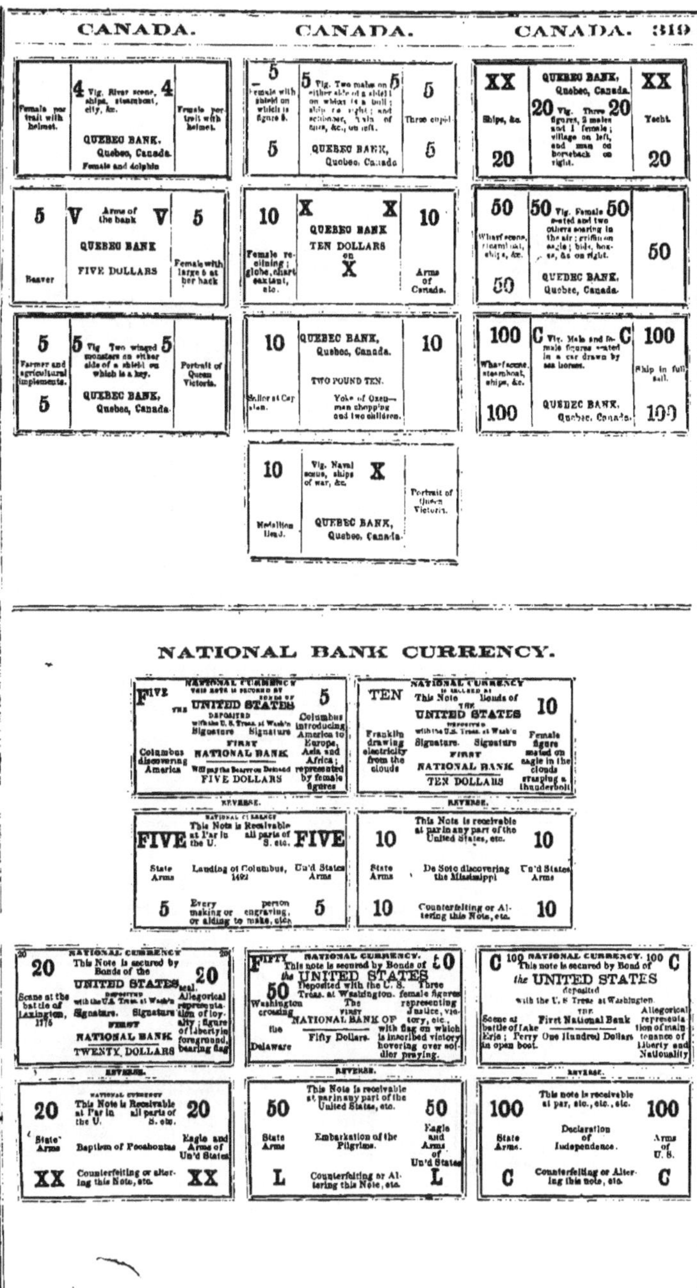

Female portrait with helmet.
4 Vig. River scene, ships, steamboat, city, &c. 4
QUEBEC BANK, Quebec, Canada.
Female and dolphin
Female portrait with helmet.

5
Female with shield on which is figure 5.
5
5 Vig. Two males on either side of a shield on which is a bull; ship on right; and schooner, bale of furs, &c., on left. 5
QUEBEC BANK, Quebec, Canada
5
Three cupids
5

XX
Ships, &c.
20
QUEBEC BANK, Quebec, Canada.
20 Vig. Three figures, 2 males and 1 female; village on left, and man on horseback on right. 20
XX
Yacht.
20

5
Beaver
V Arms of the bank V
QUEBEC BANK
FIVE DOLLARS
5
Female with large 5 at her back

10
Female reclining; globe, chart, sextant, etc.
X X
QUEBEC BANK
TEN DOLLARS on X
10
Arms of Canada.

50
Wharf scene, steamboat, ships, &c.
50
50 Vig. Female seated and two others soaring in the air; griffin on eagle; bids, boxes, &c on right. 50
QUEBEC BANK, Quebec, Canada.
50

5
Farmer and agricultural implements.
5
5 Vig. Two winged monsters on either side of a shield on which is a key. 5
QUEBEC BANK, Quebec, Canada.
Portrait of Queen Victoria.

10
Sailor at Capstan.
QUEBEC BANK, Quebec, Canada.
TWO POUND TEN.
Yoke of Oxen—man chopping and two children.
10

100
Wharf scene, steamboat, ships, &c.
100
C Vig. Male and female figures seated in a car drawn by sea horses. C
QUEBEC BANK, Quebec, Canada.
100
Ship in full sail.
100

10
Medallion Head.
Vig. Naval scene, ships of war, &c. X
QUEBEC BANK, Quebec, Canada.
Portrait of Queen Victoria.

NATIONAL BANK CURRENCY.

FIVE
Columbus discovering America
NATIONAL CURRENCY
THIS NOTE IS SECURED BY BONDS OF THE UNITED STATES
DEPOSITED with the U. S. Treas. at Wash'n
Signature Signature
FIRST NATIONAL BANK
Will pay the Bearer on Demand FIVE DOLLARS
5
Columbus introducing America to Europe, Asia and Africa; represented by female figures

TEN
Franklin drawing electricity from the clouds
NATIONAL CURRENCY
This Note is secured by Bonds of THE UNITED STATES
DEPOSITED with the U.S. Treas. at Wash'n
Signature. Signature
FIRST NATIONAL BANK
TEN DOLLARS
10
Female figure seated on eagle in the clouds grasping a thunderbolt

REVERSE.

FIVE
NATIONAL CURRENCY
This Note is Receivable at Par in all parts of the U. S. etc.
FIVE
State Arms
Landing of Columbus, 1492
Un'd States Arms
5
Every person making or engraving, or aiding to make, etc.
5

REVERSE.

10
This Note is receivable at par in any part of the United States, etc.
10
State Arms
De Soto discovering the Mississippi
Un'd States Arms
10
Counterfeiting or Altering this Note, etc.
10

20
Scene at the battle of Lexington, 1775
NATIONAL CURRENCY
This Note is secured by Bonds of the UNITED STATES
DEPOSITED with the U.S. Treas. at Wash'n
Signature. Signature
FIRST NATIONAL BANK
TWENTY DOLLARS
20
seal. Allegorical representation of loyalty; figure of Liberty in foreground, bearing flag

FIFTY
NATIONAL CURRENCY.
This note is secured by Bonds of the UNITED STATES
Deposited with the U. S. Treas. at Washington.
The FIRST NATIONAL BANK OF
Fifty Dollars.
50
50
Washington crossing the Delaware
Three female figures representing Justice, victory, etc., with flag on which is inscribed victory hovering over soldier praying.

C 100 NATIONAL CURRENCY. 100 C
This note is secured by Bond of the UNITED STATES
deposited with the U. S Treas at Washington.
THE First National Bank
One Hundred Dollars
Scene at battle of Lake Erie; Perry in open boat.
Allegorical representation of maintenance of Liberty and Nationality

REVERSE.

20
NATIONAL CURRENCY
This Note is Receivable at Par in all parts of the U. S. etc.
20
State Arms
Baptism of Pocahontas
Eagle and Arms of Un'd States
XX
Counterfeiting or altering this Note, etc.
XX

REVERSE.

50
This Note is receivable at par in any part of the United States, etc.
50
State Arms
Embarkation of the Pilgrims.
Eagle and Arms of Un'd States
L
Counterfeiting or Altering this Note, etc.
L

REVERSE.

100
This note is receivable at par, etc., etc., etc.
100
State Arms.
Declaration of Independence.
Arms of U. S.
C
Counterfeiting or Altering this note, etc.
C

UNITED STATES TREASURY NOTES.

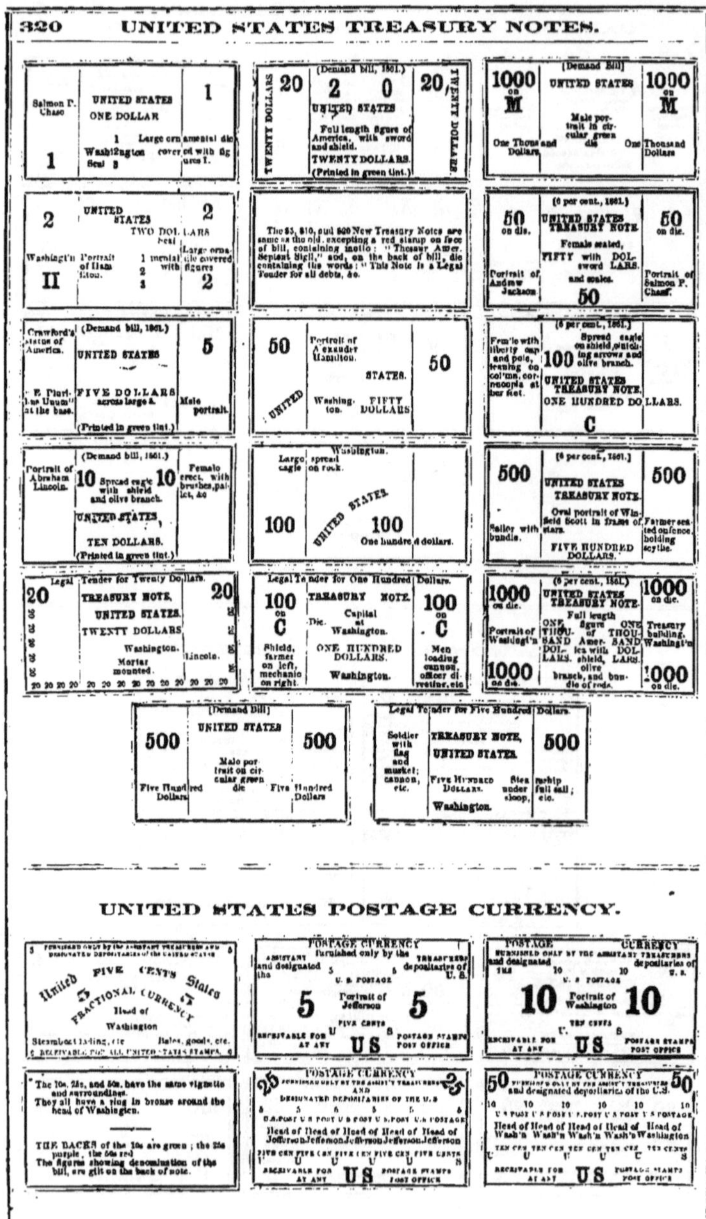
Salmon P. Chase
UNITED STATES
ONE DOLLAR
Washington Seal
Large ornamental die covered with figures 1.
(Demand bill, 1861.)
TWENTY DOLLARS
UNITED STATES
Full length figure of America, with sword and shield.
TWENTY DOLLARS.
(Printed in green tint.)
(Demand Bill)
1000 on M
UNITED STATES
Male portrait in circular green die
One Thousand Dollars
UNITED STATES
TWO DOLLARS
Washingt'n
Portrait of Hamilton.
Large ornamental die covered with figures
The $5, $10, and $20 New Treasury Notes are same as the old, excepting a red stamp on face of bill, containing motto: "Thesaur. Amer. Septent Sigil," and, on the back of bill, die containing the words: "This Note is a Legal Tender for all debts, &c.
(6 per cent., 1861.)
50 on die.
UNITED STATES TREASURY NOTE.
Female seated, FIFTY with DOLLARS. sword and scales.
Portrait of Andrew Jackson
Portrait of Salmon P. Chase.
Crawford's statue of America.
(Demand bill, 1861.)
UNITED STATES
E Pluribus Unum" at the base.
FIVE DOLLARS across large 5.
Male portrait.
(Printed in green tint.)
Portrait of Alexander Hamilton.
UNITED STATES.
Washington.
FIFTY DOLLARS
(6 per cent., 1861.)
Female with liberty cap and pole, leaning on col'mn, cornucopia at her feet.
Spread eagle on shield, clutching arrows and olive branch.
UNITED STATES TREASURY NOTE.
ONE HUNDRED DOLLARS.
C
Portrait of Abraham Lincoln.
(Demand bill, 1861.)
Spread eagle with shield and olive branch.
UNITED STATES.
TEN DOLLARS.
(Printed in green tint.)
Female erect, with brushes, pallet, &c
Large eagle
spread on rock.
Washington.
UNITED STATES
One hundred dollars.
(6 per cent., 1861.)
UNITED STATES TREASURY NOTE.
Oval portrait of Winfield Scott in frame of stars.
Sailor with bundle.
FIVE HUNDRED DOLLARS.
Farmer seated on fence, holding scythe.
Legal Tender for Twenty Dollars.
TREASURY NOTE.
UNITED STATES.
TWENTY DOLLARS
Washington.
Mortar mounted.
Lincoln.
Legal Tender for One Hundred Dollars.
100 on C
TREASURY NOTE.
Die.
Capitol at Washington.
ONE HUNDRED DOLLARS.
Washington.
Shield, farmer on left, mechanic on right.
Men loading cannon, officer directing, etc.
(6 per cent., 1861.)
1000 on die.
UNITED STATES TREASURY NOTE.
Full length figure of America, with shield, olive branch, and bundle of rods.
ONE THOUSAND DOLLARS.
Portrait of Washingt'n
Treasury building, Washingt'n
(Demand Bill)
UNITED STATES
Male portrait on circular green die
Five Hundred Dollars
Legal Tender for Five Hundred Dollars.
Soldier with flag and musket; cannon, etc.
TREASURY NOTE.
UNITED STATES.
Five Hundred Dollars.
Steamship under full sail; sloop, etc.
Washington.

UNITED STATES POSTAGE CURRENCY.

Furnished only by the Assistant Treasurers and Designated Depositaries of the United States
United FIVE CENTS States
FRACTIONAL CURRENCY
Head of Washington
Steamboat landing, etc.
Bales, goods, etc.
Receivable for all United States Stamps.
POSTAGE CURRENCY
furnished only by the Assistant Treasurers and designated depositaries of the U. S.
U. S. POSTAGE
Portrait of Jefferson
FIVE CENTS
Receivable for postage stamps at any post office
US
POSTAGE CURRENCY
Furnished only by the Assistant Treasurers and designated depositaries of the U. S.
U. S. POSTAGE
Portrait of Washington
TEN CENTS
Receivable for postage stamps at any post office
US
The 10s, 25s, and 50s, have the same vignette and surroundings.
They all have a ring in bronze around the head of Washington.
THE BACKS of the 10s are green; the 25s purple, the 50s red.
The figures showing denomination of the bill, are gilt on the back of note.
POSTAGE CURRENCY
Furnished only by the Ass't Treasurers and designated depositaries of the U. S.
Head of Jefferson
FIVE CENTS
Receivable for postage stamps at any post office
US
POSTAGE CURRENCY
and designated depositaries of the U. S.
Head of Washington
TEN CENTS
Receivable for postage stamps at any post office
US

www.ingramcontent.com/pod-product-compliance
Lightning Source LLC
Chambersburg PA
CBHW021500210326
41599CB00012B/1068

9783742800374